# Natural Law and Modern Society

# Natural Law and Modern Society

SEAN COYLE

OXFORD
UNIVERSITY PRESS

OXFORD
UNIVERSITY PRESS

Great Clarendon Street, Oxford, OX2 6DP,
United Kingdom

Oxford University Press is a department of the University of Oxford. It furthers the University's objective of excellence in research, scholarship, and education by publishing worldwide. Oxford is a registered trade mark of Oxford University Press in the UK and in certain other countries



First Edition published in 2023



Published in the United States of America by Oxford University Press
198 Madison Avenue, New York, NY 10016, United States of America

British Library Cataloguing in Publication Data

Data available

Library of Congress Control Number: 2023932469

ISBN 978–0–19–288699–6

DOI: 10.1093/oso/9780192886996.001.0001

*For Allison*

# Preface

The three main parts of this book collectively attempt to deal with the full range of issues facing the legal philosopher at the current day (perhaps any day): ethics, political theory, and law. The subjects discussed range from questions about method, the ends of legal philosophy, and moral truth, to questions concerning justice, community, the common good, rights, power, authority, law, and international community. In a book even of this length, it is impossible to give the last word on any of these subjects, but the book at least sets them within a framework in which they may be newly understood. This book is not, therefore, to borrow Hart's expression, a book about other books. It is an attempt to think through a set of problems, in a way that broadly conforms to the natural law philosophy of St Thomas Aquinas. It develops its own arguments, which stand or fall according to their philosophical coherence, plausibility, and explanatory power, rather than attempting systematic criticism of existing arguments. The reader who wishes to know more about how the book's arguments relate to the wider literature is encouraged to consult the rather lengthy endnotes, which (as it were) lift the engine-cover to display the book's sources. Nevertheless, the theories of Finnis, Raz, Hart, Gardner, Murphy, and others are given some discussion in the book's main text. Even a cursory glance will confirm to the reader the very great extent of the impression of Finnis's work on both book and author. Many discussions are initiated and inspired by Finnis's discussions. But the present book diverges from Finnis's in large ways and small, and there is virtually no aspect of Finnis's work of which the book is not critical: from principal doctrines on morality, justice, right, authority, and law, to subject ordering, to the analyses of law, obligation, and morality to the placement of theological material in the book's main argument.

The book is a contribution to natural law theory (in a sense to be defined in Chapters II and III), but its subject is, with the exception of Chapter II, natural law itself, and not its theory. It enumerates certain natural laws without which society either cannot be said to exist at all, or without which society is at least impoverished: by curtailing opportunities for human flourishing and self-determination; by reducing and regimenting cultural expression, art, and literature, especially that which opposes the state-imposed doctrine; by controlling and suppressing education, thereby ensuring that scientific advances are fewer and further between; and by introducing law into areas of private life that ought to be unregulated by the state (such as the internal economic organization of family life). The title of the book refers to 'modern society', and that is the book's focus as a context in which to raise and pursue its central ideas. I do not pretend to offer significant interpretations of modern politics, life, and society. Indeed, as I have indicated, my principal intellectual debts are to the Scholastic and Late-Scholastic writers on natural law, and on the still-older philosophies of Aristotle and Plato. But the ideas themselves are timeless (despite wide variations in attitudes, political forms, and technological progress), stable, enduring, penetrating, and constant: *Stat Crux dum volvitur orbis* (the Cross will remain while the world revolves).

In general outlook, then, the book is directed, at least in part, to recovering a moral and political framework that has been obscured, derided, and reacted against in the political circumstances of modern times. It argues against the belief that 'agnosticism and sceptical relativism are the philosophy and the basic attitude which correspond to democratic forms of political life'.[1] Those attitudes have indeed become ingrained in western political thought, but they are not the necessary nor the most natural interpretation of democratic ways of living. This does not suggest that there are no aspects of political, ethical, and legal thought that are distinctly modern and in accord with natural law. For, as all the major natural law theorists held, there are matters on which natural law is silent, or otherwise compatible with a range of values and approaches. Nor does natural law theory indicate any particular political form as the soundest, the most in tune with human flourishing, or in some other way the optimal form of human society. But those in control of political forms of governance have a *right* to rule, and thus a *right* to be obeyed, insofar as such forms are distinguishable from tyranny, oppression, or extortion. These issues are the concern of Chapters VIII–XI. Chapters III–VII present an ethical framework of concepts setting out the implications of what I call a 'core morality': a body of values that are constant and permanent in contrast to more subjective values that are relative to particular places and times. The book's opening chapters deal with 'method' (an approach to and understanding of legal philosophy), and the meaning, scope, and importance of natural law.

It should be added to Chapter I's warning that this book is not a work of philosophical theology, nor even, in a pure sense, of political theory. It is a book about natural law *jurisprudence*: answers to a set of questions of, or connected to, law. It may be described, however, as a book at least partly about ethics, for ethics is the starting point for all inquiry into law and politics: the human goods that the law protects must first be identified and illuminated.

The book attempts to answer jurisprudential questions, but confronts a set of problems that seem insurmountable. In the mid-nineteenth century, Cardinal Newman offers a sense of these problems:

> To consider the world in its length and breadth, its various history, the many races of man, their starts, their fortunes, their mutual alienation, their conflicts; and

[1] *Compendium of the Social Doctrine of the Catholic Church* II.7.8.4.407.

> then their ways, habits, governments, forms of worship; their enterprises, their aimless courses, their random achievements and acquirements, the impotent conclusion of longstanding facts, the tokens so faint and broken of a superintending design, the blind evolution of what turn out to be great powers or truths, the progress of things, as if from unreasoning elements, not towards final causes, the greatness and littleness of man, his far-reaching aims, his short duration, the curtain hung over his futurity, the disappointments of life, the defeat of good, the success of evil, physical pain, mental anguish, the prevalence and intensity of sin, the pervading idolatries, the corruptions, the dreary hopeless irreligion, that condition of the whole race, so fearfully yet exactly described in the Apostle's words, 'having no hope and without God in the world'—all this is a vision to dizzy and appall; and inflicts upon the mind the sense of a profound mystery, which is absolutely beyond human solution.[2]

I do not pretend to offer more than this litany suggests, but I do offer some hope, that at least in certain political and (especially) legal institutions one may detect the flow of God's love and mercy, of justice and right ordering. In this sense, the book offers a classical natural law theory that is attuned to the modern day, through such topics as law, justice, authority, and obligation.

The reader may perhaps be aware that there are many different natural law theories, and that they diverge on various points, ethical and theological. But with perhaps the exception of those discussed in the first chapter, the conflicts are small and there is not much in this book that would be problematical for one traditional theory of natural law rather than another. The book focuses on natural law theories of the scholastic and early modern periods, mostly Catholic (with the honourable exception of Grotius). It draws upon these figures not because they are Catholic but because the content of their intellectual systems seems to the author important and true. Likewise the book sometimes makes reference to the Catholic Church's social teaching encyclicals for their richness, sound sense, and probity, and not as such to advance a dogmatic position.

It is interesting to think that the second scholastic period was approximately four centuries after the time of Aquinas, roughly a similar amount of time between the second scholastics and the present. The time is therefore ripe for a third scholastic period, and this book is a very modest contribution to this end. It is consequent to this that I employ the term 'pre-modern' to describe philosophies of the medieval or late-medieval periods, and I use the term 'modern' flexibly to denote either the general period following on from that earlier period (i.e. the early modern period and after), or more specifically to the philosophical developments of the late twentieth and twenty-first centuries: the context makes clear which is intended.

[2] JH Newman, *Apologia Pro Vita Sua* (Penguin Classics 1994) 217.

A word, finally, about my use of the Latin abbreviation 'cf' (*conferatur*). It has become popular in recent times to use this abbreviation to refer the reader to other works that agree with one's own on some point. But I use it in its correct sense, as *contrasting* the argument in other works to the argument I am advancing. Where I wish to signal agreement or neutrality vis-à-vis other works I use the phrases 'see' or 'see also'.

This book has been a decade in the making. It was begun in early 2013. The main lines of argument were devised by 2016, when a generous period of research leave allowed the author to make swift progress in mapping out the arguments in more detail. A complete manuscript was prepared by the summer of 2022. Along the way, numerous intellectual debts were accrued, and it is my great pleasure to thank the following people for their encouragement, support, and comments: to Brian Stone and Matthew Williams at OUP and to three anonymous referees for their penetrating and very helpful comments; to Gavin Byrne, Paul Dale, Kristine Kalanges, Bob Lee, Margaret Martin, John Tingle, Bosko Tripkovic, and Fiona Smith (who generously read and commented on the whole manuscript). Each of these readers afforded me the opportunity to refine the arguments, see things differently, and gain new perspectives. Posthumous thanks also to my late father John Coyle (for comments on Chapter VII), to my mother Mary Coyle, and to Jez, Paul, and their families for constant support and encouragement, and above all to my wife, Allison, to whom this book is lovingly dedicated.

Sean Coyle
22 November 2022

# Contents

# List of Abbreviations

| | |
|---|---|
| *AJJ* | *American Journal of Jurisprudence* |
| *AL* | Raz, *The Authority of Law* 2nd edn (Oxford University Press 2009) |
| *Aquinas* | Finnis, *Aquinas: Moral, Political and Legal Theory* (Oxford University Press 1998) |
| *AV* | MacIntyre, *After Virtue* (Duckworth (1981) |
| *Catechism* | *Catechism of the Catholic Church* 2nd edn (Libreria Editrice Vaticana 2020) |
| *CEJF* | Finnis, *The Collected Essays of John Finnis* (Oxford University Press 2011) 5 vols |
| *CL* | Hart, *The Concept of Law* (3rd edn Oxford University Press 2012) |
| *CLJ* | *Cambridge Law Journal* |
| *Com Pol* | Aquinas, *Commentary on the Politics of Aristotle* |
| *Comm* | Blackstone, *Commentaries on the Law of England* (1765–69) |
| *Compendium* | *Compendium of the Social Teachings of the Catholic Church* |
| *DE* | Irwin, *The Development of Ethics* (3 vols) (Oxford University Press 2007) |
| *De An* | Aquinas, *De Anima* |
| *De Bon* | Suarez, *De Bonitate et Malitia Humanorum Actuum* |
| *De Car* | Aquinas, *De Caritate* |
| *De Mal* | Aquinas, *Questiones Disputate De Malo* |
| *De Reg* | Aquinas, *De Regno* |
| *De Ver* | Aquinas, *De Veritate* |
| *De Virt* | Aquinas, *De Virtutibus* |
| *De Virt Card* | Aquinas, *De Virtutibus Cardinalibus* |
| *De Vol* | Suarez, *De Voluntario et Involuntario* |
| *DIBP* | Grotius, *De Iure Belli ac Pacis* |
| *DINEG* | Pufendorf, *De Iure Naturae et Gentium* |
| *DIPC* | Grotius, *De Iure Praedae Commentarius* |
| *DL* | Suarez, *De Legibus* |
| *DM* | Suarez, *Disputationes Metaphysicae* |
| *DOR* | Kramer, Simmonds, Steiner, *A Debate Over Rights* (Oxford University Press 1998) |
| *ECM* | MacIntyre, *Essays in the Conflicts of Modernity* (Cambridge University Press, 2016) |
| *EE* | Aristotle, *Eudemean Ethics* |
| *EJP* | Hart, *Essays in Jurisprudence and Philosophy* (Oxford University Press 1983) |

| | |
|---|---|
| *EP* | MacIntyre, *Ethics and Politics: Selected Essays* (Cambridge University Press 2006) |
| *Eth* | Aquinas, *Sententia Libri Ethicorum* (Commentary on *NE*) |
| *FE* | Finnis, *Fundamentals of Ethics* (Georgetown University Press 1983) |
| First Principle | Grisez, 'The First Principle of Practical Reason: A Comment on *Summa Theologiae* I-II.94.2c (1965) *Natural Law Forum* 168 |
| *HN* | Allott, *Health of Nations* (Cambridge University Press 2002) |
| *In Primam Secundae* | Vasquez, *Commentaria ac Disputationes in Primam Secundae Sancti Thomae* |
| *LE* | Dworkin, *Law's Empire* (Fontana 1986) |
| *LLF* | Gardner, *Law as a Leap of Faith* (Oxford University Press 2012) |
| *Meta* | Aristotle, *Metaphysics* |
| *ML* | Porter, *Ministers of the Law* (Eerdmans 2010) |
| *ML* | Fuller, *The Morality of Law* (Yale University Press 1964) |
| *MLR* | *Modern Law Review* |
| *NDMR* | Grisez, Finnis, & Boyle, *Nuclear Deterrence, Morality and Realism* (Oxford University Press 1988) |
| *NE* | Aristotle, *Nicomachean Ethics* |
| *NLJP* | Murphy, *Natural Law in Jurisprudence and Politics* (Cambridge University Press 2006) |
| *NLNL* | Crowe, *Natural Law and the Nature of Law* (Cambridge University Press 2019) |
| *NLNR* | Finnis, *Natural Law and Natural Rights* 2nd edn (Oxford, Clarendon Press 2011) |
| *NLPR* | Murphy, *Natural Law and Practical Rationality* (Cambridge University Press 2001) |
| *OJLS* | *Oxford Journal of Legal Studies* |
| *Pol* | Aquinas, *Sententia Libri Politicorum* (Commentary on Aristotle's *Politics*) |
| *SCG* | Aquinas, *Summa Contra Gentiles* |
| *Sent* | Biel, *Collectorium circa quattuor libros Sententiarum* |
| *Sent* | Gregory of Rimini, *Lectura Super Primum et Secundum Sententiarum* |
| *Sent* | Aquinas, Commentary on Peter Lombard's *Libri Quattuor Sententiarum* |
| *ST* | Aquinas, *Summa Theologiae* |
| *TJ* | Rawls, *A Theory of Justice* (Harvard University Press 1972) |
| *TPIL* | Besson & Tasioulas, *The Philosophy of International Law* (Oxford University Press 2010) |
| *TRV* | MacIntyre, *Three Rival Versions of Moral Inquiry: Encyclopedia, Genealogy and Tradition* (Duckworth 1990) |
| *WJWR* | MacIntyre, *Whose Justice? Which Rationality?* (Duckworth 1996) |

# PART ONE

# I
# METHOD AND ETHICS IN JURISPRUDENCE

## I.1. METHOD AND POINT OF VIEW

There are human objectives and ends that are dependent upon law; and there are demands of justice and social order for which law is the only fully viable mechanism. This book will be concerned with the elaboration and defence of these ideas, and the identification of those demands and requirements. In a sense to be explained later (Chapter II), the book puts forward a natural law theory. The natural law does not encompass the whole of ethics. It extends only as far as ethical truths shared in common with all persons, even those who dispute the existence of God or an afterlife.

These remarks are liable to raise a suspicion in the minds of many modern readers, who will dispute the suggestion that there are ethical truths that are common to all persons. Instead, many at the present day believe that each person formulates his or her own truth, and that present-day society is characterized by a universal disagreement over ethical truth. In light of this, it has appeared imperative to some that jurisprudence preserve its status as a social science, founded upon neutral, value-free descriptions, even if such descriptions are of human practices or purposes. The legal theorist's descriptions, in this way, resemble those of the historian, for example in deciphering the reasoning of Cromwell's generals in their battle with rebels at Chepstow in the summer of 1648. They are purported descriptions *of evaluations*, though without sharing them, and without the intention of advancing some practical point. This reconstruction of the reasoning of another is of the kind called by Dworkin 'conversational interpretation', in which some specific meaning is communicated or discovered.[1] Indeed, there seem to be problems in *contrasting* this form of interpretation (as Dworkin does) with that involved in analysing a social practice, such as law. For if we accept (on the contrary) that meaning and purpose are imposed only by the participants, the result is a depiction of law as an instrument serving only the purposes of the day, whatever they may be, with no further practical significance.

[1] Ronald Dworkin, *Law's Empire* (Belknap Press 1986), 54–55.

*Natural Law and Modern Society.* Sean Coyle, Oxford University Press. © Sean Coyle 2023.
DOI: 10.1093/oso/9780192886996.003.0001

Jurisprudence then seeks an account of human practices and purposes. But unlike the historian, the legal philosopher does not wish to confine the account only to the practices of a particular time, or place. Here the object is: the intelligibility of practice itself. The starting-point for inquiry is therefore practical, in the sense indicated by Aristotle in contrast with reasoning that is *purely* theoretical. It is an inquiry for which possession of truth about particular human actions and particular aims and intentions is insufficient, for the aim must be to uncover the truth about human ends and purposes in general, and to reveal (a) what is genuinely good for human beings, and (b) the means to obtain it. In fact no theorist can successfully undertake the effort to describe human practice, without engaging in this form of practical philosophy. The concepts employed by the legal philosopher do not therefore have their starting-point in social science, but in ethics.

Given the wide variety of ends and practices associated with the laws of different societies at particular times and places, a principle is required to explain how and why the term 'law' is used appropriately in relation to each of a number of disparate instances. The collection of such instances can proceed only by the identification of a principal or central case, to which the other instances are related by similitude and analogy.[2] But how does one determine the essential properties of law in distinction from the inessential, the debased, or the aberrant? The methodological perspective adopted in modern jurisprudence is that of the 'internal' point of view, that is, the perspective of the participants in a practice. However, the latitude afforded to legal theory under this method is too broad: for the allegiance to the system of those who *accept* the rules and *use* them to appraise behaviour, can rest on so slender a basis as a 'mere wish to do as others do'.[3] This cannot, however, be a central, fully developed case of that *critical* and *reflective* attitude on the part of participants which sustains a legal system in existence. The standards of criticism and reflection that are appropriate to law are fully capable of generating the conditional acceptance of rules that run counter to moral duty (conditional e.g. upon their having been validly legislated by a legal body that remains in power). As a result of this duality, those same standards of criticism and reflection are capable of extending beyond the aims and purposes of this or that legal system, to consider the aims and purposes of legal systems *as such*. We may call this *the practical point of view*. Here, the theorist still understands things 'from the inside' (though only in an extended sense), but with the additional understanding that the ultimate point or function of the practice may transcend (or even oppose) the immediate purposes to which the practice is being put. There will be, then, characteristics which explain the point of the practice, that are present only in its central cases (such as directiveness to certain human goods).

[2] See e.g. John Finnis, *Natural Law & Natural Rights* (2nd edn Clarendon Press 2011, hereafter *NLNR*) 9–11, 20 (on analogy); Aristotle, *Nicomachian Ethics* (hereafter *NE*) VIII.4.1157a, VIII.6.1158b.

[3] See HLA Hart, *The Concept of Law* (3rd edn OUP 2012, hereafter *CL*) 203, also 116 ('from any motive whatever').

The analytical philosopher wishes to describe law as a type of human practice, not only in relation to present society, but of all societies and at all times. But the pretensions of 'general theory' extend beyond describing the linguistic conceptions and distinctions observed in particular cultures, or even a history of all usages. A theory is obliged to start with particular data of human efforts, in this or that cultural locality or place in time; but it will not achieve intelligibility unless it deciphers their point. Nor will it achieve generality, unless it perceives this point (and the point of similar efforts in varied times and circumstances) as an instance of the effort to pursue and secure certain human *goods*. The primary matter of jurisprudence, therefore, is the contention that there are indeed such human goods, and that they represent ends to be pursued through law, correctly and uprightly applied.

Inattention to this question—whether there are or are not objective human ends—has contributed to the dismissal of natural law theory as an antiquated relic of no relevance to modern times. For if the question of ends had been posed more directly, it would have been seen more clearly that the purpose of natural law theory is not to dispute the *fact* of disagreement over ethical truth, which after all is nothing new (although natural law theory must be able to, and indeed can, account for this phenomenon). It is rather to dispute the (live) *philosophical* claim that there is no moral truth. The response to that claim is itself philosophical and not merely historical; it is as timeless as philosophy itself, and cannot be dismissed as a relic of the past.

The purpose of this book is to defend a natural law theory. But it is possible to make here a preliminary observation: that one's moral *disagreement* with others incorporates the belief that ethical arguments belong to the same plane of discourse. When we disagree with others, it is because they (or we) are incorrect about the demands of morality, so that there really are universal moral demands even if not every person properly perceives them. If one disbelieves in the existence of universal truths, it follows that moral disagreements are only apparent disagreements: ethical arguments do not belong to the same plane of discourse. Instead, each person's view of moral demands is true in its own frame of discourse.

The methodology pursued by legal philosophers at the present day reinforces the perception that ethical truths remain true only in their own frame of discourse. For, it is assumed that legal scholars assert and defend their viewpoints *contra mundum*. In order to establish the case for their own opinion, it is necessary to refute all contrary opinions. The terms on which a theory is evaluated are, on the one hand, originality (avoiding the mere reformulation of other views), and on the other hand, rigour (in demolishing contrary views).[4] This methodology directly

[4] See Gardner's remarks in John Gardner, *Law as a Leap of Faith* (OUP 2012, hereafter *LLF*) vi.164–70.

contributes to the appearance that legal philosophy is a fragmented and pluralistic subject. There is not one truth that all scholars join in trying to formulate, but many opposing truths between which each thinker must decide. Yet the values of originality and disagreement are not so highly regarded by all legal scholars. The scholastic philosophers of the Middle Ages looked for the truth in their opponents' opinions, in the belief that every person possesses a measure of true insight into moral goodness, even if their opinion is seriously in error in some respects. As a consequence, the scholastic method emphasized continuity with textual authorities, and the effort to reconcile apparently divergent opinions. The method of formulating and responding to objections allowed an author to identify the true conditions in which an opponent's opinion is correct, and explain the reasons why it is mistaken in the context established by the specific question. For example, Aquinas holds the opinion that an innate characteristic of law is to make citizens good, but he considers the objection that tyrannical laws do not possess this quality, because a tyrant does not intend the good of his subjects, but rather his own ends. He explains that the disagreement is only partial, because even tyrannical laws aim to secure peace and order within the state, and seek to make citizens good not in an absolute sense, but relative to the aims and purposes of the tyrant.[5]

The scholastic method has an important advantage, especially in the sceptical times of the present: it helps to reinforce the fact that legal philosophers are arguing about a single truth, not proposing multiple truths. But even more, it serves as a reminder that even severe disagreements are only partial disagreements. An important purpose of legal philosophy is to articulate the common ground that exists between one's own opinion and the opinions of one's opponents. This reminds us that all legal philosophers are engaged in the same task and inquiry, not a series of separate inquiries. It also allows us to see that disagreements should not lead a philosopher to reject everything an opponent has to say, but seek to correct the limited ways in which their view is mistaken.

There is one further advantage to this approach: it shows that the philosophical thinking of earlier ages remains relevant to our own times, and is not relegated to the plane of merely historical interest. Part of the resistance to natural law jurisprudence at the present day perhaps stems from the belief that the world as it appeared to the scholastic writers is not the same as the world as we know it today. Yet there is no evidence to support this point of view. The world addressed by medieval and scholastic writers was no less at war, nor divided over values, than our own. No less than our present times, pre-modern times contained a wide range of opinions on many subjects, including ethics. Because ethics is a philosophical inquiry not an historical one, the scholastic writers regarded themselves as in dialogue not only

[5] Thomas Aquinas, *Summa Theologiae* (hereafter *ST*) I-II.92.1 arg 4; for another example see I-II.6.6c. See also Aquinas's treatment of Origen in the *Commentary on the Gospel of John* I.2.

with contemporary thinkers, but also their predecessors and even ancient, pre-Christian writers such as Aristotle and Cicero.

When they read and considered the works of the ancients, pre-modern writers of the scholastic and late-scholastic periods did not regard themselves as engaged in historical research, for they shared with the ancient writers a view that ethics is concerned with the identity of our ultimate end, and of the means it is necessary to take to secure it. Furthermore, they agreed with the ancients over the most general way to describe the end: happiness. As a consequence, pre-modern philosophers recognized that both they and the ancients were involved in the same effort: to discover and articulate truths of the human condition, and to interpret our ultimate end. By examining the opinions of ancient writers, the pre-modern writers did not think of themselves as learning only about archaic ideas of happiness. They saw themselves as contributors to the same plane of discourse: philosophical discourse.

## I.2. A COMMON STARTING-POINT FOR LEGAL PHILOSOPHY

Eudaemonist philosophies of ethics[6] share a common understanding of the task and purpose of ethical inquiry: to identify the ultimate end for human beings, and to give practical guidance on how to achieve it. Ancient moral philosophers, no less than people at the present day, disagree about the right way to characterize the ultimate end, yet they found it easy to describe in formal terms. It can be described as the end for the sake of which all other ends are sought (in Aristotle's definition), or as the good composed of all other goods (as in Plato's). For the want of a better term, it can be said that the ancient philosophers (including even the sceptics) agreed that happiness is our ultimate end or supreme good, even though they disagreed about its substance and the means to attain it.

In modern times, it has seemed impossible to suggest that legal philosophers share a common starting-point, and even less that they agree on ethics. Not only do some legal philosophers—legal positivists—think that the starting-point of inquiry does not include ethics, some also disbelieve in the existence of ethical truth. Consequently they dismiss the idea of an ultimate end for all human beings, in favour of the belief that each person invents their own end. By reference to any one of these ends, law can be characterized as good or evil; or to the extent that people agree in their ethical judgments (so-called positive morality), law can contravene accepted norms of morality. How then (it may be asked) can legal philosophy have a common starting-point in ethics?

[6] That is to say, ethics concerned with goods and ends, and with the ultimate good or end.

A promising way to begin is by examining the views of a prominent legal positivist, HLA Hart. From what we learn about his outlook on law and morals in *The Concept of Law* chapter IX, Hart *seems* to be a moral sceptic. The issue at the centre of his discussion is, whether there are any true principles of right conduct that are rationally discoverable. But a person who believed in moral goodness would not make this issue the central question for discussion. They would instead direct the inquiry to uncovering the identity of the end in respect of which the principles have their goodness and desirability. Hart's discussion is not overtly directed to the question of ends. Yet despite this, his disagreement with the classical tradition of natural law is not a complete disagreement. This is clearly evident in Hart's own admission that the natural law tradition contains an appeal for him, in spite of differences concerning metaphysics and religious belief. Because the disagreement is merely partial, it allows him to see in traditional natural law theory 'certain elementary truths of importance for the understanding of both law and morality'.[7]

Among the truths that Hart mentions include human vulnerability, equality, and limited altruism. In Hart's view they are 'of importance' for law and ethics for only one reason: they assist in determining the necessary steps human beings must take to secure an agreed end, human survival. In spite of announcing this point only in the ninth chapter of his book, the entirety of Hart's argument is implicitly concerned with this end (and as we will see, other ends). Furthermore, his argument agrees with eudaemonist ethics in regarding these ends as *goods*. Nevertheless, he rejects two beliefs about these goods. First, he rejects the belief that human goods are perfective of human nature. (As we will see, there is a grain of truth in this rejection.) Second, he rejects the belief that human beings have an ultimate end or purpose that is objectively determined for them. However, even this disagreement with the idea of perfection and end is not an entire disagreement with eudaemonist ethics, for, he recognizes that all living things are described as healthy or unhealthy depending upon their progress towards or away from their optimal condition.[8] This signals his agreement with Aristotle that the nature of a thing is determined according to a mature and flourishing condition of the thing, not the condition in which it is merely *in potentia* or in decay. Hart also recognizes that the ideas of perfection and end are the basis for identifying needs and human goods, as well as for distinguishing harms and injuries.

Hart's discussion displays a *limited* rejection of the idea of human ends. He disbelieves in the existence of higher ends than the preservation of one's existence, because such ends are 'complex and debatable'. Then he disbelieves that preservation of one's existence is naturally an end. Instead, he conceives it to be only a contingently chosen aim. This rejection *seems* to be a fundamental disregard of the very ground of eudaemonist ethics. Yet in fact, the rejection is more limited than it

[7] Hart, *CL* (n 3) 187.
[8] Ibid, 188–89.

appears. For, Hart also believes acceptance of the 'aim' of self-preservation is a *practical* necessity, because it could not be abandoned without completely obliterating every aspect of human thought and effort. Thus, no discussion regarding law and morals can proceed if it is not presupposed. Therefore, Hart concurs with eudaemonist ethics in holding that, as long as human nature remains as it is, certain moral precepts will hold true.[9]

Hart's argument is a eudaemonist argument. It supposes the existence of an end (the preservation of life) which it regards as a good. Other subordinate goods, such as law and order, are conceived as being directed to the ultimate good. But it is also a deficient argument. It is deficient not because it is false, but because of what it leaves out. Unlike previous accounts of ethics, Hart does not initiate any inquiry into the identity of the ultimate good, for he remains sceptical of the existence of more ultimate goods than survival (unless they are subjectively chosen). Nevertheless, his starting-point remains a eudaemonist starting-point.

Yet it may seem that there are some alternative approaches to legal philosophy that reject eudaemonism. For example, we can bring to mind the Kantian legal philosophy that exerted an influence on Hans Kelsen. Kelsen defines the 'criterion' of law as 'the social technique which consists in bringing about the desired social conduct of men through the threat of a coercive measure that is to be applied in case of contrary conduct'.[10] Nothing *seems* to be further from a eudaemonist point of view. We are informed that the law is a technique concerned with human *conduct* (i.e. duty) rather than human *good*. Indeed, juristic considerations extend only as far as human conduct, so that '[t]he person only exists insofar as he "has" duties and rights', without which 'the person has no existence whatsoever'.[11] However, the eudaemonistic suppositions of Kelsen's viewpoint become apparent when we ask why a specific type of social conduct is 'desired', or in other words, why it is considered as a *good*. Moreover, in a work devoted to scientific positivism where moral and evaluative considerations are supposedly eschewed, it is a good singled out as worthy of pursuit, indeed as socially *necessary* to pursue in a wide variety of societies at all times and places.[12]

Quite apart from legal order, Kelsen's discussion implicitly recognizes other kinds of human good. In discussing the same point, he observes that '[t]he evil applied to the violator of [legal] order . . . consists in a depravation of possessions—life, health, freedom or property'. By identifying human evils (i.e. harms), Kelsen implicitly agrees with eudaemonist ethics that certain incidents to human life—such as health—are human goods. Kelsen's starting-point does not spell out what is clearly implied: that legal order exists in order to secure human goods such as

[9] Ibid, 190 ('certain rules of conduct which . . . constitute a common element in law and conventional morality'); compare Finnis, *NLNR* (n 2), 34.

[10] Hans Kelsen, *General Theory of Law and State* (Routledge 2005) 19.

[11] Ibid, 94.

[12] Ibid, 19.

life, health, freedom, and so forth. Indeed he mentions only a few pages further on, a central end or purpose of legal order upon which eudaemonist ethicists would all concur: the good of peace, or internal tranquillity of the community. It is often overlooked that Kelsen even wrote a short monograph, entitled *Peace Through Law*. Because these matters form part of the 'criterion' of law, Kelsen's starting-point is a eudaemonist starting-point: it is based upon an assessment of human goods.

The 'Kantian' beginnings of Kelsen's ethical ideas (e.g. the basis of legal order and peace in reciprocity) do not present an obstacle to his implicit eudaemonism. Though it is often considered that Kant's 'categorical imperative' pursues a deontological version of ethics, by focusing on duty rather than human good, nevertheless all the considerations that could cause a person to will a certain kind of conduct as a universal law for all reach down into conceptions of human good (that one ought to pursue) or human evils (that it is necessary to avoid). The supposed contrast between eudaemonist and deontological ethics is an imaginary contrast: deontic ethics concerns what is good and bad, just as eudaemonists are concerned with our duties towards one another and to God. Indeed, Kant's antipathy towards Aristotle's ethics seems to stem from Kant's own theoretical assumptions: for his notion of 'happiness' (*Gluckseligkeit*), lies with the notion of 'inclinations', that is to say, desires, with ultimate happiness being the summation of desires.[13] Aristotle's eudaemonism by contrast centres upon the values of contemplation and practice of virtue. Kant's opposition to Aristotelian ethics is immediately hollowed out: for the actions done in the name of *eudaemonia* are not sensation-enhancing actions but those aimed at living well and doing well (or, if we were to talk in the terms Aristotle employs when speaking of the virtues, living *rightly*). And the idea of 'acting well' is connectable to Kant's concern with right action, action that is in accord with moral law. The categorical imperative itself, though constructed in terms of will and law, is re-translatable in the language of good and end: will that which is good in itself, that is, an authentic end.[14]

Kelsen's position (and to an extent Hart's position) attempts to isolate the treatment of law from inquiry into ethics. The attempt does not succeed, as we have seen. But legal philosophers have maintained the appearance of separation, because very often the *methodological* aim to offer a neutral account of law comes to be supported by a *substantive* thesis of moral scepticism. This is evident for example at the point at which Hart concludes that the substantive content of legal systems is never entirely fixed, given the contingency of all human purposes. But

[13] See E Sonny Elizondo, 'Kantian Eudaimonism' (2022) *J of the American Philosophical Association* 3–4. Murphy treats happiness as a basic good in itself, not as an aspect of the pursuit of other goods: Mark C Murphy, *Natural Law & Practical Rationality* (CUP 2001, hereafter *NLPR*) 134–35.

[14] See especially Erica A Holberg, 'Kant's Quasi-Eudaimonism' 56 (2018) *Southern J of Philosophy* 317; Robert B Louden, 'The End of All Human Action/The Final Object of All My Conduct: Aristotle and Kant on the Highest Good' in Joachim Aufderheide & Ralf Bader (eds) *The Highest Good in Aristotle and Kant* (OUP 2015) 112.

Hart's theory is neither the first nor the last to depend upon a background of moral scepticism. Another clear example of this can be found in Bentham's jurisprudence. Bentham separates the function of the 'expositor' who tries to explain what 'as it *seems* to him' the law is, and that of the 'censor' which is to state what 'as he *thinks*' it ought to be.[15] The censor holds to a form of ethics that *seems* to differ from eudaemonism: utilitarianism (consequentialism). And the 'greatest happiness' (sc. good) principle does not sit in judgment over the kinds of things that promote that happiness. Bentham is both a utilitarian and a moral sceptic: for the units of utility at the centre of the theory are intended as a neutral currency by which to avoid specious arguments about natural right, and imposters such as the virtues.[16] But the difference between Bentham's utilitarianism and a eudaemonist ethics is only apparent: for the estimation of an action in virtue of its consequences, concerns consequences that are good or bad as understood by human beings. The notion of utility stands in place of human goods for the purposes of calculation, and avoids the evaluation of which goods are real goods as opposed to apparent goods (real evils desired in virtue of the appearance of good). Yet a eudaemonist ethicist would point out two things about this calculation.

The first point is merely the practical point of who is doing this evaluating, and this measuring, and on the basis of what data. Let us put aside the difficulties of shifting attitudes, low voter turnout, and corruption, all of which act to degrade the quality of the data to be processed. The utilitarian requires a coherent procedure to generate comprehensible data; but all of the mechanisms by which populations can be consulted for their views (general elections, referendums, surveys) operate by *presenting options*, not by asking infinitely determinable questions. It is practically necessary for such mechanisms to generate only a manageable number of options. A utilitarian calculus would therefore need to define a unit of utility: in Bentham's eyes, pleasure or desire, but for his successors, preference, the avoidance of pain, and other ideas. Even where (as in the case of Bentham) a unit of utility is not based on reason, nevertheless the reason for defining utility in that way depends on what the Censor (or Hare's 'archangel')[17] would have recognized *as a good*, such as the satisfaction of a desire. This definition is independent of any aggregative calculus, despite Bentham's tendency to regard communities as aggregates of individuals.[18] Postema observes: 'Bentham suggested that it is possible to construct a powerful ethical deliberating machine capable of churning out precise, determinate, and publicly verifiable judgments and prescriptions for all moral occasions, both private and public.'[19] In this he failed. Bentham was aware of the problem: there is

[15] Jeremy Bentham, *A Fragment on Government* [1776], Preface (my emphasis).

[16] They are also agent-neutral: see Murphy, *NLPR* (n 13) 167.

[17] See RM Hare, *Moral Thinking* (OUP 1981), 46.

[18] See Jeremy Bentham, *Colonies, Commerce and Constitutional Law* in Philip Schofield (ed) *The Collected Works of Jeremy Bentham* (Clarendon Press 1995) 149: see also Gerald Postema, *Utility, Publicity and Law* (OUP 2019) 255.

[19] See Postema, ibid 73.

no common measure of pleasure and pain, and no way to measure the relative intensity of such experiences.[20] His hope that money or some other proxy might supply the ground of calculation came to nothing.[21] Nonetheless, Bentham never retreated from the idea of a mode of calculation of shifting utilities.

The second point is that a calculus of interests aggregates units of utility. It can do this only because there are some kinds of goods that all people agree on, such as preserving one's life and bodily health for example. If there were no widespread agreement on the goodness of some ends, such as attaining peace, then aggregation would be impossible.[22] If people did not agree upon the goodness of any single thing, the calculus would produce no outcomes, for the output would be identical with the input. Yet, the fact of agreement deserves some explanation: either as the collective consciousness of an end or good, or (at least) as a collective false-consciousness.

In seeking such an explanation, the ethicist does not blank out every last mote of these foregoing accounts of ethics. Instead he or she moves beyond their limitations, and rejects only those aspects of them that are incompatible with the effort to decipher the character of the good.[23] We may follow the example of John Finnis, whose account is not put forward with the intention to ignore or obliterate Hart's theory, but to supply what was missing from it: a proper discussion of our ultimate end and good. He rejects only the aspects of Hart's theory that are incompatible with this purpose. (Hart in turn does not reject everything he finds in Bentham's and Austin's jurisprudence, but retains essential elements—such as the separation thesis.)

Finnis's discussion clearly announces an intention to put the question of human good at the very centre of inquiry: 'There are human goods that can be secured only through the institutions of human law, and requirements of practical reasonableness that only those institutions can satisfy. It is the object of this book to identify those goods, and those requirements of practical reasonableness.'[24] Then, Finnis's long discussion of concept-formation and 'focal' meaning explains the faults that led his predecessors into error.[25] This disagreement is also a limited disagreement. It is not a case of one writer (Finnis) claiming that law is directed to securing human goods, and another writer (Hart or Bentham) denying that law is so directed. The

[20] Ibid, 81–82, 83.

[21] Ibid, 84–86.

[22] Aggregative philosophies also tend to annihilate community by reducing it to 'bundles of appetites': see JA Gunn 'Jeremy Bentham and the Public Interest' 1 (1968) *Canadian J of Political Science* 398. It also all but annihilates the individual, for there is essentially nothing about a person, as such, that is sacred if the balance of interests/utilities inclines to the contrary.

[23] As Murphy observes, later ethicists foreswore maximization but retained welfarism as a key feature of ethics: Murphy, *NLPR* (n 13) 145.

[24] Finnis, *NLNR* (n 2) 3.

[25] For some comment see Veronica Rodriguez-Blanco 'Tracing Finnis's Criticism of Hart's Internal Point of View' in Torben Spaak & Patricia Mindus (eds) *The Cambridge Companion to Legal Positivism* (CUP 2021) 695.

disagreement instead concerns the character of the goods that ought to be pursued by the law. Due to their scepticism that there are higher ends than the satisfaction of desire (in Bentham's case) or survival (in Hart's), they do not consider that ethics constitutes the starting-point for legal philosophy. To consider Hart specifically: he consequently lacks a motive to distinguish between numerous possible 'internal points of view', that is, ways in which a person can employ legal rules as standards for appraising or criticizing behaviour, such as those of a committed citizen versus those of a reluctant cynic.[26] In contrast, Finnis treats ethics as the correct starting-point, because he accepts that human actions and institutions are directed to ends higher than the end of mere survival. Because all our actions are directed towards realizing the *good life*, at least in the sense mentioned above, it is proper to hold an internal viewpoint that considers law as a force for human good. Any other viewpoint is 'parasitic' upon this one.[27]

Virtually all of the main part of Finnis's discussion is devoted to the topic that Hart treats in an inadequate and defective way, namely the identification of human goods and ends. Besides the preservation of life, Finnis identifies other fundamental human goods that are not mentioned by Hart: goods such as knowledge, reasonableness, and love of beauty. These are indisputably goods, on which everybody can agree (except perhaps the very unreasonable). All other human goods are (according to Finnis) particular ways of attaining or enjoying these fundamental goods.[28] This explains the wide variety in conceptions of human goodness familiar in everyday life: different people who pursue different forms of human good *appear* to disagree about what is good; but in fact they are simply choosing to give priority to certain combinations of the fundamental goods as opposed to others. Only the wicked, and perhaps the weak of will, genuinely prefer apparent goods (actual evils) to real goods.

This argument establishes that there are not different truths about goodness and happiness for different people, or even different societies, but one truth that can be pursued and realized in different ways. It can be seen from this that the recognition of higher goods than mere survival does not threaten the idea of liberal pluralism, as Hart seems to have feared. It allows different people to live their life in different ways.

## I.3. A DESCRIPTIVE STARTING-POINT?

The common starting-point proposed for the study of jurisprudence, is a practical starting-point. That is to say, it is directed to the end of advising the citizen

[26] See Hart, *CL* (n 3) 98. For Finnis's criticisms see *NLNR* (n 2) 12–14.
[27] Finnis, *NLNR* (n 2) 14.
[28] Ibid, 92.

and the state official on the ends that we ought to pursue together as a community, and on the means (e.g. law) by which we should pursue them. This does not mean selecting a starting-point that is 'complex and debatable' (as Hart put it), but identifying common goods that at least every reasonable person would recognize as the proper ends to be pursued by the community as a whole.

Modern analytical positivists assert the possibility of an alternative purpose of jurisprudential inquiry: an inquiry into the form or concept of law itself, independently of the practical ends to which it may be put. It is worth saying a word about the characteristics and limits of such inquiries. The thought that one can investigate the qualities of law without further practical ends in view, simply to arrive at a speculative knowledge of a subject, is not an inherently unreasonable one. Indeed, the possibility is conceded (inter alia) by Aristotle, who observes that certain ethical inquiries are concerned with action in a more preliminary and theoretical way.[29] In the case of legal philosophy, the concept of 'law' is sufficiently broad as to allow hypothetical studies of ways in which legal systems can realize or depart from standards of justice, as well as empirical analyses of their achievements and deficiencies. As a legal historian, for example, a scholar may have no interest in assisting lay citizens and legal professionals in their efforts to secure a common good. His or her intentions are entirely intellectual rather than practical. Such a scholar will indeed require a working conception of a 'legal order that is general enough to encompass the familiar developed systems of law of the present day, and the ancient codes and practices of primitive peoples. At least implicitly, such a concept must be capable of marking the division between primitive legal arrangements and features of what Hart calls the 'pre-legal world'; and it must explain the basis of differentiation between mature, developed instances of the concept and primitive, undeveloped instances.

Studies of this kind presuppose the practical point of view, for one cannot simply *describe* the properties of the central or principal case of 'law': the question is one of *classifying* and *differentiating between* instances. One cannot therefore avoid appealing to the (practical) considerations that call for the recognition of particular organized human efforts as instituting *legal* arrangements for a community: considerations that inevitably appeal to the point or end of the efforts, and evaluate them in terms of their degree of success or failure in attaining that point or end. Indeed, as Hart makes clear, one's reason for defining a set of concepts or distinctions in one rather than another way is their theoretical power, that is, the assistance they give to the practical deliberations of those involved in the practice. Although 'directed to action' in a less immediate way, such theorizing is no descriptive social science, however strong may be the surface resemblance. The qualitative procedures in the paradigm social sciences, economics, and human geography,

[29] Aristotle, *NE* (n 2) VI.2.1139a-1139b; *Eudemian Ethics* I.5.16–18.1216b.

involve the reconstruction of factors (such as human decisions and reasons) that lead to, and hence explain, an outcome. But the purpose of Hart's own theoretical arguments is not a mere reconstruction of the reasoning of officials; it is an attempt to understand what the practice itself is, in the light of human purposes, and with a knowledge of human needs and failings. The inquiry is thus orientated to a question ('what is law'?) that—as Hart observes from the outset—would be extremely puzzling in the context of properly scientific disciplines.

There can be no objection to Hart's own preferred way of demarcating the boundary between the legal and the non-legal: the introduction of 'primary' and 'secondary' rules.[30] This marks the outer borderline of the concept of law, one that applies to all instances of the concept whether central or qualified. But it does so only in virtue of an implicit acceptation of the terms 'primary' and 'secondary' as *relative to* the same organized human effort: the effort to realize a common end for the community. If we then add the criterion that law in the strict (central) sense aims to secure the common *good*, this is not because such efforts are historically more numerous than efforts of repression or extinction, but because this is the intelligible point of all *reasonable* human effort. Thus we arrive by a different route at Hart's conclusion, that a *minimum* point or purpose of law is to ensure our shared survival. Despite Hart's attempt to disguise the fact, this end is, as we have seen, a moral end or good for a community.

Can legal positivism yet provide grounds for postulating a descriptive starting-point? Gardner suggests that the validity of law (laws) depends on their source(s) and not their 'merits', including the merits of their sources, a proposition he calls 'LP*'.[31] The separation of these elements is easier in theory than in practice: one remembers AWB Simpson's observation that in the common law system, the legal solution of a case (that which is in accordance with the law) is frequently indistinguishable from the determination of what is the most just, reasonable or fair solution.[32] And such questions are of course questions about what is in accord with, advances or at least does not retard, the human good. Gardner's LP* entails two propositions: (1) that a norm that is morally terrible does not thereby fail to be a legal norm, and (2) that no matter how laudatory a norm is, it does not 'count as law' unless adopted by officials.[33] Let us take these in turn. The natural law theorist's position in regard to (1) is sufficiently well-known that it should not have required repetition: a norm that is announced, enforced or involved in judicial reasoning is

[30] See e.g. Matthew Kramer 'The Legal Positivism of HLA Hart' in Spaak & Mindus (n 25) 301.

[31] Gardner, *LLF* (n 4) ii.21. Those who accuse Gardner of reducing positivism to LP* should take note that he says this thesis is only one thesis of legal positivism, the only one at issue in the present argument: ibid, ii.19. Other claims, such as the separability thesis, have been carefully dropped: see Daniel Priel, 'Law as Social Construction and Conceptual Legal Theory' 38 (2019) *Law & Philosophy* 268.

[32] AWB Simpson, 'The Common Law and Legal Theory' in *Oxford Essays in Jurisprudence* (second series, OUP 1971).

[33] Gardner, *LLF* (n 4) ii.20; see also vi.161: law always has moral consequences for its subjects inasmuch as it varies their legal relationships.

of course a law in one possible sense, namely that is has been announced, enforced or involved in reasoning; but it is law only in a qualified sense because it lacks the moral authority that is part of law in the central, focal sense. Operating with an undifferentiated concept of 'counting' as a legal norm is apt to disguise these differences. The position in respect of (2) is slightly more complicated. In many ways, a natural law theorist would agree that the moral goodness of a norm is insufficient to create law; however it is precisely the justice (to take one aspect of morality) of a norm that recommends it for consideration in legal reasoning, often decisively so. It is true that judges cannot apply a norm simply because of its moral goodness. Yet they may, and often do, apply a norm as law because it conforms to a system of just principles, concepts and ideas which is more or less explicit in the preceding case law. This is not, to be clear, because legal officials 'endorse' the relevant principle, but because they *already view it as a law*, implicit in the law inchoately. They do so because the extant law is not theorizable as a body of discrete norms ('rules') or principles, but rather as grounds for decision, the character of which is therefore the reason and the rational. And it must of course thereby be added that legal officials 'endorse' such norms because and to the extent that they regard the whole legal project as directed to the human good.[34] This remains true even where the relevant conception of human good involves the infliction of misery on many, or where a highly imperfect or corrupted sense of human good is endorsed in preference to one that is even worse.[35]

This kind of positivism seeks to dissociate justice from the good, and good from civil society by reducing the good to the private realm of interests. But the individual exists in a state of self-impoverishment if she or he is not nourished by the good that gives substance to their inner life.[36] Every action of a human being is motivated by the search for some good; and every law (the product of many human actions) aims for some good: a good that may well be merely apparent rather than real, a situation which explains why any law or legal system may be evaluated by wider horizons of morality. This possibility of wider critique is the very reason positivists dissociate the content of law from its 'merits': they implicitly reduce the good that is pursued to the status of an interest, rather than a purpose.

Gardner suggests, as above, that laws are valid in terms of their content and not the 'merits' of their content. We have just seen that this distinction, though it may be apparent in some cases, is untenable as a general assumption: for the 'content' of a legal norm frequently takes shape only against assumptions of purpose, its

[34] Ibid, vi.167: one can only come to an understanding of immoral law by first experiencing or theorizing just law. See also Maria Cristina Redondo, 'Some Remarks of the Connection Between Law and Morality' 33 (2014) *Law and Philosophy* 773.

[35] For an interesting and more general discussion of the divide between Gardner and Finnis see Michelle M Dempsey, 'On Finnis's Way In' 57 (2012) *Villanova Rev* 827.

[36] See Emile Perreau-Saussine, *Alasdair MacIntyre: An Intellectual Biography* (Notre Dame University Press 2022) 5.

logical connection to other legal standards, and an indefinite range of background assumptions. (Note that Hart made clear that this dimension of legal norms applies as much to statute law as to common law.)[37] And should not the 'merit' of a legal norm consist in its harmony with other laws? But whatever the validity of Gardner's own position, he clearly believes that most laws, in the jurisdictions he knows most intimately, *have* merits, and to this extent his thoughts imply a background understanding of what is good for the human beings who created and apply this law, most often for the benefits of others rather than themselves. Even the opposite situation of a tyranny inflicting misery on its unfortunate citizens, implies a conception of human flourishing that is being perverted or stifled. To this extent, Gardner as much as any legal philosopher is tacitly concerned with the good of law.[38]

The most obvious conclusion that can be drawn from these reflections is that 'descriptive' standpoints are in fact methodologically dependent upon a prior practical standpoint. Second, it follows from this that disagreements about the 'concept' of law are in reality disagreements about the practical ends that members of a community ought to pursue together. (Hart announces this practical dimension when he asserts that higher ends than survival are 'debatable': this is an indication that the entire 'concept' of law is to be understood in such a way that its intrinsic purpose is not to enforce any particular conception of the good life.) All attempts to determine the law's essential or necessary features draw implicitly upon our familiarity with the common goods—or at least apparent goods—the pursuit of which makes such features essential or necessary. It alas does not go without saying that our conception of apparent goods is dependent upon our recognition of true moral goods: apparent goods such as the survival and flourishing of a tyrant or ruling class at the expense of others in the community, obviously qualify as 'goods' only by analogy to the principal case of survival and flourishing for all. Thus Hart's 'concept' of law is determined by his (let us say, moderate) moral scepticism, that is, his inability to distinguish between principal and peripheral ideas of good.

It is perhaps worth reiterating the purpose and aims of the present book. This book is *not* concerned with the development and defence of descriptive concepts of law, right, justice, and other ideas. Its purpose is practical: to offer guidance to officials, professionals, and citizens on the goods they ought to pursue together as a community, and the means to attain them. This involves, inevitably, some elucidation of terms such as law, right and so on. But the aim in discussing them does not

[37] Hart, *CL* (n 3) 124–35. See however Gardner, *LLF* (n 4) vi.175: morality is unlike law in its form, in numerous different ways but including its lack of systemicity. But why morality or natural law should be thought to fail to define a system is left quite unanswered. See also John Gardner, '"Law as a Leap of Faith" as Others See It' 33 (2014) *Law & Philosophy* 813. For some critical discussion around Gardner's claim that theory should not make the connection between law and morality *too contingent* see Nicole Roughan, 'The Official Point of View and the Official Claim to Authority' 38 (2018) *Oxford Journal of Legal Studies* 193 & 203ff.

[38] The same can be said of e.g. Scott Shapiro, *Legality* (Harvard University Press 2011), for we can ask the simple question: why plan?

rest with the demonstration that they depend upon, and cannot be comprehended apart from, moral 'values'. It carries them forward into consideration as the means by which certain actions are to (or can) be undertaken, and certain human goods secured. Given the book's reliance on the legal and ethical philosophies of Aquinas, Grotius, and Suarez, it may be useful to explain their continuing relevance for jurisprudential debate.

## I.4. PHILOSOPHY AND HISTORY

Medieval and early-modern philosophers were more keenly aware of the practical dimension to their inquiries, than modern writers are today. The central argument of this book draws from the eudaemonist philosophy of Aquinas, and of later Thomist philosophers such as Francisco Suarez (1548–1617) and Hugo Grotius (1583–1645). But is it not a mistake to base one's arguments on thinkers who lived in times and in circumstances so distant from our own? For example, how can such historical works contain anything of relevance for the democratic and pluralistic society of the present day?

This question conceals a number of suppositions. The first concerns the historical and cultural relativity of ideas. There are (for the relativist) no ideas that remain true throughout history and between cultures: the values relevant to today's society are different from the values that are relevant to medieval or early-modern society. Yet, the scholastic and early-modern philosophers would have responded by observing that their efforts were directed exactly to describing (i) the moral and legal values that hold in and between all nations (the *ius inter gentes*); and (ii) the values that apply to all societies at all times, irrespective of their political form (e.g. tyranny or democracy). These would include values such as peace, justice, and material prosperity: values that it is necessary for all societies to pursue, even those governed by a tyrant. The scholastic philosophers would have pointed out that a community's common good is made up partly by permanent values of this kind, and partly by those values that are chosen as the result of political agreement. Only values of this second kind are subject to historical change. Where the earlier philosophers discussed these more culturally specific norms (as in Grotius's work *De Iure Belli ac Pacis*), they were careful to observe that such matters were a particular determination of natural law, not natural law in the strict sense.

A second supposition latent in the question is that medieval and early-modern societies, as known to Aquinas and his followers, are fundamentally different from the societies we know today. The suggestion is that earlier societies were more culturally and politically homogenous than those of the present day. But there is no reason to accept this judgment. Medieval societies did not contain less disagreement or conflict than our own on matters of politics and religion, nor less awareness of opposing points of view. Political factions and religious schisms and heresies attest to the extent of disagreement in medieval societies. Furthermore, the scholastic method focused upon the existence of divergent points of view, as a means of finding out the truth.

The third supposition implied in the above question, is that the philosophical thinking of earlier eras can only be studied as a history of ideas, rather than as philosophical arguments to be seriously considered and disputed. This supposition relegates earlier thinking to the plane of history, rather than addressing it on the plane of philosophical truth. The first philosopher to take such an approach to the ethical thought of his forebears was the French translator of Grotius and Pufendorf, Jean Barbeyrac. In his introduction to the French edition of Pufendorf's *De Iure Naturae et Gentium*, he seeks to give '[a]n historical and critical account of the science of morality'. The figures of Grotius and Pufendorf are presented in a context in which their predecessors are 'found incapable of applying themselves to [moral] science with any tolerable success'.[39] Barbeyrac places Grotius and Pufendorf on the modern side of an ancient-modern divide, as the first philosophers properly to characterize the science of ethics.[40] By recognizing a watershed, Barbeyrac makes it possible to consign the entirety of pre-modern ethics to the domain of history.

Barbeyrac, and Pufendorf after him, are responsible for the creation of a new scholarly discipline: the history of moral philosophy. This innovation encourages the belief that certain philosophical ideas can only be inspected to determine their historical causes and effects, not their philosophical merit and truth. It suggests that anyone who seeks to decipher the meaning of pre-modern philosophical ideas is engaged in an historical enterprise of no direct concern to modern ideas. Yet 'modern' writers are remarkably inconsistent in their explanations of what the supposed watershed consists in: Tuck, for example, merely repeats the view of Barbeyrac, that Grotius 'broke the ice' after the long winter of ancient and medieval ethics.[41] But he adduces not one scrap of evidence for Grotius's allegedly radical departure from these earlier authorities. Alternatively, Grotius's modernity is said to consist in his recognition of the idea of subjective rights: an idea that was certainly present also in the work of Thomas Aquinas.[42]

Modern scholars must set aside the idea that the works of scholastic philosophers contain no relevant ideas for modern times. The scholastic philosophers themselves engaged in dialogue with ancient writers from whom they were separated by more than a thousand years. By considering the ancient works as living philosophical systems, they avoided two opposing tendencies to which modern writers are prone: they avoided denigrating those works as irrelevant historical footnotes, and they avoided elevating them into revered idols to be preserved in

[39] See Pufendorf, *De Iure Naturae et Gentium*, Introduction § 1.

[40] Ibid, §§ 29–31.

[41] Hugo Grotius, Richard Tuck (ed) *The Rights of War and Peace* (3 vols, Liberty Fund 2005), I.x–xi. I am grateful to Tobias Schaffner for discussion of the foregoing ideas.

[42] For references see Finnis, *NLNR* (n 2) 206–10.

their entirety from contemporary interpretation and criticism. Likewise, our inquiry must be how ancient and scholastic philosophy illuminates the practices and circumstances of the present. It must not be to 'demonstrate' the unalloyed truth of all scholastic propositions. Whether or to what extent the philosophical ideas of the scholastics do cast light upon modern conditions is shown by the account of human practices given in this book's central chapters.

## I.5. MORAL TRUTH AND KNOWLEDGE OF MORAL TRUTH

Philosophers in the tradition of Aquinas and Aristotle assert that there is moral truth; but they acknowledge that our human knowledge of that truth is imperfect, and may be severely deficient in relation to particular questions. Aristotle for example notably warns in the *Nicomachean Ethics* that the same degree of precision is not to be sought in all discussions, and that the mark of an educated person is to search only for that degree of accuracy that the nature of the subject permits.[43] In the case of political science (i.e. ethics), he goes on to say that the subject-matters with which ethics deals are so varied and diverse that they can give the *appearance* of being instituted by convention rather than by nature.

In a similar spirit, Aquinas observes a distinction between, on the one hand, eternal law, and on the other hand, divine and natural law. It is because the eternal law is known to us only to some extent (*aliqualiter*), that human beings stood in need of divine revelation.[44] But whereas the divine law reveals moral truth to us directly, natural law admits of degrees of certainty and specificity. As a consequence, our ability to determine what is practically reasonable is often limited or divested of certainty in specific cases. In Aquinas's famous example, it is reasonable and right for goods that have been entrusted to another to be returned to their owner: but only in the majority of cases (*ut in pluribus*), for in particular cases it may be damaging or ill-advised, and hence unreasonable.[45]

The questions with which we are concerned do not centre upon our ability to discern intelligible forms of goodness such as health or knowledge, but ask whether (in some particular situation) it is right or admirable to pursue certain knowledge, or prioritize one's health, and so forth. This requires us to decipher the standard by which such goods are to be commensurated: something that cannot be done in the abstract (i.e. in a thin sense), but only by including a reference to the circumstances in which one thinks and acts. Moreover, Aristotle already identifies the kind of standard we seek after: it must be that *for the sake of which* we perform our actions

43 Aristotle, *NE* (n 2) I.3.1094b.
44 Aquinas, *ST* (n 5) I-II.19.4 ad 3.
45 Ibid, I-II.94.4c.

and attain subordinate ends. This is a reference to what we may call comprehensive or all-round virtue.

Yet, even a person who is willing to live according to virtue stands in need of direction if they are to live the morally best life. Unfortunately, most manuals on ethics fail to specify what a person should do in situations where virtue seems to be compatible with numerous different courses of action. For example, should a person who is able to absorb the loss insist upon the payment of a debt by another who, though also able to cover the cost, would suffer a certain loss of position; or should he or she rather waive the debt as an act of mercy? The difficulty of such situations is made clear by considering two opposing counterfactual situations: the first, in which every person (or state) loses their desire to recover sums lent to others, as well as their intelligent grasp of justice as an end to be upheld (either for themselves or others); and the second in which every person (or state) demands the enforcement of their right against debtors in all circumstances without exception, no matter the human cost. Because neither standpoint is clearly a palatable standpoint, the needs of justice must give way to mercy on some occasions. It is the difficulty of questions such as this one that led Socrates and Plato to judge that all moral faults are intellectual faults, stemming from ignorance of moral truth.

The tradition from Aristotle to Aquinas displays an awareness of the fearsome difficulty of making right practical judgements in accordance with virtue. That is why their accounts of ethics do not simply set out the virtues, but offer detailed guidance on the operation of each virtue, explaining how each relates to the others. They do this first of all by designating some virtues as primary or cardinal virtues, literally those virtues upon whose practice the moral life hinges: justice, fortitude, prudence, temperance. Thus Aquinas advises for example that mercy is a virtuous act so long as it preserves justice.[46] This explains that mercy is perfective only when exercised reasonably, that is, with a view to the standards and precepts of its master-virtue, justice. The exercise of mercy must contribute to, rather than detract from, a peaceful and just order in the community. For example as an act of forgiveness mercy can assist a contrite wrongdoer in the task of reforming their character, by opening their heart to the possibility of good works. This understanding of mercy as an attempt to assist wrongdoers in their effort to contribute to a just order in society, recognizes the fact that a just social order is created through coordinated action, rather than by each person acting alone.

Aquinas like Aristotle remarks upon the difficulty of discerning the mean of virtue in relation to every case. For the mean and the extremes concerning actions and passions 'depend upon a variety of circumstances, such that nothing prevents something from being an extreme in relation to a virtue in one circumstance, whilst the same thing is a mean in other circumstances'.[47] This means that their

[46] Ibid, I-II.59.1 ad 3. See also I-II.66.4 ad 1 on the relation of justice and liberality.
[47] Ibid, I-II.64.1 ad 2.

advice pertaining to the demands of natural law is necessarily incomplete and at varying levels of abstraction. Furthermore, they knew that each person's disposition to attain the mean of virtue may vary due to habituation, natural disposition or shrewdness of judgment: a variation that affects moral judgment all the more considering the complex interrelationship of all the virtues.[48] They regarded the purpose of an ethical treatise as instructing willing learners in the primary or foundational moral precepts, as well as some secondary and more concrete conclusions, in order to educate the learner in how to reason correctly for themselves about moral matters. But in so doing the pupil is cast loose to face moral questions about which there is frequently not any certainty, nor apparent conclusiveness.

## I.6. NATURAL LAW

This book is a work on natural law, not theological ethics (moral theology), but it is worth pointing out early on that Aquinas's ethics, which spans the whole of the Second Part (I-II *and* II-II) of the *Summa Theologiae*, devotes only a handful of questions to natural law as part of the subject of ethics as a whole. The importance of these facts is explored in Chapter II. At present, the contrast allows me to single out the primary area of study in the present book. For it is not concerned to examine the inner life of the individual in regard to the fullest extent of their friendship with God, but instead with individuals as they relate to one another as citizens. The book's doctrines explore the social friendship (in Latin *concordia*) that exists between the members of a community, and the forms of association to which it gives rise. This focus is justified by the fact that this is a book of *jurisprudence*, not of political or moral philosophy.

The questions that provoke consideration of natural law are those that define the main questions of jurisprudence. What is the relationship of legal duties to moral truths? Can one discover the meaning and validity of those moral truths? Recognizing that positive law serves human goods, what is the nature of those goods? What is the significance of positive laws that impede or undermine such goods? Above all, how should one act, either as a public official or as a private citizen?

A theory of natural law is above all a theory of action, and of the determinants of intellect, will and passion that lead to action. Hart's division of the external and internal aspects of action proved to be an advance over the utilitarian philosophies of Bentham and Austin, which did not possess a developed action theory as such. But Hart's moral scepticism prevented him from analysing the causes of different kinds of internal attitude, such as the bad will, the innocent but erroneous conscience

[48] Ibid, I-II.66.1c; I-II.65.1c; I-II.66.2c.

and so on. More importantly, the theory lacked a means of critique in relation to various possible interior states of mind and will. The theory of natural law provides the criteria for such a standpoint, and identifies the conditions and precepts associated with virtuous (good) action.

As mentioned, I will unfold a response to these questions in Chapter II. But it is as well to set out the features of some recent theories about natural law from which this book distinguishes, indeed opposes, itself. A full presentation and response to such theories must wait for another occasion, lest this book be much too long, but here I shall set out some of their general features.

(1) Legal positivism gets its meaning from a contrast: positivism rejects natural law theory. 'But the contrast', says Finnis, 'like the rejection, is a blunder'.[49] For beyond the natural law theorist's acceptance, and the positivist's rejection, of the reality of *knowledge* of good and evil, there is 'nothing ... strategic in dispute'. George Duke writes that there is little to prevent a natural law theorist from agreeing with Gardner's form of legal positivism.[50] Similarly, Mark C Murphy claims that natural law theorists should concede the positivist separation thesis, the claim that moral reasoning is not necessarily part of legal reason.[51] And Jonathan Crowe avers that inclusive legal positivism is compatible with what Murphy has termed the 'weak' natural law thesis.[52] This capitulation fails to give due weight to the proposition that law is (necessarily) a system of practical rationality aimed at the common good, and that any system of law that is perverted away from the common good (to serve a mere section of the community or the enrichment of legal officials) is to that extent deficient and possibly (in severe cases) only a facade or pretence of law. Nor are these possibilities of equal status: as Gardner agrees, in order to understand an unjust law one must first understand just law (see Section I.3). More to the point, the system of practical rationality cannot consistently be regarded as a mere prudential pursuit of any end whatsoever, for such a mode of reasoning is nothing but a truncated and inadequate form of practical rationality, a premature breaking-off from valid and necessary considerations, openness to which would have a correcting influence on errant beliefs. Precisely because the

[49] John Finnis, 'Natural Law Theory: Its Past and Its Present' 57 (2012) *American Journal of Jurisprudence* 99. See also Dempsey (n 35) 830 (truce or methodological stalemate between Finnis's natural law theory and Gardner's positivism); Leslie Green, 'Positivism and the Inseparability Between Law and Morals' 83 (2008) *New York University L Rev* 1035; Veronica Rodriguez-Blanco & Pilar Zambrano, 'One Myth of the Classical Natural Law Theory: Reflecting on the "Thin" View of Legal Positivism' 31 (2018) *Ratio Juris* 9; David Plunkett & Daniel Wodak, 'Legal Positivism and the Real Definition of Law' (2022) 13 *Jurisprudence* 317.

[50] George Duke, 'The Weak Natural Law Thesis and the Common Good' 35 (2016) *Law and Philosophy* 502. See also 504: laws can be validated intra-systemically prior to being evaluated morally.

[51] See e.g. Mark C Murphy, 'Two Unhappy Dilemmas for Natural Law Jurisprudence' 60 (2015) *American Journal of Jurisprudence* 140.

[52] Jonathan Crowe, *Natural Law and the Nature of Law* (CUP 2019, hereafter *NLNL*) 145; see conversely Jonathan Crowe, 'Functions, Validity, and the Strong Natural Law Thesis' 10 (2019) *Jurisprudence* 237.

law is a domain of practical reason, the natural law theorist must deny the thesis that whatever emanates from a recognized source of law genuinely is a law. (See Section X.5.)

(2) Further on the topic of the relationship of natural law to positivism, Murphy contests that what he calls the 'moral thesis' (a thesis he rejects: the thesis that unreasonable laws are not to be obeyed) mistakenly moves from a question about the nature of law (validity) to one of political morality (whether unjust laws should be obeyed).[53] But it is incorrect to banish questions of obedience to a separate discipline. The law purports to be a system of rational standards for the common good. One's intellectual response to those standards is shaped by their rationality (or lack thereof), and further political standpoints are not in view. Such responses may be towards a particular legal standard, or they might be shaped by the benevolence and effectiveness (or otherwise) of the system of such standards as a whole. Such judgments are legal rather than political. But Murphy connects these questions of legal and political morality: his main contention is that the point of natural law theory is to assert a connection between the law's existence and its prescriptive force.[54] It is the 'weak' claim that a law that fails to be a rational standard for conduct is defective as law: this claim is compatible with the letter of legal positivism, for it allows that there are norms which are not derived from true principles of practical reasonableness, but which remain laws despite being defective.[55] Yet natural law theory need not capitulate to that view, or to Finnis's contention that one may speak of laws that are valid only in the lawyer's specific sense of intra-systemic validity. For it is not at all clear that *all* practically unreasonable standards remain simply defective 'as laws'; some cases of law may be so egregiously immoral that no court will or should apply them, that ought not to be considered as laws at all. The so-called German 'purity laws' are of this kind, as are 'laws' permitting invasive medical experiments on living children. For such standards are not simply failures to embody standards of reasonableness which are part of the law's innate character, but norms in opposition to and in defiance of such standards. (As to Finnis's claim regarding legal validity, I refer the reader to my discussion in Section X.6.) Murphy, unlike Finnis, more or less explicitly locates natural law theory at the question of obedience to law. Yet the classical natural law theories instead focused upon the question of the nature of law. Those authors considered the kinds and effects of law, and of the relationship between natural law and other types of law, and it is not obviously a mistake to do so. Murphy's refocusing of natural law theory on the question of obedience represents an impoverishment of natural law theory. It is, at best, only a subsidiary concern of natural law theory.[56]

[53] Mark C Murphy, *Natural Law in Jurisprudence and Politics* (CUP 2006, hereafter *NLJP*) 9.

[54] Ibid, 20.

[55] Ibid, 22. See also Crowe, *NLNL* (n 52) 137.

[56] See Finnis, *NLNR* (n 2) 351–52. Murphy may point out that his argument pertains only to 'natural law jurisprudence' (the subject of his book) and not to ethics: for which see *NLPR* (n 13). My response

(3) Another myth of natural law is highlighted by Moore, who argues that for law to be defined as serving an end, it must be an end that is served only through law.[57] Is this true? The common good of peace, for example, is served 'through law' in virtue of the precepts of the criminal law, the courts' applying legislation without challenging the will of parliament or the Constitution, their upholding valid contracts and well-founded claims of injury, and so on. But the good of peace is no less served by all members of society who act reasonably and sociably. Thus the end of peace, like a great many other ends, is not served exclusively through law, but is nonetheless an object or end of law. Moore's and (to an extent) Murphy's discussion is permeated by notions of service: yet law demands to be understood not only in terms of its function, but also its *object*.[58] The law's principal object is: justice. Thus, much legal theory must centre upon unfolding the principles and demands of justice ('principles of practical reason'), their correction where mistaken or insufficiently theorized, and their application to all members of the community. It is therefore incorrect to present natural law theory as 'descriptive' rather than 'normative': a further impoverishment.[59]

(4) As the earlier question of the common good of peace implies, it is necessary to understand what the common good refers to (though it cannot be wholly understood apart from the law's efforts to secure it). Murphy and Finnis stand at opposite ends of a single tradition. Murphy says that the common good is a complex state of affairs,[60] whereas for Finnis it is an 'ensemble of conditions'. This distinction has an important implication, for Murphy's claim that the common good is a complex state of affairs, in which the good of every individual is fully realized, is equivalent to saying that there is a situation in which every person receives their proper *due*. Finnis, by contrast, states that justice is not a situation (even hypothetical), but a constantly changing and unfolding set of sets of relationships. The latter view is to be preferred: see Section IV.3. But as Murphy says, it is necessary to show (i) that there is a common good that is truly common, and (ii) that a law is in some way related to the common good.[61] Murphy perhaps has Kant in mind when he claims that a law is a *determinatio* of a practical principle and so to act on a law is *not* merely to act in accordance with it but also *for* it.[62] This contradicts both Aristotle, for whom the law exists to encourage the recalcitrant to goodness until they no

is that these ought not to be regarded as separate subjects, but in order of explanation ethics comes first: for human goods are the object of sound law: see Chapter III.

[57] See Michael S Moore, 'Law as a Functional Kind' in Robert George (ed) *Natural Law Theories: Contemporary Essays* (OUP 1992), 223–25.

[58] Murphy, *NLJP* (n 53) 32: it is the function of law to create order; also 35: there should be harmony between all parts of the system; if certain norms are at odds with one another, this is because the *function* of the system has not been correctly described.

[59] Ibid, 26.

[60] Ibid, 61, 114.

[61] Ibid, 62.

[62] Ibid, 115.

longer require its correction,[63] and St Paul, who observes that 'Gentiles, who do not have the law, do *by nature* the things required by the law, are a law for themselves'.[64] But Aristotle, like Aquinas, would dispute the notion that laws quite generally are *determinationes*, for many legal principles and standards are more direct *conclusiones* from general principles of natural law: such as laws against murder, theft, and sexual assault.

(5) These arguments against traditional natural law theory are not the only arguments. For the very possibility of timeless universal values (i.e. that which Finnis takes as the distinctive essence of natural law theory) has come under assault by modern-day natural law theorists. It would be too strong to say that they deny moral truth, but they significantly erode it. Jonathan Crowe argues that natural law is (i) socially embodied: we reason by reflecting upon our own practices, and by contrasting others; (ii) historically extended: the best form of life changes over time; and hence (iii) natural law itself changes: as does the nature of human society from simple and small beginnings to the complex nation-states of the modern era.[65] Thus for example Crowe argues that there may be circumstances in which one ought intentionally to impede or destroy a 'basic good', for the sake of another ('greater'?) good;[66] or again, the good of sociability must be held to have altered from the close and somewhat personal relationships in the small, pre-capitalist and pre-industrial parish societies of the past, to the informal, contractual and delictual relationships of the mature nation-state.[67] Is this the case? Take the latter first: the nature of sociability does not change, but its possibilities expand. Close personal ties exist and are possible in the present just as much as they ever were (e.g. in Aristotle's time), but so are arms-length, privacy-preserving relationships (which also existed in that time), and yet others: doctor–patient, teacher–pupil, lawyer–client, priest–parishioner, prison visitor–inmate, and so on. It is, in any case, manifestly untrue that human society (the human condition) or the best form of human life, changes over time. The same set of goods—peace, justice, prosperity, safety—form the central preoccupation of human societies (including, as St Augustine reminds us, immoral ones)[68] irrespective of historical era. The same human goods (health, life, sociability, knowledge) remain the focus of pursuit at the present day as they were when mentioned by Aquinas, himself drawing upon earlier philosophical writings.

Crowe is careful to observe that it is not that human goods are valuable because they are valued, but falls short of the order of explanation of the scholastics: that

[63] Aristotle, *NE* (n 2) II.1.1103b.
[64] Romans 2:14.
[65] Crowe, *NLNL* (n 52) 6–7; see also Jonathan Crowe, 'The Idea of Small Justice' 34 (2021) *Ratio Juris* 224–43.
[66] Crowe, *NLNL* (n 52) 4–5, 9.
[67] Ibid, 28–30.
[68] Augustine, *De Civitate Dei* IV.4.

goods are valued because they are valuable.[69] Instead he adopts a different thesis: the fact that human beings value 'goods' is evidence that they are good for human beings. This proposition is true, but it is inadequate by itself to capture the sense of the term 'human good' (*bona humana*) as used in the tradition.[70] For it would support the proposition that if human beings value bathing in pigs' blood, then bathing in pigs' blood is a human good. The missing scholastic element renders the position incapable of explaining *why* human beings value the things they value; it fails to explain why certain 'goods', engaged in by multitudes of human beings over long stretches of time, are in fact false goods. To be sure, the proposition is merely that long and wide usage is only *evidence* that an object is a human good, but then a further proposition is required to explain the capacity of human beings to discover the difference between true and false goods. Admittedly, Crowe introduces a distinction between motivating reasons, which are psychological states, and normative reasons (i.e. justifying reasons), but (i) the distinction is an unhappy one if it fails to explain why some norms do not possess *motivating* force,[71] and (ii) there are many things that one is justified in doing that are nevertheless harmful for that person, such as smoking the tobacco they have just lawfully purchased. Moreover, Crowe leaves these 'normative' reasons essentially detached from the qualities of the human goods in question. Aquinas's position, by contrast, is that certain objects tend to expand or deepen human capacities to which they are fitting (*conveniens*), and are therefore potential objects of love: there is at once the power of attraction and the desire: a two-way process.[72] One can contrast this with the approach lately outlined, which culminates in a process of dialectical (reflective) equilibrium.[73] Such a process suggests, for example, that one must seek equilibrium between general universal norms (e.g. that lying is wrong), and one's particular intuitions (e.g. that one should lie to the axeman who asks whether you are harbouring his intended victim). This suggests that one must modify both one's intuitions *and* one's norms in order to arrive at equilibrium; but this contradicts the tradition's teaching e.g. on lying that it is sinful on every occasion and cannot be used as a tool for good ends.

So too is it with the other prominent writers in the natural law tradition: Jean Porter and Alasdair MacIntyre. Porter expresses doubt that there can be only one best way of living, and that general institutions such as marriage are capable of specification in numerous ways, such as polygamous or same-sex unions.[74] For the normative significance of human nature would collapse in the face of sheer variety

[69] Crowe, *NLNL* (n 52) 33; see also 53: human goods are the *product* of normative inclinations.

[70] See e.g. Francisco Suarez, *Defensio Fidei Catholicae Adversus Anglicanae Sectae*, XVIII.4.

[71] See Finnis's (rather selective) comments on Suarez, *NLNR* (n 2) 42–48.

[72] Aquinas, *ST* (n 5) I-II.51.1 & 51.2. See Peter Kwasniewski, *The Ecstasy of Love in the Thought of Thomas Aquinas* (Erasmus Publishing 2021) 177–285.

[73] Crowe, *NLNL* (n 52) 60. Unsurprisingly, Crowe adopts the idea of 'integrity' in law: 227–32.

[74] Jean Porter, *Ministers of the Law* (Eerdmans 2010, hereafter *ML*) 118, 156–57.

of cultures and practices if one single form of life were proposed.[75] It is, Porter says, impossible to resolve all moral conflicts, especially those concerned with fundamental values.[76] This may be a feature of human psychology rather than moral truth. This is perhaps why a significant figure in the natural law tradition entitled a very long book *Difficult Moral Questions*.[77] The stubbornness of the human will, or of the problem of moral truth itself, is no evidence against universal values, or of their permanence. For the new questions are essentially the old questions: Can I give up this woman and marry another; Can I take this item of another's property; Should I lie in this situation; Is it reasonable to let property at extortionate rates because the market permits it; Can I assault an enemy without provocation; May I escape harms I have committed?—and so on.

Similarly Porter argues that natural law is not in fact a set of precepts at all, but a set of capacities or principles that require to be interpreted and applied through varied human institutions.[78] (She too, then, capitulates to the sources thesis.) MacIntyre likewise laments that there *seems* to be no way to resolve difficult moral questions,[79] and thus that there is no such thing as natural rights or, by extension, human rights.[80] But it is at the level of concepts, not of ideas or precepts, that MacIntyre locates the relativity: thus he says that when we read Aristotle, for example, it is necessary to locate terms such as *arete* (excellence) in their historical and social context, or else we fail to understand their proper meaning and import. Yet, on the contrary, although if relying on Aristotle's authority we would wish to interpret Aristotle correctly, it is ultimately the substance of this interpretation, its substantive truth or falsity, that matters. And that such an interpretation is available to us is testament to the timelessness of his ideas.

But not all difficulties are difficulties of interpretation. MacIntyre further announces that it is an error to suppose that one's own morality, or the morality of one's society at a particular point in history, is applicable to all human societies at all times.[81] To which the response is: who does this supposing? Philosophical reasoning is intended to remove supposition, replacing it with clarity, honesty, and fairness. One arrives at philosophical truths in ethics precisely by examining the human condition from all directions, isolating and exploring those dimensions that are both universal and timeless, as Aquinas did with the Islamic commentators. (And indeed a flourishing ethical tradition beginning in the classical period is itself evidence of similar basic concerns, capacities, and human possibilities.)[82]

[75] Ibid, 207, 278.

[76] Ibid, 113, 118.

[77] Germain Grisez, *Difficult Moral Questions* (Fransiscan Press 1997).

[78] Porter, *ML* (n 74) 61, esp 62–64; see also Alasdair MacIntyre, *Ethics in the Conflicts of Modernity* (CUP 2016, hereafter *ECM*) 61. As I observe below, natural law is not a capacity but a set of truths *given in reason*, secure starting-points and primary precepts rather than endlessly contestable beginnings.

[79] Alasdair MacIntyre, *After Virtue* (3rd edn University of Notre Dame Press 2007) 91.

[80] Ibid, 69–70.

[81] MacIntyre, *ECM* (n 78) 114. MacIntyre himself converted to Catholicism in the early 1980s.

[82] Ibid, 79.

But are such truths subject to exceptions? MacIntyre invites us to consider two examples aimed at challenging the universality of ethical norms: (i) torture is gravely wrong, but the only way to save hundreds of people from a bomb is to torture the terrorist who planted it; (ii) killing the innocent is wrong, but the only way for a driver to avoid killing a crowd of people is intentionally to aim at another individual.[83] But any Catholic natural law theorist can dispose of these issues quickly. For he or she will point out that torture is always gravely wrong no matter what the circumstances; one may try all forms of persuasion short of torture to get the terrorist to reveal the bomb's location, but if these efforts prove unsuccessful, it is the terrorist who killed the people rather than the interrogator. And if the driver's intention in swerving is precisely *to avoid hitting the crowd*, even with the knowledge that another individual will almost certainly die, then there is nothing blameworthy in that choice.[84] The driver does not *aim at* the unfortunate individual, but if she does, full culpability attaches to the action. There is nothing in MacIntyre's worrying that precludes the existence of timeless moral norms. In short, though we should not succumb to a view of historical 'progress', nor should we subscribe to a pessimistic doubt about the ability of those under one particular political form or another to reason their way to the truth (as MacIntyre's assault first on communism, then on liberalism, frequently does).

Defenders of MacIntyre have claimed that this pessimism is qualified by a positive option for Aristotelian-Thomism as the *philosophia perennis*. Does his reading of Aristotle and St Thomas banish the consequences of his pessimism? The thrust of MacIntyre's argument is sufficiently well known: one must agree that there are divergent and mutually incompatible theories of justice in the world, because there are divergent and mutually incompatible forms of practical rationality.[85] He denies that this thesis amounts to relativism, and one can see that this is so. Divergence in theories of justice in no way implicates the suggestion that all truths are relative or culturally specific. Similarly one may posit divergence among forms of practical rationality (though this is more dubious) yet believe that there is a *possible*, yet-to-be discovered form of practical rationality from which moral truths can be securely established. But MacIntyre holds that *all* forms of practical rationality are tradition-specific. Squaring this with moral universals is much trickier, for one can ask of any reasons put forward for accepting a form of practical reason whether *they* are culturally specific. Even the natural law is, for MacIntyre, culturally determined: it consists in a law that is 'presented to human reason *by human reason*'.[86] It is no longer depicted as being presented to human reason *by an imprint*

[83] Ibid, 116.

[84] *Catechism of the Catholic Church* 1737, 1756.

[85] Alasdair MacIntyre, 'Precis' in Kelvin Knight, *The MacIntyre Reader* (Notre Dame Press 1998) 107.

[86] Alasdair MacIntyre, *Whose Justice? Which Rationality?* (Duckworth 1996, hereafter *WJWR*) 179. He does suggest that the social bonds necessary for a flourishing form of practical reason are ultimately not cultural, ethnic, or linguistic but *rational* (see 'Politics, Philosophy and the Common Good' in *The*

*of the Eternal law on the rational creature.*[87] (Note particularly that this is a form of *promulgation*, or *participation*, rather than a philosophical search.) The modern state, says MacIntyre, produces only a 'deformed and fragmented' version of the common practical rationality that constitutes the common good.[88] But given that practical rationality is a *common* rationality, how could we ever determine that our reason, collective or otherwise, is free of deformity and fragmentation? MacIntyre leaves us with a question: Aristotle or Nietzsche? But precisely as tradition-specific versions of practical rationality, one must ask: why these two, out of all possible versions? The answer cannot be, the inherent reasonableness (or unreasonableness) of the accounts, for this merely implicates *another* version to which the same questions apply. One may rephrase the question: Machiavelli (or, to take more modern examples, Hitler, Stalin, Putin, Postmodernism), or Pope Francis?

MacIntyre is not an ethical relativist. However, in the incisive words of Pierre Manent, '[Philosophical] enquiry should lead us beyond the opinions and traditions of the city, which is to say outside of the city itself. It does not seem that MacIntyre feels the slightest need or desire to accomplish this movement ... He does not dream of exiting the cave, as long as the cave is unpretentious and lit by candle light.'[89] He has been both a consistent and an inconsistent critic of liberalism: inconsistent because he moves from Marxism to Trotskyism, to socialism to Aristotelianism; consistent because the target of his attack has throughout these changes always been liberalism.

MacIntyre is correct in his belief that the moral life is not one for the individual alone, but for a community of moral thinkers collectively leading the examined life: pondering what to do, and how to act. The human being is truly a social being, and the sharing of ideas is the only way to better ideas even if it sometimes ends in catastrophic ideas. But MacIntyre's focus is much too introspective. Moral insight is not to be found by a culture looking in on itself, but by a collective effort to obtain truths which transcend all culture and cultures. It is true that Aristotle disbelieves in Plato's Forms, but he replaces them with a teleology of human nature, on the basis of which careful reflection will reveal sound truths. It is true that he believes

*MacIntyre Reader* 183. But then (for MacIntyre) forms of practical reason are on no surer ground than that of 'tradition'.

[87] See Aquinas, *ST* (n 5) I-II.90.4 ad 1; I-II.91.2c & ad 1.

[88] See Sante Maletta, 'MacIntyre and the Subversion of Natural Law' in Paul Blackledge & Kelvin Knight (eds) *Virtue and Politics* (Notre Dame University Press 2011) 190.

[89] Pierre Manent, 'Foreword' in Perreau-Saussine (n 36) xiv–xv. See MacIntyre, *WJWR* (n 86) 30: it is necessary to distinguish what is good here and now from what is really good for us here and now, and what is really good for us here and now from what is good absolutely. (MacIntyre's insistence on tradition as a final intellectual horizon for moral thinking complicates his own adherence to his intellectual hero Thomas Aquinas, for the latter cannot be said to belong either to the same linguistic or the same intellectual culture, community, or practice. Alternatively, insofar as MacIntyre holds Aquinas to be correct in the majority of his opinions, he would seem to point to moral norms that are indeed absolute and not merely *here* and *now*.)

that a central aspect of that teleology consists in humans as language-users, that is, as *essentially* communal reasoners, but it is not foregrounded in his main accounts of ethics, which centre upon undeniable human goods grounded in biological realities, and upon the appeal to what is inherently reasonable or unreasonable.[90] It is remarkable that MacIntyre, despite his most famous book's title, gives no substantial account of the virtues; instead he is eager to describe the social practices in which they appear. One is left wondering how, if virtues belong to such practices, the latter can be significantly accounted for without the former. MacIntyre has no such scruples concerning the laws of logic (and, one assumes, arithmetic).[91] They are invariant between all cultures and independent of culture (he is not an intuitionist). But if this is granted, if there are rational standards that do not depend on the cultural milieu in which they are, apparently, formed, what prevents there from being also strongly independent rational *ethical* standards?[92] Is this not an instance of Aristotle's warning not to expect the same degree of certainty in all subject-matters, and not to proceed from the realization that there *seems* to be considerable variation in cultural norms to the belief that there are no universal moral standards? ('Moral concepts change as social life changes').[93] MacIntyre suggests that 'tradition is a long argument', in itself, we might say, an artificial perfection of reason; but it is not only ethics but norms of rationality that are internal to such traditions. MacIntyre offers no definitive explanation of how diverse cultures converge upon the same such norms, nor the basis for *evaluating* those that do not.[94]

Does the burden of proof lie with the one who asserts that there are universal norms? It is not clear that it does. However we may make two observations. First, defenders of the thesis that human goods are historically changeable have made no convincing argument that human nature is changeable, historically or in other terms. Second, defenders of the thesis that moral norms are to be understood

[90] On the centrality of language, see *Politics* I.1.1253a. For an excellent discussion of MacIntyre's concept of 'good' as an 'internal relation' (i.e. non-univocal but appearing only in practices) see Perreau-Saussine (n 35) 81–82. Finnis rejects explanations based on teleology (instead focusing on moral explanation) but his own doctrine of focal meaning ought to have alerted him to the fact that the concept 'human being' has a focal meaning (a normal healthy adult, socialized and rational, in short the *spoudaios*) and various non-focal instances (the sick, the elderly, the deranged). See also International Theological Commission *In Search of a Universal Ethic* § 69: it is the *form* of human nature, not a description of it, that is required for human progress and protection of human rights.

[91] Alasdair MacIntyre, *Against the Self-Images of the Age* (University of Notre Dame Press 1978) 253.

[92] See Perreau-Saussine's summary: 'Practical reason is linked to a context: it is neither reduced to a context nor is it enclosed by a context': *Alasdair MacIntyre: An Intellectual Biography* (n 36) 97.

[93] For the strongest such statement see Alasdair MacIntyre, *A Short History of Ethics* (Routledge 1966) 1; also Alasdair MacIntyre, 'How Can We Learn What *Veritas Splendor* Has to Teach?' 58 (1994) *The Thomist* 187: '[W]e are culture-transcending rational animals'. MacIntyre veers on a course between relativism and cultural absolutism by articulating the idea of *tradition*. We could, if so motivated, draw a distinction between the 'soft' and perhaps inherently unstable form of ethical universalism championed by MacIntyre, and a 'hard' form of universalism that the present book seeks to offer. See also Alasdair MacIntyre, 'Four—or More?—Political Aristotles' in Kelvin Knight et al (eds) *Virtue Ethics and Contemporary Aristotelianism: Modernity, Conflict and Politics* (Bloomsbury 2020) 11.

[94] See Perreau-Saussine (n 36) 145.

against their historical contexts have not demonstrated the impossibility of universal moral understandings. Let us take Aristotle's defence of slavery as an example. One might argue that Aristotle's concept of *eudaemonia* must be read in light of his defence of 'natural' slavery, that is, that some people are so incapable of acting for the sake of true goods that they must be ruled by others. But whether or not Aristotle indeed meant by '*eudaemonia*' a concept inclusive of the natural slavery argument (or that such a concept was compatible with it) is of no interest philosophically. For not only is that concept detachable from the slavery argument, but it is also, when considered properly, in *opposition* to that argument. Hence the concept of *eudaemonia* can be considered purely philosophically apart from its historical associations: those associations are accidental to the concept, not part of its inherent meaning. In other words, historical components of the concept have no relevance to its philosophical meaning.

It might be thought that arguments of a different kind are required to meet the theses of Porter and MacIntyre: that (to use Porter's example), a general concept of 'marriage' can be inferred from more local and particular meanings, such as forced marriages and same-sex marriages. Now in order to regard those forms of marriage as forms of *marriage*, there must be some general concept to which they relate, in similarity to which they take on the semblance of marriage. There is in fact no historical relativity here. The priority is contrary to that proposed. If forced marriages, arranged marriages, and same-sex marriages are genuinely and legitimately forms of *marriage*, they are so not only in present times but throughout time, whether recognized or not. Nor is there ethical relativity: insofar as putative forms of 'marriage' (such as forced marriage) depart from the norm of marriage, they are not marriages *at all*. In both Eastern and Western countries, marriage has traditionally been regarded as sacred, in the Catholic Church a sacrament, and all forms of non-sacramental or non-sacred marriages are recognizable as marriages in their similarity (in form if not substance) to sacred and sacramental marriage. Indeed non-sacramental but religious marriages (such as those celebrated in the Anglican church) are given a degree of recognition by the Catholic Church, so that (for example) the parties to an Anglican marriage of twenty years' standing would not be regarded as free to marry new partners in a Catholic ceremony: for this would be regarded as an instance of adultery.

(6) The agenda set by Murphy's argument, to which I here return, is that of a choice between, or amalgamation of, the 'weak' and 'strong' theories of natural law: that law is necessarily a rational standard for conduct, and Crowe suggests that all natural law theories are versions of these theses. The strong version of the claim is that a rationally defective law is 'no law at all' (i.e. is 'invalid'), whereas the weak version, preferred by Murphy, is that such a law, when rationally defective, remains a law but is defective precisely as a law. Chapter XI will be devoted to an examination of the underpinning idea, that an unjust law is not a law, an examination which concludes that there are indeed some laws that are not laws 'at all', whereas

others are law only in a reduced sense. In fact, the idea of a 'rational' defect is wider than 'injustice' or 'moral' defect: it would include laws that, for example, are too vague or impossible to carry out: see Section X.3. But it remains to be argued that moral ideas are 'rational': an argument begun in Chapter II.2. 'Rational', of course, is not a synonym for 'moral'; there are modes of rationality that are anti-moral, as might be said of 'prudential' reasoning, in the sense that it may be prudential for someone to commit an injustice in order to gain an advantage. This kind of reasoning is precisely that denounced by Plato in the *Gorgias*. Rationality is one, but only one, determinant of law: it must additionally, as Aquinas says, be (a) explicitly laid down, (b) by one who has the wellbeing of the community at heart, (c) proportionately for the common good.[95] But this focus on the rationality of rules seems the wrong way to go about a theory of natural law. For that theory is most naturally concerned with (i) the nature of the human condition and of human flourishing, and (ii) the situation of natural law within the order of the four kinds of law discussed by Aquinas (eternal, divine, natural, and human). And it is only derivatively concerned with (iii) the means by which to bring this flourishing about, and to create the conditions necessary to sustain it. Or, in the words of Crowe, natural law theory can be 'broadly defined as the view that (1) there are certain forms of life that are intrinsically good for humans by virtue of their nature and (2) these forms of life play a fundamental role in explaining the nature and purpose of social, political and legal institutions'.[96]

(7) Another heresy is that all natural law precepts require to be interpreted in and through laws and practices of various kinds such that it is impossible to say that God wills any particular political form.[97] Crowe likewise is of the view that all human laws are a mixture of more or less *determinatio*.[98] But this thesis underrepresents the extent to which human laws and actions derive from natural law *per modo conclusio*, that is, articulate the natural law in a way that does not involve the admixture of human standards. Laws criminalizing homicides, for example, articulate (rightly or wrongly) the demands of natural law in respect of murder: but those laws, in all their fallibility, are not an *interpretation* of natural law, but an embodiment. Indeed Aquinas carefully states that not only the primary precepts, but also those secondary precepts that follow on closely from those primary precepts, are a species of *conclusio*. Correct thinking at these levels is not yet the practice of *determinatio*, and incorrect thinking is not the admixture of the natural and human but simply a failure correctly to state the relevant natural law precepts. How then can one hope to convince someone (say a far-right politician) that their moral

[95] Aquinas, *ST* (n 5) I-II.90.4c & ad 3.

[96] Crowe, *NLNL* (n 52) 2.

[97] See Porter, *ML* (n 74). There is a hint of this assumption, perhaps, in the long second part of Stuart Banner, *The Decline of Natural Law: How Americans Once Used Natural Law and Why They Stopped* (OUP 2021).

[98] Crowe, *NLNL* (n 52) 149–50.

understandings are incorrect, perhaps gravely wrong? This is a question not only of reason, of laying out correct ethics and tracing the errors, but of emotion: of re-mapping the virtues and re-educating impulses and desires. As Plato reminds us, with recalcitrant persons we must be prepared to have the argument over and over again, teasing out falsities and contradictions.[99] (This is not brainwashing, as it is essential to the process that the dialogue partner's critical faculties remain fully engaged.)

That prominent natural law theorists of the present day hold views (1)–(7), is unfortunate. They have refocused the conceptual framework of natural law theory away from much that is distinctive of the Thomist tradition. I have argued that the weak and strong natural law theses represent partial truths concerning the nature of law (certain laws are defective, some to the extent that they are not laws at all), but that neither focuses on the central issue of natural law: its role in articulating *conclusiones* of the most basic precepts of natural law, and looser but still derived *determinationes* which together bring protection and certainty to important human goods.

This book sets out a new version of an ancient tradition of natural law thinking. Today's theories dwell upon the character of ethical precepts which they take to be relative to time and place. But in fact natural law theory really concerns God's rational governance of the world, made accessible to human beings through the natural law, that is, rational standards for conduct that are distinct from both divinely revealed law (which they confirm and explain) and positive/human law (with which they are sometimes in agreement and sometimes at variance). Without this element of eternal law, one has the sheer reasonableness of the demands of natural law, but no final explanation as to why human reason is or can be an effective instrument by which to recognize those demands. Only the thesis that human reason bears God's impress, can give us the confidence to trust in reason's deepest commitments, in the possibility of 'right reason'.[100]

[99] See Plato, *Gorgias* 505d; see Sean Coyle, 'Can Natural Laws be Derived from Human Sociability?' 101 (2020) *New Blackfriars* 46.

[100] Though one should bear in mind Martin Rhonheimer's warning that natural law is not eternal law as it exists in the mind of God, but as it exists in the rational creature: in John Berkman & William Mattison III, *Searching for a Universal Ethic: Multidisciplinary, Ecumenical, and Interfaith Responses to the Catholic Natural Law Tradition* (Eerdmans 2014) 276.

# II
# NATURAL LAW

## II.1. NATURAL LAW, ETHICS, AND IDEALISM

The meaning to be given to 'natural law' throughout this book might be captured by the following initial definition: 'a set of ethical precepts that (a) are not of human making; (b) render intelligible the goodness or badness of ends towards which it is possible to direct oneself; and (c) indicate the terms (and occasions) on which such ends may be, or ought to be, pursued; resulting in (d) a theory of moral goodness'.

A theory of natural law must explain, and ultimately defend, each of these elements. The task of defending each of these elements is undertaken in the remainder of Part I of this book, and in the series of chapters in Part II. The function of the present chapter is explanative. Its subject is the nature, scope, and meaning of natural law. Its subject is not a history of every theory that can or has been called a 'natural law theory'; nevertheless a brief discussion of historical precedents is useful in refining our understanding of that term.

Use of the term 'natural law' may give rise to confusion. Both Aristotle and Plato can be said to hold a view that law is in some way natural to human beings and human society. Aristotle for example introduces the *Politics* with an argument that human beings are essentially political animals who are naturally born for life in society, and that such a life entails living under the rule of law and justice. For otherwise, the human person is 'the most depraved and savage of animals'.[1] But neither Aristotle nor Plato imagined that such law and order was by its very nature just, for they, like Plato's philosopher in the *Republic*, endured a society lived under the rule of depraved legal customs.

Perhaps the earliest image of a truly natural law theory is to be found in the Stoic political philosophy of the first century BC. There, Cicero famously stated that there is 'not one law for Rome and another for Athens, nor a law for the present and another for the future':

> Rather there is one law, encompassing all peoples and all times, that is everlasting and immutable; and there is one God who is common ruler and governor of all things, who is the creator and maker, and interpreter, of this law. One who

[1] Aristotle, *Politics* I.2.

*Natural Law and Modern Society*. Sean Coyle, Oxford University Press. © Sean Coyle 2023.
DOI: 10.1093/oso/9780192886996.003.0002

> disobeys it will be alienated from his true self, and will suffer the gravest of penalties, even though he escape all so-called punishments [in the present life].[2]

The idea of 'one law' extending across all times and places has been taken as expressing a central tenet of natural law theory. But in fact this 'one law' for all nations reflects only those elements of the common good that are essential for all communities, namely peace, justice, material prosperity, and a few other goods. Yet Cicero and his contemporaries also recognized that there are other aspects of the common good of a community that are particular to that community in virtue of its history, culture, geography, etc—for example, its rules of property ownership or the care of its cultural artefacts.

But it is only in the medieval period, in the writings of Thomas Aquinas and others, that we fully witness a doctrine of natural law that is distinct both from positive human law and from the eternal law of God (see Section II.9). Almost the first thing Aquinas says about natural law is that it is a participation of eternal law in rational creatures.[3] The separation of natural law from positive law, on the other hand, may itself encourage a false image: that of natural law as a higher, ideal form of law for the guidance (or judgment) of positive law. The image is misleading, because the demands of natural law are immanent demands, which concern fully operative duties of justice, and are not in this sense ideals.[4]

The tendency of modern moral theory to regard moral *ideas* as expressible by (or expressive of) 'moral ideals'[5] is not without a measure of justification, for there is an obvious sense in which what ought to be done is the same as what ideally should be done. If, however, moral obligation is regarded exclusively under the aspect of 'ideals', we open the door to the suggestion that all duties are 'subjective valuations' which must be opposed to present reality,[6] or else the projections of an 'ideal world' that ignores the real obstacles of recalcitrance and self-interest which characterize the real world, and thus remain 'theoretical' postulates of which the full moral force is postponed until the fulfilment of some future transformation of social conditions.[7] It is in a similar idiom that modern ethicists speak of 'moral ideology' or

[2] Cicero, *De Re Publica* III.33.

[3] See Aquinas, *Summa Theologiae* (hereafter *ST*) I-II.91.2c. His only earlier statement is that natural law is revealed to human minds by God in the form of natural knowledge: see I-II.90.4 ad 1.

[4] Alasdair MacIntyre clearly believes that morality cannot be disconnected from politics in the way suggested in this section: see Emile Perreau-Saussine, *Alasdair MacIntyre: An Intellectual Biography* (Notre Dame University Press 2022) 57. The ultimate horizons for morality would therefore appear to be *intersubjective* despite his later Thomism.

[5] See for example the essays collected in Edward Harcourt (ed), *Morality, Reflection and Ideology* (Clarendon Press 2000); also Nigel E Simmonds, *Law as a Moral Idea* (Oxford University Press 2007).

[6] See e.g. Eric Voeglin, *Order & History* III (University of Missouri Press 1957), 83; also John Finnis, 'Law as Idea, Ideal and Duty', 1 (2010) *Jurisprudence*, 246n (the danger of treating justice as 'just another value-judgment'); MacIntyre (n 6) 89.

[7] See e.g. John Rawls's notion of a full compliance society in John Rawls, *A Theory of Justice*, revised ed. (Belknap Press 1999), 244–45; Jean Porter, *Justice as a Virtue* (Eerdmans 2016) 12; cf Timothy Macklem, 'The Ideal and the Everyday' 10 (2019) *Jurisprudence* 532.

'political morality': a manner of speaking which can, if used unreflectively, suggest morality as a servant of political outlooks, not an independent perspective for the disinterested judgment of all outlooks. Plato and Aristotle were not ideologues in this sense, indulging subjective valuations in opposition to reality. Their efforts to describe the character of the just state were part of an objective inquiry into the nature of reality. For them, and for their successors in the western intellectual tradition, the subject of ethics was not simply a battleground of competing ideologies. As such, 'ideals' (considered as aspirational guides to excellent conduct) must be contrasted with the *duties* that structure moral action in the present (considered as baselines or demands).[8]

So too we must reject Alasdair MacIntyre's view that moral philosophy requires a sociology for its concepts and that ideas must be capable of expression through social contexts.[9] This is a central theme of MacIntrye's but it is quite mistaken. The fact that virtues such as justice and charity are not identifiable with any one way of living does not suggest that the expressions we give to them form part of a rootless and shifting meaning. Nor need we endorse Plato's suggestion that if justice requires a city, it requires an ideal (and thus unreal) city. We instead require Aristotle's doctrine of the mean: many of our culture-bound and time-bound expressions of justice capture something true of that concept, but each one lacks something or is wrong in part. True justice is the mean between the thousand ways in which our expressions of justice distort that value; this mean is definitely a political and not merely ethical concept, but the standard to which we have recourse is defined neither by time nor society. The task of philosophy is thus (i) to try to focus upon that mean, to determine ever more closely its true demands, (ii) to compare our varied understandings of that value to that archetype, and (iii) to apply the archetype as faithfully as possible to contemporary moral and political problems.

An inquiry into ethics and natural law is therefore an investigation neither of ideology nor of the history of moral standpoints. Such a history could only be a history of *ideas*, not of morality as such.[10] The precepts of morality do not have historical origins; their 'validity' is timeless, and does not come into being at some specific point in history.[11] Their 'origins' lie in reason, not in history. At the same time, however, moral precepts must have some extended historical presence, for they make demands upon human action, and not only upon human thought.

[8] On the distinction between a 'morality of aspiration' and a 'morality of duty', see Lon Fuller, *The Morality of Law* (revised ed, Yale University Press 1969) ch 1. At the same time, one should avoid any suggestion of a categorical division of moral thinking into 'deontology', 'eudaemonism', 'virtue ethics', and so on.

[9] Alasdair MacIntyre, *After Virtue* (3rd edn University of Notre Dame Press 2007) 23. For a similar view see Jean Porter, *Ministers of the Law* (Eerdmans 2010, hereafter *ML*) 249, 111 ('what is morally good in one society may be morally odious in another, and disputes last for centuries'); see Section I.6.

[10] See John Finnis, *Natural Law & Natural Rights* (2nd edn OUP 2011, hereafter *NLNR*) 24.

[11] Cf Jonathan Crowe, 'Is Natural Law Timeless?' 33 (2021) *Bond L Rev* 1–10; see also John Tasioulas, 'Human Rights, Legitimacy, and International Law' 58 (2013) *American Journal of Jurisprudence* 3.

Again, an account of the penetration of such precepts into the history of human action could be written; but it is not the purpose of this book to supply such a history.

Thus as against those theories examined in Section I.6, we must reject the historical view of conceptual authenticity, according to which one cannot understand ethical ideas except in relation to the contextual pressures of society and history in which they were advanced, used, reinterpreted, or rejected. It is the present usage; it is the precise sense in which the concept is being used, its substance, that makes it authentic. But the human condition through history is not unremittingly dark or evil. One should expect, therefore, that one's present ethical concepts hold true not only of present human society (or what is good in it) but also of, for example, classical or medieval society (or what is good in it). The only way in which to confute the historicized view of natural law(s) is to demonstrate that some time-independent natural laws exist: that certain ethical values are independent of political and ideological standpoints past and present. This will be the focus of Chapter III. The task is urgent: for no less a body than the International Theological Commission recently stated, in its 'new look at the natural law', that the variability of natural law precepts as one descends into the detail of moral problems accounts for the variation between the ethical foundation of different states, or that of different historical epochs.[12] Natural law lies at the bedrock of all societies, including democratic states, but does not unalloyedly favour any one of them.[13] Perhaps this proposition explains Alf Ross's well-known expression that 'Like a *harlot*, natural law is at the disposal of everyone. The ideology does not exist that cannot be defended by an appeal to the law of nature'.[14] Say rather that natural law is a *teacher* to all societies, encouraging what is good in them whilst castigating the bad.

Now it may appear as if the distinction of ethics and natural law from ideological outlooks were straightforward. For we may wonder whether the distinction consists simply in the depth and scope of practical inquiry: between those efforts of investigation and introspection which assume some basic moral ideas as axioms,[15] or which place a higher value upon the systematic coherence of belief than on critical doubt, and those introspective and investigative efforts which are all-things-considered. Certainly, it is a characteristic trait of ideologies, and of 'belief systems', to close off further inquiry before all critical investigations have been made that could be made, and all questions carefully and honestly considered which could be raised against one's foundational beliefs or ideals. But we should hesitate to draw the distinction this way, out of a real fear that human minds that are finite in capacity and subject to other time-consuming demands inevitably fall considerably

[12] International Theological Commission, *In Search of a Universal Ethic: A New Look at the Natural Law* (2004) § 53.

[13] Porter, *ML* (n 9) 207.

[14] Alf Ross, *On Law and Justice* (Stevens & Sons 1958) 261.

[15] I am of course using 'moral' here in a generic sense.

short of being able to consider 'all things' which may be of relevance.[16] A distinction between ideology and true moral principle can be sustained only if it can be shown that there are secure, rationally incontestable starting-points for practical reason concerning the good, and a fully rational means of discerning, from those starting-points, the terms upon which the good should be pursued.

## II.2. REASON AND NATURE

'Whatsoever is the object of any man's appetite or desire', Hobbes says, 'that is it which he for his part calls *good*: and the object of his hate and aversion, *evil*... For these words of good, evil, and contemptible are ever used in relation to the person who uses them: there being nothing simply and absolutely so, nor any common rule of good and evil to be taken from the nature of the objects themselves'.[17] This statement is not the first statement of the position known as philosophical scepticism (forms of which were known to Aristotle and Plato), but it is one that any theory of natural law must oppose. It must do so in two senses: both as regards the statement that nothing is either good or bad (as the Scholastics would say), *simpliciter*; and as regards the statement that the rule of good and evil is not 'taken from the nature of the objects themselves'. The latter issue is the one that falls to be discussed in this section; the former will be taken up below, Section II.5.

Hobbes's statement does not go on to explain what is meant by taking something 'from the nature of the objects', but it presumably sits in the same frame of discourse as statements of Aristotle and Plato when they claimed that ethical truths exist by nature rather than by convention, and when they asked the question whether it is (by nature) better to suffer injustice than to perpetrate it.[18] The picture of rational choosing offered by Hobbes is one based on more-or-less spontaneous, or primitive (in the sense of original) desire: one experiences a desire—for example to know something—and *then* one's reason gets to work by seeking out the means by which the desire can be satisfied. But Hobbes offers no fully realized account of how such desires arise, and of what makes them intelligible. He recognizes only three sources of motivation that are possessed by human beings 'by nature': competition, diffidence, and glory.[19] But none of these can properly be defended as a human *good* (even 'glory' is a time-wasting search for 'trifles'), and Hobbes is explicitly aware of how strange it is that 'nature' is responsible for such destructive passions. He fails to see that, in order to desire something, it must first be intelligible as a good, for the answer to the perfectly reasonable question 'Why do you desire ...?'

[16] Hence James I's reported words, 'Reason is too large. Find me a precedent and I will accept it.' Quoted (inter alia) in Christopher Hill, *The Century of Revolution 1603–1714* (Routledge 1961), 177.

[17] Hobbes, *Leviathan* VI.

[18] Aristotle, *Nicomachean Ethics* (hereafter *NE*) I.3.1094b; Plato, *Gorgias* 469b-c; also *Republic* I.

[19] Hobbes, *Leviathan* XIII.

is always finally '… Because it is good …'. For if something is agreeable, desirable, or wanted, it is because the object of want or desire must possess certain properties that make it agreeable, desirable, or wanted: for 'it is rather the case that we desire something because we conceive it to be good, than that we believe a thing to be good because we desire it'.[20]

This Aristotelian saying could equally well be said by replacing 'desire' with 'choice'. The reality of free choice is that it exists in relation to opportunities to pursue certain goods; choice cannot meaningfully be made between objects the goodness of which is a matter of one's very choosing, or which absolutely cannot be resisted. The central question of ethics—and Aristotle's central question in the *Nicomachean Ethics*—is therefore the identification of what is, truly, good. A full discussion of goodness must be deferred to Section II.5. But Aristotle's overall position is reasonably clear in treating goods or goodness as kinds of completeness or fulfilment, or (to the extent that goods are obtained through deliberate effort) as the activities that are characteristic of the human being.[21] Hence they are (if genuinely fulfilling) ways and modes of perfecting human nature.[22]

There is such a thing as human nature; and there is such a thing as that which fulfils human nature. Indeed a number of things fulfil human nature. It is possible to understand that human nature is fulfillable by certain things even if one does not (at some stage) grasp, as a matter of practical reason, what is good to have or to pursue. This is perhaps the meaning to be given to Finnis's remark that goods and speculative conclusions are 'non-inferentially' relatable. An understanding of human flourishing can guide a person to the right kind of objects, even the right kind of practical judgment, without being inferential (a state of affairs quite common in those who undergo psychotherapy) all without cancelling human freedom, the utter inderivability of one good from another. For a certain freedom exists in relation to the pursuit of goods that fulfil human nature. Aquinas speaks of the generic character of the human being as an animal, as well as the specific nature of every person.[23] Many kinds of good or goodness fulfil human nature generically, such as the desire for life or the raising of children; others fulfil human nature more specifically, such as the desire for knowledge or to live in peaceful society with others. Furthermore, a particular person may be attracted more to some of these sources of goodness, and to others scarcely at all. Human freedom exists at this particular level, in the choice and realization of certain kinds of good rather than others. But the mind is *not* free to disregard altogether the goodness of certain goods, nor to accept as 'good' things that are really bad. Does this seem strange? By analogy, the human mind is not free to regard as false certain mathematical truths

[20] Aristotle, *Metaphysics* XII.7.1072a; Aquinas, *ST* (n 3) I.5.6 & I-II.8.1.

[21] Aristotle, *NE* (n 18) I.7.1097a-b.

[22] For some discussion see Mark C Murphy, *Natural Law & Practical Rationality* (CUP 2001) 16–21.

[23] Aquinas, *ST* (n 3) I-II.10.1 ad 3; I-II.46.5c; I-II.95.2 ad 3.

(even if the computation is beyond the resources of the particular mind of one who denies the truth); so to regard a mathematical proposition is not an instance of freedom but of error. Likewise there can be no coherent denial of the goods of human nature, nor a preference for bad over good as such; such denials and preferences are instead for evils under the guise of goods: false goods.[24]

How are such human goods identified? Aquinas's answer is that human good is what accords with rational nature (*secundum naturam*):[25] an explanation also given by the natural law theorists of the second scholastic. And what is in accord with rational nature is determined by one's characteristic human inclinations.[26] Yet it is in fact impossible, as Aristotle reminds us, for ethical deliberation to be put onto a 'scientific' footing, by a kind of anthropology. Nor is it possible to begin from 'settled' ideas of good and bad. Such ideas 'involve much difference of opinion and uncertainty'.[27] But although ethical knowledge can therefore take on the appearance of mere convention, nevertheless a closer inspection proves that a significant number of ethical precepts obtain prior to and independently of, conventional standards (see especially Chapter III).

To speak of 'human inclinations' is not to speak of subjective preferences or spontaneous eruptions of desire. The relevant inclinations are those identifiable as belonging (*conveniens*) to the human animal as such: not only the inclination to self-preservation and the begetting of offspring, but to knowledge about one's situation or circumstances, to peaceful coexistence with others, and to act in accord with reason.[28] Everyone experiences such inclinations. They are part of what it means to be a human being. Aquinas's repeated references to natural inclinations are no mere 'speculative appendage' to his discussion of natural law,[29] nor are they simple 'urges'.[30] They are the 'imprint' of eternal law on the human being, the impulsion of the Holy Spirit that inclines the human being to act freely and for the right ends.[31] It is 'from [the eternal law's] being imprinted on them that [human beings] *derive* their respective inclinations to their proper acts and ends'.[32] Such 'extrinsic' inclinations are to be distinguished from 'interior' inclinations that are mere desires (*passiones*) or habits, which are 'natural' only by extension (as we speak of certain habits as 'second nature').[33] But at least some of these desires—if they are disordered or depraved—may also stem from an extrinsic source: fallen

[24] Ibid, I-II.8.1c.

[25] Ibid, I-II.31.7c.

[26] Ibid, I.80.1 ad 3.

[27] Aristotle, *NE* (n 18) I.3.1094b; also I.5.1095b-1096a; V.7.1134b; *Eudemean Ethics* I.5.1215b-1236a.

[28] Aquinas, *ST* (n 3) I-II.94.3c.

[29] See Finnis, *NLNR* (n 10) 36.

[30] Ibid, 91.

[31] Aquinas, *Summa Contra Gentiles* (hereafter *SCG*) IV.22.5–6.

[32] Aquinas, *ST* I-II.91.2c; see also *De Virtutibus Cardinalibus* II.

[33] Aquinas, *Commentary on Aristotle's Nicomachean Ethics* (hereafter *Eth*) III.17.9; Aquinas, *ST* (n 3) I-II.8.1c. See for discussion SB Cunningham, 'Inclination in Aquinas' PhD thesis CUA 2013, 107.

angels or the Devil.[34] Thus human beings are, or can be, inclined to evil ends, by turning away from their proper end.

Aquinas's use of the term 'rational nature' (and not merely 'rationality') highlights the importance of nature in the explanation of ethics: it is possible exactly in this way that natural inclinations can be spoken of as corresponding to 'natural laws'. Reason does not impose order upon human nature, but discovers an order that is already present. The orderliness of nature is matched by the inward order of reason, the capacity of each person to bring order and coherence to their reasoning about how to act. Neither kind of order depends on conventional ordering (except perhaps linguistic conventions, which can be substituted one for another without greatly affecting the structure of one's thinking), except insofar as depraved customs are likely to erode one's own natural inner understandings, leading to vicious dispositions.[35] But there is, lying below and prior to such customary influences, a form of 'natural knowledge', regarded by all the major natural law philosophers as impervious to personal and collective depravity.

Natural knowledge of this kind is not inborn, 'written on the heart' of each person. It is the result of experience of one's natural inclinations and of their fulfilment: that is, of the ends towards which they are directed. Such knowledge remains 'natural' even when it must be taught, for example to infants who lack sufficient life-experience, or the ability to frame for themselves their inclinations and needs. Nevertheless our efforts to apprehend human goods are without foundation unless we have some experience of the relevant inclinations.

Even so, the difficulty of attaining a correct view of good or goodness (and of evil) is considerable. Some forms of goodness (such as the value of life itself, or of social relationships) are easily established. Others are less easily understood: such as the virtue of truth where lies are intended to serve the good by saving a life.[36] Questions of taste are also problematic. Many such questions pertain to the way in which universal human goods are related to the specific nature of individuals, so that (for example) one person may have a stronger taste for friendship whereas another may give priority to scholarly research. But in some cases, a person may develop a 'taste' for evil, not as such but through a degenerate relationship to genuine goods: for example, a taste for cruelty is a degenerate taste for power (the opportunity to take a hand in ordering human affairs for the better). The extension of 'matters of taste' into the description or justification of evil acts helps to disguise the wrongness of certain actions even (or especially) to the wrongdoer. In such cases, the distinction between good and bad taste discloses—or ought to disclose—the human goods that are in question, which evil acts subvert. But correct reasoning

[34] Aquinas, *ST* (n3) I-II.90 prologue; compare with Thomas's treatment of extrinsic inclinations that are unnatural: II-II.157.1. (See Cunningham (n 33) 105.)

[35] Aquinas, *ST* (n 3) I-II.94.4c.

[36] Though this would amount only to a venial sin: Aquinas, *De Malo* VII.1c; Aquinas, *ST* (n 3) II-II.69.1 arg 2.

about such matters may overcome ignorance or powerful non-rational or emotional forces only in the wise, as both Aristotle and Aquinas warn.[37]

It might then be asked, how do we tell the genuine from the apparently but not really good? One initial answer to this question is offered by Aquinas, building on a suggestion of Aristotle's. In the *Nicomachean Ethics*, Aristotle notes that the pleasures of unthinking people tend to conflict with one another because they are not noble or pleasurable in their very nature;[38] hence they do not endure, whereas the noble goods of the wise are permanent and not subject to change.[39] To this Aquinas adds that it is unity among goods that confirms the true goodness of well-chosen ends, including the harmony between one's inclinations and the coherence of practical reason.[40] For, the goods that we pursue ought not to be sought randomly and unthinkingly (*passim*) but with intelligence according to reason's order.[41] Nor should the pursuit of one good undo another, in the way that, say, the actions of a drug-addict undo his or her bodily health. In so saying, we are dealing not with mere opportunity costs of pursuing one good rather than another, but of destructive interference between apparent goods.[42] It is indeed the mark of merely apparent goods that the good obtained from them is radically inadequate, and so not to be preferred in any circumstances to genuine goods.

For the moment, let us say that a good act is one that is aimed towards an end that is practically rational versus ends that are practically irrational. To avoid misunderstanding, it should be said that practical irrationality is not the sheer irrationality of the person whose acts are deranged or inexplicable. An act that is practically irrational is one that may well (and usually will) arise from instrumental reasoning from a desire to its fulfilment. To this extent practically irrational acts demonstrate a measure of rationality. Their *irrationality* consists in their being opposed to genuine, noble, or morally upright goods (*bona honesta*) that are properly fulfilling, and which are consistent with one another. For rationality and coherence go intrinsically together, whereas irrationality struggles to achieve more than the superficial appearance of consistency. Such inconsistency is ever the price for prioritizing desire or emotion above reason (itself a choice or decision).

No doubt all of these matters require further explanation, and Aquinas's response does not, without more, provide a solution to the question. But Aquinas points the way to a full explanation, an explanation that will be set out in the remaining chapters of this book.

[37] Aristotle, *NE* (n 18) I.3.1095a; Aquinas, *ST* (n 3) I-II.94.2c. Even apparent (false) goods contain some measure of good: *ST* I-II.19.1 ad 1.

[38] Aristotle, *NE* (n 18) I.8.1099a.

[39] Ibid, I.10.1100b.

[40] Aquinas, *ST* (n 3) I-II.3.5c.

[41] Ibid, II-II.96.4 ad 1. For other examples, see ibid, I-II.3.8c, I.12.8 ad 4; Aquinas, *De Veritate* (hereafter *De Ver*) 16.1 ad 14.

[42] See e.g. Aquinas, *ST* (n 3) II-II.101.4c. Perhaps an example would be the incompatibility of excess food and drink with profligate sexual performance.

## II.3. PRECEPTS AND STARTING-POINTS

It is impossible to place ethics on a par with scientific investigations; it is impossible to *derive* ethical norms from scientific, or social-scientific, data as such. The point of comparison between ethics and science is not to suggest that ethical reasoning can only hope to be vague or indeterminate, but to indicate that the mind's capacities are not here ordered, as in the natural sciences, to discerning purely 'external' things to which its ratiocinations are to be accommodated (preferably successfully). We immediately go wrong in our thinking, then, if the purpose of ethics is conceived as a principally speculative inquiry.[43] The activity of the practical intellect is from its inception concerned with some transformation of existing circumstances.

Nevertheless, it was apparent to Thomas Aquinas (and his successors in the natural law tradition) that the faculty of practical reason is in certain important respects akin to the operation of the speculative intellect. For both proceed on the basis of indemonstrable principles that are presupposed in all subsequent judgments. Speculative reasoning has its own set of indemonstrable principles, beginning with the principle of contradiction (that something cannot both have being and non-being at the same instant), and including certain axioms of logic and mathematics. The primary principle is indemonstrable because human powers do not extend as far as the ability to verify this principle for all atoms in the universe; but the principle is not less secure or less readily believable for that.

In the case of practical reasoning, which is concerned with action (i.e. with changing existing conditions in some way), the foundational precept is concerned not with being, but with good, or equivalently, the end of action. For if a person bestirs themselves to move, in order to bring about some end through the exertion of their labour (or their deliberate omission), it can only be because they consider the end to be, on some level and in some way, good. Hence the original precept of practical reasoning is that of aiming for or securing the good, and avoiding whatever is contrary to the good.[44] This precept is again indemonstrable, but nonetheless intelligible. There is no reason why such a precept should be considered more in need of demonstration than that concerning being, or indeed any of the foundational principles of physics or mathematics. Instead, their validity is presupposed in any discussion we care to have within the relevant field of discourse.

The relevant confirmation of the soundness of practical reason's original precept is discovered by understanding the requisite processes of intellect and will in aiming for some end: processes that are scarcely intelligible unless the end is desired *as good*, even if (in reality) the goodness is only surface appearance. To put the point in the form of a precept, we can say that: insofar as an agent, when

[43] See GEM Anscombe, *Intention* (Blackwell 1957), 57.

[44] For all, see Aquinas, *ST* (n 3) I-II.94.2c.

reasoning practically (i.e. deliberating about ends), (a) elects to activate his or her mental and, perhaps, physical powers and capacities in pursuit of some end and (b) continues consciously and deliberately (wilfully) to exert those powers for the sake of securing that end, (c) in conditions where other alternatives, including the alternative of inaction, are available, then the agent's actions are explicable (just as rational actions) only on the following terms:

(i) that the agent conceives of that end to be, in some way, *good* so as to be not only abstractly worthy of hypothetical pursuit, but actually to be pursued/obtained; and
(ii) that all of those things that are contrary to that end, or that impede or reduce its fulfilment, are understood as things to be avoided, and conceived as *bad(s)* or *evil(s)*.

This statement of the original practical precept requires some elaboration of course, and its connection to other precepts of ethics must be explained: an explanation that will be given in later sections of this book. For the moment, let us deal with one immediate objection.

The assumption in recent times has been that each individual has their own conception of what is good for them, and that all so-called human goods are contentious and debatable.[45] This is no doubt a considerable exaggeration of the level of disagreement. Despite his own belief that human goods are 'complex and debatable', HLA Hart was not prevented from pointing to a 'modest but important minimum' of goods that derive from an undeniable human good: survival.[46] Such human goods include the suppression and punishment of criminality, regulation of property, civil responsibility for wrongs, and the operation of commutative justice: in other words, those aspects of the common good that are essential for all communities.

None of this is to call into question the fact that, as Hart says, a great many forms of goodness are complex and debatable. Indeed, as we have seen, Aquinas emphasized that there are precepts both of speculative and practical reason that are known only to the learned and the wise.[47] But such contestable ideas are not found among the most general precepts (*principia communia*) of natural law, which can by no means be eliminated in their entirety (*in universali*) from the human heart.[48] They form part of every human being's 'natural knowledge', their comprehension of their natural inclinations. These most generic, primary precepts are those that

[45] To be sure, a number of modern writers dispute this in whole or in part. See e.g. John Tasioulas, *Cambridge Companion to the Philosophy of Law* (CUP 2020) ch 6.
[46] HLA Hart, *The Concept of Law* (3rd edn OUP 2012, hereafter *CL*) 193.
[47] Aquinas, *ST* (n 3) I-II.94.2c; also I-II.100.1c: some matters are known only after careful consideration (*subtiliori consideratione*).
[48] Ibid, I-II.94.6c.

identify forms of good (such as the raising of children or living peacefully in society) as *human goods*, that is, as good not only for the one reasoning but all others, insofar as they share in one's humanity, and so as giving rise to duties of justice in regard to those others. Nevertheless there are various secondary precepts, that are moral implications of the primary, first-order precepts, and even the most fundamental of these can be obscured or subverted by individuals or entire communities through bad customs or malignant practices.[49] It may turn out that certain individuals who are in possession of these precepts nonetheless fail to apply them properly in concrete circumstances, much as it is possible for a mathematician to commit an error in calculation from known general theorems.

The primary precepts of natural law are not axiomatic assumptions, however, but known truths confirmed in thought and action. This has produced some confusion amongst critics of natural law theory. Hart, for example, complains that natural law philosophers derive from statements of regularly recurring events a claim that a certain thing *ought* to happen.[50] But this is a confusion of Hart's, not of natural law theorists, all of whom would point out that properly good actions recur all too infrequently, and that the most recurrent actions are not a reliable guide to what ought to be done. Still, Hart is correct to the extent that practical reason relies at least in part on speculative truths, for one's desire for some human good, say friendship, is possible only because 'human nature' is as it is, so that the order of precepts of natural law follows the order of natural human inclinations:[51] an order that is discoverable by reason, but is not the result of reason imposing its norms upon a mere chaos: see Section II.5.

The effect of Hart's suggestion that all desires are 'contingent' is to push all values into the sphere of negotiation, that is, of politics. This makes him blind to levels of reasoning that are by nature pre-political. The primary first-order precepts are not political in nature; they are instead the fundamental ground upon which all reasonable political philosophies or outlooks are built. As a result, natural law precepts leave open a wide space to matters pertaining to social ordering and political arrangements. So long as certain precepts are observed (including but not limited to those of justice), human societies can accommodate, in Grotius's words, a wide variety of different ways of living.[52]

The extent to which norms of natural law guide and underpin human political communities will be discussed in Section V.2. But it is worth observing that the most basic values of promoting life and the development of natural capacities and potential (aptly termed 'human flourishing') are at the heart even of terrible forms of political order, though they may be radically curtailed or repressed, or given

[49] Ibid, I-II.94.6c, I-II.94.4c (even theft can have a superficial appearance of good among certain peoples).

[50] Hart, *CL* (n 46) 191.

[51] Aquinas, *ST* (n 3) I-II.94.2c.

[52] See Grotius, *De Iure Belli ac Pacis* (hereafter *DIBP*) I.3.8.2; *De Iure Praedae Commentarius*, 229.

effect only in a highly partial or delinquent way, or withheld from specific groups of citizens. Recognition of this in no way blunted the ability of natural law philosophers to point to depraved forms of human community, and to condemn repressive regimes.

## II.4. THESE PRECEPTS ARE KNOWN TO EVERY PERSON

The primary precepts of natural law, thus described, are known to all persons: they are universal,[53] and are incapable of being wiped out by the effects of depraved habits or customs. These most general precepts are knowable without reference to any other principle (*per se nota*), and hence are not among those things that are knowable only to the learned.[54] Any person who possesses the appropriate linguistic and intellectual development is capable of grasping such truths, provided that they have a modicum of life-experience in pursuing ends or wants under their own action: see Section II.7(b).

There are, however, levels of depth to which one can know these precepts. Anyone can grasp that the destruction of life is, other things being equal, an evil to be avoided. But it is evident that people can have different understandings of the reference of this precept, based upon the relative extent of their self-knowledge as a being. One who subscribes to the idea that the human being is a conjunction of body and soul, and that personhood is a matter of soul (or spirit) rather than bodily reality, will likely see no difficulty in performing abortions of early-stage foetuses or assisting the death of one who is bodily alive but no longer able to exercise their mental powers. A correct understanding of the human organism, as a unity of body and soul, is required in order to understand the range and reference of the primary precepts; and such knowledge is not possessed by every person.[55]

Some natural law theorists, MacIntyre among them, have disputed the classical picture. Permit me therefore a little further discussion of some themes introduced in Section II.1. MacIntyre says that the primary precepts remain the same in every society and culture, but the socially and culturally embodied forms through which they receive expression do not.[56] This would appear to admit of the existence of universals, but MacIntyre undercuts this reading by saying that the facts of moral disagreement are incompatible with the idea of principles that all persons *know*.[57] But the question is not of actual knowledge (though Aquinas does indeed believe that certain norms are implicitly part of every person's reason), but of *knowability*. Take mathematics: all dimensions and fields of mathematics are *knowable*, but are

[53] Aquinas, *ST* (n 3) I-II.93.2c.
[54] Ibid, I-II.94.2c; I-II.91.2 ad 2.
[55] Ibid, I.75.4c; I.90.4c & ad 1.
[56] Alasdair MacIntyre, *Ethics and Politics: Selected Essays vol 2* (CUP 2006) 65.
[57] Ibid, 68–69. For a stronger statement of this view see MacIntyre (n 6) 393.

only very partially *known*. Yet everything we know about mathematics would lead us to believe that it is objective and universal.[58] Likewise, but to a greater extent, the primary norms of natural law (and many secondary ones) are *knowable* to all, and everything we know about natural law and ethics should lead us to believe that its norms are objective and universal. Notice in this respect the two metaphors of light in the text of John 1:9: 'The Word of God is the *true light* that *enlightens* many persons.' Christian natural law theorists would additionally speak of the Holy Spirit's gifts to human beings, each of which is a form of *knowledge*: love, joy, peace, patience, kindness, goodness, faithfulness, gentleness, and self-control.[59] The preceding two sentences assert more than can be achieved by philosophy alone. But MacIntyre himself recognizes the universalizing aspect of ethics when he observes that to say that someone's life is impoverished because they lack a virtue, is to say that *anyone's* life would be impoverished if they lacked that virtue.[60] Likewise, and as Aristotle affirms, no one can flourish alone: the possibilities of human wellbeing and of virtue are impossible if human beings act alone and without a tolerably just *polis*. My acts of virtue depend upon your acts of virtue and those of others lest we become, in the medieval figure, wolf to our fellow human beings. Similarly, my wellbeing ('happiness') depends upon your happiness and that of others, for it is all but impossible to formulate and pursue ends of any description without a community which knows something of justice, fairness, legality, and internal tranquillity. Indeed something of the sort seems to have been on Aquinas's mind at *ST* I-II.14.3c,[61] where he observes that reasoning on one's own is more apt to errors, whereas the counsel of many brings more certainty. These are the lessons of even the one who is frequently depicted as the arch-anti-Aristotelian, Hobbes, whose litany of cultural prizes which are impossible in the 'natural condition' is the antithesis of the opening sentences of Aristotle's *Ethics*.[62] This duality of self and community allows us to understand how a person simultaneously acts for their own good and for the common good in all their morally good actions.

## II.5. GOODNESS AND MORAL GOODNESS

Thus far, we have been using the terms 'good' and 'evil' in relatively broad terms. But what exactly is the character of the good? When Aquinas tells us that 'the good is to be done and pursued, and the bad is to be avoided',[63] is this a reference to

[58] The exceptions are the views of those described as 'realists' and 'intuitionists', but I will not enter into that discussion here.

[59] Gal 5:22–23. See *In Search of a Universal Ethic* (n 12) § 3.

[60] Alasdair MacIntyre, *Ethics in the Conflicts of Modernity* (CUP 2016) 218, 51, 53. See also Alasdair MacIntyre, *Dependent Rational Animals* (Duckworth 1999) 140.

[61] See also Aquinas, *ST* (n 3) I-II.14.1 ad 3.

[62] See Hobbes, *Leviathan* XIII.

[63] Aquinas, (n 3) *ST* I-II.94.2c.

*moral* good and evil, or only to natural good and evil?[64] The context here is one of action: of *doing* good, in the practical sense, 'pursuit' referring to efforts not yet complete or fully achieved. But it is nevertheless necessary to ask how this precept relates to the goods that Aquinas names specifically in the same Article, namely, preservation of life, begetting and raising offspring, having knowledge of God, and living peacefully in society.

Goods such as 'life' and 'sociability' are moral goods in the classical (i.e. broad) sense, because to act against any of them as such is morally wrong. But it is also clear that to comprehend something as a moral good in the strict sense, one must first identify it as good simply. In this sense, it is because life is good that the destruction of life is a morally wrong act. Consequently it is necessary to ask what is the basis of (our grasp of) moral goodness? Post-Reformation writers such as Locke, drawing upon the authors of the second scholastic period, said that our grasp of moral realities depends upon our grasp of God as a law-maker.[65] And indeed our comprehension of our natural inclinations involves the realization that God is the final end towards which all such inclinations tend. But in fact there must be natural, as well as supernatural, grounds of moral belief. Part of our natural grounds of belief is the realization that so-called 'natural goods'—such as life — are good not only for the one reasoning, but also for all others shaped by the same natural inclinations and the same bodily and spiritual realities. Yet while this explains that we must act morally towards others, it does not explain why we ought not to act against forms of goodness even in ourselves: why is it immoral to extinguish one's own life?

One possible answer is as follows: preservation of one's life is in one sense a natural, rather than a moral, good because it is an end that we share with all animals (indeed all living substances), which do not possess moral agency; whereas goods that are particular to human beings (e.g. sociability, fidelity, candour, charity, the obligation to educate oneself...) are intrinsically moral because of their value and importance in a distinctively human form of common life. A Social Darwinist could perhaps support these views. It would not then be difficult to regard goods such as life as imbued with moral implications because of the distinctively human way in which they are pursued: animals are not, but human beings are, provident *for themselves*, as well as being subject to Divine providence.[66] But for a Social Darwinist, morality is reduced to the status of an instrument, a means of securing the continuation of the species.

The idea that the human being is provident for itself, and thus capable of choice—of pursuing certain inclinations rather than others—is not opposed to the very idea of 'natural inclination' (cf reflex) but in fact explains the distinction between

[64] See e.g. Germain Grisez, 'The First Principle of Practical Reason' (1965) *Natural Law Forum* 168; Finnis, *NLNR* (n 10) 59, 76n.

[65] See John Locke, *Essays on the Law of Nature*, W von Leyden (ed) (Clarendon Press 2002), Essay IV.

[66] Aquinas, *ST* (n 3) I-II.91.2c; see also I-II.1.2c and especially I-II.31.7.

inclinations that are in conformity with, and those that are contrary to, human nature. Thus the part of human nature that is rational must work in conjunction with sensate nature (desires, urges, etc); reason is not the governor of an unruly 'lower' nature, but is part of a single unified organism. The precepts of natural law reflect the natural hierarchy of natural human inclinations. As mentioned earlier, Aquinas and other natural law theorists thus refer to 'rational nature' rather than 'reason' alone. Applying reason to one's situation, it is apparent that acts intended to extinguish one's life are always morally wrong because they run counter to a fundamental natural inclination to be provident for oneself, which is connected to God's providence. Of course the person who attempts, or commits, suicide is perfectly clear about the goodness and value of life, which is why the decision to end one's life is such a momentous and serious matter. Reasons to end one's life are more often to do with extremes of mental or physical anguish from which the person can see no other escape. Such a decision is made either because the person cannot see any way of improving their situation, and thus regards him- or herself as no longer provident, or else because they lack the moral virtue of fortitude which is a firm persistence in the face of danger.[67] The human being acts more naturally when acting according to the 'form' of human nature than when acting only in accord with bodily or material substance.[68] Thus, Hart's assumption that human beings value their lives only contingently, and could perhaps as well be members of a 'suicide organisation', radically mistakes the character of human natural inclinations, and the human goods that are their end.[69]

Knowledge of one's nature as an animal and as a rational human being is important if one is to act morally and avoid evil. Aquinas clearly says:

> Love of oneself is common to all, in one sense; in another way it is proper to the good, and in a third way it is proper to the wicked ... [B]oth the good and the wicked love themselves inasmuch as they desire to preserve themselves ... Now the good regard their rational nature (or the interior human being) as being the most significant thing in them ... whereas the wicked esteem sensate and corporeal nature (or the exterior human being). Because they [the wicked] do not have a correct knowledge of themselves, they do not love themselves correctly but only love what they think themselves to be. But the good know themselves correctly, and thus correctly love themselves.[70]

[67] Ibid, II-II.166.2 ad 3.

[68] Aquinas, *De Malo* (n 36) V.5c.

[69] Hart, *CL* (n 46) 192.

[70] Aquinas, *ST* (n 3) II-II.25.7c. See also Aquinas, *De Malo* (n 36) IV.2 ad 1. It is worth noting that proper knowledge (*studiositas*) is not to be mistaken for the vice of curiosity by which a person inordinately pursues knowledge of trivial matters or of the private business of others: see Aquinas, *ST* (n 3) II-II.167.1c; cf Finnis, *NLNR* 60 (knowledge of 'some gossipy rumour'). In contrast to *NLNR*, Aquinas notes that a person should seek only knowledge that fills a person rather than that which drains away: i.e. is specifically *not good*: Aquinas, *Commentary on the Gospel of John* § 849; Aquinas, *ST* (n 3) II-II.166–67.

Let us recall that these teachings on natural law have in recent times been rejected in favour of an account which views the primary precepts of natural law as being concerned with non-moral goods.[71] It has been suggested, for example by Finnis (after Grisez), that one can develop from the primary precept (to do and pursue good, and avoid evil) a set of non-moral 'basic' goods (e.g. life, knowledge, sociability, play) in relation to which, exactly because such goods are not virtuous goods, it matters relatively little to our ultimate end or good exactly in which order, combination or selection such goods are sought or realized.[72] Accordingly, the life devoted to knowledge above all else is not inherently superior or inferior to the life lived for friendship. Virtue can be cultivated in many different modes of life: most obviously in a life of service to others, but *equally* through (for example) the scholar's contribution to the common good by publishing important works. Thus natural law calls for a life of virtuous goodness, no matter which primary ('basic') goods are otherwise pursued. But Aquinas in fact sets out a hierarchy among the primary precepts of natural law, ranging from the most fundamental (protection of life) to those which call out to human excellences (sociability, peace, intellectual relationship to God).[73] These steps are necessary in order to create a reasonable, distinctively human existence. They impose ever more demanding moral duties on the person (e.g. childcare, forming relationships, avoiding contention, contemplating fundamental questions about life), but at the same time, ever richer and more rewarding goods. The injunction to pursue good and avoid evil is therefore not merely a prudential, but also a moral, precept.

The idea that natural law's primary precept ('the good is to be done') is concerned with non-moral goods or excellences constitutes a fundamental misreading of Aquinas's intentions in his main article on natural law (*ST* I-II.94.2c). For whilst natural law precepts correspond to natural human inclinations (to preserve one's life, etc), they are not identical with those inclinations. In each case, it is not the inclination, but rather what is to be done '*by reason* of this inclination', that 'belongs to natural law'; for example 'whatever is a means of preserving life, and of defending against threats to one's life'. Thus, the relevant range of precepts of natural law would include being at peace with others, creation of and participation in mutual forbearances, defence of the weak against the violence of the strong, suppression of criminality, and so forth. In the case of the inclination to raise offspring, the relevant precepts would naturally include raising the child not as the property or object of the parents but as an independent being, one to be given the treasury of knowledge and wisdom of parents and teachers, including moral training. The

[71] See e.g. Porter, *ML* (n 9) 91.

[72] See especially Finnis, *NLNR* (n 10) 59, 76n. But cf Aquinas, *ST* (n 3) I.60.1 ad 3. For a position in all respects the same as that of Finnis and Grisez see Robert P George, *In Defence of Natural Law* (OUP 2001) Part One.

[73] For some discussion see Mark C Murphy *Natural Law & Practical Rationality* (CUP 2001, hereafter *NLPR*) 190–98.

inclination to live in society is naturally associated with precepts of sociability, harmony (not unison) with others, forgiveness for trespasses, reasonable assistance at need, civility, compassion, and other such precepts.[74] Thus, on the most natural reading of these passages, Aquinas's natural law theory is best understood as being grounded in biological realities and corresponding needs, however it is identical not with those needs but with the precepts that arise from them.

Those who assert that the primary precept of natural law is non-moral also point to Aquinas's acknowledgement that even very evil people reason in accord with the primary precept; for they still aim at something they consider to be good, even if in reality it is a false good. Two responses are possible here. (1) Evil people certainly do reason in accord with the primary precept when they pursue a wide range of goods—such as preserving their own existence, achieving peaceful and cooperative relationships with (at least some) others, exercising their own agency, and so on. (2) But they reason in accord with the precept only in a defective way when they pursue false goods. Aquinas is very clear about this: sinners make use of the primary precept only in a defective *way*, they do not use it perfectly yet in relation to a defective *good*.[75] Such a good is knowable as defective because, despite its delectability or usefulness, it is radically inadequate and incompatible with the ultimate end of a properly good (*eudaemon*) life. For Aquinas can hardly be interpreted as saying that *false* goods should be done and pursued.

A further point should also be considered: in the doing and pursuit of even very evil ends, there is some measure of true self-knowledge on the part of the actor. For even without practical wisdom (*prudentia*) a person still has the very basic stirrings towards the good supplied by *synderesis*[76] (see Section II.9). It remains possible for such an actor to choose against these promptings, by acceding to vices the attraction of which is much greater in that actor; but those vices can never completely obliterate the promptings towards the good and the reasonable. Indeed for both the virtuous and non-virtuous person, goods are valued simultaneously (i) for themselves and (ii) as constituents of *eudaemonia*.[77]

What, then, of human goods the value of which may seem to depend on the use to which they are put? For knowledge can be gained for bad use (knowledge of how to construct a terrorist bomb) as well as for good use (the bomb disposal expert's ability to render such devices safe).

A little clear thinking will dispel any misconceptions. Neither Aquinas nor Aristotle, nor any of the subsequent commentators in the Scholastic tradition made the error of assuming that, if X is a (human) good, then all instances of X must be pursued. In medieval terminology, a good such as knowledge can be good

[74] Some of these values are at work in e.g. Nigel E Simmonds, 'Constitutional Rights, Civility and Artifice' 78 (2019) *Cambridge Law Journal* 175.

[75] See Aquinas, *De Caritate* 12 arg 16; See also 12c; *ST* (n 3) I-II.8.1c.

[76] See Alasdair MacIntyre, *Whose Justice? Which Rationality?* (Duckworth 1988) 196.

[77] Cf ibid 108.

*per se* but bad *per accidens*. It was well understood that one and the same good (e.g. knowledge) could be viewed under various aspects: as something useful or of strategic value, or as the delightful knowledge of a secret, or yet as something that is appropriate and edifying to know for its own sake or for the sake of a noble end. The bomb-maker's knowledge of how to construct an explosive device is comprised of scientific principles of physics and of chemical reactions, which in other circumstances it is good to know, not only for practical reasons (bomb disposal, or any of a great variety of practical purposes) but for their own sake. Other examples would include the scientific knowledge of human (or even animal) cloning, or attempts artificially to extend the natural human lifespan. These kinds of knowledge are dangerous even if they lead to incidental medical advances, for such advances are not the end sought but mere side effects. Nor are these kinds of knowledge good in themselves and only bad *per accidens*, for the knowledge of how to clone a human being is achieved only through the execution of the practical steps that are required to bring the relevant end about. Not all knowledge is good, therefore, but must be related to and in harmony with the broader ends of human life (as per Aristotle's principle above),[78] even perhaps as an alternative to simply wasting one's time . . .

Furthermore, Scholastic philosophers were aware that certain human goods are not strictly speaking ends at which it is possible for a human being deliberately to aim. They fall outside the domain of practical reason as such. Thus whereas I can choose to obtain some piece of knowledge, I cannot choose to pursue a life free of disease. The Scholastics (and indeed Aquinas)[79] therefore understood the term 'moral' (*moralis*) to refer to the whole domain of practical reason, that is, the field in which one deliberates about, chooses, and pursues ends. Under this assumption, health is a non-moral good to the extent that I cannot (for example) control or 'aim at' my body's ability to defend against disease; though I may of course be able to deliberate and choose to pursue actions that are likely to lower the risk of contracting disease, and to this extent health—the prudent care for one's physical and mental wellbeing—*is* a 'moral good', that is, a moral *choice* in the classic sense.

Moreover one must not disregard Aquinas's teaching that the central case of goodness (not the most frequent case!) applies to the *perfection* of being,[80] that is to say, the qualities of being that advance a person towards their ultimate end and good. The fact is that, in order to make any sense of the distinction between good and bad, the notion of 'good' must eventually meet with some restriction if it is to be opposed to bad ends and choices. Even at the very abstract level of first principles, 'good' cannot be equated with 'end' to the extent that there are no 'bad' ends.

In the case of the absolutely first precept and the first-order precepts of natural law generally, then, the references to 'good' and 'evil' are in the primary (focal)

[78] The idea that truths harmonise with one another, whereas falsehoods contradict: see Section II.2.

[79] Aquinas, *ST* (n 3) I-II.6.7 ad 3, I-II.10.3, I-II.20.1–3, I-II.56.3; Aquinas, *SCG* (n 31) III.114.

[80] See Aquinas, *ST* (n 3) I.5.3, I.5.1 ad 1, I.48.1, I.60.3, II-II.64.5; *De Virt* 2.

sense to moral good(s) and evil(s); they range over apparent goods and non-moral goods only in a secondary, extended sense.

The reader may notice that I provide no finite list of basic goods; such lists strike me as unproductive in ethical theory, and fail to explain the manifold but often mysterious ways in which a person acts for some combination of the basic goods:[81] how for example the combination can reduce down to one act, and the basis on which truly incommensurable goods are presented hierarchically to the reason.[82] This of course is a question for all ethical theories, and will receive some explanation in Chapter III. For the present, I would like to quote Rhonheimer's observation that reason without natural inclinations would be like shining a light into the void.[83] It would similarly derail judgments about the fittingness and order (*convenientia*) of goods to nature.

## II.6. NATURAL LAW AND POSITIVE LAW

The subject of natural law's relationship to positive law will be taken up in more detail in Part III of this book, but a few preliminary observations should be made. The dominant perceptions of natural law at the present day, in the writings of legal positivists, cling onto some distorted and misleading notions which were never a part of the Aristotelian–Thomist tradition. Perhaps the most persistent of these concerns the view that natural law theory is a theory of the validity of positive law: if understood as a theory that holds 'that by its very nature, law successfully reconciles the duality of morality and power', rather than regarding the relationship as one of contingencies and 'political realities', this image is false.[84] The origins of these views are perhaps traceable to the writings of late-seventeenth and early-eighteenth century jurists who wrote in a way that could suggest that the common law is articulative or declaratory of natural rights, such that positive laws that contradict such rights are of no validity. Something of the declaratory view can be glimpsed, for example, in the Introduction to Blackstone's *Commentaries*, one of the main sources of Bentham's attack on natural rights doctrines. But natural law theories were never, in reality, declaratory theories of this kind.

Yet for natural law theorists, natural law is indeed a source of positive law: a source from which principles of justice can be drawn apart from, and sometimes in despite of, positive laws. But this does not mean that natural law theory 'successfully

[81] See e.g. John Finnis, 'Reflections and Responses' in John Keown & Robert George (eds) *Reason Morality and Law* (OUP 2013); see also Murphy, *NLPR* (n 73) ch 3.

[82] Martin Rhonheimer, 'Natural Law as a Work of Reason' (2010) *American Journal of Jurisprudence* 70.

[83] Ibid, 69.

[84] Joseph Raz, *Between Authority and Interpretation* (OUP 2009), 1; quoted also by Finnis, *NLNR* (n 10) 437. See also JG Moore, 'Hart, Radbruch and the Necessary Connection Between Law and Morals' 39 (2020) *Law & Philosophy* 691.

reconciles the duality of morality and power'. It certainly sets *de iure* limits with which parliaments or legislatures and the courts *ought* to comply, but it does not set or favour any particular constitutional forms to which a legal order must conform. Natural law does indeed provide standards against which positive laws can be adjudged valid or invalid. But it is important to note that natural law theory does not claim to render all unjust laws as invalid. So for example, the advice of Aquinas to a citizen faced with loss due to an unjust law is to obey it, if failure to do so would cause scandal or disturbance in the community.[85] The relationship between natural law and positive law is complex; but one should not fly to the opposite extreme of holding that natural law theory carefully distinguishes between positivists' (systematic) sense of conformity to whatever criteria of 'recognition' happen to obtain in a given community, and validity in the unrestricted, primary sense, which is a moral sense.[86] On the contrary, natural law passes judgment on positive law, even where the judgment is that the positive law is valid.

Thus some care must be taken in representing natural law as a moral critique of positive law, lest this lead to further misconceptions. For positivists could easily take away the message that, in this case, their positivism is correct: the law is one thing, with its own systemic principles of validity, and morality is another. Indeed, even Finnis argues that the attempt to contrast natural law theory and legal positivism is a 'blunder' and that beyond the question of moral scepticism, 'there is really nothing strategic in dispute'.[87] But, whilst we must guard against the caricatures of the declaratory theory, it must be remembered that the law is (above all) a domain of *practical reason*. So although there are standpoints, interpretations and systems of reasoning that are more or less insulated in their intentions from the broader, unrestrictive flow of ethical deliberation, nevertheless they are never wholly thus insulated, either in substance or in form. The question of substance was explored only in limited ways, mostly by common lawyers who objected to the positivist (mis)characterization of common law 'rules'. It was therefore necessary for an historian of the common law to remind modern positivists that '[i]n the common law system no very clear distinction exists between saying that a particular solution to a problem is in accordance with the law, and saying that it is the rational, or fair, or just solution'.[88] Nor was the substance of Finnis's theory historically one held by any of the major natural law theorists. Such theorists believed (i) that positive law is only one type of law that applies to human beings as part of their official legal systems, and (ii) that positive law can be classified as valid/invalid

[85] Aquinas, *ST* (n 3) I-II.96.4c.
[86] John Finnis, 'Natural Law Theory: Its Past and Its Present' 57 (2012) *American Journal of Jurisprudence* 99.
[87] Ibid.
[88] AWB Simpson, 'The Common Law and Legal Theory' in Simpson (ed) *Oxford Essays in Jurisprudence* (2nd series, Clarendon Press 1973) 79.

on the basis of (a) the extent of its conformity to natural law, and (b) whether non-compliance with it would bring about greater injustices.

In the twentieth century, considerable attention was devoted to the question of form, that is, the extent to which 'legal forms' (in Lon Fuller's expression) serve an inherently moral purpose. These reflections, which Fuller later acknowledged to have been foreshadowed in Aquinas, are aptly celebrated for the light they bring to the issue (which positivists take to be the central concern of natural law) of modes of governance that so radically depart from the central, primary case of the law's *substantive* aim, of securing freedom, peace, and justice, that the subverted forms are no longer recognizable as 'law'. This of course is very far from the doctrine of *lex iniusta non est lex* that positivists have falsely identified as a tenet of natural law theory. But it is a reminder that Thomist natural law theory is not confined *in extreme cases* to acknowledging the existence of legal obligations, whilst maintaining that they are not binding *in foro interno*. It is able to distinguish between legal obligations that are unjust, to which some form of obedience is nevertheless necessary, and those pseudo-obligations that are really nothing but subjection through intimidation or violence of individuals to organised state power. In the latter case, some laws that are 'valid' in the positivist sense are adjudged by natural law theorists as intrinsically lacking the essential characteristics of law. (See Section X.3.)

## II.7. THE PURPOSES OF NATURAL LAW THEORY

In recent years, natural law theory has been dominated by the 'natural law thesis': that 'a norm or system of norms that does not serve as a rational standard for conduct is necessarily invalid or defective as law'.[89] This names the thesis, with little adjustment, demarcated by Finnis as a subsidiary thesis of natural law theory. It is a thesis not concerned with the relationship of law and morality, but with the issue of the law's rationality.[90] Jonathan Crowe, taking inspiration from Murphy, points out that it is possible for a law to be morally defective yet sufficiently rational to require compliance, or morally sound yet insufficiently rational to require compliance.[91] He admits that the distinction between the two ideas of morality and rationality is 'subtle', but it rather leads back to the positivist concern with the relationship of law and morality: the central reason for Hart's employment of that distinction was to avoid the dangers in holding that anything immoral is not legally binding, and anything that is moral must be a legally binding matter. Crowe's

[89] Jonathan Crowe, 'Clarifying the Natural Law Thesis' 37 (2012) *Australian Journal of Legal Philosophy* 159.

[90] Jonathan Crowe, *Natural Law and the Nature of Law* (CUP 2019, hereafter *NLNL*) 147; see Mark C Murphy, *Natural Law in Jurisprudence and Politics* (CUP 2006) 3.

[91] Crowe, *NLNL* (n 90).

example does not advance matters: imagine that a legal norm is more rational than existing social norms but 'fails to gain salience as a matter of social practice'.[92] The example is ambiguous: is the law simply stricter, so that one's observance of it puts one behind those who flout it? Or is it morally more excellent in that it fosters the good of individuals and the community? In any event, from the most reasonable perspective one should actually obey the morally more excellent law. The example Crowe seems to have in mind is one in which the question of obedience is a political rather than legal matter. And the only example that comes to mind of this kind is the widespread non-compliance with the community charge which the UK Government sought to introduce in 1989. But here the law was in fact far from morally more excellent, and the riots that followed its introduction were not riots against a moral law. Crowe suggests a different example: that of a morally sound norm that is procedurally defective. But a procedurally defective norm may again be of various kinds, yet in many cases a procedurally defective law is not a law, or is not a law with which it is possible to comply: see Section X.3. Of his remaining example, that one ought to obey even unjust laws, is straightforwardly a well-known thesis of natural law theory, serving to connect writers who endorse the 'natural law thesis' with the mainstream of that tradition.

Consider the very different, but classical, argument that human positive law is law only insofar as it captures moral duties between citizens, and is not law insofar as it stands against those duties. The most important phrase is 'insofar as': for we can distinguish law in the primary, focal sense, in contrast to law in a deficient, degraded, or reduced sense. Some who oppose this doctrine do so because they point to a range of possible 'attitudes' that citizens may have towards the law (from the criminal and enemy of the state to the fully committed model citizen), and insist that all of these are relevant to an understanding of law. And they further insist that the distinction between good and bad law (rather than good law and non-law) assists the deliberations of those who must decide which of these attitudes to possess. These are the purposes of legal positivism. But they are blunt purposes so long as the terms 'focal' and 'non-focal' are remain unspecified. For when they are fully unpacked, these terms accurately express the range of values that the positivists seek to account for, and to this extent natural law theory is indeed, as Crowe suggests, concerned with the question of whether a given law is a rational standard for conduct. But both Crowe and positivists overlook other purposes and theses of natural law theory, prominently including the positive law's articulation of natural law. What, then, are the purposes of natural law theory? Why hold a theory of natural law in addition to one of ethics? There are a number of reasons, explored below.

[92] Ibid, 147n.

## (a) Inclination and revelation

In the first place, the purpose served by natural law is to explain why individuals or entire peoples who never possessed the revealed truths of Scripture, nonetheless possessed a knowledge of virtue. The pagan philosophers, above all Aristotle and Plato, wrote and taught extensively on ethics, in ways which obviously anticipate Aquinas's own discussions, without the benefit of revelation. As a eudaemonist, Aquinas believes that there are not several ultimate ends but only one. All other goods except the one ultimate end are subordinate to that end, and remain good only insofar as they do not point away from the end.[93] It was therefore necessary to explain how pagan philosophers like Aristotle could possess moral *truths* even though they possessed an incorrect idea of the ultimate end.[94]

The explanation required two things: it needed to call attention to the goodness *per se* of the things which derive their goodness from the final end, that is, that they are genuine goods even when taken on their own terms—Aquinas does this in his treatise on ultimate end, and to a lesser extent in the treatise on law,[95] and it needed to show how pagans could have knowledge of these truths whilst not possessing revealed truth. Aquinas says that there is an exterior (as well as an internal) principle by which God moves human beings to the good, consisting partly in direction through law (*instruit per legem*) and partly in the assistance of Grace.[96] He does this by endowing human beings (and other creatures) with characteristic inclinations by which they naturally incline to their good, and—in the case of human beings—by 'placing [a law, i.e. the natural law] into human minds so that it can be naturally apprehended'.[97] Irrational creatures are subject to eternal law entirely only through the operation of their natural instincts, whereas human beings participate in eternal law in a free and self-directed way. Aristotle and Plato could therefore be participants in this way, without having the benefit of divine revelation.

## (b) Universal truths and modes of life

The second purpose fulfilled by natural law is to explain the relationship between universal moral truth and the many different ways of living in a community seen across the world. The teachings of Christ and the Apostles in the New Testament concern the duties to love God and to love one's neighbours, but they

[93] See Aquinas, *ST* (n 3) I-II.1.5c, I-II.1.6c, I-II.13.3 ad 2, I-II.90.2c; also I-II.12.3 ad 2.

[94] See Mary Keys's illuminating discussion of the ways in which Aquinas adds to Aristotle's ethics, so that Thomist natural law is not a mere copy of Aristotle: *Aquinas, Aristotle and the Promise of the Common Good* (CUP 2006) 23 & 67.

[95] Aquinas, *ST* (n 3) e.g. I-II.1.5c, I-II.5.3–4, I-II.94.2c.

[96] Ibid, I-II.90, preamble, but see also especially I-II.63.1c & 63.2 ad 2.

[97] Ibid, I-II.90.4 ad 1.

do not prescribe any single form of political society as morally the most excellent. Indeed the Gospels are careful to separate the duties owed to God from those owed to Caesar. Because the perfection of earthly communities is not our last end, moral theology does not specify particular political forms as objects of work to be achieved in this life.

Natural law—that is, that part of ethics which deals with our natural ends—pertains to matters of virtuous actions ordered to the common good of the community.[98] First among all the matters essential to the common good is peace (*pax*), consisting of sociable or benevolent dispositions to one's fellow citizens (*harmonia, concordia*),[99] tranquillity of internal order within the state (*temporalis tranquillitas civitatis*), as well as justice (*iustum*) and prosperity (*affluentia*).[100] The attainment of these ends also demands the good of a stable legal order,[101] proportionate government, and impartiality in settling disputes,[102] enforcement of bargains and remuneration for work, as well as the restraint of negligent acts (*reparatio*)[103] and punishment of crimes (*retributio*).[104] These are necessary goods for all societies. Without them, there is anarchy rather than society.

One aspect of these goods (or equivalently, ends) looks towards the responsibilities of state government in securing them for its citizens. I will deal with this in subsection (c) on unjust law, below. But it would be a mistake to regard them only as duties of the state, for they are also responsibilities for every citizen. All except the most wicked can agree on the need to maintain peaceful and just relations with one's fellow citizens (e.g. to refrain from inflammatory behaviour, to perform one's contractual duties, render what is owed etc). Even people with highly divergent views of our ultimate end can agree on them, just because they are not the ultimate end but subordinate ends that must be obtained no matter what one's individual conception of the ultimate end. Of course for the Christian, it is necessary not only to deal justly with one's neighbours but also to love them: to exhibit not only the virtue of *iustitia*, but also of *caritas*. But natural law—the part of ethics divested of moral theology—also indicates why it is important to acquire *iustitia*. Most societies (unless they are deficient or very wicked) place citizens under positive *legal* duties of justice, like the observance of contracts, payment of taxes, compensation for harms etc. It is possible for the citizen to perform these duties very unwillingly, under protest or through enforcement by the courts. Such a person will not have happiness, because they act against their will, and in spite of their inmost wishes. It

[98] Ibid, I-II.90.2c; I-II.94.2c.

[99] See references in John Finnis, *Aquinas: Moral, Political and Legal Theory* (OUP 1998, hereafter *Aquinas*) 85n & 227n; Aquinas, *ST* (n 3) I-II.94.2c.

[100] Aquinas, *ST* (n 3) I-II.96.3, I-II.98.1, II-II.77.4; *De Regno* I.2–3.

[101] Aquinas, *ST* (n 3) I-II.90.4, I-II.95.3, I-II.96.1.

[102] Ibid, I-II.97.2, I-II.97.4, & II-II.120.1.

[103] Ibid, II-II.62.4, I-II.105.2 ad 9.

[104] Ibid, I-II.87.6.

was clear even to pagan philosophers therefore that a prerequisite for a happy life was the acquisition of virtuous habits.

Modern legal philosophers are aware that effective legal order needs the voluntary compliance of a majority of citizens, who willingly carry out their legal duties of justice. Likewise, Aquinas noted the natural propensity of human beings to a life of peace in society.[105] But although all societies are founded upon natural law precepts of (at least minimal) peace and justice, there will be a wide variety in the specific laws and arrangements by which each society pursues these ends. He acknowledges this for example in the *De Regno*, '[i]t is clear that a people can only be considered as one community (*multitudine*) if they are under the same laws and the same government'.[106] Some requirements of justice, such as the restraint of murder and fraud, or (on the other hand) acts of restitution or compensation, are directly spelled out in the positive state law of all communities, and this common content was hence often referred to in classic writings as the law of peoples (*ius gentium*) or the European common (civil) law (*ius commune*). But many other matters concerning, for example, the specification of punishments, the method of determining title to property rights, distribution of risk in contract, the form of pleading in litigation, the constitutional powers of the prime minister or the president, and so forth, are all more or less matters for reasonable determination (*determinatio*) rather than direct derivation from moral precepts.[107] In the most extreme cases, on morally indifferent matters, positive state laws derive all of their authority from their enactment (e.g. whether to drive on the right or the left).[108]

This leads naturally on to the third purpose that is served by natural law, its explanation of when one should obey even an unjust enactment of the positive state law.

## (c) Unjust enactments

Natural law explains the basis for obeying positive state law: since positive law is enacted for the common good of the community (*bonum civile*), it would be unjust to prioritize one's private interests over one's legal duties of justice. The basis of positive state law consists in the necessity to safeguard the common good. Private individuals do not possess the detachment or the coercive authority that is necessary to protect or oversee the common good. Only a ruling authority (*princeps*)

[105] Ibid, I-II.94.2c; he agrees with Aristotle on the naturally political nature of human beings: I-II.96.2c, I-II.99.2c, II-II.26.3c, II-II.29.1 ad 1, II-II.47.10 ad 2, II-II58.8c, II-II.58.9 ad 3.

[106] *De Regno* I.15.106 (Aquinas adds, 'being directed to live well'); see also *De Reg* I.2.10–15; Aquinas, *ST* (n 3) I-II.95.4c.

[107] See esp Aquinas, *ST* (n 3) I-II.104.1c: they get their force not from reason alone but (also) from their enactment (*non habeant vim obligandi ex sola ratio sed ex institutione*).

[108] Ibid, I-II.95.2c.

governing through law can hope to secure internal order (*ordo per legem*) and the organized defence of the community against external enemies.[109] All political forms of government are rooted in these necessities, which explain the citizen's obligation to obey the state laws.

But natural law also gives reasons for disobedience to positive law, which are not political reasons. Political disagreement is not a sufficient basis for disobeying the positive law of the state. A person may conscientiously disobey the law only in the gravest circumstances: as we have already seen, Aquinas remarks that it may often be necessary to give up one's just rights by offering obedience to an unjust law, in order to avoid disrupting civil order (*turbatio*) or occasioning public outcry (*scandalum*).[110] This is a reference to unjust provisions that might exist in a legal system which commands willing obedience due to being orientated to the common good. The loss to one's rights does not permit illegal resistance which endangers the broader common goods of peace, harmony, concord, and the like.

But there are other kinds of unjust law which are not conscientiously binding. An example would be a law which commands the performance of an immoral act: such as murder, or taking more than one's proper share. In this case, one denies another's right as a means of unjustly extending one's own right. Acts of this kind damage an important component of the common good: justice (the virtue which ensures that each person will obtain what is theirs by right).

This encompasses another possibility, that is, laws that are unjustly burdensome to all subjects, or laws that are orientated away from the common good of the community and instead towards the lawgiver. Laws of these kinds are not conscientiously binding upon the subject, because their enactment exceeds the authority of the lawgiver (*ultra vires*), which is restricted to upholding the common good.[111] They are not 'licitly laws' but more like violent interventions.[112] They retain a resemblance to law in the proper sense only because they carry out a similar social function, but in a perverted way: they direct citizens to goodness, though not simply but relative to that particular government.[113]

## (d) Articulation of values

Natural law theory concerns the derivation, and mode of derivation, of natural law precepts, both primary and secondary, to human positive law. This includes

109 Ibid, I-II.104.1 ad 1 (detachment), I-II.90.3 ad 2 (authority); *De Virtutibus Cardinalibus* 4.4.

110 Ibid, I-II.96.4c & ad 3, I-II.97.1 ad 2, II-II.117.6c.

111 Ibid, I-II.96.4c.

112 Ibid; I find Scott Shapiro's claim that natural law theory is untenable because it 'rules out the possibility of evil legal systems' to be somewhat bizarre: Scott Shapiro, *Legality* (Belknap Press 2013) 49.

113 Aquinas, *ST* (n 3) I-II.92.1 ad 4.

the positive law's function in articulating and concretizing natural law precepts. It includes the purpose of positive law in defining, shaping, and upholding the common good. And it explains the consequences of positive law's failure to embody and express those standards, and the consequences of contravening the natural law.

All of these matters are available to careful ethical reflection, without the need of revealed truths (e.g. the outlines can be found in Books V and IX of Aristotle's *Ethics*). But they do require the operation of natural law within us, as a participation of eternal law. The treatment given to these issues by Aquinas, particularly in the 'treatise' on Law, makes clear that human beings have every reason to accept and practise the virtues, even if they reject the truth of revelation. The 'natural law thesis' of Murphy and Crowe is subordinate to these purposes.

## II.8. LAW-LIKENESS

Natural law is not law merely by analogy or in some metaphorically extended sense.[114] Aquinas states that natural law is a rational *participation* of eternal law in the human person, and he makes clear that this mode of participation is the development in a person of a critical and reflective internal attitude (to use Hart's expression).[115] For it is a share in the directivity of the law-maker,[116] and not mere moral advice to oneself, which would be without compulsive force.[117]

The central thesis for a Thomistic jurisprudence is that every law, insofar as it is a law, is a work of reason, a *regula*.[118] It therefore follows that *natural* law is a work of *natural* reason, that is to say, human reason insofar as it acts with the 'spontaneity and necessity of reason'.[119] As a work of reason it is not prior to that reason; it is not an *object* of moral knowledge but a *kind* of moral knowledge.[120] And such reason is found in us due to the light of understanding infused by God.[121] And natural reason can be distinguished from non-natural, conventional reason by simultaneously (i) operating on a level that is pre-political and pre-ideological: see Section II.1; and (ii) reaching farther than those other uses of practical reason in (a) its critical detachment from all such uses and (b) its self-criticism.

114 Cf Finnis, *NLNR* (n 10) 280–81.
115 See Aquinas, *ST* (n 3) I-II.90.1 ad 1.
116 Ibid, I-II.90.3 ad 1.
117 Ibid, I-II.90.3 ad 2, I-II.90.4c & ad 1.
118 See Rhonheimer (n 82) 41; Aquinas, *ST* (n 3) I-II.90.1c.
119 Rhonheimer (n 82) 43.
120 Ibid, 75; Aquinas, *ST* (n 3) I-II.94.6c.
121 Rhonheimer (n 82), 43; Aquinas, *ST* (n 3) I-II.91.2c.

## II.9. SACRED OR SECULAR?

The idea of natural law's secular character reaches back at least as far as St Augustine's *De Civitate Dei*, where he remarks, in that book's nineteenth chapter, that he will, 'for the sake of unbelievers, make as much use of reason as possible'.[122] Perhaps the most famous equation of natural law with 'secular' reason is found, much later, in Grotius's *De Iure Belli ac Pacis* [1625]. There, he states that propositions concerning natural law, and natural right, 'would retain the same status to some extent [*locum aliquem*] even if we were to concede that which cannot be conceded without the uttermost wickedness, that there is no God, or that human affairs are of no concern to Him'.[123] Certainly, Aristotle and Plato were able to point to moral truths without the benefit of revelation, not indeed by sheer chance, but on the basis of rational insight. Yet Grotius's famous statement goes further than his predecessors were prepared to go in supposing that human reason (and the rest of Creation) would be in other respects unchanged even in the highly counterfactual situation that God does not exist. By no means shy of quoting Scripture in support of his arguments, Grotius fails to quote those important passages of the Bible in which God warns of the danger and disaster which follow on from His people's decision to define good and evil for themselves, rather than trusting God's definition of good and evil. The warning, unheeded for the most part, is first given to Adam in the Garden of Eden (Genesis 2:15) and repeated often in the Old Testament books (see e.g. Judges 17:6 & 21:25; Proverbs 14:12).

Secularism is not, of course, a synonym for atheism; it is best understood as making an epistemological point (how human beings come to know the good) whilst leaving unaffected the ontology of good, the nature of which depends ultimately upon God's nature as expressed through His will. This raises the complicated question of how human reason gains access to truth, independently of recognizing the source of that truth. The ontological dimension to the problem is resolved through a faculty the Scholastics called *synderesis*. That is the inward disposition (*habitus*) through which human beings are able to grasp, or have an intellection of, the primary foundations of human action: the pursuit of good and avoidance of evil. Synderesis may cause me to understand that a particular action is morally wrong, and ought to be avoided. But, it might be asked, what reason do I have to regard myself as *obliged* to do what I *ought* to do? Later Thomist writers such as Francisco Suarez therefore drew a distinction, upon which Aquinas himself was insufficiently clear, between *debitum* (what is owed or ought to be given) and *obligatio* (legal obligation in the proper sense).

This brings us back to Grotius. For what Grotius 'had been saying' immediately prior to his famous passage is that the basic precepts of justice arise from an *internal* rational principle, which makes clear that the attainment of all that is beneficial,

[122] Augustine, *De Civitate Dei*, XIX.1.
[123] Grotius, *DIBP* (n 52) Prolegomena §11.

and the avoidance of all that is harmful (*quae delectant aut nocent*) requires abstention from one another's property, restoration of that which belongs to another, as well as any profits from its use, keeping one's promises, giving compensation in respect of culpable harm, and punishing the wicked.[124] These basic precepts of justice are known (at least in some form) to all human beings irrespective of whether they possess a knowledge of God. But 'as Christians', we also understand that these internal principles are testimonies of His will. Hence even though natural law necessarily derives from principles that are internal to human beings (*ex principiis homini internis necessario profluit*), it is also rightly attributed to God's will, which is the cause of those principles in us.[125]

The point of the counterfactual concerning God's inexistence was not, as first appearances might suggest, to establish *motivational* grounds for obedience to moral demands. The Scholastics and early-moderns were not, of course, in possession of Hart's distinction between 'having an obligation' and 'being obliged'; but they (and Suarez in particular) tended to speak of *obliging* in the context of the one instigating the obligation, and *obligation* in the context of the one to whom it is directed. Thus 'obliged' as translated from the Latin sources means 'obliged *to*' and not 'obliged *by*'.[126] The counterfactual premise of God's inexistence served a number of interrelated purposes, of which the most significant (in the present context) is its bearing on the fact, pointed out by ancient as well as modern writers, that Aristotle managed to give an account of ethics and of the intricate workings of the polities of the ancient world without ever invoking religious considerations. But the reception of Aristotle's natural philosophy by the Scholastics did not blind them to the fact that Aristotle nowhere offers a fully and properly conceived account of natural *law*. They marked this distinction by explaining that moral precepts are 'laws' only in a qualified and extended sense, to which they applied the term *lex indicans*, whereas natural law in the proper sense (i.e. possessing the necessary characteristics of law) is prescriptive, and is thus a *lex praeceptiva*. In observing this distinction, the Scholastics could draw upon passages in Aquinas in which he affirms variously that the law is 'a kind of yardstick and measure of acts, by which a person is either *led* to action or is *restrained* from acting',[127] and that it is 'a kind of *precept*' or 'command'.[128]

[124] Ibid, § 10.

[125] Ibid, § 11–12; I.1.10.1–2. For some interesting remarks see Mark C Murphy, 'Suarez's "Best Argument" and the Dependence of Morality on God' 5 (2014) *Quaestiones Disputatae* 136–42.

[126] See e.g. Suarez, *De Legibus* (hereafter *DL*) I.5.17: 'Obliging by a law produces a moral situation [*effectus moralis*].' The view about motivational grounds is held by Finnis (and is repeated by Grisez): *NLNR* (n 10) 47, and seems to have been given encouragement by the Carnegie Endowment translation of *De Legibus* on which he frequently relies, and in which the meaning of the quoted passage is reversed: 'binding by means of law is a moral effect'.

[127] Aquinas, *ST* (n 3) I-II.90.1c & ad 1, I-II.90.2c; *De Ver* (n 41) 17.3c & ad 1; see also Aquinas, *ST* (n 3) I-II.19.5; *Commentary on the Sentences of Peter Lombard* (hereafter *Sent*) 2.39.3.3 ad 3; *De Ver* (n 41) 17.4 ad 2; Suarez, *DL* (n 126) II.10.6.

[128] Aquinas, *ST* (n 3) I-II.92.2 ad 1 ('every law is a kind of precept'; also I-II.96.1 ad 2 & I-II.92.2 ad 2 ('Provision of advice is not a proper function of the law, though this lies with the competence even of a private person, who cannot make law ... and is not considered as an effect of law').

Thus Aquinas's discussion of natural law is marked by a distinction between (i) the guidance that is offered to action by practical reason's grasp of the significance of natural inclinations, which is 'law' by virtue of the subject's participation in the law-giver's directivity;[129] and (ii) those precepts, originating in the divine will, which command or enjoin human beings to virtuous forms of action, and is 'law' considered as a command.[130] The standard response to the distinction amongst Aquinas's successors in the Scholastic tradition was essentially the same as that of Grotius, to indicate by means of the counterfactual that the goodness and badness of certain acts would remain unchanged even if God had not commanded them as law. But there was some disagreement throughout the Scholastic tradition about the implications of this admission for the 'legal' character of natural law.

On one hand were those, of whom the most prominent was perhaps Vasquez, who asserted that *natural law* therefore did not depend upon any judgment of God, but only on the intrinsic goodness or evil of certain actions, in the absence of which indeed God cannot come to any *judgment* (and certainly cannot judge the bad to be good).[131] Vasquez even goes as far as saying that 'the term "law" [*lex*] does not accord with the natural law as much as it does with positive law'.[132] These remarks are reminiscent of similar sentiments expressed by John Finnis, who repeatedly stresses that 'natural law' is just another term for moral principle, and is 'only analogically law'.[133] In the brief passages in which he discusses the late Scholastics, Finnis presents Suarez (and Vasquez!) as inferior imitators of Aquinas, who succeeded only in overlaying the latter's subtle exposition of ends and goods with the crude rationalist principle that one should 'follow nature', eked out by a voluntarist reliance upon divine injunction to supply its normative force.[134]

And where does Suarez stand in relation to these issues? With Vasquez in mind, he observes that there are some who hold that rational nature is itself the natural law.[135] And he concedes that intrinsic rightness and wrongness must arise from (i.e. be an attribute of) the facts themselves, not from reason's judgment of those facts, since it is the facts in virtue of which the judgment of reason is right or wrong.[136] But he holds that rational nature is in the end only a yardstick or measure

[129] See e.g. Aquinas, *ST* (n 3) I-II.90.1 ad 1 ('so that any inclination that arises from a law is not to be called 'law' in the fullest sense, but only by a kind of participation'); also I-II.91.2c & ad 3 and I-II.91.6c ('every inclination or ordination that may be found in things subject to the law is called a law *by participation*).

[130] See Aquinas, *ST* (n 3) I-II.92.2c, I-II.92.1c ('law is a dictate of reason in the ruler through which he governs those subject to him'), I-II.90.4 ob 1 ('the natural law more than anything else has the character of law'), & ad 1 ('the natural law is promulgated precisely in that God instilled it in us, in the form of natural knowledge [i.e. inclinations]').

[131] Vasquez, *In Primam Secundae* 150.3.22 (for the claim), 150.4.30 (for the point about God's judgment).

[132] Ibid, 150.3.26.

[133] Finnis, *NLNR* (n 10) X.5, 274; X.6, 280–81.

[134] Ibid, II.6, esp 46–47.

[135] The key passage is Suarez, *DL* (n 126) II.5.2.

[136] Suarez, *DL* (n 126) II.5.5.

for the assessment of good and bad, not a *law*, the characteristic of which is (inter alia) prescriptiveness.

In these passages, Suarez regards himself as an interpreter and expositor of Aquinas, and an innovator only to the extent that he is seeking to resolve matters that Aquinas's discussion leaves ambiguous. And indeed, on Suarez's side is the fact that Aquinas differentiates between divine (i.e. directly revealed) law and natural law as modes of human participation in eternal *law* (*lex aeterna*), God's creative and ordering act which remains, as a totality, otherwise unfathomable and inaccessible to human reason.[137] Suarez glosses the point by observing that, whereas both the divine law (in being divine) and the natural law are *from* God (*ex Deo*), and thus require God's judgment, the natural law is also *dependent* on God (*pendere ex Deo*) as Creator, and is thus also prior to His judgment, as a lawgiver's command is prior to his or her judgment.[138] That is to say, the intrinsic goodness and badness of certain acts (attributes which God cannot even in principle controvert) arises from the creative act itself, in making things as they are. Thus goodness comes from God as Creator, not as legislator.[139] But Suarez holds that it is additionally necessary for God to *command* the good and prohibit evil, since it would be contrary to human good merely to indicate the good as a *possible* path for human beings to take.[140] This (thinks Suarez) is the intention that lies behind Aquinas's observation (*ST* I-II.91.2) that the rational capacity of human beings to distinguish between right and wrong is necessary for the natural law *in us*, but it is not constitutive of (i.e. does not explain the existence of) that law.[141] And thus, Suarez says that the rational capacity in humans which indicates what is good and bad *also* (therefore) indicates that it is in accord with the divine will to do good and abstain from evil: *honestum est faciendum, parvum vitandum*.[142]

Running throughout the Thomist tradition, then, was the realization the divine law itself, as revealed in the Decalogue and elsewhere, would lose any force as a guide to *reasoning* if, in addition to electing to obey or disobey it, human beings could not also arrive at an understanding of *why* murder, adultery, theft etc are wrongs. But because reason is capable of comprehending the associated forms of good (being, fidelity, prosperity ...) as *human* goods, and thus as subject to

[137] See esp Aquinas, *ST* (n 3) I-II.91.2 & 91.4.

[138] Suarez, *DL* (n 126) II.7–8; (cf Terence Irwin, *The Development of Ethics* (OUP 2007) II.9, who treats the two terms as equivalent).

[139] Suarez, *DL* (n 126) II.6.2.

[140] Ibid, I.3.3 & II.6.6 (the passages Finnis seems to rely on); but also crucially II.6.8–10.

[141] For Aquinas treats natural law as a *precept*, thus requiring *imperium*: Aquinas, *ST* (n 3) I-II.17.1, 17.3 ad 1; II-II.47.8 & 50. Cajetan, in his commentary on I-II.17.1, characterizes *imperium* as an act of intellect not (exclusively) of will, which is preferable to Suarez's interpretation. But Suarez is correct to say that, in any event, one cannot 'bind oneself' (give oneself the law) for then the obligation is to oneself, not to others or to God.

[142] Suarez, *DL* (n 126) II.7.5 ('the [moral] good is to be done, and wrongs avoided'); this is Suarez's attempt to represent the first precept in light of the knowledge of the foregoing matters; elsewhere he reproduces Aquinas's preferred formulation: II.7.2 & 15.2.

demands of justice (giving what is owed, refraining from that which belongs to another) which those wrongs violate, it is possible to arrive at the relevant moral knowledge independently of revelation.[143] One can therefore properly direct oneself to very many of these goods without accepting Christianity.

But Christians, possessing knowledge of God, understand that many of the moral norms that practical reason identifies as to be done or pursued, are also *laws* requiring obedience. They are not mere theorems of prudence or Darwinian evolutionary traits. This does not mean that the concepts of good and end are left behind at any point (per Finnis's accusation): loving God and obtaining heavenly beatitude are genuine goods![144] But it remains that Christians are also *commanded* to worship God, and to take no other god but Yahweh; and likewise, it is a commandment to love one's neighbours (enemies . . .). This love-of-neighbour is not an emotional, ecstatic love, but precisely the operative working of the virtues (justice, mercy, etc) in one's dealings with others. Whatever the questions and complexities which surround the operation of the virtues in practice (and there are many), they retain, for Aquinas as for Suarez, the character of true obligations,[145] and failures to live up to these standards, as these writers tirelessly remind us, are not mere faults, but sins (*peccata*).

## II.10. NATURAL LAW AND PHILOSOPHY

In a famous passage in his book *A History of Western Philosophy*, Bertrand Russell advanced the following criticism of Thomas Aquinas, which could stand as a criticism of Christian philosophy as a whole:

> There is little of the true philosophic spirit in Aquinas. He does not, like the Platonic Socrates, set out to follow wherever the argument may lead. He is not engaged in an inquiry, the result of which it is impossible to know in advance. Before he begins to philosophize, he already knows the truth; it is declared in the Catholic faith. If he can find apparently rational arguments for some parts of the faith, so much the better; if he cannot, he need only fall back on revelation. The finding of arguments for a conclusion given in advance is not philosophy, but special pleading. I cannot, therefore, feel that he deserves to be put on a level with the best philosophers either of Greece or of modern times.[146]

143 The exception is possibly the Commandment to love God, and to take no false gods: see Aquinas, *ST* (n 3) I-II.100.1.

144 See e.g. Aquinas, *ST* (n 3) I-II.3.5, 3.8, 4.2.

145 See Suarez, *DL* (n 126) II.6.10.

146 Bertrand Russell, *A History of Western Philosophy* (George Allen & Unwin, 1946), 463. See also Graham Oppy, 'On the Lack of True Philosophic Spirit in Aquinas' 76 (2001) *Philosophy* 615.

Russell observes a few pages earlier that 'Aquinas is glad, at the end of a piece of reasoning, to quote texts showing that reason has led him to a conclusion in harmony with the Scriptures, but he does not appeal to authority until his result has been reached.'[147] But he goes on to say that 'The appeal to reason is, in a sense, insincere, since the conclusion to be reached is fixed in advance.'[148] He cites by way of example a text in which Aquinas, discussing monogamy within marriage, says that monogamy is required if the husband is effectively to educate his offspring.[149] Russell says that the argument does not work, but that Catholic thinkers would not be thereby induced to abandon the doctrine of monogamous marriage, for the 'real' ground of the argument is revelation.

This is a significant misrepresentation of Aquinas's argument, and of the method which underlies his response. Aquinas's word *educatio* is better translated as 'raising' or 'rearing', as distinct from the *doctrina* or *disciplina* of the classroom that Russell has in mind. Furthermore, he overlooks the other grounds of Aquinas's reply which argue that whilst polygamy is normal for animals generically, the specific nature of the human being is fitted for monogamy (like the turtledove), and that the great good of matrimonial fidelity (so absent from Russell's own life, and therefore also special pleading?) stems from the secondary precepts of natural law which are grounded upon an account of the basic principles of practical reason, which were extensively discussed in the *Prima-secundae*.

More generally, Russell is incorrect in his estimation of Aquinas's method. He fails to cite any example of Aquinas 'falling back' on revelation having failed to support his position with rational arguments. More importantly, he misrepresents the status of 'fixed' conclusions (the validity of which are assumed in advance) both in Aquinas and in philosophy and human inquiry generally. For we typically do not believe only one thing at a time, in any subject matter, and suspend our judgment until we have followed our thoughts wherever they lead. Beliefs ordinarily form a system, in which some, indeed many, of our beliefs are held on the basis of their coherence with others the truth of which are either proven or otherwise assured.[150] Philosophy is partly concerned with interrogating our beliefs, and is not always driven by the method of doubt: for there must be reasons for doubt, as well as for belief. In common with other natural law thinkers, Aquinas is not motivated by doubt, but he nevertheless wishes to find reasons for his beliefs. In fact, Russell too pursued this method in his perhaps most celebrated work, *Principia Mathematica*:

[147] Russell (n 146) 460.
[148] Ibid, 462.
[149] Aquinas, *ST* (n 3) III Supp.65.1c.
[150] See e.g. Willard Van Orman Quine, *The Web of Belief* (2nd edn McGraw-Hill 1978).

> [In mathematics] the greatest degree of self-evidence is usually not to be found quite at the beginning, but at some later point; hence the early deductions, until they reach this point, give reasons rather for believing the premises because true consequences follow from them, than for believing the consequences because they follow from the premises.[151]

Hence Russell is perfectly content in pursuing a philosophical investigation into the validity of the equation '2 + 2 = 4' which one assumes he treats as valid in advance, and which if his investigation contradicts, it is the latter and not the former that must be given up.

## II.11. IN SUMMARY: FALSE IMAGES

The foregoing sections of this chapter hopefully supply sufficient grounds for rejecting most of the false images of natural law that are advanced by opponents as the object of criticism. But one further example might usefully be considered in brief, as it summarizes well the central contention of opponents of natural law, that its doctrines, methods and assumptions ought to be consigned to history, of interest only to the historian and not the moralist. In a recent essay, Nigel Simmonds says that:

> The pre-liberal view [of politics] assumed a single right ordering of conduct directly informing every aspect of social and political life. Merchant, prince and peasant were to act upon a shared idea of Christian virtue, grounded in the teachings of the Church. The social order was conceived of 'as a highly articulated organism of members contributing in their different degrees to a spiritual purpose'.[152]

This passage is incorrect in almost every particular. Natural law does not assume a 'single right ordering' of social and political life. There are many respects in which, as we have seen, natural law is indifferent as to norms that structure social and political life (extending to indifference regarding the kind of political structures within a state, excepting tyranny and forms of cronyism, etc); and neither does natural law determine 'every aspect' of social and political life: many of the rules we ordinarily encounter are mere conventions, *determinationes*, which can take one form or another. Very far, then, from the notion of a 'single right ordering'.

[151] AN Whitehead & Bertrand Russell, *Principia Mathematica* (Cambridge University Press 1910–13), v. Ironically, Russell's core belief—that mathematics could be reduced to logic—proved to be false.

[152] Nigel E Simmonds, 'Constitutional Rights, Civility and Artifice' 78 (2019) *Cambridge Law Journal* 176.

Furthermore, as should be apparent from the foregoing discussions in this chapter, the natural law precepts discussed therein do not in any way dictate a single form of life, but are compatible with a great variety of forms of life, all of which are capable of instantiating the virtues in different ways, whether in the sweat and dedication of the marathon runner, the workings of the brush of the painter, or the ascetic life of the scholar. Nor is it true to say that every person, 'merchant, prince and peasant', acts or ought to act upon a shared idea of Christian virtue. As we will see (Section III.4), the 'virtues' demanded by the levers of government are distinct and distinguishable from the ordinary virtues which pervade private and social life. Even ostensibly identical virtues, such as integrity and justice, are raised to a higher register in public life, in which different vices are at work, and different opportunities to act for the good are present. Within the private realm, natural law philosophy draws distinctions between the range of virtues demanded of people of different social standing, so that (for example) the person in poverty lacks the material means by which to exhibit virtues that are available to the rich, such as generosity, magnanimity, and mercy.

A similar misunderstanding pervades the second half of the same sentence just explored. The core teachings of virtue were and are grounded in reason, not doctrine, and belong as much to the Aristotelian-Thomist tradition as to the Church: the Church does not 'own' those teachings but expresses them as truths of reason confirmed by divine law. It is true that the specifically theological virtues of faith, hope and charity (or love) 'infuse' the other virtues, so that the latter are in some sense 'grounded' in Church doctrine, but again virtues of the latter kind are and remain intelligible without reference to or knowledge of the former.

Finally, the 'social order' was emphatically *not* conceived by natural law the theorists as orientated towards a 'spiritual purpose'. As Aquinas makes abundantly clear, the purpose of law (and thus state coercion) is not to bring people to perfect virtue, but must be 'proportionate to the common good', the common good itself 'is comprised of many things' (*constat ex multis*).[153] The purpose of human law (presumably the kind of law Simmonds has in mind) falls short of eternal law: it is concerned, again, with the common good and not the perfect spiritual wellbeing of each person.[154]

So much for particulars. Taking the quoted passage as a whole, in calling this view 'pre-liberal', Simmonds implies that natural law jurisprudence is incompatible with liberal political theory, which is not the case, as the preceding sections hopefully demonstrate; and he infers, by his use throughout of the past tense, that the natural law theory is of merely historical, not moral, interest: an implication that the arguments of the present chapter have sought to expose as utter falsehood.

[153] Aquinas, *ST* (n 3) I-II.96.1c; see also and especially I-II.96.2 ad 2.
[154] Ibid, I-II.96.2 ad 3.

Let these remarks, which require considerable further elucidation, stand for the present as part of the outline conception of natural law. Later chapters of this book are devoted to their development; but since it has not yet been established precisely what freedom, peace, and justice (and other moral demands) require, it is necessary to preface a specifically legal philosophy with a moral and political theory.

# PART TWO

# III
# MORALITY AND HUMAN GOOD

## III.1. HUMAN GOOD

Chapter II set out a general theory of natural law, and thus of human good. In this chapter, it will be shown how the basic precepts of natural law are carried forward into action, resulting in a fully fledged commitment to basic moral values.

The term 'human good' is not abstract or mysterious. Any person who has experienced an inclination to some particular thing, and has pursued and attained satisfaction from it, understands (even if only implicitly) what it means for something to be a human good. This does not mean that human good *derives from* those reflexive experiences; instead, those experiences are made possible and intelligible by the goodness of the objects sought.

Sometimes, traditional orders of priority may impede our understanding of the way in which concepts, categorical values or forms enter into human thinking and practical deliberation. One such case concerns the topic of human good. For, in practical human thinking and judging, contrary to what one might expect, 'human good' is prior to 'good' *simpliciter*. To recognize that a thing is good one must perceive *in one's mind's eye* that it possesses beneficial properties. Before one can recognize that something is good for, say, fish, it is necessary to understand what 'good for' is, and in order to comprehend this one must know first hand what it is to experience fulfilment. Part of the judgment that a certain thing is good, or worth pursuing, then, is the intellection that it is *appropriate* for one, unlike, say, drinking poison or mating with other species. This is the necessary prelude to any understanding of good-for-a-thing.

Ethics, then, begins with the realization that it is possible to talk of the 'human being': a shared humanity and series of characteristics and inclinations possessed in some measure by all members of the species. It is true that unlike other forms of life, human beings possess the freedom to act against their natural inclinations, and to act in favour of ends that undo their human nature. Both classical and modern discourses reflect the fact that not every inclination is a natural one: paedophilia and incest name two vices that are commonly recognized as unnatural, for example. In such cases, the very wicked or perverse are capable of conceiving themselves as acting in a natural and reasonable way (even though in reality they are not).

Philosophical ethics has the ability to distinguish the natural from the unnatural. Aristotle provides one such test: genuine goods exist in harmony within the person, and reinforce one another, whereas the false goods and coarse pleasures

*Natural Law and Modern Society*. Sean Coyle, Oxford University Press. © Sean Coyle 2023.
DOI: 10.1093/oso/9780192886996.003.0003

of the unreasonable tend to clash and conflict within the person, one source of pleasure (e.g. drug-taking) cancelling out another (e.g. wealth). Thus in determining whether something is truly good, rather than a simulacrum of goodness, the first and foremost consideration is whether an alleged good harmonizes with one's other inclinations. This is a further instance of the general principle that the truth harmonizes with all data, whereas falsehoods clash and contradict one another. (For example, the thief wishes to take property unjustly, but does not himself want to be the victim of unjust taking.)

Human striving after goods is a subset of total human activity, for there is also sleep and rest, and many forms of activity are only indirectly connected with the pursuit of human goods: such as the work one does simply in order to pay bills and taxes, or to sustain oneself. The precise percentage of actions that possess some high degree of proximity to overarching goals of life (such as, perhaps, having a satisfying career, or raising a family), as opposed to daily chores (e.g. brushing one's teeth) need not be exactly specified. Furthermore it is well known that certain goods, such as bodily health, are valuable for their own sake as well as prerequisites for further kinds of goodness. Nevertheless, it needs to be explained how the notion of human good, understood as the satisfaction of one's rational inclinations, is connected to the phenomenon of moral goodness.

The nature of human good is such that it belongs to all human beings, and not just the one immediately reasoning about them.[1] All reasonable human beings—those capable of reflecting upon their own needs and desires, as well as the needs and desires of others, and the potential for conflicts in interests—can grasp that life, for example, is a human good. The origins of this grasp do not lie in theoretical reason, but rather in the practical intellect, and 'spring naturally and immediately from basic insights of practical reason: in the "appetitive dynamics of natural inclinations"'.[2] But the pursuit of moral truth also requires the cooperation of the speculative intellect, for one's basic nature *and* the nature of others, and understanding of the world are required to be known sufficiently to formulate and pursue ends.[3] In this respect therefore, human beings are moral creatures. (We are also, as participants in the eternal law, creatures of God: the possibilities of the natural inclinations are infused in us at the point of creation.)

As an object of practical reasoning, then, a given human good is reflectively taken up not exclusively from a first-person perspective, but from the point of view that it is valuable in ways that go beyond one's own present or future interests. The

[1] For a recent account see Christopher Tollefsen, 'The Good of Play in John Finnis's Natural Law and Natural Rights' 83 (2020) *Persona y derecho* 575.

[2] See Martin Rhonheimer, 'Natural Law as a Work of Reason' (2010) *American Journal of Jurisprudence* 54.

[3] See Aquinas, *Summa Theologiae* (hereafter *ST*) I.79.11 ad 2. Cf Rhonheimer (n 2) 59: Theoretical reason can say nothing about whether a good should be pursued. But it can give us information *about* the object and its likely consequences; it simply cannot say *why* it is worthy of pursuit or avoidance.

recognition of human goods therefore immediately raises all the classic questions of interpersonal morality, such as what is owed or due to each person. Because of this grasp of human good, there is no 'pre-moral moment' in one's thinking. The recognition of an object as (humanly) good implicitly calls into play the full range of duties and virtues which govern one's pursuit and attainment of human goods. Recognition of these questions does not require the device of a primordial state of equality (as in Hobbes), nor any pre-social commonality of goods (as in Grotius or Locke) for, to reiterate, recognition of *human* goods involves the insight that such goods are the goods of persons, not of any specific individual or group of individuals: an insight that is available at any time and in any society advanced enough to possess the necessary linguistic resources.

It might be asked, nevertheless, why the resulting insights are moral as opposed to merely prudential? The answer is that the notion of 'human good' offers no basis for the individualistic reasoning that grounds the prudential calculation that 'if *I* am to have it, then so must others'. There is no implicit reference to agent-centricity at all.[4] One does begin one's ethical thinking by identifying human goods, goods which apply to oneself as well as others; we first learn about many such goods by coming to know ourselves, but the *reason* for adhering to ethical norms is not reciprocity of respect but is rather based on the love of charity: that one should not act against human goods wherever they may lie. This is not to deny that relationships of reciprocity exist as part of the human striving after primary human goods. But as Aquinas observes, the assistance that each one needs in order to secure such goods is more readily and fully available if human beings love one another appropriately:[5] a form of amity that explains why one human being will assist a stranger in need or distress, without thought of reward. For a person 'loves the good not because it is his own, but because it is good; for the good as such is the object of the will'.[6]

These truths are not falsified by the fact that some, even many people, will assist others either not at all, or only on the basis of narrow reciprocity. Such individuals are called 'prudential', but in reality the intellectual virtue of prudence (*prudentia*) exists in them only in a stunted or misshapen form, not the fully-fledged form in which it guides and unites the other virtues within the person: virtues that include justice, regard for others (*societas*; *humanitas*) and so forth. So the so-called 'prudential' standpoint involves a misconstruction of the nature of primary human goods; they are treated in a way that regards them as open to pursuit first and foremost for oneself, as if they were one's own, without thought for the needs of others. A standpoint of this kind not only disfigures the primary goods, but directly undermines and degrades one of those goods: the establishment of amicable social relations between persons.

[4] See Aquinas, *ST* (n 3) II-II.58.2c.

[5] See Aquinas, *Summa Contra Gentiles* (hereafter *SCG*) III.117.

[6] Aquinas, *Sent* II.3.4.1 ad 2.

Nor does it falsify these phenomena that some, perhaps many, people either fail to comprehend certain forms of human good, or else act contrary to them. It does not alter their truth that newborn human beings have no innate knowledge or understanding of them, or that children have to be taught to value them. Finally, it does not matter whether some human beings are incapable, through mental or physical impairment, of experiencing certain types of human good. All such questions pertain only to the extent to which human persons, societies, or legal systems recognize or participate in forms of human good, not to goodness *per se*.

It will be rightly said that, at least in mature political societies, there will exist myriad customs and laws for the determination of who has access or title to goods of all kinds, and on which terms. These are complex issues that it is best for the moment to defer. They will be taken up again in this book's treatment of justice (Section IV.3), and common good (Section V.2). But many of the goods of which we are speaking are in any case not subject to limitations in this way. The good of being able to make music is a good that, at least in the abstract, is open to all persons with the appropriate skills. One person's possession of such skills does not imply or result in another's not having those skills. For the moment, then, it is best to consider the human good in abstraction from the positive laws of the community.

## III.2. INCLINATION AND PERFECTION

Let us call goods such as sociability, and knowledge and care for human life 'primary goods', because they are not reducible to further types or modes of goodness, and because they are presupposed in many other forms of good that human beings typically pursue or seek to realize. Elsewhere in the literature on natural law, such goods are referred to as 'basic goods', but that term is avoided here as it suggests a lack of complexity which certainly is not a feature of primary goods. (Sociability, for example, is not an uncomplicated inclination in any of its manifestations.) The goods just mentioned are not the only primary human goods: there is willingness and diligence in undertaking meaningful work; the discovery and appreciation of beauty in one's life, the love between friends, and others besides.

The reader will have noticed that the account of goods here does not begin from a listing of primary 'basic' goods. But there is no need to produce an exhaustive list of primary human goods (See Section II.5).[7] Yet even a partial listing must work

[7] See Mark C Murphy, *Natural Law and Practical Rationality* (CUP 2001, hereafter *NLPR*) 100–137 for such a list. His category of 'excellence in play and work' might seem to correspond to my mention of meaningful labour, but this is not the case: what makes labour meaningful is not only its productiveness but that it is in the service of others. One's work in purifying heroin for sale is not an instance of meaningful labour. But see his assumption (ibid 112) that manual work hammering rivets on a production line is not intrinsically valuable because it is 'instrumental': this overlooks the dimension of service to others, which makes a person's efforts worthwhile because they assist the wellbeing of others. This is

according to some principle of what is to be included in or excluded from the list. Therefore let us say that a presumptive human primary good must be (i) irreducible to any other good, (ii) the subject of a natural inclination, and (iii) not merely good but also perfective of human beings.

Of these three, irreducibility is easiest to understand. It amounts to the claim that primary human goods are basic and performatively unquestionable. Primary human goods are basic in that they cannot be reduced into further component parts, nor to the status of a mere instrument to the attainment of other goals or ends. When we act to preserve our lives (for instance in checking the traffic before crossing a road), we do so for the sake of life as a human good as such. It may be true of any person that they have any number of future plans, goals, semi-fulfilled ideals, etc, but the act of prudentially caring for one's ongoing existence is not explicable by reference to any of these desires, even though life is included in the good of all of them. For there may be considerable doubt as to whether any of one's future plans can be brought off; one may believe in a mechanistic world in which the satisfaction of desires is of no greater significance, all things considered, than an early but painless (instantaneous) death. For all we know, present health may be compromised in future by illness or disease, or by degrees of pain and suffering that make life intolerable. We operate, in such conditions, in blindness if also in hope of, future measures of happiness. In acting to preserve one's life, therefore, in the moment of acting, one acts for the sake of one's life understood as a good thing in itself.

Performative unquestionableness requires a longer explanation. This category corresponds to Aquinas's *per se nota* principles, that is, principles of which the truth is grasped through an understanding of the relevant component terms. In the case of speculative principles, understanding involves a grasp of the meaning of terms, as in the proposition that the angles of a triangle add up to 180 degrees: in this case the concept of angles and natural numbers. The description of such principles as *per se nota* (or known in themselves) is not entirely satisfactory, and leads Aquinas to remark that some self-evident propositions are known to be true only by the relatively learned, whereas for others their self-evidence or even truth is unknown. The idea of performative unquestionableness has the advantage that it applies alike to the learned and unlearned. It asserts that a person who is involved in acting for the sake of some good, *X*, cannot consistently deny or bring into question the goodness of those goods that are presupposed in aiming for *X*. The prudential care for one's ongoing existence is such a good, since it is presupposed in all actions whatever: to perform such actions is to *assert*, through those actions, the value of that good. Such practical assertion does not necessarily involve, and will usually not involve, any *explicit* assertion that one's existence is a good. But such an

not to eliminate the distinction between intrinsic and instrumental value, but to reveal a dimension of meaningfulness that Murphy (and Finnis) overlook.

assertion may come into the foreground whenever one's life is threatened: for example on the battlefield, or when involved in a life-threatening accident. In short, one comprehends the goodness of some end of action in one's pursuit and experience of it.[8] In continuing to pursue some end, we cannot deny its goodness (or at least apparent goodness) for us.

In all such circumstances, the statement that human existence is a good is not open to denial. This can be seen, for example, in Hart's treatment of human existence (survival): in order to deny this good, one would have to give up, one by one, as matters of indifference or aversion, all the linguistic structures (and thus structures of thought) that talk of harm, injury, risk, and of needs, wants, safety (etc), of practices of medicine, and all of one's efforts and choices in which preserving one's life, or the lives of others, plays a part. All such thoughts and efforts are performatively inconsistent with the denial that preservation of one's existence is a good.

It may be thought that the example of suicide contradicts the idea of life as a good. But in fact, it is confirmation that there are other goods besides the good of existence, that are humanly necessary: that existence on its own is not a sufficient basis for a genuinely human form of life (for animals and plants have life). The reasons that accompany completed and attempted suicides are not typically addressed to the evilness of life as such, but to circumstances that in combination have made life unliveable: unrequited love, painful or terminal illnesses, lack of friendship, loss of livelihood, despair, and so on. All of these factors are negations of the human goods that make a life distinctively human, as opposed to purely vegetative or bestial.

Still, it might be pointed out that an individual may indeed bring into question their commitments and courses of action, sometimes with salutary results. But this does not call into doubt performative unquestionableness. When we reflectively question, doubt, or otherwise have misgivings about a course of action, this is generally as a precursor to abandoning the action as leading to some (now-) foreseeable evil. In the case of life (to continue the example), one's continued efforts to preserve one's life, during and after the time spent in questioning such efforts, contradict the attempt to regard as true the proposition that one's life ought to be abandoned. In this sense, life is a special case. For the case of other primary human goods stands differently, as one may very well judge it to be necessary to abandon one's quest for knowledge, or one's friends, in certain situations: perhaps the knowledge one seeks is too advanced for one's efforts to obtain it, or perhaps other priorities entail its abandonment. But in all such cases, there is no performative inconsistency in one's choice to abandon a good, here and now, in the face of countervailing priorities. One's action in such contexts is not the action of bringing into question the statement that (for example) 'knowledge is a human good'; it is

[8] See John Finnis, *Natural Law & Natural Rights* (2nd edn OUP 2011, hereafter *NLNR*) 63–64; Jonathan Crowe, *Natural Law & the Nature of Law* (CUP 2019, hereafter *NLNL*) 53.

simply the recognition that such a good does not have permanent priority over the other goods of life, that it would be imprudent or impolitic *here and now* to pursue it, though one does not rule out taking up again the quest for knowledge in future. In that sense, the good remains unquestioned when considered in the abstract, and nothing in one's present actions and decisions asserts the opposite.

Let us make the following observation: that 'disposition' (*habitus* in St Thomas's works) describes the general category under which particular *inclinations* are subsumed. Our dispositions are indeed shaped by the inclinations we experience (and the extent to which they fall under the governance of prudence). This helps to explain why our dispositions can become corrupted and changed for the worse: giving in to bad inclinations gradually, but surprisingly quickly, corrupts dispositions, and the dispositions are thereafter hard to correct because one's present inclination must work against the pull of the range of inclinations which fall under the disposition. Our dispositions, as MacIntyre says, sometimes depend upon those of others, either because we wish to please them, or because we fear or love them.[9] This raises a significant question about the relative strength of different dispositions, and their relative merit. I defer discussion of this question to Section III.6.

It should be mentioned that primary goods can be experienced in different ways, but this is not (as Crowe seems to suggest) a matter of free choice.[10] Goods are not products of whatever our inclinations happen to be; rather, we experience inclinations in a variety of ways due to the complexity and multifaceted nature of the goods themselves. Take, as one example, sociability: one may be a naturally sociable person with a wide circle of friends, or one may experience deeper friendships with only a few. Alternatively, one may reserve love to, and feel connection only with, one's immediate family, or one may possibly experience friendships with the same persons over the course of one's life, or drift between old and new friends with the years. To be clear, these are not matters of free choice into how to engage with primary goods, but genuine differences in inclination which indicate different possibilities for realizing the goodness of those goods.[11]

To say that such primary human goods are the objects of natural human inclinations (such as a thirst for knowledge, or desire for society), is not to *reduce* those goods to any more basic terms. But the implied contrast that gives sense to the term 'natural inclination' is not the relatively narrow category of 'unnatural inclinations'; it is instead the broad though imprecise category of conventional inclination, those inclinations that are traceable to culturally and historically evolved practices.

[9] Alasdair MacIntyre, *Ethics in the Conflicts of Modernity* (CUP 2020, hereafter *ECM*) 7.

[10] Crowe, *NLNL* (n 8) 53 (basic goods are *products* of normative inclinations); MacIntyre, *ECM* (n 9) 5.

[11] As MacIntyre points out, the main features of Finnis's account of friendship can be found as far back as Plato's *Lysis*: see Alasdair MacIntyre, *After Virtue* (3rd edn University of Notre Dame Press 2007) 152.

Additionally, original sin, the first effect of which was to deprive humans of sanctifying Grace, produces disharmony between reason, will and the emotions: a disharmony curable only by the acquisition of the cardinal virtues.[12]

Order among the natural inclinations is what it is, not solely by virtue of human reason, but no less in virtue of 'nature'. Practical reason's rule does not establish or impose its authority upon pre-existing anarchy; so intellections of human goods are ontologically, and to a degree epistemically dependent upon human nature. This is not the case with socially conditioned inclinations, such as the inclination to maintain elements of privacy in one's life, away from the gaze of society, or the inclination to be self-determining in decisions about education, career, and so on. Such inclinations (though reasonable) are not natural, but are brought into existence and shaped by one's community. Reason responds to such inclinations, but is also responsible for determining the order that exists between them.

Both the presence and the fulfilment of natural inclinations are obviously matters of importance in the attempt to identify primary human goods. For if these were different, so also would be the goods that satisfy them. This counterfactual should not however be allowed to mislead us. Human nature does not, and has not, deviated from what it was in the times of the most ancient philosophers. It is not chosen or mutable. Neither Darwinists nor Social Darwinists nor any end-of-history philosophers can point to substantial shifts in human nature, and therefore in natural inclinations. The instincts of so-called *homo economicus* are secondary, conventional inclinations which represent particular ways of aiming to secure more basic primary human goods (such as peace and survival). Indeed, in the Darwinian slogan of the 'survival of the fittest', the notion of 'fittest' does not invariably mean 'strongest' but rather 'most fitting'. To this extent Darwinists are alive to the fact that certain moral practices are most in-keeping with human nature and with successful strategies to obtain and secure fundamental human goods such as life. They articulate, in effect, a natural law theory by another name.

Another current but mistaken image is that of 'reflective equilibrium'. Some natural law theorists account for our relationship to 'basic' or primary goods by reference to reflective equilibrium. The term originates with Rawls but has been taken up by, for example, Crowe.[13] The general idea is that one oscillates between one's immediate intuitions and one's abstract moral principles, in order to arrive at a stable equilibrium point between the two. There are many reasons for rejecting this idea of moral judgment (for instance, it denies the existence of strict, universal moral wrongs: I must never lie, even if I am asked by the murderer if his intended victim is inside; I must not give any weight to my immediate inclination to lie in such a circumstance). But in the present context we can focus on a different aspect of the problem. For at the most basic level, inclinations are *not* intuitions; they are

[12] See Rhonheimer (n 2) 74.
[13] Crowe, *NLNL* (n 8) 62.

felt needs, attractions, or repulsions. The most general precepts of natural law (to which, presumably, Crowe refers) *inform* one's more immediate judgments, they are not mere *counters* to be modified or balanced in argument. To be sure, Crowe adapts Rawls's idea of reflective equilibrium into a model of 'dialectical equilibrium', but the issue is not with the reflectivity of Rawls's idea but its concern for equilibrium.

In the act of seeking for and obtaining human goods, a person's capacities, powers, or potentialities are awoken, activated, and developed. The development of these potentialities (that is, bringing certain capacities or powers into actuality) is a contribution to the proper fulfilment of the person, and therefore represents the numerous ways in which the person grows towards their ultimate fulfilment or perfection. This cannot be the case with 'goods' that are merely apparent (false), such as the taste of tobacco, but only those goods that are genuine, such as the benevolent and careful custodianship of one's life and the lives of others: since it is only through deliberate *action* that one's potentialities are made actual. Indeed a person is perfected exactly through their actions.

The good ordering of one's reason is one of the primary sources of perfection of the human being, for without this there can be no distinctly human action, action that is fully chosen and deliberated. Of course it is possible for a person to be possessed with the appropriate capacities, but only to bring order to reason in some narrower or more minor way: in this sense, a person possesses the relative (but wholly inadequate) goodness of the good *statesman*, or the good *sportsperson*, or even the good *thief*. Thus the scholastic term 'perfection' should not be taken in any obscure, metaphysical sense. If I diligently practise the piano every day, I will gradually perfect my playing until I become an excellent piano player. Similarly, someone who carefully undertakes many surgical operations will eventually perfect the techniques of surgery. But it is only by bringing order to the full range of one's considerations that one attains to complete perfection, to be a good *person* in an unrestricted sense, and to possess Aquinas's *prudentia*.

The Greek term *eudaemonia* and the Latin terms *beatitudo* and *felicitas* are used to describe the highest good of human life: the happy contentedness of the truly fulfilled person. But the subordinate goods that are steps on the way to complete fulfilment are radically incomplete if they include only so-called 'natural' primary goods, such as bodily health or skilful knowledge, for true complete fulfilment also requires virtuous goods such as fortitude and justice.[14] A healthy body and good mind assist a person who strives to become virtuous, but they are nonetheless peripheral in relation to absolute contentment, and may *per accidens* impede virtue: consider the person who clings to life at any price, or the one who seeks a knowledge of how to pick locks. Such persons can no doubt attain measures of

[14] See esp Aquinas, *ST* (n 3) II-II.47.6c: 'the end of the moral virtues is human good'.

'happiness' through their gains, but they do not approach the beatitude of one who remains at ease with their conscience and rests in their fulfilment.

Finally, Crowe suggests a distinction between inclinations (learnt, revisable) and reflexes (innate, unchangeable).[15] If correct, this would mean that there are no *natural* inclinations. The discussion appears to follow Aristotle who claims in Book II of the *Ethics* that intellectual virtues are inborn whilst moral virtues require to be learnt.[16] But the route of learning is not of the essence of inclination, as Crowe's discussion implies. If in one's learning one discovers natural inclinations (we are not talking here of natural inclinations such as hunger and thirst, but of inclinations to pursue primary goods), then one has uncovered (a) something about one's nature as a human being, and (b) characteristic modes of living which satisfy and develop one's nature. There is no sense of conventionality here: the learning mentioned in Crowe's bracketed couple should be paired with the object of that learning: a natural inclination that is *conveniens* to one's nature. As it is, that learning is coupled with revisability; but this is not of the essence of inclinations. The inclination to choose and pursue goods is not revisable, nor is the inclination to act reasonably with all the knowledge that is available to one at the time. There are some inclinations which one might decide to act against, in relation to specific goods that are in view. But to act against an inclination is not to *revise* that inclination, but to act for the sake of *another* inclination that competes with the first. And this is simply to recognize the fact that there are (i) other ranges of goods that one might reasonably pursue rather than others to which one has a natural inclination, and (ii) false goods to which a person may be more attracted, in this moment, to goods that are genuinely fulfilling and promotive of wellbeing.

Nonetheless, Crowe rightly states that the task of natural law theory is to reflect on human practices with a view to uncovering their common elements and thus our common humanity.[17] I will begin this task in Section III.3, and provide a substantively new account in Section III.4 and onwards.

## III.3. RECIPROCITY AND MORAL DUTY

The question of moral goodness can be approached, as the foregoing discussion does, from the question of inward perfectibility. Such a perspective focuses upon the ultimate good for the person, and the outward actions, and inward states of mind, of the person. But there is another, no less important, perspective from which the question of morality must be approached: namely, the outward facing

[15] Crowe, *NLNL* (n 8) 25.
[16] Aristotle, *Nicomachean Ethics* (hereafter *NE*) II.1.1103a.
[17] Crowe, *NLNL* (n 8) 38.

question of one's moral duties towards others (see Section IV.1). Central to modern jurisprudential thinking is the idea of reciprocity.[18]

Such outward facing duties arise directly out of the recognition that there are human goods: goods that are worth obtaining or striving after not only for you or me, but for all human beings. This judgment (or series of judgments, since there are many forms of human good) does not depend upon, and is not qualified by, the notion of reciprocity that played such an important role in early-modern thinking, in the writings (for example) of Hobbes, Locke, or Adam Smith. In Hobbes for instance, the reader will learn that all human goods are attainable (by me) only if I willingly lay aside my natural right of self-determining thought and action *insofar as* others do the same. Reciprocity is capable of giving me reasons to show restraint towards, and care for, others, but such reasons are not moral reasons. They are instead a species of long-term instrumental rationality. Locke's philosophy, in this respect more sophisticated than that of Hobbes, yields a theory of commerce: the passing back and forth of rights between equals, for mutual advantage, that have an ultimate foundation in common patrimony, a situation (of equality) that only a divine mandate could alter.[19] But for all its sophistication, Locke's account remains one of reciprocity.

Reciprocity is not the foundation of morality. But there is inevitably an element of reciprocity in social relationships within a community, for reciprocity is a (one) demand of justice. This is glimpsed most clearly in the context of commutative justice, which in Aristotle's terms requires an arithmetic proportion. But it is an error to suppose that a reverse polarity also (or instead) holds: namely that justice is a demand of reciprocity. For there are many occasions on which reciprocity is qualified or suspended in the name of justice, for example in cases where bad faith is present or where it was reasonable to suppose, and to rely upon the supposition, that a particular transaction was a gift. In short, reciprocity may be present in human practices, and may even be a requirement of certain practices, but it is not primary, and is not the basis of an explanation of morality.

Justice is for obvious reasons the clearest example of an outward facing (other-regarding) duty; but both classical and early modern philosophers also recognized that the form of so-called 'general' justice could be associated with the whole range of virtues, including those that are not considered as other-regarding in themselves. Thus, having intercourse with another's wife is an act of intemperance, but it is also an injustice perpetrated on the husband (and the wife). The coward or the

[18] See Finnis, *NLNR* (n 8) 136–39 (but observe that Finnis's account of true friendship—the highest in a sliding scale—is not based on reciprocity as such; there has been no exploration of how this affects the more imperfect modes of sociability. Note too how the 'natural progression' in Aristotle is the reverse, *beginning* with family love and proceeding to more diluted forms of association); also 272–74; also George Klosko, 'Fair Play, Reciprocity and Natural Duties of Justice' 33 (2020) *Ratio Juris* 335; Robert Axelrod, *The Evolution of Cooperation* (Basic Books 2006); Lawrence Becker, *Reciprocity* (Routledge 1986). The view reaches back at least to Plato's *Crito* and *Republic*.

[19] John Locke, *Two Treatises of Government*, II.2.(4).

heedless risk-taker are alike in performing unjust actions in times of war or battle, again because such actions affect not only that individual but also fellow soldiers or citizens. In this broader sense, justice requires the performance of all the virtues, as matters directed to the common good of the community; and, when understood in this way, all virtues are relevant to, and required for, the common good.

Justice generates complex issues that must be addressed on their own (see Sections IV.2 and IV.3). But it should be acknowledged that human beings do *in fact* frequently operate on the basis of reciprocity and for no more noble cause; but (to repeat) neither this fact nor the 'fact' that reciprocity is a powerful and useful aid to social cohesion and order, detracts from the truth that such actions are not moral actions in the proper sense. Actions of this kind may be explored and studied by social historians or social scientists, but they are of scarce relevance to the moral philosopher.

What, then, is the basis of properly moral duties towards others? How does one get from a narrow self-regard to a perspective in which others matter? A number of candidates have been proposed to explain how this gap is to be traversed: for example, the harm principle, or the principle that one ought to love one's neighbour as oneself. Both principles are sound, but are unlikely to convince a person who is wedded to a belief in reciprocity. The point must be instead that there are no reasons in principle why one matters more than other human beings so far as allocations of human goods are concerned. Such goods are capable of nourishing, assisting, fortifying, and fulfilling each person with the same range and type of capacities as oneself, so that there are no permanent reasons of priority why one (anyone) ought to take precedence over others. This is not to deny another venerable moral precept: that each person should (and is best placed to) act in their own interests rather than for the interests of others. This principle (of reasonable self-preference) holds not because one's interests and wellbeing are more important than anyone else's, but because our own welfare is naturally the first and most intimate consideration in each person's practical intellect. In short, I am best placed to know and understand my own interests, and others are likewise in the best position to know and understand theirs.[20] A civilization in which each person acted always by interpreting the interests and needs of others, would be a history of mistake and cross-purposes, and of waste.

The very idea of a moral absolute denies the relevance of reciprocity. It is something that holds in *any* circumstances, including circumstances in which others do not conform their behaviour to it. Crowe rightly says that the idea of a moral absolute should not be sought in the doctrine that one ought never intentionally to harm another's pursuit of basic goods.[21] This is undoubtedly correct. Moral absolutes are better defined in terms of baselines beyond which the state cannot

[20] Finnis, *NLNR* (n 8) 146–48.
[21] Crowe, *NLNL* (n 8) 97.

regulate the lives of individuals or families, and that there are permanent features of the human being that (a) such beings must be free to explore and develop and (b) cannot be lawfully transgressed.[22]

The argument for genuine moral duty is best, and historically, made through the use of a counterfactual: the counterfactual situation in which no set and stable human laws, or social institutions, exist or ever existed, to determine questions of ownership and right. In such circumstances, there would be no reasons why one person rather than another should assert title to natural goods, that is to say, no natural hierarchy among persons concerning the moral right to those things necessary for survival and wellbeing. In other words, there would be a natural equality between all persons: an equality that may subsequently be developed and understood in different ways (by, for example, a Hobbes or a Rousseau), but which explains why (i) each person is most suitably placed *themselves* to pursue, in a self-determining way, those ends that are essential to life and fulfilment; and (ii) no person can claim any priority over the needs and interests of others by reason of any arbitrary self-preference.

Of other ways in which philosophers have attempted to account for the force of moral propositions, I shall briefly mention only two: Kantian and neo-Kantian philosophy. Kant's categorical imperative, with its aim of universalizing moral propositions, is an inadequate way in which to understand the other-regarding quality of moral norms; for the rule is in fact self-regarding: can *I* will consistently a universal moral law such that others, following that same moral law, can act towards *me* as *I* wish to act towards them? Similarly, the conservative thinking of the members of the Original Position, in Rawls's modern Kantian theory, is essentially an adaptation of this same self-regard: what must I decide, so that *my* position is not made insufferable, when the veil of ignorance is removed? Such theories proceed on the assumption that genuinely other-regarding thinking is an impossibility, for the reason that they have no fully worked-out and sensitive theory of human good.

For many modern theories of ethics, the central problem to be overcome is that of partiality or personal bias. Rawls's Original Position is one attempt to overcome this problem, by having the inhabitants of that condition deliberate to produce agreement on basic principles of justice. This device fails to heed Aquinas's warning that many of the primary and secondary precepts of ethics are known only to those who are wise enough to understand the relevant matters, who have benefitted from a stable upbringing amongst practices that are morally good, and who possess sufficient experience of life in order to comprehend the difficulties faced by practical reason's bearing upon contingent facts and particulars. But it is nevertheless knowledge of human good that grounds ethics, including the interface between public and private good. No amount of fairness in procedure could produce the relevant

[22] This position draws on Grotius, *De Iure Belli ac Pacis* I.I.XIV; I.2.

knowledge, any more than agreement can (of itself) constitute the nature of human goods, which instead follow the order of natural inclinations.[23] Indeed, the exclusion of fully fledged 'theories' of human good from the Original Position has a correspondingly suppressive effect upon the recognition of schemes of justice that are regarded as 'fair'. Such schemes are obliterated from the account before they can be heard.

No genuine account of moral duty, therefore, can be derived from a theory of reciprocity, no matter how elaborate. It must instead arise out of a sober consideration of human goods as something other than mere private interests or predilections. In this sense, all of one's moral thinking is directed to the *common* good or goods, the complexities of which fall to be discussed in later sections of this book.

## III.4. A THEORY OF MORALITY

Let us make an entirely new start. An account of human primary goods raises various moral questions. It is morally necessary to act prudently to protect one's life (or the lives of others) rather than seek its extinction. A life lived in opposition to sociable friendship (the denial of peace and justice) is an immoral life. A life spent in pursuit of false or apparent goods is a culpable waste of one's life. In this sense, moral questions surround the pursuit of non-moral excellences: see Section II.5. But exactly because there are many, perhaps infinite, ways in which a person might pursue or attain primary goods, questions about the moral life do not centre upon the combination of the goods thus pursued. Hence Aquinas, who possesses a highly complete moral theory, mentions in passing only a few primary goods; and Grotius (for example) refers to none.

An indispensable aspect of one's moral thinking is a knowledge of one's circumstances. In line with the classical and medieval sense of 'morality', which concerns *all* free human action as such, the pursuit of various primary goods enters into moral thinking only by reference to what is reasonable in the circumstances. If all things are equal, the choice to attain some item of knowledge (or knowledge *tout court*)—rather than, say, learning to play a piece of music—is of no moral significance. But things are not always equal. Circumstances may render the attainment of some piece of knowledge the more prudent course of action, or the more edifying, when compared with other ends or actions that it is possible to perform. Alternatively, to strive after some piece of knowledge that is hopelessly beyond one's intellectual powers, is neither prudent nor reasonable, for it is a waste of one's time and talents. These are practical questions—questions of practical reason—but

[23] Cf John Rawls, *Theory of Justice* (revised edn Belknap Press 1999) 54–55.

they are also moral questions as they relate to the question of how one's life should be lived both in the present and when contemplated as a whole.

There are however also moral questions that are not thus dependent upon circumstances. They give structure to the total field of one's choices. Thus a theory of morality must distinguish between those principles, standards, and demands that hold true of all human societies and at all times, and those principles, standards, and demands that are a product of social or historical conditions, and which hold only among certain peoples: between what we shall call a *core morality* and those standards that have been reasonably determined by human minds pondering specific problems of social coordination or social peace.

Failure to distinguish between these two moralities has been responsible for many of the relativist arguments of present times. For there are indeed many divergences between practices across the world which, if we are not careful, can give rise to the impression that *all* moral ideas lie in the realm of determination, the creative yet rational response to specific moral issues. For example, sentencing is often paraded as one instance of such determinative reasoning, for it is clearly a moral issue, but not one upon which natural law is conclusive. The creative freedom that the lawmaker has in this respect is one that is limited by other precepts of natural law (pertaining for example to the dignity of human life); but that same freedom may obscure those limits to such an extent that the death penalty may be put forward as a moral and justified punishment for serious crimes. Thus it will *appear* that divergent practices in different societies are entirely matters of convention.

More generally, the demands of social morality—of moral determinations made by and within a given community—are capable of being mistaken or unjust. Both Aquinas and St Augustine, for example, were concerned with social morality as a source of depraved practices.[24] Again, such practices can in time obscure or distort the demands of the core morality. Nevertheless, those demands are always available to prudent individuals in any society. They express the derived precepts of natural law. Here I list seven principles which make up the core morality. This list does not intend to be exhaustive of moral principles, but maps out the most basic principles from which finer moral judgments must proceed.

(a) *Never intentionally harm another person.* This principle is a venerable principle of morality, most famously stated by Mill in the first book of *On Liberty*.[25] There, Mill states the principle as one of prudent government, and as a duty of the state: 'The only purpose for which power can be rightfully exercised over any member of a civilized community, against his will, is to prevent harm to others.' But this specification of the principle goes wrong in two senses. First, it is a principle that applies not only to officials of a legal system or system of government, but to each individual citizen within the state. There are no reasons for believing

[24] See Augustine, *De Civitate Dei* XIX.5 & 21, IV.4.

[25] It is also present in Aquinas, *ST* (n 3) I-II.100.3c.

that the harm principle affects only official actions, nor that (therefore) individual citizens comply fully with the harm principle simply by obeying the law. It is up to each individual person's judgment to limit their behaviours to those which do not knowingly harm other persons: a judgment which is anyway needed due to the law's generality.[26] Secondly, Mill is in error in supposing that the harm principle is the *only* principle by which action is to be limited. Below I suggest at least six additional principles that must be given effect in action in order to render that action morally right.

Of course, our actions as individuals affect others in ways that we cannot anticipate and of which we may remain ignorant. Hence it is necessary to add to Mill's formulation of the principle the caveat that (subject to principle (g) below) only intentional harm is singled out as immoral. Our actions frequently have effects in the world of which we are not aware: each action creates a new circumstance, and the change we bring about in action is always greater than the change we intend. Without this limitation on the principle, life would become a kind of moral paralysis, with the additional thought that one's *omissions* may also, for all one knows, create indirect harm.

A further corollary of this principle, however, is that one ought to be willing to compensate victims unintentionally harmed by one's actions. Typically, it will not be clear to the individuals involved in such situations precisely what kind or amount of compensation is justified or necessary. Tort law therefore provides appropriate (conventional) measures of compensation in order to clarify the rights and duties of those concerned. Principle (a) thereby expresses an aspect of justice, and a dimension of the common good (mutual forbearance, mutual restraint).

There are of course limits to the notion of 'harm' that must be taken into account in the operation of this principle. For these purposes, 'harm' certainly and obviously includes harm to the person (i.e. bodily harm), but also to their interests. But not all interests are reasonably counted as reasons against a given course of action. For example, my decision to open a restaurant next door to your restaurant might be said in some sense to 'harm' your interests; but it would be patently unreasonable to suggest that I have acted immorally by opening a rival establishment. Equally, our competing with one another for a prize or a promotion does not mean that I harm your interests if I win. In both cases, the other person has no reasonable (moral) right to regard his or her interests as more important than, or prevailing over, mine. In any large and complex society, the interests of individuals will clash or compete. The purpose of this principle is then to outlaw intentional injuries to others' legitimate interests. The content of 'legitimate' for these purposes is spelled out conveniently in private law, but will be obvious enough most of the time to rational judgment as such.

[26] See HLA Hart, *The Concept of Law* (3rd edn OUP 2012, hereafter *CL*) 124.

(b) *Act with integrity*. The second principle, here stated positively as an aspiration, is also capable of being stated through a catalogue of negative precepts, such as that one should not lie to deflect blame, or bear false witness. But in more general terms the principle demands that action is honest (in the sense of stemming from pure motives), sincere, and informed by conscientiously clear moral principles. In the context of work, this requirement means that one should not willingly perform less than one's role, nor exceed it by encroaching on the role of another person or stepping beyond one's legal power. In other contexts, it means acting fairly and with decency, and in accord with one's principles.

In other words, this requirement demands that one follow one's conscience. But conscience can also be mistaken either in relation to a single event or regarding general principle. There is thus a need, in order to satisfy this principle, to educate one's conscience as far as one can. This means (for example) working out and holding a system of articulated moral principles, rather than facing each new situation one by one, *de novo*. But at the same time one should be reflectively open to doubt about one's principles, to avoid clinging to dogmatism in the face of contrary evidence.

(c) *Seek out ways of living peacefully in society*. This is a many-sided principle. It is the main principle by which citizens contribute to the common good. It obviously involves avoiding occasions of violent affray, and seeking to resolve disputes peacefully (possibly through the courts). But it involves too the effort to forgive minor faults, and to avoid acts that occasion what Aquinas calls 'outcry or public disturbance' (*scandalum vel turbatio*).[27] Indeed, as Aquinas also says, there may be times when one ought to forgo one's rights in order to avoid destabilizing the governing regime and threatening the breakdown of law and order. (This may involve, for example, paying an unpopular or unfair tax.) Acts contrary to social peace can also be in the form of words rather than deeds, so that for example hate speech in all its forms is immoral, as also are words that are intended to incite violence or exploit social divisions.

It was quite obvious to the scholastic philosophers that the effort to impose and uphold peace is not the responsibility of officials alone, but depends also upon the efforts of every citizen. For there will be no peace unless each person observes their legal duties and refrains from criminal acts. At the same time, it is impossible for any one citizen to achieve peace on their own; it requires the common will and effort of the people as a whole. This means that the majority of one's actions in seeking peace are directed to only a relatively few: maintaining peace with one's family and friends, and having amicable relations with the others that one meets. This includes, for example, the willingness to enter into agreements with others,

[27] Aquinas, *ST* (n 3) I-II.96.4c & ad 3, I-II.97.1 ad 2, II-II.117.6c.

even for one's own enrichment, but sometimes into more complicated political or commercial arrangements to produce common goods such as schools or hospitals.

(d) *Carry out one's promises.* This principle, which is stricter than is typically to be found in the law of contract, requires that one's *lawful* (non-criminal) agreements be fulfilled unless some intervening act prevents performance of the duty. It is stricter than the rule of *restitutio in integrum* because it recognizes that, most of the time, the performance is more valuable than being restored to the pre-contractual position. Notwithstanding this, the actual laws of contract of mature societies (including for example doctrines of consideration, frustration, and fraud) are intended not just to facilitate the making of economic bargains but also to inject a minimal morality into the market.

The performance of one's promises (whether contractual in nature or not) clearly contributes to the above principle concerning peace, for it avoids the contention which would arise were the promise not performed. But the principle of carrying out one's promises goes beyond the desire for peace as such; it serves the common good in powerful further ways. To see this, we need only consider the counter-factual situation in which promises are regularly broken, so that no person is able to trust or rely upon the word of any other. In such a condition, there could be no infrastructure (roads, bridges, aqueducts ...) and no major common endeavours (hospitals, schools, public transport...). There would be no economic institutions, such as banks or shops, and no marriage in the form with which we are familiar. Thus the principle that promises should be carried out (where possible) is a distinct principle with its own links to the common good of the community.

(e) *Honour one's debts.* This is the principle that one should return to others what is owed to them, a key principle of justice as recognized since the most ancient times. Broadly interpreted, this principle enjoins one to respect the property of others, not merely by returning borrowed items but by refraining from taking without permission. It recognizes the property rights of others. Again this principle is sometimes an aspect of principle (d) above, but not always: for not all debts arise through promise or contract.

Aquinas (amongst others) recognizes that there are exceptions to this principle. He specifically mentions the case of the return of a weapon to an enemy, whom one thinks will use it against one's community; or to a drunk or madman who has diminished their judgment and who is thus a danger either to themselves or others.[28] In these cases there are intervening acts or states of affairs which make it unreasonable to repay the debt *at that time*. One should therefore perhaps say that the principle is to honour one's debts *in good time*, the 'good' time being relative to the circumstances that have arisen meanwhile. But these exceptional circumstances

[28] See ibid II-II.120.1c.

should not be allowed to deflect the general judgment that debts are normally to be repaid promptly.

Not all debts are monetary however. For it has long been a principle of western thought that one owes a debt to the state in which one has been raised and nurtured. When we think about duties to the state, we think primarily about taxation. But there are other types of duty that may be said to be owed to the state: such as national service, voting in elections, or (not to be overlooked) the duty to obey the state laws.

(f) *Work*. In the first place this principle demands that those who can should work for a living; but in a wider sense it relates to the need to be of use to others throughout one's life. Those who rejoiced at Scrooge's grave in *A Christmas Carol* express the moral outrage one feels against one who lived exclusively for their own interests. Often, the work that one does for a living will also be of service to others: even the self-employed may, for example, generate jobs or opportunities for others. But this will not always be the case: in such cases, one's care for others must find other outlets and modes of expression. It ranges over noble instances of self-sacrifice as well as minor acts of kindness or forbearance. It is present whenever one bestirs oneself to assist another.

Economists from Adam Smith onward possess the notion of an 'invisible hand', by which the effort to enrich oneself or improve one's position has the collateral (and unintended) effect of enhancing the situation of others. For present purposes it is not necessary to examine the reality of this notion. The present principle does not deny that there is a rational self-preference to care for one's own needs, nor does it deny that much of one's resources and energy are expended for the sake of one's close family and friends. It does not outlaw the making of profit as such, though it recognizes that much work generates profit only because it produces useful products (e.g. food, housing) or useful services (e.g. clean facilities, good education) that benefit others. By contrast, the invisible hand is concerned only with the distribution of wealth, not of products or services. Further, however, just as this principle recognizes rational self-preference, it outlaws *unreasonable* self-preference: the carrying on of work that seeks to enrich only the worker, by any means, or by ignoring or harming the interests of others. It therefore condemns forms of work-for-profit in which the interests of others 'form no part of [the] intention' to assist others to a better position.[29]

These matters raise questions of justice that must be postponed until Section IV.1. For now, we may perhaps accept that work is a significant moral need at least for all those in society who are fit to undertake it.

(g) *Act with reasonable foresight*. This discrete principle enters into all of the principles (a)–(f). All persons are more-or-less able to act with foresight, so that

[29] See Adam Smith, *The Wealth of Nations*, IV.2.9.

they can anticipate likely consequences of their actions. To act with blithe disregard for the consequences of one's actions, or deliberately to deprive oneself of the knowledge of such consequences, is an immoral act. Indeed no act can be moral that is not guided by the likely consequences of the action.

To highlight the importance of reasonable foresight is not to adopt the utilitarian philosophy that the 'moral' goodness of an act is measured by its overall consequences. For there are other measures of an act's goodness that relate to motivation and substantive rightness: consider principles (a)–(c) for example. Yet the likely consequences of one's action are an important ingredient of one's judgment to act in one way rather than another, or to employ one means rather than another: the avoidance of waste is equally a consideration of morality. Let us therefore include efficiency in means as a subordinate consideration of this principle.

Another term for reasonable foresight might be 'prudence', in something like the classical sense of Aquinas's *prudentia*. For it involves the good ordering of thought in relation to the other principles of core morality. For example, prudence might dictate that one not take on any debt that one cannot easily repay, or enter into a promise or contract that one suspects one will not be able to perform. Equally, prudence or reasonable foresight relates not only to single acts which lie immediately in one's judgment, but also to how the presently contemplated action relates to other actions either past or in view. To operate without this sort of prudence, one's life would be a mess: one action undoing or rendering impossible another. To avoid such chaos in one's life, to bring coherence to one's impulses and choices, requires a high degree of reasonable foresight. Thus, as Aristotle observed, one's immediate goals tend to be subsumed under more general ends, and they under some single unifying end of happiness. Such order in one's life is made possible by foresight: specific courses of action are undertaken for the sake of a general end, because one foresees that their completion will bring one closer to the fulfilment of the general end.

But reasonable foresight also matters in terms of the lives and interests of others. To this extent, foresight is an outward-facing principle. To act without such foresight is to treat others as so many potential casualties along the way to one's own goals. It is therefore to ignore potential harm to others (principle (a)), not to mention to treat with disregard those with whom one is supposed to live in harmony (principle (c)). At the same time, reasonable foresight is distinct from the sort of catastrophizing that, at the limit, could end in a kind of moral paralysis (see principle (a) above). Nor does it (therefore) eliminate the possibility of all risk, and it does not deflect the thought that certain risks are well taken. Clearly, many cases will exist along the borderline between reasonable and unreasonable risk: here one's moral duties need to be carefully and sensitively calculated.

Each of these seven principles reinforces the others, and as such an aspect of each principle is realized through others. But no principle entirely reduces to any other. Taken together they set out a core morality: one that applies to every person, irrespective of culture, history, or time. The core morality is therefore also a *universal* morality. This is obviously not to deny that individuals or even whole peoples are capable of departing from these principles: Aquinas, for example, observes that (according to Julius Caesar) among the 'Germanic tribes' theft was not considered to be evil.[30] But such principles are always ready to hand in the practical reason of all persons and all peoples, at least those of sufficient linguistic sophistication to draw the relevant distinctions.

It must be remembered however that the core morality binding upon each person is only a minimal morality. It represents the least that a person must do in order to act morally. For example, it does not extend as far as demanding that every person exercise beneficence towards others. This is not because such moral virtues are less universal in character (they are not), but because it is impossible to attain moral excellence before one is thoroughly accustomed to acting in line with the core morality. For instance, one cannot exercise liberality until one has *already* honoured all of one's debts. The core morality is the starting point for all moral excellences, but it does not include them.

It is often said that morality is essentially other-regarding, and the core morality is no exception. But since the earliest times, it has also been said that acting immorally is also a harm to the person acting. Thus Plato, for example, warns that it is better to suffer injustice than to do it. The harm to oneself in acting immorally consists in detracting from a properly *eudaemon* life, that is, that the immoral agent can never be truly fulfilled. But to this it must be added that acting immorally directly affects one's inner being: it causes a stain on one's soul.

The core morality is binding on all individuals no matter what their status in society. But there are in addition principles of core morality that apply particularly to state officials in the performance of their office. Perhaps one should rather say that the demands of core morality are raised to a new register in the case of officials. As Aquinas says, there is a special virtue for governing well.[31] Thus, for example, the principle that others should not be deliberately harmed is extended not just to other individuals with whom one happens to come into contact, but to all individuals affected by one's policies or judgments. Clearly new laws and governmental policies (not to mention prison sentences) will not affect all citizens in the same way, to the same extent, and in some cases will have a negative rather than positive effect on certain sections of the community. Some of these will be reasonably foreseeable whereas others will not. Occasionally, tough choices have to be made for the sake of the common good. But it is a principle that all such judgments and policies must seek to ensure the protection of the least well-off members of the community, or to provide safety nets for those negatively affected by policy decisions. These and other demands of justice will be discussed later.

[30] Aquinas, *ST* (n 3) I-II.94.4c; see also I-II.94.6c.

[31] Ibid, II-II.47.12c.

Officials are also under a special duty to act with integrity when carrying out political offices. They must act consistently and without corruption; they must not allow allegiances of class, race, or friendship to deflect their aims; and they must not act out of personal interest. They must strive to maintain the peaceful order of the community at the level of laws, policies, and sentences; and they must put in place legal frameworks for the governance of bargains and debts (including debts brought about through accident). The work that they do is specially directed to the common good of the community, but they can only do this insofar as they operate with reasonable foresight of the ends of their actions.

These principles of morality represent the deep structure of our moral thinking and acting. They are the principles that inform and give content to the virtues: for the virtues demand that one act for the *right* reasons, at the *right* time, in the *right* way, and for the *right* ends. They are implicit in the account of the virtue of justice, and are presupposed in our obligations to the common good, of which account is given in the chapters that follow.

## III.5. GENERAL MORALITY

The core morality discussed above can be contrasted with what we might call the 'general morality' of a community. Whereas the core morality is directed to those elements of the common good that apply to all societies and at all times, the precepts of general morality pertain specially to those elements of the common good that are culturally or historically specific. For instance, liberal societies perhaps more than any other require a general morality, for principles such as 'live and let live' are insufficiently definite to offer proper guidance to state officials and citizens. But all societies have a common good that goes beyond the requirements of peace and justice, for which governing arrangements need to be made. Such arrangements are for the welfare of citizens beyond the benefits of justice and peace. An example of a matter of general morality is taxation and public spending.

Taxation represents a legal transfer of property from the individual person to the government, in order to sustain the community.[32] It can be reckoned, as in Section III.4 above, as an aspect of the debt citizens owe to their community. But the kind and measure of taxation is (within reasonable limits) a matter of variance between different communities and in different times and circumstances. The specific rate of taxation is one of those matters that is, in Aquinas's words, substantially or wholly determined by their having been laid down or decided. Similarly (and again within reasonable limits) the question of public spending on the basis of tax revenue is one to be determined by particular governments at particular times and in particular

[32] See Alejandro Chafuen, *Faith and Liberty: The Economic Thought of the Late Scholastics* (Lexington Books 2003) 58.

circumstances. In both of these cases, individuals and governments (as well as officers of the law) carry out duties to the wider common good, the common good that is specific and particular to that society at that time.

There are many respects in which a tax system must correspond to reason. It must be comprehensible to those who must administer the system and to those who must pay; it must be at least relatively stable, yet respond to particular issues or circumstances; it must be fair yet not stifle entrepreneurship; it must exclude tax-dodging efforts of individuals and corporations; it must enact civil and/or criminal liability for those who avoid payment; and its demands must not be random but correspond to prevailing social needs. Similarly, a tax system must pursue coherent ends: redistribution from rich to poor, discouraging or penalizing certain behaviours (such as smoking), stimulating growth in certain sectors of the economy, and so forth. In all such cases, tax law pursues means and ends that are connected to the common good in a broader sense, specific to a certain community at a certain time. Even matters that derive from natural law through creative determination must therefore be rational, and not arbitrary. Whilst fundamental aspects of government, law, and order have to be paid for, both the exact nature of the payment and the specific constitutional forms are matters of general morality, to be worked out in that community's legislation.

There are many other matters of general morality than that of tax. State officials, as has previously been noted, have a core moral duty to ensure peace, law, and order for the community. But the exact terms of this peace and order will vary depending upon a range of circumstances, such as levels of natural resources or population growth, and may change over time. Thus, a state's general morality must include decisions about the allocation of resources, goods, opportunities, and offices: matters in other words of distributive justice. Integrity (lack of bias or discrimination) is a basic aspect of distributive justice, but it is not the whole, and cannot answer every question that is likely to be posed about particular distributions. Here, specific distributions must not only be reasonable, but must also do justice to the historic rights of the persons whose property or wealth is up for redistribution. Clearly, these questions inherently pull in different directions, making the question of distributive justice one of the most difficult tasks faced by state officials. More will be said about this in Section IV.1.

Another wider moral duty of the state is to act as carer and custodian of a community's culture, including its arts treasures and its scientific advances. Not only must the state protect these cultural objects, it must also ensure that they are available to the nation (to whom they ultimately belong). This availability is one facet of another of the state's responsibilities to the flourishing of its members: education. For liberty depends upon an understanding of options, and choosing between options demands, inter alia, an understanding of their attractiveness and their cost. Without literacy and numeracy, many doors that lie open to individuals in pursuit of a good life would become closed. Thus it is incumbent upon the state to divert a proportion of its tax revenue into schools, colleges, and other educational institutions.

To say all of this is not to suggest that general morality is in some way inferior to, or less important than, core morality. It is not an optional extra, but a fully binding moral order of duties that apply to a community in virtue of its particular kind and circumstances. Thus for example, in a country in which there is (for some good reason) food rationing, it is a duty of general morality that rationing be observed, not circumvented, obstructed, applied unfairly (i.e. applied to some and not others) or otherwise subverted. The set of moral duties hence applied to state officials, corporations, and private individuals are, again, fully binding and incumbent on all persons. They are every bit as important as core moral duties of peace and justice, for indeed such duties are required for justice and social peace in that community at *that* time and in *those* circumstances.

General morality should also inform and direct the lives of individuals, beyond their core moral duties. For general morality goes beyond the requirements of the common goods of peace and justice; it transforms the merely good *citizen* into a good *person*. One's decision for example to get married is a matter of this kind. Once married, both spouses owe one another fidelity, alongside duties of affection and love, and material assistance; and these are instances of the core moral duty to keep one's promises. But the decision to marry is not itself a core moral duty, for it is possible without immorality to remain unmarried all one's life. Yet marriage itself is a morally excellent condition, one that shapes one's life in profound ways, as well as that of one's spouse. Not all aspects of general morality are chosen in this sense. In addition, one can also mention such life-shaping norms as the avoidance of greed and lust, willingness to care for dependants, and all modes of liberality and benefaction. Then there is beneficence: doing good to others, even those who are not one's responsibility. This consists partly in action, such as in rescuing and assisting (even at some risk to oneself), and in being forgiving; and partly in omission, such as in not vandalizing public property or wilfully destroying assets.

It should be clear from this partial list that not all duties of general morality are supererogatory; avoidance of greed for example is not so. Neither can it be presumed that general moral duties are essentially personal virtues, for many such duties are other-regarding (as with caring for the sick). Indeed there is an other-regarding aspect to virtually all general moral duties: even greed has repercussions for the stock of common goods. Thus general moral duties can be distinguished from core moral duties by their relationship to the common good. For as already stated, the core moral duties of persons represent a minimal morality principally concerned with the common goods of peace and justice. General moral duties by contrast are concerned with the common good (the good between persons) in a further way, and thus presuppose the bedrock of core morality.

The reference here to 'common good' is to be understood as identifying modes or kinds of fulfilment that arise, or are capable of arising, between two or more individuals, including but not necessarily referring to, the common good of the whole community. Indeed, the scholastic philosophers were accustomed to dividing morality into three parts: individual, domestic, and political. The second of these, domestic, refers to the good of households as they seek together the good of their members, by taking thought about how to pursue and obtain human goods. The division is not rigid, for such pursuit of goods requires households to participate in political community and to engage with other members of the community; equally, political morality should be directed to the flourishing of households and individuals. But the division is useful in highlighting the existence of a broad range of moral duties at the level of domestic *oeconomica*.

Finally, general morality is not, as some sceptics like to think, arbitrary. Moral scepticism entirely overlooks the core morality, but also mischaracterizes the general morality of the community as something wilfully asserted or chosen, so that all values are relative to a particular community. But there is no link between cultural relativity and arbitrariness: nothing in the general morality is arbitrary simply because it relates to specific circumstances. Some general moral duties are indeed in one sense contingent, depending upon the particular historical, cultural, and social circumstances of the community. But their contingency is not an indicator of arbitrariness. Such duties (mostly duties of the state) are a reasoned response to particular circumstances and challenges facing a community. Furthermore, not all parts of the wider common good are relative to particular communities at particular times: many of the individual moral duties mentioned above are recognized at least implicitly in mature societies as values to be respected.

## III.6. THE PRIORITY OF GOOD

A person may ask, what is the point of morality? Why should I act morally? The question is an invitation to sublimate desire, which can be wild and inordinate, and to relegate reason to an instrumental role in satisfying desires, avoiding one's obligations and so forth. Why is this situation worth avoiding? Several answers can be given, drawing upon the preceding discussion. (i) A life devoted to selfishness and self-preference is unlikely to be marked by genuine and true friendship, one of the most important human goods. Without true friendship, life is immeasurably impoverished. (ii) The virtuous life is the only wholly happy life; one can pay one's taxes willingly and with joy at the thought of redistributing a part of one's surplus wealth to the poor or to the common good; or one can pay taxes unwillingly and with anger at the loss of one's wealth. (iii) The immoral person is ignorant of what constitutes genuine happiness: he or she acts for the sake of false goods rather than true goods, and is consequently unfulfilled and can achieve only fleeting measures of happiness. (iv) To act immorally out of habit is to accept the tyranny of desire over reason, and to put oneself into the position of a slave to one's emotions; but a properly human life is one in which reason is in the driving seat, ruling over the emotions. (v) The immoral person's soul is put into jeopardy by their actions: every religion has at its core a series of moral teachings laid down for the faithful to follow. Many such teachings are not aspirational but instead set out duties to be observed by all in present time. To act against such duties is not to ruin one's character at some future point, but rather here and now.

Each of these reasons has been offered, at one time or another, by philosophers seeking to overcome the objections of sceptics; but all are valid. Each is an appeal to (rational) self-interest, as distinct from the unreasonable self-interest of immorality. For morality is good not only for those affected by one's actions, but also for one's own wellbeing. We may speak in this sense of the priority of good. For (equally), as outlined in Section III.3 above, the basis of morality is the realization that the goods in which one shares are *human* goods: good not just for the agent but for all others too. There are simply no reasons for believing that one's own interests are more important than, or take priority over, the needs and interests of others.

MacIntyre raises the question of the relative priority of dispositions and desires. We need good reasons for our desires, and sufficient reasons for action (reasons that are superior to other, competing reasons): see Section III.1.[33] But how (we might ask) are we to measure the competing strength of reasons when the goods to which they adhere are themselves incommensurable? A partial answer is available to those who support the current orthodoxy in natural law theory (i.e. Finnis's and Grisez's account). For they will point out that, although goods are strictly incommensurable, they nonetheless take on shifting priorities as circumstances dictate or make appropriate. One can go to a lecture *or* be sociable with one's friends; keep on reading one's book *or* flee the library which is currently burning down around one; become lost in wonder and appreciation at a moving art exhibit *or* catch one's train (and so forth). Some of these trade-offs are obvious, others less so. But the partial answer on its own is not satisfactory. For we might well wonder how or whether it is possible to orchestrate our dispositions over a lifetime, or whether there is more to existence than moving from one disposition to the next? The partial answer is completed by acknowledging a general teleology of the human being (one who is healthy rather than sick, reasonable rather than unreasonable, and virtuous rather than vicious). Why should one be any of these things? As Cicero said (see Section II.1), to be lacking in virtue is to be divided, alienated from one's true self; is to be divorced from the deep and true friendships of those who understand the satisfactions that come from giving of oneself, one's things, one's time and effort; is to be incapable of understanding the whole of art because high art seeks to communicate truth; and is to be a destroyer of goodness in those around him or her, for he or she will wish the good of those persons according to the good as they see and

[33] MacIntyre, *ECM* (n 9) 8, 14. See also George Duke, 'Natural Law's Normative Point' 38 (2019) *Law & Philosophy* 1.

experience it (or, if they do not, but wish them true good, will be even more divided against themselves). Such a person will fail to grasp that virtue is its own reward, that there is, amongst all the true goods it is possible to pursue, a rational form of life not only suitable but also beneficial for all human beings, centred upon the virtues, which may be sought and realized in numerous ways and which open further horizons for human good and human endeavour the more they are practised. They will fail to understand that while goods such as pleasure, power, and honour are genuine goods, they are not the final good.[34] This is the human *telos*.

As both Aristotle and Plato were aware, unreasonable persons are not readily persuadable by arguments, but require further persuasion in the form of legal punishments. Thus Aristotle admits that immature persons (in attitudes if not in years) are not fitted to listen to arguments about morality.[35] Perhaps the archetypal immoralist in this sense is Plato's Callicles, who differs from other reprobates in openly despising the good. Callicles resists Socrates's arguments (that it is better to suffer wrong than to do it) to the bitter end. His retorts have little to do with the argument, but simply do not take it very seriously. But Socrates is alive to the illogic of Callicles's position: 'If we argued the issues over and over again, you would be persuaded.'[36] (See Section I.6.) Why? Because Callicles's position is incoherent: the behaviour he wishes to get away with (e.g. stealing) is behaviour that he would not wish others to engage in at his expense. The two situations, wishing to steal from others but not wishing to be stolen from, can be reconciled (but only on the surface) by treating one's own interests as intrinsically more important than the interests of others. But there is simply no basis for such a position; indeed the attempt to generalize such a position would end in contradiction.

The relevant standard for action is supplied by the *spoudaios*, or person of practical wisdom. In the same way as food tastes as it should to a healthy person but may have a bad taste for an ill person, so true goodness, the correct measure of good and bad in action, is apparent to and is known by the *spoudaios*, who must for these purposes be the standard for our practical judgments.[37] Correspondingly, the unwise judgments of lovers of pleasure, who (Aristotle suggests) are to be found in society in far greater numbers, are to be shunned.

Morality does not presuppose what Rawls calls a 'strict compliance' society, or what Raz calls a 'society of angels'. Real situations of moral judgment arise in circumstances in which one cannot presume upon other people acting morally in their various dealings, even towards oneself. Indeed, they take place in circumstances in which even good people disagree about the demands of morality. This does not render one's moral obligations any less pressing, nor does it license

[34] MacIntyre, *ECM* (n 9) 53.
[35] Aristotle, *NE* (n 16) I.3.1095a.
[36] Plato, *Gorgias* 513c.
[37] Aristotle, *NE* (n 16) III.4.1113a.

reciprocal immorality: Hobbes's stark depiction of the 'natural condition' of humankind perhaps illustrates the logical conclusion of such policies. The moral citizen must therefore be prepared to suffer setbacks and endure certain hurts in order to stay true to the requirements of morality. For the real challenge of morality is not that of coming to know what good morals are, but rather the effort to put those moral principles into effect in the real world.

# IV
# JUSTICE

## IV.1. SOME DISTINCTIONS

In Chapter II commented that the 'natural law thesis' (that the purpose of law is to provide decisive reasons for action) is incorrect, or at least subordinate to other aspects of natural law theory (see Section I.6).[1] Traditionally, the point of law is to administer justice: a point illustrated by the continued focus on the doctrine *lex iniusta non est lex*: whether decried or defended, the focus is not usually upon *immoral* law in general, but upon *unjust* law in particular. This narrowing of debate testifies to justice's importance, but it unfolds a variety of contested theories as to what justice is, and what it demands. In an effort to cut through some of these complications, and to describe in outline what justice *is*, and what it *truly* demands, I propose to return to first principles. I begin with some distinctions.

Justice, according to the classical definition, is 'the constant and perpetual willingness to give to each person what is *due* or *owed* to them'. But what exactly is owed to each person, and how are we to determine what is owed? Since the very earliest times, philosophers of justice have begun their inquiries by observing that the inquiry into justice is not one inquiry, but many. Thus we find Aristotle, for example, distinguishing between what is owed to each person in terms of the distribution of common stock, and what is due to those same persons by virtue of their direct relationships with other individuals, by way of 'corrective' (or later, commutative) justice. This basic distinction gave rise to difficulties, however, as it relates to another distinction of Aristotle's, which came to dominate thinking in the Aristotelian–Thomist tradition: the distinction between so-called 'general' (or 'legal') and 'particular' justice.[2]

General justice is Aristotle's term for the obedience (to laws) that each citizen owes their community, or in modern terms, the state; it represents each person's orientation to the common good. At the same time, however, general justice also signified what is morally owed to others in a broad sense, beyond the confines of justice understood as a distinct ethical virtue. Thus, the commission of adultery is a vice by which one fails to moderate or control one's desire (and hence pertains to temperance), but it is also undeniably an injustice to the husband with whose wife one has had an affair. Or again, a deserting soldier displays cowardice

[1] See Mark C Murphy, *Natural Law in Jurisprudence & Politics* (CUP 2010, hereafter *NLJP*) 34.
[2] Aristotle, *Nicomachean Ethics* (hereafter *NE*) V.1.1129b.

*Natural Law and Modern Society*. Sean Coyle, Oxford University Press. © Sean Coyle 2023.
DOI: 10.1093/oso/9780192886996.003.0004

by running away from battle, but his actions also form an injustice to the community he is meant to defend. In the classical schema, general justice is distinct from particular justice (justice understood as a distinct virtue apart from other ethical values), and particular justice is divided into commutative and distributive justice. Not without a measure of justification, scholastic commentators in the centuries after Aquinas interpreted the classical writers as proposing a threefold understanding of justice: (1) general justice, governing the relationship of individuals to the state; (2) distributive justice, governing the state's relationship to individuals; and (3) commutative justice, governing the relationship of individuals to one another.[3] This realignment of the classical schema is however problematic. On the one hand, the state owes its people not only just distributions of resources but also certain obligations of commutative justice, such as the provision of a safe social environment, defence against external threats, and so on (see Section V.3.) On the other hand, the obligations that individuals owe to the state might well, on the basis of law, include distributive elements: for example, the property of a person who dies intestate will be distributed according to certain proportions among the surviving relatives (so in either case a distribution must be made). Furthermore, forms of distributive justice obtain between private individuals, for example when any privately owned assets are distributed among two or more individuals. This confusion over the identity of general justice is plain from Aquinas's discussion, where he states that general justice gets its name from the fact that it is possible for one's act to be directed towards other people in general, and not to particular individuals; and such directiveness is therefore a general virtue, whose proper object is the common good.[4] Now, the common good is the object of the state, which acts as custodian of the common, not the individual, good.[5] Thus individuals can only act for the common good in a fully adequate way through their acts of obedience to the commands of that very custodian. Hence, 'general justice' can also be called 'legal justice'. Completely absent from these ruminations on the character of general justice is any sense of justice as a general virtue implicated in moral or immoral acts directed towards other individuals, such as the cuckolded husband.

Another distinction that might structure our inquiries into justice is that between what we might call political and civil justice. Political justice relates to all those matters of justice that result from the political process; civil justice pertains to interpersonal relationships structured by the operations of the civil or common law. But the boundary between these two aspects of justice is at best difficult to discern. Clearly, a state's provision of health services, educational opportunities, industrial infrastructure, and so on belongs to the political realm rather than the

[3] For some useful discussion, with slightly different emphasis, see Finnis, *Aquinas* 215–17n; John Finnis, *Natural Law & Natural Rights* (2nd edn OUP 2011, hereafter *NLNR*) 184–88.

[4] Aquinas, *Summa Theologiae* (hereafter *ST*) II-II.58.5c.

[5] Ibid, I-II.90.4c.

realm of private rights, but there are many examples where the contrast is much less clear. For example, the state may legislate numerous provisions creating rights in and to property, but the character of those rights is private: though dependent, like all rights, upon the state's ultimately coercive authority, they belong to the civil realm of horizontal rights between citizens and other legal persons. It is also worthy of notice that the political/civil distinction is itself distinct from that between distributive and commutative justice. Any statutory system that institutes and determines ownership must in that sense create a particular distribution, or pattern of distributions, of rights to property. But the pattern of rights thus created is adjudicated in commutative justice, for example through litigation on trespass, privacy, saleability, and so forth. Thus the political/civil distinction has little effect on the way that the resultant rights are ultimately adjudicated. Even a right such as the right of free speech, paradigmatic of political rights, is largely rhetorical unless and except insofar as it is given determinate legal effect by the courts.

Should we, then, recast the political/civil justice distinction as one between vertical relationships of entitlement between citizen and state, versus patterns of horizontal entitlement obtaining between private citizens and other legal persons? Certainly, such rights arise in different ways; but the determination that a right is vertical rather than horizontal in character does not alter the more fundamental characteristic of such rights which remain due to the right-holder in either distributive or commutative justice. In recent times, the language of 'horizontal' and 'vertical' effect has been co-opted to describe the intended effect of human rights instruments and other directives, in particular the question of whether private as well as public bodies and persons have standing under the relevant provisions.[6] But the question of who has standing, though obviously important in the context of the exercise of rights, does not disturb the underlying patterns of *justice*, which remain either distributive or commutative: there is no illuminating distinction to be made between 'private' and 'public' or 'vertical' and 'horizontal' justice.

A further distinction that might be made is that between 'perfect' and 'imperfect' justice. The distinction derives from some passages in Grotius's *De Iure Belli ac Pacis*, in which he equates a faculty (*facultas*) with justice strictly so called, and an aptitude (*aptitudo*) with justice in an imperfect sense. The former case he identifies with the example of rights under contract, in which something is owed to another, strictly defined. In the latter case, Grotius appears to have in mind claims an individual might have to some subject-matter in some sense, but falling short of being strictly 'due'.[7] His chosen example of this kind of justice (as a kind of deservingness) gives some sense of what he means: a person has an aptitude to receive a legacy from another's estate.[8] But Grotius then obscures the distinction by aligning it with

6 See e.g. *Ghaidan v Godin-Mendoza* (2004) UKHL 30; (2004) 2 AC 557, II.
7 Grotius, *De Iure Belli ac Pacis* (hereafter *DIBP*) I.1.4.
8 Ibid, I.1.8.

Aristotle's distinction between distributive and commutative justice, or in Grotius's somewhat idiosyncratic terminology, attributive and expletive justice. The alignment in not a happy one, however, for there are clearly occasions on which we would say that a person is entitled to (and not merely deserving of), a distributive share: an obvious example is that of the creditors of a bankrupt who stand to be recompensed *pari passu* or *pro rata*. More generally, we regard certain individuals as being *owed*, and not merely deserving of, benefits drawn from public resources, such as unemployment and housing benefit, healthcare, and education. Questions of desert certainly do factor into determinations of who is owed what in terms of distributive justice; but that is merely part of the decision-making process which ends in a rationally arrived-at understanding of distributively just shares. Thus the perfect/imperfect distinction is for the most part a distracting and defective gloss on the distinction between commutative and distributive justice.

Still other distinctions should be mentioned: the distinction between justice as a virtue, and justice as a series of principles that establish what ought to be done. Typically, the ethics of the virtues is portrayed as a rival 'tradition' of moral thinking to that of rule- or principle-based, or 'deontological', ethics. But from the very beginning, justice is deemed by the classical natural law theorists as a virtue of the *will*, not of the affective appetites, and it is dissimilar from other virtues also in being directed at one's actions towards others, and only in a metaphorically extended sense inwardly to oneself. As a virtue, justice prevents one's reasoning from becoming deflected by desires; but unlike fortitude (which prevents one from committing acts of cowardice) or temperance (which prevents greed), justice pertains to the reason implicated in inter-personal relationships. As a consequence, justice is necessary not because it controls vicious inward passions, but because it is demanded by the love of neighbour that is of paramount importance to a fully ethical life.[9] Justice is classically associated with certain precepts of rightness: one must perform the right act, at the right time, in the right way, and so on. These precepts of rightness take the form of conventions that structure both act and intention. By 'convention' here is *not* meant a subjective standard resulting from the practices of a given community, as opposed to natural principles that bind everywhere. It is intended to signify a series of standards that hold 'for the most part' (*ut in pluribus*), but which may have to be qualified, adapted or even abandoned in specific situations as reason demands.[10]

The uniqueness of justice as a virtue of the will is emphasized by Aquinas on various occasions, for example where he insists that justice is a real, not a rational, mean: that is to say, a rational mean differs according to different persons, who may have different metabolic rates meaning they will require different amounts of food,

[9] See Jean Porter 'The Virtue of Justice' in Stephen Pope (ed) *Essays on Aquinas's Ethics* (Georgetown University Press 2014) 284.

[10] Aquinas, *ST* (n 4) II-II.51.4, 120.1c; Suarez, *De Legibus* II.13.8.

and have different amounts of tolerance of alcohol, and so what is temperate for one person is different to another; but justice is a real mean because irrespective of one's physical size, taking more than one's share of the cake is the same in every case, or taking without permission is the same commutatively unjust act for all.[11] Justice therefore requires both (a) the relevant internal attitudes, specifically the *willingness* to give another his due or right; and (b) an understanding of what is 'due' to or 'rightly' belongs to another. And this understanding of what is due must be in the form of stable principles, not one-off judgments. An appreciation of what is owed to one individual is, implicitly, an appreciation of what is owed to others (perhaps oneself). It pertains not to sentiments felt towards the other, but to the 'right determination of reason'.[12] But if stable principles are needed, it is necessary to ask what sort of principles are relevant to the determination of what is just: principles concerning life, liberty, property, and other holdings, offices, and advantages, or perhaps all of these in some measure and order of priority? These questions will be considered below: see Section IV.5.

One final distinction that is typically drawn is that between civil and criminal justice. The types of criminal justice are mostly well-known: retributive, deterrent, reformative, restorative ... But these 'types' are in reality terms describing the motives behind the infliction of punishment: motives which may, to be sure, affect the severity of punishment inflicted. Again however, this differentiation in motive does not affect the essential *character* of criminal justice, which remains an element of the state's commutative justice to its citizens. (The exception is possibly deterrence, which might be considered distributive rather than commutative in that the level of punishment exceeds what is deserved by the one who committed the crime, extending into disincentives to those who might be otherwise tempted to commit similar offences.) The classic rationale behind punishment is stated in clear terms by Aquinas, who says that punishment consists in the suppression of the wrongdoer's will, as a means of redressing the injury done to the common good by the wrongdoer's *excess* in willing what did not belong to him.[13] This suppression of will can be brought about through the wrongdoer's own remorse, but also (more usually in imagination) imposed by public officials. The sentencing of malefactors is typically a more complex and more difficult matter than, say, computing damages due in tort. (There is no natural relationship between crime and the level, or kind, of punishment; it is a clear example of *determinatio*.)[14] But the justice involved is nonetheless 'corrective', that is to say, a kind of commutative justice.

We return, then, finally to the original distinction between commutative and distributive justice. Doubt, too, can be (and has been) entertained in relation to

[11] Aquinas, *ST* (n 4) I-II.19.6, 72.1, 78.1 ad 2; see also Jean Porter, *Justice as a Virtue* (Eerdmans 2016) ch 2.

[12] Aquinas, *ST* (n 4) II-II.60.2c (*secundum rectam rationem prudentiae*).

[13] See e.g. ibid, I-II.87.1c & ad 3 ('inordinate affection').

[14] Ibid, I-II.95.2c.

this distinction. For even contractual obligations, ordinarily a paradigm of commutative justice, can be reinterpreted as actions under a limited form of partnership in which the risks of frustration or non-performance are distributed between the contracting parties. Similarly it has long been a debated question in tort law whether the outcome of an unintended accident should be viewed in terms of the distribution of risk, particularly in the case of systems of national insurance which allocate some of the financial costs associated with an accident (such as the provision of emergency healthcare) on the taxpayer rather than the individual who committed the harm. Indeed, even the act of adjudication itself, insofar as it apportions the relevant rights and obligations of the litigants, has been regarded as an action of distributive justice.[15] Are the relevant risks, liabilities and actions correctly understood in this way?

In fact none of these examples minimize, let alone erode, the importance of the distinction between distributive and commutative justice. To interpret a problem as one of distributive justice is to impose upon the problem certain patterns of thought and questions of responsibility that are alien to the treatment of the problem as one of commutative justice. For, to take the contract example, the question in commutative justice is A's responsibility for B's loss (or vice versa) and hence A's obligation in commutative justice to render restitution to B. If B has not contributed to the breach, B bears *no* responsibility for it at all, and is not liable to render a percentage of restitution to A. This is not to say that the law cannot interpret contracts as joint enterprises, and cannot insist upon distributing the risks and consequences of frustration or non-performance. But to do so is to treat those issues *as a different kind of problem*, and imposing *a different solution* to the situation.

The example of tort raises more complex questions, for although it is rightly taken as a paradigm of commutative justice, there is no doubt that, at least in certain legal systems, it also contains distributive elements. Typically, though not inevitably, the tortfeasor is not legally liable for all of the real costs of the accident: including, as mentioned, hospital treatment but also, for example, ongoing care and care costs of the victim. This may or may not be a determination in justice: it may be a simple pragmatic realization that the average tortfeasor cannot afford to compensate for all of the harm caused to the victim; or it may be that matters such as healthcare are anyway freely provided by the state no matter what the cause of the harm. But the fact that healthcare etc is funded through taxation and national insurance demonstrates that there is a distributive principle in play, namely that, as a society, we should all contribute to the costs of accidental or negligent acts that, just as easily, might be committed by us. Nowhere is this more evident than in the context of the use of motor vehicles. Accidents involving such vehicles tend to cause expensive damage beyond the pockets of most persons. Through the use of (usually

[15] See Finnis, *NLNR* (n 3) 180–83, 460–61.

compulsory) motor insurance, the individual motorist typically does not pay directly for the damage he or she caused; the costs are effectively distributed amongst all motorists, perhaps in recognition of the fact that all drivers are engaged in a potentially risky activity and that accidents, when they do occur, often involve contributory negligence. When A and B have a collision, it is often difficult to ascertain, or prove, exclusive liability. Nevertheless, there are commutative elements in play in such situations, reflected in the fact that the parties to the accident (or one of them, if liability can be established) will see their insurance premiums rise, and indeed rise faster and by a greater margin than the rise in insurance premiums generally. Here again, there are sound reasons why such accidents ought to be treated at least in part as issues of distributive justice, over and above the commutative justice of A's relationship with B.

What, then, of the adjudicative act itself? John Finnis argues that, while the judge's duty to award a decision that fulfils the rights and obligations of the litigating parties is a matter of commutative justice, the judicial act is also conceivable as an issue of distributive justice, insofar as the judge is required to apportion the costs associated with the *lis inter partes* such that a decision in favour of A is a loss to B.[16] But this is not persuasive. For to possess a right is to be entitled to a decision at law which upholds and satisfies that right: there is no question of distribution of costs and benefits *between* the litigants. A right is not an entitlement to the *greater part* of the award that upholds it, part of it being diverted for the benefit of the other litigating party. Aristotle somewhat unhelpfully tries to describe the difference as involving an arithmetic, rather than geometric, proportion.[17] But the fact is that to treat adjudication as a distributive matter (and not merely addressing a problem of distributive justice between the parties, say beneficiaries under a will) is wholly alien to its essential character in determining and upholding legal rights. Hence we must reject the claim that the distributive/commutative distinction is a hindrance to clear thinking, yielding 'no really clear and stable analytical pattern.'[18]

## IV.2. JUSTICE BETWEEN CITIZEN AND STATE

In thinking about justice, we can fruitfully employ Cajetan's distinction between three types of relationship: (1) between citizen and state, (2) between state and citizen, and (3) between citizen and citizen. We can do so without repeating his confusion of associating distributive justice solely with (2) and commutative justice exclusively with (3). In this section we can briefly examine (1).

[16] Ibid, 179–80. This agrees with Aquinas, see *ST* (n 4) II-II.63.4 ad 1.
[17] Aristotle, *NE* (n 2) V.3–4.
[18] John Finnis, *Aquinas: Moral, Political and Legal Theory* (OUP 1998) 188; Finnis, *NLNR* (n 3) 460.

The relationship of the citizen to the state of which he or she is a member, is in Aristotelian terms one of 'general justice' or, as he sometimes puts it, 'legal justice'. He so refers to it because he equates this form of justice with obedience to law: such obedience is each person's contribution to the common good of their community, by (for example) refraining from acts of violence, vandalism, serious dishonesty, treason, trespass, and so on. More generally, we might say that general justice involves respect for the rights of others, and thus helps to ensure internal peace within the community.[19] Such respect for rights is by and large negative, in that it involves abstaining from certain types of behaviour on certain occasions.[20] But citizens also possess a positive orientation towards the common good, directed either towards the state itself (such as payment of taxes) or towards other legal (public or private) actors. The fulfilment of society's basic needs (the realization of public goods such as transport, infrastructure, industry, communication, housebuilding, and so forth) depends largely upon the voluntary efforts of private citizens to cooperate with one another in a spirit of peace and common purpose (see Section III.4(c)). It is obviously true that cooperative relationships of this kind are entered into for mutual profit above all, but their underlying orientation to the common good cannot be denied. In all such cases, the private pursuit of profit depends first of all upon the identification of a public *need* which it is the aim of the activity to fulfil. In the absence of private enterprise, it would be necessary for the state or other public body to undertake and manage such projects.[21] And the state itself, understood in the broad sense, requires men and women willing to serve in public office, especially (in Plato's view) if they do so only reluctantly.

It is, as we shall shortly see, part of the state's function to create conditions that make possible, or (in the case of, say, employment law) enhance, the sort of collaborative efforts required for the common good. There are however other, less appealing ways of ensuring citizens act for the good of the state: for example by minimizing or forbidding private enterprise and requiring at least a majority of citizens to labour in state-run industries for meagre benefit, as bees work not for themselves but for the good of the hive; or by forcing free labourers to yield up their product in the national interest. Plato's *Republic* offers one particularly dreadful image of such a society, but the relatively recent history of communist societies provides ample evidence of the plight into which states of this kind plunge their citizens. (Witness for example Stalin's seizure of the wheat and, finally, farmland of

[19] As Alasdair MacIntyre aptly puts it, legal justice is the virtue by which we judge all the other virtues correctly: Alasdair MacIntyre, *Whose Justice? Which Rationality?* (Duckworth 1988, hereafter *WJWR*) 106.

[20] See Thomas Nagel, 'The Problem of Global Justice' 33 (2005) *Philosophy & Public Affairs* 113; See also TM Scanlon, *What We Owe to Each Other* (Harvard University Press 1998) 295; Iris Young, *Responsibility for Justice* (OUP 2011), 3ff.

[21] I ignore, for present purposes, the phenomenon of selfishness and the problem of greed: see GA Cohen, *If You're an Egalitarian How Come You're So Rich?* (Harvard University Press 2000) 117; GA Cohen, *Rescuing Justice & Equality* (Harvard University Press 2008) 27.

the kulaks in January of 1930.) The question of obedience to state laws, especially of unjust or repressive laws, is a topic to be taken up later (see Chapter XI). But it should be noted that general justice imposes at least a *prima facie* obligation to obey the laws of the state even where they are unjust.

Nevertheless, it is important to observe that the directiveness of general justice is not, ultimately, towards the state itself, but in reality towards the good of all others within the community: that is to say, the common good. This understanding helps to explain away what might be regarded as an inconsistency or even contradiction in Aquinas's treatment of general justice, the object of which he states to be, at various points, the common good, but at other points, right.[22] The direction towards the common good consists of the individual's determination to act not only for himself or herself, but also for the good of other persons in society. One acts this way when one pursues one's chosen ends peacefully and lawfully, recognizing that other people also have rights that must be respected and which may, in any given situation, block the way to the end one is seeking after (see Section III.4(c)). The shift in the last sentence discloses the connection Aquinas intends to reveal between the common good and the right. For the extent and scope of the duty to act for the good of others (or in many cases, refrain from acting) is given definite shape and expression through the *rights* that are held by those other persons. Typically, of course, such rights are substantially the same as the rights oneself possesses. Equally as importantly, however, rights define the effective *limits* to one's duty to promote the good of others; for none of us is fully responsible for, or a mere means to, the fulfilment of others. It would therefore be more correct to state that general justice pertains to the common good, not in the fullest sense of that term, but insofar as it is defined by rights. The rights we are speaking of here do not amount to the full range of rights that each individual may happen to possess: a full range that may include any number of contractual entitlements, property rights and so forth. Rather the relevant range of rights is restricted to the rights that *all* persons possess *as members of a community*; generic rights of both positive and natural law.[23] Furthermore, acknowledgement of the common good requires that the rights of particular individuals are not fulfilled at the expense of the rights of others: Aquinas's chosen example being that one should not return a sword to its owner if he is insane, or an enemy of one's community.[24]

The same analysis also indicates why unjust acts are against the community as such. For according to Murphy, one manifests one's consent to be governed by one's continued efforts to obey the law; if one commits a crime, one signals one's objection to living on the terms on which people are members of their community to the

[22] See e.g. Aquinas, *ST* (n 4) II-II.57.1 & 60.1c (the object of justice is the right); II-II.58.5c (the object of justice is the common good).

[23] Ibid, II-II.122.6c.

[24] Ibid, II-II.51.4c, 62.5 ad 1, 120.1c.

extent that one resists (or evades) their lawful punishment.[25] For Aquinas such a situation represents a double injustice: first the crime, followed by the avoidance of that suppression of the will that is essential to lawful punishment.

Having examined the character of general justice as one's orientation to the common good through obedience to state laws (and hence synonymously 'legal' justice), it remains to mention briefly Aristotle's other account of this term, as being synonymous with general virtue. Not all immoral acts are acts of injustice: for example, greed, whilst immoral, may have no negative effects at all towards others, if food and drink are plentiful. Similarly, a disposition towards cowardice will be unjust to no one if the coward is never put in a position in which bravery is demanded for the good of others: for example, intervention to defend another from assault, or carrying out one's duty as a paid soldier. But Aristotle is right to say that many failures of virtue are also acts of injustice. (Let the earlier example suffice: an adulterer exhibits a failure of temperance, but also perpetrates an injustice to the cuckolded husband or wife.) Justice in this general sense requires the exhibition of all the virtues: not, as Aristotle says, absolutely, but in relation to others. How does this connect with the first characterization of general justice, above? Building on Aristotle's treatment, Aquinas observes that (general) justice directs all virtues to the common good. But the instance of adultery is not an example of this kind, as it is a harm directed to the cuckolded spouse, not to society in general; unless perhaps in the secondary sense that acts of secrecy and dishonesty tend to weaken the fabric of a community. However, Aquinas then goes on to say that general/legal justice is principally a matter for the head of state, to secure the common good, and only secondarily for private citizens.[26]

The solution to this problem lies in the thought that general justice is all-round virtue exercised in relation to others. We might recall that, for Aristotle, the purpose of the law is to force the unwilling to act virtuously.[27] Moreover, Aquinas says that the purpose of law is to command the act, not of all virtues, but only those that are required for the common good.[28] Hence, the legislator's duty (in general justice) is to enact just provisions that protect and foster the common good; and the citizen's duty (in general justice) is to obey the laws, which require the kind of virtuous behaviour demanded by the common good. General justice does not therefore demand that people are good men and women, but only that they are good *citizens*.[29] It is in this sense that general justice demands the orientation of citizens towards the state.

[25] Murphy, *NLJP* (n 1) 93.
[26] Aquinas, *ST* (n 4) II-II.58.6c.
[27] Aristotle, *NE* (n 2) II.1.1103b.
[28] Aquinas, *ST* (n 4) I-II.96.3c.
[29] Aquinas, *Commentary on Aristotle's Ethics* (hereafter *Eth*) V.3.926.

## IV.3. JUSTICE BETWEEN STATE AND CITIZEN

We have already begun to trace the state's responsibility to the citizen in the last paragraph: to legislate and publish laws for the care of the common good. Aquinas calls this concern for the common good 'architectonic': the state laws establish a scheme for the common good; individuals put it into effect through their obedience.[30] The state's obligations can be divided into two broad categories: (1) to provide for the common good in both commutative and distributive justice, and (2) not to exceed the limits of its lawful power. In considering the first of these, it is necessary to note that the range and extent of state power (for a long time royal or imperial power) during earlier periods in history is much less than it is today. Consequently, my following remarks are directed principally to modern societies.

In any society of considerable size, a key function of the state will be to distribute wealth, resources, medical care, official positions, opportunities for employment, housing, and so on, across the full range of society. None of these matters can be left entirely to private initiative even when it is the policy of the state government largely so to leave them. For example, it is a concern for the community whether a given company gives women equal status to men; and it is also a matter of justice how these decisions are made and by whom. Similarly, it is a concern for the community whether workers' unions should be allowed to operate or be made illegal; whether the poor should be given assistance with the costs of medical care and housing; and a whole host of other matters. In general, it is a function of the state to divide up and mobilize into effect the common resources of the community. It is important to stress, as Aquinas does, that the duties of the state in distributive justice are owed not to 'the community' undifferentiated, but to 'every single person'.[31]

Furthermore, it is the duty of the state in distributive justice to distribute not only the goods of social life but also its burdens, principally the costs associated with such goods, punishments and, in some cases, the defence of the community against external enemies. So far, the discussion has not touched upon the question of whether these goods, and these burdens, are a matter only of politics (the realm of what is practically possible), and thus of *determinatio*, or whether they are based in clear principles of natural law. I take up that discussion in Section V.4. But we should pause to note that such 'burdens' are not always unwelcome or, even if unwelcome, not always un-beneficial. Criminals of course do not desire punishment, but the state's punishment of crimes is in fact a form of justice *to* the criminal, who is otherwise immune from (i.e. not subject to) harm from private individuals seeking revenge.[32] And there are those who willingly and profitably partake in national service.

30 Aquinas, *ST* (n 4) II-II.58.6c, 60.1 ad 4; *De Regno* XVI.117.
31 Aquinas, *ST* (n 4) II-II.61.1c (*singulas personas*).
32 Ibid, II-II.64.3 ad 2.

There is an important difference between the state's distributive responsibilities and its commutative obligations. When Aquinas says that distributive obligations apply to 'every single person', he presumably means that the state must take everyone into account in determining the reach of its obligations, not that every single person actually deserves, or is owed, some percentage of some common resource. So we can say that whereas distributive justice pertains to the division, after some scheme, of common resources amongst a population, attaching to some groups but not others, the state's commutative obligations are owed to every single person *absolutely*. Whether particular state responsibilities are distributive or commutative in character to some extent depends upon the technological and fiscal resources open to the state. Healthcare offers a useful example of this. Prior to the creation of the National Health Service in Britain, the National Insurance Act 1911 extended free medical care only, in effect, to those who had previously depended upon charities or the Poor Law. This limitation was partly ideological, but partly reflected the extent of the state's ability to fund such healthcare. One such limitation pertained to hospital care, which was excluded even from the very poor. Leaving aside questions of affordability, certain cures, vaccines, and immunizations are owed (in principle) to every person who may benefit from them, once they have been invented and proved to be safe. But actual conditions interrupt the abstract demands of justice, such that (1) even developed states, with flourishing medical research facilities, do not 'owe' their citizens a cure for their common colds, for one does not yet exist; and (2) when such a cure is invented, its expense will partly determine whether it is distributed only to areas of greatest need (i.e. those most at risk of complications, such as the elderly) or freely available for all. In general terms, then, we can say that there are different ways of distributing common goods depending upon different types of social order.[33]

These remarks cast doubt on one of the most influential principles in modern thinking on justice: Rawls's difference principle. All of Rawls's principles of justice (the principle of equal liberty, of equality of opportunity, and the difference principle) are distributive in aim, leading to the claim that distributive justice is prior to commutative justice: commutative justice is largely employed to 'correct' disparities that may creep into a given distribution so that the original distribution is restored.[34] But the difference principle is compatible with the suggestion that an increase in the fortunes of the most wealthy is permitted if it will lead to some (how much?) improvement in the lot of the worst off, *even if the lot of the worst off remains below a subsistence level*. This ignores the state's obligations in commutative (not merely corrective) justice: obligations owed to each person in turn and not to some social sub-group rather than another. Such obligations, to be clear, obtain not because a certain inequality requires correction (restitution), but because

[33] Ibid, II-II.61.2c.

[34] See also MacIntytre, *WJWR* (n 19) 104.

something is owed directly to a specific person and not to individuals identifiable only due to their inclusion within some given sub-group.

In terms of the state's responsibilities in commutative justice, perhaps the greatest—those that take priority in spending of revenues—are health, education, public safety, and order. Order, for these purposes, includes laws relating to contracts, torts, property rights, and so forth, and the regulation of economic life and activity: in short, of injecting at least a minimum morality into the marketplace. As employed here, the difference between distributive and commutative justice is not that between a geometric and an arithmetic proportion, but between a benefit that is owed to some sub-group (more specifically, to the individual members of some sub-group) and something that is owed, absolutely, to one person who has suffered, or would suffer, loss, or is otherwise entitled to the relevant benefit. But these two distinct kinds of justice are often found together. Once it has been determined that a certain quantum of social security payments will be given to those at or below a certain level of income, a group that includes a person, A, then A has a right in *commutative* justice that B, the relevant official or agent of the state, pay A the relevant amount.

The question of the relative priorities of distributive and commutative justice is a complex and difficult one that I do not propose to answer here (this is not a book on justice). But it is obvious that they can, at a basic level, run into conflict. We can ask, for example, whether the state should effect some redistribution wherever there is an historical injustice? Certainly, it will not be in all cases possible to do so without introducing a commutative injustice, for this will involve disturbing settled entitlements. For example, should tenth-generation settlers of land be removed in favour of the ancestors of those original inhabitants who were forcefully displaced? Or should the redistribution be effected by a compensation scheme funded by taxpayers as a whole? It is sometimes said that legal justice is historical, in that it considers a situation by reference to how the situation came about (e.g. was there an offer? Was there clear acceptance? Was there consideration?). But how much history is relevant, and what, precisely, is the normative value of history or histories? Let us say that A produces a product which is sold in shops belonging to B (B having bought in a particular level of stock), and C buys a unit from B. Now suppose that A's production line involves the use of child labour or that A's workers labour under terrible conditions and are inadequately remunerated. Does C owe A's workers in corrective (commutative) justice? Would it matter whether C actually knows about A's working practices? Many reasons can be brought to bear in order to show that C possesses no such duty: for example that C lawfully bought the product from B; that to interrupt people's proprietary rights in such a way would cause chaos and insecurity that would unravel the marketplace; and so on. (But note that if B had *stolen* the product from A, or some other person B', matters would stand differently, as would they if C received property in knowing receipt from B). In general, modern developed societies prioritize security of property rights over re-distribution; in doing so they prioritize commutative justice over distributive justice. Or, perhaps it would be more correct to say that in modern societies the question of distributive justice is *shaped by* entitlements in commutative justice: for it is impossible to say who should pay what (in terms of taxes, fines, insurance premiums...) unless it is clear who owns what.

Another way in which commutative justice may override distributive justice is made clear in the following example. If food is scarce in a particular community, the state may introduce rationing as a method of ensuring that every person is fed: this represents an attempt to be distributively just, and may indeed involve variation in entitlement depending upon the characteristics of the persons that must be fed. Thus we might expect that a child's rations will be proportionately shorter than that of a grown adult; or perhaps those in active service in defence of the community may be entitled to greater rations than those of ordinary men and women. However, if food is extremely scarce, it might be that a proportionately smaller ration is simply insufficient to keep the child alive. Depending upon the amount of food available, a child may perhaps have a claim in commutative justice to rations equal to that of adults. Such a claim would override the norms of distribution that would otherwise produce a just outcome. The use of the term 'equal' here is somewhat unfortunate, for it is endlessly pliable. In the example just given, the relevant ratio of equality is 1:1 (having worked out what is due commutatively to each person, an appropriate distribution must be made), and giving equal shares is an obvious way of treating people as equals. But in another way, once relevant factors (such as size and weight, or perhaps nutritional need) are factored in, we might find that it is not a satisfactory measure of equality, and that a ratio of, say, 1:1.5 or 1:2 would reflect better the true equalities involved. Equality is then an important residual characteristic of justice—it is impossible to do justice without it—but it is not the only, or even the main, criterion by which judgments of justice are made. This invites a question, to be taken up in Section IV.5, as to what the other determinants of justice are. For the moment however I am concerned only with an outline of the state's duties in justice to its citizens.

It should be apparent that societies are full of injustices that cannot be practically resolved, given the tensions between the state's commutative responsibilities and its distributive aims. From the radical origins of property rights to problems of access to affordable justice and legal representation, there is no route from the present predicament to a fully just society. Finnis is therefore correct to say that justice is not a situation at which to aim, but ongoing series of relationships and transactions.[35] Nevertheless it should be observed that present arrangements achieve *some* degree of justice; lack of recognition of this lies at the heart of most critical theories of modern society: see for example Unger's *What Should Legal Analysis Become?*

[35] Finnis, *NLNR* (n 3) 175.

and Crenshaw's *Intersectionality*, which seek a radical overhaul of existing entitlements.[36] For we might ask: why prioritize the needs and interests of one's immediate family over strangers within our community? Why prioritize the wealth and needs of our own community over that of others across the globe?[37] A full answer must await discussion of subsidiarity (Section V.3). One could appeal to facts about psychology as shaping the horizon from which we view rights and interests. But this would not provide a moral reason to prefer interests closer at hand. The fact is rather that pursuit of *all* interests (even within one's own community) would drag everything down to the same low level. Nor is such a vision possible: one cannot have a single global community: it will be hopelessly at odds with itself (for wars and perceived causes of war would not disappear), citizens across the globe would wish to migrate to temperate and productive lands, and how would one orchestrate the harmonization of political systems that are the antithesis of one another: for example oil-rich theocratic states and Western liberal consumption societies? Every problem and cause of instability in the world would continue to exist under a putative single world state.[38]

The second of the matters mentioned at the start of this section is the duty of the state not to overstep its legal authority. But again, there are no hard and fast measures here, as circumstances and levels of technology that create new horizons for state activity, vary across communities and over time. Nevertheless, there are certain precepts of natural law that cannot be overridden except by perpetrating injustice.[39] Thus, any attempt by the state to interfere in the procreative act (except of course by outlawing sexual assault, the use of children for sexual gratification, and incest) will in general be unjust: it is no part of the state's function to limit the number of children conceived within a family, and the state cannot justly require any two specific people to engage in (or refrain from) sexual relations, for example as part of a programme of eugenics. This is not to say that the state cannot interfere in family life at all: it may do so, for example, to remove vulnerable children from abusive parents, or, more positively, to provide financial assistance in the raising of children and by creating rights to protected maternity and/or paternity leave. But the principle that there should exist zones of privacy, of private life and decision-making, is a precept of natural law. Very roughly, the state should allow its citizens the freedom to make their own moral decisions except in relation to (1) the moral content of the criminal law, (2) the morality of the marketplace, (3) the ,morality of torts; and (4) the morality of public office.

[36] See Roberto Unger, *What Should Legal Analysis Become?* (Verso 1996); Kimberley Crenshaw, *Intersectionality* (The New Press 2022).

[37] Murphy, *NLJP* (n 1) 175.

[38] See Jean Pórter, *Ministers of the Law* (Eerdmans 2010) 340: it is impossible for the peoples of the world to form themselves into a polity.

[39] Aquinas, *ST* (n 4) II-II.94.5c; see also II-II.104.6 ad 3.

How should the limits of the state's interference in private life be drawn? There is no easy answer. For example, should the state's scrutiny of private affairs and private transactions (including monetary transactions) be increased in order to offset a relatively remote but serious threat to public safety? Here, the natural law precept of privacy comes into conflict with another natural law precept, that the state should protect the lives of its citizens. In potentially many cases, not just of this kind, the requirements of justice might not be immediately clear. For there may be a number of different paths to upholding the good of the community, none of which is obviously the best, or the only rational, approach, consistent with both distributive and commutative justice. This does not mean that the alternative proposals must be 'weighed up', for the values promoted by each proposal may be incommensurable with those promoted by the others: freedom and safety, for example. A theory of justice must necessarily involve an inquiry into such values (i.e. human goods) if grave errors or dangerous social experiments are to be avoided. Thus at least a very 'thin theory of the good' is required in order to make progress in such an inquiry, though there are grounds (explored in the extant literature and briefly set out in Section IV.5) for believing that a very thin theory is inadequate.

The natural law precept that the state owes duties of justice to protect and nurture the common good must be carefully differentiated from a spurious principle trading on an ambiguity in the term 'common good'. For we can understand the common good *either* as a reference to the good of all persons within the community, *or* as an agglomeration of all citizens, or even, as in utilitarianism, an agglomeration of *most* citizens. Thus, to borrow the example of the preceding paragraph, the state may move to protect 'the common good' by placing all of its citizens under minute surveillance; or it may seek to promote the common good by absorbing all labour, or all property, into common enterprises.[40] Such an understanding of the 'common good', as the good of the *polis* itself, often at the expense of the good of individual citizens, is a mistake of the kind Plato makes in the *Republic* book V,[41] when he says that citizens should 'have nothing in private possession but their bodies, but all else in common'. The ambition behind this remark is an error because it is radically mistaken about, and in contention with, the character of human good. The opposite error is perpetrated by Crowe, who argues that practices such as contracting would still continue even if the state ceased to exist.[42] This is of course an untested hypothesis, but it touches upon an important truth that contracting and other practices are not owned by the state even if the state orchestrates them through legislation, and enforces them through the courts. They form part

40 See Finnis, *NLNR* (n 3) 194n; Aquinas, *De Reg* I.4.7.27.

41 *Republic*, V.457c-d, 459d-460d, 462b-464d.

42 Jonathan Crowe, *Natural Law & the Nature of Law* (CUP 2019, hereafter *NLNL*) 118.

of a *common law*, a *ius commune*, which belongs to the community in which they have a history and long practice.[43]

Having made these very brief remarks, let us now turn to the third dimension of justice, that between citizens. Here the discussion relies upon mostly classical sources, which shall nevertheless be related to the problems of the present day.

## IV.4. JUSTICE BETWEEN CITIZEN AND CITIZEN

On the classical definition of justice, there are two distinct forms of injustice: there is general injustice, which opposes the common good, and particular injustice, which is concerned with the relationship between one person and others, whereby a person seeks for more good than his or her due, or for fewer evils and harms.[44] In relation to the latter kind of injustice there must be, in appropriate circumstances, an act of restitution: both because such an act restores equality, and because injustice is an act, and thus requires an act to rectify it. Accordingly, the natural law theorists laid emphasis on the fact that in cases of injustice, penitence alone is insufficient to remove sin; there must also be the act of restitution.[45] Without restitution, one's penitence is insincere (see Section III.4(b)). Furthermore, because virtue demands that the right act be done, at the right time, in the right way, for the right reasons, etc, the act of restitution must be immediately connected to the injustice, and not for example performed at some remote date.[46] At the same time, not all detrimental acts are to be treated as acts of injustice, for nothing prevents an act from having two ends, one intended or direct and the other unintended or indirect. Where the harmful act is not directly intended, there is technically no injustice,[47] though an act of restitution may still be required. Now, all of these concepts (justice, injustice, restitution) depend upon the ability to determine what is due or owed to, or what belongs to, each person. Thus, speaking in general terms, Aquinas says that since the human being is a social animal, one person naturally owes to another whatever is required for the preservation of society.[48] If we want more determinate guidance, however, it will be necessary to explore the justice and limits of private ownership of property. This will be explored below and in Section IV.5.

[43] Crowe also states that if the state were to wither away, people would by and large continue to obey the law: ibid 126–27.

[44] Aquinas, *ST* (n 4) II-II.59.1c; see also II-II.58.7 For an interesting discussion see Shelley Kagan, *The Geometry of Desert* (OUP 2012).

[45] See Aquinas, *ST* (n 4) II-II.62.4sc; II-II.62.6 ad 6; on relativity to circumstances, see II-II.62.5 ad 1.

[46] Ibid, II-II.62.8 ad 3; II-II.106.4 ad 1.

[47] Ibid, II-II.59.2c; II-II.64.7c. Aquinas here may be thinking of justice as a sin, for the act remains 'materially unjust'.

[48] Ibid, II-II.109.3 ad 1.

One supposition to be made is that all citizens are free (and do not merely enjoy freedom) at the level set by Grotius and affirmed by Rawls: no person is naturally the slave of another: they have the status of those who possess the capacity (sometimes tragically missing) to engage in social cooperation over a lifetime. Unlike Rawls, however, it must be affirmed that all persons are *not* equally rational and reasonable. Citizens confront citizens with an inbuilt inequality of bargaining power, for some possess inherently superior commercial abilities than others; still others possess or inherit greater riches than fellow citizens, can afford to take more risks and can more easily insure themselves against the tribulations of bad investments and loss of capital. (It will be remembered that Rawls's theory is an 'ideal' theory, not one premised upon the reality of concrete inequalities.)

I began this section with a discussion of injustice. Acknowledgement of injustice is one of the fundamental differences between the classical discussion of justice and modern theories of justice such as that of Rawls. For whereas Rawls's theoretical innovations are situated within the framework of an imagined 'full compliance society', in which each person follows the demands of justice, the tradition of thinking stemming from Aristotle's treatment of justice makes no such unrealistic assumption. With a more astute understanding of the human psyche, Aristotle himself contrasts the thinking of the practically reasonable person from the reasoning of 'the masses', the latter tending to identify the demands of justice with their own self-fulfilment or the pursuit of pleasure.[49] Such people do not perform acts of virtue spontaneously, but require the force of law to direct them to good actions.[50] The reasoning of this rather unsatisfactorily defined group is not wholly estranged from the ordinary practical reasoning of the wise; the failure lies rather in applying such reasoning to the emotions and desires. We must therefore accept that our thinking about justice takes place in an imperfectly just world; it is carried on by imperfectly rational persons; and so the task of justice does not consist in the creation of a just state of affairs, but in the description of just actions, or more narrowly, those actions we might call *dealings*. Among the things we have to accept is that the present state of property holdings in a given society will have come about at least partly through a complex web of unjust dealings. The point of justice is not, at least not invariably, to try to unravel such dealings back to their beginning. This does not prevent people from identifying instances of injustice in their communities, but it does mean that it is necessary to distinguish between those injustices that are subject to legally enforced restitutionary acts, and those that must simply be borne.

This distinction is not without justification and criteria. For (1) we typically do not know, and cannot identify, all of the transactions made by ourselves and our ancestors that led to our present impoverished position; (2) there must be a

[49] See e.g. Aristotle, *NE* (n 2) I.4.1095a. See generally Richard Kraut, *Aristotle* (OUP 2002) ch 4.
[50] Aristotle, *NE* (n 2) II.1.1103b.

presumption against depriving others of their proprietary rights if these have persisted for a long (conventionally determined) time; (3) the unravelling of a line of dealings is likely to lead to, or at least to require in justice, the unravelling of dealings more generally; and (4) a thorough investigation of the litigants' situations is likely to expose dealings that are at once distributively just but commutatively unjust, or at once distributively unjust but commutatively just, and particular resources thus implicated may well extend across numerous dealings which may in the case of a particular resource be (for example) commutatively unjust in one dealing and commutatively just in another. Thus the law of a community will typically (1) restrict restitution to cases in which it is possible to identify the tortfeasor, contractual party, etc; (2) restrict standing to raise an action to those directly involved in the dispute; (3) limit the inquiry to the relevant rights and obligations of the litigants, and not, for example, to their respective wealth or property holdings in general; (4) confine inquiry to the way in which the *present* situation came about, as between the litigating parties, and not extend it to a more general investigation of the justice of the litigants' respective situations. (One may also reflect upon the impossibility, in a modern society, of being a truly ethical consumer, avoiding altogether products implicated in unjust labour practices.)

Cajetan, it will be remembered, conceived of the relationship of citizen with citizen as a matter of commutative justice alone. But this is not the case: there are many situations in which private citizens face questions of distributive justice. For example, an interview panel of a private firm in deciding to whom to offer a job acts in accord with distributive justice when making the offer to the most suitable candidate. A contract between private citizens (including of course commercial entities) secures distributive justice when it provides explicitly for the extent of the respective liabilities of the contracting parties in the event the contract is frustrated or not performed.[51] And, as mentioned earlier above, an insurance company acts in distributive justice when it calculates the premiums of members of the scheme based on factors of risk, experience, and number of claims made. Private citizens invoke questions of distributive justice whenever the matter before them concerns the division of common assets between two or more individuals, or where opportunities must be allocated between persons more or less suited for those opportunities (for example, the parents of a badly-off family deciding which of their four children to send to university). Typically, it will not be in accordance with distributive justice to decide such questions by lottery, blind choice or other random decision procedure. So to decide the question is an avoidance of justice, an attempt to treat the question as one not of justice at all. Such a procedure is an injustice to *all* of the persons who have some claim to be considered for some benefit, office, position, or opportunity.

[51] A provision sometimes inserted by the state.

The final sentence of the preceding paragraph is not intended to be taken as claiming that in all possible contexts of decision the candidates for a given distribution can be commensurated. There may be situations in which, for example, two candidates for the same position are equally suited to the role. This will only in extremely rare circumstances mean that both candidates are equally suitable in exactly the same way. More likely, candidate A will have particular appeal in relation to *x* and *y* but not *z*, whereas candidate B will have strength in *x* and *z* but not *y*. Such decisions can be very difficult but are not, usually, arbitrary. More likely, the process of reasoning will fix upon a discussion of which of the essential characteristics *x*, *y*, *z* are the most important or valuable, perhaps only in this instance: a ranking that may not have been conceived of ahead of this current decision.

Other subject-matters, too, involve an element of distributive justice. As adverted to earlier, the commutatively just claims of the creditors of a bankrupt are converted into distributive shares when the value of the bankrupt's assets are less than the combined value of the claims. As Finnis points out, the law of contract is sometimes interpreted as adjudicating agreements reimagined as limited partnerships in which the risks of frustration and non-performance are shared in some measure between the parties.[52] This is not a sign that distributive and commutative justice are interchangeable, but that the treatment of contracts by the courts has changed over time. Similarly, the law of tort contains distributive elements in that the costs of personal accidents are distributed across the community through schemes of national insurance and freely available healthcare: whilst the tortfeasor remains liable in commutative justice, he or she is not liable for the full costs of care and assistance to the victim which may be unreachably high.

But let us turn to consider commutative justice. In fact many of the duties that individuals owe to the state in commutative justice are also owed to fellow citizens, for they aim at the common good of the community: obligations such as dealing peacefully with others; upholding the law; avoiding contention and causes of violence, fraud, and dishonesty; avoiding negligent acts that put others in danger of harm, etc. We may summarize these requirements by saying that each person owes a duty of civility to every other person. In addition, each citizen owes to others what we might call a duty of cooperation. Very little in life would be achieved without private cooperation, that is, cooperation between private individuals and corporations. Very few indeed would be the buildings, hospitals, systems of education, and of economic life if private citizens did not cooperate with one another in the pursuit of ambitious ends. This duty needs to be understood carefully and is difficult to pin down precisely. No particular private individual is under a direct obligation to enter into contractual or other obligations with any other specific person.

[52] See Finnis, *NLNR* (n 3) 181–82.

But without a *general* duty to cooperate, very impoverished would be the society that resulted (see Section III.4(d)).

Commutative justice presupposes some form of ownership. It presupposes ownership when questions relating to the passing of assets from one person to another are in play (such assets including goods, obligations, time, the right to be compensated, etc). The majority of obligations in commutative justice cannot be fulfilled except where the duty-holder actually has assets to bring to bear: little sense can be made of the claim that something is *owed* or *due* to some person unless there is a general framework of *rights* to property of one kind or another. But equally, the determination of *these specific rights* is made through the operation of commutative (and sometimes distributive) justice.

We need not, as some have proposed, have a theory of the way in which notions of private ownership come out of an original commonality of property. Grotius, for example, makes the attractive argument that as small nomadic tribes grow larger and larger, their ability to move from place to place is progressively restricted to the point where permanent settlement becomes necessary. At this point, a scheme of property rights, of one kind or another, becomes necessary. Typically this will have to involve recognition of private property in at least such things as clothing and living space. But in a second argument, Grotius observes that private property is not created by an act of will: it comes about not by deliberate invention but by gradual recognition of patterns of living that have been around already for some time, and which have grown out of necessity.[53] Similarly, the condition that exists prior to the recognition of private ownership is not one of a conscious system of common property, but rather of pragmatic use of resources that come to hand. The justice of private property rights is therefore not preceded by justice in common holdings. Grotius, like other natural law theorists, asserts a right to take from others, at direst need, but he is careful to attribute this not to a radical commonality of property, but to necessity.[54]

Grotius explicitly acknowledges the fact that different societies may develop in different ways, and with different structural responses to questions of ownership. But Aquinas, and after him the full weight of the Catholic tradition, holds that a system of private property is a requirement of human flourishing, because private ownership alone provides (1) that property will be used effectively and efficiently, (2) a more orderly society and social certainty, and (3) social peace, in which only the few are tempted to identify as theirs what does not belong to them.[55] I follow Aquinas here in regarding private property as a requirement of justice.

No property, of course, is held *absolutely* privately. The doctrines of eminent domain, of adverse possession, and increasingly environmental laws, place

[53] Grotius, *DIBP* (n 7) II.2.2.5; cf *ST* II-II.66.2 ad 1.
[54] Grotius, *DIBP* (n 7) II.2.6.2; *ST* II-II.66.7c.
[55] Aquinas, *ST* (n 4) II-II.66.2c.

restrictions on the rights associated with ownership of private property. Property and income taxes also represent qualifications to the private ownership of property, but it would be a mistake to think that their purpose is redistributive. The maintenance of society, the creation and administration of schools, hospitals, parks, and community centres, investment in infrastructure, police and army services: public goods such as these must be paid for, but their object is not redistributive. Thus, as Finnis observes, there is a point beyond which what is private becomes again common property,[56] but his chosen examples lay the whole emphasis on the redistribution of resources to the less well off. But the purpose of taxation is not to make the poor more equal to the rich (and if this were the purpose it would have utterly failed); rather it is to ensure that the poor have access to many of the same basic social goods as the rich: education, doctors, unemployment, and child benefits, and so forth. It is to ensure that the poor have access to such goods *despite* their poverty, not to make the poor wealthy per se. The question is, then, through what means, if not these, are the poor to become wealthy, the wealthy to maintain their wealth, or conceivably to lose their wealth? And the answer is: through their dealings.

Now the justice of individual dealings requires, inevitably, a market. But what kind of market? According to the encyclical *Centesimus annus* (§ 34), a free market economy is the most efficient instrument for using resources and responding to needs, but only when in accord with justice.[57] To this end, as stated above (Section IV.3) we can think of the law of contract, property, and commercial law more generally as not merely aimed at facilitating economic transactions, but more fundamentally as imposing a minimal morality on the marketplace: by, for example, offsetting inequality of bargaining power (through statutory consumer rights), outlawing acts of serious dishonesty (such as fraud, insider dealing, misleading advertising), and so on. Perhaps this is part of Rawls's intention in stating that justice is the *first* virtue of social institutions: institutions that would on any definition have to include the market. Indeed, as Rawls later observes, the market should not be regarded as autonomous in this respect, for we must examine 'the way in which the major social institutions fit together into one system, and how they assign fundamental rights and duties and shape the division of advantages that arises through social cooperation'.[58] Those who regard justice or just holdings as being determined primarily by the market have failed to understand the integrated nature of law, and the integrated nature of rights and obligations. To be clear, we are talking of an institutional basis that *promotes* justice, not one that embodies justice.[59] As a glance at Book I of Aquinas's *De Regno* confirms, all social institutional forms have their

[56] See Finnis, *NLNR* (n 3) 174–75. In the opposite direction, see the claim by Allan Thomas that if you are a Rawlsian, you have to be committed to a property owning democracy (at least an egalitarian version): see Alan Thomas, *The Republic of Equals* (OUP 2016) 70.

[57] See also encyclical *Populorum progressio* § 59.

[58] John Rawls, *Political Liberalism* (Columbia University Press 2005) 284.

[59] See Amartya Sen, *The Idea of Justice* (Penguin 2010) 82.

dark, repressive, or unjust side (monarchy and tyranny for example), therefore no social structure can be taken as the embodiment of justice. It is worth noting in passing that it is not a principle of justice that the most basic needs of society (health, education ...) must be met before 'lesser' social goods, such as funding for the arts or pure scientific research. This is not the case because there will never be a point at which the basic needs are fully met; a society must allocate spending across the whole spectrum of social needs, and the question of allocation is itself a question of justice.

It will be noted that the two kinds of justice considered here and throughout this chapter, are both essentially other-regarding. As Aquinas never tires of remarking, justice cannot be towards oneself except as a kind of metaphor.[60] Its function is not self-constitution but, at least in part, benefitting others. Furthermore, he emphasizes that at least the basic precepts of justice, although directed towards others, are capable of being grasped by every person.[61] The injustice of theft, rape, murder, should be clear to anyone, whatever else they believe. But there are perhaps matters of justice that are only available to the learned, or else available only after significant sober reflection. A particularly difficult example is *truth*.

The possibility of living together in close proximity with others, that is, as *social animals*, depends upon relations of truth between persons[62] (see Section III.4.(b)). It is an act of friendliness[63] owed to all persons, not only in court proceedings[64] and other solemn occasions (such as swearing an oath, advising a client, making a promise) but in all of social life: our common life would fall apart if no one could be believed. But what of cases in which the lie is uttered in order to protect a third party, for example a Jewish family hiding in the cellar when the Nazis come knocking at the door? Aquinas's reply is at first uncompromising: it is unlawful to tell a lie even to protect one's neighbour from any danger whatever.[65] Now it might be argued that the Nazis are not *owed* the truth about the Jewish family; but Aquinas observes that the lie's injury to (the interests of) one's neighbour is only one reason for the lie's unlawfulness; the other is its misdirection, its unsuitability (*inordinatione*) for any end no matter how grave.[66] The most that one can do is refuse to reveal the truth. But in some cases, such as the present example, refusal to reveal the truth is tantamount to admission of guilt. Therefore Aquinas, with perhaps a similar example in mind, appears to soften the judgment, stating that the greater the good intended, the more the sin is diminished in gravity,[67] and that lying to protect one's

[60] See e.g. Aquinas, *ST* (n 4) II-II.57.4 ad 1; II-II.58.2c & ad 1; II-II.58.5c; Aquinas, *Eth* (n 29) V.1.885–86; V.12.1098 & 1106–107.

[61] Aquinas, *ST* (n 4) II-II.100.1 & 3.

[62] Ibid, II-II.109.3 ad 1.

[63] Ibid, II-II.114.1c.

[64] Ibid, II-II.109.3 ad 3.

[65] Ibid, II-II.110.3 ad 4. See also I-II.19.6, I-II.72.1 & I-II.78.1 ad 2.

[66] Ibid; also II-II.64.3 ad 3.

[67] Ibid, II-II.110.2c.

neighbour is not a mortal sin.[68] To be sure, Aquinas never wavers from his view that the end cannot justify the means. But his chosen example (that one should not steal in order to give alms) seems unsuitable, since it involves injury to an innocent, which is not the case with lying to the Nazis. Perhaps we should say that, although lying remains wrong in such cases, it is nevertheless excusable. But this admission comes with a cost: for if one's *policy* is to lie in order to evade or frustrate unwanted ends, one is more likely to employ it in more trivial cases where honesty is indeed the best policy. And, if lying is typically so employed by others in society, we find to our detriment that we cannot trust our politicians, police, media, neighbours, and that our dealings generally are made less secure.

This section has pointed out some of the rights and obligations that hold between citizens within a state. A fuller consideration of these points will be undertaken in Chapter VI. But we are not quite finished with the idea of justice, for we must face a question left over from Section IV.3: are the citizens of the state owed a particular form of government, and what are the fundamental institutions through which states deliver on their obligations in justice?

## IV.5. THE PURPOSE OF SOCIAL INSTITUTIONS

When considered from the perspective of natural law, Rawls's assertion that justice is a property ('virtue') of social institutions,[69] must be understood to invoke justice only in an analogical sense; for justice is first and foremost a property of actions, not institutions. But institutions are important in terms of the way they put principles of justice into action. Two questions are therefore important: (1) the identity of such institutions, and (2) the range of their operation. For if justice pertains to exchanges (more broadly 'dealings' in my terminology), it is necessary to ask with what subset of exchanges social institutions must be engaged.

Turning to the first question, one key factor of Rawls's theory of basic institutions is its artificiality: not simply the artificiality of the original position and attendant assumptions, but the fact that it represents a fresh start, a new beginning for a community, rather than the complex and difficult attempt to address the problems of an existing community burdened by historical injustices. But which social institutions belong to the basic structure of society? The market is plainly one such institution, but as already seen it cannot operate fairly without legal regulation. But which areas of the law are relevant to the basic structure? Clearly the law of contract and commercial law; but there seems no reason not to include tort law, public and administrative law, criminal law, and the constitution. The difficulty here (for Rawls) is that none of these areas of law seem to be primarily concerned

[68] Ibid, II-II.110.4c.

[69] John Rawls, *A Theory of Justice* (revised edn Belknap Press 1999, hereafter *TJ*) 3.

with pursuing the greatest system of liberties for all citizens. For other, perhaps more important, aims include avoidance of fraud, compensation, definition and limitation of public powers, accountability, punishment of the guilty, and so on. Each of these represents a concern of justice that Rawls's theory entirely ignores. Similarly, the courts (surely another basic institution) do not take, as their highest governing principle, the creation or maintenance of a scheme of liberties, but rather pursuit of justice in all of the senses just mentioned. Neither do such institutions seek primarily to secure the difference principle: that economic inequalities should be tolerated only when this leads to the advantage of the least well-off. For not all even of private law is orientated towards distributive justice: the right not to be harmed is not governed by any distributive principle, even if the question of liability for costs is so.

Obviously, Rawls could argue that his principles represent the proper, not the actual, function of law. But it is difficult to understand what, for example, contract law would look like if made to serve the difference principle. Clearly there would be no question of giving legal effectonly to those contracts that benefit the worse off. But the question of how some particular contract, between these particular litigants, is related to the fortunes of the least well-off, and how distribution is to be effected, is entirely unclear. What constraints would have to be placed on contract law in order for it to serve the difference principle? Would the doctrines of consideration and of privity continue to hold? Moreover, once we dispense with the fantasy of a 'full compliance society', it would quickly become clear that a flourishing black market would develop and run alongside the legally regulated one. Indeed, even in a legally regulated market society, goods 'are not in the hands of the state in the first instance [for] the allocation of goods is a result of millions of individuals' decisions in the marketplace'.[70] But if we assume, as Aristotle does in his treatment of justice, that a great many people cannot be counted on to be disinterested and reasonable, then the very attempt to derive a theory of justice from rational agreement between persons, who are loyal to it because it is *theirs*, is doomed from the beginning. And there is no reason to suppose, as Rawls does, that those in the original position would obey the maximin principle,[71] for we should not exclude the possibility that some in that position are less risk-averse than others, and more prepared to gamble on being a member of some favoured group, especially if this is a large group such as the middle-classes. It should be noted, too, that the thinking in the original position is entirely ego-centric, not moral (what can I choose or accept that will not disadvantage *me* once the veil has been lifted?).

What other aspects of society are to be included in the 'basic structure'? For example, what is the position of the family? Although Rawls counts the family as part of the basic structure, he has no reason to do so: it is not orientated towards the

[70] Jeremy Waldron, 'The Primacy of Justice' 9 (2003) *Legal Theory* 278.
[71] Rawls, *TJ* (n 69) 150ff.

difference principle, or of equality of opportunity (indeed it favours its own members) or basic liberties. Come to that, the deliberators in the original position do not know whether they have a religion, or what it might be, and thus could just as easily favour the inclusion of polygamous or open relationships. The fact that the deliberators have knowledge of 'the laws of human psychology'[72] is completely inadequate to rule out such possibilities. Even if such laws might be thought to favour the family, for they include the biological affinity between parent and child, Rawls would presumably want to reject any such assertion, for 'it would amount to conceding that human nature embodies a particular conception of the good, and abandoning the liberal notion that justice is wholly neutral among such opposing conceptions of the good'.[73]

It is worth asking how the worst-off in society are to be identified, and whether such identification is made on the basis of the sort of institutions we currently possess (which is doubtful) or whether some new institution is required. Certainly, the category of the 'worst-off' is not to be regarded as referring to a single flat level. For even those on equivalent incomes, and with equivalent benefits, are not necessarily equal in terms of sources of family assistance (e.g. with childcare), or in terms of the number of hours worked, exposure to hazardous substances at work or at home, and so forth. There is, moreover, no single measure or yardstick by which given disadvantages can be summated so as to produce equalities. Governments at the time of writing do not have the capability or the resources for comparative analysis between the sort of cases just mentioned, even if we suppose that different forms of disadvantage are commensurable. Furthermore, as I shall argue below, any social institution (presumably bureaucratic) that is able to gather the amount and kind of information on individual citizens required for these purposes, is likely to pose a threat to the very liberties Rawls so passionately defends.

The problem of varying capacities and responsiveness has taken the form of a rival theory to that of Rawls: the so-called 'capabilities approach', developed by Sen and popularized by Nussbaum.[74] Nussbaum in particular suggests a range of capabilities that are essential to the human being; these read similarly to the lists of basic goods propounded by Finnis and his later imitators: life, bodily health, bodily integrity, senses, thought and imagination, emotions, practical reason, affiliation, different species, play, control over one's environment.[75] This appears to me to fall into the same trap as other lists of goods: they are not exhaustive of human potentialities, nor do all potentialities reduce to them. Human capacities are of course finite, and it is tempting to try to discover a finite list of basic goods or capabilities.

[72] Ibid, 119.

[73] Justin Schwartz, 'Rights of Inequality: Rawlsian Justice, Equal Opportunity and the Status of the Family' 7 (2001) *Legal Theory* 92.

[74] See in particular Martha Nussbaum, *Frontiers of Justice* (Harvard University Press 2007; Martha Nussbaum, *Creating Capabilities: The Human Development Approach* (Harvard University Press 2013).

[75] Nussbaum, *Frontiers of Justice* (n 74) 76–78.

But the temptation should be resisted. Human capacities, as well as the kinds of good they engage in, admit of a myriad of fine distinctions, and shade off into a bewildering array of possible forms: the knowledge of complex formulas of pure mathematics (knowledge does not appear on Nussbaum's list) is simply different as an experience to the theorizing of the social scientist or the location of a fault in an undersea cable by an electrical engineer. These experiences are subsumable under a single kind (knowledge/thought and imagination) only at a hopeless level of abstraction, one that is singularly uninformative as an insight into the relevant range of practices. But subtracting them from the general approach, the capabilities theory offers a greater insight into justice than a purely institutional/economic one. Whilst we should not be tempted by the thought that 'everyone experiences the world differently' or that 'everybody has their own troubles', there is no doubt that there is a variety of problems that are better resolved at the level of capabilities than at the level of institutions (hence the temptation to reduce all problems to a list). The list approach is also explained by the simple fact that capabilities theorists want to allocate public money, and such allocations are effected en bloc, not to individuals. A defender of Rawls will point out that his theory can take account of such finer textured needs, for each person behind the veil of ignorance must deliberate about possible forms of disadvantage and how (or whether?) the state needs to respond to them. But there is a genuine problem to be faced, for the purpose—or underlying paradigm—of Rawls's measures is to allow persons to exercise autonomy, to become fully autonomous agents within the law. Yet the notion of an autonomous agent simply does not describe the person of deep mental illness, or of the very poor person who lives hand-to-mouth, day by day; or the person who is of below average intelligence. In an inventory of character traits of such persons, 'autonomy' would not be at the top; it is (at least for such persons) an unhelpful abstraction.[76]

This brings us back to a question with Rawls's theory. There is little doubt about the form of society favoured by Rawls's theory. But standing back, we can ask whether people are owed a particular form of government? The teachings of natural law do not implicate any particular form of government as the most optimal (all have their repressive, unjust manifestations). Nevertheless, there are certain traits that societies ought to have if they are to treat their members with justice. Openness, transparency, free traffic in ideas, are perhaps typically associated with democracy, but they extend beyond democratic rule. Censorship, rule through fear, intimidation, a stranglehold on information, and so on: these are methods of governance that are to be shunned not only within democratic politics but in all societies. The independence of the courts and of the press, uncoerced public discussion, and free speech and movement are among the matters that the state

[76] See Martha Albertson Fineman, *The Autonomy Myth* (The New Press 2005).

owes in justice to its people. It is for these reasons that the Catholic Church's social teachings, begun in *Rerum novarum*, are generally hostile to communism, which it regards as allowing individual persons too few opportunities to flourish. At the same time, democracy will not flourish unless it pursues such goods, shuns such evils, and extends educational opportunities to every member of society: without these goods, voting in general elections counts for very little. But Catholic tradition is likewise hostile to rampant capitalism, the prioritization of money over persons, the monetization of all corners of life. Capitalist societies, as much as communist societies, tend towards corruption. Once the idea of divine entitlement to the thrones of Europe waned, so too did any measure of certainty about the best form of government. One can but oppose the demands of justice to the prevailing forms of government of the day, and notice their fundamental incompatibility with the worst forms of society: see Section VIII.2.

What, then, of the range of operation of basic institutions? The question we are here asking is: precisely what matters are suitable for distribution? As we have seen, many of the goods that the state owes to its people, as well as the goods mentioned in the preceding paragraph (openness, transparency, etc) are owed in commutative justice, that is, to all persons within the community. Health, security, social peace, and justice itself are all goods of this kind. We might initially want to restrict the category of goods open to distribution to what Nozick and Griffin call 'holdings': money, services, legal powers, material things. For these are easily transferable, can be amassed in excess of need, and are usually traceable to some person's work.[77] But the connection with work highlights one limitation of focus on holdings: whilst the industrious person's greater wealth in holdings than the idle person seems reasonable and just, the greater wealth of the more intelligent person, who has a high-paying, highly skilled job, than that of person of low intelligence, who works in a manual job for subsistence wages, is more troubling, for people do not deserve their natural intelligence or other natural gifts (or deficiencies).[78] Of course, 'gifted' individuals will not prosper unless they diligently work to develop their gift, often for many years of secondary and tertiary education, and at considerable expense and opportunity cost. And, further, the gifted person with the high-paying job typically pays more in tax than lower-earning workers. Nevertheless, holdings seem an unnecessarily narrow restriction on what can be distributed.

The connection to education is an important one. I have said that the state's duty to offer educational opportunities to every person is a commutative one, and so it is. But beyond a certain level, not every person will benefit from further education, and so the duty of the state becomes at that point distributive, providing grants to universities that will open their doors only to the relatively few, and perhaps

[77] See e.g. James Griffin, *Well-being: Its Meaning, Measurement and Moral Importance* (Clarendon Press 1986), 284.

[78] See AP Simister & Winnie Chan, 'On Tax and Justice' 23 (2003) *Oxford Journal of Legal Studies* 718.

bursaries, loans, or funds to students on the basis of merit or potential. Similar sentiments hold in the case of food, which in times of desperate scarcity may be rationed; or to health or to policing, which may be concentrated in areas of high crime rates, whereas others, nominally entitled to the same treatment, suffer from a lower police presence and detection rate.

In a society with a range of abilities and talents, and a sufficiently developed framework of institutions to assist in developing those abilities and talents, a progressive income tax will generally be a demand of justice. For the high-flyers will, in most but not all circumstances, have gained their skills from the basis of society's common stock of ideas, techniques and skills, and specifically from teachers who have themselves developed their skills from the inherited stock of skills. Each and every person has been favoured or assisted by their community in some way (schools, police, orphanages), and are therefore notionally at least obliged to support the common good not only through their behaviour (by abstaining from violence, etc) but through their wealth via taxes. Although horizontal relationships between individuals are rightly limited to dealings (for anything else would be too indirect), the justice of dealings alone is insufficient to give to others what is rightfully theirs. *Ceteris paribus*, my qualification for some state benefit does not affect your qualification for the same benefit, so there is no dealing between us. But my receipt of the benefit might mean (a) that more state resources are spent on the relevant benefit to the detriment of spending on other social goods, (b) that the overall value of the relevant benefit is diminished for all, or, perhaps, (c) that the threshold of qualification for the benefit is raised so that fewer qualify. In normal circumstances, it should be the judgment of the state, and not of individuals, to decide how common tax resources and other modes of revenue are to be distributed, except in the very limited context of general elections on the basis of party manifestos, for the very obvious reason that individuals will tend to favour themselves first and foremost in patterns of distribution. But, as my examples (a)–(c) show, the state cannot decide matters of distribution one-by-one. It cannot work out the extent of its obligation to provide healthcare unless it also works out how much it should spend on matters such as education, industry, and the arts, to name only a few.[79]

So what can and cannot be distributed? First of all, privately owned land is in general immune from amalgamation and redistribution by the state except in two circumstances: eminent domain and adverse possession. This reflects the fact that people will in general not flourish securely unless they own, or can rent, property on a stable basis. Healthcare, though (as previously stated) a right of every person in commutative justice, requires distribution of resources to the most serious cases (or, perhaps, most realistically successful outcomes), where resources

[79] See also Griffin (n 77) 297.

are scarce: triage is a principle of distributive justice. Questions of justice may appear to concern levels of equality, but this is a very abstract measure. Difficult questions remain. Once extraneous characteristics (such as race, gender, and social class) have been removed from the market, as being irrelevant to productivity, service, trustworthiness and so on, it might seem as if we are approaching equality of opportunity—or at least a meritocracy of opportunity. But suppose my ambition, and dearest wish, is to become a conductor at the major opera houses around the world. Am I owed, as a matter of distribution, the long and expensive training in music required? Few, probably, would be prepared to say yes: after all, this seems like a desire rather than a basic need, and needs should be fulfilled, to the extent possible, before desires. But the distinction between needs and desires is not as clear-cut as it might seem. Work—meaningful labour—is a basic human good, a source of human fulfilment. To equate sincere vocations with mere desires is too easy. But unless I can get by on bursaries and scholarships, I will be less likely than my better-off contemporaries to make it to the stage (or for that matter, into academia, or to the Bar, or into high office). Unless a community is very rich, it will be most unlikely to be able to create an equal playing field, and equality of opportunity is in any case unobtainable unless the mechanism of distribution (in this case, the state) holds a staggering and intrusive level of information on each person's wants, desires, and natural talents. The same is true when we factor in an individual's collateral obligations, such as caring for a dependant relative: these are essentially hidden costs, preventing the carer from competing on an equal basis in the job market. Such a person is likely to have a greater expenditure but also a lower income than those who are not burdened in this respect. Providing relief from at least some of the costs of care would appear to be a principle of justice: after all, a community has to take care of its elderly and sick people, and if such care is to be privatized it would nevertheless seem reasonable for the whole community to contribute to the costs.

I am suggesting, then, that justice requires the distribution of more than 'holdings'. The primary goods for distribution in at least a modern, complex society include: provision of basic needs (housing, clothes, food), that is, a minimum level of prosperity for each individual, promotion of wellbeing (medical treatment, inoculations, care, education . . .); and fairness in appointments to offices and positions in political and economic life (derivatively, exclusion of irrelevant characteristics such as race and gender). These are minimum requirements. A flourishing, modern society will require investment in infrastructure, oversight of the banking sector, free traffic of information, contributions to the arts and to scientific research, among other things.

Other questions, not perhaps recognized enough as matters of justice, require to be factored into our analysis. What kinds of distribution would be consonant with motivation or even social peace? Would for example a very large percentage of the state's revenue spent on rehabilitating drug addicts be tolerated by the rich and the middle classes, or even by the poor whose benefits are proportionately reduced? Would most people accept a pattern of taxation and social spending derived from some philosopher's scheme? Should most people's self-interest, and preference for causes that they hold dear, be used to shape the state's policy of tax and spend? These matters, though not much discussed in works on justice are nevertheless relevant to the real world in which principles of justice are to operate. In thinking of the range of operations of social institutions, another paradigm we might use is that of *recognition*. States owe duties of justice in this regard too. Each citizen within a state is owed formal recognition of their birth and death, of their right to schooling and medical treatment, of their marriage (including ongoing tax status and allowances), and so forth. The state owes us such recognition when it provides us with child benefits, driving licences, examinations, qualifications, and transcripts. It recognizes us even when it sets out our tax and social security contributions. The state also accords us recognition when it treats us as the owners of our actions: either in a positive sense (as with marriage or voting in elections) or a negative one (trying and convicting us of our crimes). Without such recognition, we suffer social death. And, because we are social animals, such recognition is a requirement of justice. And recognition is also the basis on which the state calculates each person's contribution to the common good, most obviously through income tax.

## IV.6. THE REALITY OF JUSTICE

The foregoing discussion may convince the reader that justice exists and has a certain content. But even natural law theorists, such as Crowe, have argued that any theory of justice must be 'small' in that it focuses upon the relationships between persons as they belong together historically. It therefore encapsulates an idea of justice, but one which depends on the particular society and the terms of its historical emergence: a universal concept of justice but one which differs between communities, and which proposes no general principles.[80] It is not clear what such a hollowed-out vision of justice is supposed to achieve. To the extent that philosophers such as Aquinas and Grotius observed that there are many distinct forms of polity, each with its own internal laws and organisation, there is nothing new in Crowe's proposal. But neither Aquinas nor Grotius envisaged a form of justice that differed between communities in their general principles: the primary precepts of natural law and the secondary precepts which follow closely on from them. There is no suggestion in Crowe that the practices of theft associated by Julius Caesar with the Germanic tribes, constitute any kind of justice, and that norms of justice are entirely relative.[81] Clearly such practices (if they ever in fact existed—Aquinas

[80] Crowe, *NLNL* (n 42) 240; see also Jonathan Crowe, 'The Idea of Small Justice' 34 (2021) *Ratio Juris* 224; Porter, *Ministers of the Law* (n 38) 207.

[81] See Aquinas, *ST* I-II.94.4c.

merely states that Caesar reported them) could not be reconciled with any universal norms. Where and how, then, is the line to be drawn between the universal and the particular? Or (in other words) what are the universal principles of justice, and what is their extent? My discussion above aims to highlight some such principles, and to convey a general outline of the demands of justice irrespective of particular political realities. For the most part, differing particulars (insofar as they are just or reasonable) will constitute determinations of the general principles rather than radically new forms of social order, utterly peculiar to a given society. Aquinas and (in particular Grotius) carefully enumerate the general principles; Crowe gives to them a relatively cursory treatment. Thus it remains unclear on his account how exactly the cultural particulars are to be condemned or defended by the universal precepts which form the backbone of the theories of natural law philosophers from the medieval period through to early modernity and the present day.[82] Furthermore, it entirely overlooks the core morality (for both individuals and state governments) expounded in Chapter III. To be similarly avoided, then, is Porter's argument that anyone who has experienced injustice can comprehend that universal moral norms are true of any and all communities.[83] For perhaps many people have an inflated or mistaken sense of their own entitlements, and their and our feelings of harm cannot be trusted to disclose moral truths of justice: they and we can approach justice insofar as we are reasonable.

But so far I have said relatively little about how people can learn to be just. MacIntyre suggests, correctly, that we first learn justice from other people.[84] But since those other people are not perfect in justice—their actions consist of norms of justice admixed with error and self-interest—is it not highly difficult to learn about justice from that source? How do we know that what we are learning is true, secure? The answer must be that a solid grasp is available to us of first the primary, then the close secondary, precepts of natural law, which include principles of how we ought to act towards others, and that at least part of our inner life is shaped by eternal law, for the natural law is a participation in eternal law of the rational creature, whereby the light of God is infused in us. The divine light is one of learning how to connect premises to conclusions across a vast range of cases. Thus it not only discloses the most general principles, but indicates how those principles must be applied as *judgments* of facts (though as Aquinas warns, this task becomes progressively harder as one descends into detail). But what Aquinas and the scholastics do not say very clearly, is that while (a) acts of individuals in the private sphere are generally capable of achieving justice to a high degree,[85] (b) the actions of government, both internal and external, are much more difficult to assess and typically

[82] See e.g. Porter, *Ministers of the Law* (n 38) 169. For a damning account of rhetoric, only partially redeemed by Aristotle, see Plato's *Gorgias*.
[83] Ibid, 210.
[84] MacIntytre, *WJWR* (n 19) 110.
[85] See e.g. International Theological Commission, *In Search of a Universal Ethic* § 31.

involve a complex interweaving of just and unjust associations. They, more than is the case with acts of individuals, face situations which require action where no action is even moderately just.

Clearly much else could be said about the nature of justice, and I have limited myself here to the most pressing concerns that are relevant to a natural law understanding of modern society. Some important residual matters are discussed in the following two chapters, concerned respectively with the common good and individual rights. It is to these that we now turn.

# V
# THE COMMON GOOD

## V.1. THE COMMON GOOD AND THE GREATER GOOD

From justice we turn now to justice's object, the common good. As remarked upon in earlier sections of this book, the common good of a community can be divided into two parts: the part of the common good that is or must be present in any society, in order to be sufficiently formed into a society, and the part of the common good that is particular to specific societies on the basis of their cultural, geographical, and economic situation. This chapter shall be concerned only with the first, universal, part of the common good, and shall attempt to enumerate the conditions required by the common good in this sense, and to explore its limits.

To begin with, it is necessary to clarify the meaning of the phrase 'common good' by distinguishing it from an alternative concept with which it is sometimes confused: 'the greater good'.[1] For the common good is not a mere amalgamation of individual goods, which numerically outweigh the good of a particular individual and so require the forfeiture of that individual's interests to the 'greater good'.[2] Numerical priority is in any case an opaque and unsatisfactory basis for ethics, for it is implicitly the numerical superiority rather than goodness that provides the real grounds upon which the various interests are thus weighed and measured. But if the majority of the community wish to exterminate or deport those of Jewish race from their society, what viable concept of the good underpins this? The good is not an aggregate: one cannot (and not merely ought not to) justify collective action, in any robust sense of 'justify', on the basis of numbers. The aggregative conception of the common good is in effect just another form of utilitarianism, as discussed in Section I.2. A society whose major ethical decisions are settled by referendums is, in an important sense, one that is morally impoverished. You may say, referendums are carried out by thorough and often lively debates for and against, pro and con, but the reality is that the arguments, being political, tend to be one-sided rather than disinterested, emotive rather than fully reasoned, prone to rhetoric, exaggeration, and unsubstantiated fears rather than measured, subtle, complex. Moral action is not rationally arrived at by counting votes; it cannot be justified by ballots.

[1] See Jonathan Crowe, *Natural Law & the Nature of Law* (CUP 2019, hereafter *NLNL*) 5.
[2] See Adrian Vermeule, *Common Law Constitutionalism* (Polity 2022) 7, 14, 37.

*Natural Law and Modern Society.* Sean Coyle, Oxford University Press. © Sean Coyle 2023.
DOI: 10.1093/oso/9780192886996.003.0005

But there is another meaning of 'aggregative' by which the common good is held to consist in the full flourishing of every member of the community.[3] Here the numerical aggregate does not override the interests of the individual, for each individual's good is relevant to the aggregate. This is in opposition to the 'instrumentalist' view that the common good consists of the creation of conditions that are necessary or conducive to every individual's pursuit of their own good.[4] But even if the merits of the aggregative view were positively established, it is far from clear that the situation it describes is realizable even in principle. Murphy argues that if a community has a reason to favour or promote A's flourishing, it has an even greater reason to secure A's flourishing *and* B's flourishing.[5] But this supposes that A's flourishing is actually compatible with B's flourishing, and both with C's (and so on). Even if this was a coherent proposal, it is one that can only be achieved by creating opportunities and liberties which allow every member of the community to pursue their own flourishing in their own way, and by supplementing such naked liberties with forms of good that can reasonably be attained by those people. We thus seem to fall back on the 'instrumentalist' concept.

Further specifications of the aggregative view are possible: for instance that the common good is a situation in which all members of the community stand to one another in relationships of practical reasonableness. But such a concept ignores fundamental facts of the human condition (e.g. emotive reasoning, imperfect altruism) and would require quite repressive adjustments to mechanisms of public and political life, seeking to exclude emotive decision-making.[6] Moreover, concepts of this kind tend to regard only one aspect of human flourishing (practical reasonableness in this case) as relevant to the mechanisms designed to bring the common good about; and these and other proposals wrongly regard their preferred metric of flourishing as primary and prior to others: they fail to perceive that, although any one aspect of human flourishing can reasonably take priority in certain situations, no aspect of flourishing can be maintained as prior and primary to the others across all actual or potential human situations. There may be situations, for example of national emergency, in which the human good of (preservation of) life takes priority over the maintenance of institutions maximizing reasonableness between citizens. Such would be the case where members of a community are deeply divided about what practical reason demands: in such cases, social solidarity may be of greater importance, from large concerns such as referendums to smaller *affaires Dreyfus*.

[3] See e.g. Mark C Murphy, *Natural Law in Jurisprudence & Politics* (CUP 2006, hereafter *NLJP*) 3. See also Crowe, *NLNL* (n 1) 89.

[4] See George Duke, 'Finnis on the Authority of Law and the Common Good' 19 (2013) *Legal Theory* 46.

[5] Murphy, *NLJP* (n 3) 63.

[6] See ibid, 60: the purpose of law is to close off some of the normative openness that generates practical conflict between even fully reasonable agents.

Murphy contends that the 'instrumental' concept is, however, troubling. For Finnis in effect treats the common good as an instrumental, rather than basic, good.[7] But the concept, like the description ('instrumental' and 'instrumentalist'), is misplaced. We may introduce instead the concept of a 'non-basic component good'. Human goods that are non-basic are not by definition instrumental. They may be (1) aspects of a number of more basic goods, such as sociability and practical reasoning, (2) generalizations of more specific goods (such as civility from friendship), or (3) specifications from more general categories (e.g. marriage from sociability). And a 'component' good is simply a good that is a required part of a target-good, as peace is a component of commercial transactions. It is therefore far from clear (whatever the specific merits of Finnis's position) that an account of his kind treats the common good as an instrumental good. Indeed Murphy highlights the key aspect of Finnis's account: that of the requirement of practical reasonableness to favour and foster the common good of one's community.[8] But practical reasonableness is not an instrumental good, the important criticism being that Finnis regards this aspect of practical reasonableness as self-evident, for which he (therefore) offers no equivalent discussion. That practical reasonableness involves commitment to the common good may or may not be *per se nota* (I believe it is), but its consequences for the common good are at least capable of reasoning *per modo conclusio* from the most basic precepts of natural law, and as such ought to be untroubling.

It should come as no surprise, then, that the discussion of the present chapter largely avoids both terms, 'instrumental' and 'aggregate'. But we are not finished with the idea of the 'greater good', from which the discussion above started. Another aspect of the 'greater good' is that it is typically invoked in order to justify an evil of some kind. The legitimate interests of some individual, or group of individuals, are to be denied in favour of the interests of a numerically greater group or class of individuals. To be sure, we sometimes invoke the *common good* as a reason for sacrificing certain individual interests, but in this case the sacrifice is not for the sake of some other *group*, a group that does not include the relevant individual whose interests are sacrificed, but rather for the benefit of the whole community *including* the individual. Such instances are comparatively rare: a billionaire is accidentally injured by the negligent act of a pauper; it would cause scandal and outcry if the billionaire, who can absorb the loss, enforced his rights against the pauper, who is unable to pay. The billionaire certainly loses out if he waives his entitlement

[7] Ibid, 67. See also George Duke, 'The Weak Natural Law Thesis and the Common Good' 35 (2016) *Law & Philosophy* 485. Finnis himself conceded, perhaps unnecessarily, in his Postscript to John Finnis, *Natural Law & Natural Rights* (2nd edn OUP 2011, hereafter *NLNR*) that his account of the common good in the original text was too instrumental. See also Mark C Murphy, *Natural Law and Practical Rationality* (CUP 2001, hereafter *NLPR*)) 129.

[8] Murphy, *NLJP* (n 3) 66–67. Crowe also classifies Finnis's account as instrumentalist: *NLNL* (n 1) 89, citing Finnis, *NLNR* (n 7) 156.

(he does not get what he has a right to recover), but he avoids becoming the object of moral opprobrium, and he lives in a community that cares sufficiently for its worse-off citizens and vocally upholds a sense of justice, matters which enhance the lives of all the community, including the billionaire. But on the majority of occasions, the demands of the common good do not come at the expense of individual rights: the demands of peace and justice, for example, require individuals to forego committing crimes, but not their lawful activities. The common good of prosperity in community requires individuals to engage with the market, and enter into contracts, which they would in any case want to do, for they are generally advantageous.

The idea of the greater good is also misleading in other ways, for example by implying that the good of the community consists of one single thing or state of affairs; yet 'the common good' is really a shorthand way of referring to many *common goods*. We have mentioned some of these goods (peace, justice, security) already. No single, fixed state of affairs arises from such goods, and a political community will find itself over time promoting (i.e. expending political time, money, and effort on) various goods in various relationships of priority in the name of 'the' common good. Agents of the state who are tasked with promoting common goods have finite time and skill: thus, a police force will be obliged to shift its priorities away from, for example, the detection and foiling of external terrorist threats, in order to restore peace in the wake of large-scale riots. The special responsibilities of holders of public offices are all directed to the common good, or common goods, in this sense. But is there some point in referring to 'the common good' of a community as signifying some overarching political aims or more-or-less permanent values, such as liberty? As already mentioned, perhaps it can be employed as a shorthand way of referring to various common *goods*, but the term is misleading when it is used to refer to some monolithic or unified set of aims. We need only recall to mind the many ways in which liberty (for example) conflicts with other common goods, such as security, or indeed, sometimes, fairness. There may be many ways of balancing values such as these, and typically such values are of shifting priority. Common good is not the same thing as singularity of purpose: a community is typically held together by many more or less shared intentions, none of which need be universally shared by all the members of the community. Indeed, Aristotle observes that unity ought not to become the purpose of a community even where it is possible to fulfil.[9] Only in times of war, for example, where defence of the nation is a common aim, or in times of constitutional crisis when defence of parliamentary elections are at stake, can one point to a universal aim. In normal conditions, the function of the state is one of management, not the pursuit of some overall achievement.

[9] Aristotle, *Politics* II.2.1261a.

It is not the purpose of public officials to bring about some specific state of affairs. It is, as Aquinas reminds us, part of the common good to facilitate the prudential reasoning of citizens in making their free choices in private life.[10] Such choices have a consequent effect upon the political values and priorities that are the subject of governmental policy at any given time. But such choices are also partially shaped and affected by those values and priorities (through minimum wages, pricing controls, equality legislation, and so on), so that there is a dynamic relationship between the two parts of the common good: on the one hand, the individual choices and actions of citizens, and, on the other hand, decisions taken by public officials directed to the collective welfare, or (in other words) to the entire body of individual choices and decisions considered as a whole. The phrase 'as a whole' should not be taken in an aggregative sense, as meaning any sum of individual choices. It should be understood as a reference to the maintenance of the whole edifice of rules and conditions that make individual choice possible. Again, not all of these conditions are necessarily fixed (although some are: such as the suppression and punishment of crime); hence the conditions in which individual citizens choose and act shift and change depending on, for example, the health of the economy, the supply of competent teachers and facilities, solidity and sophistication of infrastructure, etc.

So it seems, then, that the common good consists of two interrelated parts: (i) the flourishing of all citizens within a community (that is to say, the flourishing of each and every person as, in Kant's terms, an end in themselves), and (ii) all those actions and measures necessary for the good/flourishing of individuals that those same individuals cannot bring about by their private actions unaided and/or unorganized or uncoordinated. Obviously, (ii) can limit (i), and vice versa. But it should not be forgotten that (iii) private individuals can also act for the sake of the common good directly (and not only indirectly through the operation of an 'invisible hand'), so that their actions are explicable as contributions to some common good aside from their own good.[11] An example of (iii) is: the intellectual life of a university department. Consider the case of X, who attends a seminar delivered by his colleague Y, not because he wishes to learn anything (the subject might fall outside his teaching and research interests) but to ensure a good crowd for the sake of Y and other colleagues present, by contributing to the intellectual life of the department. X does this by acting for the sake of the common good: a department that is friendly and integrated, and in which members are mutually interested in one another, and one another's work, is a better department to work in for everybody, including X. But although X benefits from this broader common good, it is achieved (through X and the other members of the department) at the expense

[10] Aquinas, *Summa Contra Gentiles* (hereafter *SCG*) III.71.4.[2470].
[11] Aquinas, *Summa Theologiae* (hereafter *ST*) I-II.96.3c.

of other goods that may well be more important to X himself: in particular, time-costs; time which could have been used for research, preparation for classes, or simply rest.

The importance of (iii) is brought out in the implication of the foregoing example: that the common good cannot be understood as an instrumental conception, as referring exclusively to the establishment of conditions for the realization of human primary goods.[12] Thus neither the aggregative nor the instrumental conceptions of the common good adequately explain its inner complexity. An alternative conception might be proposed along the following lines. Aristotle identifies the intrinsic goodness of the common good as a kind of *friendship*, which is still required even by one who has in his possession all other goods.[13] In his ensuing analysis, Aristotle sets out the basic characteristics of this form of social friendship. It is a state, not an emotion;[14] it is, like justice, a kind of equality;[15] it is a kind of concord (political friendship);[16] nevertheless, it is distinct from true (paradigmatic) friendship, which can only be extended to a few;[17] and thus one naturally owes more to one's spouse, family and close friends than to strangers.[18] The good that is specific to individuals, and that which is specific to families, are not part of a continuum that runs from the private to the common good: they do not form part of one single ethical framework. Rather, the good of the household is the subject of domestic ethics (*oeconomica*) as distinct from political ethics;[19] the question of how one should live or structure one's life is (within obvious limits) a discrete topic for ethics.

The reference to friendship, or more broadly, sociability, is particularly significant in relation to the last-mentioned field of ethics, that of the individual. Despite Aristotle's suggestion that concord, or social friendship, resembles friendships of utility rather than true friendships, the maintenance of peaceful and friendly relations with others is intrinsically valuable and not merely instrumental in pursuit of human primary goods: it is such a good. It is therefore intelligible for a person to

[12] See Duke (n 7) 67. Various passages in both Aristotle and Aquinas can be superficially read in this instrumentalist way: perhaps most clearly in *De Regno* (hereafter *De Reg*) I.15.103: the purpose of government is to lead the thing governed to *its* proper end (and therefore not that of the ruler or a mere aggregate of persons). See also *Gaudium et spes* § 25; Aquinas, *ST* (n 11) II-II.58.5c.

[13] Aristotle, *Nicomachean Ethics* (hereafter *NE*) VIII.1.1155a. See Aquinas, *Commentary on Aristotle's Ethics* (hereafter *Eth*) VIII.4.1594: all friendship is to be understood by reference to perfect friendship (i.e. to the archetypal or 'focal' conception of friendship between two *individuals*). Aristotle's remark must therefore be understood in relation to his analysis of friendship at *NE* VIII.3: specifically, it is not the focal instance of friendship discussed at 1156b, but rather resembles friendship of utility.

[14] Aristotle, *NE* (n 13) VIII.5.1157b.

[15] Ibid, VIII.5.1158a; but the mode of equality is different: VIII.6.1158b.

[16] Ibid, VIII.6.1167a–b.

[17] Ibid, VIII.6.1158a; see also Aquinas, *Eth* (n 13) IX.12.1921.

[18] Aristotle, *NE* (n 13) VIII.9.1160a; for exceptions to this doctrine see Aquinas, *Eth* (n 13) IX.2.1774–79.

[19] Aquinas, *Eth* (n 13)VIII.12.1725; see also VIII.9.1660. Indeed it is only because of the diversity of private means and ends that a directive principle (the common good) is necessary: *De Reg* (n 12) I.1.3.

act out of concern for concord without tracing back its benefits to personal interest. Living in a society in which people meet on friendly terms rather than hostility; knowing that if one were in danger, strangers may well come to one's aid rather than passing by with indifference; realizing that violence and assault are the exception in social contexts rather than the norm: all of these and other factors explain why it is not unreasonable to regard the common good (or certain common goods) as intrinsically valuable (see Section III.4(c)). Such factors are also at play in other specific contexts that a society must face (and must face collectively). A soldier, for example, is precisely a cog in the machine, who must act on behalf of his unit, battalion, battle group; his merit to the army lies in submerging private interests for the good of the whole. More generally, during a time of famine or short commons, citizens must quell their desire, even need, of more food, and must not subvert through dishonesty or claims of special friendship (let alone violence) the system of rationing that is put in place for the benefit of all. At the same time, although acting for the common good sometimes requires one to sacrifice one's own interests, the common goods of peace, security and concord nurture and reinforce one's own private good: for (as Aristotle again suggests) the human being is a *social* animal by nature, and so such common goods are constitutive of and not merely instrumental to the good of individuals.[20]

The general question of the relationship between common good and private good will be explored and unfolded throughout this chapter. The question we have been pondering is: are all actions for the sake of the common good thus also beneficial to the one who acts? And do all acts in pursuit of private good also have a positive effect on the common good? A useful introduction to the issue is offered by Suarez, in the context of his discussion of common good. After a crime has been committed, it might seem that the penance of the sinner is for the sinner's sake alone, for it reconnects the sinner with the ultimate source of all wellbeing, God. But Suarez notes that the penance also enhances the common good, by additionally making the truly repentant sinner into a good person who will henceforth not act wickedly towards others in the community[21] (see Section III.4(b)). In common with other late scholastic writers, Suarez wishes to extend this mutuality of benefit to all aspects of common good. He observes that certain matters pertain to the common welfare of all (such as open meadows, churches, magistracies), whereas other aspects of common good favour the private good of individuals *which is itself an aspect of common good* because the individual is part of society.[22] An example, purportedly of this kind, is provided by Finnis. A farmer is prevented by law from polluting a stream; but the same legal system that prohibits pollution also provides

[20] I lack a satisfactory name for this theory of the common good: perhaps 'constitutive' or even 'virtue' capture something of it.

[21] Suarez, *De Legibus* (hereafter *DL*) I.7.3.

[22] Ibid, I.7.7.

the farmer with security against trespass, and all the benefits, rights, and liberties that the law extends to all citizens. Hence not polluting the stream is also to the farmer's own good. But is the Suarez–Finnis view tenable? The farmer may have no interest in an unpolluted environment so long as his own land remains free of pollution; he is not contaminating water that will ultimately pour from his taps; and by continuing to pollute the stream he may not sacrifice any of the benefits, rights, and liberties that he values (perhaps he pays a fine, which he can easily afford). So there is no discernible private benefit to the farmer's ceasing to pollute the stream. Perhaps in light of circumstances such as these, Suarez later qualifies his doctrine, for he says that in the event of a conflict between the private good of an individual and the common good of the community, the common good must prevail.[23] This is, of course, potentially a dangerous doctrine, and subsequent sections of this chapter will attempt to indicate its scope and limits.

It is customary to distinguish between the limited *political* common good of a community (goods such as peace and justice) that are owed by the state to its citizens, and the broader common good (or common goods) that lie outside the state's responsibility, and which, if the state did pursue them, would end in oppression: these are goods that individuals and groups of citizens should strive to procure for themselves. Aquinas almost certainly held such a view.[24] The discussion in this chapter supposes something akin to this view, but is concerned to illuminate other aspects of the common good, and thus employs a different intellectual framework.

## V.2. THE RELATIONSHIP OF INDIVIDUAL GOOD TO COMMON GOOD

The preceding section began an investigation that will be pursued further in this section. The question of the common good's relationship to individual good is endlessly complex; what follows is an attempt to trace the relationship in broad outline. The question of priority (of common good over individual good, or vice versa) is not a static one, for circumstances, such as resisting enemy invasion, may temporarily elevate aspects of common good (defence of the realm) above that of individual goods (such as freedom)

The scholastics employed various images to explain the priority but also subsidiary function of the common good: that the common good of the community is not the organic unity of the body, neither in terms of workers all labouring for the

[23] Ibid, I.7.14; see also Aquinas, *ST* (n 11) II-II.32.6c; John Finnis, 'The Authority of Law in the Predicament of Contemporary Social Theory' (1984) *Notre Dame J of Law, Ethics & Public Policy* 133ff. We might of course note that the farmer *benefits from* the relevant common goods even if he does not *value* them. For a similar example see Suarez's account in *DL* (n 21) II.7.7.

[24] See John Finnis, *Aquinas: Moral, Political & Legal Theory* (OUP 1998) 222–27; see also Mark C Murphy, *Natural Law and Practical Rationality* (CUP 2001, hereafter *NLPR*) 127–28, 130.

benefit of the ruler nor in terms of collective pursuit of some utilitarian aggregation or epitomization of the community, nor that of harmony among citizens turning into unison. The human being is the foundation and purpose of political community;[25] but although the common good is the good of all persons in the community, there can be collisions between the requirements of the common good and the narrower (yet legitimate) interests of particular individuals. Take a simple example:[26] X, a student, has an interest in attending tutorials given by the university, and also an interest in articulating her views; but X cannot say all that she wants to say. For the common good of the tutorial group, there are times (perhaps many) where she must remain silent and let others speak. Indeed, if X were continually to interrupt and talk over other members of the tutorial group, and perhaps the tutor, the tutor may remove X for the sake of the common good of the group. Alternatively, consider the case of the individual who has to be evicted from their land in order to make way for some public building project, such as a road. The compensation (if any) is not as satisfactory to the individual as remaining on the land they call 'home'. And, as a more extreme example, Aquinas states that the common good of the community might require the death of one of its members if they are dangerous to others.[27] Individual good and common good can, therefore, conflict.

Aquinas observes that law does not concern the private good of individuals, but only those acts that are relatable to the common goods of peace and justice.[28] This broad statement obscures the complexity of the relationship of private and common good explored in this section.[29]

Individual citizens have both rights and responsibilities in relation to the common good.[30] It is not difficult to point to basic rights of this kind. Such rights encompass (i) a functioning legal system,[31] (ii) fairness in official procedures and decisions, (iii) a regulated market to buy and sell goods and services, and opportunities for gainful employment, (iv) social peace and safety, (v) some degree of privacy from the state and other citizens, (vi) as broad a scope of freedom to live one's life in one's own way as possible,[32] and (vii) certain basic necessities and material resources, especially (though not only) food and shelter.

This is no mere wish-list; a society lacking in any of these regards is seriously unjust in ways that are too obvious to require statement. But it is worth dwelling on the last of these: for is it really true that all citizens have an *entitlement* to a

25 *Gaudium et spes* § 25.
26 Inspired by Finnis.
27 Aquinas, *ST* (n 11) II-II.64.2c; see also II-II.64.6c.
28 Ibid, I-II.96.3.
29 Suarez's rather intricate account in virtually all respects remains close to Aquinas, with only limited departures; he cites Aquinas more than any other author, but explores the legal situation of contemporary Europe in some greater detail, relying in particular on the *Decretum* and other legal sources: see Suarez, *DL* (n 21) II.7.
30 Crowe, *NLNL* (n 1) 92.
31 On requirements of the rule of law see Section X.3.
32 Aquinas, *Commentary on Aristotle's Politics* (hereafter *Com Pol*) II.1.

minimum level of prosperity? (Is it not said, 'If anyone will not work, let him not eat'?)[33] As one might imagine, the doctrine of the scholastics on this matter is subtle and multi-faceted. They took pains to point out that a person can at times of extreme necessity, when starvation would otherwise result, take resources from their owner in order to succour themselves. Such an act would normally be contrary to natural law,[34] not to mention positive law; and so of course there are conditions that have to be met: (i) the starving person must be in dire need; (ii) they must have exhausted all other alternatives; (iii) the person whose goods have been taken must be affluent, or at least in better condition than the taker, and left with enough means to live; (iv) the goods must be 'at hand'; and (v) no more should be taken than the absolute minimum required to succour the desperate man. Where (i)–(v) are met, the action of the starving person is not an act of theft (which it otherwise would be), for all property becomes common at necessity.[35]

This doctrine, limited as it is, is contrary to the first and most important duty of individuals to the common good of their community: that of obeying just positive laws. For the state is the custodian of the common good, and individual citizens can only act in a fully adequate way for the common good by obeying the standards enacted by that custodian:[36] by conforming their behaviour to the requirements of the law, by engaging in behaviour made licit by the law (e.g. by entering into contracts, marriages, use of property, and so on), and occasionally by waiving their rights in acknowledgement of the imperfection of those same enactments. But Aquinas is able to differentiate, of course, between what is required by positive law and right, and what is required or allowed by natural law; so as we have seen, he remarks that taking another's property out of dire necessity 'is not, strictly speaking, theft'.[37] Thus if positive laws include within the definition of theft the taking of another's property at dire need, this is an example of an unjust positive law that does not morally require obedience. The scope of this doctrine has considerably narrowed in modern affluent societies, which often establish welfare schemes and safety nets to answer the needs of the hungry, the destitute, and the sick: homeless shelters, soup kitchens and hostels, and state benefits of various kinds. Hence the person in need who resorts to theft without having exhausted other opportunities for assistance—or who shows no willingness to work—commits an offence against the natural as well as the positive law: see Section III.4(f).

The duty to obey just positive laws is the central means by which individual citizens contribute to the common good of their communities (see Section III.4(e)). First and foremost, performance of this duty favours the common goods of security, stability, and peace. Now, these are truly common goods, good not only for

[33] 2 Thessalonians 3:10.
[34] Aquinas, *ST* (n 11) I-II.94.6.
[35] Ibid, II-II.32.7 ad 3.
[36] Ibid, I-II.90.4c.
[37] Ibid, II-II.66.7c & ad 2.

others in the community but oneself also. But it is sometimes necessary to waive one's right in order to uphold those goods, as was the case in the example of the billionaire in Section V.1.[38] Thus in a certain sense individuals are sometimes called upon, by natural law, to sacrifice their immediate interests for the sake of common goods that are more important. Such self-denials reach beyond the individual herself: part of the common good of the community is friendship, a disposition to benevolence towards others, even strangers, that can, in cases of desperate need, override one's responsibilities towards one's family and close friends.[39] But it is necessary to give out of one's own resources: stealing from X to sustain Y is an offence against natural law in all but the most serious cases.[40] Yet it is evidently impossible for one individual to relieve the needs of every person,[41] and in normal conditions one's moral obligation to assist others pertains first and foremost to the ones for whom one is in some measure responsible: family, friends, those around one. But it is not irrational for a person to contribute to relief efforts to assist those dying of hunger in a famine-struck country far away, just as it is not unreasonable to pray for the souls of those whom one has never met. Given the inexhaustibility of causes to which one could in principle contribute, there are no firm or conclusive principles of justice or common good to guide one's liberality. Such principles as there are admit of too many variations and exceptions to be applied determinatively. In such cases, it is necessary to resort to casuistry. But the casuistry does not alter the fact that any contribution to a good cause (even if there are greater and better causes) is an action for the common good.

Are there other ways in which individual citizens can and ought to contribute to the common good(s) of their community, beyond obedience to positive laws, exactly *as* positive laws? Certainly, there are aspects of justice (itself a common good) that must be observed, such as refraining from acts of violence and wanton destruction, from invading another's rights, and from serious forms of dishonesty such as fraud, libel, and slander (see Section IV.2). More generally, individual citizens must *participate in community*, that is, interact with other individuals and groups in a positive way in order to bring about or enhance common goods (see Section III.4(c)). This can be achieved, inter alia, by transacting business, teaching, writing novels, painting, etc, by medical practice, or by working in one's capacity as an ambulance driver, fire officer, police officer, civil servant, or as a producer of useful goods; by writing works of history, economic theory, law, and by being a responsible parent, guardian, sibling; in short, one must pursue an active life, not one of passive inactivity. One must, in some shape or form, contribute to one's community. Aristotle famously reduced the possible alternatives to just two forms of

[38] Ibid, I-II.96.4c.
[39] Ibid, II-II.31.3c & ad 3; also Aquinas, *Eth* (n 13) VIII.12.1725.
[40] Aquinas, *ST* (n 11) ad 3.
[41] Ibid, II-II.32.5c.

life: one of active political service, or one of contemplation and virtue (the exercise of virtue requiring, of course, active engagement with others);[42] but there seems no reason to follow him in this. Yet, among the individual citizen's duties to the common good, aside from any operation of 'invisible hands', must be counted *the active life itself*. (Even the money-maker who only seeks to enrich himself benefits the community in a minimal way by not being a drain on common resources.) One must help oneself.

Murphy observes that the common good is not only or even chiefly to be characterized in downward terms (the individual deriving benefits from the community), but must be understood also in upward terms: in terms of the individual's contribution to the common good. It may seem as if Finnis neglects this trajectory in his account of the common good, for he describes it in terms of an 'ensemble of conditions' that enables persons to flourish in the basic goods. Yet it must in fairness be stated that many of the citizen's duties towards the common good—their contributions to peace, justice, public safety, transactional honesty, and so forth—are plainly stated in the various dimensions of practical reasonableness set out in Chapter V of *NLNR*. The obligations of each person to the common good form an intrinsic part of the determination of things to do or to avoid. Finnis probably obscures this connection by (1) failing adequately to acknowledge that his 'basic goods' are themselves aspects of the common good, and (2) providing an overly individualistic picture of practical reasonableness, as structuring the pursuit of those goods, in which the demands of reasonableness are reserved to a discrete and late section: see *NLNR* V.8. Murphy is thus wrong to characterize Finnis's theory as one that is entirely top-down, but he is correct to maintain that a theory of natural law must also account for the individual's contribution towards (i.e. duties to) the common good.

Murphy has long criticized Finnis's conception of the common good as being 'instrumentalist' rather than 'aggregative'. For (he says) Finnis describes the common good as the 'whole ensemble of material and other conditions, including forms of collaboration, that tend to favour, facilitate and foster the realisation of each individual . . . of his or her personal development'.[43] Murphy's own conception (the aggregative) begins from the premise that, if A's flourishing is a fundamental reason for action within A's community, then the situation in which both A and B are flourishing is an even stronger such reason.[44] Murphy appears to overlook the fact that Finnis defines the common good as the material *and other conditions* that tend to foster the common good of all individuals within the community. For those other conditions may well include the understanding that the flourishing of A and B is a stronger reason for political action than that of A alone. And that stronger

[42] Aristotle, *NE* (n 13) I.5.1095b-1096a.
[43] Quoted by Mark C Murphy, 'The Common Good' 59 (2005) *Review of Metaphysics* 139.
[44] Ibid, 137.

reason must incorporate the understanding that if A and B are to flourish, there must be limits to both A an B's pursuit of their flourishing: that is to say, an 'ensemble of conditions' that differ from A's and B's unbridled flourishing, but which can nevertheless be said to 'favour or foster' their flourishing. For that ensemble will have to include such matters (goods) as sociability, solidarity, and cooperation in preserving and extending the community's inventory of goods. (This parallels Finnis's treatment of friendship, in which each friend has a reason to favour and foster, beyond theirs and their friend's flourishing, a third thing: the common good that exists between them.)

We have been speaking of the duties of individuals to the common good(s) of their communities. But we should also observe the way in which those common goods have a collateral or reinforcing effect on the good of individuals. As we have already noted, the common good of sociability, or social friendship/friendliness, is intrinsically good for all persons. But sociability also grounds and supports human primary goods: knowledge, prudence, and other goods are vastly impoverished if one must live by the limit of one's own reason alone.[45] Sociability is therefore a human *need*, a need that is more precise than the mere general need to live in a multitude with those who share a common nature. For human beings also require the more specific form of communality that they share as members of the same political union, with shared customs and social life.[46] They require a shared language or languages, a shared history and the shared struggles that define a particular community: the ability to *express oneself* (sometimes idiomatically) and be *understood*, both in terms of what one is, at the time, *saying*, but also in terms of shared assumptions, values, and ideas to which ordinary patterns of discourse tacitly appeal. This shared background of assumptions etc does not usually require to be stated, but is present in everyday contexts of human interaction. For example, there is no reason why one would need to appeal explicitly to the rules of contract law when buying goods in a shop, and no need (in normal circumstances) to appeal explicitly to the moral canons of promise, performance, lack of threat, or dishonesty, and in general doing what one says that one is doing, that underpin those contractual rules.

It is perhaps necessary to tease out something that is implicit in the foregoing remarks about the relationship between individual good and common good. For certain general aspects of common good are an intrinsic part of the individual's good, and do not merely reinforce such goods. Thus the *Compendium* of the social teachings of the Catholic Church refers to the private, familial, and associative aspects of the good of the person as dimensions of that person's flourishing.[47] Language,

[45] *De Reg* (n 12) I.1.6; see also I.2.14.

[46] Aquinas, *Eth* (n 13) VIII.1.1541.

[47] *Compendium of the Social Teaching of the Catholic Church* (hereafter *Compendium*) II.1.61; see also Aristotle, *NE* VIII.9.1160a.

and hence knowledge and prudence, and opportunities to understand and participate in further forms of human good, are social constructions: not in the sense of being mere subjectivities, but in the sense of being necessary requirements to uncover truths and realities that are essential to human flourishing. For one cannot promote the good of the individual person without promoting the good of families, groups, associations, or local territorial realities.[48] Each of these groups (let us so-call them) has its own characteristic needs, ambitions, and forms of the good; each, as a matter of common good (not only the common good of their members), deserves to be made the object of ethical attention, and to be considered and resourced, whether by private or public means (or more usually a combination of the two: thus the raising of children within a family is often supported by both the income of the parents and state-derived child benefits).

Throughout this section and the one previous, I have referred to the common good of the *community*. But what does this reference mean? In fact 'community' is an abstraction with no fixed reference or form of its own, and hence has no fixed form to develop or express.[49] Liberal democracies are not 'the end of history'; they do not have a unique right to view themselves as the final embodiment of the common good. Scholastic and early-modern writers made no such claims. Hence, Grotius wrote that there are as many ways of living in society as there are peoples (see Section XII.3–4).[50] Community, then, is a state of affairs: it consists not only of all individuals within a given locality, but also of the various groups, associations and fraternal structures that are ongoing in that locality.[51] As these groups and organizations shift, change, become more powerful, or fade away, so the reference of 'common good' changes too. Furthermore, the individual citizen can act for the common good at any of these levels. By acting for the common good of their academic community, an individual scholar contributes to the wider common good of the community, for a well-functioning academic department is more productive and successful than one riven by internal discord and factional interests. If the members of a family get along with one another, and act for the good of their association, the family is less likely to require outside assistance (e.g. social services interventions or child custody battles). The common good is the good of the relationships that make up a community. And what is 'good' for a particular relationship or set of relationships is not necessarily, at any given time, what is beneficial to the narrow self-interests of particular individuals who benefit from those relationships: such a benefit being itself a personal, as well as a common, good. Let us refer to this conception as the 'relational theory of the common good'.

48 *Rerum novarum* § 102–103, 213.
49 See Porter, *Ministers of the Law* (Eerdmans 2010, hereafter *ML*) 155.
50 Grotius, *De Iure Belli ac Pacis* (hereafter *DIBP*) I.3.8.2; see also Proleg § LIV.
51 See Aristotle, *NE* (n 13) VIII.5.1157b, discussing friendship as a state.

It is entirely possible, in terms of this structure, for an individual to act for the sake (that is, for the common good) of a group or association of which they are not a member, and from which they do not derive any benefit. An individual does this when, for example, giving alms to a good cause from which he or she does not him/herself benefit. Such actions are intelligible because it is possible for an individual to perceive the good of that association, and to regard it as worth supporting aside from any personal forms of gain. And this, in turn, is an action for the common good of the community in general (of which the individual is part), for a community is better off with such groups or forms of association than without them. By contrast, an individual who contributes to the flourishing of a criminal organization acts against the common good of the community. The criminal organization possesses a 'common good' only in a qualified and inadequate sense: when it flourishes, its members become more affluent; but in every other measure the flourishing of such an organization is to the detriment of its members, by embroiling them in injustice, anti-social, and destructive behaviour.[52] Let it be said, in sum, that it is essential for the common good that members of the community are sufficiently in tune with one another that they (1) subscribe to basic moral values that are shared by all (NB this sharing need not in practice amount to actual compliance); (2) are aware of, and can see the point of, values, projects, and goals, even if they do not themselves subscribe to them; and (3) recognize that sometimes they may have to give way, when pursuing their own goals, in order that another is not unduly impeded in securing theirs.

Murphy argues that some acts, that are not other-regarding but self-regarding, are so debasing or repugnant that they are worth restraining even though they do not harm the common good.[53] On the relational theory, however, such acts *do* harm the common good, for they change the relationship of the individual to others in the community who are in some way debased as a result. This is not because others may be disgusted by the action(s), but because their own status as citizens and human beings is impacted in some way. Aristotle gives the example of engaging in depraved acts in the marketplace. Lewdness generally has this quality, whether performed in public or in private. The courts tacitly evoked the relational theory (though misapplied) in the obscenity trials of the mid-twentieth century: reading a lewd book, essentially a private act, would cheapen the human being's understanding of the human being.[54]

Finally, it should be noticed that sociability, that is, social friendship in community, is *proper* to the human being, not something that merely happens to be beneficial.[55] The foregoing dimensions of common good represent permanent,

[52] See Augustine, *De Civitate Dei* IV.4. For the argument that experiencing an injustice is preferable to acting unjustly, see Plato, *Gorgias* 469c, 527b.

[53] See Murphy, *NLJP* (n 3) 72.

[54] See e.g. *R v Penguin Books Ltd* [1961] Crim LR 176.

[55] See Aquinas, *ST* (n 11) I-II.94.2c; cf. Hart, *The Concept of Law* (3rd edn OUP 2012, hereafter *CL*) ch IX.

not temporary or conditional, truths of human association. They give content to Aristotle's statement (in *Politics* I.1) that the human being is a *political* animal.[56]

## V.3. THE STATE AND THE COMMON GOOD

The previous section's division of the common good into personal, familial, and associative good, concentrated upon the way in which individuals can and do further each of these kinds of good, and how these kinds of good are also, in a definite sense, individual goods. But there are aspects of these goods that individuals *cannot* bring about through their own unaided actions, either singly or in collaboration with other individuals, without further assistance. The scope of individual powers to act for the common good is also limited to actions (for some common good) that do not adversely affect the good of others. Hence actions that are harmful to others can only be morally carried out by the governing authority, whose competence extends to determinations of what is to be taken from individuals for the benefit of all.[57] This does not imply that all state action is *ipso facto* legitimate: there are limits even to the state's power to override individual interests in the name of the common good. Such limits stem from the very nature of political authority (see Section XI.1; XI.2). It is in all other cases the person(s) to whom an end belongs that direct resources to that end; hence the governing authority possesses the competence to direct individuals and groups only insofar as it acts as the agent (*vicem*) or personification (*personam publicam*) of the people.[58]

The source of the state's directive power lies in the fact that, given the plurality and diversity of ends and means, individuals require a directive principle to structure their actions and interactions.[59] But this must be understood in a minimal sense: though Aquinas in his treatise *De Regno*, composed around the same time as the *Summa Theologiae*, uncautiously observes that the purpose of government is to assist individual citizens to their proper end,[60] he straightaway qualifies the remark, stating that it is *not* the function of government to lead people to their *final* end (heavenly beatitude), for this is the function of divine law, not human law.[61] Thus human law is confined to establishing an ordered and peaceful society among persons, focused on the needs of peace and justice and not the inculcation of virtue more generally.[62] It would be easy, if unsatisfactory, to read this statement

[56] Indeed, for Aquinas, not merely political but conjugal: Aquinas, *Eth* (n 13) VIII.12.1720.

[57] See Aquinas, *ST* (n 11) II-II.64.3 ad 3.

[58] Ibid, I-II.90.3c. On the character of the political common good, see e.g. Richard Ekins, 'The State and Its People' 66 (2021) *American Journal of Jurisprudence* 54–55.

[59] *De Reg* (n 12) I.1.3.

[60] Ibid, I.15.103.

[61] Ibid, I.15.108; Aquinas, *ST* (n 11) I-II.100.2c.

[62] Aquinas, *ST* (n 11) I-II.96.3c; *De Reg* (n 12) I.6.37, also I.3.17.

as implying an instrumental conception of the common good. But George Duke offers a salutary reminder:

> If the common good of a polity is simply an instrumental means for the instantiation of the more basic goods, then it is difficult to see how it can be legitimate to regard the state as having an authoritative role to play that extends beyond a framework for the realization of minimal liberal goods such as liberty, fair distribution, equality of opportunity, and so on ... A more robust conception of the common good, by contrast, would seem to suggest that the state has a role to play in promoting a particular conception of the virtues of citizens, considered in terms of those forms of human excellence that allow for the fulfilment of [basic human] goods. Yet this in turn seems to presuppose some form of comprehensive doctrine regarding human excellence and the conditions of human flourishing.[63]

Indeed, a conception of justice (which scholastics identify as a primary common good) would seem to depend upon the proper end and functioning of the human being. Consider for example the resources put in place in order to protect young children and babies from the desperately sad cases of neglect and physical or sexual abuse. Such matters require a clear understanding of the proper development, flourishing, and moral status of persons. Or again, take any of the central provisions of the criminal law of modern societies (those that define what is *mala in se*, not *mala prohibita*): these articulate the relevant forms of moral uprightness that are proper to the human being as a sociable animal. Hence, while the state's function is not to demand comprehensive virtue from its citizens, its purview goes beyond securing the minimal standards required for the functioning of, for example, *homo economicus*. Although it is a central duty of the state to create conditions in which individuals can exercise their talents in the marketplace,[64] this does not extend to facilitating the activities of the pimp or the arms dealer.

Let it then be said that individual citizens are owed *limited* impartiality by the state as to how to define the good life, not complete impartiality about what is good. It is, of course, a matter of great difficulty as to how the line should be drawn. A useful example is the state's policies on sexual ethics. In at least some jurisdictions, prostitution is illegal despite being otherwise an instance of economic exchange. In virtually all jurisdictions, sexual intercourse between siblings, or between father and daughter etc is a criminal offence, and the ban is not held in place by fears about the welfare of any children born from such a union (for such couplings could easily involve contraceptives), but because of the intrinsic wrongfulness of the act (i.e. its contrariness to proper human functioning). Neither

[63] George Duke, 'Finnis on the Authority of Law and the Common Good' (2013) 19 *Legal Theory* 55–56; see also George Duke, 'The Distinctive Common Good' (2016) 78 *Review of Politics* 227.

[64] See *Compendium* (n 47) II.72.334.

are provisions of the criminal law, which make economic life possible, intelligible solely on that basis. Laws prohibiting serious fraud defend the mechanisms of the market (although fraud itself is just another process that contributes to supply and demand), but fraud also tends to undermine the normal social nature of human action. The popular principle of modern times, that 'political decisions must be, so far as possible, independent of any particular conception of the good life'[65] is therefore inaccurate. If we want to understand the proper limits of state action, and the legitimate exercise of state powers, we must give up the idea, popular since the early-modern period, that one can identify a minimal social framework that is neutral between opposing conceptions of the good. For a decision *not* to resource or foster some particular human good is not 'independent of any particular conception of the good life'; there is probably no kind of human good that could be considered as a neutral baseline common to all individual 'conceptions of the good'. There are probably individuals to be found who would dispute the goodness of any given human good, such as sociability for example: such individuals would regard state policies and laws promoting sociable interaction as precisely favouring a particular vision of the good life.[66] Indeed from the perspective of the anarchist, *all* common goods necessary for the existence of a peaceful and ordered society favour a specific conception of the good life. The state's impartiality with regard to defining the good life cannot therefore extend as far as throwing all dimensions of human good into question.

Modes of governance inevitably depend upon a conception of human flourishing: the atrocious forms of governance in Nazi Germany and Stalin's Russia are predicated on intolerably erroneous conceptions of the human being; those of enlightened states on a more accurate insight into human flourishing. Nor then is the common good a matter of popular consensus.[67] Certain views—for example racist views—even if held by the majority in society are not to be fostered, as if they were part of a reasonable vision of a good life, even at the cost of social peace. But such views demand not only to be suppressed by the enlightened, but to be denounced by policies and ideas of the common good that can be rationally explained and defended to racists and others, in principle if not in fact, regardless of relative numbers of adherents. Finally, a state favours or fosters a specific conception of the good through its allocation of resources to one project rather than another: the creation of zones to protect the natural human environment rather than the building of roads, for example.

[65] Ronald Dworkin, *A Matter of Principle* (Harvard UP 1985) 191.

[66] Life? Well, one can imagine a small society whose members are brought up to ignore risk, who are capable of throwing their lives away in pursuit of (not the merest whim, but) intelligible ends, and generally act recklessly. They possess life, for as long as it lasts, but are ignorant of the idea of life as a value. The high mortality rate would keep the population small.

[67] See Vermeule (n 2) 48–49; also Suarez, *DL* (n 21) III.1.11: authoritarianism for its own sake is inimical to the natural law; also II.7.1–2.

Some of these questions about the scope of the state's duties to specify the content of the good life are answered by the doctrine of Catholic social teaching known as 'subsidiarity'.[68] This consists of (i) a positive principle (that the state should assist smaller social units such as the family, or various fraternal associations, to flourish in ways that those social units cannot bring about by their own unaided actions); and (ii) a negative principle (not to regard those smaller units as mere means to higher-order activities).[69] What the principle of subsidiarity does not say, but ought to say, is that it is likewise wrong (seriously unjust) (iii) to elevate a smaller unit to control higher-level operations (for example, giving a private corporation control of significant public assets without oversight); (iv) to force same-level groups to merge for the sake of the common good; or (v) to give control of public assets to organizations (e.g. organized crime syndicates) that are unlikely to foster the common good. John Stuart Mill captured some of the reasons underlying the principle of subsidiarity in his 1848 work on *The Principles of Political Economy*:

> [T]he mischief of overloading the chief functionaries of government with demands on their attention, and diverting them from duties which they alone can discharge, to objects which can be sufficiently well attained without them; the danger of unnecessarily swelling the direct power and indirect influence of government, and multiplying occasions of collision between its agents and private citizens; and the inexpediency of concentrating in a dominant bureaucracy all the skill and experience in the management of large interests, and all the power of organized action, existing in the community; a practice which keeps the citizens in a relation to the government like that of children to their guardians.[70]

Aristotle, too, cautions against pursuing too much unity for the state, as this will stifle families and other associations.[71] Concomitantly, it is against the basic purposes of the state to seek to suppress or eliminate legitimate forms of human association. Such forms are, as we have already seen, dimensions of the common good of persons: forms of speech and association are themselves goods, not adjunct realities instrumental to the pursuit of good. Nor is the pursuit of human good in general a wholly individual affair; it depends for its realization in one life a connection with other lives, as when one experiences fulfilment by reading a novel that another has written, which is in turn shaped and made possible by shared linguistic forms.[72] Individuals are not subject in all their lives and belongings to the

[68] For a longer treatment, see Finnis, *NLNR* (n 7) 144–46.

[69] *Rerum novarum* § 101–102, 123; Catechism of the Catholic Church § 1882–83.

[70] John Stuart Mill, *The Principles of Political Economy* [1848] V.11.11; also quoted at greater length in John Finnis, 'Subsidiarity's Roots and History' 61 (2016) *American Journal of Jurisprudence* 139.

[71] Aristotle, *Politics* II.2.1261b.

[72] For some discussion, see David Hollenbach, *The Common Good and Christian Ethics* (CUP 2012), 83; also Yves Simon, 'Common Good and Common Action' (1960) *Review of Politics* 203.

state's purposes; hence the state should not intervene to prevent people from acting according to their obligations, except in grave emergencies.[73] The principle of subsidiarity resembles the elevation to the political sphere of Kant's principle that the human person should be treated as an end and not merely as a means; but the present principle lacks the abstraction of Kant's formula, the implications of which it brings out in detail.[74]

The principle of subsidiarity raises a more general question: who decides what is the common good? As the preceding discussion should have made clear, this cannot be a matter for determination by the state alone, for the state is not equipped to discern what is in the best interests of millions of individual citizens. Moreover, the state could become so equipped (and then imperfectly) only by amassing detailed information about the lives and preferences of its citizens, a course of action stifling even if well-meaning, likely to lead to totalitarian abuses, and is entirely *ultra vires.* Hence Aquinas reminds his readers that a positive law lacks the necessary characteristics of law to the extent that it pertains to individual matters [*opere*] rather than the common good of all.[75] Nor can the determination lie wholly in the hands of citizens, due to the difficulty of discriminating between self-interest and the true demands of justice and common good. The answer can only lie in a sound ethics; but whose ethical judgments should count? The solving of this last question depends upon proper distinctions between different common *goods.* If you and I collaborate, be it only by refraining from action, in pursuit of some common end, then it is correct to say that a common good exists between us. For example, common goods of this kind exist between the listeners at a concert, and between the musicians who all play from the same score under the direction of the same conductor. The silence at the concert is not perhaps the perfect silence that might be enforced by the presence of the state's agents with powers to inflict punishments, but it is fit for purpose, and action by the state in this context is obviously disproportionate to the end, and proportionality is a precept of justice. Similarly the ordinary functioning of the family is a matter for the members of that family and not others; only where the law is being broken should the state interfere directly in its affairs.

This principle can in theory be extended to all associations within the community, but in practice it is not. For example, workers' unions and trade unions have powers only to the extent permitted by law, and there is nothing obviously illegitimate in the state's curtailing such powers for the sake of the broader common good for which it is responsible. In times of war, the community's need for munitions

[73] Aquinas, *ST* (n 11) I-II.21.4 ad 3; *SCG* (n 10) III.71.4.2470.

[74] For some recent discussion of the principle see the long symposium on subsidiarity in 61 (2016) *American Journal of Jurisprudence*; also Maria Cahill, 'Subsidiarity as a Preference for Proximity' 66 (2021) *American Journal of Jurisprudence* 129; and Michael Plaxton, 'Subsidiarity and the Criminal Jury' 67 (2022) *American Journal of Jurisprudence* 33.

[75] Aquinas, *ST* (n 11) I-II.90.2c.

will generally outweigh the rights of workers to strike over long hours or unpaid overtime. But when we refer to the 'broader common good', we mean only a particular subset of actions for the sake of the common good. The first and foremost demand is the creation and maintenance of a legal system, for it is only in the presence of a system of laws (governing behaviour, prohibiting crimes, facilitating exchanges, and protecting property) that individual citizens can take those steps that are necessary for their own good. The encyclical *Gaudium et spes* lists a number of common goods for which the state is responsible, including food, housing, work, education, sound judicial procedures, organized political power, peace, protection, care of the environment, access to healthcare, transportation and infrastructure, culture, freedom of communication and expression, and freedom of religion.[76] At least the majority of these common goods are realized through private, as well as public, efforts: food is grown, packaged, transported, and sold, in a market economy, through a series of private transactions. But such transactions are only possible on the basis of legal forms, and often facilitated through public subsidies and grants. Moreover, it is the state's responsibility to see that food is placed in the mouths of every citizen, not only those who can afford to pay the market price. These mechanisms and processes do not lie exclusively in any particular pair of hands, but take the form of continual practical reasoning between the members of a community.

Real-world judgments about the scope of state action—what lies within or outside the sphere of competence of government—are typically partly constitutional, partly cultural, partly technological, and partly political. The question of how far the state should go in seeking to promote the common good of interpersonal associations, otherwise of private character, depends therefore upon the particular circumstances and resources of a given community. Payment of child benefit for example depends upon the existence of bureaucratic institutions charged with investigating and processing individual claims, as well as upon suitably established income streams out of which the benefits are to be paid. A community without a well-developed infrastructure could hardly be said to possess such obligations. In general, the greater the level of technical development within a state, the greater will be the opportunity for government to interfere, for better or for worse, in the lives and dealings of its citizens. We are rightly uneasy about such developments. But the fact is that there is no single or comprehensive means by which a state government can be prevented from trespassing beyond its proper sphere of competence in pursuit of the broader common good.

The principle of subsidiarity enables us to draw a distinction between governmental *interference* in the affairs of individuals, families, or groups, and *assistance* by government to those groups. Forms of assistance (in the shape of tax-cuts,

[76] *Gaudium et spes* §26.

benefits, provision of services ...) though governed by justice (i.e. distributive and commutative fairness) should be presumed to be valid exercises of state power; forms of interference should be presumed to be morally invalid. But whether an instance of government action is to be regarded as assistance or otherwise depends upon its point. Removal of an abused or neglected child from its family is obviously a form of interference in the family's affairs, but the intention is to give assistance to the child, its development and future wellbeing; interference is a necessary means. Sometimes, state efforts to improve the common lot, to raise the general status of people, will count as assistance even if some interference with individual interests is an inevitable means. Conversely, interference with individual lives (actions, responsibilities, rights) for the purpose of better aligning them to state priorities and agenda, is an invalid exercise of state power.

How should a people respond to a government that trammels the rights of individuals in pursuit of the good of the state itself? The standard answer given by Aquinas and other scholastics (given above) is that, as long as the state does not coercively require an individual to commit an immoral act (e.g. informing against one's innocent neighbour; denouncing one's religious beliefs), that individual probably ought to bear the injustice to their interests in order to avoid greater destabilization and not to present the state power with further opportunities to take direct action against its people. But it has long been recognized by natural law philosophers that there are occasions upon which it is justified, perhaps even morally required, to overthrow a tyrannical regime. There are conditions: (a) the tyrant is oppressing the entire people or sizable portion of the people; (b) there is a grave and prolonged violation of individual rights; (c) all other means of changing the tyrant's mind have been exhausted; (d) the resistance will not cause even greater disorders; (e) the resistance has a well-founded hope of success; and (f) it is impossible to foresee any other solution.[77] And, as Aristotle reminds us, rebellion against tyranny cannot get underway unless citizens have confidence in one another.[78]

## V.4. LIVING IN COMMUNITY

We have been exploring the concept of the common good, and what this entails in terms of the duties of the state and the good of individual citizens. Let us now turn to the converse subject of what living in community demands of citizens if they are to experience any of the goods appropriate to their nature as political animals. The conditions required for living in community appear in Christian philosophy as the virtue of charitable love (*caritas*). Now, Christians are called to exhibit charitable love as a theological virtue (directly ordained to God), and to aim at the

[77] For (b)–(f), see Catechism of the Catholic Church § 2243.

[78] Aristotle, *Politics* V.11.1314a.

perfection of virtue. But it is perfectly possible for non-Christians to exhibit charity without directing their efforts to God, and, in no doubt many cases (Christian and otherwise), practicing charity in various less than perfect forms. The beginning of charity is the realization that many or all of the goods one seeks are appropriate not only for oneself, but for others who share one's nature, capacities, and characteristic inclinations. No theorem or principle of ethics is relatable to oneself alone, and no form of human good is due or owed to oneself more than to others: see Section III.1. The term '*human* good' already implies limits on the permissible scope of individual action to pursue such goods. But, according to the scholastics, a reasonable form of self-love is both compatible with, and foundational to, love of others, for others are (a) equally made in God's image, (b) like one in all relevant ways, and (c) effectively 'other selves'.[79]

The injunction to love the other 'as oneself' should not be misunderstood. It does not signify a need to love the other *to the same extent as oneself* (even were such a thing psychologically possible), but *in the same way as oneself*: no person is born into the world less entitled to life, and to the possibility of flourishing, than any other person, oneself included. No person's good acts should be disparaged, or their bad acts approved, any more than one's own. We should censure and blame others as we censure and blame ourselves: not more severely or unforgivingly.[80] But there are natural psychological limits to love. We do not love everybody in society, or across the world, with the same kind of love and with the same amount of affection. Thus the scholastics observed that love relates to *community*. Within one's own extended family, one loves one's immediate family most; within one's neighbourhood, one loves one's near neighbours and friends to a greater extent than more distant neighbours and acquaintances. In one's spiritual life, one loves more those who form one's immediate spiritual community (e.g. church, prayer group ...) than the whole body of the church throughout the world.[81] But we are moved by compassion and the need to take action (for instance, by giving alms) for the sake of those in desperate need anywhere in the world; where need is great, one should give priority to the needs of the hungry and distressed, even above the needs of one's own father.[82] We ought, in such emergencies, to be prepared to love our neighbour more than our own body.[83]

The term 'self-love' can easily be mistaken for more venal forms of self-interest. When the classical and medieval philosophers employ the term, they do so with the sense not of a search for more material goods and comforts, nor for seeking greater power or prestige, but as the effort to increase in oneself what is good, rational and noble.[84] Above all such goodness is that of friendship, for a life lived

[79] Aquinas, *ST* (n 11) II-II.44.7c; Aristotle, *NE* (n 13) IX.4.1166a; Finnis, *Aquinas* (n 24) 112.
[80] Aquinas, *ST* (n 11) II.II.44.7c.
[81] Ibid, II-II.31.3c, II-II.32.5c, II-II.44.8 ad 2; Aristotle, *NE* VIII.9.1160a, IX.10.1171a.
[82] Aquinas, *ST* (n 11) II-II.31.3c & ad 3, II-II.44.7c.
[83] Ibid, II-II.44.8 ad 2.
[84] See e.g. Aristotle, *NE* (n 13) IX.8.1167b-1169a.

even in abundance of all other goods is deficient and unhappy if it contains no friendships.[85] A person who 'loves himself' in the sense of loving his friend only for the sake of what the friend can benefit him does not experience true friendship and possesses only a diminished form of good.[86]

The general outline of Aristotle's and Aquinas's treatment of friendship is fairly well known. Friendship is akin to a form of justice,[87] but is greater than justice;[88] one's friend's good is an aspect of one's own good (and vice versa);[89] social relationships more generally are embryonic forms of the concord between friends,[90] but to seek to elevate all relationships to the level of friendship results in sycophancy;[91] friendship is above all else a common good; it is not an emotion but a state.[92] Friendship may be the greatest social good, but it is not to be sought everywhere and indiscriminately. But the obligations one has to one's friends and to one's family and others in society possess a great deal of complexity. Aquinas asks, ought we to pay back our father, a friend in need, or a benefactor, if we are unable to afford all three?[93] His answer is that, although one may lay down general rules, they admit of too many variations and circumstances to provide any definitive guidance. One must, again, fall back on casuistry to resolve the dilemmas of particular situations, but with the rules of justice always in the background.

The charity and love that characterize true friendship and self-sacrifice also admit of extraordinary forms and excellences. But as Aquinas and other scholastics were aware, the Christian injunction to love one's enemies and to do good to one's persecutors lies beyond the ability of most people, Christians and non-Christians alike.[94] There are however limits to this injunction. By doing good to one's enemies and persecutors, one is not to assist them in doing evil to one, or indeed undertake anything evil at all. One's actions may therefore be legitimately aimed at frustrating the enemy's evil intentions. The good that one does to one's enemy is primarily to persuade or direct them back to goodness. It is, secondarily, to ensure their wellbeing in terms of basic need; for all persons are due the primary human goods that are necessary for life. A society's criminal proceedings (if they are just and incorrupt) and its prisons (if they are reformative in aim) embody the good that is done not only to society but to the criminal, for the effort is to turn him into a good citizen. By contrast, police procedures, legal advocates and criminal trials that are characterized by bribery, trumped-up evidence, false witnesses, and penal

[85] Ibid, VIII.1.1155a.
[86] Aquinas, *Eth* (n 13) VIII.5.1604.
[87] Aristotle, *NE* (n 13) VIII.1.1155a; Aquinas, *Eth* (n 13) VIII.2.1559.
[88] Aristotle, *NE* (n 13) VIII.6.1158b.
[89] Ibid, IX.4.1166a; Aquinas, *Eth* (n 13) VIII.5.1605, IX.11.1909.
[90] Aquinas, *Eth* (n 13) VIII.4.1594.
[91] Ibid, IX.12.1923.
[92] Aristotle, *NE* (n 13) VIII.5.1157b.
[93] Ibid, IX.2.1774–79.
[94] *De Reg* (n 12) I.11.78.

policies by which criminals are thrown into prison and forgotten about, serve neither justice nor the common good.

Charitable love is not often discussed in works of social or political theory. But in fact, no legislative act or line of argument can persuade people to live in unity and peace: only love can do this.[95] Love in this sense is not mere emotion, but involves an intellectual act, the act of discerning the truth of interpersonal relationships, of justice and common goods. This love is sustained by a shared intellectual life, one that can identify primary forms of human flourishing, and a shared commitment to virtue in the form of a steady appreciation of one's own good and the good of others:[96] this is the point of saying that the object of justice is the common good. It is true that the overwhelming majority of people act without a thought for the virtues, but that is the right term to describe reason's governance of the appetite when, for example, sharing limited rations rather than hoarding them for oneself, refraining from thefts of items one desires, missing our train to assist a stranger, and generally not living a life centred entirely upon one's own interests in which others are treated as a means to one's satisfactions. Those for whom 'charity' signifies a response to an immediate need of another person, rather than a standing attitude or disposition to acknowledge the good of others, fail to understand the true underpinnings of social and political life.

In the foregoing paragraph, I adverted to the intellectual activity of discerning the truth of interpersonal relationships. But the value of living in community goes far beyond truths concerning justice and common good. For part of the common good itself is the ability to discern between truth and error in all matters, but especially matters of the morally sound and unsound. Without community, there is no language or rich set of concepts in which to phrase and explore one's thoughts; and without cooperative intellectual inquiry, carried out by many minds in relation, there is very little chance that mistaken conceptions or errors of reasoning could be overcome, or many truthful discoveries made. Technological progress is only possible due to the intellectual efforts of many; and moral questions pertaining to the use of technology, and the ever-expanding field of human skills, require sustained conversation and (if decisions are to be taken) consensus of many minds.

This spirit of shared action can, and ought to be, extended to all areas of social life. Without cooperation between citizens, there can be no contracts or valuable, mutually beneficial arrangements; no respect for private or public property; no educational establishments; no hospitals; no armies; no enforcement of laws … One's actions, as Aquinas points out, cannot help but be beneficial or injurious to the common good; so the moral measurement of actions must extend beyond the persons immediately affected to encompass the community in general.[97] All human

[95] See *Compendium* (n 47) I.8.207. See also David Decosimo, *Ethics as a Work of Charity: Thomas Aquinas and Pagan Virtue* (Stanford University Press 2014) 177.

[96] *Solicitudo rei socialis* § 26.

[97] Aquinas, *ST* (n 11) I-II.21.3c, I-II.74.2c.

goods must therefore be sought within the context of the broader common good of the community, at least so long as that common good is genuinely the good of all citizens. Mary Keys provides a useful illustration of this dynamic relationship. A student on a field trip abroad is captured by a hostile regime, which offers to release him in exchange for the release of twenty convicted terrorists who are being held in the student's home country. The student's family will naturally demand the release of the student, and may petition their own government to agree to the exchange. But both the government and perhaps the family will recognize the danger to society of releasing the terrorists and the emboldening effect this would have, and that there is a greater common good at stake (safety and security).[98] This provides a neat illustration of a remark by Aquinas, to the effect that, whilst common goods are rationally to be preferred to personal goods, the order of one's affections is the reverse.[99] The answer to this problem lies in the virtues. Because virtues order one's appetites, the virtuous person (especially the person of practical wisdom (*prudentia*)) will generally find it easier to reconcile the drive for personal goods with broader common goods.[100] Perhaps for this reason, Aquinas observes that the immediate end of human life consists in the good of reason *in common*.[101]

## V.5. PRIVATE PROPERTY

The preceding discussion in this chapter made a handful of references to property in general, and to private property in particular. It is now time to examine these concepts more closely. For the arrangements for the division of assets among the members of a community, and the state, is a pressing matter for the common goods of justice, peace, prosperity, and the opportunity for personal development. The necessity of private property and private resources was well understood by the medieval- and late-scholastics, Grotius pointing out, for example, that whilst the apples on the apple tree are common property, the apple that one takes and eats becomes irrevocably private property, along with the water one drinks from a common source.[102] But the concept of property, private, public, or common, is a development of patterns of human action, something that is given definite form only in retrospect, as an attempt to make sense of, and to explore the implications of, an already-existent social practice.[103] Even a nomadic people, as it grows to a large size, becomes less mobile and must develop practices of agriculture, and hence generate questions of ownership of land and products: we might call this 'the

[98] Mary Keys, *The Promise of the Common Good* (CUP 2006), 121–22.
[99] Aquinas, *ST* (n 11) I-II.19.10c.
[100] Ibid, II-II.47.10c & ad 2.
[101] *Sent* III.33.2.3c (*finis proximus humanae vitae est bonum rationis in communi*).
[102] See Grotius, *DIBP* (n 50) II.2.2.1.
[103] Ibid, II.2.2.4–5.

circumstances of ownership'. Grotius was aware that the circumstances of ownership do not invariably favour the development of private property, but one system or another of property must develop for uncertainty over property is a direct cause of war.[104] These arguments even pertain to aboriginal peoples who regard land in a spiritual way, as a 'connection' rather than 'ownership': for there are still boundaries, customs, and usages . . .

The terms 'private property', 'public property', 'common property' and so on, need to be understood and defended, or derided, in context rather than universally. The aim of defending, say, private property, should not be understood as a defence of such arrangements in all cases, but with respect to certain types of property or certain ranges of rights.[105] We are asking not whether private property is valid without qualification, but whether it best serves justice and the common good for some assets to remain or be placed in private hands; similarly, we want to know whether certain types of property ought to lie in public ownership, for the sake of the common good. For natural law theorists, property is natural, because the circumstances of ownership are natural; but the precise shape of property *rights* is a matter of convention. The view of property explored here takes its inspiration from these scholastic and early modern natural law theorists.[106] Property, for the purposes of the present discussion, is a series of relationships between persons with respect to things. Private property centrally involves the right to exclude others from use of the property, the right to transfer ownership to another or others, and the right to utilize the property within the limits recognized by the law. Property laws also create certain expectations, in terms of enforcement against trespassers or thieves, and in relation to peaceful possession.[107]

The circumstances of ownership demand a regime of property, but what of private property, in particular? The reader will already have gathered, from what has been said in previous sections of this chapter, that a good many things and actions (such as charitable giving, repaying debts, paying for goods and services) demand private property in at least some things.[108] More broadly, one needs resources in order to meet one's obligations and responsibilities (such as child-raising), and

[104] Ibid, II.1.11.1; see also Proleg §§ 8 & 10.

[105] For some discussion, see Hanoch Dagan, *A Liberal Theory of Property* (CUP 2021) 42–66.

[106] See Edward Feser, 'Classical Natural Law Theory, Property Rights and Taxation' 27 (2010) *Social Philosophy and Policy* 21. The most significant modern natural law theory of property is that of Finnis (*NLNR* (n 7) 169–73), though it is very short; for a contemporary work see e.g. Thomas Russman, 'Balancing Rights: The Modern Problem' 26 (1981) *The Catholic Lawyer* 296. Finnis situates his analysis of property within a discussion of justice; Russman couches his analysis in a treatment of rights: he enters the trap of supposing there to be a meaningful distinction between the classical notion of a 'right' and the modern 'subjective' notion: 296–98. For a more recent work see Francis Feingold, 'Is the Institution of Private Property Part of the Natural Law? *Ius gentium* and *ius naturale* in Aquinas's Account of the Right to "Steal" When in Urgent Need' 92 (2018) *Proceedings of the American Catholic Philosophical Association* 189; also Stephen Buckle, *Natural Law and the Theory of Property: Grotius to Hume* (OUP 1993) esp ch 1.

[107] On the general idea of expectations see Stephen Munzer, *A Theory of Property* (CUP 1990) 28.

[108] See ibid, 127; *De Reg* (n 12) I.6.118.

what are considered to be necessaries for life, and thus private in character, will vary depending upon one's situation: a person responsible for the wellbeing and support of many mouths will require more resources than the person responsible only for himself.[109] Now it might be objected that such resources could be obtained directly from the state, or from some communal group. But this is neither efficient nor practically possible: even if private individuals (or more likely, families) obtain their food from a common harvest, it would be practically unworkable and disastrously inefficient for each person to receive their share on a meal-by-meal basis. Instead, it would be much more likely and beneficial for private persons (or especially families) to receive a weekly—or monthly allowance of food which is then—as now a private asset—divided according to need or domestic prudence.

There are various psychological reasons why certain assets ought to lie in private hands, some of which are well known. To call these 'psychological' does not imply that they are in any way subjective, for they can be accounted as more-or-less permanent features of the human condition, at least as the human drama is played out in a society of any great size or complexity. Certain types of asset are likely to be neglected if left in common with no particular person(s) responsible for their cultivation or management.[110] Such an arrangement promotes inefficiency; more seriously, the absence of a clear owner/manager and structure of use-rights is more likely to lead to discord and squabbling.[111] And fundamentally, as Antonio de Escobar y Mendoza observed in his *Universae Theologiae Moralis* [1662], an arrangement of this kind is endemically unjust, for when all is left in common wicked people will contribute less but take more.[112]

Conversely, recognition of private property has a number of important advantages. Private property facilitates increased production, which contributes to the common good. It reduces neglect, destruction, and waste (though does not eliminate them altogether). It provides the certainty that is necessary for useful cultivation and productive use. It makes possible the design and building of expensive things, and of great works of art. For even the shipbuilder and the weaver must have their own material to work from.[113] Plato's reasons for excising private property from his ideal state are, as Aquinas points out, radically mistaken: for though Plato wished to create a social order characterized by the highest friendship, and regarded private property as a source of division and strife, Aquinas reminds us that the strife is not referable to the lack of commonality but to human wickedness, which the institution of a domain of communal property would do nothing

[109] *Sent ST* (n 11) II-II.32.6c (the illustration is not Aquinas's).
[110] Ibid, I-II.105.2c & ad 3; Aristotle, *Politics* II.3.1261b.
[111] Ibid, II-II.66.2c.
[112] See A de Escobar y Mendoza, *Universae Theologiae Moralis* [1662] 3, 4; quoted in AA Chafuen, *Faith and Liberty: The Economic Thought of the Late Scholastics* (Lexington Books 2003) 37. See Hanoch Dagan, *Property: Values and Institutions* (OUP 2011) ch 2; Larissa Katz, 'Exclusion and Exclusivity in Property Law' 58 (2008) *University of Toronto Law Journal* 275.
[113] Aristotle, *Politics* VII.4.1325b-1326a.

to extinguish.[114] You may ask, should the state not institute a system of *equal* property? But it is people's desires, not their possessions, that need to be equalized.[115] Equal property would only succeed in reducing violence if every person feels entitled to the same as others, and not more.

Property that has been recognized by the state as privately owned, nonetheless has a public dimension to it. Owners of land are not free to cause nuisance; they are not exempted from their ordinary legal obligations while on their property; they are not lawfully able to employ their private property to commit crimes; and they are not (through mechanisms of adverse possession and eminent domain) allowed to let their landed property fall into decay and disuse. Furthermore, the constant teaching of the scholastics, Aquinas in particular, is that once private assets have adequately nourished and provided for the owner, the owner's family and perhaps close friends, any remaining assets (those assets, we might say, that are left over once prudent savings, investment, insurance and future need have been taken into account) should be directed to relieving the needs of others.[116]

Many theories have been put forward in order to justify the institutions of private property, perhaps the most famous of which is Locke's Labour theory. But what would it mean to 'justify' private property? Does this entail a search for principles such that one can demonstrate that no injustice has been committed at any stage in the development of property, particularly property in land? Such an approach is impossible, for it is usually impossible, in the case of landed property, to trace a full and complete title to land back to the first owner or holder, and in the case of personal property, to ascertain the contribution of every person in its production against their remuneration (if any), and the origin of the materials used in its construction. We may in light of this distinguish between *justice* and *justification*: the latter is an attempt to offer sound reasons for preservation of the status quo with respect to some item of property (i.e. to determine conclusively, for practical purposes, the present owner of the asset) or, on the other hand, to find sound reasons why the asset should be differently transferred or distributed. We might therefore *justify* X's present holding of A, whilst not being able to ascertain who first made, developed, or held A; and the originator of A must normally be assumed to *own* what s/he *makes*. We may do all this whilst at the same time acknowledging that we have failed to prove that X *justly* holds A. For one thing, the whole edifice of a modern politico-economic order is not itself flawlessly just, but transactions must still take place, and take place with confidence and certainty. Perhaps Christ's warning that His 'Kingdom is not of this world' should be interpreted as a recognition of the fact that all earthly political orders contain endemic injustices,

[114] *Com Pol* (n 32) II.4.9; Aristotle, *Politics* II.5.1263b.
[115] Aristotle, *Politics* II.7.1266a-b; also 1267b.
[116] Aquinas, *ST* (n 11) II-II.32.5c; see perhaps Finnis, *NLNR* (n 7) 175.

which cannot be unravelled, and the promise that we shall see the just society only in heaven.

A telling illustration of this situation is the case of aboriginal land disputes, too well-known to require extensive rehearsal. Unlike the case of, say, modern-day ownership of buildings financed and erected through the slave trade, modern-day owners of houses built on ancestral lands are involved in an ongoing injustice. Their ownership is commutatively just (let us suppose) in terms of the politico-economic system that supports the housing market, but is commutatively unjust when examined against the broader strokes of history. Now, it could reasonably be argued that it would be prohibitively expensive and against the common good to demolish an entire city and evict its residents, in order to return ancestral lands to their original inhabitants, but unjust to those original inhabitants not to do so (see Section IV.4). (Let us assume that monetary compensation and alternative dwellings could not replace the value of the spiritual connection of those inhabitants with their ancestral lands.) But it would, equally, be unjust to evict the present owners, who may themselves have formed a sentimental attachment to their homes, and built a life and community in that place, and who after all paid the market rate for their land and houses. It is therefore practically impossible to avoid injustice to at least some groups of people; some historic injustices cannot be entirely undone by later actions (or inaction).

A coda to the present discussion: we have been examining the relationship of private property to the common good, and noting that a defence of private property is not defensible without qualification but only in relation to particular ranges of assets. What, then, are we to make of Aristotle's and Aquinas's extension of private property to the case of persons, in the form of slavery? After his rather desperate defence of slavery in *Politics* I.6–7, Aristotle begins to break through this argument early in I.13, in relation to the status of both slaves and women: he admits that slaves and women seem to exhibit virtue, the supposed lack of which is the basis for their being ruled by another. But he does not pursue his thought to its logical conclusion. Likewise, Aquinas mentions the views of those who think that slavery is immoral or unjust, but he fails to condemn it himself.[117] Thus anti-slavery arguments are not distinctively modern, any more than slavery itself is of the past. Modern western societies have not eradicated slavery but have merely outsourced it to other countries in which both adults and children are forced to work long hours on monotonous tasks for very little pay, and under appalling conditions, in order to supply affluent countries with both luxury goods and necessities. Aristotle and Aquinas at least attempted to provide an ethical framework for the moral treatment of slaves, but it awaited the social teachings of the Catholic Church in the late nineteenth century to acknowledge that slavery is itself immoral.

[117] *Com Pol* (n 32) I.4.5–10.

## V.6. WIDER HORIZONS

The common good of the community, in the writings of Aristotle, refers to the common good of the *polis*, or city-state. The present discussion extends that treatment to the political communities of today, that is, to nation-states. But we can now ask whether there are any common goods that surpass the boundaries of nation-states, and can be articulated at the level of the global community of human beings? (See Section XII.1.) Aquinas observes that the common good extends 'to the entire human family';[118] the encyclical *Pacem in terris* states that the good of a nation is inseparable from the good of the entire human family.[119] What kind of community is this 'entire human family'? It is 'akin to one single community'; the relation between the common good internal to nation-states and that of international society is to be understood as analogous.[120] The matter of how international community should be understood is one that has been in development since the beginning of recorded Western thought. Many of the natural law theorists, notably Grotius, made decisive contributions to the subject. Both he and the scholastics conceived of what we now call the international community as every bit a natural community as that internal to states. States are akin to brothers, and their relations fall under the natural law: just as one would rebuke a brother for wickedness, so the actions of states may be subjected to moral criticism.[121] Just as one might restrain or punish a brother in virtue of their evil actions, so certain kinds of state-action should be met with resistance and force. Like the common good of the state, the common good of the international community is ultimately related to the good of human beings. Hence, just wars can be waged not only against aggressive states but also those who oppress their people. For when a state turns on its own people and annihilates its own internal common good, who else but other states, or the international community at large, can defend that common good? (See Section XII.6.)

To speak of the global common good is in part to speak of global common goods such as peace and security: without these goods, the lives of all persons in all communities are worse off. But to speak of the global common good is also to speak of the good of all societies. Because each state is a member of the community of nations, each bears some responsibility for the flourishing of all. Such flourishing requires internal peace and security, justice, and institutions to secure it, some sharing of knowledge to improve the infrastructure of developing nations, practical assistance including advanced crop growing techniques, pest control, and so forth. Clearly then, affluent and developed states owe duties in aid, trade, and investment to developing states, along with duties to receive refugees fleeing murderous

[118] *De Malo* (hereafter *De Mal*) IV.1.
[119] *Pacem in terris* § 55.
[120] *De Mal* (n 118) IV.1 & *Solicitudo rei socialis* § 39 respectively.
[121] For the doctrine of *correctio fraterna* (brotherly correction) see Aquinas, *ST* (n 11) II-II.33.1c.

regimes where there is a real chance of inhuman treatment or death[122]—and even an obligation to share their wealth. But these duties are defined by the need for the developed state to safeguard its own borders, protect and defend its own common good, prioritize the wellbeing of its own population, and generally not to go backwards in terms of development in pursuit of a uniform worldwide condition (which would be at a much lower level): see Section XII.7. In broad terms one state both is and is not responsible for the common good of another.

The question of when a state, or group of states, must intervene in the internal affairs of another country, without that country's invitation, is an immensely thorny problem of international law and global ethics (see Section XII.6). In practice of course states limit their interventions to contexts of removal of a threat, or of securing ongoing access to some precious commodity such as oil. Most states do not acknowledge the duties mentioned in the preceding paragraph. Nevertheless the common good of all persons, and of all communities, is pursued, attained, or lost, promoted or suppressed, misidentified or protected, in a global context which, increasingly, depends upon relations between states. Two points should immediately be clarified, however. First, the duties spoken of here do not refer to the *ius cogens* norms of international law, conventions, treaties, or human rights instruments, all of which are positive legal instruments. We are speaking here of what is necessary according to *natural law*, and to natural rights (see Section XII.1). Second, not all internal injustices provide adequate grounds for intervening in the affairs of a state; for as we have seen, no state can claim to be entirely just in its internal affairs. It is probably impossible to provide a threshold criterion beyond which action is permitted, and the journey towards any such threshold should be marked by constructive dialogue in which it is the role of the international community of nations to seek to persuade a state to reverse its assault on the common good of its citizens: a constructive dialogue that must not, however, fail to include clear condemnation of the abuse or abuses in issue.[123] Chapter XII will explore in more detail the complexities and challenges facing international action for the common good.

Let us note, finally, that there is nothing inherently wrong about groups of states, short of the entire international community, coming together in mutual defence of their interests. These interests—these common goods—refer not only, in the West, to liberty and free-market institutions. They concern the amassed stock of knowledge, arts and technical skills, all manner of infrastructure, of cultural works from buildings to the stained glass iconography in church windows, and to wealth. There is nothing inherently wrong in regarding an attack on one such state as an attack on all, that is, on a shared way of life. There is nothing wrong with maintaining an arsenal of weapons and trained personnel in times of peace, ready to defend

[122] See Convention on the Status of Refugees 1951.

[123] The same is true of the domestic level: see Vermeule (n 2) 47.

the state if the occasion arises. It may be thought, moreover, that there is nothing wrong with stockpiling deadly weapons to be used as a deterrent against similar weapons possessed by hostile nations.[124] But there is, as Hobbes points out,[125] an overarching and permanent duty to explore all possible avenues to peace and good relations with other states, resorting to armed conflict or economic—and other sorts of—warfare only as a last resort. States party to groupings of this kind must also be aware that the very existence of such alliances is inherently threatening to other nations or blocs; and hence the members individually and the groupings collectively ought as far as possible to refrain from overtly hostile words or actions, of a kind that disrupts the peaceful order of the community: in other words, of the global common good.

[124] Though see Section XII.2.

[125] Hobbes, *Leviathan* XIV (Hobbes is speaking of war between individuals rather than commonwealths).

# VI
# NATURAL RIGHTS, LEGAL RIGHTS, HUMAN RIGHTS

## VI.1. SOME IMPORTANT PRELIMINARIES

Rights form the final element in a trinity of concepts that began with justice and the common good.[1] Rights, in the technical sense shortly to be outlined, correlate with duties on the part of another or others, but so far the discussion has talked of duties only in a loose way: whether of the state, of associations, or of the individual. But the preceding discussion of justice and the common good deliberately avoided the language of rights. This illustrates the fact that moral claims of the sort centrally at stake in politics and ethics (see Section III.4) are not inevitably or even best conceived in terms of rights. The discussion in Section III.4, which did not employ the language of rights, sets out a core morality that structures our understanding of the object of rights. Nevertheless many rights, including certain positive rights and human rights, are expressive of the general morality of a particular community.

Numerous controversies attend the subject of rights: about their existence conditions, the nature of the protection they afford, about the nature of their correlation with duties, and about their ultimate significance in ethics and political thought. For example, is it significant that classical and medieval philosophers explored the subject of ethics from the standpoint of the virtues, rather than of rights? Can one identify a definite point at which the 'language of rights' came into being and into common currency? Let us take these matters in reverse order.

Now, the Latin term for right, *ius*, was in use in Roman law texts stretching back into antiquity. But it is often said that classical and medieval writers possessed a notion of *objective right* [*ius obiectum*], but possessed no concept of *subjective right* [*ius subiectum*], or 'right' in the distinctively modern sense, as a kind of instrument for securing one's due, or what one is owed or, equivalently, one's right. The plausibility of this claim is bolstered by the fact that the established Roman law usage regarded the plaintiff as having the *ius* of performance by the defendant, but also the defendant of having the *ius* of performing the requisite actions for the benefit of the plaintiff. Clearly, this sense of '*ius*' is not equivalent to our modern usage: we would ordinarily speak of *A*'s right to uninterrupted flow of water from *B*'s property, but

[1] See *Evangelium vitae* § 71.

*Natural Law and Modern Society*. Sean Coyle, Oxford University Press. © Sean Coyle 2023.
DOI: 10.1093/oso/9780192886996.003.0006

not of *B*'s 'right' to ensure the flow.[2] This broader conception of 'right', generalizable to 'whatever the law demands', is reflected in patterns of ancient and medieval thought in which the terms '*ius*' and '*lex*' [law] are considered as interchangeable. Yet in fact when Aquinas turns to the subject of right, he is careful to observe that this sense of 'right' is only one of a number of distinct meanings of the word 'right', which also include the just thing itself (the central meaning of the term), the forum in which judgments are handed down, and the content of the judgment itself, even if it be unjust.[3] (Later, Hobbes would write that 'those who speak of this subject' habitually confused *ius* and *lex*, evidence that Aquinas used these terms interchangeably: but only with respect to one of its meanings, a qualification Hobbes ignores.[4]) Commenting upon Aquinas, Suarez observes a distinction between two senses of 'right': (i) that which is fair and in conformity with reason and (ii) the equity that is due to each person as a matter of justice.[5] The references to 'his due' or 'their due' are references to 'right' in the modern sense, merely expressed in different terminology. Suarez notes that 'right' in the second of these two senses corresponds to Aquinas's primary signification of the term. In subsequent remarks, Suarez develops further the second sense of 'right', in a way that extends, but remains in conformity with, Aquinas's account. For he states that 'right' can be understood as a moral capacity [*facultas*]—i.e. fitness—that every person has over the things they own, or over those things that are due to them, so that the owner can be said to have 'a right' to those things, and a worker is entitled to (i.e. has a right to) his or her wages, the *ius* being the ability to *claim* what one is owed;[6] and thus a right is properly held to be an *effect* of law [*effectum legis*], not its rational basis.[7]

Yet it is not necessary to pinpoint exactly when the concept of 'right' first emerged in juristic thought. For that issue says nothing about the usefulness of rights-talk, nor about the two most important implications of such talk: (a) the existence conditions of rights, and (b) their effects: matters which will be explored, to the extent necessary for the present discussion, below.

The fourth of the controversies about rights mentioned above—that of how the language of rights contrasts with an ethics of the virtues—can be dealt with fairly quickly. Rights are the proper object of justice, and justice is the virtue that specifically concerns one's relations with others. Here we must mention one of the characteristics of rights upon which there is widespread agreement: their conclusivity (or at least their quasi-conclusivity). Rights are distinctive in moral thought in that an

[2] See Charles Donahue, '*Ius* in Roman Law' in John Witte & Frank Alexander (eds) *Christianity and Human Rights* (CUP 2010) 64; also William A Edmundson, *An Introduction to Rights* (2nd edn, CUP 2012) 3.

[3] Aquinas, *Summa Theologiae* (hereafter *ST*) II-II.57.1 ad 1.

[4] *Leviathan* XIV.

[5] Suarez, *De Legibus* (hereafter *DL*) I.2.4.

[6] Ibid, I.2.5.

[7] Ibid, I.2.6; see also II.17.2: *ius* is the moral right to acquire or attain something, and is the proper object of justice.

appeal to one's right(s) is generally to be taken as a conclusive or peremptory reason for action (or inaction) on the part of others in the discourse. If I have a right to delivery of consumables, to peaceful possession of my land, or to be free from your interference in some matter, then that is sufficient reason for you to deliver, refrain from trespass, or from interfering, and so on. This holds even where other courses of action, in defiance of the right, might otherwise have been morally preferable (e.g. donating goods to the homeless that would otherwise have been delivered to another). So long as we lack the notion of a right, it might be difficult, in certain cases, to know what is the most virtuous course of action. Should I respect your claims to exclusive possession of land that you swindled or coerced out of another, or purchased with money that came directly from the slave trade? Is it more virtuous to put oneself at risk for the sake of a noble cause by forcibly occupying, along with others, the private land of a wicked baron? It is scarcely possible to entertain such examples without calling rights into service (what else is a 'claim' in this sense; what else is exclusive possession but a kind of right; how else can one determine what is private?). Studious avoidance of right-claims in such situations is possible, but it would not be an aid to clear thinking. Hence it is necessary to distinguish between private sins (failures of virtue in general) and social sins, which pertain to one's relationship with others, in which rights, and not virtues broadly defined, are in issue.[8] It will, in most circumstances, be preferable to live in a society with a clear structure of rights, even if such rights are unjustly obtained, than to live in a benevolent community in which claims are made, waived, or enforced on the basis of broader ideas of justice; for questions of justice can always be re-opened, re-explored, and decided differently on the basis of circumstances, the value of which may be perceived only dimly or imprecisely: not all questions of justice, to be sure but many that, in the absence of clearly defined ethical principles, must be decided through positive definition [*determinatio*].

As will become clear in the discussion that follows, this attribute of conclusivity is by no means as clear-cut as the previous paragraph perhaps suggests. But that matter will have to wait, as it is first necessary to consider the third of the controversies mentioned above, that of the relation of correlativity between right and duty. Specifically, do all rights correlate to duties (and vice versa), and what is the nature of this relation? Any conception of rights, in order to be fruitful and precise, must take account of Hohfeld's famous disambiguation of the term 'right' into distinct elements, and no analysis of rights will be successful that is not mindful of those distinctions. Given the fame of Hohfeld's analysis of rights, only a very short account will be given here. Hohfeld divides the concept of 'right' into relationships of jural correlatives, and jural opposites. In the table below, the columns represent

[8] See the Apostolic Exhortation, *Reconciliatio et paenitentia* § 16.

relationships of correlation, and the diagonals of the first two columns and again of the second two columns represent relationships of opposition.[9]

| Right | Permissibility | Power | Immunity |
|---|---|---|---|
| Duty | No-right | Liability | Disability |

(I have here re-named Hohfeld's 'privilege'—itself often recast as 'liberty'—as 'permissibility' since both extant terms, but especially liberty, invite confusion between an actual form of legal relationship and the kind of residual liberty possessed in cases where the law is silent.) Of immediate importance is that there is no logical relationship between the pairs in either the top or bottom row: possession of a right does not entail possession of a permission (one has a right to free expression at Speaker's Corner in Hyde Park, but one cannot avail oneself of that right—one is not permitted to exercise it—if one is in prison), and possession of a permission (e.g. to carry on a business) in no way implies the existence of a right that others either assist or refrain from interfering with you, for example in relation to that business: for, obviously, one may set up a rival establishment charging lower prices in the same street.[10] Right and duty can be inter-defined: if *A* has a right that *B* assist him with regard to some endeavour, then *B* has the corresponding duty to assist *A* (and not *C*, *D*, *E* ...) in that endeavour. Similarly, possession of a permission with respect to another implies that that other possesses no right (i.e. has a 'no-right') towards the holder of the permission, that the holder do or refrain from doing something in relation to some specified subject-matter. It follows from this that right and no-right, and permissibility and duty, are 'jural opposites' or contradictories of one another: they cannot hold of the same person(s) at the same time in respect of the same endeavour or subject-matter. Turning briefly to the second two columns, a 'power' in Hohfeld's terminology represents the legal ability to change another's relationship to oneself, that other person having the correlative *liability* to have their legal position changed in some way. Not all liabilities are disadvantageous: when *A* makes a contractual offer to *B*, she changes *B*'s legal position by creating another power, this time of *B*'s, either to waive or accept the offer. Indeed not all legal powers are advantageous: *A*'s negligent conduct, resulting in *B*'s injury, changes the legal relationship between *A* and *B*, for now *B* has the right to sue *A*

[9] The arrangement of the relationships is borrowed from Matthew Kramer's excellently clear presentation: Matthew H Kramer, 'Rights Without Trimmings' in Matthew H Kramer, Nigel E Simmonds, & Hillel Steiner, *A Debate Over Rights* (OUP 1998, hereafter *DOR*) 8. See also Andrew Halpin, *Rights and Law: Analysis and Theory* (Hart Publishing 1997); cf Andrew Halpin, 'No-Right and its Correlative' 65 (2020) *American Journal of Jurisprudence* 147.

[10] For a useful though more complex example, see Hohfeld's discussion of *Quinn v Leathem* (1901) AC 495, in his 'Fundamental Legal Conceptions as Applied in Judicial Reasoning' 23 (1913) *Yale Law Journal* 36–37. See also Edmundson (n 2) 71.

in damages. Finally, a legal immunity (from having one's legal position changed) correlates with a disability to effect such a change. Hence to possess an immunity is the opposite of being liable to some change, and to possess a legal disability is the opposite of possessing a power to make some change.

A feature of rights (in the general sense) is that they always hold between two individuals, one of whom possesses the right (or power, permission, immunity) whilst the other holds the corresponding duty (or liability, no-right, disability); and it is a further feature of such rights that they pertain to a specific act-description. Logically, then, rights take the following form: $A$ has a right that $B$ shall refrain from interfering in (or shall assist) some endeavour $\varphi$ if and only if $B$ has a corresponding duty to $\varphi$ (or not to $\varphi$) in respect of $A$ (and thus also for the other kinds of Hohfeldian right). Does this mean, as many interpreters of Hohfeld have alleged, that Hohfeld's analysis cannot successfully account for real rights, but only rights *in personam*, except by the clumsy expedient of positing a near-infinite scheme of particular rights held by $A$ against $B$, $C$, $D$ ... ? No: there is nothing preventing a reference to a *class* of persons, $A$ having a right against $\{B\}$, members of whom are determinable by their possession of certain definable qualities. In terms of the act-description $\varphi$, it should be said that the relevant act might, as Finnis observes, be a 'legal act' (e.g. of buying, selling, leasing, marrying...), as will typically be the case in relation to exercise of powers and immunities; whereas in the case of rights and liberties, the act will typically be a 'natural act' (such as walking, fishing, speaking, taking...), though itself requiring legal definition.[11]

The clarity that Hohfeld's terminology brings to discussions of rights cannot be underestimated. However, very few legal rights indeed are instances of these simple, basic forms. Actual legal rights tend to be a portmanteau of such elements, permissions for example being protected by what Hart calls a 'perimeter of protection' afforded by other rights, powers, and immunities, which are nonetheless logically distinct from them. But the presence of such rights ought not to mislead us into thinking that permissions are themselves protected by duties on the part of others: outside of contractual or statutory rights, there is no duty on the part of others to assist me in the things I am merely permitted to do; and there is likewise no duty for others to refrain from acting in such a way that interferes with or frustrates my pursuit of a certain endeavours, except insofar as I possess rights against assault, false imprisonment, theft, etc—rights the purpose of which is not to facilitate my pursuit of the permitted activities, but which protect other aspects of my person, such as my bodily integrity. The purpose of the Hohfeldian disintegration of 'right' into these four components is not intended to exclude other possible ways of regimenting our talk of rights: it remains possible, for example, to talk of $A$'s right *to* some particular thing, whether this thing be a sum of money

[11] See John Finnis, *Natural Law and Natural Rights* (2nd edn, OUP 2011, hereafter *NLNR*) 200.

under contract or a piece of land or to bodily integrity, the need for disintegrating the 'right' into its more basic components becoming necessary only at the coalface of adjudication or in drafting legislation, when the logical consequences of possession of the 'right' need to be specified with precision.

Among these consequences, the correlativity between 'right' and 'duty' requires further analysis. We can ask whether rights of all kinds (legal, moral, political) are logically associated with duties, or whether the correlativity between rights and duties only holds within some narrower domain, such as law?[12] For example, the moral duty to give alms may seem to correlate with the moral right of those in need to receive alms. This may seem to furnish an example of the principle discussed above, that rights can be generalized by referring to a *class* of person, members of which can be identified by virtue of their possession of qualifying characteristics. But what, in the case of those in need, would those characteristics be? Can they be defined with any precision? Furthermore, the moral duty to give alms does not seem to correlate with the right of any specific person to receive alms (let alone a right to receive alms *from A*). Casting aside further worries about the proportion of relief to be given to different categories of the needy, we might observe that correlativity breaks down in the case of a monetary donation that is made to a particular charity, which goes into a collective fund but as a single donation might reach only a fraction of the lowest denomination of currency when divided per person. These questions must be confronted; but they will be confronted in the context of discussions of legal rights, human rights, and moral rights later in this chapter.

On a superficial glance, all of the Hohfeldian elements seem to possess the same logical character, defined as they are in terms of correlations and opposites. But in fact there is some variation amongst them: *permissions*, for example, are unilateral. They either give the holder permission *to do* something, in which case they are said to be 'positive', or *not to do* something, in which case they are 'negative'. The conjunction of two permissions (one positive and one negative) is called a *bilateral* permission. But legal *powers* are inherently bilateral: to exercise a power is to change one's legal relationship to some other person; not to exercise it is to leave one's position unchanged.[13] This gives rise to a difficult question, whether *rights* (in the strict sense) are of unilateral or bilateral character. Should rights, in other words, be understood as enforceable but not waivable, and to become waivable only when conjoined to a Hohfeldian power, or should they be thought of as possessing their own bilateral nature, by which they can be enforced or left unenforced? This apparently technical question is in fact fundamental to the nature of legal rights. For, more generally, we can ask, what is the principle that underlies

[12] Some writers for example believe that the correlativity applies only to private law rights; others that it does not extend to moral rights: for a classic statement see Joel Feinberg, 'The Nature and Value of Rights' 4 (1970) *Journal of Value Inquiry* 245.

[13] See Nigel E Simmonds, 'Rights at the Cutting Edge' in Kramer, Simmonds, & Steiner, *DOR* (n 9) 156.

the various Hohfeldian elements, that makes them instances of *right*? For despite Hohfeld's insistence that powers, permissions, and immunities are only rights *secundum quid*, to be distinguished from 'right' in the strict sense (the reference to those secondary meanings as 'rights' being exactly the sort of imprecise and misleading talk Hohfeld's analysis is intended to discourage), they remain jural relations of a kind united to 'rights' in the strict sense in terms of the character of protection they afford. Hence we are confronted with the first and second controversies mentioned at the outset. Are the various Hohfeldian components treatable as 'rights' because they each, severally or in combination, bestow (or are apt to bestow) a benefit upon the right-holder? Or do they confer their protection upon only one interest of the right-holder, among possible others: that of choice? The first of these options is known generally as the 'interest theory' of rights; the second is the 'will theory'. A discussion of these opposing views of rights will be the subject of the next section.

## VI.2. INTEREST, WILL, AND RIGHT

Hohfeld himself considered that the term 'right' should be restricted to the first of his disintegrated elements, 'right' (or in his preferred terminology, 'claim-right'), as opposed to powers, permissions, and immunities.[14] But in fact it is important to ask how all of these elements protect the well-being or flourishing of those who hold such entitlements: what is their underlying and uniting purpose? Do they protect a sphere of self-determination, constituting a domain in which a person is enabled to act without being subject to the will of others, as the notions of 'right' and 'permissibility' and 'immunity' seem to suggest, and to exercise choices with respect to other citizens, as that of 'power' seems to indicate? Or, are 'rights' in all of their basic significations concerned with the interests of the holder more generally, touching upon almost every aspect of human life and growth? Such might be the case in relation to 'rights' under the criminal law, against assault, theft of property, fraudulent dealing and so on, which do not seem to be concerned with protection of choice on the part of the holders of those 'rights'. Searching for a metaphor, we might regard the 'will theory' of rights as a boundary wall, of significance only

[14] To this litany Margaret Gilbert adds the concept of a 'demand-right': see Margaret Gilbert, *Rights and Demands: A Foundational Enquiry* (OUP 2018) 56–78. The focus of the theory is on the standing of the right-holder to demand an action be performed by some other. While this explains the nature of rights, it is unclear how this concept improves on that of claim-rights in Hohfeld's terminology. Furthermore, the issue of standing attaches to all four forms of entitlement examined by Hohfeld, making it a far more subtle account than one focused on demands. The demand theory is somewhat stronger than legal rights actually tend to be: in most cases a right-holder is entitled at most to performance *or* damages, i.e. *restitutio in integrum*: to be restored to the position s/he was in *prior to* the contract (for example), not *after* the performance. On claim-rights specifically, see Alec Walen, *The Mechanics of Claims and Permissible Killing in War* (OUP 2019) esp 83–96.

when one's own will comes into conflict with that of others, whereas the 'interest theory' is a lush meadow within, protected, at least in part, by measures over which one has no effective control.

Neither the will theory nor the interest theory consistently reflects ordinary usage, even amongst legal professionals and those tasked with administering the law. They should be considered as inviting us to regiment our discourse on rights in differing ways. Such a regimentation is needed because it is necessary to understand what rights are, and how and when they come into existence. But it is probably safe to say that modern discourse—especially human rights discourse—has tended to favour the interest theory over the will theory.[15] For it seems obvious that human rights protect human interests: not only self-determination or self-constitution, but many other interests besides, such as the interest human beings have in not being politically oppressed, the interest in receiving appropriate medicine and health care, and the interest in not being tortured, to list only a few examples. The interest theory likewise appears to steer closer to ordinary usage in drawing a distinction between rights that are waivable by the holder (such as rights under contract and in private law generally), and unwaivable rights (such as those protected by the criminal law), whereas the will theory (it is said) regards as rights only those legal instruments that are coupled with a power of waiver on the part of the holder. Thus (it seems) the will theory must deny that children, those with dementia or other serious mental problems, animals, cultures, and so on, possess rights, though they may possess other forms of moral and legal protection. But the suspicion is (in the present rights-based culture) that such other forms of protection lack the power, certainty, or dignity of rights.[16]

How should we understand these criticisms? Take rights under the criminal law against assault, theft, fraudulent dealing, and so forth, which (I said) do not appear to be concerned to protect the choice of the holder, but other (perhaps more pressing) interests, such as being free from pain and injury. But in fact such provisions do have a relationship to the will of the holder, for one's range of choices depends upon one's bodily health and wellbeing, is frustrated by fraud, theft, coercion, and can often be overborne by inequality of bargaining power. Certain 'unwaivable rights', such as employment rights, protect the employee against threats or financial

[15] See for instance Jonathan Crowe, *Natural Law and the Nature of Law* (CUP 2019, hereafter *NLNL*) 99; see Joel Feinberg, *Rights, Justice and the Bounds of Liberty* (Princeton University Press 1980) 159–82; John Eekelaar, 'The Emergence of Children's Rights' 6 (1986) *Oxford Journal of Legal Studies* 161; also Mark McBride, 'Preserving the Interest Theory of Rights' 26 (2020) *Legal Theory* 3 (on the problem of the intended beneficiary); Visa Kurki, 'The Interest Theory of Rights: Still Standing' 27 (2021) *Legal Theory* 352. Cf Rowan Cruft, 'Rights Beyond Will and Interest Theory' 23 (2004) *Law & Philosophy* 347; Mark McBride, 'The Tracking Theory of Rights' in Mark McBride (ed) *New Essays on the Nature of Rights* (Hart Publishing 2022) 149.

[16] See Saskia Stucki, 'Towards a Theory of Animal Rights' 40 (2020) *Oxford Journal of Legal Studies* 533; Patrick Lee, 'The Basis for Being a Subject of Rights' in John Keown & Robert P George (eds) *Reason, Morality and Law: The Philosophy of John Finnis* (OUP 2013) 238; Gopal Sreenivasan, 'A Hybrid Theory of Claim Rights' 25 (2005) *Oxford Journal of Legal Studies* 257.

inducements to bargain away their protections, and in this sense serve the will of the employee against subjection by the will of the employer. It might be tempting to suggest that what we have here is a Hohfeldian 'right', unadorned by a Hohfeldian 'power', and that the distinction between waivable and unwaivable rights corresponds to the presence of absence of such a power.[17] But this view should be rejected. For the Hohfeldian 'right' is itself a specialized form of power: the power to waive or seek enforcement of the corresponding duty. Like all powers, Hohfeldian 'rights' entail liabilities (a vulnerability to change in the duty-bearer's legal position), but as a specialized form of power, entail a special form of liability: duties.[18]

When legal philosophers talk about powers of waiver, they do not very often distinguish between the exercise of such a power (a decision to waive the right) and simple non-enforcement, which might stem from a multitude of motives, mistakes as to the extent of one's rights or simple ignorance that one possesses such-and-such a right at all. When legal professionals talk about waivers, they typically have in mind a formal decision to set aside one's right, very often by signing a document of waiver or some other formal instrument, such as a disclaimer or other kind of prospective waiver. Sometimes also, one can be said to have waived one's right when one has acted in a way contrary to the substance of a right, as with an absentee landowner who makes no effort to interrupt the adverse possession of a person or persons occupying his land.[19] These technical senses of waiver derive from possession of the right itself, and do not arise out of a separate power that is distinct from the right in question. (And let us interject here: the overwhelming majority of one's 'rights' are sophisticated complexes of various Hohfeldian elements, including certain ranges of immunities from having one's legal rights disrupted or nullified, rights to seek compensation or damages, permissibilities to act in ways consistent with the exercise or non-exercise of the right, and so on.) Now in the case of rights under criminal law, which are often considered to be a paradigm of unwaivable rights, such formal exercises of waiver are indeed not present. They can be considered 'rights', as the preceding paragraph claimed, on the basis of their protection of aspects of the individual's will which would otherwise suffer some impediment or impairment. But how does this relate to the idea of Hohfeldian 'rights' as specialized powers of waiver? Typically, when someone is made the victim of a crime, they contact the police not because (in the victim's consciousness) their rights have been infringed, but because they have suffered a wrong. But this is nevertheless a first step in securing one's rights: not usually to compensation (which is often a matter

[17] See Kramer in Kramer, Simmonds, & Steiner, *DOR* (n 9) 68; see also Matthew Kramer & Hillel Steiner, 'Theories of Rights: Is There a Third Way?' 27 (2007) *Oxford Journal of Legal Studies* 281.

[18] This suggestion was originally advanced by HLA Hart, 'Bentham on Legal Rights' in AWB Simpson (ed) *Oxford Essays in Jurisprudence 2nd Series* (OUP 1973) 196; see also Simmonds in Kramer, Simmonds, & Steiner, *DOR* (n 9) 221–23, though here the right is said to imply both a liability *and* a duty.

[19] See Land Registration Act 2002 Sched 6, paras 1–5.

of insurance or private law remedy), but to see that the offender is caught and punished appropriately. Such rights may be said to offer a more limited protection of the will of the victim, being coupled as they are with a *disability* against altering the legal relationship between perpetrator and victim,[20] though in many cases there will be a parallel right to pursue damages, return of property etc in the civil courts. Persons in the United Kingdom can refuse to testify (e.g. against one's spouse) and/or become a hostile witness, and in this way provide a limited waiver of their right, but the police and prosecuting authorities do not require the consent of the victim to press charges. Within criminal law, there is a general duty upon the state to prosecute and punish offenders, so far as is consistent with other factors such as time, quality of evidence, proportionality, and cost, which correlates with a general political right on the part of all citizens, and not just the victim, that criminals be punished, that society be made safe, and that justice be done.[21] This political right is non-Hohfeldian in character since it is not a right either to assistance or against interference, but a right *that* a certain situation be brought about. It is political rather than legal because it is shaped by necessities, public policy, pragmatism, and party politics: for example the police in times of overstretch or underfunding may as a matter of public policy be ordered to prioritize investigation of certain crimes and not to pursue others; in such a case the victim lacks in real terms a legal right to have their crime investigated. Its enforcement is likewise broadly political in character, although possesses legal dimensions, such as appeals, parole board decisions, and judicial review.[22]

This line of thinking can be broadened further still. The will theory is said to be unable to account for children's rights, and the rights of the mentally infirm. But there is no very good reason why rights, in the sense of a specialized power, should not be invested in such groups of persons who, through some impediment, are incapable of exercising them. Could we say, for example, that such persons cannot own or possess property (actually a right of non-interference by others), in virtue of a lack of capacity? In many cases, the rights of persons lacking legal capacity are rightly not to be thought of as being adorned with an additional power, vested in the parent/guardian of the infirm person, to exercise the rights on that person's behalf. Instead, *the infirm person's right* is itself temporarily vested in their responsible guardian, to be exercised *as if* the infirm were acting in that situation. Such relationships amount to a trust or other fiduciary relationship, the duty not to defraud or annihilate the infirm person's estate but to administer it on behalf of that person: a duty correlating with that person's (claim-) right not to be so defrauded, a right which is again enforceable not by the person themselves but by

[20] See e.g. *Smart v HMA* (1975) JC 30.

[21] The victim may not, after all, wish to pursue the case, e.g. in a rape trial where the victim may be disinclined to expose herself to cross-examination.

[22] See e.g. *The Queen on the application of DSD and NBV & Ors v The Parole Board of England and Wales & Ors and John Radford* [2018] EWHC 694 (Admin).

some appropriate power-holder such as the state, ombudsman, or social services.[23] But is this not a concern for the person's welfare, rather than their will?[24] On first sight this seems like a valid objection: most obviously so in relation to babies or the unborn. But of course a legally competent person typically exercises their rights *in their best interests*; thus there is no difficulty in saying that a trustee exercises *the infirm's rights* in the infirm's best interests, whatever they may be. Such cases are no more problematic than godparents affirming the Baptismal promises on behalf of the child at the font. Perhaps both are problematic? It does not seem so, since ordinary thought and action, including every action that a parent takes to ensure that the child grows up to be an autonomous person (and not, for example, a slave or puppet of its parents), offers countless examples of what it means to act for the sake of another who is unable to exercise their will to the fullest extent. The separate but combinable nature of the Hohfeldian elements should alert us to the fact that a person's otherwise waivable right can be rendered unwaivable due to its association with other elements: the prisoner's lack of liberty to assert or waive her right to vote, the child's disability from exercising entitlements due to non-age, and so on. To be clear: we are speaking of a right (i.e. a special kind of power) coupled with a disability which (a) interrupts the exercise of that power, but (b) does not cancel or throw into inexistence that power. The association of right with disability does not alter the right's character as a special kind of power, however its normal range of operation is limited.

In light of the above, Visa Kurki generalizes the argument against the will theory. He argues that a 'hard' will theorist can scarcely account for the relationship between rights and harms, whereas the 'soft' will theorist alienates the defining concepts of the will theory such that it collapses into the interest theory.[25] Since the argument above would identify as a 'soft' approach, I will concentrate on Kurki's account of that theory. His argument is that while the will theory can account for the rights of the infirm and incapable (by vesting the rights in guardians who exercise those rights on their behalf), it would seem that such rights cannot exist in a person in a permanent state of infirmity, for if the will theory connects rights with exercises of will, such persons could never have possessed rights in the first place.[26] Moreover, uses of such rights could not be uses in the name of the infirm's will, for that, at least in law, does not exist. If the will theory nevertheless asserted that such persons possess rights, held by guardians, it would have collapsed into the interest theory, for the guardians could only be said to exercising the rights in the *interests* of the infirm. This seems to me an error. For the key fact is that the rights are

[23] See Catechism of the Catholic Church § 2266.

[24] See Kramer, Simmonds, & Steiner, *DOR* (n 9) 226.

[25] Visa Kurki, 'Rights, Harming and Wronging: A Restatement of the Interest Theory' 38 (2018) *Oxford Journal of Legal Studies* 446–50.

[26] Ibid 449. Cf Mark Osiel, *The Right to do Wrong: Morality and the Limits of Law* (Harvard University Press 2019) 110.

exercised by an act of *will* on the part of the guardians, and such exercises are intended (ideally) to correspond to the mature, well-functioning, and balanced mind that the infirm would have, were it not for their infirmity. The will of the person lying in the hospital bed in a coma may never be known, but the will of the person of practical reason and mature experience can be known, particularly in relation to questions of consent to medical procedures designed to restore that person to full consciousness and flourishing, or perhaps only to be kept alive or free of pain. The will theory does not collapse into the interest theory.

The above discussion's division between legal and political rights and—as I shall shortly add—natural rights is reflected in the discussion that follows. There is no reason to expect the latter two categories of right to exhibit the same Hohfeldian structure as legal rights. But perhaps out of a desire for symmetry, holders of the interest theory of rights have tended to argue that the entire range of rights, legal or otherwise, admit of Hohfeldian analysis, or possess a Hohfeldian structure. In this sense, legal rights would represent the central or focal case of rights, against which other rights are measured. Yet the interest theory itself is vulnerable to the difficulty of specifying the party or parties who possess *locus standi* since many persons may possess an interest in a particular legal state of affairs (say, a contract) without having standing to enforce the corresponding duty: for example, it may be in *A*'s interest that *B* inherit property from *C*, since *B* intends to let *A* stay on the property without charge or rent. Different versions of the interest theory propose more and fewer plausible methods of identifying the right-holder, yet the overwhelming bulk of adjudication is taken up, not with the identification and balancing of interests, but with the application of well-defined legal concepts, such as causation, consideration, foreseeability, possession, and so on.[27]

This section's arguments are extremely schematic. But they, and the previous section, have the limited purpose of clarifying some preliminary ideas that it is essential to hold in mind in the discussion that follows. That discussion will explore the nature and importance of, respectively, natural, legal, and human rights, and their relationship to the broader themes of this book.

## VI.3. NATURAL RIGHTS

Are there, as Hart once asked, any natural rights?[28] It will be helpful to begin the enquiry with Aquinas, who sets out the general structure of concepts in which rights take their place. In particular, it is necessary to understand how rights fit into the moral universe of law and justice. According to Aquinas, justice is special among the virtues in that its object is not the performance of an action in a

[27] See Kramer, Simmonds, & Steiner, *DOR* (n 9) 163.

[28] HLA Hart, 'Are There Any Natural Rights?' 64 (1955) *The Philosophical Review* 175.

particular way, but a kind of equality consisting in 'the just thing', which is identical to 'the right'.[29] He goes on to explain that the right is justice's object. Though Aquinas does not say so, his discussion clearly implies that rights are instruments of justice: significant stages in practical reason by which one discovers or articulates what is *due* or *owed* to another person. Right is further linked to law, not only as a possible synonym, but as the rational underpinnings of the law, or—as Aquinas puts it—law is a kind of system of right [*ratio iuris*].[30] Such a system is intrinsically an interpersonal one: it relates not merely to the organization and harmony between one's own rights, but the interplay of one's rights with those of many others. Hence Aquinas says that 'the right' and 'the just' are a work that is sufficiently adjusted to another according to a particular mode of equality.[31] Is it the case, as Hart says, that equality between persons is the only natural right, all other rights being created by voluntary human action?[32] The previous two chapters IV and V offer a number of reasons for the recognition of many other natural rights: rights that are 'natural' in virtue of being the product of reasoned reflection on the human condition, the requirements of which go beyond formal justice to matters such as peace, prosperity, suppression of crime, just punishment of the guilty, and so forth. These are substantive matters of justice, the object of which is 'right'. The extent to which such rights represent Hohfeldian 'rights' against interference or for assistance (as some at least clearly are) need not be determined here. The important issue is that such rights are woven into the moral fabric of human existence and do not depend for their recognition on widespread acceptance; acceptance (which may be for different reasons) that is all too often absent from human societies.[33] New arguments need not be advanced for the existence of such rights: they are the implications of the previous discussions of natural law, morality, justice, and the common good.

Nevertheless, the issue of natural rights raises some new questions. For example, do all moral duties correspond to natural rights? As noted in Section VI.2, neither the will theory or the interest theory of rights, nor Hohfeld's analysis of rights, entail that all duties correlate to rights (though all rights correspond to duties). In the case of the will theory, rights add to duties a measure of control over the duty: the power to release the other from the duty or to enforce it. And this measure of control is not present in moral codes such as the Decalogue which, as Hart observes, is not readily convertible into a set of human rights.[34] Hart rightly says that it would be a surprising interpretation of the Commandments that regarded them as conferring rights, even if the breach of (some of) them would constitute human

[29] Aquinas, *ST* (n 3) II-II.57.1c; Suarez, *DL* (n 5) II.xvii.2.
[30] Aquinas, *ST* (n 3) II-II.57.1 ad 2.
[31] Ibid II-II.57.2c; see also arg 2: 'the just and the right are the same' (confirmed in corpus).
[32] Hart (n 28) 175–76.
[33] Cf Julio Montero, 'Do Human Rights Derive from Natural Rights? The State of Nature, Political Authority and the Natural Right to Independence' 47 (2016) *Philosophical Forum* 151.
[34] Ibid, 182; but see Aquinas, *ST* (n 3) II-II.122.6 ad 1 & 2, I-II.99.2c.

wrongs. But Hart commits an error here, for whilst the Decalogue does not *confer* rights on human beings, it readily *implies* the existence of such rights: rights that are articulated through reason's reflection upon those forms of wrong as violations of forms of justice.[35] The failure of Hart's example does not, however, alter the fact that not all moral duties correlate with rights. Feinberg, for example, discusses the difference between moral pressure and the sort of conclusive force possessed by rights: as he observes, in the absence of a natural right to vote in elections, women might still have demanded a legal right based on moral arguments; but they could not have laid claim to it as rightfully theirs.[36] And Aquinas, in thrall to traditional assumptions about family life, states that there are strictly speaking no rights of son against father, or slave against master, since the former in each case is a kind of possession of the latter, except that which is due to them as human beings.[37]

We might then wonder what are the existence conditions for natural rights, if the presence of a duty is not a guarantee of right. The answer lies in Aquinas's doctrine that rights are the object(s) of justice. His subtle remarks on this relationship are worth quoting:

> There are two ways in which something can be adjusted to another human being. The first way is by the very nature of the thing in question, as when a person gives so much in expectation of receiving the same amount in return: and this is called *natural right*. The second way is when something is adjusted to another either by [private] agreement or by common agreement, such that a person regards himself as compensated by such-and-such an amount ... and this is known as *positive right*.[38]

Aquinas's example of a natural right is but one such example, but the basic pattern underlying the example is nevertheless true of all natural rights: for natural rights secure what is owed or due to a person (and thus adjusts their position) as a matter of justice rather than by agreement. In terms of the former, Grotius follows Suarez in referring to natural rights as a kind of capacity, though he expresses the relation in rather vague terms as the possession of a 'moral quality' of or 'attachment to' the person. He also distinguishes between a moral capacity [*facultas*] to receive some benefit, and a mere deservingness [*aptitudo*], the first relating to what is, in some sense, 'one's own', the latter to what is a reasonable claim upon the wealth of others (e.g. through almsgiving).[39] The framing of natural rights in terms of what is owed or due is generally preferable to the somewhat unsatisfactory and misleading

35 See Catechism of the Catholic Church § 2070.
36 Joel Feinberg, 'In Defence of Moral Rights' 12 (1992) *Oxford Journal of Legal Studies* 153.
37 Aquinas, *ST* (n 3) II-II.57.4 ad 1 & 2, II-II.104.5c.
38 Ibid, II-II.57.4c.
39 Grotius, *De Iure Belli ac Pacis* I.1.iv-v. See also Aquinas's not-quite-similar distinction between absolute and qualified justice: Aquinas, *ST* (n 3) I-II.114.1c.

notion of an 'equality', a concept more difficult to grasp in cases such as the natural right to peace and security where transactional mechanisms are not (or at least not directly) in play. It is the idea of *facultas* that seems to inform Nozick's explanation of rights in terms of that which is required if a human being is to live a long and uninterrupted life: that is to say, rights prevent such interruptions and upheavals.[40]

But does reference to natural rights add anything to moral discussions of justice and the common good? In fact neither of these phenomena can be adequately protected without a sense of rights. This is not, as has often been supposed, due to the special conclusive force of rights (for moral demands, as Aquinas's discussion above makes clear, are very capable of conclusive force), but rather what might be regarded as their firmness of edge: for whereas (as Aquinas tells us) moral precepts encounter more defects and exceptions as they become more specified,[41] rights possess a hard-edged firmness such that their content remains stable at whatever level of specificity they are employed. A community without rights (whether recognized as such in specialized terminology or not) thereby also lacks a clear understanding of wrongs: not indeed in central cases of wrong, but at the margins where assessment of wrongs is less clear. Ought a person to be compensated where they have undergone only marginal loss, the other party's financial situation being precarious? Can they, or ought they to, cancel the debt? These questions are difficult to resolve and even to state except in the language of rights. For if we fall back on general moral considerations (i.e. the virtues) we will be inclined to be misled by the internal perspective of disposition and attitude and of locating 'the mean', even while recognizing that justice's *act* differs markedly from the other virtues.[42] But rights make clear, for example, that *A*'s waiving of *B*'s debt, though an act of goodness, perpetuates an injustice: *A* does not get what *B* owes him. More generally, the erasure of rights from legal discourse would all but eliminate the category of *damnum absque iniuria*, the means whereby to tell the difference between actual instances of illegal harm from attributes of another person, or their actions, that are merely annoying or offensive to the complainant. Adjudication of such claims would be impossible without calling attention to general features of the act complained of, which are to be always or in most cases counted as illegal harms (or, conversely, always or mostly harmless): a process which would, over time, result in

[40] See Robert Nozick, *Anarchy, State and Utopia* (Basic Books 1974) 50: the 'ability to form a picture of one's whole life' with the 'overall conception of the life one wishes to lead'. But Nozick's theory goes too far in presenting an overly robust theory of self-ownership, which would permit abortion, euthanasia, and suicide, for example. For cautious support for Nozick see Jonathan Crowe, 'Explaining Natural Rights: Ontological Freedom and the Foundations of Political Discourse' 70 (2019) *New York University Journal of Law & Liberty* 70.

[41] Aquinas, *ST* (n 3) I-II.94.4c.

[42] Note Aristotle's warning: 'Now "justice" and "injustice" seem to be ambiguous, but because their different meanings approach near to one another the ambiguity escapes notice and is not obvious as it is, comparatively, when the meanings are far apart.' *Nicomachean Ethics* V.1.1129a; also see the warning that justice is not a mean in the same manner of other virtues: ibid, V.5.1133b-1134a.

the development of a detailed body of doctrine that would amount implicitly to an organized system of *rights*.[43]

The discussion in this section has so far purposely avoided references to 'human rights', for such rights are distinct from natural rights in the proper sense. However, Finnis argues that the concepts of 'natural right' and 'human right' should be used interchangeably.[44] But this is a dangerous doctrine, for human rights are *positive law* instruments, the existence of which is often controversial due to the need for *consent* between nations. Thus, the Church warns that it must be the guardian of the forgotten and unacknowledged rights of the poor and needy, left behind by the doctrines of established human rights.[45] Furthermore, such natural rights cannot correctly be understood as a product of human *will*, but rather of human *being*. They cannot be waived or alienated, for to do so would be an injury to human dignity and to the human person (indeed all persons).[46] Such natural rights are in part based on the biological realities of human beings, basic needs such as access to clean water and nourishment, the physical freedom of the body, and freedom from assault and battery; but also upon what might be called moral aspects of the human being, such as the development of capacities, freedom from coercion, and involvement in sociable relations with others (as opposed to suppression or expulsion from the community). The severe restriction of the body's freedom to move, and isolation from the society of others (e.g. through imprisonment or solitary confinement) are punishments precisely because they run contrary to ordinary human capacities and needs. But even such punishments can be said to respect the moral aspects of human beings, for punishment respects human agency by holding to account a person's own voluntary deeds, and by not attributing responsibility to innocent parties who were not the authors of those deeds.

Natural rights therefore form a broader category than human rights, including as they do the right to develop unmolested in the womb from conception, the right to a family or moral community in which to be raised, and the right to freedom in seeking and knowing the truth.[47] But it is important not to overestimate the range of natural rights. For example, Finnis argues that natural rights may be inferred from Aquinas's (partial) list of wrongs, for the latter are implicitly a list of natural rights. But this is improbable for rights do not correlate with *wrongs* but only with *duties*; to suggest otherwise is to hold that all wrongs are correlated with rights, whereas in fact many forms of wrong do not correspond to duties (and thus correlate with rights), as my previous argument suggested. If a mother suggests a trip

[43] Hence Crowe's argument that rights are either absolute or prima facie, and that the majority are the latter, is intensely problematic: *NLNL* (n 15) 100, 104.

[44] Finnis, *NLNR* (n 11) 198. See Montero (n 33) 153–56; Charles Beitz, *The Idea of Human Rights* (OUP 2009) 49–58; Alan Buchanan, *The Heart of Human Rights* (OUP 2013) 5; Martti Koskenniemi, 'Rights, History, Critique' in A Etinson (ed) *Human Rights: Moral or Political?* (OUP 2018) 41.

[45] *Gaudium et spes* § 76; Apostolic letter *Novo millenio ineunte* §§ 50–51.

[46] *Pacem in terris* § 55; Hart seems to recognize such rights too: 'Bentham on Legal Rights' (n 18) 201.

[47] *Compendium* § 155.

to the cinema (without promising), but does not act on the suggestion, one might say that the child has been *wronged* (especially if, for example, she cancels arrangements to meet with a friend) or is very upset or disappointed. But it would be very odd to say that the child had a *right* to the cinema trip, or that the mother breached a *duty*. Yet the example does force upon us another question, that is, how does one derive rights from the most basic moral precepts? Aquinas begins from the most basic of all moral precepts, that of loving one's neighbour as oneself.[48] A number of more detailed general precepts flow from this most general one: such as not killing or harming the innocent, refraining from verbal or physical contention, exercising due care and attention when involved in potentially dangerous activities, assisting one's neighbour *in extremis*, avoiding untruthfulness, compensating injuries, and more generally, exhibiting willingness to sort out disagreements peacefully, if necessary through the courts, and to abide by decisions of the court and to treat such decisions (if necessary, on appeal) as dispositive of the issue. It is not difficult to see how this schematic list of moral precepts gives rise to recognition of natural rights, all of which in some measure assist the human good of sociability. Of course the detailed provisions of, for example, tort law represent instances of *determinatio*, reason's work in filling out the general natural rights into a comprehensive and complex body of specific rights, duties, and principles, the exact nature of which may vary from one society to another. But the law recognizes many natural rights directly, without the mediation of positive determination: such as the right of parents to possess and raise their own children. This right is not given distinct recognition but is recognized implicitly in, for example, rules on eligibility for child benefit, and the graveness of circumstances in which a child is taken from its natural parents and placed into foster care.

The majority of the basic moral precepts mentioned in the preceding paragraph are, despite their surface appearance, negative in character: only the duty to assist one's neighbour is positive. (Thus, for example, compensation for injuries is the negative duty to leave no injury uncompensated for which one is responsible.) Such negative duties hold 'forever and always' [*semper et ad semper*], they are exceptionless moral precepts, and hence exceptionless natural rights. But positive duties, such as the one mentioned, hold only 'forever but not always' [*semper sed non ad semper*], leaving room for practical judgment to determine their role and significance in particular contexts of time and place.[49] Aquinas's favoured example is that of returning a weapon, something that should normally be done and not avoided lightly, but on certain occasions must not be done, as when the recipient intends to murder someone. Similarly, rescuing one's drowning neighbour is normally a moral duty, but there is no culpability in avoiding the attempt if

[48] Aquinas, *ST* (n 3) I-II.99.1 ad 2.
[49] *Sent* III.25.2.1.2 ad 3; Aquinas, *ST* (n 3) II-II.33.2c; also John Finnis, *Aquinas: Moral, Political & Legal Theory* (OUP 1998) 164.

circumstances make it likely that one would join or replace the neighbour in that predicament.[50]

There is a stark difference between these last two examples. For whilst the return of the weapon would ordinarily be a duty under the positive laws of the state, correlating to the right of the owner to receive it in due time, the assistance to one's neighbour is typically not a duty under positive law. More generally, therefore, it becomes necessary to distinguish between natural rights that are (or ought to be) enshrined in positive law, and natural rights that are not (or ought not to be) part of positive law. For not all of the ways in which one ought to love one's neighbour are suitable subjects for positive lawmaking. Natural law philosophers usually concentrate on rights of the first kind, but typically neglect or ignore rights of the second kind. This is unfortunate. One's neighbour can be said to possess a natural right, for example to be warned of an impending attack, to compassionate aid when severely sick, or to relief from starvation either by sustenance of one's own, or by reporting the case to the relevant authorities or charities. But a legal system that enforced such rights would be stifling and intolerable. Furthermore, a system that aimed to enforce as many aspects of neighbourly love as possible would leave no room for spontaneous love of neighbour or other good acts. Let us therefore say in summary that natural rights that bind 'forever and always' are part of the natural law that underpins all civilized systems of positive law.

## VI.4. LEGAL RIGHTS

Before examining human rights, it will be useful to examine the general characteristics of legal rights, for human rights are a special kind of legal right. In considering legal rights, it must be remembered that at least some legal rights are also natural rights in the sense explored above in Section VI.3. Legal systems generally do not name or uphold these rights directly, but establish and enforce them through numerous provisions (such as provisions of criminal law and constitutional law) which, taken together, constitute the relevant rights. The doctrines of criminal law, for example, along with provisions for punishment and those of civil liability, together uphold the natural rights of peace and security, without directly referring to those rights. Rules of contract law and commercial law, together with criminal liability for fraud, support the natural right of morality in dealings in the marketplace, without ever announcing that right directly. Other legal rights, insofar as they are just, are determinations of more general principles that can be specified in different ways, and in that sense give force to natural rights: such as rights over property. Particular systems of property law vary from place to place,[51] but all

[50] See Aquinas, *ST* (n 3) II-II.140.1 ad 2 (what is due in times of danger is not reducible to a general precept).

[51] Grotius's argument is roughly the one in the text, but see also Crowe, *NLNL* (n 15) 113.

aim (insofar as they are just) to determine the general conditions of ownership and honesty and fairness in dealings. Another reminder is necessary: a community that does not possess, at least implicitly, the concept of rights will leave all important matters hopelessly uncertain: in virtue of this, legal rights are one component in the necessary conditions for the rule of law (see more generally Section X.3). It is sometimes said, for example, that the traditional common law was conceived as a system of remedies, or heads of pleading, rather than of rights. But the notion of right is implicit in such a system, for the courts must decide who, in a particular case, is *entitled to* the relevant remedy, or to a judgment in their favour in virtue of having selected the correct head of pleading. The presence of legal rights, then, ensures that citizens are subject to the law, and not to the will of others.

To these reminders of the character of legal rights, another consideration must be added. This is the claim that a system of legal rights reflects, or ought to reflect, neutrality between opposing conceptions of the good life, allowing each person to decide such matters for themselves, and act upon them to the extent permitted by the law: namely without unduly impeding others' rights to pursue their conception of the good in their own way.[52] But even if it could be fulfilled in practice, neutrality is neither empirically nor morally viable. When the state endows artistic works out of public money, it does so because of the value of art, not on the basis of neutrality, but as a beautiful object, as something enriching and uplifting, that it is *good to have*; when the state prohibits public nudity, outrageous conduct, and obscene language and images, it does so not out of a desire for 'neutrality' but on the basis that such acts are indecent.[53] Patterns of legal rights uphold not only one's freedom (Hohfeldian permissibilities, adjoined by Hohfeldian rights and immunities and powers) but also a basic scheme of morality in various aspects of social life and dealings.

But are legal rights expressions of moral conceptions of the good life in this way? According to Raz, the law 'is not a system of practical reasoning, but of operative action-guiding rules. An explanation of rights in terms of their role in practical reasoning is, therefore, incapable of explaining legal rights ... That the law is a system of practical reasoning means no more than that belief in the normative force of some of the legal rules commits one to belief in the normative force of some of the others'.[54] Two responses seem necessary to this. First, practical reason is both 'operative' (i.e. practical) and 'action-guiding' (i.e. moral); and, if we consider practical reasoning as systematic, operative, and action-guiding, it will certainly require at least a proportion of its outcomes to be expressed in the form of 'rules'. But, secondly, the characterisation of legal reasoning as commitment to

[52] See e.g. Nigel E Simmonds, 'Between Positivism and Idealism' 50 (1991) *Cambridge Law Journal* 309.

[53] See George Sher, 'Rights, Neutrality and the Oppressive Power of the State' 14 (1995) *Law and Philosophy* 192.

[54] Joseph Raz, 'Legal Rights' 4 (1984) *Oxford Journal of Legal Studies* 6.

certain rules on the basis of others, does not seem reflective of the actual character of legal reasoning in adjudication (which is presumably the context addressed by Raz's statement). For again, adjudication more usually concerns the correct interpretation and application of doctrine, the implication for the facts of the case of, for example, the reasonable person's perspective, foreseeability, the *bona fide* purchaser, duty of care, negligence, and so forth, and care in stating and characterizing the facts of both the instant case and the precedent cases. Such dimensions to legal thought are not rules, but they are laws. A system of legal rights implicates a whole range of moral considerations, informed (on some level) by a conception of the good life. But are such rights equally held by all, and therefore *neutral* as between richer, more varied conceptions of the good life? They are not: equality is not the same as neutrality. The conception(s) of the good life that are supported by equal legal rights may be many, but do not include, for example, the conception of the good favoured by the habitual criminal or the paedophile. The hardened criminal and the paedophile both, of course, have equal rights with the rest of society to be, for example, free from assault, fraud, and to enter into legal contracts; but beyond these basic rights the law does not assist, and seeks to prevent, the kind of life desired by them. Furthermore, the idea of equal legal rights is a false abstraction. Certainly, *some* rights are possessed by all. But we do not, for example, hold equal rights to property or to enforce or waive contractual duties. We do not all qualify for the right to the same state benefits; we do not all have the same right to tuition at university; we do not possess the rights that come with certain offices; and children do not possess the same range of rights as adults. The notion of 'equality' is at best a pliable idea.

It might seem as if an assumption is being made in the foregoing discussion. Does not the conclusive character of rights entail that rights cannot conflict? Are we committed to the conclusion that, whilst permissibilities may conflict (my permissibility to run a business conflicts with your permissibility to run a similar business so that we compete for customers), rights cannot and do not conflict within the same legal system? Must all potential or actual clashes between rights be adjudicated so that *A*'s right is understood and defined in relation to *Y*'s right, one against another, until the conflict is resolved? In fact, the conclusivity of rights does not entail that rights cannot conflict. For example, the rights of creditors of a bankrupt may be said to conflict with one another when there is insufficient capital to cover their losses; the operation of the *pari passu* principle does not *define* one creditor's right in terms of another's, but decreases the value of the remedy *pro rata* with the others. At the same time, conclusivity itself is not an absolute property of rights. We might think, for example, that rights settle an issue either permanently or quasi-permanently, but a few examples illustrate the converse: the level of entitlement (i.e. threshold) and value of state benefits may fluctuate; one's property may be subject to a compulsory purchase order; the level of income tax raised by the government may increase or decrease; changes may be made to the extent of legal liability, etc. Rights are in general not dead-letters but living instruments, open to an ongoing process of *determinatio*.

What does all of this mean for the general character of legal rights? Rights are conclusive in their force, but they are themselves conclusions. A great deal of 'legal reasoning' concerns, not rights, but analyses and comparisons of grounds of decision, doctrines, principles, and rules. But often the outcome of those analyses and comparisons assist in defining the scope and substance of legal rights. Rights are, in a sense, the end-points of adjudicative reasoning, since the conclusion of the judgment is the upholding of *A*'s right against *B*, or of *A*'s no-right against *B*, or alternatively *B*'s liability or disability in respect of *A*, or *B*'s immunity against or power with respect to *A*, and so on. Rights are not absolute; yet nevertheless a right that is not consistently upheld but is given legal effect only on some occasions but not others, can scarcely be classified as a right. The quasi-permanence of rights is a key feature of rights. The reasons that defeat rights tend not to be interests that conflict with the right, nor general considerations of utility (for otherwise rights would simply merge into open-ended debate about what ought to be done); they tend instead to be well-defined occasions, of the kind Aquinas has in mind when he speaks of the non-return of a weapon to one who is deranged or who will use the weapon against the innocent. Similarly, the subjection of property rights to compulsory purchase orders does not (usually) imply a quite general and ever-present threat to property interests, but rather a highly exceptional and specific case. One could perhaps insist on reading such examples as involving a competition between interests, but that is not their point or force.

The latter example is complicated by a further distinction, one that very often goes unnoticed. For the right to property typically figures in practical reasoning as both a legal right and as a political right. As a legal right, the right to property consists of certain well-defined entitlements and various implications (e.g. the right to alienate and the power to exclude trespassers). As a political right, the right to property is typically conceived in terms of an aspect of human flourishing and independence, as against others and against state interference in one's private affairs. Because the latter invites examination in terms of the interests involved, it is easy to conclude that legal reasoning represents an attempt to weigh and balance competing interests,[55] when in fact the well-defined *legal* implications of the right are very often (though not invariably) sufficient to adjudicate the issue at hand. Alternatively, legal disputes may centre upon the application of one body of law to another, as in cases where a tort of nuisance is alleged against an owner of land by, for example, causing undue noise and disturbance on the neighbouring land.[56] Such forms of reasoning, again, do not resemble a stark weighing and balancing of interests, but an attempt to explore the characteristic implications of rights already

[55] The term 'actual occupation' is political in this sense: it is primarily shaped by policy considerations.

[56] See e.g. *Sturges v Bridgman* (1879) LR 11 Ch D 852.

possessed. This perhaps explains the scholastic and medieval equation of 'right' and 'law': for it emphasizes the fact that the substance of 'rights' is that which is just *according to law*, and when viewed from the perspective of the beneficiary of the court's ruling. The *political* right to property, on the other hand, does not involve any such reasoning. It is predicated upon basic requirements of human flourishing, on the one hand, and upon fundamental attributes of known human behaviour, such as free-riding, on the other. Failure to observe the distinction between the two levels of discourse, legal and political, is fatal to the clarity that is essential in the handling of instruments of such high importance in the collective consciousness.

The preceding discussion has been somewhat lax in its discussion of rights. Political rights are, in general, non-Hohfeldian in character. Legal rights, on the other hand, demand to be expounded in Hohfeldian terms especially in the context of litigation. One may indeed talk in a loose way of 'rights to property', for example, by which is meant a series of complex Hohfeldian relations between a person, *A*, and a person or class of persons, *B*. But to speak of legal rights in exclusively Hohfeldian terms is both tiresome and unwieldy, for the sheer number and complexity of Hohfeldian entitlements that make up the humble right of ownership obscures rather than clarifies legal discourse. Legal rights do, and should, admit of division into Hohfeldian components, but this is useful only at what Simmonds calls the 'cutting edge' of law: the determination of the judgment in adjudication, or in statutory interpretation. Elsewhere, the need for economy to aid understanding permits the looser talk. We need to beware of that looser talk, however, for the tendency to think of such rights, especially political rights, as 'interests' that are held *against* 'considerations of general welfare or utility' can itself obscure the importance and nature of rights. For rights are not held *against* the common good, but form part of the common good. Rights, especially legal rights, are the expression of what is just [*iustum*]; and, since justice is an aspect of the common good, so rights are part of the common good. As part of the common good rights are subject to other aspects of the common good such as public health and public order.[57] But if, as increasingly is the case, we regard other such components of the common good as rights also, as being *due* or *owed* to every person, then there is no real, deep opposition between rights and common welfare or common good.

An extension of this argument is possible. For it is the duty of the ruling authority to secure the common good for the people: a duty grounded in what is just, and therefore in right. But if the ruling authority trespasses beyond this function, in an attempt to lay down a quite comprehensive moral system, then it exceeds its lawful authority, and hence invades basic natural rights of self-constitution and free will.[58] A people, we might say, has a right to be governed, but to be governed well.[59] Good governance is also *limited* governance. Exceeding lawful ruling power

57 See Finnis, *NLNR* (n 11) 218; Aquinas, *ST* (n 3) suppl 65.4c.
58 Aquinas, *ST* (n 3) I-II.96.2c & ad 1–2; see also I-II.90.2c.
59 See ibid, I-II.95.1c.

is one way in which such a right can be breached; but the right can also be breached by the use of organized power to enforce an unjust law: a (necessarily positive) law that is of lesser[60] or no moral effect because and insofar as it invades a natural right.[61] Aquinas goes so far as to say that corrupt positive law 'has a greater resemblance to villainy [*iniquitas*] than to law'.[62] Aquinas's caution may be said to play out in the following way: where the requirements of common good, natural right, and positive law come into conflict, it is presumptively the common good that triumphs, depending upon the importance and gravity of the natural right that has been infringed. One must, as Aquinas says, be prepared to give up one's right—to what is justly one's own—if reliance upon it would lead to general scandal and disturbance in the community.[63] In all other cases, natural right is superior to positive law: hence a ruling authority which oversteps its authority, by creating onerous obligations or unjust laws, is acting essentially *ultra vires* and in conflict with natural right: see Section XI.2.

This brief discussion of legal rights forms the necessary backdrop to an account of human rights, for human rights are instruments of positive law in terms of their *creation*; the question is how and according to what canons we can *derive* them. Even so, it is important not to lose sight of the fact that it is ultimately agreement between states that informs that second issue.

## VI.5. HUMAN RIGHTS

As previously mentioned, it is important to remember that human rights are by nature *positive* rights, and the attempt to enumerate such rights in the major human rights documents, treaties, and transnational constitutions is not the attempt to expound fundamental moral truths about human beings and their needs, but rather the attempt to have as many human rights recognized and ratified by as many nations as possible. Thus human rights are useful only to the extent that they are enshrined in positive law, and where violations of such rights are the basis of sanctions or exclusions.[64] Nevertheless, it is often claimed that human rights are a modern idiom for natural rights, such that 'the notion of universal human rights has been present in "pre-modern" and "Roman Catholic" thought, expressed in statements to the effect that all human beings are protected by the duties of justice, duties that are owed to, for example, the newborn child who might by custom be

[60] Ibid, I-II.96.4c.
[61] Ibid, I-II.92.1 ad 4, I-II.96.4c.
[62] Ibid, I-II.90.1 ad 3.
[63] Ibid, I-II.96.4c.
[64] Cf Patrick Macklem, *The Sovereignty of Human Rights* (OUP 2015) 3–28. See also Christopher McCrudden, 'Common Law of Human Rights?' 20 (2000) *Oxford Journal of Legal Studies* 499.

left to die on the mountainside . . .'[65] But there is simply no direct historical derivation from the natural rights doctrines of the twelfth century and beyond to the human rights doctrines that emerged in the twentieth century. Natural rights have their origin in a worldview in which human beings and human nature have incalculable significance and value, for human beings are the *imago dei*. By contrast, the human rights Commissioners, under Eleanor Roosevelt, and under pressure of time and circumstance, simply announced a list of protected rights, leaving the question of foundations 'for another day'.[66] The Commissioners were not engaged in philosophical dialogue, in which no subject or facet of discussion is off the table, and in which time is not a factor, but in political discussion, in which the number of topics is highly circumscribed and in which certain matters, having been discussed, are not eligible to be brought back into discussion.

It must be emphasized that these remarks pertain to the *origin* of human rights as instruments of positive law, as announced in treaties and legislation such as the UDHR or ECHR, rather than their *justification*. Yet the circumstances in which human rights gained recognition, coupled with a certain commitment to value-pluralism, led so influential a thinker as Rawls to argue that human rights are grounded in no more than a political conception of justice founded upon an 'overlapping consensus'. Thus human rights doctrines are said to rest upon no foundational insights into human nature but upon political norms that are agreed and affirmed for different reasons, human rights having no justification independent of that overlapping consensus.[67] Such a domain of discourse is fundamentally political rather than ethical: it does not undertake to consider carefully all matters germane to the subject, but cuts off discussion at a much earlier stage.[68] One might justifiably call the outcome of such a discussion an ideology of human rights (see Section II.1). An example of this overlapping consensus can be found in the circumstances surrounding the 'Smuts draft' at the San Francisco conference, which originally contained a reference to the 'sanctity' of human life, but which was replaced by the concept of human 'dignity': a concept the meaning of which was not at all agreed upon by the delegates, and indeed those same delegates carefully avoided any systematic discussion of its significance.[69] Unlike most legal norms, however, the import of human rights norms is not constrained by (a) legislative

[65] John Finnis, 'Grounding Human Rights in Natural Law' 16 (2015) *American Journal of Jurisprudence* 218.

[66] Mary Ann Glendon, 'Foundations of Human Rights: The Unfinished Business' 44 (1999) *American Journal of Jurisprudence* 1.

[67] See Jon Mahoney, 'Liberalism and the Moral Basis for Human Rights' 27 (2008) *Law and Philosophy* 165. For a similar sentiment see David N Stamos, *The Myth of Universal Human Rights* (Routledge 2013); Allan Gewirth, *The Community of Rights* (University of Chicago Press 1996) for the 'principle of generic consistency'.

[68] On the institutional character of human rights see Mark Retter, 'The Road Not Taken: On Alasdair MacIntyre's Human Rights Scepticism' 63 (2018) *American Journal of Jurisprudence* 189.

[69] See Charles Beitz, 'Human Dignity in the Theory of Human Rights: Nothing but a Phrase?' 41 (2013) *Philosophy & Public Affairs* 266–68.

intention or past practice, but can be interpreted according to (b) that meaning that is likely to be supported and upheld by the greatest number of nations, *or* (c) sound ethical theory. We may refer therefore to the (a) intention-, (b) saturation-, and (c) ethical-interpretations of human rights norms. This section shall be concerned almost entirely with (c).

There is some similarity between the views stated here and those of MacIntyre, who in a famous passage in *After Virtue* likened the belief in rights possessed by humans simply in virtue of their humanity, to belief in unicorns.[70] For he excludes from his scepticism the existence of positive rights created by positive law. But the similarity is only superficial. For I have stated that human rights are creatures of positive law, and that their origin lies in the history of human practices, unlike natural rights which humans possess, not 'simply' in virtue of their humanity, but through a natural law which transcends that nature by ordering human practices towards the divine. MacIntyre's scepticism towards human rights is tempered by his Aristotelianism, for he elsewhere states that 'human rights' are in fact to be articulated through the social practices and historical traditions that define ethical and moral concepts. Belief in rights or any ethical ideas that lie outside or 'beyond' those practices, he believes, is indeed like searching for unicorns.[71] This denies any transcendent source of insight into ethics, i.e. that there can be, in the strictest sense, natural rights. As I stated in Section I.6, MacIntyre is no relativist, nor is he a nihilist,[72] but his work gives encouragement to the atheist, to anyone who wishes to deny the transcendent aspect to human life. His ethical norms remain human norms, theorized on the human plane, amid human traditions. Thus although we agree upon the essential positivity of human rights, we diverge starkly upon the character of natural rights. Vitoria's thought betrays a similar fluidity, between notions of *ius gentium* and *ius naturale*.[73] But in at least one respect, the difference is clear: the natural law concerns right and just relations between all persons, whether in war or in peace; but any deviation from the natural law, whether intentional or no, can only establish human-imposed laws, the *ius gentium*. The latter are historically extended norms, the former timeless: see Section I.6.

Those who assert a kind of historical relativity of human rights are in consequence closer to MacIntyre than appears. For it has already been stated that human rights do not have their *origin* in sound ethical theory; but a great many writers on human rights seek a *justification* of human rights norms by appealing to ethical theory, in particular an ethical understanding of the human person and of human needs. In contrast to the framers of human rights norms, academic writers are not

[70] Alasdair MacIntyre, *After Virtue* (Duckworth 1981) 69.

[71] Alasdair MacIntyre, *A Short History of Ethics* (Routledge 2002) 1–3.

[72] See Bill Bowring, 'Misunderstanding MacIntyre on Human Rights' 30 (2008) *Analyse & Kritik* 206.

[73] See Brian Tierney, 'Vitoria and Suarez on *ius gentium*, natural law and custom' in Amanda Perreau-Saussine & James Murphy (eds) *The Nature of Customary Law* (CUP 2007) 103, 112: *ius gentium* must be intellectually separated from *ius naturale* (commenting on Aquinas, *ST* (n 3) II-II.57.3 on justice).

constrained by time and political realities (even if both of these matters are taken into account), and arguments that have been judged to have been defeated can always be restated and reaffirmed, or defended, in a new form. Some writers who have taken this ethical approach to the subject, for example Tasioulas and Griffin, have argued that although human rights norms are absolute, they are nevertheless relative to time and place: that rights held in virtue of one's humanity must nevertheless be sensitive to the effects of time and circumstance upon that humanity.[74]

A brief glance at the UDHR, for example, seems to confirm this view, for the Preamble of that document first of all makes reference to the role of human rights in providing a foundation for freedoms of speech and belief, and other unspecified 'fundamental freedoms', a series of concerns that appear to be both distinctively modern and particular to developed societies. But the view that human rights are therefore relative to time and place is nevertheless a mistake, for it fails to distinguish between human rights that are indeed relative in these respects (such as freedom of the press: a freedom only possible in developed societies that possess a media infrastructure) and human rights that are founded upon permanent human needs: needs such as emancipation from tyranny and oppression (Preamble), justice and peace (Preamble), life, liberty, and security (Art 3), freedom from torture or degrading treatment (Art 5), equality before the law (Art 7), and many others besides. The rights that arise out of these needs are not temporary or relative to certain conditions, but give expression to universal and timeless facets of the human condition. Tasioulas seems to acknowledge the distinction, for he observes that the timeless quality of rights is not plausible in relation to 'many items in the Human Declaration', and that human rights in the strict sense (Arts 3–18) should be distinguished from mere 'liberal aspirations' elsewhere in the document.[75] But this is obviously too narrow a view of what constitutes a timeless human right. The very next article (Art 20.1) mentions the freedom of peaceful assembly and association, a fundamental ground of human sociability, and Art 23.3 incorporates the right to meaningful and just remuneration for work, a necessary right (though not the only one) to secure against slavery or forced labour (Art 4).

But if the UDHR secures fundamental human rights and freedoms, it also throws doubt upon the extent to which such rights can be, or should be, given effect in positive law. For Art 29.2 famously states that 'In the exercise of his rights and freedoms, everyone shall be subject only to such limitations as are determined by law solely for the purpose of securing due recognition and respect for the rights and freedoms of others and of meeting the just requirements of morality, public order and the general welfare in a democratic society.' This clause makes clear the

[74] See John Tasioulas, 'Human Rights, Legitimacy, and International Law' 58 (2013) *American Journal of Jurisprudence* 3 & 8<; see Raffael Fasel, 'Simply in Virtue of Being Human? A Critical Appraisal of a Human Rights Commonplace' 9 (2018) *Jurisprudence* 461.

[75] Tasioulas (n 74) 8 & 11.

difference between human rights, which are creatures of positive law, and natural rights. For the limits of human rights are said to be 'determined by law' upon the listed grounds. The first of these, 'the rights and freedoms of others', is straightaway problematic in holding that the right or freedom (Hohfeldian permissibility) of *A* must be exercised only in ways that do not disrupt the *freedoms* of *B*. But as we saw earlier, every person possesses freedoms that can disrupt another's freedoms, such as the freedom to run a business or to speak in public (for I might simply speak more loudly than others who wish to speak). And few are the occasions on which my natural right to $\varphi$ will disrupt any natural rights of yours, for no person possesses a natural right to commit an immoral act, and contravening another's right (i.e. what is due to them in justice) is an immoral act. Hence also the second ground mentioned in Art 29.2 is applicable only to *positive* right, for natural rights are expressions of moral precepts and not opposed to such precepts. The third of the mentioned grounds is the only one to apply to both natural and human rights, bearing again in mind Aquinas's warning that it may sometimes be more important to uphold public order than to uphold one's right. Yet the extent of the doctrine is not clear: should one allow oneself to be put to death for the sake of avoiding scandal? But it is the final ground of restriction in Art 29.2 that causes most trouble. For what does it mean for considerations of 'general welfare' to override one's right? As previously noted (Section I.2), utilitarian and other aggregative conceptions of individual interests are not merely senseless, but are impossible to carry out. As a result, references to 'general welfare' and similar terms are frequently no more than political intuitions dangerous in their openness to oppression. These mistakes are repeated, even amplified, in other human rights documents that follow on from the UDHR. For example, the ECHR (Art 10.2) states:

> The exercise of these freedoms, since it carries with it duties and responsibilities, may be subject to formalities, conditions, restrictions or penalties as are prescribed by law and are necessary in a democratic society, in the interests of national security, territorial integrity or public safety, for the prevention of disorder or crime, for the protection of health or morals, for the protection of the reputation or rights of others, for preventing the disclosure of information received in confidence, or for maintaining the authority and impartiality of the judiciary.

Here the problem is compounded, for what exactly is the difference between a 'condition' and a 'restriction'; and what is the difference between those terms and 'formalities'? Formalities are essentially a restriction upon form; conditions a restriction upon range of application. That the Article states that exercise of freedoms '*may* be subject to formalities, conditions, restrictions' suggests a potentially wide competence for domestic systems of law to restrict such freedoms in any of the ways stated, those ways themselves being capable of a range of moral interpretation. For who determines what constitutes a crime or offence against public safety, disorder, etc.? Could a potentially wide array of freedoms to demonstrate against the state government be included within such a restriction? Could the protection of 'health' and 'morals' justify a restriction of homosexual activity, for example? To be sure, the ECtHR strives to achieve a universal jurisprudence around such questions, but there is nothing in the provisions themselves to exclude oppressive interpretations that limit freedoms or their exercise.

But what of conflicts between *rights*, as opposed to *freedoms*? Is there some principle or set of principles by reference to which such conflicts can be successfully and clearly adjudicated? Finnis writes of such conflicts—of one person's right with that same right possessed by another, or of one right of one person with another right of another person—that there is 'no alternative but to hold in one's mind's eye some pattern, or range of patterns, of human character, conduct, and interaction in community, and then to choose such specification of rights as tends to favour that pattern, or range of patterns.'[76] This is, he goes on to say, equivalent to defining some conception (or conceptions?) of human good and human flourishing, and determining a system of rights that promotes that flourishing. But this is not, I think, Aquinas's method. Rights for Aquinas are not jigsaw puzzle pieces, to be fitted together as best can be done in light of the facts of human nature and human flourishing; they are conclusions of practical reason from universal precepts of natural law. Such precepts are based on human good, and more especially upon alertness to actions which subvert those goods. Thus it is a universal precept of natural law that one must not harm the innocent. From this we can readily derive *rights* against certain types of behaviour that would cause harm to the innocent (whether deliberate or negligent), rights which specify what is *due* or *owed* to human persons. Crucially, we can define and specify such rights without 'hold[ing] in one's mind's eye some pattern, or range of patterns' of human character or interaction. To the extent that morality is coherent and consistent, we should expect that rights—natural rights—are likewise coherent and consistent; but nevertheless we should not expect morality to be fulfilled by 'a range of [different] patterns' of rights, except at the level of *determinatio*, that is to say, *positive* legal (human) rights. More generally, then, natural rights are not in general derived from their coherence with other established natural rights, but from universal precepts of natural law.

This short detour into natural rights was necessary due to Finnis's insistence that 'human right' and 'natural right' can be used interchangeably. But Finnis is not alone in regarding human rights as resting upon moral foundations. The encyclical *Pacem in terris* § 55 clearly states that the ultimate source of human rights is not in human will but in human *being*. As Aquinas makes clear, human persons possess dignity (a trait mentioned very often in human rights instruments) intrinsically

[76] Finnis, *NLNR* (n 11) 219.

and not as a status conferred by positive law.[77] Thus human rights are not waivable or alienable by any person, for to do so would be to injure the dignity of *all* persons.[78] For to fail to respect one person's human right is to deny the absolute priority of the dignity that is the foundation of the rights of all others.[79] Despite these teachings, I have argued that human rights are products of *positive law*, rather than of natural law, in terms of their *origin*. But they require, as I have said, *justification* and thus a moral defence. (If human rights are regarded as pragmatic in averting wrongful acts against human beings, they nevertheless depend upon a concept of 'wrong', and thus have a moral basis. If human rights are nothing but western hegemony, they are nevertheless an imposition of *value*.) In a recent work, Griffin takes a similar approach to Finnis in suggesting that one must discern a pattern of rights, a number of which might be viable, but in this case not from conceptions of human good or human flourishing, but instead from an examination of existing human rights to a more general justification.[80] The former approach is said to be too abstract, seeking to derive concrete norms from abstract general principles that are inevitably contentious. This worry is misplaced, however, for the human goods that lead to human flourishing are themselves perfectly concrete. Griffin likewise argues that human rights should be regarded as protecting, not human good or human flourishing, but only human *status*.[81] But the central values that status demands—life, autonomy, security of person, freedom of belief, etc.—are themselves aspects of human flourishing. An understanding of the person, no matter how austere it aspires to be, cannot avoid making assumptions about what it means for a human person to flourish in any of the concrete ways readily inferred from one's own daily life and actions.

Griffin recognizes a distinction between universal- and derived human rights: the latter, such as freedom of the press, depending upon certain cultural, historical, and social conditions.[82] In much the same way, I have distinguished between natural rights that hold at all times and places without exception, and those natural rights that are more specific to particular times and conditions. But Griffin regards human rights of the former type (universal) as not ahistorical.[83] Griffin is right to regard *all* human rights as historical artefacts, but not for the reason he gives: that human nature is itself historical and malleable. Rather, they are artefacts because they are creatures of positive lawmaking. But their underlying *justification* is indeed timeless, ahistoric, universal. It is however the rights, and not the justification, that forms much of modern human rights practice (as the Roosevelt draft

[77] Aquinas, *ST* (n 3) I.29.3 ad 2.
[78] *Pacem in terris* § 55.
[79] *Compendium* § 154.
[80] James Griffin, *On Human Rights* (OUP 2006) 29.
[81] Ibid, 34.
[82] Ibid, 38.
[83] Ibid, 35.

makes clear). This process of justification is highly likely to step beyond the realm of acknowledged human rights as expressed in the various human rights instruments. Thus the Church acknowledges that it is the defender of 'forgotten and unacknowledged rights', especially of the poor and needy.[84] Human rights documents raise natural rights to a new importance; for they pose the question of how and by whom natural rights should be upheld or enforced. Certainly there are new avenues for the enforcement of natural rights than before the advent of human rights legislation. Nation states, as well as domestic actors such as governments, parents, adult children of the elderly, at different times have the standing to enforce such rights. In the case of acknowledged human rights, it may sometimes be a necessary means of enforcement by another state, or group of states (acting for the 'international community') to intervene in the internal affairs of a state: a new kind of rights-enforcement, although one also counterbalanced by grave reasons for not intervening, such as the need to avoid destabilizing a geopolitical area or posing a threat to international peace.[85]

The UDHR and other legal instruments contain and give expression to numerous natural rights, which they enshrine in provisions of positive law. But they also contain a number of human rights to which there is no corresponding natural right. Such an example is Art 21 UDHR, which establishes a right to rule by democracy. The right to democratic rule cannot be a natural right: it is simply not available as a possibility except in (a) the limited political domain of the classic city-state, or (b) modern technologically advanced societies with sufficient infrastructure to ensure mass and rapid spread of information, more-or-less simultaneous with events, scrupulous electoral procedures, institutionalized mechanisms for peaceful transfer of power, and so on. But it can be a human right, for although controversial, this right can be said to follow from the underlying justification of human rights, as the context in which alone many other human rights can flourish. Many so-called 'welfare rights' fall into this category. But does it follow from this that no human right is 'absolute'?[86] Here, 'absolute' can be taken to mean (1) permanent, (2) without exception, (3) not subject to limitation by any other rights, and (4) not outweighed by any other considerations, such as military advantage, even in a just cause. And the answer is that, yes there are absolute human rights: typically those that are expressions of natural rights. A pertinent example is the right of the innocent not to be severely harmed or killed. For on what consideration could such a right be outweighed? And if the right could be outweighed at all, then it could be outweighed only by some determination that is of greater importance than the sanctity of the innocent person's life. Typically (and whatever the real motivations) the taking of innocent life is defended on the basis of public order or of reclaiming

[84] *Gaudium et spes* § 76.
[85] Griffin (n 80) 183–84.
[86] For Griffin's affirmative answer see ibid 138.

geographical, ancestral, or cultural rights (ethnic cleansing). But such interests are only important because they are interests of other human beings; and no interest, even the gravest of interests, can outweigh those same interests in another. Hence it is absolutely wrong for one person in a famine-struck community to feed her children on the flesh of another child, for both have an inalienable right to life. The example can readily be scaled up: there is no legitimate justification for ending the lives of thousands or millions of innocent civilians by bombing or other means in order to procure military advantage which will lead to the security of more millions of lives in one's own society. The interest of one group simply cannot outweigh, or be balanced against, a similar interest in another group. Nor even can one group's interest be weighed against 'lesser' interests of others: it is not permissible, to secure military advantage, to maim or impair the lives of innocents through, for example, chemical attacks, use of landmines in civilian areas, etc.

To be clear, these examples do not depict a *conflict* between the human rights of one group and those of another. Griffin states that, where the only means to protect the human rights of one group *A* that are being threatened by another group *B*, is the rounding up of all members of *B*, knowing that caught in the net will be some innocent persons, then there is a conflict between the human rights of those innocents and the rights of group *A*.[87] But this is entirely wrong: there is no conflict, for the rights of group *A* do not extend as far as extinguishing the rights of innocent members of group *B*. If the cultural, linguistic, historical, or religious heritage of group *A* is threatened, then they had better find an alternative means of securing their rights, if not by persuasion then by passive resistance. Indeed, while the Church recognizes human rights to one's culture, language, etc.,[88] this cannot be extended to *all* cultures, such as German national socialism's quest for supposed cultural purity: for rights are ultimately justified by human goods, and are thus relative to what is good or at least reasonable in one's culture.[89] Conversely, whilst human rights violations are correctly judged as very grave matters, the commission of atrocities, genocide, chemical attacks on the civilian population, and so forth, appear to demand stronger condemnation than a mere infringement of rights. For rights are, as previously argued, merely an apposite and powerful way of expressing the demands of justice; but there are times at which those demands are better expressed in the language of justice and natural law itself.

Human rights are determined and defined not only at the level of international institutions, but at the level of states also: in this sense, the working-out of the potentially rich content of abstractly expressed human rights, a form of *determinatio*, represents an aspect of the principle of subsidiarity:

[87] Ibid, 63.

[88] *Compendium* § 157.

[89] There is a threshold consideration here, for obviously no culture is based entirely on what is good or reasonable. But I do not propose to discuss the threshold for present purposes. See also Tasioulas (n 74) 5.

> The margin of appreciation doctrine recognizes that there may be a range of different but justified interpretations of international human rights law depending on the domestic context. As a result, the Court should defer to the judgment of domestic authorities that are better placed to decide on what these are. That deference or self-restraint is not absolute, of course, or else the review and supervision power of the Court would be pointless.[90]

Besson's example of this, reminiscent of Aquinas's own example of *determinatio*, is that of remedial enforcement, a matter to be determined by states themselves.[91] But this power of determination must necessarily be subject to norms of natural law, norms that are largely excluded as relevant to the meaning of human rights from the world's major human rights charters. Hence responses to human rights abuses will typically be regarded as strategic and 'political'. A society that uses torture or inhumane treatment entirely loses its moral authority to challenge the conduct of states that act in the same way. Any enforcement measure taken against such states—diplomatic and economic sanctions, exclusion from international organizations, political pressure, humanitarian intervention[92]—will appear as surface pretexts for the advancing of self-interests that, apart from such pretexts, would take on the character of unlawful intervention.

## VI.6. RIGHTS AND CORE MORALITY

The language of rights defines modern legal and political discourse, and is often said to lend precision to questions of justice and common good. But the language of rights is not inevitable: one could, for example, imagine a community orientated around a universal scheme of national insurance in which the central concept is not with fault but with harm, legal reasoning being chiefly concerned with demonstration of the claimant's having fallen within a legally defined form of harm, and with the scope and extent of types of harm. Thus the language of rights is but one possible discourse for the orientation of thought; but the deep structure of legal, political, and moral thought is represented by the core morality (see Section III.4), where harm is indeed a key component of thought, but not the only or even the chief component. The principles of the core morality (derivations from the secondary precepts of natural law) structure and inform the 'surface' moral discourse. To follow the same example, legal notions of 'fault' hinge upon assessments of harm; concepts of fraud, misrepresentation, inducement, etc., hinge upon

[90] Samantha Besson, 'Subsidiarity in Human Rights Law' 61 (2016) *American Journal of Jurisprudence* 81.

[91] Ibid, 83.

[92] See Evan Fox-Decent & Evan Criddle, 'The Fiduciary Constitution of Human Rights' 15 (2009) *Legal Theory* 304.

questions of authenticity (integrity); the definition of criminal laws hinges upon principles of social peace, and very many legal concepts are informed by the need to exercise reasonable foresight; and so on (see Section III.4). Insofar as legal concepts conform to, or derive their content from, core moral principles, they are to be reckoned just and in conformity to natural law. Insofar as such concepts depart from, are in tension with, or oppose those principles, the law is to be reckoned unjust and against natural law. The question of the status of such laws is addressed in Chapter XI.

It is time to bring this long discussion of human rights to a close. The discussion has served to emphasize two main points. (1) Human rights, in terms of their *origins*, are essentially positive law instruments. (2) In terms of their *justification*, human rights must derive from or articulate natural rights, either in substance or through a reasonable determination of such rights as they may apply in diverse contexts. The failure to distinguish between these two kinds of derivation lies behind many of the modern sceptical concerns about the true status of, for example, economic rights, or of rights to democratic rule, etc. But we must also be aware of the distinction between the justification of human rights (in an absolute sense) and particular projects of justification undertaken by international organizations, states and scholars. The context for many of these projects is political rather than ethical. They have the aim of, for instance, getting as many states as possible to subscribe to putative human rights, or of defending or promoting this or that right as a human right, or of pushing certain rights on or off the discussion table. These conversations are carried on under pressure of time, of circumstance and the ebb and flow of political will. As with all political discussion, conversations about human rights are expressions of conflicting ideologies, which fall short of the honesty and scope of ethical reflection into natural rights, where one must follow the argument wherever it leads and for however long the enquiry takes (see Section II.1). For this reason, the subsequent sections of this book, insofar as they involve reference to rights, will refer to natural rights and positive rights rather than human rights. For the book is one long unbroken argument about natural law in modern times, and largely excludes extraneous matters of politics and ideological debate.

# VII
# THE CULMINATION OF NATURAL LAW

## VII.1. THE REACH AND SCOPE OF REASON

The theory of natural law, of justice, of common good, and of natural right can be comprehended by reason to be both true and superior to all alternatives, especially those of positivism and scepticism. Of the truth of the network of propositions set out in Chapters III–VI, it is incumbent on the reader to determine, for him or herself, just as it is the duty of all persons to determine, for themselves (though seldom without assistance), sound guidance for living well. In doing so, each person engages their faculty of reflection and practical reason, building upon what Aquinas and other scholastic philosophers termed '*synderesis*', our spontaneous capacity to comprehend at least certain acts as indubitably wrong, or as indubitably right.[1] Reason is our highest capacity, capable of grasping aspects of reality as well as practical ethical truths, and it is the summation of all human decision-making. In one sense, then, reason is sufficient to determine the good from the bad, the politic from the impolitic, and the wise from the unwise course of action. The long process of reasoning in the chapters just mentioned is (it is hoped) sufficient to demonstrate the truth of the conclusions at which they arrive. In this sense, nothing else is wanted: neither Aristotle's nor Plato's ethics depend upon, or make reference to, supernatural phenomena or theories, for example. Furthermore, the natural law theories of the scholastic period down to the present day are presented as works of reason rather than of faith. With very few exceptions, such theories depend entirely upon the powers of natural reason to establish their conclusions. But the reader who is familiar with, say, Aquinas's philosophy will want to point out that, although that august philosopher's *natural law* theory depends upon 'secular' reason, the same is not true of his wider ethics, which is teeming with references to a divine Creator, nor of his account of human nature and the human being as such, which are set within a cosmological order that includes God's creativity. To what extent, if any, is it necessary to probe into such matters, and how does this affect the doctrines presented in the previous chapters?[2]

1 See e.g. Aquinas, *De Veritate* (hereafter *De Ver*) 16.1c.

2 For a similar sentiment see David MacIlroy, 'What is at Stake in Natural Law?' 89 (2008) *New Blackfriars* 508; EF Rogers, 'How the Spirit Moves the Law' *Aquinas and the Supreme Court: Race, Gender and the Failure of Natural Law in Saint Thomas's Biblical Commentaries* (Blackwell 2013) 247; cf Martin Rhonheimer, 'Natural Law as a Work of Reason' (2010) *American Journal of Jurisprudence* 53 & 61–62 (natural law is the only basis for a universal ethics).

*Natural Law and Modern Society*. Sean Coyle, Oxford University Press. © Sean Coyle 2023.
DOI: 10.1093/oso/9780192886996.003.0007

For the limited purposes of the present work, it is not necessary to inquire at length into such matters as the existence of angels and the mystery of the Holy Trinity. But the reader is owed some further explanation of natural law, since Aquinas, in common with all philosophers in the Thomist tradition, places 'natural law' in a framework of other kinds of law: positive (human) law, divine law and eternal law. In particular, natural law is held to be natural reason's ability to comprehend a small part of eternal law, otherwise mysterious and closed to human comprehension, and to determine through its own efforts the truth of precepts of divine law, and to elaborate on those precepts as they apply in sometimes complex and difficult situations (see Section II.9). But so far, we have not established the existence of eternal law, so the reader might wonder why more should be advocated than a social Darwinist conception of the most fitting: of why natural law (however understood) stands in need of further, revelatory, confirmations. The need for revelatory confirmations is the topic of the present chapter. To confront such questions is to accept that practical reason alone is *in*sufficient to underpin our knowledge of natural law: for we might wonder, if there is no God, no eternity, no heaven, no ultimate meaning to human life and the goods that shape human existence, why our attempts to do good and avoid evil are of any final significance. The individual, recognizing the 'truth' of Social Darwinism, may nevertheless pursue a life of recidivism on the basis that their own pursuit of self-advantage does not after all threaten to any appreciable extent the path of collective human flourishing, and that the only imperative worth following is the avoidance of capture and punishment. The argument of Chapter II was, in part, devoted to a demonstration that social Darwinists in reality commit themselves to an impoverished version of natural law that is, in practical terms, inadequate. But that chapter nevertheless left unanswered questions about the ultimate significance of moral values, beyond their practical necessity. Thus, this chapter is devoted to arguments of a speculative nature which examine the extent to which natural reason can establish the existence of God, His attributes, and further the reasons why it is rational to accept the other mode of revelation, God's direct communication of moral imperatives through divine law.

Furthermore, the theory of natural law thus far presented has, in common with Aristotelian ethical theory and Aquinas's natural law theory, rested only upon merely those aspects or characteristics of the human condition and human being that are observable or quantifiable by reason.[3] The primary precepts of natural law relate to human characteristics such as the desire for, and preservation of, life, the safeguarding and education of one's offspring, and the desire to live peacefully in society (see Section II.5). Such principles, then, relate to realities of human life that are equally open to Darwinism, Gnosticism, or merely atheism.

[3] For an account centred upon virtues and love, see EF Rogers, 'Aquinas on Natural Law and the Virtues in Biblical Context' 27 (1999) *Journal of Religious Ethics* 29.

But those realities are not the only realities of human life and human thinking. Nor are they fully adequate as an explanation of ethics, without further investigation of the ultimate source, and ultimate end, of human striving. Very roughly speaking, we may ask: what shapes these realities, and what significance do they have when confronted with the question, why do anything at all? This question leads us to theology as a possible explanation of the ultimate significance of human actions. Murphy reminds us that natural law on Aquinas's account of it is not voluntarist, so that his general statement on the nature of law, as necessarily having been promulgated by a superior, does not supply a ground for thinking that natural law is law due to God's command.[4] This is debatable, for the fact that Divine command is not the only or the principal ground of natural law, does not entail that it occupies no place in Aquinas's theory of natural law, and there is no reading of Aquinas's account that can altogether eliminate the role of the Divine will in natural law (see Section II.9). For nothing that is can be without Divine will.

There exist (so I will argue) rational arguments for the existence of God, in particular the Christian God, that is, the three Persons of Holy Trinity. But what is a rational argument? Rational arguments come in various forms. The most obvious is that of first-order propositional logic whereby the conclusion implied by true premises must also be true. But there are many other forms, including inductive arguments of various strength: from the claim that some large proportion of a group G has quality Q, and that A is a member of G, to the conclusion that A has (or probably has) the quality Q; or (less readily) that all observed instances of G have Q, therefore all Gs have Q. The natural sciences depend fundamentally upon inductive arguments of the first type. The arguments to be explored in the present chapter more closely resemble those of logic. They proceed not from generalizations but from concrete empirical facts, though they easily give rise to more general inductive arguments. Most people, of course, derive their belief in God not from philosophical arguments as set out in this chapter, but from authority, often the authority of inherited belief, although such belief requires ongoing support if it is not to fade away, be left behind in childhood, abandoned in difficult circumstances, etc. For those people to whom the philosophical arguments are inaccessible difficult, there is nothing amiss about the derivation from authority, just as it is not contrary to reason to believe that one's neighbour's wife is dead solely on the testimony of one's neighbour himself. Such persons would similarly derive all of their knowledge of science not directly from experimental technique and evidence, but from the authority of scientists past and present.

The arguments set out in this chapter do not, I believe, conclusively prove the existence of God. Were that the case, there would be no need of faith. Rather, the arguments give us good reasons to believe in God, and to remove apparent obstacles

[4] See Mark C Murphy, *God and the Moral Law* (OUP 2011, hereafter *GML*) 76–79.

by, for instance, demonstrating that belief in God does not contravene or require the abandonment of scientific technique or scientific theories that are highly confirmed by available evidence. Conversely, scientific theories cannot establish the inexistence of God, for the most that they can do (and set out to do) is to explain observable phenomena on the basis of material causality. Even a comprehensive and consistent scientific explanation of all observable phenomena could only yield a deflationary agnosticism: an agnosticism that is not, as I shall argue below, tenable. But the present chapter does not as a whole seek to present all possible (valid) arguments for the existence of God, nor, for reasons of space, to defend them. Nor is it a discussion of the secondary commentaries on the philosophical arguments outlined herein; rather, it is a substantive discussion of propositions that must be evaluated, challenged, scrutinized, accepted. Finally, the following discussion is heavily indebted to, amongst others, Thomas Aquinas, Edward Feser, Germain Grisez, and Francisco Suarez.

Before proceeding to the arguments, let me make one highly important observation: the argumentative forms, both in this chapter and throughout this book *do not* proceed from the supposition of God to the character and content of morality, but on the contrary from the character of moral or practical reasoning, and ultimately to the widest reaches of theoretical insight about the universe and the things in it, *to* the existence of God.[5] As I have indicated, these arguments are unlikely to persuade those who are not open to their broader intellectual possibilities;[6] but they are worth stating in any case for they provide an ultimate grounding for a natural law theory that does not simply collapse into Social Darwinism.

## VII.2. FIRST ARGUMENT

In line with my observation above that faith is still required to supplement reason (but not fight against it), Aquinas refers to his arguments as 'five paths' (*quinque viae*) to knowledge of God, not as 'proofs'; and Suarez, commenting at length on Aquinas's arguments, observes that although they are subtle and convincing to the open-minded reader, they will fail to persuade the stubborn and the unreasonable.[7] In order to set the scene for the arguments that follow, we may begin with some (hopefully non-contentious) observations: (1) The 'Big Bang' model, the most prevalent cosmological model for the observable universe, fails on its own terms to explain how something (a whole universe no less) can be created out of nothing at all. (2) Subsequent theories which attempt such an explanation are unable to account for the origin of the quantum matter (or more likely energy) that is said to

[5] See e.g. Murphy, *GML* (n 4) 1–2.

[6] As Murphy agrees: see ibid, 6.

[7] Suarez, *Disputationes Metaphysicae* (hereafter *DM*) XXIX.3.8, also XXIX.3.32.

cause the Big Bang. (3) Such subsequent theories, concerning a dense energy-state immediately prior to the Big Bang, are difficult to square with that theory for which matter and space can only exist in time (space-time) so that discussion of prior energy-states is metaphorical, but without clear sense of what it is that the metaphor stands for. (4) The postulation of a universe coming into being out of nothing is just as plausible or difficult to believe as the existence of a creator God living from eternity, outside of space-time. (5) A theological explanation of the universe is the only explanation in which the universe can be explained in terms of causality from its very beginning. These propositions are perhaps sufficient to dismiss the idea that speculative theology can only hope to provide an explanation for present gaps in scientific theory, and that as such gaps diminish through successive scientific discoveries, the theological arguments are proven to be of no value. In fact, theology is not especially concerned with current unknowns; its focus is on the explanation of perfectly familiar events and states of affairs: an explanation that is required for a full and properly adequate account of observable phenomena.[8]

There are limits to speculative theological arguments. As Aquinas makes clear, our participation in the life of the Creator is only ever incomplete: either through our exercise of *prudentia* in living the morally correct form of life and in the forms of speculative arguments we are about to explore, through prayer, or (very infrequently and to only a few) through our direct communication with angelic messengers or the Blessed Mother. Clearly, other animals and plants, insofar as they also have a mode of participation in eternal law, do not do so through the natural law.[9] Nevertheless, our rational participation in eternal law in no way implies that we can in any great measure 'comprehend' God, or His purposes. More can be deduced of God than His existence alone (as will become evident below), but the limits of human knowledge of God are nevertheless severe.[10] Indeed, the first of Aquinas's preliminaries to his 'five paths' acknowledges that the proposition that God exists, while self-evident in itself, is *not* self-evident *to us*, who know God not as He is in Himself, but through His effects on substantive matter.[11] Thus, when Aquinas concludes each of his five paths with the statement that 'everyone' calls the primary cause (or mover) God, he is probably referring to his fellow Dominican brothers and not literally to all persons, for the very undertaking to establish God's existence through argument implies that this question was contested in Aquinas's time as in our own. So to the first 'path'.

The first argument is based on movement (*motus*).[12] We are used to everyday objects and phenomena changing around us: we begin to feel hot because the air is warm; the air becomes warm because the clouds have evaporated, allowing

[8] Ibid, XXIX.1.2; Aristotle, *Posterior Analytics* I.10.76b.

[9] Aquinas, *Summa Theologiae* (hereafter *ST*) I-II.91.2c, I-II.93.5–6, I.79.4c.

[10] See Suarez, *DM* (n 7) XXVIII.1.19.

[11] Aquinas, *ST* (n 9) I.2.1c.

[12] The following argument is a mixture of Aquinas's at *ibid* I.2.3c, and that of Feser.

sunlight to break through; the clouds disperse because of the heat radiating from the sun; heat radiates from the sun because of the nuclear reactions and processes going on in the sun, and so on. The English term 'movement' is not fully adequate to encompass all of these events and processes, and the Latin term '*motus*' spans both the sense of 'movement' and of 'change' or 'process'. Let us however stick with 'movement' for a moment. Nor are all instances of movement entirely linear: the tea in my cup is going colder because the air in the room is lower in temperature; it is lower in temperature because ambient conditions are such-and-such; those conditions hold because the Earth's axis is tilted away from the sun, etc; but the tea is also getting cold because I left it on the table; I placed it there because I bought it in a coffee shop; I was able to buy it because (a) I possessed sufficient money, and (b) I decided to (and actually did) walk to the shop to obtain it, and (c) because an employee prepared it, and was able to do so because (d) someone grew it and transported it, etc. Each of these explanations (a)–(d), and other relevant conditions that can be readily imagined (this particular tea-plant received just the right amount of water, shelter, sun, etc) is a linear sequence by itself, and it will often be impossible to trace precisely all of the events and conditions for the obtaining of a particular current movement. But we may perhaps ignore such complexities by viewing them as discrete strands within an overarching sequence that we can still call 'linear' since it extends backward in time, and because one can identify the steps—movements—that lead to the current state of affairs. In principle, we could trace such linear sequences back to the origin of the universe itself; in fact we could entertain the hypothesis that the universe resulted from the rapid implosion and heat of a previous universe, and so on to infinity, so that there never was a first mover.

A linear sequence of this kind is essential to our understanding of the given state of affairs. There is, however, another dimension of explanation that is required if we are truly to explain the given situation. We may term this a 'hierarchical sequence': the cup occupies its place in the room because it is held up by the table; the table is held up by the floor, which is held up by the walls of the room below, which are held in place by the ground, etc. Unlike a linear sequence, a hierarchical sequence must of necessity have a first member, what we might call a *prime mover*. Why is this? First, it might be objected that a hierarchical sequence does not seem to involve *change* (i.e. one synonym for *motus*). But, applying Aquinas's terms, it can be said that each member of the hierarchical sequence (and of a linear sequence) *actualizes* a *potentiality*—brings about in some object something that was potentially true of it—and is in turn actualized by some other. It therefore does not matter whether the sequence is simultaneous or extended backward through time. Second, it is important to mention that the potentialities of an object are not limitless. A cup has the potential to be hot or cold, cracked, or undamaged, dirty or clean, here or there, and so on, but it does not have the potential to be converted into a gorilla, or to fly under its own power, to be incapable of destruction, etc.

Now the fact that the table actualizes a potential in the cup to occupy a certain space within the room cannot be the end of the explanation, for the table in itself has no power to actualize anything; it does so only because it is itself actualized (in part) by another object (the floor), which is in turn actualized by the walls below (and so on). But nothing can hold up anything unless there is an ultimate foundation, an actualizer that is not itself actualized by anything else. Thus the Earth itself is not the terminus of the sequence because it is not, to use Aquinas's expression, 'pure actuality': something which contains no potentialities, for the Earth's position in space and time, its composition, etc, have to be explained by a *further* object, and thus would not be the prime mover.[13] The hierarchical series that explains how the potentialities of numerous objects are actualized in order to bring about a certain state of affairs, therefore requires a first term which consists of actuality alone.

All linear sequences, whether finite or infinite, depend upon a hierarchical sequence. For the teacup to exist at all, and for it to *subsist* in a stable manner, certain atomic material and processes (e.g. of atomic bonding) must obtain, which in turn depend upon the existence and characteristics of subatomic particles as they are arranged in a certain way. But the existence of such particles, and their subsistence, must also be explained. Moreover, it must be explained not only what caused an object to exist, but also why it continues in existence *now*. We therefore require to identify a term that not only exists but is not brought into being by the existence and actualizing power of anything else. And this prime mover can be called 'God', for it has all of the characteristics associated with God in the Judeo–Christian tradition. For, since the prime mover gives actuality to all other things, it is omnipotent (all-powerful). The prime mover also lacks evil, not because it is incomplete, but because evil is a privation, whereas the prime mover lacks nothing (otherwise it would possess potentiality, which was ruled out above). Hence, the prime mover is perfectly good.[14] The prime mover exists outside of time and space (space-time in modern scientific terminology), and is thus eternal and incorporeal. The prime mover also actualizes objects and processes according to physical, chemical, and biological laws that are capable of being isolated, studied, comprehended, and experimentally verified, so that the prime mover must be said to be intelligent. Thus, the existence of God is not inferred from the fact that He is the cause of the whole universe and everything in it (though this is all true), but from the ordinary properties of any random object, as small as a teacup.

In attributing these properties to God, we must be understood to be speaking analogically, when compared with the intelligence, agency, and goodness of human beings. We have, for example, a range of distinct though related meanings of the concept 'good': someone could be a good person, or possess a good

[13] Aquinas, *Summa Contra Gentiles* (hereafter *SCG*) I.22.7.

[14] Ibid, I.28.3; see also e.g. Grisez, *God? A Philosophical Preface to Faith* (St Augustine's Press) 256.

house, or drink good wine. These differences are not the differences between focal and non-focal cases of a concept and are not, strictly speaking, defined by comparison of any kind: moral goodness and good wine are not comparable even if the same term seems appropriate in some way. But the analogous concepts here have at least the advantage of being understood: a wine is called 'good' when it has a pleasing taste, whereas the goodness of God cannot be properly comprehended, though is still conceived of in analogy with human goodness. The biblical image is apposite: we 'see through a glass darkly'.[15] It must also be mentioned that God's omnipotence is not the indiscriminate ability to bring forth impossible objects. God cannot make 2 + 2 = 5, or make a round triangle, for these are not the actualizations of any potentiality; they are not genuine potentialities (of, say, the number 5) but simply incoherent ideas.[16] Neither is God's incorporeality to be understood as a deficiency or lack of material form; rather materiality is a limitation to which God is not subject. Nor is it possible to equate primal movement with Platonic forms; for such forms are pure idea, and in no way *actualize* anything, even those objects that tend towards those forms. By contrast, God can be said to be *in* the objects He actualizes, as the cause of their being. (But this is to anticipate the second argument.)

The divine attributes (omnipotence, omniscience, perfect goodness, etc) might give rise to a concern that God is therefore a composite being rather than a unity, and thus not of pure actuality but of potentiality (to actualize some parts and not others).[17] But this objection supposes that those attributes refer to different qualities that God possesses, whereas in fact they are a reference to the same thing, merely understood in different ways. Divine omnipotence simply is divine omniscience, perfect goodness etc: the perception of difference is the result of analogical thinking based on the fact that in human beings there is sight without action, action without understanding, and without moral goodness. We can thus be confident that God is One and not many; indeed if there were a pantheon of gods we should expect to find differences in matter, and in natural laws of gravity and motion across local areas of the universe, contrary to all experience.[18] Despite the fact that God is One, and that certain attributes might be analogically predicated of God, Aquinas warns that human knowledge of God by reason alone is scant, and that our knowledge of God is as nothing compared with the reality of God.[19]

[15] 1 Corinthians 13.

[16] Aquinas, *SCG* (n 13) I.84.2.

[17] For a catalogue of confusions on the attributes of God see John Gardner, *Law as a Leap of Faith* (OUP 2012) ch 1.

[18] See Richard Swinburne, *The Existence of God* (Clarendon Press 2004) 147; Aquinas, *SCG* (n 13) I.42.3, I.42.5 (the same argument from motion) I.42.8 (from necessity).

[19] Aquinas, *SCG* (n 13) I.4.4, I.14.2.

## VII.3. SECOND ARGUMENT

Aquinas's second argument is based on causation, in particular efficient causation (i.e. a cause brought about by the action of a mover).[20] The world of experience discloses not only that there are efficient causes of things, but that there is a certain order of efficient causes. Typically, we attach (or at least seek for) a cause for every event we experience. If the train is late, we wonder what the reason is, which is another way of saying that we seek to determine the *cause* of its lateness, and this is so whether or not we ever find out what the cause was. Similarly, if police detectives find a murdered corpse, they attribute its demise to some cause, indeed some agency, even if they never find the culprit. The world of experience likewise discloses a *linear* order to efficient causes: in no experience do we ever find a case of something causing itself, for nothing exists prior to itself. We therefore expect, and find, causes of things extending backward into the past. It follows too that the cause of *A* must be some *B*, and of *B* some *C*, and so on. At this point, Aquinas argues that any such series must have a *first* cause, that is not itself caused by anything prior (or else that prior cause would be the genuine first cause). Now, the hypothesis was entertained in the preceding section that a linear sequence may extend backward to infinity, if we regard a universe-creating event as being caused by the heat and energy of a prior universe imploding, that prior universe having been brought into existence by a yet previous universe (and so on). This hypothesis is vanishingly unlikely, and to discard it at this point would give support to Aquinas's argument that there is a first cause.[21] But we do not need to discard it, for to speak of a 'first cause' is not to say that it is at the head of a sequence, but rather that it is the cause by which every other member of the sequence (currently) derives its characteristics and attributes.[22] Again, reference to a 'linear' sequence does not capture the complexity of causal series, which usually depends upon numerous series of causes: in addition to the causes mentioned above in relation to the teacup, we may include, for example, the manufacture of the cup from its chemical elements; the labour, materials, and organization required for the existence of the production process; the education of those who designed the cup; a shared English language and culture which enables a practice of trade in goods to exist, and so on. Linear series therefore resemble more of a cone, whose point is the present event and whose widening sides extend back into the past, than a line.

Thus Aquinas's conclusion holds: that the removal of the first cause (or, preferably, *primary* cause) would take out of existence everything that depends upon the primary cause for its existence, which is to say, the whole universe. As before,

20 See also Aquinas, *De Ente et Essentia* IV.80; Suarez, *DM* (n 7) XXIX.1.20–22.

21 Suarez is aware of the argument: he argues that the proof remains valid even if the universe existed from infinity: *DM* (n 7) XXIX.1.25; XXIX.1.31.

22 See Edward Feser, *Five Proofs of the Existence of God* (Ignatius Press 2017, hereafter *Five Proofs*) 133.

the argument does not begin with the claim that there is a cause of the entire universe, but only that there is a cause of some *A*, such as one person's sipping tea from a teacup. The claim that the primary cause causes the entire universe is rather the conclusion of the argument. And Aquinas ends the argument with the claim that the primary cause is God. It is not difficult to see, for example, how the primary cause should be omnipotent, for it is the cause of absolutely everything. It is pure cause, since there is no effect in it (nothing causes the primary cause for otherwise that thing would be the primary cause). It is one rather than many, for otherwise we would need to posit many causes; but this is not supported by experience, the stability and explanation of which is based on natural physical, chemical, and biological laws that are apparently universal rather than subject to local change by hypothetical demiurges. Indeed, if there are many uncaused causes, none could be said to cause *everything* let alone one another, and many uncaused causes could not be perfect, for each would be lacking in a property possessed by another. The primary cause is intelligent, because the caused physical realm is capable of coherent explanation. And it is omniscient because the divine intention is not withdrawn from any element of the universe, at least insofar as it is known to us, but is rather being caused at every moment: from being the cause of all things and maintaining all things in existence, God cannot fail to know all things. Again, these attributes must be understood analogically rather than literally, for any proposition that God is *X* implies a knowledge of what God is in Himself, which in turn would require knowledge of the things that are required for God to be as He is; but lacking such knowledge, all such propositions are literally false.[23]

An objection presents itself at this point. If God is the cause of all things, then God is the cause of horrific diseases, such as bone cancer in children; but this is incompatible with the idea of a perfectly good God, for children are innocent of any sin that would merit the incurring of such a disease. There are a number of answers to this objection, of which I shall mention only three. First, there is an ambiguity in the term 'cause'. In one sense, God is indeed the cause of all things, in the sense of maintaining all aspects of reality in existence at any given moment. But (in another sense) God cannot be said to cause, for example, the decision of a human person to assault another. The thoughts in our heads are ours, not God's, and God's existential causation of all things in no way compromises the reality of genuine freedom of the will. In a similar way, the explanation of horrific diseases, on the part of the Christian apologist, is essentially the same as the explanation given by biologists: human beings are made of cells, and it is natural, if unwanted, that certain cells may have a disposition to become cancerous and indeed do so in certain individuals.[24] God in no way 'causes' such diseases any more than He periodically

[23] See Grisez (n 14) 243.

[24] This naturalness is to be contrasted with the impossibility of, say, a person transforming into a donkey: for by no transformation can human DNA become donkey DNA, thus no way in which a person could so transform and continue to be that person: Aquinas, *ST* (n 9) I. I.25.3c.

'gives' us common colds or minor injuries. The second answer relates to the tracing of causal effects. It is a principle of causation that the effect, in some object, must be in the *total* cause, and not merely one member, or indeed the first.[25] That total cause includes the presence of genetic material created through the sexual act of the parents, and its conditioning by environmental effects, which might include unhealthy food, poor choices, and a host of other factors. It also includes random chances and perhaps causes that cannot be practically discerned. Thus, to say that God 'causes' terrible childhood diseases is simply a misunderstanding of causation. The third answer pertains to the Christian doctrine of original sin: corruption of the body is an effect of original sin, as mentioned in Genesis. This is in no sense a *punishment* for a past transgression, but rather a *consequence* of it. Hence diseases, like the rain, fall indiscriminately on the good and the bad alike. Atheists, of course, will reject such an explanation for they do not believe in original sin. But the idea that one's ancestors—even or perhaps especially those whom one does not know and to whom one is not related by blood—may commit wrongs and injustices that the present generation (and future generations) of humans inherit, is not at all difficult to understand. Each generation is bequeathed by the previous one a flawed criminal justice system, an unjust distribution of property rights, etc, and it is the duty of present-day humans to work to correct, if not undo, those flaws and injustices, simply because they are the only ones who can, and because, existing within a framework of flawed institutions, they are already embroiled in its injustices. Moreover the theist's explanation of terrible childhood diseases is essentially the same as the atheist's: genes mutate.

Before leaving the second argument, it is worth noting (as Anthony Kenny does) that the first and second arguments both deal with efficient causality but in diverging directions. The first argument focuses on the effect of movement (or actualization) in the object being moved; the second pertains to the agent or means by which an object is moved. As will become apparent, the five paths in fact correspond to the four causes enumerated by Aristotle: the third argument pertains to material causality, the fourth to formal causality, and the fifth to final causality.[26] These terms will be explained at the appropriate place. For the moment, it should be said that the primary cause of the second argument, and the prime mover of the first, do not point to separate beings, but rather to different dimensions of the same being, God; for they possess attributes that are identical.

[25] See Feser (n 22) 173.

[26] See Anthony Kenny, *The Five Ways* (Routledge 2008) 36.

## VII.4. THIRD ARGUMENT

The third argument explores the nature of necessity and contingency, and is concerned with material causality, that is, movement that is determined by the material substance of which moving or causing objects are composed. In the world of our experience, objects exist, fail to exist (i.e. never came into existence), and cease to exist. For all such things, if it is possible for them not to exist, then there must be some time at which they did not exist. Everything of this contingent kind requires a cause in order to exist. Since the cause of their existence does not lie in themselves, there must be some time at which nothing existed. But if this is so, then nothing could ever have come into existence, and nothing would exist now, for anything that does not exist comes into existence by virtue of the existence of something else. Hence this argument reduces to absurdity. It is therefore necessary to say that not all objects are contingent or merely possible, but there exists something the existence of which is necessary. Now it would seem that necessary objects must have the character of necessity either because they were created by another necessary object, or because they are their own necessity. In order to avoid an infinite regress, we must say that some necessary object (a) is its own necessity, (b) does not derive any element of necessity from another, and (c) causes the necessity of all other necessary objects. Such a necessary object is God.

It should be observed that Aquinas's avoidance of an infinite procession is premised upon the highly probable claim that the universe does not (or previous universes do not) exist from infinity, a claim about which Aquinas is consistently agnostic. But there is no need to depend on the truth of this proposition, for the series Aquinas has in mind applies as much to a hierarchical sequence (in which God is, currently and at all times, causing the necessity of other necessary objects) as to a linear one. The proof itself is premised upon the idea, constant in Aquinas's thinking, that material change (change of substance) can take place only in the physical world: something that materially corrupts or perishes nevertheless leaves behind matter of some kind.[27] His argument can therefore be interpreted in two ways: (1) as stating that not every object can be contingent (i.e. depend for its existence on some further object), and (2) as stating that if all objects were contingent, nothing would exist now. The sense of 'necessity' here is not, again, the Platonic 'idea', for no such abstract entities could *cause* material objects to exist or materially conform to the ideal. Yet neither is necessity located in the substance of material objects (if necessary material objects can be said to exist: perhaps the matter throughout the universe *must* exist, however it is locally distributed or changed). Necessity, if it exists at all, must exist even if the world or human minds never

[27] See Brian Davies, 'Aquinas's Third Way' 82 (2001) *New Blackfriars* 452.

existed. It must therefore exist in some intellectual way, and this can only be in the Divine mind, the only object that can actualize what is necessary.[28]

Among necessary objects might be numbered, for example, propositions of mathematics and (though they cannot be demonstrated) principles of logic. These hold necessarily, and cannot be other than they are. But they exist at all only because of existence as such. Though '2 + 2 = 5' could never have been true, the proposition '2 + 2 = 4' is valid only because existence itself exists. In this way, God can be said to be the source of the necessity of other necessary objects, objects that could not possibly fail to exist or be other than they are, but which are distinct from the higher-order necessity of God's existence. We cannot ask of such truths (unlike e.g. stars, galaxies, atomic particles) how they could be different than they are, but neither can we use the term 'necessity' in the same way when speaking of such objects and in talking about God's existence. For God's existence is outside of all contingent and necessary sequences. We are, again, reduced to speaking only analogically of God's necessity.

This third argument from material causation depends upon a principle first coherently articulated by Leibniz, often known as the 'principle of sufficient reason': that anything that exists must have a sufficient reason for doing so. The principle has been disputed by many—some Thomists as well as atheists—but if the principle did not hold, the world would be very different from the way it actually is, for we seem to be able to explain the existence of objects on the basis of material causes, and indeed such explanations are the bedrock of the coherence of our experience of the world.[29] Objects do not appear out of nothing, nor disappear without trace. When we see a magic trick performed, even though we may not understand how the trick worked, we know that there must be some explanation that conforms to ordinary experience. We know that we have experienced an illusion, not a genuine alteration of the laws of material causality. Science can describe this world because of its intrinsic *order*. To deny the principle of sufficient reason is to undercut any possibility of rational inquiry.[30] It is to render the apparent ordering and explicability of physical processes entirely illusory. At most, it would render all causal explanations dependent upon unintelligible givens.[31] But we require an explanation of the existence of a contingent sequence, which cannot be based upon (a) nothing, or (b) a further contingent object, for the principle of sufficient reason can only be satisfied if there is some *necessary* cause of that entire sequence, which explains not only the existence of the sequence but also the ongoing existence of all the members of that sequence. We thus arrive at the same conclusion as before.

[28] Adapting from Feser (n 22) 102–103.
[29] For a Thomist denial of the principle of sufficient reason see Grisez (n 14) 71.
[30] See Feser, *Five Proofs* 148–50.
[31] Ibid, 151.

As also before, the necessary term that causes the entire contingent sequence exhibits the attributes normally associated with the Christian God. Such a term would have to be pure actuality and contain no potentialities, since if it did possess potentialities, some prior and outside force would be required in order to combine those potentialities.[32] Such a term must be a *being* and not something inert, for it imparts consciousness to other objects. Since time and space are among the contingent things caused by such a being, that being must exist outside space-time and is thus eternal. Since it contains no potentiality, and thus no privation, and is caused by nothing, that being is perfectly good. Similarly, this being is One and not many: if there are two such necessary objects, they must be distinguished by either one or both possessing some feature that the other does not. Yet such additions render those objects composite. But no composite being can cause its own necessity; hence it is impossible that there could be many necessary beings (in this way), and thus neither can there be many gods.[33] Finally, this being must be omnipotent, since a cause is a kind of power, and God is the material cause of all things.

## VII.5. FOURTH ARGUMENT

The final two of Aquinas's arguments are less impressive than the preceding three—at least they will appear so to one whose tacit metaphysical position holds that science exhausts our knowledge of and ability to explain the world and its processes. But they are nonetheless worth stating. The fourth argument concerns formal causality. As we have already noted, the sense of 'form' here does not conform to Plato's use of that term, for Platonic 'forms' (*eidos*) possess no genuine causal power. In fact, form and matter go together, as the early Church insisted against the Gnostic heresy: confronted by a statue, we see, for example, a man. But we cannot perceive the matter (the stone, marble, steel) without simultaneously seeing its form, its arrangement into the shape that it is; nor can we perceive the form except through the matter, since if we subtract the matter we see nothing.[34] This is perhaps clearest with geometrical objects: one cannot conceive of a triangle without at least picturing one with one's inner eye; in the external world, there are no triangular forms that are not embodied by material objects or at least inferred from the space framed by other material objects. However, the material triangles of experience are, every one of them, imperfect in some way. No building materials or slabs of marble are entirely without blemishes, raised protrusions or pits, at least on a microscopic level, and thus fail to attain the precision and perfection of the geometer's form. But the material triangles or statues can be said to fulfil

[32] Ibid, 159.
[33] Aquinas, *SCG* (n 13) I.42.8.
[34] See Edward Feser, *The Last Superstition* (St Augustine's Press 2010) 57–59.

those abstract forms to some degree, sufficiently in order to be spoken of as statues or triangles. Aquinas talks of these imperfect specimens as having been *caused* by the perfect abstract form. This should not be misunderstood. He is not suggesting that, for example, the perfect triangle of geometry is the cause of some given triangle, rather than the craftsman's hands. Rather, he is pointing out that a purely *material* cause can only account for the state of the matter (e.g. whether it is rough or smooth, hot or cold, etc), whereas the *formal cause* accounts for its being hammered into its particular form. When the artist has in mind a particular artistic object, he or she perceives, with their inward eye, not only formless matter but also the shape, the form, that is to be created, and it is in this sense that there is a formal, as well as a material, cause of objects.

There are other forms besides geometric forms. There is, for example, the form of truth, which is the formal property of certain propositions, and there is the form of goodness, which pertains variously to perfections, acts, beings, substances (such as good wine), and other objects understood as good analogically. These objects too approach or incline away from their formal causes: a proposition can be a near-truth, a mistake or an outright lie; an act can avoid evil but not reach moral perfection, and so on. In the case of persons and other beings, each can approach its characteristic maximal states, their goodness and perfections; thus such beings can be said to have many forms that are either *essential* to them (such as rationality in a human being, speed in a cheetah, etc) or else *accidental* (such as skin colour, tallness, smoothness). But 'form' and 'matter' are abstractions when considered apart, and are both aspects of reality that cannot be separated. And the formal cause of such perfections, goodness etc can be shown to be God.

Forms, as just mentioned, cannot exist alone and without matter. The cause of a human person is the cause of (a) its characteristic matter, blood cells, skin, bone, muscle, and so on, and (b) its form, its capacity to reason, understand, etc. 'Rationality', the essential formal property of human beings, is an abstraction from the rationality of human persons, the capacity that all human beings possess and exercise. A human being cannot be *caused* without (a), or without (b). Moreover, in a human being, (a) cannot exist without (b) nor (b) without (a). Neither a human being nor any other contingent object can be brought into being only through a material cause, without its formal cause, nor a formal cause without its material cause. Hence, if the argument from material causality (argument three) is accepted, then so must the present argument, the argument from formal causality.

We have been speaking about 'rationality' as the characteristic form of a human being. But it would be more correct to speak of the 'rational soul' (*anima*). Building on Aquinas, Suarez speaks in this context of 'mixed objects', objects brought into being partly through material causality (the role of procreation and gestation in the creation of a child), and partly through God's intervention (the creation of a soul) as formal cause.[35] The constant teaching of the Church has therefore been that the soul comes into being with the human body, at conception, and is only severed from the body at death. The *anima* of plants—that which animates them—and of animals is, on the other hand, traditionally held to become extinguished upon the death of the corporeal body. Mention was made above of 'essential cause', in the sense that rationality is the essential (formal) cause of the human being *as* a human being, as opposed to accidents such as eye-colour, height, and so forth. This was to avoid the term 'essence', or to invoke the doctrine of 'essentialism', which modern philosophers regard as discredited. The avoidance of the term was necessary in order to allow the argument to proceed without being abandoned at that point due to instant scepticism about the argument's intellectual commitments. But the time has now come to face the issue directly.

There is nothing very mysterious about the notion of an essence; indeed our everyday usage, in which we call things essential ('it is essential to complete the task on time'; 'he is essentially wrong about that') seems inescapably wedded to the distinction between essence and accident. An 'essence' is not a thing, separate from an object's essential properties, but is a shorter way of referring to those properties when there is wide agreement on what they are. I adverted above to this distinction, in saying that rationality is an essential property of human beings, whereas properties such as tallness, colour of skin or hair, eye-colour, and so forth are accidental properties: (formal) properties that a person has contingently rather than necessarily. The 'essence' of what it is to be human, that is, the essential properties that make human beings the creatures they are, as a species, are what divide us from other identifiable animals and inert substances, each of which is again determined according to its relevant essential characteristics, such as the fact that gold is the element with the atomic number 79. Rationality is of course not the only essential trait of human beings, but it has the advantage of being unique to humans by contrast with traits such as bipedal locomotion, tool-use, and so forth. Aristotelian metaphysics therefore distinguishes, in relation to any given object, (a) its essence, or essential characteristics; (b) its properties, those things that are proper to the object, such as a questioning mind in humans; (c) its accidents, that is, accidental qualities of the object, such as blue eyes; and (d) its relations, such that, for example, Plato was the teacher of Aristotle.[36] The loss of any one of these categories results in an incomplete description of the object in question. Most especially, it is necessary to distinguish between an object's *existence* and its *essence*: in other words, the fact *that it is* should not be confused with the fact of *what it is*. It is a necessary truth that, of any human being, they have the capacity of rationality; but *that* any given human exists is a contingent fact. The existence of a contingent object is distinct from *what* makes it the kind of thing it is.[37] If we wanted to eradicate

[35] See Suarez, *DM* (n 7) XXIX.2.13.
[36] See Feser (n 34) 193.
[37] Feser (n 22) 123.

'essentialism' from our intellectual life (though not our experienced reality), we would need to give up not only all permutations of talk of 'essentials', 'essentially', etc, but much of the scope and power of our explanations of the nature of things around us, and ourselves.

Assuming now that it is safe to proceed with the argument, with its appeal to essences, we can begin to elaborate on the idea of God as ultimate formal cause. For we require an explanation of how the ordinary formal causes (some of which are essential) are themselves caused, and how such forms are retained and present at any given moment. We need, that is, an account of the ultimate formal cause. God is the only being for whom essence and existence are one: that is to say, our understanding of *what* God is, is identical with understanding *that* He is: God is pure essence and actuality.[38] Since there are forms in the world, of whom God is the ultimate formal cause, of truth, goodness and perfection, it follows that God is perfectly good, perfectly true, and a perfect being, lacking nothing. Therefore God is all-powerful, for He lacks no power. Therefore He is also omniscient, for He lacks no knowledge of states-of-affairs. There is likewise no beginning or end in God, or else He would at one time or another lack existence, or possess fewer traits and thus unrealized potentialities, and He is thus eternal. And such traits are hallmarks of the Christian God, as known by and revealed to human beings.

## VII.6. FIFTH ARGUMENT

The fifth argument of Aquinas pertains to 'final causation', that is, with the ends of various objects. It runs roughly as follows. All of nature seems to be end-directed, with each kind of thing existing in pursuit of its proper end. Such an end is a cause of the object's actions, motion or being, and the object's essence can be said to rest in, participate in, or incline towards its end (e.g. as a plant literally inclines towards the sun in order to engage in photosynthesis). Objects participate in their ends not inconstantly or through mere chance, but regularly and deliberately (*ex intentione*).[39] But there is a difference in the way in which different objects pursue or attain their end: some do so intelligently and with deliberation; others not with rational deliberation but with purpose and intelligence; still others without intelligence but by the power of their nature (as with the case of planets and heavenly bodies). Conscious striving is thus only one way in which objects can participate in an end. Those objects that lack intellectual knowledge of their proper end must be said to be moved by another object that possesses intelligence and is capable of moving those objects towards their end, or in fulfilment of it. Thus a being of

[38] Aquinas, *SCG* (n 13) I.22.7.
[39] Aquinas, *ST* (n 9) I.2.3c.

intellect must be held to exist by which all natural objects are directed to their end, and this being is God.[40]

This passage in the *Summa Theologiae* is perhaps the source of Hart's dismissal as 'somewhat comic' the idea that a stone falling to the ground is realizing some end,[41] and it is almost certainly one source of the much-derided 'argument from design' that forms the focus of the majority of atheistic critiques of religious belief. Now, neither Aquinas nor (so far as I am aware) any other natural law theorist, would equate a stone's falling to Earth with its proper end, unless by (a somewhat lame) analogy with the ends of living things or human artefacts. But they, and we, would presumably want to rule out, as not being *natural* properties of the stone, the stone's singing, turning into a dog, or moving under its own locomotion: hence ruling out any ends of this kind as ends of the stone (for it has none). More generally, Aquinas, in agreement with other medieval philosophers, regards the relationship of an object to an end as consisting in 'dispositions' to the end. An object possesses a number of developmental potentialities, some of which realize the full actualization of the object's natural properties, and some of which (in a non-moral sense) corrupt or distort the object's actualization.[42] Aquinas (as we have already seen) states that there are three types of developmental properties: vegetative (mere living), animal, and rational.[43] But it is perfectly obvious that a stone possesses none of these developmental properties: it possesses no developmental properties at all: it is inert, incapable of development. (The stonemason 'develops' the stone into a brick only in a highly colloquial and misleading sense, if any sense can be made of this at all.) It is only correct to say that stones and other inert objects are subject to chemical and physical laws, or human or animal interventions, that are external to the object, and thus not among *its* developmental capacities. Hart's comment therefore illustrates his own ignorance of Scholastic metaphysics, a metaphysics that is entirely reasonable and sensible. Hart's misguided comment therefore in no way impugns the fifth argument advanced by Aquinas.

These remarks, it is hoped, go some way towards correcting the view that the argument from final causation is 'somewhat comic'. Indeed the argument from final causation underpins the theory of natural law in the following way. The human being is a rational animal. The proper end of reason is the pursuit and, where possible, attainment of truth, and the avoidance of error, mistake, confusion, superstition. Thus the final end of reason, and the possibility of attaining it, indicate that

[40] See Aquinas, *SCG* (n 13) III.135.24–25.

[41] HLA Hart, *The Concept of Law* (3rd edn OUP 2012) 189–90.

[42] One might distinguish 'developmental potentialities' in the focal sense from 'developmental potentialities' in a secondary sense: the latter case is the sheer possibility of a living thing's properties to 'develop' into malignant forms which prevent the thing's capacities from achieving completion (development in the focal sense). A stone, or any inanimate object, possesses no innate developmental processes and thus no 'end' or 'complete' state irrespective of what might happen to it so that it is changed by being subject to external forces.

[43] Aquinas, *ST* (n 9) I-II.94.2c.

there is a natural law to seek truth and to avoid error, falsity, and the like.[44] Natural law represents a special way in which only human beings participate in eternal law; other creatures and unconscious living things participate in eternal law in another way.[45] In general and (again) analogical terms, it is the stirrings of natural appetite that incline each being to its proper end. But even if the notion of ends can be rescued from the scepticism of Hart and others, what is to be said about the powerful arguments against intelligent design?

In fact by the most natural reading of Aquinas's fifth argument, he is not offering an intelligent design argument at all. The argument is based on final cause, that is to say, a metaphysical theory of teleology, and a teleological theory does not of itself support an argument for intelligent design. Those who suppose that Aquinas is offering such an argument are perhaps led to do so by a sentence in the most widely available translation of the *Summa Theologiae* (the Dominican Fathers edition) which says that 'natural bodies' are directed to their proper end 'not fortuitously but designedly'. But the most natural reading of the phrase '*ex intentione*' is not that of design but of tendency or inclination, as the flower inclines towards the sunlight. The proposition that *all things* incline to their proper ends makes no reference to the idea that the universe as a whole exhibits purposeful design. This is for two reasons: first, a teleological picture of the universe is consistent with the idea that created matter is left by the Creator to find its own place and form according to ordinary physical laws such as that of gravity, and is not in that sense 'directed' in an ongoing way as part of a complex overall design in the manner in which the parts of a watch fit together to form the whole; secondly, and more importantly, the argument from final causation, like the arguments before it, makes no claim about the state or foundations of the universe as a whole, but proceeds only from individual objects, such as a flower or a cheetah or a human person, which cannot be said to incline towards the same end. Indeed, unlike the watch analogy, the argument from final causation is compatible with the fact that ends may conflict. It is not the cow's proper end to become beef for human consumption, any more than it is the end of the fly to become food for a spider (that is why the fly struggles for its life when caught in the web). Neither is it always the case that the lower-order being dies for the sake of the higher: the bite of a venomous snake paralyses and kills the human being. The argument from final causation does not, of course, imply the falsity of the argument from intelligent design (if suitably amended). But neither does it depend upon any such argument. It depends merely upon the insight that, if (for example) human beings act for the sake of an end—to bring some desired state of affairs about—then that end can be said to be a *cause* of such action. It would

[44] Ibid.

[45] Ibid, I-II.91.2c & ad 3; the 'ought' of ontological good in relation to animals or stones is not a *moral* 'ought', since their 'actions' are necessary rather than free.

be immensely difficult to account for the intelligibility of, and reasons for, action without such an assumption.

Aquinas's argument refers specifically to natural objects (*res naturales*) and not to intelligent creatures who, to one extent or another, are provident for themselves. We therefore need not ponder the complex case of human beings in relation to final causality. Instead, we can briefly enumerate the attributes that the intelligence directing natural objects must possess if the preceding argument is valid.[46] First, intelligence implies being, not something inert. Second, since this being directs *all things* to their proper end, it can be described as omnipotent and omniscient. Third, it must be a perfect being since it is by itself that it draws all things to their characteristic perfections.[47] Fourth, since it is the final cause of all finite things, the intelligent being must itself be infinite (or else it would form one more finite thing whose existence needs to be explained and caused), and thus also eternal (since time itself is finite).[48] Finally, since 'end' and 'good' are synonymous, the intelligent being who is the source of all ends and which inclines all things to their respective ends, is therefore perfectly good. But, again, the being who possesses all of these attributes is the Christian God.

## VII.7. THE EXISTENCE OF EVIL

All of the preceding arguments can be supplemented by other arguments of a roughly similar kind. For example, one could argue from the relativity of all objects to the existence of a non-relative object which is required to explain them. Since this is not a book on metaphysics or natural theology, I have presented the foregoing arguments only very briefly and in outline. But the conclusions of those arguments raise a question, touched upon in Section VII.3, that must be faced in the present section: that because there is evil in the world, either God is evil or He does not exist. 'Evil' in the first occurrence in this question is not restricted to moral evil, but includes all evils understood as harms, such as disease, death, natural disaster, and so forth. In its second appearance, however, 'evil' in that question refers to moral evil, but few posers of the question investigate the complexities involved in moving from one sense of evil to the other, and we shall not do so here.

The two senses of 'evil' are connected in being privations of what is proper to an object. Disease is a lack of good health, a malfunctioning of organs whose operations have been in some way impaired or qualified. A natural disaster such as an earthquake is a loss of habitat and also of life. Ignorance or mistake is a lack of knowledge. These are obviously natural (i.e. non-moral) evils; but moral evil is a

46 Aquinas, *SCG* (n 13) I.71.4.
47 Ibid, I.28.3.
48 Ibid, I.7.2sc, I.10.1c, I.10.2 ad 3, I.10.4c.

lack of goodness, a perversion of rational intelligence away from its proper and full functioning so that it operates in an impaired way. Anyone who has ever given in to idleness or temptation is aware of this impairment. One *knows* what is good, but chooses not to do it. But evil is, as just mentioned, an impairment of what is *proper* to the object: the lack of wings in a tree is not a privation, but the lack of healthy roots is.[49] It follows that good is an actuality, and evil an unrealized potentiality. This is not to argue that evil is unreal or an illusion: any person who has suffered hurt of any kind, or who has been mistaken about, for example, the loyalty of a friend, or who has been the victim of a crime, has experienced evil. Nor is it possible to rationalize certain evils as goods, for (a) good is seldom regarded under the guise of evil, and (b) human beings lack a sufficiently lofty vantage point from which to assess the ultimate significance of choices and events. But the classification of evil as a privation does not eliminate the question posed at the outset of this section, for we can ask, why does God permit states of affairs of which privation is a part? The question about the existence of evil posed above invites two conclusions: that either God is evil or He does not exist. The second of these conclusions asks whether and how God can exist alongside evil; the first asks whether God is *responsible* for evil.

In answer to the first question, one must again distinguish between natural evil and moral evil. In both cases, it must be said that a world without evil is an impossibility. Just as God cannot make 2 + 2 = 5, neither can He logically obliterate all evil. For the same geological processes that make life possible also cause earthquakes; the same sun that warms and illuminates our planet will also one day devour it, due to the very same nuclear reactions that take place within it, and which cause skin damage and cancers in the here-and-now. The water that floods and destroys habitats is part of the water cycle that sustains all life, and so on. The same physical, chemical, and biological laws that make life possible are the reason for cataclysmic destruction on a planetary scale across the universe. Such laws cannot be suspended or altered by God without unravelling the entire universe as it exists here and now. The case of moral evil is similar and quite well-known: moral evil cannot be eradicated without altogether eliminating free will. But the goodness of free will (in virtue of which human beings are the *imago Dei*) is greater than even the most terrible acts of evil.[50] Such acts of evil, great or small, are directed at other human beings irrespective of whether those persons are themselves good or evil. God cannot redirect such actions without cancelling free will not only in the perpetrators, but in all human beings insofar as they deliberate morally. Hence, bad things happen to good people. Certain goods (such as free will) thus presuppose certain evils (immoral choices). Indeed, the good acts of mercy, compassion, forgiveness, courage, all presuppose an antecedent evil.[51] Furthermore, enduring

[49] See Feser (n 22) 219–221.
[50] See Aquinas, *De Malo* (hereafter *De Mal*) III.1 ad 1–8.
[51] Feser (n 22) 296.

such evils as physical pain is useful in evolutionary terms and in promoting care of vulnerable extremities.[52] This does not turn evils into goods: although the phenomenon of pain can be educative, so that for example one avoids putting one's hand in the fire, the sensation of pain is an evil to be avoided, and indeed must be so in order to perform its function. But as Aquinas remarks, the greatest good does not presuppose, or correlate to, the greatest evil; it in fact implies the least evil.[53] Christians also have two further responses to the existence of evil. The first is that of original sin: it is through human choice that evil—both moral and natural—was brought into the world, not indeed as a *punishment* for sin, but rather a *consequence* of sin. The second is that the evils suffered in this life are utterly outweighed by the goodness of the next life, so that one should prioritize the eternal destiny of the soul rather than the comforts of the body.

These brief remarks are sufficient to demonstrate that evil is compatible with the existence of God; what then of the second question, whether the existence of evil implies that God is *responsible* for evil? The answer must again be no. In the case of what we are calling natural evils (monsoons, earthquakes, famines, etc), such evils are produced by natural laws of matter and energy that must hold true if there is to be anything at all. God does not inflict such calamities upon innocent human beings by any deliberate positive act, but tolerates them as unwanted consequences of sustaining in existence the whole created universe which exists because of those same laws of matter and energy. Natural evils *are* evils; they ought not to be explained away as indifferent brute happenings. They are, or are at least capable of being, contrary to the good of human beings, of animals and of natural objects. But they are not deliberate evils, and they are inevitable: and of what is inevitable, it makes no sense to ask whether it should or should not be. Thus whilst God upholds the laws of matter and energy throughout the universe, and sustains all things in existence, He does not use His agency to bring natural disasters about. God is therefore not responsible for such phenomena. There is again a specifically Christian response to the problem of evil: that perfect good, and perfect rest, can be attained only when in the direct presence of God in the afterlife. The forms of good experienced in the present life cannot come close to the perfect good of God's presence; human experience by nature cannot measure up to that perfect goodness, and must in comparison with the eternal destiny of the soul seem impoverished and inadequate. To speak of privation is therefore not to speak of any *positive* quality imposed on human life, but simply something that defines the human condition.

Thus, God is not responsible for natural evils. The same argument holds true in the case of moral evil. Moral evil, as we have seen, is the result of evil choices and perverted reasoning, and of human agency. God neither enforces those choices nor

[52] See Grisez (n 14) 288–89.
[53] Aquinas, *De Mal* (n 50) III.1 ad 14.

compels such actions; they are radically free and are not determined by any outside agency. Just as one must not blame one person for another's bad actions, neither must God be blamed for the bad actions of human beings. It is true that God causes and sustains free will, but He is not indifferent to the exercises of such will, and further does not leave human beings to themselves to determine what is right and wrong, good and evil. For He gives human beings (1) natural inclinations (desires and aversions) that, when not deflected, incline all persons towards what is genuinely good, and away from what is naturally bad, (2) a potent disposition capable of determining the good from the bad, *synderesis*, and (3) a faculty of practical reason through which the goodness or badness of putative ends may be rightly evaluated. In other words, human beings have access to the natural law, in terms of which they may guide themselves to a knowledge of good and evil. Now it might be objected that one person may *cause* another to commit an evil act, though not in any of the senses of 'cause' outlined in Section VII.2–6 above. A person may, for example, hold a gun to another's head, or seek by ingenious arguments to persuade or tempt another person into sin. Or one may place the person in a situation in which an immoral act seems to be the only way out (e.g. lying to the soldiers at one's door about the location of the family that one is hiding in the house). But it should be clear that God does not cause or tempt towards sin in any of these ways. For again, evil is a privation, a lack of goodness, and the preceding arguments in the present chapter concluded to God's perfect goodness. Moreover, neither participants nor observers of the predicaments just mentioned typically regard God as the source of their temptation to do wrong. They, like we, put the existence of the predicament down to human agency.[54]

Everybody, then, experiences evils both moral and non-moral, startling and mundane, in their everyday lives, without attributing their occurrence to Divine agency. Nor indeed do we always have an explanation as to why the evil is happening to *us*, and it is perhaps natural, if obvious human agency is not apparent, to ascribe the misfortune to God's agency. In this, we resemble the child who resents attending school, but is made to do so by the parent, not understanding why it cannot be absolved of the evil it hates. We also do not understand all evils that befall us. But there is something perverse, even dishonest, in laying the blame for the world's evils at the door of Divine agency, for this is typically an argument advanced by those who do not believe in God, and who disdain all forms of religious belief. So, like the theist, they do not really believe that God is the source of evil. This divests the argument of much of its credibility.

A word ought to be said about religion, however, for it is frequently claimed that religion is a source of many evils in the world: of superstition, false belief (e.g. about faith's ability to heal the body without medical intervention), hatred, oppression of

[54] I ignore for convenience some of the complexities introduced in Aquinas, *De Mal* (n 50) III.2.

women and persecution of homosexuals, bloody wars and conquests, and genital mutilation. There are two things that may be said of this. The first is that the practice of specific religions, including the Christian religion, does not always live up to the message that those religions seek to impart and realize within the world: a message above all of peace and of the eternal destiny of the soul. Both matters, it is true, demand action as well as words—sometimes violent action in pursuit of a just war, such as a war to overthrow a tyrant who is oppressing his people and abolishing religious observance. But—secondly— 'wars of religion' are seldom only about religion, but include matters of security, honour, politics, empire-building, etc. Insofar as 'religion' incorporates a doctrine of just war (and not merely holy war), then it can indeed be said to be a source of evils, for the evils of war are evils indeed, no matter how just the cause. But religions teach, and very many non-religious persons believe, that just wars must be waged *despite* the evil (e.g. loss of life) that is their inevitable result. The evil is not, as it were, religious, but is born out of the circumstances of the world and the human beings who shape them.

As to the charges of superstition and false belief, examples indeed abound. But one must distinguish between true religion and error. Of course each religion regards itself as the one true faith; but if there is indeed a God, only one of those religions can be actually true. The preceding discussion offers some arguments for the defence of the Christian religion (specifically Roman Catholicism); it does so not by impugning the doctrines and beliefs of other religions such as Daoism or Islam, but by reasoning from everyday objects to the existence and properties of God, as He is understood within the Christian religion. Much more indeed needs to be added to those arguments in order to give those doctrines a rigorous defence, but such a labour lies beyond the scope of the present book. But reason is only one source for belief in the Christian God. For we also have revelation: God's direct disclosure to human beings through Biblical texts. To the content and significance of these we now must turn.

## VII.8. THE DIVINITY OF JESUS

The five arguments for the existence of God outlined in Sections VII.2–6 offer reasonable grounds for the conclusion that God exists. The evidence they offer is inductive: we move from what is seen in everyday experience, to the unseen. But because what is unseen, by definition, cannot be perceived by the senses, those arguments leave room for doubt in the minds of those who regard the natural sciences as the only paradigms for knowledge, and for whom any metaphysics must be confined to the metaphysics implied by science. For science does imply certain metaphysical and epistemological commitments: such as an external world, order and regularity in physical, chemical, and biological processes, the ability of the mind to grasp those processes, and the view that scientific explanation is the only valid sort of explanation as regards those processes.[55] But there are in fact other kinds of evidence aside from scientific evidence that can contribute to a demonstration that God exists. There is, for example, historical evidence, witness evidence, and prophetic evidence. In this short section, I will present some of this evidence, to supplement that already offered. Again, such evidence is not likely to convince the hardened atheist, but it does offer further confirmation of the evidence set out in the preceding sections. The evidence I mean to present pertains to the divinity of Jesus. The overwhelming majority of historians of the near-east agree upon the historical existence of Jesus.[56] But they disagree about His divinity.

The first body of evidence relates to the impressive fact of Jesus's fulfilling of prophesies that were made and committed to writing centuries before His birth. Such prophesies are not enigmatic mystical sayings, but are surprisingly specific. These range from a prophesy that the Saviour would be born in Bethlehem,[57] to the specifics of Jesus's Passion, such as that He would be scourged,[58] pierced,[59] that He would suffer without complaint or justifying words,[60] and that despite His many terrible injuries, no bones of His would be broken.[61] It was prophesied that His hands and feet would be pierced,[62] that the soldiers would cast lots for His garments,[63] and that He would be betrayed for thirty pieces of silver.[64] His Resurrection was foretold.[65] Now it is barely conceivable (but conceivable nonetheless) that a person with knowledge of these prophesies could seek to model their life upon them so as to 'fulfil' them. The cost of so doing would be hideous pain and suffering. But it is wholly *inconceivable* that such a person could manoeuvre his enemies into fulfilling their side of the prophesies, for over that he could have no control. Furthermore, the number and specificity of the prophesies make it in the highest degree unlikely that they could be fulfilled by chance. Thus, the fulfilment of the prophesies gives to us a powerful reason to believe in the reality of Christ's divinity, and the truth and sincerity of His teachings. But Jesus prophesied Himself, notably that the Temple in Jerusalem would be destroyed, as indeed it was at the hands of the Romans in 70AD.

The second body of evidence is that of witnesses who knew Christ in person. The Gospels are the written record of an oral tradition passed on by Christ's apostles. What reasons do we have for believing in the truth of their testimony? The first

55 See Feser (n 34) 274.

56 For a survey see Robert Van Voorst, *Jesus Outside the New Testament: An Introduction to the Ancient Evidence* (Eerdmans 2000).

57 Micah 5:2; Jeremiah 31:31; Isaiah 7:14.

58 Isaiah 53:5.

59 Ibid; also Zechariah 12:10.

60 Isaiah 53:7.

61 Psalm 34:20.

62 Ibid 22:16.

63 Ibid 22:18.

64 Zechariah 11:12–13.

65 Isaiah 53:11, 52:13–15.

reason is that each of the Gospels portrays the apostles in a bad light, constantly misunderstanding the nature of Christ's message, and abandoning Him after His arrest. The second is that the apostles do not seek to claim any divine power for themselves, but preach solely about Christ's teachings and Resurrection. Perhaps this second consideration merely shows prudence on the part of the apostles, gaining influence over others by convincing people of an unseen power? But influence to what end? Not to riches or adulation, but rather to persecution. The most compelling evidence of the truth and sincerity of the apostles' testimony is that all but one of them were martyred for their beliefs; even in the face of hideous torture and ordeal, none of them recanted their faith or denied the truth of their teachings. Indeed St Peter, at his own request, was crucified inverted since he felt unworthy to meet the same death as his Lord. Other apostles were variously crucified, burned to death, stoned, sawn in two, or beheaded. This ought to be seen as powerful evidence of the sincerity of their teachings.

It is sometimes thought that the Gospel writers were the *only* witnesses to Christ's ministry and miracles. This is incorrect on two counts. First, the four canonical Gospels are the written record of an oral tradition deriving from witnesses to the events they describe: up to 500 at one time.[66] It stands to reason that a nascent religious movement, not seeking the overthrow of any state, could not gain any traction with only a dozen adherents. But secondly, the argument misunderstands the New Testament which, like the Old Testament, is not one book but a number of books and letters penned by different writers, and must hence be considered (as it is by Biblical scholars) as affording a multiplicity of sources detailing aspects of Christ's ministry, death, and Resurrection. Nor are these the only written sources detailing aspects of Jesus's life. They are the only *canonical* sources, as determined by the Early Church, who ultimately, and over time, discarded others on grounds of their heterodoxy.

The importance of prophesies is that they reveal truths that are not available to philosophical reflection. But there is a further question: if we therefore believe in the divinity of Christ, we must presumably believe that He worked the miracles as attested in the Gospels, most notably His Resurrection; but what attitude should we take to modern miracles, such as miraculous cures or apparitions of the Blessed Mother? No doubt not all of these are genuinely miraculous happenings, and the Church has been rightly exceedingly cautious in confirming the existence of a miracle. But as Germain Grisez observes, if one petitions God to cure the terminal illness of one's child, and the child does indeed recover, both more rapidly and more widely than natural laws of physics and biology can explain, then it is reasonable to believe that one's prayer has been granted.[67] Why then does God not grant all such prayers; why are miracle cures the remote exception to the general course of

[66] I Corinthians 15:6.
[67] Grisez (n 14) 338.

events? The answer must remain conjectural, for we do not have knowledge of the Divine plan. But it seems reasonable that the existence of normal laws of biology and physics would be rendered meaningless if many exceptions or suspensions of them were to occur in everyday life. Furthermore, corruption of the body is an effect of original sin. For both of these reasons, miraculous cures and reversals of bodily corruption must be the rare exception rather than the norm in human affairs. They should be seen as exceptional rewards for deep faith, or for the strengthening of faith in, or conversion of, others.

It can be seen, then, that the scriptural disclosures of Christ's divinity are not a matter of faith only, but instead of faith informed by rational reflection upon the circumstances of the texts, and of the reliability of the writers and witnesses, and those who acted to spread Christ's message in the first century AD. From these considerations, we can conclude that the miracles ascribed to Jesus in the Gospels, and in particular the Resurrection, are likely to be authentic.

## VII.9. NATURAL LAW, ETERNAL LAW, AND DIVINE LAW

The present chapter's discussion has been necessary in order to bring completeness to natural law ethics. For natural law, as remarked above, is the rational creature's participation in eternal law, and eternal law encompasses God's divine plan for all things. It is correct to speak of eternal *law*, for God's governance (as can be inferred from His knowable characteristics) has the necessary form of law: by it and through it all creatures are orientated towards their proper end. A few remarks are however necessary on the relationship between the natural law and divine law. It is usual to observe that many of the truths of the divine law can be arrived at, independently, by natural law, that is, by the light of ordinary practical reason. The injunction not to murder is an obvious example of this kind, as is the prohibition on theft. But there are some matters for which unaided practical reason is insufficient, such as the injunction against coveting another's wife or husband, which, on the basis of reason alone, we might not have considered to be wrong unless acted upon. Similarly, practical reason alone is unlikely to have come up with the demand to love one's enemies, a moral excellence that can be understood only through the possession of Christian love (*caritas*) which infuses and raises to a new register the ordinary moral virtues. The discussion of the present chapter, then, brings to its culmination the long exploration of ethics in Chapters II–VI.

It is worth observing, however, that the Gospel teachings do not abolish the findings of ordinary practical reasoning. Practical reason is capable of discovering moral truths about the human person and the human condition that remain in force. Similarly, practical reason offers its own grounds for obedience to moral norms which do not make reference to the will of God or to the so-called theological virtues of faith, hope and charity. In fact, at no point did the discussion of the present chapter advert to God's will. But the attributes of God, which reason can discover (Section VII.2), provide an additional dimension, though not additional force, to our ordinary moral precepts. Christians do not obey such precepts solely *because* it is the will of the Father that they do so, or to avoid eternal damnation. They do so because God *is* love, and the heavenly experience of love of blessed souls is prefigured in the love of neighbour and of enemies in the present life. It is, in other words (or at least ought to be), due to a love of the good that people act well, and not for reasons of prudence or material gain; and God as the ultimate good is the highest end for which human beings ought to strive.

Jonathan Crowe nevertheless wonders whether the image of God's agency as 'static' (in works such as Finnis's) should not be replaced with an image of His agency as evolving over time. Thus different laws were given to the Israelites than to other peoples, and thus we might see natural law as evolving over time, with certain precepts belonging to different eras.[68] But the evidence does not bear this out. The Levitical laws were indeed given to the chosen people, but they were almost entirely ceremonial rather than moral. And the Decalogue, which is moral, was clearly applicable not only to one people but to all peoples, and condemned forms of behaviour not only of the present and future, but which held in any case to all persons and in all eras: this is why we can condemn Cain's murder of Abel, not excusing it as happening at a time when murders were not immoral.[69] Similarly exhibiting the timeless quality of natural law, Jesus observes that He comes to uphold the law, not to abolish it.[70] No passage of the Bible supports Crowe's position. Nor do the arguments of the present chapter: as a perfectly good, omnipotent being who lacks nothing and is qualified by nothing, God's agency cannot be regarded as evolving over time.

The present chapter sets out the main arguments for belief in God, in particular the God of Christianity and of the Bible. It does not purport to defend those arguments against the many challenges that are thrown at them by philosophers and scientists, both ancient and modern. To do so would require a substantial volume by itself. The aim in presenting those arguments was simply to set out the grounds on which a substantial defence of Christian theism, and thus a further ground of natural law ethics, can be undertaken.[71]

This ends the second part of this work. The third part is devoted to matters more strictly of jurisprudence and law, to which we now turn.

[68] Jonathan Crowe, *Natural Law & the Nature of Law* (CUP 2019) 244–45.

[69] See Genesis 4:1–12.

[70] Matt 5:27.

[71] For an interesting alternative approach to the themes of this chapter see Yujin Nagasawa, 'A New Defence of Anselmian Theism' 58 (2008) *Philosophical Quarterly* 577. For one of the great debates concerning the existence of God (not pursued here) see Alvin Plantinga, *Does God Have a Nature?* (Marquette University Press 1980) and most recently *Knowledge and Christian Belief* (Eerdmans 2015).

# PART THREE

# VIII
# LEGAL AUTHORITY, POLITICAL AUTHORITY, AND MORAL AUTHORITY

## VIII.1. NATURE, POWER, AND AUTHORITY

The next two chapters discuss the same subject from opposite ends. The first concerns authority, specifically the authority of the law; the second deals with obligation, or, as I prefer to call it, *commitment* (see Section IX.1). The subject also concerns matters such as the rule of law and of obedience to unjust laws, which will be considered separately (see Section X.3 & XI). Three types of authority fall to be discussed: legal authority, political authority, and moral authority. Each of these kinds of authority depends to some extent on the other two, since for example political authority can scarcely exist without control of lawmaking processes, and cannot subsist without moral authority, but legal authority is impossible without political authority (control over governmental organs of state), which is mere tyranny except for the possession of moral authority, but moral authority is a mere abstraction unless grounded in legal and political authority. At the same time, these kinds of authority have a degree of self-standing, for the authority of law (the authority of past legal decisions and customs) is not invariably traceable to past political authority, and political authority can be manifested, at least in the short term, without the possession of moral authority. Nevertheless, one may posit a relationship of priority between these types of authority, one that is based on practical priority or necessity: we can assert the practical priority of political authority over legal authority, and both legal and political authority are ultimately explained by (but historically prior to) moral authority, or its semblance: for there to be moral authority there must first be authority. To talk in these terms is to talk of logical priority.

It is necessary at this point to speak briefly about power. Power is distinct from authority, and can certainly be exercised without the presence of authority of the kinds mentioned above, especially moral authority. Power comes in various forms: political power, managerial power, physical power, the power to set and teach a syllabus, and so on. Power is inherent in society and in human relationships. Contrary to the efforts of political philosophers such as Hobbes and Locke to ground power and authority in an originary agreement, power within society has

*Natural Law and Modern Society*. Sean Coyle, Oxford University Press. © Sean Coyle 2023.
DOI: 10.1093/oso/9780192886996.003.0008

no origin, no beginning. The strong possess a 'natural' power over the weak; there is even a dynamic of power between close friends: the power to upset one's friend, to induce emotional suffering, to please, and so forth. The question for political philosophy is not where or how such power originates (for it does not); it is rather how and in what manner it is, or should be, harnessed for political purposes. As the example of friendship shows, there can exist power without the authority to wield it.[1] But there can be no authority without power, for authority is the *socially recognized* power to create and enforce laws, or to make and carry out managerial decisions, or to determine limits for one's child's behaviour, for example. This element of recognition (for no authority can exist if unrecognized) has traditionally been associated with the idea that the ultimate authority within the state rests not with a sovereign power, nor with the forces of law and order, but with the people as a whole, so that a breach of the limits within which that authority is recognized brings into existence a right of rebellion against that sovereign power.[2] But this is a mistake, for authority is not delegated by the people to the sovereign power, for the mode of authority possessed by persons, even considered as a unified multitude, was never political in nature. It was necessary for Grotius therefore to remind the political philosophers of his day that human beings do not, as a matter of natural law, possess political authority over one another's bodies, actions, and what naturally belongs to them *suum ius*.[3]

As there is strictly speaking no 'origin' of political power in human societies, it is impossible to trace present political authority to an ultimate source, nor to state exactly in what way political authority came about. But one could plausibly point to crude forms of political power as an evolution from basic forms of managerial or even financial power, more or less organized, which exist in any human society worthy of the name. Such forms of managerial power may include organized military power, but need not do so: tribal societies for example may venerate tribal elders, a kind of status-authority. But the general fact remains: just as power is inherent within human societies, so too is a somewhat uneven *distribution* of power, and it is this unevenness from which political power and authority grows. For a great many things in society have to be *organized*, and such organization cannot be effectively left to the ad hoc actions of individuals who deal with one another. Such matters include the most basic issues a society faces (basic both in complexity and in importance): recognition and protection of property, suppression and punishment of aggression, creation of units of exchange, responsiveness to

[1] See Joseph Raz, 'Authority and Justification' 14 (1985) *Philosophy & Public Affairs* 4; see also Adriana Placani, 'Jospeh Raz's Service Conception and the Limits of Knowability' 34 (2021) *Ratio Juris* 208–13; Hillary Nye, 'Finnis's Divided View of Law: Problems for Adjudicative Theory' 11 (2020) *Jurisprudence* 503.

[2] See e.g. Lee Ward, *The Politics of Liberty in England and Revolutionary America* (CUP 2004).

[3] Grotius, *De Iurae Praedae Commentarius* [1604] § 19; Grotius, *De Iure Belli ac Pacis* (hereafter *DIBP*) II.1.2.1, II.5.23.1.

natural disasters (famines, hurricanes, crop failures), and defence against outside attackers, to name only a few. Necessity is indeed the mother of invention when such issues arise. But, to repeat, the 'invention' of offices of power is not a matter of deliberate creation; instead, the recognition of authority takes place gradually and in retrospect once individual persons or groups have begun exercising that authority, normally (though not inevitably) for the public good.[4]

A consequence of this is that power and authority are in some sense *natural* to human communities, and may thus be said to form part of the natural human condition. Aristotle, for example, famously recognized that the human being 'is a political [not merely social] animal'[5] and of those in authority as great benefactors, that is, advancing and securing human flourishing, which is what it is in virtue of the reality of the human being as a political animal. Again, not all human communities are 'political' in this sense: a small prayer-group, devotional community, social club or academic organization, is not a political community, even if they are prone to 'office politics'. Thus when Aristotle speaks of human communities as inherently political, he has in mind what he elsewhere calls 'complete community', in modern terms the nation-state. But the description is also easily applicable to smaller political communities within the nation-state, so that there is such a thing as local government, the priorities of which may or may not conform to those of 'complete community'. (Indeed Aristotle's *polis* resembled more a city-state than any modern conception of national government.) Two factors seem to distinguish political communities in the relevant sense from other types of organization. First, the members of a political community possess many and varied (and sometimes opposing) interests, and are not all striving to advance some finite and particular end such as the flourishing of an academic department. But secondly, the members of a political community do not in any proper sense *consent* to a constitution or set of rules that govern the community in which they live. An account of authority must therefore proceed without the assumption of consent. Similarly, the possession of moral authority cannot be traced to any original transaction or originary act, but must derive from a set of moral norms that become apparent only after authority has been established. Even the history of authority within some state can be relevant to its ongoing warrant only if moral weight is accorded to past practice.

Political authority, then, is an evolution from the practice of political power (this sort of power being distinguishable from other forms of power by reference to its purpose in governing a political community, in the sense just outlined).[6] Its

[4] Cf Mark C Murphy, *Natural Law in Jurisprudence & Politics* (CUP 2006, hereafter *NLJP*) 92, arguing that a natural law theory of political authority requires the assistance of consent theory. For a different account see Anna Stiltz, *Liberal Loyalty: Freedom, Obligation & the State* (Princeton University Press) 2009) 27–50.

[5] *Politics* I.1.1253a. See also Andres Rosler, *Political Authority and Obligation in Aristotle* (OUP 2005) ch 1.

[6] This may perhaps be regarded as a prior term in the argument of Finnis that political authority is necessary in the face of no unanimity: see John Finnis, *Natural Law & Natural Rights* (2nd edn OUP

inherent purpose is, as Aquinas said, the promotion of justice and the common good: in other words, it is to take a situation in which relationships of power exist between the various members of the community, relationships that arise due to certain inequalities (such as inequality of wealth or physical strength), and to orientate them by reference to norms of justice. Recognition of this purpose does not, of course, obscure the fact that political authority can be exercised for immoral or repressive ends. But a regime possesses *moral* authority to the extent that it aims to protect and promote justice and the common good. The question of moral authority raises many issues to be explored later. But it is worth observing that broad disagreement persists in relation to the range of power dynamics which are to be reorientated to conform to justice. In particular, questions arise as to whether the state's approach to the distribution of wealth should be *laissez fare*, for example, or as to the existence and level of state benefits to those who are sick, unemployed, or with caring responsibilities. To speak of the state's moral authority is, then, to speak of the attainment of a threshold: the avoidance of repression, commitment to social justice, observance of human rights, and the fulfilment of certain basic needs. But we must return to these questions in due course.

This exceedingly schematic account of authority perhaps allows us to isolate for the purposes of analysis the three kinds of authority previously mentioned: legal authority, political authority, and moral authority. These divisions are artificial, in seeking to separate that which cannot be truly separated. In particular, the focal meaning of authority is a moral one. But there is value in attempting to subject each of these kinds of authority to scrutiny, as far as possible, in isolation. The logical place to begin is with the subject of political authority, and then to move to consider the particular kind of political authority that we call legal authority. This is not to suggest that political authority as such always establishes itself or becomes viable prior to the establishment of legal authority, for it may be that certain kinds of primitive political authority are at the same time primitive legal forms. But the distinction allows us to observe in modern, developed societies a distinction between, for example, questions or policy manoeuvres in Parliament from acts of legislation or decisions of the courts (the latter of which may frustrate the ambitions of the former). Lastly it will be necessary to examine the phenomenon of moral authority, and raise some of the issues attendant upon it.

## VIII.2. POLITICAL AUTHORITY

Power is either organized or disorganized within a community; there is, as we have seen, no such thing as the origin of power. Distinctively political power arises from

2011, hereafter *NLNR*) IX.1; George Duke, 'Finnis on the Authority of Law and the Common Good' 19 (2013) *Legal Theory* 47.

those acts in which one person, or group of persons, seeks to order the activities of others for some purpose that is in some sense desirable or good. Such acts are classifiable as 'political' even if the good to be secured is that of the governor rather than the governed. But this broad notion of political power, it should be mentioned straightaway, does not illuminate fully the central or 'focal' meaning of the concept, which (like the other concepts examined in this book) are depicted by reference to the flourishing or complete sense of the term. Thus, when Suarez asks what justifies (and thus grounds) the ability of certain persons to exercise authority over others, his answer is rooted in Aristotle's *Politics* (I.5.1254b), and in Aquinas's *De Regimine Principum* I.1: it is that the human being is a social animal but cannot achieve the state required for proper human development without temporal rules and judges.[7] But he is clear that human governance does not arise 'from nature' (though it is not contrary to nature), but results from the inability, due to human weakness and corruptibility, of human beings to establish such conditions spontaneously and in good order.[8] Hence, the ruler derives his or her power from the community, not in the sense of a Hobbesian transfer of right from governed to governor, but from the fact that such governance is *required* by human societies and is in this sense a *natural* or essential feature of any human society.[9]

Political governance is essentially *organized* power within a community. It is organized in the sense of attaining a high level of coherence in the use of power, and in seeking to organize in various ways the lives and actions of members of the community. In this sense, a governing regime can be classified according to the purpose that animates its use of power for organization. Totalitarian societies are characterized by excessive pursuit of organization for purposes other than the self-constitution of individuals and groups. Liberal societies typically use organization for the purpose of allowing and encouraging responsible self-constitution. But the ambition and purpose of all forms of government is to organize, to one extent or another. One particular mode of organization, upon which much focus rests in modern political philosophy, is that of coordination.[10] It is said frequently that the main purpose of authority is to resolve coordination problems that exist between members of a community.[11] Examples of coordination problems are indeed not difficult to find: laws governing road traffic present an obvious case in point. But it is not clear that even a majority of authoritative actions relate to the resolution of

[7] Suarez, *De Legibus* (hereafter *DL*) III.1.3–4. The *Regimine* is of disputed authorship, but the first part, from which this proposition is drawn, is reliably attributed to Aquinas. See also *Compendium of the Social Teaching of the Catholic Church* (hereafter *Compendium*) § 168.

[8] Suarez, *DL* (n 7) III.4.1 & III.1.12.

[9] Ibid, III.4.2.

[10] See e.g. John Finnis, *Collected Essays of John Finnis* (OUP 2011, hereafter *CEJF*) IV 66; Leslie Green, 'Authority and Convention' 35 (1985) *Philosophical Quarterly* 340–42; Joseph Raz, 'Facing Up: A Reply' 62 (1989) *Southern California Law Review* 1153; Joseph Raz, *Between Authority and Interpretation* (OUP 2009) 341–42, 346–47, 383–86; Murphy, *NLJP* (n 4) 122; Jonathan Crowe, *Natural Law & the Nature of Law* (CUP 2019, hereafter *NLNL*) 188.

[11] See e.g. *Compendium* (n 7) § 394.

such problems. Command of military forces, which of course involves the coordination of materials and effort, does not have coordination as its end, for the end of military action is defence of the realm or pursuit of foreign interests. Equally, the laws of contract or of tort are not ordered first and foremost to coordination, but seek to uphold standards of justice. The concepts employed by the criminal lawyer are both apparently and substantially concerned with moral precepts rather than with coordination. Regulation of the economy has as its principal aim the stimulation of growth and the avoidance of force or fraud. Even property law, which surely involves the coordination of all individuals in a community with respect to conceptions of ownership and trespass, is not orientated to coordination as a primary end, but rather to the maintenance of at least a minimal morality with respect to a fundamental resource. Can all of these activities really be understood as efforts to resolve coordination problems? It is not clear that they even amount to problems of coordination, as opposed (for example) to problems of the finitude of human foresight, of the propensity to act either immorally or without due consideration of the rights of others, or the tendency of free markets towards monopoly or exploitation. The need for coordination is thus typically either a sub-problem or side-effect of problems of a different nature (see further Section X.2.)

Murphy suggests that the central case of 'law' (that is backed by decisive reasons for action) cannot be explained by reference to coordination alone.[12] Yet there are a great many instances in which action can be decisive *only* when it coordinates with other actions. One cannot unilaterally bring about the great common goods of peace and justice. One cannot enhance the common good by pressing ahead with a radical proposal to which no one else assents. Furthermore, it is surely a hallmark of genuinely good acts that they harmonize or coordinate with those of others. The central aim of law is not coordination, but neither is it 'decisive reasons for action': it is, as mentioned in the preceding paragraph, the introduction of morality into areas of public and private life. Such laws are not decisive descriptively, but nor is it clear that they are invariably decisive normatively: the final arbiter of my actions is (or ought to be) my conscience. To suggest that law is backed by such reasons is to articulate a legal vision that is uncomfortably Hobbesian: see the long endnote to Section I.2.

I made reference above to the central or focal meaning of authority. But is there such a meaning, that is extractable from cultural or historical conditions? For, as Raz asserts, *our* concept of authority is distinguishable from its historical ancestors, and indeed might itself undergo change.[13] One might, for example, venture to suggest that structures of authority among early humans differ significantly from those characteristic of a mature and modern society, or that the exercise of authority in

[12] Murphy, *NLJP* (n 4) 111. See also George Duke, 'The Weak Natural Law Thesis and the Common Good' 35 (2016) *Law & Philosophy* 490; see also Duke (n 6) 53.

[13] Raz (n 10) 133. See also Leslie Green, *The Authority of the State* (OUP 1988).

medieval times, when news travelled slowly and mechanisms for effective control of large populations did not exist, must be different from those of a technologically advanced society. But the very recognition of such structures as structures *of authority* depends upon their relationship to some central, stable concept to which they owe some 'family resemblance'. Thus an 'ancestor' concept cannot be quite unlike our own if it is to be recognizable as a concept of authority: perhaps the social structures of early humanity are not those of authority at all? If, as I am suggesting, the central meaning of authority is a moral one, it follows that historical conceptions of authority are more or less valid depending upon their conformity to a set of universal moral norms, which have yet to be spelled out, but which have a special relationship to justice and common good (see Sections VIII.4–5).

When discussing the character of political authority, it is necessary to bear in mind the warning in Section VIII.1 above, that such authority cannot be traced to any originary act. It is true that certain passages in natural law writings seem to suggest or suppose the existence of such an act: Grotius, for example, famously asserts that:

> Just as, in fact, there are many ways of living, one being better than another, and out of so many ways of living each is free to select that which he prefers, so also a people can select the form of government which it wishes; and the extent of its legal right in the matter is not to be measured by the superior excellence of this or that form of government, in regard to which different persons hold different views, but by its free choice.[14]

But what Grotius is proposing here is an analogy with personal choice, such that the subject of the analogy (authority of the state) exists only in an imperfect correspondence to its object, personal choice. This much is made clear by the fact that this sentence must be read in the context of Grotius's immediately preceding remark that 'the opinion of those must be rejected who hold that everywhere and without exception sovereignty resides in the people, so that it is permissible for the people to restrain and punish kings whenever they make a bad use of their power.'[15]

Rejection of the doctrine that political authority emerges from an originary act or consensus of the people may seem to invite the conclusion that such authority can only be seized and (through some process of political alchemy) attain legitimacy at a later stage of social development: that might, at least in the beginning, makes right. Something of the sort appears, at least, to be Finnis's position, in which 'raw power plays a pivotal role in both the right to rule and the duty to govern ... [even if] only in a context in which it is actually orientated toward the common good and in which all the fundamental goods, such as life and religion,

[14] Grotius, *DIBP* (n 3) I.3.8.2.
[15] Ibid, I.3.8.1.

are properly respected.'[16] Now, there are certainly kinds of what we might call pre-political power that seem to be based on might: such as the power of the strong over the weak, and the rich over the lives of the poor. But many of the human acts which manifest power over others, prior to the evolution of governmental organs, are not instances of 'raw power'; they are instead forms of managerial power, such as one finds in employment relationships, contracts for services, household arrangements, and proto-political structures of authority beyond the household (perhaps the matriarch of an extended family). They include, for example, forms of military discipline. Such forms of power are intrinsic to the human condition. They reflect the social/political nature of human beings by their centrality to the secure flourishing of those beings. Political power in the proper sense does not replace such proto-political forms of power, but rather evolves from them. The legitimacy or moral standing of present political authority does not depend upon its genesis, however, but upon its standing conformity to and ongoing embodiment of norms of morality and justice. But this is to anticipate questions to be discussed further below. It is worth observing, however, that what I have been calling 'proto-political' forms of power are also made intelligible by their orientation to the promotion, creation, or defence of human goods; and they are rightly judged as degenerate, evil, and secondary when they lead away from, extinguish or render more vulnerable those same goods. Thus for example, a father can beat his children, or a military commander can order soldiers to fight an unjust war, or to engage in atrocities.

A word ought to be said about the relationship of authority to autonomy, for many political philosophers of the present day, not only anarchists, feel troubled by the fact that authority seems to diminish the scope for autonomy. (Such philosophers frequently call upon Kant, whose conception of the political state places autonomy at the centre, although Kant himself believed that human beings are not truly autonomous.)[17] But this view rests upon a fundamental mistake: the forms of proto-political power, and the political forms of power that flow from them, in fact create and enhance spheres of personal autonomy that, but for them, would either not exist or would exist only in a severely diminished form. Hobbes's *Leviathan* is often taken as a theory that shows how the advent of political power considerably restricts the scope of personal autonomy (the 'right of nature'); but it performs this illusion only by assuming that individuals in the 'natural condition' (prior to the founding of the political state) are already capable of reflecting philosophically and politically about their situation and its dreadful limits and disadvantages. In fact (and as the *Leviathan*'s subtext hints), it is through the structures of power and authority from which political power is derived that autonomy is increased: through, for example, education both within the family and outside, through the division of labour that civilization makes possible, and through the creation of markets and

[16] Leslie Green, 'The Duty to Govern' 13 (2007) *Legal Theory* 169 & 171.

[17] See Sean Coyle, *Dimensions of Politics and English Jurisprudence* (CUP 2013) ch 6.

social conventions, recognition of property, and so forth. An educated person is, typically, more capable of making enlightened decisions, and has many more options, than one who has never been educated. The whole range of civilizing influences made possible by political authority creates and enhances the scope of personal autonomy and (where exercised benevolently) limits autonomy only where it is necessary in order to secure autonomy, or where important common goods are at stake. Of course, where political authority is misused, it can considerably diminish personal autonomy, by stripping away the structures and forms of civil society. But while anarchists and others rightly fear such developments, they are wrong to suggest that the limitation of personal autonomy is the effect, still less the goal, of all political authority.[18]

There is another way in which the anarchist impulse is mistaken. For the assumption that restriction of personal autonomy is in itself an evil, is fallacious. The decision whether an enemy lives or dies ought not to be made by the person who has been wronged. The decision whether and how to compensate the victim of an accident is rightly made by someone other than the perpetrator of the accident. In general, any determination of the requirements of justice should not be decided by the victim or the perpetrator of the relevant harm. This principle can be extended: it is *good* for a parent to make the decision to educate, and/or provide for the education of, their children. It is right that such decisions are made in the child's own interests, and not influenced by the child's immediate preferences. One's autonomy must—and should—often give way to other values, either in one's own interest or in that of another, or of the community. No society has a perfect record is these regards, but this fact should not be taken as suggesting that there is something inherently wrong with or bad about political authority. Essentially the same argument can be invoked in order to answer the question of how broad the scope of political authority should be: are there any limits in principle beyond which authority cannot go; any areas of life to which it should not be made to apply? Raz makes the following argument:

> People differ in their knowledge, skills, strength of character and understanding. Since the main argument for authority depends on such factors it is impossible to generalize and indicate an area of government regulation which is better left to individuals. But regarding every person there are several such areas.[19]

[18] For a thesis of 'political anarchism' (vs philosophical anarchism) see Bruno Leipold, 'Political Anarchism and Raz's Theory of Authority' 21 (2015) *Res Publica* 309. It seems to me that philosophical anarchists (and by extension more extreme forms) fail to understand that power is always a facet of human dealings; that political institutions *regulate* power across the community in the sense of smoothing out inconsistencies in, and abuses of, power; and that the removal of such regularities in the name of calling into question the authority of state power is not only catastrophic but entirely muddled.

[19] Joseph Raz, *Morality of Freedom* (Clarendon Press 1988) 77–78.

There is truth in this argument: no general area of life is outside the competence of political authority. But it is a truth that must be strictly limited, to allow people to flourish in their own way with the resources that they have. Consider for example the domain of friendship. It is not the place of political authority to dictate who ought to be friends with whom, and how or to what extent they should share resources, including time, or the projects they devise and pursue. But the state will rightly prohibit and punish criminal enterprises which friends might concoct between themselves, and will step in where one friend intrudes on the private life of the other by, for example, stalking them. Similarly, a person's religious observances are not matters in which the state should be directly interested, but can become so if those observances include the grooming of potential suicide-bombers. The image of political authority as a 'brooding omnipresence' is therefore not wholly false. Yet all of this needs to be understood in the context of Aquinas's warning that the state (and the law) should not seek to prohibit all vices nor compel the performance of all virtues.[20]

This delimitation is less clear than it might seem. Governmental authority extends into all areas in the same way: there is a general competence to legislate that is the same in all cases, except those of constitutional change. The governing authority's competence to legislate on climate controls is not independent of its competence to reform the tax system. We do not ask whether the government has the authority to change the one but not the other, or whether there are limits upon competence in one area that do not apply to another. We do not ask whether governmental oversight can extend into new areas of social life, such as online computing. Political authority in the focal sense is exercised for the common good, for the sake of the all-around flourishing of the people, but it also belongs to the focal sense for political authority to be used for the sake of the community itself to the potential detriment of individual flourishing. This is exemplified most clearly in military conscription in times when a nation is threatened by external enemies. The lives of conscripted individuals are placed in jeopardy, and many of their choices and others forms of good are taken away for the sake of the nation. Much smaller such sacrifices are made every day: the money I might use in order to purchase a fine painting is redirected by the tax system for many purposes that are not connected to my own flourishing in any meaningful way. Now, the good of all individuals within a state cannot be secured or maintained viably except through measures that are taken for the common good of the community as a whole. Can natural law theory offer no guidance as to where the line ought to be drawn between community interests and private flourishing? The answer is that it can, although not in every detail. All of the main social teaching encyclicals of the Catholic Church deplore the evils of communism, in which the people are made

[20] Aquinas, *Summa Theologiae* (hereafter *ST*) I-II.96.2–3.

the servant of the state, not the state the servant of the people. This priority (of state over people) can occur in small ways as well as large; systematically as well as in particular cases. Whilst the systematic abuse of power to subjugate the citizen is obviously contrary to natural law, the assessment of particular cases of abuse of power in an otherwise benevolent state is more difficult, and depends upon many conditions. For example, the seizure of property by the state (eminent domain) for the purpose of enabling a large infrastructure project such as a railway, or even for the building of a new state-run power plant, is not by itself unjust, unless the profits from the project go to line ministerial pockets; but seizure of property for the purposes of erecting a palace for the ruler, or some other folly, will in general be contrary to justice.[21] The need to rest content with 'general' principles of the kind just outlined does not in any way suggest that natural law theory is of no assistance in concrete cases and in light of particular circumstances. For the generality of principle is merely a recognition that the process of practical reasoning in specific cases involves a casuistry that cannot be stated in universal terms, but requires further elaboration due to the need to consider conditions and circumstances that vary from case to case. This in no way implies that practical reason is entirely indeterminate in such cases, or cannot make inferences on the basis of observable facts and instantiated values. In this way, practical reason in such cases bears a considerable similarity to legal reasoning in common law jurisdictions.[22]

The scope of political authority is not only a moral question but one of practicality. In a technologically advanced state, government can extend into virtually all areas of life, not only coercively but through incentives and disincentives, public advice, and information campaigns, and much else. In that of a historically more primitive age, government will be accordingly restricted to military spending, court matters and taxation, with many more decisions taken at local level, and an absence of procedural consistency and sophistication. This raises the question of what form of government, from a natural law point of view, is the most preferable? The answer of the medieval scholastics and early-modern writers is that monarchy is in principle preferable, but since human frailty leads to tyranny, a 'mixed' regime is to be preferred in which there is some element of popular rule.[23] That writers such as Aquinas and Suarez should prefer monarchical government should come as no surprise: for they had constantly in view the examples of King David, of Christ's claim to be a king, and of God's Kingdom itself. But the reality is that political communities of any size cannot be governed effectively by one person or even

[21] Aquinas somewhat narrowly says that the only considerations that allow public good to outweigh individual good are those of peace and justice: Aquinas, *Sent.* III.30.1.4.

[22] All of these observations hold true of domestic legal authority, and set aside for the moment the complexities introduced by international law, e.g. a government's authority to change taxes to incentivize firms to shift to pro-environmental policies may be constrained by international treaties: see Chapter XII.

[23] See Suarez, *DL* (n 7) III.4.1; Aquinas, *ST* (n 20) I-II.105.1c; Aquinas, *De Regimine Principum* (hereafter *De Reg*) I.7.42.

a few. There is always need for advisors, for ministers to execute specific policies in specific places, of courts to apply the law, of bureaucrats (or courtiers) to interpret legislative will and systematize it with existing statutes, etc. In general, there is a need for many persons to *ensure the king's will be done*. This last proposition leads to a further requirement of political authority: that it be effective in holding the political community together, in exercising its authority, and in enforcing compliance with the law. The 'government' (let us call it) must speak with one voice, not many opposing voices.

Finally, therefore, it is necessary briefly to discuss the psychological (as opposed to moral) basis of political authority. A typical view of political authority is offered by Hart, who observes that the sovereign's will is 'intended to preclude or cut off any independent deliberation by the hearer of the merits pro and con of doing the act'.[24] But as Raz points out, such a position is absurd:

> Surely what counts, from the point of view of the person in authority, is not what the subject thinks but how he acts. I do all that the law requires of me if my actions comply with it. There is nothing wrong with my considering the merits of the law or of action in accord with it ... For there is no objection to people forming their own judgment on any issue they like. Nor does one surrender one's judgment if that means acting against one's judgment. For an authority is legitimate only if there are sufficient reasons to accept it, that is, sufficient reasons to follow its directives regardless of the balance of reasons on the merits of such action.[25]

The general point made by Raz is surely correct. But political authority is scarcely alone in providing what Raz calls 'exclusionary reasons' for action, that is, reasons which exclude the operative force of any other reasons in regard to some matter. Religious articles of faith as propounded by the Church function in a similar way, as do, perhaps, arithmetic functions in mathematical problem-solving and civil engineering. But there are a great many facets of thought in which reasons for action are not exclusionary. For the balance-sheet conception of practical reasoning implicit in the quoted passage's final sentence is simply not an accurate depiction of the process of practical reasoning in any sphere. Reasons for action are (at least when true and not simply mistaken) based on believed realities. Thus one's reason for attending Mass is based on one's belief in the reality of God. (We must also acknowledge the presence of false reasons for action that are grounded in false beliefs.) These underpinning beliefs, as with the reasons themselves, are not all equal; they differ not only in weight but in terms of their centrality to one's theoretical and practical thinking. Such beliefs are not 'exclusionary': no belief, perhaps, is entirely beyond revision or rejection in the light of new knowledge, including knowledge

[24] HLA Hart, *Essays on Bentham* (Clarendon Press 1982) 253.
[25] Raz (n 19) 39.

about the validity of certain inferences; and reasons based upon them do not exclude a lively internal discussion of what is to be done in light of all reasons, with a commitment to sincerity and truth. Such reasons are therefore not monoliths but are constantly confirmed and renewed in one's practical deliberations. The point about such processes is that they in no way resemble a balance-sheet method of reasoning; they resemble more a dialogue than an accountant's spreadsheet. The pronouncements of political authority, though they do comprise of exclusionary reasons, in light of which many of our other reasons and beliefs are rendered null, do not possess this balance-sheet quality. For example, a court's determination of damages for negligence excludes further reasoning on the part of the defendant as to how much compensation should be paid to the victim. The same thought lies behind Finnis's remark that it is not only the presence of the wicked and the dull that necessitate acts of political authority, but also that of the intelligent and the good, for they will have a great many ideas for how the common good may be advanced.[26]

## VIII.3. LEGAL AUTHORITY

The above remarks on political authority make passing references to legal authority, the development of which is the concern of the present section. There are in fact two matters that require explanation: the authority of law considered in itself; and political authority's use of governance through law in order to achieve its ends. We may begin the second of these topics with the observation that the law is only one instrument through which political authority is exercised. In certain societies (perhaps some medieval communities) it is not even the principal means by which the state is governed. For there is the regulation of the market, political support of a rigid class system such as that of feudalism, and the upholding of religious doctrine, amongst other means. There is the official recognition of the realities of conventional family life, of parish, of workers' guilds, and of local arrangements. Yet governance without law is scarcely conceivable. Thus both Hart and Fuller deem legal rules to be essential for good governance, Hart for example drawing a distinction between the legal and the pre-legal world, but neither writer offers a detailed description of what a pre-legal world would look like. One might assume that, whilst there is no origin as such of political authority within a state, there must be an origin of legal authority: for there either is law, or there is not. But legal practices are social practices, and like many important social practices, they do not arise deliberately or through the mind and will of a few persons of insight and influence. Such practices take shape on the intellectual landscape only after they have developed over time. Thus in a recent study of primitive law, the account

[26] Finnis, *NLNR* (n 10) 232.

*ends*, rather than begins, with the Code of Hammurabi, the first great legal text, produced in 1752 BC.[27]

It might be thought that the judgment that a certain political community 'has law' depends upon a prior definition of the term 'law'. I may perhaps be spared the search for the origin of such a concept, given the present book's focus on law in modern, largely liberal, societies. Forms of legal authority in such societies, although still the focus of jurisprudential controversy, are nonetheless clearly observable in the generic sense intended in this section. Therefore, whilst we may regard as unresolved the question of whether judges 'make law' or merely apply it, the structural characteristics of law are sufficiently well known and shared among modern positivists and non-positivists alike (centred around Lon Fuller's criteria of legality: see Section X.3) to enable a discussion of legal *authority* (i.e. the form of governance through law) to be discussed even in the presence of open questions in the theory of law.

As with political authority, consent on the part of those subject to law is not a source of legal authority, nor is any definable state of consciousness the origin of such authority. No kind of consent could possibly function as the origin of legal authority since there is no second option, no alternative against which authority can be set. But there is nevertheless a state of consciousness of legal subjects that constitutes *now* their ongoing relationship to the law taken as a whole, which is perhaps best captured by the term Hart frequently employs: acceptance. We accept that laws apply to us, whether or not we approve of them, and whether or not we intend to break them: the acceptance of law by those who break the law is manifested in their acknowledgment (to themselves) that they are *running the risk* of lawful punishment if they are caught. This attitude of acceptance is not a single, datable act of will, but an ongoing state of mind that is necessary for the law's very existence.[28] Some of its complexities are discussed in Chapter IX. Furthermore, the state of mind that I am calling 'acceptance' is not merely acceptance of 'the law', but also of legal authority itself: the recognition that such an authority can change, amend, and annul laws, and introduce new ones, some of which may be (from one's individual standpoint) unwelcome or even unjust. So, the state of consciousness that we *now* manifest, and which extends back in time in a series indefinitely, is the phenomenon that explains legal authority. But from whence does such a state of consciousness arise? What are *its* origins?

The answer is best explained by a seemingly innocent sentence in Grotius: 'This maintenance of social order, which we have barely outlined, ... is the source of

[27] AS Diamond, *Primitive Law, Past and Present* (Routledge 2004) 5.

[28] See also Raz (n 19) 94. For an excellent discussion see Margaret Martin, 'Raz's The Morality of Freedom: Two Models of Authority' 1 (2010) *Jurisprudence* 63; also Kenneth Ehrenberg, 'Critical Reception of Raz's Theory of Authority' (2011) *Philosophy Compass* 1. For a rebuttal of Raz's criticisms of his conception of legal authority see Finnis, 'Law's Authority and Social Theory's Predicament' in *CEJF* (n 10) IV.2 46.1.

law properly speaking.'[29] Forms of social order, as before observed, tend to arise and develop long before they strike the mind as distinctive and important. Nor is there a time at which such forms of order are regarded as voluntary: only once we have lived according to them does their nature and import become clear to us.[30] As their nature and force begin to become clear, so does our understanding extend to the recognition that such forms of order are neither static and unchanging nor changeable by oneself or one's neighbours. Only legal *authorities* can vary or interpret them. In the beginning, the relevant range of social practices may be rudimentary and local, spreading and becoming entrenched through conquest or other historical peculiarities. For legal authority can only extend to what it can control, in terms of both the substance of laws and the people to whom it is applied. But the substance of law is itself a function of the size and distribution of the people to which it applies. The precise nature of these social practices was contemplated by the natural law theorists of the medieval and early-modern periods, and will be explored in Section VIII.4. Legal authority is nevertheless a *necessary* feature at least of complex societies; perhaps there are small human communities that maintain peace and other social goods through familial and friendship relations rather than on the basis of stable rules, and perhaps there are large and complex societies that can descend so far into anarchy that no settled legal procedures are any longer effective within it. But otherwise legal authority is, in Aristotle's term, a *natural* part of human society, that is, part of what a society *is*.

But let us turn for a moment from the origin of acceptance to consider what it actually involves. What does it mean to 'accept' legal authority? One plausible suggestion is advanced by Finnis: it is that a person acts according to legal standards not because of what they say, that is, not in virtue of their substance, but (1) because they were duly enacted by legal authority, and (2) despite other, contrary reasons for action that one should not so act. There are a number of ways in which this suggestion fails to capture the complex yet recondite notion of 'acceptance' of law. First of all, whilst the suggested explanation fits well the motivation of the person who is at least strongly tempted to break the law (whether for good reasons or bad—to avoid an injustice or to commit a crime),[31] it scarcely accounts for the thinking of the good or reasonable person who does not contemplate illegal acts, and comes into explicit contact with the law only through the law of real property, or through contract or tax law, or even for that matter the bad person who plans to commit specific crimes and accepts that legal punishment will follow if she or he is caught. The attitude of 'acceptance' includes these two examples, but must also encompass (a) those who are ignorant of the law, even when acting in accord with it, for

[29] Grotius, *DIBP* (n 3) Proleg. § 5.

[30] For an opposing point of view see Matthias Brinkmann, 'Coordination Cannot Establish Political Authority' 31 (2018) *Ratio Juris* 49.

[31] Or both: one might refuse to commit an unjust act required by the law and therefore commit a crime under that law.

instance by stopping at the scene of an accident, or paying for goods in a store, and (b) those who simply do not entertain thoughts about the law in their daily lives. For such persons, and for most persons most of the time, 'acceptance' of legal authority is the constant but background awareness that they live in a society that is governed by identifiable persons holding recognized offices, for whom legislating and applying the law is a principal means of maintaining the order of society. There is nothing mysterious about such an attitude, the dynamics of which are present in many forms of activity. For example, the mechanic possesses knowledge of how to mend engines even when not drawing upon that knowledge (when asleep or engaged in other tasks); a philosopher remains a philosopher even when not philosophizing or thinking about philosophy. This selective but temporary forgetfulness, the brain's ordering of awareness, is an important aspect of practical reasoning: for practical reason requires an ordering of theoretical knowledge such that only what is relevant to the context of practical choice is brought into awareness at the necessary time. Only when we are tempted to steal, and thus faced with that practical choice, does the intellect recall to attention that such an act is immoral and a crime. But with these caveats in mind, it is possible to define acceptance of legal authority as the constant but background willingness to regard oneself as subject to the law.

The acceptance of legal authority, an attitude as I am calling it, raises other questions. Is it (1) obedience to legal rules simply because they emanate from the ruling authority? Or is it (2) obedience based upon the substance of legal rules and the prudential recognition that one cannot decide selectively to obey only those laws that one considers to be just, or in one's own interests? Or yet (3), is it obedience to legal rules in virtue of the law's connection to the common good of the community? As Hart observed, all of these attitudes are possible for persons to have; but we are concerned not with merely *possible* conceptions of acceptance, but with the central or focal conception that is characteristic of the right-thinking person's orientation to the law. Option (1) is clearly unfit for consideration, for it represents an emptying-out of the critical and reflective attitude that Hart insists is the distinctive characteristic of a legal rather than pre-legal society. Option (2) is inadequate for it is based on the idea of reciprocity (we should all obey because otherwise we are all worse off), and is compatible with obedience to heinously unjust laws for personal advantage. Only option (3) can be considered the central conception of acceptance of legal authority.[32] It too is compatible with the toleration of unjust laws, for the sake of the legal order as a whole, but never for reasons of personal advantage. Indeed, even in an unjust and repressive or murderous society, the authority of law is not entirely extinguished, so long as theft, assault, and other crimes continue to be forbidden amongst ordinary citizens, and so long as the regulation of matters such as contract and property remains effective.

[32] See Suarez, *DL* (n 7) I.7.1–2.

One of the main accounts of legal authority in modern times remains that of John Finnis. Here I simplify that account for the sake of brevity and without creating misconceptions that could not be corrected by reading the original. The account is focused upon custom. It says that the formation of a customary rule requires the following elements: (i) convergent practice; (ii) the absence of force, fraud; or mistake; and (iii) *opinio iuris*. But the classical account of *opinio iuris* amongst international lawyers is paradoxical because the customary practice cannot become a law on the basis of an erroneous belief that it is already law.[33] Instead, two propositions underlie the creation of a customary rule: first, that there is a need for some definite rule to govern a given set of circumstances; and second that some particular practice is suitable for resolving the problem and would, *if recognized* and generally adopted, be a good customary rule.[34] These are practical, as opposed to empirical, judgments; but a further practical judgment is necessary to be made by an international body to the effect that the conjunction of (i) and (ii) is a warrant for asserting that a new customary rule has formed. The relevant consideration for the goodness of the customary rule is that it serves the common good—either of the international community as such, or of certain states. A final practical judgment is needed: that customary rules of this kind are beneficial to the international community. This 'framework' custom is not implied by another yet more general custom, but from the opportunity to promote the common good.[35] As Finnis acknowledges, this account of custom raises various questions, which in light of the above discussion can be bracketed out from the present discussion: how widespread must the practice be? Which acts (or forbearances from acting) constitute evidence of *opinio iuris*? Can there be local customs or local variations in a general custom? And so on.

An obvious difficulty with the above account, if employed as a theory of legal authority, hides in plain view: it is an explanation of custom-formation in *international law*. There are at least three problems such an account must face as an explanation of domestic systems of law: (1) in international law, the subjects of law—those to whom the law applies—are also the authorities who create and recognize that law; we have already seen that this is not the case in domestic systems of law; (2) the international community is a smaller community than that of domestic systems, since there are under two hundred actors within the global community of states; the formation of new customs is relatively easy to discern as compared with the practice of millions in the domestic realm; and (3) *opinio iuris* is only possible where the phenomenon of law already exists; for one cannot recognize a customary practice to be a *legal* requirement, even a nascent one, if the category of 'legal' has no presence in the intellectual landscape. There seems no alternative

33 Finnis, *NLNR* (n 6) 238; see Duke (n 6) esp 44–49.
34 Finnis, *NLNR* (n 6) 239–40.
35 Ibid, 244–45.

than to consider that law comes to be recognized as a distinct form of ordering within in a community when its distinctive methods are employed by political authority as primary modes of governance. This is no tautology: the law's most basic requirement is that of a system of rules and penalties applying to at least the central requirements of human society, and the recognition of such a system as one of law develops only once such a system of rules exists; recognition of law cannot precede the presence of rules and penalties of those kinds. At the same time as a system of laws is recognized by its subjects, those subjects will typically recognize (or if they do not, are in a position to recognize) 'legal authority' as being the exercise of political authority through those laws and legal forms. This explanation obviates the need to locate the foundation of authority in the community itself, or in the consent of the governed, for as Finnis points out, authority is required precisely due to the lack of coherent will or unanimity in the people.[36]

Aquinas, Finnis suggests, offers no account of the genesis of human political societies, nor of their passing away.[37] This is incorrect: Aquinas offers an extended discussion of Aristotle's arguments concerning the generation of authority in his commentary on Aristotle's *Politics*.[38] As with any concept, legal authority must be understood by reference to its end, and the end requires to be understood by reference to human nature. Both Aristotle and Aquinas regard human nature as essentially sociable. This nature is expressed first of all through friendship with others: one's family members, one's neighbours, one's immediate community. Its central feature is that of being at peace with others. The characteristics of friendship among those with whom one is in a close relationship are obviously diluted in relation to those with whom one is less close: affection is replaced with disinterest; the common values, beliefs, and shared topics of conversation are diluted into good manners; the absence of aggression and a general willingness to assist. Political and legal authority have as their proper end the maintenance and promotion of these sociable characteristics. Legal authority formalizes some aspects of these relationships, defining obligations and rights in regard to contract, property, public safety, and so forth. Good authority—legal authority in the focal sense—is orientated towards these matters as its end; pernicious authority—legal authority only in a secondary sense—is orientated towards some perversion of this end: a perverted, or inadequate, understanding of basic human needs and ends, or the relegation of those needs and ends to some radically non-social end such as power or wealth. These thoughts lead Aquinas to the following two claims: (1) that legal and political authority are neither absolute nor indefeasible; and (2) even in very oppressive or evil regimes, the obligation to obey the law is never fully extinguished, for there will be potentially many laws (such as those prohibiting theft,

[36] Ibid, 248.

[37] John Finnis, *Aquinas: Moral, Political, and Legal Theory* (OUP 1998, hereafter *Aquinas*) 220.

[38] *Commentary on Aristotle's Politics* (hereafter *Com Pol*) I.1.31–41; see also *De Reg* (n 23) I.2.14.

murder, looting, etc) that continue to require obedience in view of their justice.[39] Legal authority therefore depends upon *both* the extent of its justice (too great or systematic an injustice erodes recognition of its legitimacy) *and* its formal features (such as notional comprehensiveness, an independent judiciary, procedural formalities for creating law, etc).

The discussion has centred so far upon legal authority in the sense of the exercise by a political authority of certain formal and procedural means, directed towards a certain type of end. But the authority of law is not confined to such acts, for there are kinds of law that stem not from legislation nor adjudicative decision, but from customary norms. Indeed, some of the structural features of law itself—including, for example, the judiciary's competence to articulate limits upon the Executive's prerogative power—derive their force from custom.[40] A largely unwritten constitution depends for its force upon an ongoing customary practice of regarding it as supreme; even a written constitutional code is sustained by a widespread practice which regards the relevant documents as having legal force and consequences. But whatever the precise relationship between the law and the state, the fact is that the law itself is commonly held as possessing authority, distinct from the authority of the ruler currently in power. Thus, a change of government does not render invalid all of the legal measures enacted by its predecessor, nor of the pre-existing common law. Nor do, for example, revisions to the *Code Napoleon* cause that document to cease being the *Code Napoleon*. Fidelity to law, furthermore, on the part of the citizen, does not necessarily involve fidelity to the current government, which one might after all deplore. What Hart aptly calls a 'critical and reflective attitude' to the law does not equate to a critical and reflective attitude towards actions of government. There are thus many laws the authority of which does not depend upon having been issued by authority. But the authority of law and legal customs should not be considered to have been conferred by those subject to them; for again, there is no datable origin of such authority.

Much of the jurisprudence of authority is addressed to the question of how and under what circumstances that authority arises. The above discussion was obliged to adopt a similar focus in view of this fact. But the question of the origins of authority, as I have already pointed out, is both unprofitable and unanswerable. There is no defining epoch, no historical moment in which authority comes into being. No single act or collective will creates it. The jurisprudence of authority is better devoted to an alternative question: what *sustains* authority, here and now? What set of norms underpins its ongoing existence? It is necessary to speak of norms, and not mere facts; for like the law itself, authority (particularly legal authority) must

[39] See Aquinas, *ST* (n 20) II-II.60.5 ad 2, I-II.96.4c; *Com Pol* (n 38) III.5.390; see also Joseph Raz, *Ethics in the Public Domain* (Oxford University Press 1994) 215.

[40] See e.g. *Bancoult (No 2)* [2008] UKHL 61; [2009] 1 AC 453; and the helpful discussion in Mark Elliott & Amanda Perreau-Saussine, 'Pyrrhic Public Law: *Bancoult* and the Sources, Status and Content of Common Law Limitations on Prerogative Power' (2009) *Public Law* 697.

be understood from the inside, from what Hart calls the 'internal point of view'. And if it is correct to suggest that authority gives one reasons for action, no mere set of facts can give rise to reasons without some evaluative reflection upon those facts on the part of the one over whom authority is being exercised: for, whatever the facts may be, the question is why one *should* or *ought* to obey or recognize that authority. This raises the question of the morality of authority, a subject over which we have so far glossed, but which we now turn to consider.

## VIII.4. MORAL AUTHORITY

The central case of legal authority is that of the use of law for the common good of the community, in all of the facets and complexities discussed in Chapter V. But the natural law philosophers were aware of various exceptions to this guiding principle. Thus, for example, Aquinas observes that laws consist of (1) legal precepts that declare and articulate various moral precepts, or quasi-deductions from those moral precepts, and (2) determinations the force of which derives from moral precepts in a non-deductive way, and in the limiting case derives from authoritative pronouncement alone, even if unjust.[41] Furthermore, according to scholastic doctrine, even tyranny must be endured, at least *pro tem*, if the collapse of the tyrannous regime would further erode common goods.[42] Laws can therefore be unjust in two different ways: either because they are in substance unjust, or because they exceed the boundaries of legitimate authority (see Section XI.2). These claims establish a principle, that in either case the ordinary citizen may remain bound to legal authority, but they do not clarify the distinction between legitimate and illegitimate authority.

Some clarification of terms is therefore required. An authority can be regarded as illegitimate if it seizes power from a pre-existing legitimate authority, that is to say, one that is characterized by the use of law and political power to further and protect the common good of the community. The use of conquest to expand the scope of ruling authority over peaceful nations is therefore always illegitimate. However, if such an authority subsequently acts consistently for the common good of the conquered people, it may in time come to be regarded as legitimate. This is not to suggest that the historical realities of conquest should be taken as markers of legitimacy, but rather that the legitimacy or illegitimacy of a governing regime is to be measured by a series of moral norms, to some extent independently of the origin of that regime. It matters little to the present-day legitimacy of a governing regime that its historical origins are or are not traceable to, for example, the Norman conquest. But it matters decisively that a present-day regime originally

[41] See Aquinas, *ST* (n 20) I-II.95.3c, II-II.57.1 ad 1, II-II.60.5c.
[42] *De Reg* (n 23) I.7.44.

established itself by acts of genocide or ethnic cleansing, regardless of whether it subsequently pursued the common good of the whole (purged) community. Thus while authority may gain legitimacy by a kind of prescriptive period (though one of indefinite length), its title to be regarded as such depends upon the extent of its fulfilment of a series of moral norms. There may, of course, be disparities between internal and international perspectives upon a regime's legitimacy: the acceptance by a people of a regime as legitimate is not a sufficient condition for international recognition of the regime's legitimacy. An authority can be judged illegitimate in another way, if it deliberately and routinely acts against the interests or rights of its citizens, or against their common good. Of course certain kinds of political act can be said to run contrary to a nation's common good without affecting the regime's legitimacy: entering into a costly or unwanted foreign war can be said to be contrary to the interests of a people, but this does not render legal authority illegitimate. But removal of the right to education, building of government palaces at the expense of public needs and infrastructure, ending freedom of speech, and so forth renders an authority illegitimate, for it runs contrary to the series of norms by reference to which legitimate authority is measured. Finally, authority can be illegitimate in a third way, by extending legal regulation into areas that properly belong to the private choices of individuals: for example, by instituting a compulsory breeding programme, adopting a one-child policy, or restricting who can marry.

What, then, are the norms by reference to which authority is to be considered legitimate? (1) First of all there are matters of subsidiarity such as those mentioned at the end of the preceding paragraph: authority cannot properly be extended over matters in which the individual is directly related to God, such as those sinful actions that are properly only confessed in the confessional.[43] These matters concern not only what Aquinas calls 'interior movements of the will' (e.g. covetousness), but also encompass aspects of the body's natural realities, such as the begetting of children or making binding promises concerning the body in matrimony.[44] For obedience to authority is not all-encompassing but only within the proper scope of authority. (2) Similarly, it is not the function of legal authority to direct human beings to their ultimate end, for this concerns divine, and not human, government.[45] The function of legal authority is to order human beings only to those virtues that concern one's actions towards others: so-called general justice (see Section IV.1). (3) But it *is* the function of legal authority to direct human beings towards social virtues as the proper *end* of government; all other matters, such as the wellbeing and health of the body, or the amassing of wealth, are subordinate to that proper end. Neither doctors nor economists should have the final word in policy-making or law enforcement. A natural law theory of legal authority therefore rejects the

[43] Aquinas, *ST* (n 20) II-II.33.7c & ad 1, II-II.88.8 ad 3.
[44] Ibid, II-II.104.5c; *Compendium* (n 7) § 234.
[45] *De Reg* (n 23) I.15.108.

'economic analysis of law'. (4) Fourth is the principle that legal authority should not be oppressive in the demands made on individuals or groups. Excessive taxation is an obvious example of an oppressive law, but there are many others. Thus any set of laws that place so many duties on a person that they are prevented from flourishing, or which deny any space or time for private and family life, or which plunge the people into poverty exceed the natural boundaries of legitimate authority. Aquinas does discern that even oppressive laws should be observed, but there is a moral difference between an oppressive law (such as excessive taxation) in a legal order that is otherwise orientated to the common good, and an entire legal system ordered to the oppression of the people. The moral difference in question is in the nature of each person's obligation to obey the legal authority. It does not necessarily lie in ceasing to recognize or 'accept' that legal authority, for governance of any kind is to be preferred to lawlessness. A further warning is needed: the recognition of a legal authority within a state as illegitimate does not automatically entail a moral right to rebel against that authority or to seek to depose it, even where the tyranny is unbearable.[46] (5) Legal authority should not be orientated to imperial ambitions, either for tactical reasons or aggrandizement—since foreign warfare is costly in both monetary and human terms, and diverts resources away from the community—such warfare is an acceptable end of legal authority only where it (i) is necessary to eliminate or diminish an immediate threat, (ii) will intervene militarily in the internal affairs of another state in order to prevent genocide or war crimes, or (iii) in certain circumstances, will be effective for the purposes of peacekeeping (see Section XII.6). (6) In no way must authority be employed to use the person for ends foreign to his or her own development, nor as a means to public, social, economic, or political purposes, even for the sake of the good of the community.[47] (7) Legal authority must be exercised in order to contribute centrally to the development and maintenance of public goods, such as education, healthcare, infrastructure, economic stability, and peace. The extent of a state's obligation to secure and contribute to such goods depends upon the level of its technological progress. (8) At the most fundamental level, and in summary of the principles set out above, government is for the governed.[48]

Another way of summarizing these principles is to say that the purpose of authority is not domination but *service*.[49] A recent and influential version of the so-called 'service conception' of authority is provided by Joseph Raz. But his account

[46] Ibid I.7.45–46 (we must obey not only the mild and the good, but also the oppressive); 1 Peter 2:18–19; also Grotius, *DIBP* (n 3) I.3.9.1 ('If those who are of this opinion claim that wrongful acts should not be performed just because the ruler so commanded, their claim would be both true and widely acknowledged among good persons. Yet this refusal does not imply any curtailment of power or right to exercise authority'). For an honest account of what life would be like outside of moral authority see Russell Blackford, *The Mystery of Moral Authority* (Palgrave 2016) ch 7.

[47] *Compendium* (n 7) § 133.

[48] Grotius, *DIBP* (n 3) I.3.8.18 (though, he observes, this is not always the case in fact).

[49] *Compendium* (n 7) § 383.

differs in a number of ways from the notion of 'service' found in Catholic literature and as summarized above. For while Catholic social teaching, for these purposes quite secular, considers that authority be used in service to the *interests* of the people (i.e. to what promotes and secures human flourishing), Raz's central thesis is that authority must be employed to serve the *reasons for action* that apply to persons independently of that authority.[50] Indeed, he points out that reasons for action that apply to a subject of authority need not be in their interests: a military commander issues battle orders that are in the interests of the country, not the soldiers.[51] The force of the example is unclear, however, for it is difficult to see how soldiers would have reasons for engaging in battle independently of the orders issued by military authority. Likewise, it is less than straightforwardly true that individual citizens have an independent reason to pay tax, or obey speed limits on motorways, other than for reasons of authority. Nevertheless, the 'service conception' consists, inter alia, of two conditions: (1) that the subject would more perfectly conform to reasons for action that apply to him or her independently of authority, if he or she intends to be guided by authoritative directives than otherwise (Raz calls this the normal justification thesis); and (2) 'that the matters regarding which the first condition is met are such that with respect to them it is better to conform to reason than to decide for oneself, unaided by authority' (Raz calls this the independence thesis).[52] As its name implies, the normal justification thesis articulates the *normal* way in which authority is justified,[53] thus for present purposes I shall restrict my focus to this central case of authority, and shall not consider unusual or peripheral justifications.

Regarding the independence thesis, Raz makes clear that no surrender of personal judgment occurs or is required, for individuals retain the ability to form their own judgments on all matters; it is their actions that are governed by authority.[54] In the same way, deference to authority does not imply surrender of judgment even if this means acting against one's judgment, for as Raz points out, authority is legitimate only if there are sufficient reasons for accepting it, that is, sufficient reasons to follow its directives 'regardless of the balance of reasons on the merits of such action'.[55] Earlier (in Section VIII.2) I cast doubt upon the balance-sheet conception of reasoning, the process of weighing up what to do resembling more a dialogue than a reckoning. But this does not nullify the idea of an exclusionary reason which lies at the heart of Raz's conception of authority; however there may be many occasions upon which an otherwise law-abiding citizen will not treat authoritative directives

[50] See e.g. Raz (n 39) 214.
[51] Raz (n 19) 48.
[52] Raz (n 10) 136–37.
[53] For one criticism of this thesis see Scott Hershovitz, 'The Role of Authority' 11 (2011) *Philosopher's Imprint* 1.
[54] Raz (n 19) 40. See also Catherine Wilson, 'Moral Authority and the Limits of Philosophy' in Sophie Chappell & Marcel van Ackeren (eds) *Ethics Beyond the Limits* (Routledge 2020) 238.
[55] Raz (n 19) 40.

as exclusionary, for example when deciding to break the speed limit, or in withdrawing from a contract which the other party will find too expensive to litigate, or in fraudulently claiming more state benefits than those to which they are entitled. So it is necessary to regard the exclusionary character of authoritative directives as a general thesis to which there are exceptions: a disposition to obedience to authority in most matters does not entail obedience in all.

Returning to the normal justification thesis, Raz acknowledges that there are moral limits to authority, kinds of action that are not to be regulated but left to individual choice.[56] More generally, while it must be possible for legal authorities to enact unjust laws which continue to provide exclusionary reasons for action (e.g. unjust tax provisions), there are certain immoralities that no government has the authority to commit.[57] In this respect, Raz's theory of authority resembles the scholastic accounts of authority to which reference was made above. One clear way in which government exceeds its authority is by acting in opposition to the interests of the people: 'If [an official directive] is binding on individuals it has to be justified by considerations which bind them. Public authority is ultimately based on the moral duty which individuals owe their fellow humans ... It entails the subordination of political reasons to ordinary individual morality.'[58] This statement is only partially correct. Political and legal authority are rightly said to be subordinate to the principles of core morality explored in Section III.4. But I went on to highlight further principles of core morality that apply to offices of authority. Such principles define limits to those offices in addition to those captured by ordinary core morality: limits which if transgressed by legitimate authority are lawless and by virtue of which the holders of the relevant offices act *ultra vires*.

One striking feature of Raz's theory of authority, which in key respects resembles those of the scholastics, is that he claims that it supports legal positivism. Specifically, he makes the following claim:

> [N]ecessarily law, every legal system which is in force anywhere, has *de facto* authority. That entails that the law either claims that it possesses legitimate authority or is held to possess it, or both. I shall argue that, though a legal system may not have legitimate authority, or though its legitimate authority may not be as extensive as it claims, every legal system claims that it possesses legitimate authority. If the claim to authority is part of the nature of law, then whatever else the law is it must be capable of possessing authority. A legal system may lack legitimate authority. If it lacks the moral attributes required to endow it with legitimate authority then it has none. But it must possess all the other features of authority, or else it would be odd to say that it claims authority. To claim authority it must

[56] Ibid, 46–47.
[57] Ibid, 79.
[58] Ibid, 72.

> be capable of having it, it must be a system of a kind which is capable in principle of possessing the requisite moral properties of authority. These considerations . . . create a weighty argument in favour of the sources thesis.[59]

We may begin by asking, who is doing this claiming and holding? The claiming is presumably that of legal officials, or those who possess the relevant offices of authority. The holding must be that of officials and citizens alike; for despite the disjunction in the quoted passage's second sentence, officials and officers can hardly regard their own rule as illegitimate, whatever the citizens may think. Thus a legal system has de facto authority, for example, if its officers claim to possess legitimate authority but the citizens regard it as illegitimate. In such a case, the legal system must exhibit 'all of the other features of authority' in order to maintain de facto authority. In this way, the legal system must sufficiently resemble the central case of (legitimate) authority in order to be the kind of system capable of possessing the moral properties typically (centrally) associated with authority. How then does this support legal positivism? It presumably does so because a de facto authority must *actually* be based only upon legal forms such as legislation and precedent, and not upon the moral substance of its provisions: morality being an entirely contingent feature of legal systems. But this is at least highly implausible, for any legal system in a complex society must make arrangements to regulate the economy, to create and enforce bargains, to adjudicate cases of accidental harm, to punish wrongdoers, to maintain the internal peace of the state, and so forth, and it is implausible to suggest that it is possible for all such arrangements to be instituted on any but moral concerns. Both regulation and non-regulation of, for instance, the economy presuppose certain moral viewpoints (not least a viewpoint as to whether regulation is desirable or otherwise). Furthermore, such arrangements and provisions require to be interpreted by the courts in order to be applied. Such interpretation is likely to make reference, at least tacitly, to the intended purposes and values of the laws, and the relevant sources of positive law are not the only well from which such interpretations are drawn. For the presumptive values that the law is intended to serve (even if repressive) demand to be fleshed out and defended (if justice is an overt aim of law) according to broad ethical precepts, judgments of common sense, desire to avoid floods of litigation, and so forth, which are not given full and unalloyed expression in the positive law. Even a pragmatic judiciary in an oppressive state must interpret the law as forming an important social good, and its requirements as moral requirements. Thus the creation and administration of law even by a merely de facto authority does not conform to the sources thesis. Indeed, as Finnis makes clear, the very exercise of authority itself is morally superior to lawlessness, and is in this sense a contribution to the common good.[60]

[59] Raz (n 39) 215.
[60] Finnis, *NLNR* (n 6) 251–52.

There is however one important reason, in addition to those above, for rejecting the 'service conception' of authority as outlined above. It is that (as Aquinas makes abundantly clear) it is not the purpose of law to compel *all* the modes of behaviour that are in a person's best interests. For many such modes of behaviour relate to matters of perfection that it is beyond the competence of secular government to uphold. Law should neither seek to enforce all virtues nor suppress all vices.[61] Under normal circumstances, it is not a legitimate function of law to enforce moderation, to outlaw lust, or to criminalize greed or avarice, except where these matters impinge upon 'general' justice. Such matters are matters of private conscience, and are not the proper focus of law even though their pursuit is in the best interest of human beings, and even though the law in promoting or enjoining their pursuit would be creating 'exclusionary reasons' which are reasons 'that apply to the subject already, independently of the law'. It is true that legal authorities do typically seek to regulate matters of private choice, for instance by raising high taxes upon unhealthy goods such as tobacco and alcohol, or by offering incentives to encourage people to adopt healthy lifestyles, but such measures are not, crucially, *exclusionary reasons*, and as such are not the topic of the service conception of authority. The moral authority of the state is instead to be found in the eight principles set out earlier in this section, and in the reality that authority (especially legal authority) is preferable to anarchy.

## VIII.5. SUBSIDIARITY AND SOLIDARITY

The purpose of legal authority, then, is to protect and uphold the common good of the community, and to facilitate people in pursuing their *freely chosen* ends and purposes, and in their law-abiding activities.[62] It must therefore allow people to make their own mistakes, as these after all teach more effectively than authoritative injunctions. In this way, legal and political authority must be exercised in accordance with the principle of subsidiarity. But there is an additional principle at work in authority, and that is solidarity. Neither principle should be sacrificed to the other, for the presence of one without the other leads to injustice.[63] Subsidiarity without solidarity leads to dissolution and the unravelling of society. Solidarity without subsidiarity stifles individualism and individual freedom. Having discussed subsidiarity earlier in this book (Section V.3) I here offer some very brief remarks on solidarity.

[61] Aquinas, *ST* (n 20) I-II.96.2–3.

[62] See NW Barber & Richard Ekins, 'Situating Subsidiarity' 61 (2016) *American Journal of Jurisprudence* 5; John Finnis 'Subsidiarity's Roots and History: Some Observations' 61 (2016) *American Journal of Jurisprudence* 133; Dominic Burbidge, 'The Inherently Political Nature of Subsidiarity' 62 (2017) *American Journal of Jurisprudence* 143.

[63] *Compendium* (n 7) § 351.

What exactly solidarity involves will depend upon the kind of community that is in question. In a very basic and small society, kinship ties are likely to provide the foremost means of realizing solidarity between its members. But in a large and developed society, various possible types of social structure will contribute to the feeling of solidarity amongst the members of a community. Thus, for example, a class system reinforces personal identity, not across the whole of society, but within each social class. The members of the community will tend to identify themselves as belonging to a particular social class, often with pride at that belonging, even in the face of a desire to belong to another class. But the class-system or any measure of socio-economic status is not the only possible source of solidarity within the community. Since the present chapter is concerned with authority, it is necessary to mention a significant source of solidarity: the law. Legal rules, principles, and doctrines embody values with which the vast majority of citizens can identify, not necessarily at a high level of detail, but in broad terms. People agree that the law should uphold justice, that criminals are captured and punished; that trespassers be excluded and property rights upheld, that compensation be awarded where legal blame can be identified, and that commercial dealings be regulated and honesty demanded. For, in a benevolent society, the law gives expression to basic moral values that the majority of society identifies as *its* values. Where the law is used as an instrument of oppression, the reverse is the case: an oppressive legal order, or a society in which the rule of law has been abolished, annihilates solidarity since the only thing the people now share is the likelihood of suffering, of which each individual person wants less than others and, by and large, would prefer some other person suffered in their stead.

In recent times, the Catholic Church has articulated a conception of solidarity that is international: the affluent nations of the world ought to show solidarity with the poorer parts of the world.[64] For the most fundamental means of fostering solidarity is through distribution of goods and remuneration for labour;[65] such distributions reinforce solidarity at various levels of society: between the poor themselves, and between the poor and the rich, between workers, and between employees and employers.[66] Solidarity is ultimately reinforced by (1) social structures in which each person gets what is due to them, and (2) shares in spiritual as well as material goods, including the good of faith.[67] Thus the extent to which legal authority is used to uphold solidarity or to destroy it, is at the same time the extent to which legal authority upholds justice or fails to uphold it. Solidarity reinforces justice.

64 See especially *Sollicitudo re socialis* § 39.
65 *Catechism of the Catholic Church* § 1940.
66 Ibid, § 1941.
67 Ibid, § 1941–42.

It is not necessary, in the context of this short afterword on the subject of authority, to examine the various theories of solidarity that have developed both outside and within the Catholic Church's social teachings.[68] Suffice it to note that part of the proper function of legal and political authority is to promote solidarity and seek to contain as far as possible the forces within society that range against solidarity: exploitation, inequality, sectarianism, indifference to suffering, and so on. This is, of course, to uphold central aspects of the common good. But while political and legal authority can promote solidarity, by creating the right political conditions in which it may flourish, authority cannot create solidarity: for solidarity is essentially the struggle of a people to attain justice and peace; it is not a struggle *against* but rather *with* others, and is thus primarily a facet of civil society rather than of law.[69] Law itself is an especially apposite source of solidarity, however, for it is a perpetual reminder to individual citizens that the basic obligations, duties, permissions, and rights that apply to themselves also apply to others, so that one does not regard one's obedience to the law as something of which others can take advantage.[70]

It might appear that solidarity conflicts with subsidiarity, the state's withdrawal from areas of private life and private ordering. But this is not the case. Solidarity complements subsidiarity for it is *enabling*. It values efforts that enable vulnerable individuals to help themselves through connection with others, not managerial actions taken for the benefit of the vulnerable. One's neighbour is a person with whom one should work alongside, not manage. Legal and political authority should not seek to coerce solidarity; the coercive power of the state fosters solidarity *indirectly*, through its prohibition of certain forms of injustice and dishonesty, but does not do so *directly*, by forcing individuals to work together on social projects. An authority that so seeks to bring about solidarity coercively exceeds its lawful authority. Thus solidarity is best revealed in the very numerous private transactions, public bids and franchises, contracts and corporations, that are required to erect hospitals, build road networks and schools, churches, concert halls and opera houses, and fund and apply scientific research, maintain the public stock of knowledge, and so on.

One further consideration about legal authority before closing the present chapter: such authority can be limited by both positive law (including constitutional provisions or norms), and by natural law. Authority can be limited by positive law because the authority of the law itself is distinguishable from the political authority that creates, amends and interprets the law. This is a central premise of the rule of law, not of men. But natural law places numerous restrictions upon legal

[68] For one (secular) theory see Roger Cotterrell, *Sociological Jurisprudence: Juristic Thought and Social Inquiry* (Routledge 2018) 153–55, 173–203, 220–27 (an account perhaps rather too close to the Hobbesian notion of 'security').

[69] See *Sollicitudo rei socialis* § 39.

[70] See Finnis, *CEJF* (n 10) IV.68–77.

and political authority, the most important of which is that such authority is illegitimate if not exercised for the common good of the community. This present chapter has explored some of the numerous aspects of a natural-law theory of authority. The following Chapter IX explores an issue which throws further light upon questions of authority: the idea of obligation.

# IX
# OBLIGATION AND COMMITMENT

## IX.1. COMMITMENT IN GENERAL

Chapter VIII discussed some issues around the idea of authority—political, legal, and moral. The present chapter concerns a concept that is closely associated with authority, that of obligation, or, in my terminology, *commitment*. Commitment is a wider concept than obligation, for it can always be asked how one is to discern one's obligations (legal, political, moral) and how issues of priority are to be decided amongst them. There are, for example, obligations to one's closest family members, to assist neighbours or strangers in need, one's legal obligations in contract (for example), to the political party of which one is a member, to one's employer, and many more besides. The issue of commitment is that of how these various obligations are presumptively prioritized. For example, one's legal obligations will ordinarily have a high degree of priority, but if one's wife goes into labour at the very time one's contractual duties fall due, driving one's wife to hospital and remaining by her side is obviously more important: it is a deeper commitment (the commitment one makes during one's marriage vows). Another example: one's duties to one's employer will usually have priority over many things, but if the employer demands of one the commission of (what one suspects is) an unlawful act, one acts rightly by disobeying the demand, even calling attention to it to organs of the state. Now it is possible to analyse such examples according to the peremptory character of legal rules: in the latter case, the lack of a legal defence against complicity in one's employer's illegal schemes is well-known and established, and the duty to inform the authorities thus takes priority over other legal duties, such as one's contractual duties to one's employer (and is reflective of precepts of natural law). Contracts of employment which are otherwise valid are invalid insofar as they involve a criminal enterprise, and any contractual provisions, for example word-of-mouth management decisions, that breach the law are of no operative effect. In the former case, one can attempt to reconcile one's position with the thought that one is not, by driving one's wife to hospital, disobeying a peremptory rule, for the relevant peremptory rule is that one should *either* perform one's contractual duties *or* pay the corresponding damages. But this is unpersuasive, for in relation to the second proposal just mentioned it is an open question whether rules of contract are structured in such a way: for that is scarcely the *point* of such rules, and the proposed interpretation of contractual rules scarcely makes sense of damages as a *remedy*. That is, the modern tendency to regard contract law as a branch of commercial law (that a

*Natural Law and Modern Society.* Sean Coyle, Oxford University Press. © Sean Coyle 2023.
DOI: 10.1093/oso/9780192886996.003.0009

contract is, in effect, a *price*) is not only lamentable but fundamentally at odds with the nature of contractual obligations as forms of *commitment*. In any event, the peremptory character of law can itself be challenged: one's moral commitments at least sometimes (and arguably always) override the law. Consider the case of wickedly unjust laws with which one should not comply (Section XI.2–3) and those cases in which one accedes to an unjust law not because it supplies an exclusionary reason but because one values the common goods of peace and social order (Section IV.2).

Commitment is a more versatile concept than obligation. One's earliest commitments in life are to one's family: if one is lucky, one is born into a good family; if unlucky, into a bad or even criminal one, or into foster care or an orphanage. These early influences shape one's moral psychology. They determine to a high degree one's expectations of life, of what one is really or ideally entitled to, of one's treatment of other people and one's attitude to the relative wealth or poverty of others as it affects one's own actions. This formative effect on one's moral psychology will very often extend to questions about one's family members themselves. It is exceedingly hard to be disinterested in one's family's affairs, whether licit or otherwise. One concerns oneself with the character of the person one's child proposes to marry; and one concerns oneself about one's sibling's dishonest schemes. We can express our *commitment* to our relations in these situations, in distinction from our *obligation* towards them. For just as there is a reasonable self-preference involved in moral decisions, so there is reasonable priority in attending to one's relative's interests over those of strangers. This does not, of course, amount to aiding one's relative in defrauding or assaulting the stranger, or with attempting to cover up the crime; but it does involve continuing to give emotional support and kindness to a relative when the state-of-affairs makes this difficult or unpopular. One remains *committed* to them when ordinary language and ordinary forms of expression would indicate that one is not *obligated* to them. Lest it be thought that commitment pertains to emotional attachment, there is similarly a distinction between obligation and commitment in relation to doctrinal areas of law. For example, I lay down my money, because of which the bus driver implicitly promises to issue me with a ticket, this being an obligation by reference to a complex practice to which all parties *commit* themselves. Similarly, commitments do not refer exclusively to long-term relations, for, as the family example shows, certain states-of-affairs bring our commitments to the cutting edge of our reasoning. I do not owe money to a close relative who is an inveterate gambler, to enable him or her to meet essential costs of living (I am not obligated to him or her) but I do so—here and now—out of a commitment to their general wellbeing as a family member.

Contrariwise, it is equally obvious that one can have or assume obligations that have nothing whatever to do with commitment: if I injure another person through my own negligence, I have an obligation to compensate them. Now it could be said that the requisite commitment is to established practices of tort law, and perhaps (less directly) to legal practices of obedience and submission to a court's or tribunal's decision. But the difference between these examples and those of the bus ticket, is that (for the overwhelming majority of people), there is no previous history of dealings, and little if any knowledge of the relevant practices. Such practices then do not form part of the moral psychology of the individual in the way that ordinary contracting does. In most cases, one might well have obligations that one does not know about, but one cannot have a commitment about which one does not know. This is far from suggesting that commitments are purely psychological: a commitment once made is as real as any obligation. Every obligation represents one of our commitments, objectively speaking. But it is important to consider how commitments feature upon the intellectual and psychological landscape.

Commitments can be made or broken at specific points in time; some, once made, cannot be broken. Most obviously, one makes a number of commitments, in Church, to one's marriage partner: to devote oneself 'for better, for worse', 'in sickness and in health', and 'for richer, for poorer'. Commitments of this kind can be made but not broken: they are made through human agreement, but they cannot be unmade by human agreement. Purely civil ties of this sort can be undone, of course; but the example of religious marriage is apposite because it serves to explain that whilst one undoubtedly owes one's spouse various obligations for example of fidelity and justice, such obligations are held in place by one's originary (and ongoing) commitment to one's marriage vows to one's spouse. It is not generally the case that one's commitment only lasts so long as one intends it: a commitment to be at a particular place at a particular time in order to meet one's friend continues even after one has decided against the meeting, or if one has simply forgotten it.

Normally, the depth of a commitment depends upon the depth or seriousness of the matter concerned.[1] A commitment to meet, as above, is fairly trivial; if forgotten or ignored the situation is annoying to the friend, perhaps temporarily wounding to the friend's feelings, but little more. By contrast, reneging upon one's marriage vow of fidelity is a much more serious matter, and correspondingly concerns the breaking of a far deeper commitment. Observe that the depth of the commitment is not relative to the emotional seriousness and maturity with which the vows were in fact exchanged. Generally speaking, one's commitments to the law are not related to the content of particular legal rules or processes, but to legal institutions themselves. A person regards themselves as bound by the law (committed to doing whatever the law requires) even if they do not know or understand its content. We might call this a level-one commitment, the commitment to be a law-abiding citizen of one's community. But there are many instances in which, quite aside from this general commitment, a person is committed to uphold, or not to transgress, legal rules themselves in virtue of their substance. Legal rules against violence and fraud, and those regulating contracts, are examples of rules of this

[1] For an alternative bur interesting use of 'commitment' see Margaret Gilbert, *Joint Commitment: How We Make the Social World* (OUP 2013) 37ff.

kind: we might call these level-two commitments. It may be the case that a person can have an ongoing level-two commitment to particular legal rules even when she or he no longer has a level-one commitment to the legal institutions that administer the law, for these might be embroiled in corruption or in violation of basic premises of legality, for example that the law as it is enforced and applied should be the same as the law on the statute books. Thus one may continue to be committed to legal rules prohibiting violence even if the judiciary actually allows the use of violence against certain social groups.

It is, of course, possible for one's commitments to conflict. On a trivial level, if I commit to meet two different people at different places but on the same occasion, I generate a conflict of commitments. Less trivially, if I am installed as a judge by the ruling political party, of which I am a member, and am instructed (contrary to existing legal rules) to exonerate all party members involved in violence against some hated social group, there is a conflict between my pledges and allegiance to my political party, on the one hand, and, on the other, my pledge, on being sworn in as a judge, of allegiance to the law. How should one weigh these conflicting commitments? The solution in this case ought to be obvious, but there may be a great many situations in which the solution is not obvious. Suppose for example that I am a judge in a community whose law and legal system is by and large benign, contains no more than usual amounts of corruption, bias, and so on. Suppose further that I am faced with a case in which the application of the clear legal rules that apply to the case would produce an outcome that is, according to my considered sense of justice, substantially unjust. Here, my level-one commitment is called into question, especially in light of Aquinas's teaching that one should often obey laws even if they are unjust. For in failing to uphold an unjust law, I—and by extension others—may create uncertainty and potential turbulence within the community, contributing to a general loss of the social order and peace to which I and they are also *committed*. Here it would be a mistake to think that the solution is obtained by weighing or balancing the relevant commitments. A judge as much as any person must not commit an immoral act that a greater good should flow from it: his or her options are either to engineer a solution to the case that is substantively just, based on other legal materials, or to resign from the bench. No weighing or balancing of commitments takes place: the deeper commitment takes priority over the lesser. Similarly, an individual faced with a question of obedience to an unjust law which deprives them of their proper rights, does not (ought not to) seek balance between his or her commitment to justice and his or her commitment to obedience. The natural law teaching is quite specific: one should yield one's right for the sake of the social goods of peace and stability, which are otherwise threatened by the citizen's decision to pick and choose which laws to break and which to obey. Here again there is no weighing of potential benefits, with the decision hanging upon which course of action is deemed to promise the greater benefit. There is instead a relation of priority and of depth, a ranking (not weighing) of goods in practical reasoning.

But is there not a suspicion of tacit weighing in practical reasoning? For we are told, by Aristotle and his successors, that in ethics one may only aspire to as much certainty as the subject is capable of providing. Does this uncertainty not disclose a gap between one's deliberations in ranking certain goods, and the final conclusion reached, a gap that is bridged by a weighing of one good against another? Here the sense of 'uncertainty' must be clearly understood. When Aristotle says that the domain of ethics is uncertain, he does not mean that *every* ethical argument lacks certainty: for he goes on to insist that certain actions can never be anything but evil.[2] Nor should other ethical arguments be considered inconclusive, for uncertainty is not the same thing as inconclusiveness. In the overwhelming majority of ethical deliberations, one finds an argument based on rational grounds to which there is, indeed, a conclusion. But like any subject-matter, the truth of a conclusion depends upon the truth of the premises, and there may be some reasonable disagreement about the truth of the premises, for certain human goods are contestable and disputed. However, the deliberations undertaken with respect to those goods do not, perhaps contrary to appearance, consist of weighing one good against another, a suspicion that arises wherever there are multiple goods involved. The process consists in the identification of the goods involved, followed by a *prioritization* of them in respect of an inclusive ethical framework. Such a framework includes the principle above, that certain actions are always evil and can never be done well: such as adultery with one's neighbour's spouse. It includes the principle that one's pursuit of the good life must not unduly and directly injure other persons in their pursuit of their reasonable conception of the good life: I should not defraud my neighbour so that I and my family live well. And it includes the principle that one's actions should not directly impoverish the common good: I must not destroy Rembrandts so that no one but I shall see them.

Let us return, however, to the line of discussion lately begun: the question of obedience to unjust law. What we are confronting in the question about unjust law is not a substantive principle coming into contact with another substantive principle, but rather a substantive principle brought into conflict with a formal principle with which it is usually in conformity: namely that of obeying a legal precept not because of its substantive justice or injustice, but because it has been officially laid down by the state in accordance with proper authority. Now, the attractiveness of that formal principle is premised upon the assumption that the law or legal order in question is, for the most part, substantively just and reasonable. This is the reason why the questioner may regard ethics as inconclusive, and moral reasoning a matter of weight: for sometimes the substantive justice of the law is such that it ought to be followed to one's cost, and sometimes its comparative lack of justice yields the conclusion that one should refuse to obey. However, these opposing

[2] Aristotle, *Nicomachean Ethics* (hereafter *NE*) II.6.1107a.

conclusions have nothing to do with the *strength* of the opposing interests but rather their ranking. This ranking partly involves a further consideration: that of the substantial contribution to the common good of a system of laws the content of which is insulated from the broader activity of moral reasoning about important affairs. There is no weighing of the common good against the good of the individual (for in such 'weighing' the common good would always win), but rather the respective *priorities* of common and individual good fall to be inspected and ranked. For let us suppose (a difficult hypothetical) that an apparently lawful command addressed to A, to inflict some moderate but illegal harm on B, is for the benefit of the common good. Should A harm B? Not at all! The central principle that one ought never to perform an evil act that good may come of it, is exactly a refusal to *weigh* the harms and benefits involved.[3] As before, the language of commitment is appropriate in realizing that one may be committed to law and legal institutions, yet not obligated (in the moral sense) by unjust laws. But, finally, it is necessary to differentiate between our commitment to law and legal institutions, on the one hand, and our commitment to the state and organs of government on the other. It is conceivable that one may lose confidence in the government but maintain one's trust in the law, exactly because the law may be used to restrain the government from unlawful action, or, if this fails, remain a force for civility by condemning governmental actions where these are organized for the purposes of oppression. Much more should be said about the topic of legal injustice, but this must be postponed to a later chapter (see Chapter XI).

## IX.2. THE PSYCHOLOGY OF COMMITMENT

Our commitments are many and varied. It has been said that promissory obligations are the paradigm of obligations (commitments in the narrow sense).[4] But this is not the case. Many of our most important commitments are not of this kind: our commitment to the law, for example, (a level-one commitment) is based on no promise that we make, or even implicitly make. To be sure, we have legal obligations (level-two commitments), but these obligations are likewise based on something other than on promising. On what? In the broadest sense, commitment depends upon agency, so an account of agency (insofar as it relates to commitment) is therefore required. But agency in this sense should not be understood exclusively as some active power (such as filling out one's tax returns: an obligation similarly not based on promising), for in the relevant sense a person's agency can also include passivity (such as not committing fraud or acts of violence). This kind of passive obedience to the law—at levels one and two—more resembles a 'state'

[3] See Romans 3:8.

[4] John Finnis, *Natural Law and Natural Rights* (2nd edn OUP 2011, hereafter *NLNR*) 297.

than an implicit promise. For most people, obedience to the law develops naturally with one's agency. There is no specific point at which it begins, any more than one can point to a specific time when one's agency is separated from that of one's parents or guardians. Supposed milestones on the way to adulthood are simply unhelpful abstractions in this regard. Thus there is no determinate point at which any promise, implicit or otherwise, comes into being. We should instead speak of a state developing in a person, which is only fully developed when a person reaches maturity.

The idea of a 'state' ought to be familiar to anyone versed in Aristotle's *Ethics*, for he argues that virtues are not feelings, rational choices or appetites but ongoing states.[5] But Aristotle says very little about states, other than that they are 'those things in respect of which we are well or badly disposed in relation to feelings', and that the states of which he is speaking (those of the virtues) are only one kind of state.[6] Aquinas goes further than Aristotle, and it is to his account of action that we must turn. A 'state' can be conceived as a central plank of one's total life, or a central part of the trajectory of one's life. One's level-one commitment to the law, for example, is a basic foundation of one's total life: the projects one pursues and chooses, the major decisions one makes, the relationships one enters into, and so on. This central (focal) state can be contrasted with the conscious obedience of the person to an oppressive legal regime, living in a state of constant fear. In the latter case, one's central commitment is to one's preservation, with commitment to law (particularly at level two) pushed into the foreground of one's thinking. In a benevolent regime, self-preservation remains an objective but is typically not the highest objective one pursues: we act for the sake, not merely of life, but for the good life. But we might ask how the psychology of commitment works in cases of ongoing commitments that are largely unconscious: particularly those of level-one commitments to legal and social order. Now as Aquinas points out, to will to bring about an end is to will all of the things that are necessary for that end, not necessarily consciously: whatever is moved by an internal *principium*[7] (that is, is moved by its own principle of action) must be moved by *some* knowledge of the end (*aliquam notiam finis*).[8] It is always possible that some of the things that are necessary for the end may prove unpalatable when they come to light; in which case one's basic orientation shifts to alternative priorities. But one's commitment to the law, foundational though it is in many respects, is not the only or even the principal determinant of one's life and choices. Familial and other close relationships define

[5] Aristotle, *NE* (n 2) II.5.1105b-1106a. See Philippa Foot, *Natural Goodness* (Clarendon Press 2001) 52ff; Howard Curser, *Aristotle and the Virtues* (OUP 2012) 1–3; Sylvia Berryman, *Aristotle on the Sources of Ethical Life* (OUP 2019) 76–78 & 161.

[6] Aristotle, *NE* (n 2) II.5.1105b, II.6.1106a.

[7] That is, origin/principle.

[8] Aquinas, *Summa Theologiae* (hereafter *ST*) I-II.6.1c.

one's life to a great degree, and require an ongoing commitment, although for many purposes can be taken for granted except when in crisis.

To have a commitment is not invariably to commit oneself to pursuit of a goal; one's commitment to the law for example is not for the sake of some goal, but often for the sake of deeper values that structure one's life. Such values may be termed as 'foundational', 'axiomatic', or 'ultimate'. Must the analysis rest there? Fortunately not: the nature and the mechanics of commitment to political, legal and social order are capable for further explanation. To acknowledge an obligation or commitment to forms of social order is to give partial expression of an underlying wish to be at peace with others; it is an expression and instantiation of sociability. A person desires their form of life, and thus has an ongoing commitment to its primary components. Commitment is not, therefore, intrinsically a relationship of inferior to superior: such a relationship, as of ruler and subjects, may form part of the social realities of order and peace, but one's commitment to a ruler in this manner is only to a part of the entire social realities to which one is committed as sustaining one's present form of life. This is not to say that a 'vertical' commitment to a ruler produces 'horizontal' commitments to one's fellow citizens, but rather that one's commitment to the entire fabric of social and political life is prior and more fundamental. Furthermore, one's commitment to the social fabric is not for the benefit of the ruler, but rather one's commitment to the ruler is for the benefit of the total social order of which such a commitment is only part and subservient. You may say: tyrannies typically involve commitment to social order for the sake of the tyrant, but (1) this is far from obviously the case: subjects of tyranny are committed to a repressive social order for the sake of what was once good and just about it, and the vestiges of goodness and justice that survive the repression, and (2) tyranny is in any event a pathological political reality which ought not to form or call into serious doubt the features of the central, focal, case. With that focal case in mind, however, further questions can be raised about the nature of (level-one) commitment to legal order and society. What is the psychology, what are the mechanics, of commitment to a form of life?

The question was asked by John Austin, for example, who analysed the matter in terms of a generalised 'habit of obedience'.[9] But that analysis is famously insufficient as an account of what we might loosely call 'social commitment'. (I use this term in a general sense to include commitment to relevant social, political, and legal orders.) Yet the notion of 'habit' (Latin *habitus*) is not without some interest. For it helps to explain the complex interworkings of the human mind in relation to some of its most profound commitments. Reference should thus be made to the notion of 'habit' as it is found in Aquinas's theory of human action. This is not the place for an intricate account of Aquinas's understanding of human action and

[9] See Scott Veitch, 'The Sense of Obligation' 8 (2017) *Jurisprudence* 415.

its components. It will be useful, nevertheless, bearing in mind the purposes of this section, to have resort to Aquinas's teaching on habits and dispositions. The following remarks, however, can be taken as an explanation of commitment as based upon St Thomas's theory. A commitment is not a habit, but the two concepts are related. A long-term or ongoing commitment can be said to be habitual if it becomes unconscious or automatic. This is particularly the case with negative commitments, that is, commitments to lack of action or agency.[10] It is easy to forget the decisive quality of inaction, or more precisely of one's choices in any number of situations where one has, so to speak, removed certain choices from the table altogether before deciding between acceptable alternatives. Choice is shaped by commitments of such kind in large ways and small. By forming a habit of (that is, committing oneself to) kindness to a particular person, one removes certain possible actions from one's reasoning altogether, such as acts of spite. Such ideas 'never enter one's head'. In a larger way, possible actions such as burglary, violence and fraud do not form part of one's deliberations in daily life. They are for the most part never entertained, and where entertained, not entertained seriously. But habits can also be conscious, or become the subject of conscious thought for a space of time (a moment, a few minutes, an hour, etc). In such cases—and in the vast majority of people—one recollects and reaffirms one's commitment to act as one usually does, or (equivalently) not to act as one does not. Aquinas's word for such phenomena is *habitus*, but his usage is distinct from the way Austin employs the English word 'habit'. For Aquinas's word is often used in conjunction with another term, *dispositio*. Aquinas at various points equates habits with dispositions; however he occasionally (and correctly) distinguishes the two concepts.[11] Neither concept has a lasting priority over the other: as both Aquinas and Aristotle attest, the inculcation of virtue in a subject is to enforce a habit through legally coercive measures, with the hope that this will create a *disposition* in the subject to act virtuously independent of the coercive measures. Here, habit precedes disposition (though continues as long as the disposition lasts). Alternatively, we can imagine a case in which a subject is disposed to act virtuously, but through weakness of will habitually acts in ways contrary to the virtue. The hope is then that the subject, through the disposition, forms a *habit* corresponding to the virtue, but the disposition continues as long as the habit lasts. Indeed, one may retain a disposition for something for a while after losing the habit: such as the disposition to practice the piano even after one falls away from the habit.

Commitment, to repeat, is not the same as a habit. Its beginnings in a young child are more to do with what is *not* done (stealing, fighting, lying) in which it is

[10] Aquinas, *ST* (n 8) I-II.6.3 ad 3: negative actions are as much a matter of choice as positive ones; for a lengthy account see Michael Tomasello, 'The moral psychology of obligation' 43 (2020) *Behavioural and Brain Sciences* e56, 1; also Stephen Darwall, *The Second-Person Standpoint* (Harvard University Press 2009) 151–79.

[11] See Aquinas, *ST* (n 8) I-II.50.2c, I-II.49.2c & ad 3, I-II.49.3c, I-II.50.1c, I-II.49.4c.

much harder to detect a *habit* than in a pattern of positive action. One does not normally say that one has a 'habit' of *not* smoking, for example. But these negative patterns of behaviour (that is to say, what one does *not* do) nevertheless involve a disposition. Commitment to law and order is therefore both behaviour and mode of thought. To be clear, I am not for the moment focusing on the complexity of one's 'internal attitude' to the law, after the work of HLA Hart. My purpose is to observe that even one's patterns of non-activity are (by implication) chosen forms of activity. The fact that the reasons for refraining from certain types of behaviour are seldom explicitly called to mind does not imply that such behaviour is merely automatic or unchosen. As Aquinas makes clear, voluntariness requires an act of cognition (intellect) just as it requires an act of the will; and just as it is possible not to will or act at the appropriate time, so it is also possible not to think (*cogitare*) about it.[12] Indeed the will has an indifferent relationship to many sorts of thing.[13] But let us proceed to examine commitment largely without the concept of habit, in order to get a clearer view of the intellectual landscape.[14]

First of all, to commit oneself to something (or someone) is to decide not to commit oneself to other things. A commitment to meeting one's friends (a relatively trivial instance of level-three commitments—voluntarily assumed non-legal commitments) is to decide against committing oneself to studying at home. Commitments can be to such things as times, efforts, and persons. From the point of view of commitment, each of these can take priority in one's thinking. Any commitment to persons or to exertions of effort requires investment of time: a commitment to use one's time for one purpose rather than another. But one could equally begin from persons: to exert oneself, on behalf of another, is the basis for one's decision to spend one's time in this way rather than that. Equally, one's investment in times or persons is made actual only through effort: the effort to do something, or not to do something. Can there be commitments to *things*? It does not seem so: one can have a commitment to *retain* some object, X, or to *defend, acquire* or *possess* X, but these are types of *effort* in relation to things rather than a *commitment* to things themselves. Such things are naturally spoken of as treasured or valued, but not objects of commitment. Here therefore we refer to the above types of commitment (of times, persons, and efforts) as level-three commitments. Level-three commitments are often in this way more pervasive than level-one (background) commitments in a person's lived experience. But one's commitments to family etc are nevertheless

[12] Ibid, I-II.6.3 ad 3, I-II.6.4sc (what is done wilfully even in such cases is not done out of necessity).

[13] Ibid, I-II.10.4c.

[14] Contrast Sylvie Delacroix, *Habitual Ethics?* (Hart 2022) 1.III: habits are internalized because our capacity to process elements of the external world is extremely limited; the habit is a 'short cut' (*Habitual Ethics?* 30). Aquinas's natural habits are very different: they arise in us naturally and are a natural part of human development and functioning. They are not 'short cuts' to understanding, nor are they especially held in order to facilitate understanding of the external world. They arise in us before the point at which we are able to articulate their significance.

more basic than these, and are further instances of level-one commitments (for institutions of the common good are not the only institutions basic to human life).

Though less pervasive, level-one commitments are *politically* or *socially* more important than level-two and level-three commitments: for there can be commitments to states of affairs, to communities (such as the Church, worker's unions) and to processes. Some of these commitments will be more or less in the foreground of thinking, at least some of the time; others will lie largely in the background. Commitment to the law, and its effects, will for most people be a background commitment. It is something that is willed (all commitments are willed) on the basis of a commitment to the good of persons, including oneself, and to the efforts required in upholding and maintaining that good. The term 'effort' as employed in this context should not be mistaken for onerous activity: the term applies equally and indeed especially to those actions, and refraining from actions, the ultimate end of which is more or less unconscious. One does not think of contract law when buying food; nor, if one does think of law and legal processes, does one typically remember the ultimate end of law in upholding the common good. The same is true of one's forbearance in the face of trivial harms, and of treating others with politeness and what Hart calls 'disinterested interest in others': that is to say, dealing justly with one's fellow citizens. Thus the background (level-one) commitment to the common good is referable to a concern with *efforts* and *persons*. It is further the case that, because justice and other social goods must be performed at the due time, this background commitment is also referable to a concern with *time*. The reference to the background condition is useful—even essential—however, as not all of one's commitments to persons, efforts and times are concerned with the common good. One's love for one's spouse, for example, or for one's children, does not take the common good as its object (even if it contributes to the common good). It is time therefore to explain how the commitments the average person has to social, political, and legal order are referable to basic sociability.[15]

'Sociability' in this context stands for that complex of actions, inactions and intentions that have the common good as its object, even if largely unconscious. However, as Aquinas observes, there must be some ends that a person wills that are not referable to any previous choice, but that are prior to all choices. The act of will that underlies all choices in this way can be called a 'natural appetite' or 'natural inclination', in relation to which the will is moved naturally and not out of 'free will'.[16] (When one looks for traffic before crossing a road, this is often unconscious, reflective of a natural appetite to preserve one's life.) What is thus willed naturally is what is suitable (*conveniens*) to human nature. In this respect, natural human

[15] For an interesting perspective see Marisol Garcia & Michiel Tegelaars, 'Sociability' in Anthony Orum (ed) *Blackwell Encyclopedia of Urban and Regional Studies* (Blackwell 2019) 1880–88; see also 2246–61.

[16] Aquinas, *ST* (n 8) I.82.1 ad 3, I-II.1.5, I-II.10, I-II.10.4c.

inclinations resemble animal inclinations (over which animals have no choice), but there is yet a *degree* of freedom of will, in human beings, even in relation to such inclinations.[17] For example, one may engage in actions that are anti-social, or which consciously harm the common good: theft or violence are of this nature. But even in committing such acts, one also remains committed to the general state-of-affairs—social peace, punishment only of crimes, stability, and order—in which those acts take place. Furthermore, one would also continue to be committed to such commonalities as one's use of a shared language, autonomy of will, and education (of whatever sort). Thus, even the criminal engaged in anti-social activities upholds and embodies sociability albeit in a reduced sense. It is impossible except to value sociability, even among those who pretend otherwise. One is steeped in sociability when one eats and prepares food and when one retires to one's hermit's lair, adapted to human needs; one is immersed in sociability when one learns and masters a skill and when one speaks and makes oneself intelligible to another; above all, when one relies upon the teachings of others, teachings that are themselves dependent upon other minds and previous generations who participated in sociable relations; upon the society at least of one's parents, for there never was a baby that could fend for itself.

Aquinas's mature view is nevertheless that the human being always wills from freedom rather than necessity, so that there is no object to which a person may not act out of hostility.[18] But it is impossible to rage against all of what sociability naturally entails. Only perhaps the evil one would seek to undermine all aspects of human social existence. Criminality is on that path, but not all of the way down. Anti-social tendencies are nonetheless real, and represent a threat to or erosion of the value of civility. Ordinary civility requires many things. One's adherence to such objects requires to be constantly reaffirmed in one's actions or inactions, that is, insofar as one continues to will those things. For sociability consists not merely in the negative actions of refraining from crime and civil wrongs, but also in the positive actions of politeness, agreeableness, and (in general) the forms of civility. Sociability is not willed of absolute necessity, for only beatitude is willed absolutely because it is integral to the very structure of the will, but sociability has the status of certain other ends that are willed 'with the necessity of an end' insofar as they are necessary for the ultimate end.[19]

So, sociability is a general commitment, inclusive of many things to do, to pursue and to avoid. It is a natural inclination, a deep form of commitment to which all persons are in some measure drawn. It involves level-one commitments to efforts

[17] Ibid, I.81.1c; see Candace Vogler, *Reasonably Vicious* (Harvard University Press 2009) 26ff. Some philosophers diminish the gap between human and animal cognition: see e.g. Kristin Andrews, *The Animal Mind: An Introduction to the Philosophy of Animal Cognition* (2nd edn Routledge 2020).

[18] Aquinas, *ST* (n 8) I-II.26.1c: only brute animals lack free judgment; humans too have necessary appetites but 'has some participation of freedom to the degree that it obeys the reason'.

[19] Ibid, I.81.2c; but see I-II.50.3 ad 2.

and persons, and (secondarily) to states of affairs. And it is for the most part a background commitment, coming into the foreground of attention only when its component acts or inactions are visibly threatened, as when the actions of a notorious criminal are brought to light. But the ground of sociability, is a central and profound instance of the most important of life's commitments: *love*. The motivating factor in all cases of human willingness is love (for the object that one loves): there is no (other) passion of the soul that does not depend upon some specific instance of love, and every movement towards something or rest in something proceeds from some relationship of connaturality with or conformity to that thing.[20] Love is the most basic element of any action, and all motions of the appetitive powers are based on the most basic affection of love. This is especially true of love of friendship (*amor amicitia*).[21] All of the moral life therefore hinges upon relations between persons.[22] The love of friendship is prior to love of all other goods, since one cannot love any goods except their being destined for those for whom those goods are good.

Kimberly Brownlee has nonetheless argued that there is a tension between the human need for 'associative control' (i.e. control over social relations) and our need for sociable connections:[23] 'Having considerable control over our decisions to associate or not is important for self- respect, autonomy and well-being.'[24] This paves the way for an analysis of social interaction structured by various well-known dilemmas such as the 'prisoner's dilemma'. The inspiration for this idea is Kantian: Can I will that everybody do what I do? This translates into concrete dilemmas such as this one; if every fisherman uses larger nets he will catch more fish irrespective of what others do, but if every fisherman uses larger nets the stock of fish will diminish and every fisherman will catch fewer fish.[25] Brownlee observes that the appearance of dilemma depends on a number of assumptions such as that there are sufficient fishermen to deplete the stocks, and that catching fewer fish is in fact a worse outcome for each fisherman. 'These dilemmas arise when we use our social resources in ways that, if everyone does the same, lead to indefensible allocations of social resources.'[26] This line of thinking can be traced back to Aristotle's criticisms of Plato, that in extending all social resources (of persons, property, affection ...) we radically dilute those resources and the mechanisms of that dilution become hideously oppressive.

[20] Ibid, I-II.27.4c, I-II.49.2 ad 1; see also J Budziszewski, *Commentary on Thomas Aquinas's Treatise on Law* (Cambridge University Press 2016) 21, 261 (on connaturality).
[21] Aquinas, *ST* (n 8) I-II.28.6c.
[22] David M Gallagher, 'The Will and its Acts' in Stephen J Pope (ed) *The Ethics of Aquinas* (Georgetown University Press 2002) 84.
[23] Kimberley Brownlee, 'Ethical Dilemmas of Sociability' 28 (2016) *Utilitas* 54–55, 57–58.
[24] Ibid, 57.
[25] See Derek Parfit, *On What Matters* (OUP 2011) 303; see Brownlee (n 23) 59.
[26] Brownlee (n 23) 60.

From the opposite perspective consider the following dilemma: 'If A shuns everyone, then he will feel safe and contented and will not incur the burdens of interpersonal duties whatever other people do. But, if everyone makes that same misanthropic decision, then the result will be socially worse for all.'[27] The underlying Kantian thought here is misleading for the possibility it alludes to is not a part of the human condition: the vast majority of human beings are not misanthropic and would not act as such whatever A decides. If a philosophy is to be useful (illuminating rather than confusing) it must throw light upon the human condition.[28] Brownlee suggests conditions that would need to be put in place in order to dissolve such dilemmas, such as claim-rights for children as a 'prerequisite for future associative control', respect, dignity, and meaning for all, reciprocity and the capability to make a social contribution.[29] But the worry that we will thus truncate associative freedom is entirely misplaced, for unrestricted associative freedom never existed in the first place. Such freedom must be theorized as expanding as a community comes under the rule of law and government, not as contracting, for the law makes space for protected personal choices in the form of freedom from the will of others (and the state). Obviously, law can also be used for repressive ends, in which associative freedoms are diminished, outlawed, or devalued. But even in such cases, the basic freedoms that the law establishes continue to provide protection to certain personal choices, as long as the state government continues to adhere to the rule of law: see Section X.3.

In the end, sociable commitment to law, order and stability is no more difficult or easier to understand than other commitments that unfold with time: such as love of one's spouse, one's commitment to one's friends, commitment to gaining a university degree, or to realizing a lifelong ambition. In all of these cases, there will be times when the underlying commitment is in sharp focus; at other times in the background almost forgotten. Thus Aquinas distinguishes between willing an end and intending an end habitually.[30] Virtue (which has been thus far left out of the discussion) is nothing other than a good habit that has become 'as it were natural' (*quasi-naturalem*):[31] that is, *second nature*. Sociability is a virtue in this sense; but there are also cognate virtues, such as obedience: for example, one's paying one's taxes, or (even) obeying an unjust law for the sake of peace.[32] As previously discussed, the virtue of justice is also connected closely to social peace, one element of sociability. Yet other virtues, as was noted earlier (Section V.1) can take on a dimension of justice insofar as they impact on other people: moderation, for example, is an important social virtue in times of rationing or panic-buying of

27 Ibid, 62.
28 Ibid, 62–63.
29 Ibid, 64–65.
30 Aquinas, *ST* (n 8) I-II.1.6 ad 3.
31 Ibid, I-II.58.1c.
32 Ibid, I-II.96.4 ad 3.

essential products, and is at any time essential in tempering one's desire for profit at the expense of honesty, fairness (as opposed to ruthlessness), and avarice (e.g. money-lending to the poor in society at usury), and so on. Similarly, by exercising fortitude one refrains from inflaming tensions within the community by not taking one's neighbour to court for trivial injuries or wrongs.

The psychology of these commitments has been set out in some detail. Questions of commitment to law and legal order were discussed because these are more difficult from the standpoint of explanation than the obvious cases of commitment to family and friends. Thus, in short, one's deepest commitments to law, social order, and to positive bonds of civility, are entirely natural, and are part of natural law. But discussion of this general aspect of sociability has barely touched upon the question of one's *obligation* to law: commitment in the narrow sense. The questions of one's obligations *in* and *to* the law are the subject of the next section.

## IX.3. OBLIGATION: COMMITMENT IN THE NARROW SENSE

The preceding section dealt with the ordinary person's commitment to legal, social, and political order. In doing so it was mostly concerned with level-one commitments.[33] This section is also concerned with level-one commitments, the commitment to be a law-abiding citizen of one's community, but also with a level-two commitment to substantive legal provisions. It examines both of these aspects of commitment to law and legal order by introducing a new concept: that of *obligation*. Commitment to legal, political, and social order, at both levels, can be explained as an aspect of sociability. As such, sociability is a human good. But it is not the only human good. Commitment to social order can be understood also as an implication from one's commitment or attachment to other human goods, which include one's personal freedom, availability of stores of knowledge and learning, systems of education, distribution, and economy, and so on; in other words, settled social conditions which constitute a complex state of affairs. Commitment has to do with the psychological dimension of social order, but there is also a moral dimension of social order, which hinges upon the issue of obligation—commitment in the narrow sense. An account is needed of legal, political, and moral obligation. The present section introduces the idea of obligation, and considers the example of legal obligation and of the obligation to obey the law.

Let us begin with the second of these subjects, the obligation to obey the law. It has indeed been suggested that no obligation to obey the law exists: that one's

33 As indicated in the preceding section, commitment to law and order is not the only kind of level-one commitment: for law is but one basic institution of society, which also includes the family, kinship groups, class-identity, worker's guilds, the economy and so forth.

ultimate reasons for action are moral rather than legal, so there is no distinctive *legal* obligation to obey the law.[34] One should, it is said, obey the law because it is *good*, not because it is the *law*. Such is not the case with natural law theory: as we have previously observed, Aquinas says that there are cases in which one is morally bound to obey even an unjust law,[35] and he regards citizens of a state as having a general obligation to obey the law owing to the legitimate authority of rulers.[36] Furthermore, Aquinas obviously believes that human beings are bound by natural law, at all times and in all places. But let us first examine Raz's influential argument that there is no general obligation to obey the law, as this helpfully brings into focus some of the issues that require discussion.[37]

There is an immediate problem: just as there are different kinds of law, so one might expect there to be different forms of obligation. In particular, one might expect a different form of obligation to hold in respect of the law of voluntary obligations than one finds in respect of public law, or criminal law. The term obligation to obey '*the law*' may prove an unhelpful abstraction. (In what sense, for example, do ordinary citizens 'obey' public law stipulations in relation to complaints procedures for consumers, of the implementation of human rights in domestic law, or of the assessment of welfare claims?) Now it is not possible for subjects of law to obey certain branches of law and not others: acknowledgement of the authority of one area of law involves recognition of the authority of law quite generally, not least because the law presents itself, and often in reality is, an interconnected *system*. The law of fraud presupposes the law of property, for example, and property that of contract. However, it proves difficult to state in precise terms the nature of one's obligation to bodies of law of which one has no conscious thought. For, to repeat, obligation is a moral, not a psychological, question. In one sense, the moral question would appear to be easier: a long explanation was necessary to cast light upon unconscious commitment to law and order, whereas it is clearly possible to have obligations of which one does not have knowledge (otherwise rule by law would collapse). How then do we specify the obligation to obey bodies of law of which one is unconscious? Such obligation cannot be to other branches of law 'whatever they may contain', for we have already observed that there is at most a qualified obligation to obey unjust laws. Perhaps: 'one has a general obligation to obey all laws save those that are unjust'? But people do not have that kind of relationship to the

[34] Joseph Raz, *The Authority of Law* (hereafter *AL*) (OUP 2009) 233. For a later statement see Joseph Raz, 'The Obligation to Obey: Revision and Tradition' 1 (1984) *Journal of Law, Ethics & Public Policy* 139.

[35] Aquinas, *ST* (n 8) I-II.96.4c.

[36] Ibid, II-II.104.5 (NB the limitations which will be discussed below).

[37] See Thomas May, 'On Raz and the Obligation to Obey the Law' 16 (1997) *Law & Philosophy* 19; see also Scott Hershovitz, 'The Role of Authority' 7 (2011) *Philosopher's Imprint* 16; Stephen Darwall, 'Authority and Second-Personal Reasons for Acting' in David Sobel & Steven Wall (eds) *Reasons for Action* (CUP 2009) 134; Stephen Darwall 'Authority, Accountability and Preemption' 2 (2011) *Jurisprudence* 103, esp 110–19.

law; they normally, and with considerable justification, consider themselves bound by all laws, good and bad. These are not the only problems with obligation: can one be said actually to *obey* or be *obligated by* the laws of contract? Certainly one must adhere to the rules of contracting in order to create a valid legal agreement, but as Hart points out, the nullity that results from a failure to observe the rules of contract cannot be theorized as a sanction for disobedience.[38] Nor does one breach an obligation by not contracting at all. Contract law is of course one part of 'the law of obligations': but this refers to the substance of the legal rules of contract and not the relationship of the legal subject to the body of law considered as a whole. For to whom is the obligation actually owed except the other party to the contract? Even in the law of tort, the 'involuntary obligation' is owed to the injured (and presumably litigating) party: the state's specific concern with enforcing the award of damages, if the defendant does not pay, is with contempt of court and not a breach of a (tortious) obligation towards the state.[39] That the concern of tort law is with obligations to the injured rather than to the state is demonstrated by the horror and falsity of the hypothesis that the basic rule of tort is: *either* take care to avoid injuring others *or* pay damages. Such a rule could never form a principle of justice.

But in spite of this, it seems possible to define a general obligation to obey the law as a whole: namely, that all persons, natural and legal, and all groups and organizations, are bound by the law *as it applies to them*. The sense of the word 'applies' here is not simply another word for 'binds' or 'obliges'. The law of contract, for example, 'applies' to a person whether or not they 'have applied it' to their present situation. The law of tort 'applies' irrespective of whether any accident has occurred. The idea of application emphasizes the law's *potentiality*. The areas of law just mentioned *potentially* apply to an ordinary person, but public law rules concerning standards of reasonableness in public authority decisions do not. The law of criminal attempts potentially applies to a person (if they act or contemplate acting in certain ways) but rules relating to jury selection do not. And so on. One can have a general obligation to obey the law in light of all those bodies of law that apply to one. One does not and cannot have an obligation to those areas of law which do not even potentially apply to one. But obligations in this respect can obviously change. One may become a judge, or a police officer, or a local authority planner. In each of these cases and many others besides, one may be subject to bodies of law *ex officio*. Such obligations arising out of offices are, in effect, *promissory* obligations, for the person entering office is normally required to promise to undertake certain duties of office, and to promise to discharge further duties as may from time to time be imposed on the office. They typically promise to do so faithfully and justly. But it

[38] HLA Hart, *The Concept of Law* (3rd edn OUP 2012, hereafter *CL*) 33–35; James Gordley, *Foundations of Private Law: Property, Tort, Contract, Unjust Enrichment* (OUP 2006) 159ff.

[39] See John Gardner, *Torts and Other Wrongs* (OUP 2020) 2–5, 10; on strict liability see 173ff and Gordley *Foundations of Private Law* 182–215.

remains that the majority of ordinary legal obligations are not promissory in this sense. Promissory obligations do of course arise in law, and the nature of such obligations will be outlined below. But for the moment let us continue to consider the 'general' obligation to obey the law.

A preliminary question suggests itself: if we have an obligation to obey the law, to whom is the obligation owed? To the entire community? To the organs of state and government? To the law as such? To those affected? The answer is that all breaches of law weaken the peace and order of the community, even when the specific harm is to some person or group of persons: if I commit an assault on another person, I have broken an obligation not to harm that very person (of all persons); if I breach a contract, it is to the other party to the contract that I owe the damages. But both breaches of the law weaken the fabric of the community in real ways. Contracting becomes more uncertain the more people that break their contractual agreements. One specific home invasion affects the sense of security of all households. My breaking the speed limit with apparent impunity emboldens others to do so in turn. All breaches of law erode the trust that each person places in other people that they will conform to the law (and thus to expectations). This suggests that the obligation to obey the law is one that is directed to the community as a whole, as well as to the specific persons affected by one's unlawful actions. There is no reference to organs of government or to law itself in such reasonings. This seems right: organs of government and of the state generally, including law, are a service-industry. They are for the common good, not the good of themselves. But there are clearly actions one can take that directly harm such institutions (contempt of court for example), and it is at least arguable that *any* action committed contrary to the law is an offence against legal order as such.

Some more initial remarks: it is sometimes said that there is no absolute obligation to obey all laws, and thus no real obligation to obey laws simply in virtue of their status as laws.[40] That there is no absolute obligation to obey the law is beyond argument; no person possesses an obligation to obey the laws of an extremely evil regime, and may indeed possess an obligation to break them (see Section XI.2; XI.7). But the consequence does not follow. One may possess a conditional obligation to obey the law, just as one may possess a conditional (though no less real) obligation under the law of contract. The difference between the two examples is simply that, in the case of contract, one's obligation is annulled if the other party to the contract fails to perform his or her side of the bargain, whereas in the case of obligation to law in general, the precise point at which one's obligation ceases in the face of a substantially unjust or persecutory legal order cannot be precisely told. The other suggestion that is sometimes advanced is that obligation to the law is of an exclusionary character. To be sure, there are certain features of legal order that

[40] I take this to be the point of Raz's discussion in *AL* (n 34) 236.

add weight to this suggestion: the law (it is said) cuts off moral debate (presumably about liability) by laying down a rule (or: ruling) accepted as final. But there are two reasons for rejecting this suggestion: (1) legal rules are not, as is well known and understood, self-interpreting, the question of their bearing upon and significance for each instance of application can be a matter of complex reasoning, and (2) in common law systems, the law is regarded not as a system of rules artificially grafted onto a community's practices, but an 'artificial perfection of reason', that is, a perfection of just that moral thinking that the objection regards as to be replaced: legal reasoning is a kind of moral reasoning. As such it is relatively rare for the law in a common law system to be expressed as a finite and final rule, immune from further revision.

The rules of a legal order are not exclusionary, they are *authoritative*. Except in the case of divine commands, authoritative rules are never absolute; their strength depends upon the factual and moral power of the law-maker(s). If the ruling authorities are benign in their purposes, and are factually in control of both law-making power and law enforcement, then the positive law will be strongly authoritative in character; if benign and lacking in control of law-making and law-applying instruments, weakly authoritative; if malignant, of no real authority for such governance is by terror rather than by law in the focal sense. Of course, there are degrees of legal authority just as there are degrees of malignancy or benignity in rulers, and of factual control of the law-making and law-applying machinery. A malign power may seek to govern scrupulously through institutions of law, in which case such laws would possess more than merely nominal authority: see Section VIII.3. But in all cases, authoritative rules *as they apply in the practical reason of reasonable people* are qualified rather than absolute. Unlike exclusionary reasons, they are *presumptive* and *defeasible*. They are defeasible because all such rules can be overcome by strong reasons to the contrary in one's sincere and careful practical reasoning: driving a dying family member to hospital, one may decide to break the speed limit; on the point of starvation, one may steal some food. But in every case, even that of the malign ruling power, legal rules are presumptively those rules by reference to which one guides one's conduct, not least because one may face the realities of punishment for one's transgressions. They are presumptive because society depends upon rules that are laid down, enforced, and obeyed, and thus carry more weight prima facie than one's own judgments on one's behaviour.

Raz rightly says that a reason to do that which the law requires does not entail an obligation to obey the law.[41] This is obviously true: I may have reasons to do what the law requires that are entirely prudential (in the non-moral sense). But neither does the prevalence of such reasons exclude an obligation to obey the law. Raz also conjectures that an obligation to obey the law implies that the reason one should

[41] Ibid, 233; see also Nikolas Kirby, 'The Service Conception: Just One Simple Question' 32 (2017) *Law & Philosophy* 255.

act in accordance with the law is because of the very fact that it is so required.[42] This Raz disputes; but in fact that very reason to obey the law is owed to the presumptive character of law. If Raz's argument were to succeed against legal authority, it would have to extend to all authority, including parental authority: if a child's reason for obeying his or her father was based on nothing other than the rectitude, practical and/or moral, of every command of the father's, then there would be occasions on which the child should rightly refuse to conform to them; indeed the true measure of conduct would then be the child's rather than the father's. But in fact children obey the commands of their parents precisely because those parents stand in relation to them as authorities.[43] Likewise, if the measure of an organization's rules (whether this be a worker's union, a bridge society, or a priest's relationship to his bishop) were nothing other than their acceptance on prudential or moral grounds, or through pressure of conformity, there would be no authority at all. But this is not the case. As Aquinas points out, the presumptive authority of laws extends even to unjust laws,[44] which should be obeyed except in the most grave circumstances.[45] Nor does defeasibility divest the law of its presumptive authority: any kind of defeasibility must employ considerations from outside the normative system which has the presumptive authority. As before, if such defeasibility cancelled out presumptivity, no kind of authority could exist. Similarly, any normative system that has some aspect of the welfare of persons at its centre (be it a concern with persons *as* persons, or with fair play at bridge) corresponds to an order of practical thinking, and a set of issues and concerns, that express and promote those aspects of welfare on their own terms, and perhaps even go beyond them. None of this is incompatible with the presumptive but defeasible authority possessed by such social institutions; nor does this mean that people act for the sake of those norms rather than that of authority: a driver impatient to get home, and impatient of the speed limit, may nevertheless drive at a safe speed under or at the limit *because* that is what the law demands. (The driver's actions need not be fuelled by the desire to avoid lawful punishment, but simply out of a desire to be law-abiding in all areas of life and law, consciousness of the law—a speed limit sign—reminding the driver that *this* action *now* must be integrated into a general attitude of obedience to law.) Raz's specific argument against the obligation to obey the law therefore fails.

One has legal obligations. But not obligations to adhere to those obligations (and further obligations to adhere to those obligations, potentially to infinity). This does not mean that there is no general obligation to obey the law, for the above examples demonstrate that the general obligation is grounded in a moral

[42] Raz, *AL* (n 34) 234.

[43] See Aquinas, *ST* (n 8) II-II.10.12sc, arg 1 & ad 4. Richard Dagger also rightly opposes 'anarchic' accounts of legal obligation as misunderstanding the nature of obligation, albeit on different grounds: see Richard Dagger, 'Authority, Legitimacy and the Obligation to Obey the Law' 24 (2018) *Legal Theory* 77.

[44] Aquinas, *ST* (n 8) II-II.57.1 ad 1.

[45] Ibid, I-II.96.4c.

commitment, not simply to the common good, but to the common good *as defined* and *upheld* by the specific instrument: the law. The heart of the obligation to obey the law is that law (in the focal sense) is the pre-eminent way in which a society can organize its efforts for the common good of the whole community.[46] There are many ways in which people can damage that common good: by eroding the ties of politeness, gentleness, and civility; by acts of spite and unkindness; by demeaning or degrading women in advertising; by mocking religion or being intolerant to the political views of others. But to damage the primary instrument by which the common good is promoted is rightly regarded as a more grave offence. Raz casts doubt upon this, observing that (a) perhaps certain people, such as the Archbishop of Canterbury, may have a moral duty to refrain from breaches of law, since they have a profound influence on the attitudes and behaviour of many people.[47] But (b) the majority of people do not have that visibility or influence,[48] and in any case many such offences are scarcely detected at all. This argument is misconceived. First and obviously, the factual effects of non-compliance have no bearing on the *moral* issue of obligation. There are no moral exemptions to the obligation to obey the law based on class, economic status, or invisibility of person or crime. The high visibility of the Archbishop and the moral example he sets are entirely collateral to the main issue of obedience which stems from the law's preeminence as a force for the common good. Likewise, the invisibility of a crime to detection is entirely beside the point, for the crime retains its damaging effect (however small) on the common good. One is reminded of Plato's comment in the *Gorgias* that it is better to suffer an injustice than commit one, and, if one has committed an injustice, that it is better that one's injustice is brought to light and that one should be punished for it.[49] Raz admits that a 'public atmosphere of respect for law rests on the cumulative effect of individual behaviour'.[50] This is certainly true, but this is not the *point* of obedience, which is to make one's due contribution to the common good of the community. Of each person in the community, there are no moral grounds for exempting oneself from this duty: there are no special reasons why I, rather than you, should possess such a duty.

Raz entertains the idea that the obligation to obey the law is entirely prudential rather than moral.[51] However this cannot be the central reason why all people within a community conform to the law; it is not the central case of that critical and reflective attitude that most people have in respect of the law.[52] Furthermore, Raz

46 For an account similar in some respects to the present one (but which focuses not on organization but the law's educative function in communicating to people how to act for the common good) see Daniel Mark, 'The Failure of Joseph Raz's Account of Legal Obligation' 61 (2016) *American Journal of Jurisprudence* 217.

47 Raz, *AL* (n 34) 237.

48 Ibid, 238.

49 Plato, *Gorgias* 469a–479e.

50 Raz, *AL* (n 34) 237.

51 Ibid, 244. See also Frederick Schauer, *The Force of Law* (Harvard University Press 2015) ch 5.

52 See Finnis, *NLNR* (n 4) 6–17; Hart, *CL* (n 38) 57.

appears to misunderstand the nature of prudence when he remarks that '[e]ven those who consider prudence a moral virtue will agree that on most occasions it is at best praiseworthy but not obligatory to exhibit it in one's behaviour'. Now as Aquinas demonstrates, prudence (*prudentia*) is both an intellectual and a moral virtue.[53] Prudence is 'a kind of intellectual aptitude' that enables a person to make judgments in accord with their proper end; and it is also a moral virtue by which right reason is applied to matters of direction (*consilium*).[54] But considered as a moral virtue, prudence is not concerned only with excellence, but also (as with all virtues) with the minimal demands of duty. The virtue of prudence is thus relevant to the everyday decisions of every person. Virtues on the classical definition 'make a person good and their works good': in other words, they enable the person to stand in the right relation to themselves and others, and to conform their actions to standards that are reasonable, sociable, politic. Hence even if the obligation to obey the law were based on no other virtue than prudence (say, justice), then it would remain a moral and not merely a cynical motivation. Furthermore, neither this last consideration nor any other above depend upon a principle of mutual restriction of conduct: mutuality is not mentioned at all.[55] The obligation is not to do as others do, but to do as the law commands, or enables.

More recently Crowe, like Raz, adopts the position that whilst there might be good reasons to recognize the binding quality of some laws, there is no generic obligation to obey the law.[56] Nobody argues that law, as a social institution and set of realities, is perfectly moral. But as will shortly be argued (see Section IX.4), there is nothing preventing a person from having a commitment or obligation to imperfect social institutions, so long as these sufficiently serve the common good of the community. There are many reasons for this, including (i) that the law is the preeminent way in which citizens act for the common good, sometimes singularly, sometimes in peaceful cooperation with others; (ii) that law and legal institutions channel and limit governmental use of force, coercion and penalties; (iii) that law brings certainty to personal dealings; (iv) that law brings certainty to mechanisms for the peaceful resolution of disputes; and (v) that law provides continuity in government and peaceful succession of political power.

It will be noted that I have made no mention of the law's coordinating function. In relation to this function, Finnis has this to say: 'Attempts to absorb the individual or particular groups into a vast overall co-ordination "solution," so as to eliminate all private purposes and all enterprises launched for reasons other

[53] Aquinas, *ST* (n 8) II-II.47.2 ad 1–2, II-II.47.4c, I-II.57.5c.

[54] Ibid, II-II.47.2 ad 3.

[55] See for contrast HLA Hart, 'Are There Any Natural Rights?' 64 (1955) *Philosophical Review* 185.

[56] See most recently Jonathan Crowe, *Natural Law and the Nature of Law* (CUP 2019, hereafter *NLNL*) 18, 208; also from a different perspective see Alasdair MacIntyre, *After Virtue* (Duckworth 1981) 25.

than the advancement of the public co-ordinative scheme, confuse the idea of a national common good with the idea of a national common enterprise or scheme of co-ordination. Such attempts, indeed, thereby do grave damage to the common good.'[57] But the law also coordinates in a second sense, of equal importance with the first: it enables joint ventures by coordinating individual actions through the requirements of legal instruments such as contracts, deeds, equitable transfers, and so on. Without such instruments, and without such coordination of action, no joint projects are viable, at any level of complexity. At the same time, the law's primary function is not that of coordination: see Sections VIII.2 & X.2.

This brings the discussion around to substantive legal obligations: what is their nature? Like any obligations, legal obligations are a kind of commitment. We have already had cause to mention that certain trends in contract law view contractual obligation as a disjunctive obligation: *either* one must perform the contract *or* else pay damages.[58] The logic of this interpretation of legal obligation can be carried into any area of law: one must *either* take reasonable care to avoid accidents *or* compensate the victim(s); one must *either* avoid committing crimes *or* face the threat of detection and punishment; one must *either* execute a valid will *or* frustrate one's own posthumous wishes/disappoint one's relatives; one must abide by a court ruling *or* face contempt of court, etc. These examples are perhaps sufficient to demonstrate that this logic simply fails to capture the essential features of legal obligation. And what are such features? The obligation (1) is defined in law; (2) has legal effects; (3) is (therefore) predictable in its operation; (4) demands or enables some defined activity (or inactivity); (5) concerns a relationship between defined parties or groups (including the whole community); (6) cannot in general be waived or enforced by third parties, except where the law specifically provides (see Section VI.2); (7) requires demonstrable agency (legal personhood); (8) can create or modify other legal obligations; (9) affects the legal position of another (or others); and (10) is enforceable by a court or by order of court. This list of features is not, and does not intend to be, exhaustive, but legal obligations will ordinarily exhibit these features, as opposed to 'mere' moral obligations. Legal obligation is therefore a special case of commitment, as outlined above. It has the further feature that if one is legally committed (i.e. obligated) to some action when the result is in one's favour, one must also be committed to the outcome when against one's interest. The fact that one's legal obligations (for example, one's duty non-violently to cooperate with prison staff while in detention) may weigh against one's interests (at least one's immediate or perceived interests) is the final nail in the coffin of the

[57] John Finnis, 'Law as Co-ordination' 2 (1989) *Ratio Juris* 97–104.

[58] The point is reinforced by the fact that one may claim damages against a partially performed contract to the extent of the loss.

disjunctive view of legal obligation. Few prisoners indeed regard their incarceration as the 'price' of their criminal act.

It should be interjected here: although legal obligations are *presumptive* in their force (moral reasons overcoming e.g. a legal obligation unjustly to deprive another of their property), such obligations are absolute from the intra-legal perspective. Hence, when lawyers are faced with a legal obligation that is overburdensome or unjust *in the circumstances*, their response is to define more precisely the extent of the obligation in line with competing legal considerations or with public policy. This preserves the absolute character of legal obligations at the expense of their scope. The result is that all legal obligations are of equal force, or in other words, one legal obligation is not more binding or less binding than another. Thus, when a person acts in contravention of a legal obligation on grounds that it is unjust, their reason for doing so can only be extra-legal; it cannot be harmonized with intra-legal considerations (see Section IX.6).

The burden of the preceding long discussion has been upon the generic obligation to obey the law. As we have seen, this kind of obligation is both moral, and specifically legal, in character. It is moral insofar as it concerns the common good; but it is specifically legal in that law is the preeminent means by which the common good is secured. But the obligation to obey the law is only one kind of moral obligation. To continue the discussion it is therefore necessary to examine moral obligation in general, and this will be the burden of the next section. (I will return to the issue of legal obligation below.)

## IX.4. MORAL OBLIGATION

Commitment is a certain voluntary act: it is, or involves, a constant willingness to act, or refrain from acting, in a particular way. Obligation, by contrast, is in most cases non-voluntary. Aside from the special case of voluntary obligations in contract law and elsewhere, obligation is not a matter of willingness except in the sense that acts (or inactions) carried out to fulfil the obligation require the activation of free will, the possibility of breaching the obligation always being present in that same will. In fact the legal category of so-called voluntary obligations would be better described as *voluntarily assumed* obligations; once the obligation comes into existence (due to an act of will, or perhaps many acts of will) it is likewise non-voluntary, and actions incompatible with the obligation thus voluntarily assumed are (1) wrongs, both legally and morally, and (2) enforceable against one. At the same time, commitment is required if one is to carry out one's obligations. The very act of will by which we fulfil our obligations is nothing other than our commitment to those same obligations. Similarly, any commitment at variance with an obligation is a refusal to shape one's actions in accord with that obligation; it is (if carried forth into action) a breach of that obligation. This section is concerned with our moral obligations: what it means to have such an obligation, what it means to breach them, and how they relate to our obligation to obey the law.[59]

As aforementioned, the fulfilment of moral obligation depends upon a certain kind of willingness, so that obligation is a special form of commitment. Our moral commitments are many and varied: some of them come into existence at certain points in time, last a particular length of time, or are timeless and bind us throughout our lives. Promises, for example, are made at a certain time and can be of indefinite length: the promise to meet with one's friend that evening is fulfilled or breached in that moment; whereas a promise made to one's dying mother that one will look after one's father is of indefinite length and can be breached at any time. To have an obligation is to have a strong reason for carrying out the particular act(s) that fulfil the obligation. It is not an exclusionary reason but a presumptive reason. For moral obligations do not exclude reasoning contrary to the obligation at any stage. A judge has a moral obligation to discharge to the best of his or her ability the requirements of office in applying the law as it is written; but a subsequent order of the state (validly enacted) which requires judges to divest Jewish members of the community of their legal rights and protections, overturns that strongly presumptive moral obligation. Less extreme examples abound. It is frequently said that a commitment to do X implies a commitment to do whatever it takes to bring about X. But this is untrue from the psychological standpoint: one may discover, after having committed oneself to X that part of the efforts one must undertake in order to bring X about involves an illegal act. In that case, one may revise one's commitment to do X. If not thus shielded from countervailing reasons, are moral obligations then cast back onto the 'balance of reasons'? By no means. The imagery of weighing and balancing reasons is not a happy one. Commitments shape one's life in numerous and intricate ways, and are not simply 'balanced' by reasons *pro et contra*. One's commitments can be hard to break: consider the perspective of a person who has been law-abiding throughout their life, but faced with a gravely unjust law decides to break the law.

Van der Vossen hypothesizes three lines of argument in relation to obligations to unjust institutions: (1) the 'exclusion thesis': it is impossible to incur obligations to unjust institutions; (2) the 'balance thesis': obligations to unjust institutions must be balanced against other moral commitments; and (3) the 'limitation thesis': it is possible to incur obligations to unjust institutions but there are moral limits to what such obligations can require.[60] We have already seen that (1) is false: natural law theory holds that at least some unjust laws, and unjust institutions, oblige in conscience; a position further discussed in Chapter XI. For certain aspects of the common good require such obedience. (3) is a reasonable formulation

[59] See generally Farbod Akhlaghi, 'On Moral Obligations and Our Chances of Fulfilling Them' 23 (2020) *Ethical Theory and Moral Practice* 625.

[60] Bas van der Vossen, 'Consent to Unjust Institutions' 27 (2021) *Legal Theory* 237.

of a principle of natural law, for unjust laws and unjust institutions damage the common good in small ways and large. (2) is an expression of the balance sheet conception of reasoning lately criticised (see Section VIII.2). But it is correct to say that (a) one's obligations to unjust authorities—i.e. one's political obligations—must be placed into dialogue with one's moral obligations, to which those obligations sometimes yield; and (b) one's moral obligations do not affect the political realities of these political obligations, such as decisions of the criminal courts, sentencing and so on. Duke makes explicit what is implicit in these observations: that one's obligation to unjust institutions such as law cannot reduce to an obligation to obey each law on its merits, but is rather a genuine obligation to the institution, that is to say, an obligation to obey all laws independently of their substance: a commitment that ensures the common goods of predictability and stability.[61]

Now it is true that the obligation to obey the law is only one of the central moral obligations that shape a person's life. There are one's obligations to one's family members: parents, spouse, children. There is a teacher's obligation to his or her students (as opposed to some other set of students), and there are one's obligations to one's neighbours and to strangers in need. What would make a law-abiding person break the law? It must be that the law in question is unjust, either to oneself or to others. In either case the injustice must operate to deprive oneself or another of certain human goods that are absolute and overriding. Such overriding goods represent one's deepest commitment. Their importance surpasses even that of one's family members (one must prefer justice even to one's parents), although many such goods cannot be obtained to any great extent without commitment to one's family, since they centre upon familial love and affection. Thus for example, if one's child commits a crime, obtaining justice for the child (criminal punishment) must be preferred to shielding the child from the law. In such circumstances, one cannot dissemble to the lawful authorities concerning one's child's whereabouts, or provide a false alibi; but out of parental love one can withhold one's cooperation from the legal processes, act as a witness for the defence, provide an impact statement, and so on. Again, by doing so, one is not 'balancing' or 'weighing' one's commitments to law and family, but rather giving reasonable priority to the law, in the face of seemingly counterposed interests which continue to provide reasons for action. Such judgments of priority are based on the characteristic forms and implications of human goods, and upon reasoned judgments as to how they should be given effect in the concrete circumstances in which one finds oneself. The good of sociability clearly indicates that the guilty must be brought to trial and subsequently punished; it also indicates that familial love and support continue to be given to the guilty person, and that any criminal trial must be fair, with a presumption of innocence until guilt is established, an unbiased jury, truthful witnesses, uncoerced

[61] George Duke, 'Finnis on the Authority of Law and the Common Good' 19 (2013) *Legal Theory* 48.

confession, etc. The good of sociability of course also demands that the imbalance created by the crime be restored to balance: stolen goods recovered, punitive damages awarded, and so on.

A teacher or lecturer's obligation to his or her students can also form a central moral commitment of their life. For this involves *finding out* and *passing on* the *truth*, not leading students into error or fanaticism, not misleading them or leaving out important matters, not failing to equip them with the knowledge they require both for examinations and their future life. One must expend one's time and energy on one's own students, and one must be diligent in reading and scoring assessments to produce a *just* result. Similar obligations define the world of business and manufacturing. One's efforts must be focused on one's employer's benefit, and should not be directed at a rival's benefit by leaking trade secrets or designing products for competitors. One's employer is owed the truth about the product's strengths and limitations, and important information must not be left out. Mistakes should be confessed rather than covered up or hidden. There is such a thing as 'best practice' in all areas of human endeavour, associated not only with excellence, but with moral and sometimes legal obligations that are basic, central, essential.

None of this implies that obligation is the result of one's will being *moved* by fear of penalty or sanction, nor that it is moved by the superior will of a ruler acting upon the will of the inferior.[62] The reasons for obedience to law occasionally stem from such fears, but for the vast majority of people their commitment to the law arises from neither source. Yet obligation implies, as mentioned above, a species of *voluntary* action. If one cannot but perform an action or omission, if one cannot voluntarily assent to act or not to act, there is no obligation. In fact, the will's being moved by fear or by superior will is precisely the opposite of voluntary action. But the will *is* set in motion by something; voluntary assent does not come from nowhere. What, then, is the source of the will's impulse? The impulse comes from the mind itself, from the intellect's final *consent to action* (*imperium*). Obligations represent *ends* in human thought: that which must be done. It is Aquinas's constant teaching that the will does not formulate ends but only the means to those ends, namely those things that are towards the end: 'that the precise fact that the reason moves by its command is because of the power of the will. It thus follows that command is an act of reason which presupposes an act of the will, by the power of which reason impels movement, through its command, to the performance of the act'.[63] In relation to any voluntary act, then, it is an internal principle rather than an external principle that effects movement. But there are limits that affect our ability to will. One cannot, for example, will the impossible: one cannot will 2 + 2 = 5; nor can one will what is practically impossible, as in counting all of the grains of sand on the beach.[64] It is likewise impossible to will a contradiction, that is, to will both

62 See Finnis, *NLNR* (n 4) 348–49.

63 Aquinas, *ST* (n 8) I-II.17.1c; see also I-II.9.1c.

64 Nor, interestingly, can one technically will the necessary: one cannot will 2 + 2 = 4.

a proposition and its antithesis. In practical terms, one cannot consistently will two contradictory courses of action. Consequently, our acts of will take place within a web or matrix of commitments, many of which will limit future acts of will for it is impossible to commit oneself to contradictory propositions. One always has the capacity to revise or even abandon former commitments, if they turn out to be incompatible with one's present analysis of one's commitments, but this cannot occur very frequently, or else one's life would unravel, one would not be able to commit oneself to long-term projects, and one's practical reasoning would be almost entirely without structure. You or I may revise our beliefs about important matters such as climate change, but we cannot constantly change our commitment to our deepest core values.

The language of commitment ranges across a number of subject matters. Our moral obligations extend to questions of promising, to matters of justice and to matters of (moral or legal) right. These topics are to some extent interchangeable: in many cases of promising, it will be unjust not to perform on the promise; the subject of legal and moral rights are often promises of some kind; and right is intrinsically concerned with justice. But there are differences: one's legal rights in a society where the rich get richer at the expense of the poor, or at the expense of the legal protections of some ostracized group, obviously do not square with the value of justice. Similarly, there are many forms of promising which are not legally protected in the form of rights. As a result, moral obligations extend over a larger terrain than that of legal obligations as discussed in Section IX.3. Clearly the obligation to obey the law will ordinarily represent our largest (though not most fundamental) moral obligation; the question of how and when our (other) moral obligations take precedence over this obligation is a difficult question, one that I attempted to answer in part above, and will take up again in Chapter XI.

A brief word must be spoken about the language of obliging and obligating. HLA Hart famously distinguishes 'obligation' from 'being obliged' as part of a conceptual analysis of legal concepts.[65] The gun-man *obliges* rather than *obligates* the cashier to deliver the money. It may appear as if the foregoing discussion steps lightly over this distinction. But in fact the distinction that Hart draws displays the limits of conceptual analysis as a useful tool; for there are equally many cases in which the two supposedly separate concepts are equivalent. This will be the case in any instance in which the mode of speech refers to 'oblige *to*' rather than 'obliged *by*': 'I am obliged to you' means exactly 'I am under an obligation to you' and/or 'I recognize that an obligation has been created in me to you'. Similarly, there are many cases in which it is linguistically and conceptually appropriate to treat the concepts as equivalent, that is, as different perspectives of the same linguistic unit: I have an *obligation* to pay my taxes, and am therefore *obliged* to pay them; I have an *obligation*

[65] Hart, *CL* (n 38) 18–20.

to obey the law, thus I am *obliged* to do as it requires. The context in which Hart distinguishes the two meanings is a limited context that should in no way prevent us from using the terms interchangeably in other contexts. For as Suarez observes, an obligation is an *imposition* of a moral necessity of action,[66] the necessity of which consists in *obliging* the subject to perform the action. Now in this context (of moral action in the strict sense), it is correct to speak of an obligation. In other contexts (of moral action in the broad sense, 'moral' being synonymous with 'practical'), although there is an *obliging* (the gun-man gives the cashier a choice—explicit or implicit—*either* to hand over the money *or* be shot, a choice that is 'moral' in that broader sense) one would not normally use the word 'obligation'. But one is *obliged* to tell the truth because one has an *obligation* to the truth. Hence there is no difficulty, in the contexts outlined above, in referring to obliging and obligation interchangeably. Nor does this interchangeable usage create difficulties by suggesting, contrary to what was mentioned above, that obligation is a matter of fear of reprisal or punishment. Suarez is perfectly clear that the *vis directiva* of obligation is due to the rationality of the demand, not the evil (that may be) threatened.

We should not leave the subject of obligation without considering obligations in a field closely related to moral obligation: that of equity. In particular, it is worth considering the concept of estoppel. The structure of this concept is as follows: a person A's voluntary actions ('unequivocal promise by word *or conduct*'), when person B is induced to rely upon them, produce a situation whereby A cannot now retract (is estopped from retracting) the promise, for it would be unconscionable and inequitable to do so.[67] (A similar doctrine of legitimate expectations is to be found in administrative law.) For example, a creditor who tells or otherwise represents to a debtor that the debt is cancelled, cannot subsequently seek to enforce payment of the debt by the debtor. So-called promissory estoppel is in effect a working-out of the principles of justice, focusing on the behaviour or state of mind of A in relation to B. More broadly, estoppel(s) by representations in all their forms expound the implications of unconscionability, being one form or element of injustice. The subject is interesting because in most contexts, one thinks of justice as a matter of conforming one's *actions* to the common good: it matters not whether one pays one's taxes with fury in one's heart or with pity for the poor whom one's taxes will assist. One does not commit an injustice by merely thinking of or imagining assaulting an innocent person, but only if one carries out one's intention by one's actions. But the very definition of justice betrays its internal aspect: it is the constant and perpetual *willingness* to give to others what is due or owed to them (that is, a comprehensive and thoroughgoing *commitment*). And what is 'owed' to people includes their bodily integrity and freedom from violent acts which diminish the

[66] Francisco Suarez, *Defensio Fidei Catholicae Adversus Anglicanae Sectae*; see also *De Legibus* I.1.8.

[67] Let it also be mentioned that promising by word is itself an action (a speech-act) with all of the consequences this entails.

human goods that each person enjoys. Justice for example demands that one refrain from lying: people are on most occasions *owed* the truth, and are not to be duped or mislead by *actions* or *promises*, devious or sincere. Of other forms of estoppel (so-called 'reliance-based estoppels') I pass over since they are famously impossible to reduce to a single set of principles. Each is nevertheless an aspect of justice insofar as they restrict and/or eliminate A's access to remedies when his or her unethical conduct dupes or provokes B into acting to his/her detriment.[68] Equity's famous doctrine, that one must approach the court with clean hands, is similarly an aspect of justice's interior component, the willingness that drives and controls the actions one performs. The doctrine is not the same as justice: it is famously limited to claims of equitable remedies, common law damages being continually available. There are thus senses in which the operations of justice disregard the interior states of mind of the litigating parties, for example, A can successfully sue B for damages for breach of contract whether or not A is a morally bad person/undeserving/unprincipled. But the doctrine excludes from the remedies available to A those that would otherwise arise from his or her morally unscrupulous (and thus unjust) actions with respect to B.

Why is A excluded only from equitable and not from legal remedies? The answer is that there are other dimensions of justice besides those of conscience. In particular, the law of property depends upon certainty of title, a principle that can only be maintained if there is a limit to which searches into the root of title are required to be made. Thus, even if title to land originally arose out of an historical injustice (or even fraud, misrepresentation, force), there is a strong sense in which the present holder of the title should not be divested of that title by heirs of the party originally wronged. If all titles to property were required to be investigated to times beyond the necessary legal 'good root' of title, no person's title to property would be safe and secure. Such a situation would of course result in a great deal of economic uncertainty to the detriment of all, but that is not the only or principal reason why that situation would be unjust: for the innocent holder of the title is not *responsible* for the historic injustice, and nor—crucially—is the previous holder of the title (and so on to some indefinite point). You say: should not the purchaser of a title investigate the root of title to its beginning? But this is frequently impossible, the historical injustice often coming to light only at some later stage. You ask: does not the 'innocent' holder of the title share in the guilt of the previous owners, for the original who has seized the title is guilty, as is the purchaser from that original, as is the purchaser from that first purchaser, and so on in an unbroken line to the present holder of the title? The answer is no, the problem having similar features to that of the 'problem of the bald-headed man': the unbroken line does not have the same force everywhere along the line, even if a measure of the original

68 Damages would be available if A could demonstrate promissory estoppel.

injustice is present. This is why the present title to the property is *in a way* unjust (as are perhaps all rights which arise otherwise than out of a perfect original distribution/creation), but in an important sense *not* unjust for the transmission of guilt is blocked by the ignorance of the present title-holder and the previous generations of true heirs' failure to raise an action for recovery. The Limitation Act is therefore a kind of moral principle: it operates to exonerate holders of property from being divested of their ownership and/or shielding them from lawsuits for damages against originary 'owners', whilst recognizing at least in principle the justice of the latter's claims. The maxim that an unjust initial situation produces unjust rights has therefore only limited force.

Breach of a moral obligation, ordinarily, does not involve the threat of an evil imposed by a higher authority. (In a great many cases, the 'higher authority' who bestows the obligation is simply oneself. Even if one 'imposes' a negative consequence for failure to act for the obligation, this can obviously be rescinded at any stage, and one is aware of this.) The consequence of a breach of a moral obligation may be a matter of one's own guilt only, and thus essentially private, or it may be a matter of public shame or disapprobation. Which of these is the more keenly felt depends upon the circumstance and upon the person. But it is one's own guilt or shame that is more important, for, to seek to minimize or downplay the significance of the transgression to oneself is to open the door to further transgressions, and the seemingly gradual, but in fact quite rapid, ruination of one's character. This is confirmed in everyday experience: to take immoral action, to give in to temptation, the first time is a significant event, as one has to overcome one's good character; subsequent actions of the same sort are considerably easier. In both private shame and public humiliation, Plato gives the same advice: to do an injustice is worse than experiencing it; and if one is guilty of injustice, it is better to face punishment than to evade it. For Christians, penance and Confession give institutional expression to this need to be truly remorseful for what one has done, and to swear not to do it again. But this is a first stage after which must come (if appropriate) confession of guilt to the secular authorities, surely part of the penance for without this, there is not true sorrow for sin.[69]

The moral obligations that one may breach range from the fairly trivial (though perhaps hurtful to others: the failure to meet the friend as promised) to the seriously wrong. Some are voluntarily imposed, whereas others represent moral precepts that are not chosen but natural. Furthermore, it should not be assumed that the one type of obligation is lesser than the other, for voluntarily imposed obligations may be made in respect of grave matters. For example, natural obligations not to cheat in relation to small amounts of money with which one is entrusted can be contrasted with the assumed responsibility to care for an elderly relative (e.g.

[69] On the need to engage with secular authorities see Aquinas, *Sent.* II.44 ad 4.

the father on the death of the mother). To neglect or withdraw the care is vastly more blameworthy than to be dishonest with small things, though both, to be clear, are serious matters. It is at this juncture that one would normally mention conscience. According to Aquinas, conscience is an act (*actus*) of the person, although it is sometimes, not altogether inaccurately, confused with the very first principles of understanding in practical reason, under the Latin name of *synderesis*, which is neither act nor potency/power (*potentia*) but disposition (*habitus*).[70] But unlike *synderesis*, which can never be in error, the voice of conscience can be overborne by misguided loves (*concupiscentia*), or be genuinely but innocently mistaken about the secondary precepts of natural law.[71] Nevertheless it is our conscience which is the main voice of moral probity concerning our actions and inactions, and there is hence an obligation to educate our conscience about truly moral action, and about the glamour or ever-so-tempting nature of immoral action. It is this same conscience in virtue of which we elect not to obey unjust laws, that is, by which we put morality as such ahead of the perverted morality of secular institutions. It is even this conscience which leads us, as Aquinas says, to obey unjust laws where the detriment is to us, and where scandal and disturbance would follow if the law were broken.

Having a conscience does not of course imply the necessary traits of character required to follow it, particularly where the detriment to oneself is great. Lies beget lies, and moral evils lead to further moral evils. The traits of character necessary for obedience to conscience are none other than the virtues: moderation to curb excesses and greed; fortitude to avoid temptation, and where tempted, not to succumb; compassion (*misericordia*) not to ignore one's (moral) obligations to the poor; justice, not to permit injustice in one's actions and, where injustices have occurred, not to allow those injustices to continue unchecked; and prudence, to ensure that one is led by one's rational intellect and rational appetite (will), rather than one's unchecked desires, feelings, etc. Without the virtues, one would be in the position of knowing what is right, but unable to follow it, to bring that morality into one's desires and actions. Every person experiences the contrary pulls of conscience and desire on certain occasions, but only in the lives of those addicted to illegal substances, or to gambling or drinking, do we come face-to-face with persons who are almost entirely without virtue; who would not hesitate to steal from their own family in order to finance their habit; and who can live with their immorality only by muting the voice of conscience, at the cost of depression, anxiety and other forms of mental ill-health.

[70] Aquinas, *ST* (n 8) I.79.12–13. See CL Lowe, 'Thomas Aquinas on Our Freedom to Use Our *Habitus*' in Nicholas Flaucher & Magali Roques (eds) *The Ontology, Psychology and Axiology of Habits (Habitus) in Medieval Philosophy* (Springer 2018) 167; Brian Green, 'Habitus in the Roman Catholic Tradition: Context and Challenges' in Gregory Peterson et al (eds) *Habits in Mind* (Brill 2017) 41.

[71] Or culpably: see Aquinas, *ST* (n 8) I-II.94.6c, I-II.19.6c.

Aquinas makes the comment that conscience and reason are the same.[72] But our reason, or at least our *reasoning*, it may appear, is a product of social conditioning, especially by parents. The child that is brought up to believe that stealing, fighting, and dishonesty are permissible, perhaps even necessary, and that the law is a coercive structure, something to be evaded if possible, is overwhelmingly likely to exhibit erroneous conscience, a malformed faculty of practical reason. But such a child, and anybody, has always the capacity to challenge accepted norms: they perceive the inadequacy of those malformed teachings reflected in the battered faces of their victims, and in the recognition that one has no claim to one's amassed stolen goods. This is not to say that transformation of an erroneous conscience is an easy matter, or that it is effected in every case (far from it). Many people, perhaps all people, are not fully reasonable; we need think only of Aristotle's injunction that mere *arguments* are insufficient to turn a person away from their bad habits and bad reasoning. Nothing less than a full character transformation is required.[73] But once the seed of doubt has been sown, however small, fragmentary, or suppressed, the following of one's erroneous conscience is no longer reasonable but culpable. Contrarily, if one's erroneous conscience has been formed negligently or unreasonably, then (i) action stemming from it is culpable, but (ii) if unqualified by doubt, it is necessary nevertheless to follow one's conscience and perform the culpable action for it is always unreasonable not to follow one's reasoning.[74] One potent source of custom and influence in community is of course the law itself. It follows that unjust laws or bad laws can foster or reinforce an erroneous conscience.

Finally and briefly, we must distinguish, as other philosophers have done, between obligation and counsels of perfection. Now it is an obligation to seek to perfect oneself in virtue, but aside from that obligation, the perfections of character and of action are not in themselves matters of obligation: for example, one's volunteering at a homeless shelter, donating half of one's income to charity, adopting an orphan child, and the like. Equally, one is obliged not to pursue such perfections if in doing so one neglects one's other responsibilities, such as one's spousal duties or one's paid employment. Counsels of perfection are counsels to perfect oneself once one has met all of one's existing obligations, not at the expense of those obligations. One does not perfect one's character by failing to perform basic obligations.

This wraps up our long discussion of moral obligation. Such obligations are not essentially promissory: there is a wide variety of types of obligation of which only a narrow range are promissory in nature.[75] Nor are all obligations onerous, difficult, or felt as restrictions. One's spousal duties for example ought not to be difficult to

[72] Ibid, I-II.19.5c.
[73] Aristotle, *NE* (n 2) I.3.1094b.
[74] Aquinas, *ST* (n 8) I-II.19.6c & ad 3.
[75] Cf Finnis, *NLNR* (n 4) 295–308.

carry out. Indeed, as 1 Corinthians 13 reminds us, the carrying out of our obligations is as nothing, and we ourselves gain nothing from their performance, if these actions are not suffused with love: love here referring not to romantic love or the love of concupiscence, but *caritas*, charity. Such love is ultimate virtue, inseparable from and infused in all our actions. Nevertheless, it must be confessed that the foregoing discussion prescinds from many matters that could be raised (such as a detailed analysis of kinds of non-promissory obligations), which are not essential for present purposes.

## IX.5. POLITICAL OBLIGATION

The reader may have noticed that the foregoing discussions of legal and moral obligation have not used, or invoked, the concept of an 'ought'. Obligation has less, etymologically, to do with compulsion, than with the idea of 'binding' (from the Latin *ligare*). Nowhere is the notion of binding more difficult to fathom than in the context of political obligations. To define the question precisely: we are examining the obligation not to the law but towards political systems. In speaking of political obligations, various topics or subject-matters present themselves: the nature of the obligations that uphold civic life; obligations to forms of government; and obligations to political parties. Discussions of political obligation typically centre upon the first two of these topics, but entirely neglect the last. The last topic may appear to be niche or even irrelevant to the large questions of political society, but politics, and political forms, cannot exist without politicians, and politicians cannot get anything done except by joining with others in movements that seek after political power, and upon obtaining it, attempt to rule. I defer for a few moments consideration of the obligations of those who join political parties, to discuss briefly the case of ordinary voters in a liberal democracy.[76] Such voters do not typically engage with politics except at election times, except by keeping abreast of political developments, as best they can, through available media. Indeed it should be said that voters have an *obligation* to inform themselves, at a minimum, of the manifestos of the relevant parties, their track-record in government and in opposition, voting records of members on important issues, and the personal morality of those members in and out of the relevant Chamber. Nevertheless, voting is a complex issue, and I do not intend to go into questions of tactical- and protest-voting, self-interested

[76] For two recent accounts, see Jason Brennan, *The Ethics of Voting* (Princeton University Press 2011) and Scott Althaus, *Collective Preferences in Democratic Politics* (CUP 2003). See also Julia Maskivker, *The Duty to Vote* (OUP 2019) esp ch 4 and (on the responsibilities of the active citizen) Massimo Renzo, 'Political Obligation' [2021] *Oxford Research Encyclopedia of Politics* <https://doi.org/10.1093/acrefore/9780190228637.013.197>. See also Andres Rosler, *Nature and Normativity* (OUP 2009) esp ch 2 (on the nature of the human being as intrinsically political), and Judith Shklar, *On Political Obligation* (Yale University Press 2019) ch 4 (on friendship).

voting, or single-issue voting (e.g. voting Republican in order to promote a pro-life agenda when otherwise hostile to Republican policies or leaders). Instead I merely point out that voters almost never have a straightforward choice between a set of policies they believe in, and a set of policies to which they are hostile. Often voting is a matter of choosing the least worst option, of voting for policies one does not believe in, or to which one is actively hostile, in order to cast one's vote for one's preferred policies. I raise this point because it seriously weakens the bridge between voting and political obligation to the chosen regime: the fact that I vote for party X does not give me a straightforward *obligation* to that party, when in government, to accept that government. For then what about those who voted against the party of government, or who did so reluctantly, mistakenly, confusedly? If we want to understand obligation to political government, we must look elsewhere.

Single-issue voting, as just mentioned, undercuts any argument that obligation to political government stems from the substantive laws and policies pursued or enacted by that government. Furthermore, coalitions, minority governments, and those with slim majorities can rarely press ahead with policies as originally intended. Onora O'Neill has pointed out the 'Christmas tree effect', whereby government Bills become weighed down with amendments, often only tangentially germane to the subject which the Bill is intended to apply.[77] Thus voters seldom know what they actually voted for until the relevant policies are hammered into law. It can also be the case that governments are ambiguous over the point of the legislation they enact. For example, most governments place taxes on gambling. Is this intended as a potential source of revenue-raising, or is it a hope to discourage a certain form of behaviour which the government deems detrimental? Or again, is it intended as a piece of morals legislation to curb a social vice? Perhaps these alternatives represent shifting sands, the government itself not being absolutely clear which is being pursued at any given time. Our obligation to political governance, then, must be sought elsewhere.

The second question (that of obligation to a political party) admits of a shorter answer: one's membership of a political party brings with it a host of obligations, to advance the party's aims, abide by the whips, to vote with the government in all but free votes, to attend the Chamber and to minister to one's constituents by representing their interests. In addition, there is one's obligation to justice and fairness. Obviously, and poignantly, these obligations can pull in different directions. Political casuistry is often employed to provide at least a veneer of consistency, but the facts are that (1) no political party, especially in government, is wholly just in its ends and means, and (2) if there were no political parties, and especially governments, nothing of any value would get done, with catastrophic results for the common good. It follows that politicians sometimes (often?) pursue unjust policies

[77] Onora O'Neill, 'Making Laws Better or Making Better Laws?' 3 (2012) *Jurisprudence* 1–12.

in order to carry just projects into legislation. Now this is not very satisfactory from an ethical standpoint, for it violates the directive that evil should not be done that good may come. And nor can it be argued that politicians in each case *aim* for the good whilst *tolerating* unwished-for side effects. For the unwished-for policies are not side-effects at all, but distinct policies deliberately carried into legislation. It is all too easy to write off such legislation as the price to be paid for the good. But there seems no easy way to rationalize the injustice as anything other than directly willed, and as part of the intention formed in pushing through the benevolent laws. Many responses may be made to this situation: that members of the Chamber are not precisely voting *for* the unjust policies; that without such votes no government business would pass, to the detriment of all; that politicians and especially ministers must not sacrifice political progress for the sake of their own moral purity; that to defend benevolent laws politicians must defend the government that makes them; that any revision of these practices would entail a massive shift in our idea of government; or that politics simply is the art of the possible, and not the morally perfect. Each of these responses seems to me to fail. But they are not germane to the present work. Perhaps the short, but hopelessly idealist, solution is that politicians and policy makers must take much greater care that their policies do not violate norms of justice, and must not create policies the appeal of which is not moral but popular, vote-winning, etc.

To return to the earlier question: the basic question of political obligation is an ancient one.[78] How or why are we obliged to political authority? Various answers to this question have been proposed: that it is based on consent (real or hypothetical), gratitude or, in Rawls's case, fair conditions and fair institutions.[79] Each of these proposals can be interpreted as being concerned with discovering the *origin* of political obligation. But just as we saw in Chapter VIII that political authority has no beginning, neither does political obligation, that is, obligation to that form of government, whatever it may be. However, those same proposals can be interpreted as asking about the *nature* of our (present) political obligation. If so interpreted, they are false. No act of consent, real or hypothetical, has ever been given, and has never formed the root of our obligation to political governance. There never was fair play; there never were fair conditions. Expressions of gratitude to political authority, to one's community, are not made alongside growth in mature personal agency, or in many cases at all. In other words, there were no datable acts of any of these kinds. But the central reason for their falsity is simply that they assume political obligation begins with a voluntary act. Why should this be assumed? Once political obligation is understood as a non-voluntary obligation, the problem disappears: it then becomes clear that political obligation can be explained by a re-working of

[78] See Dudley Knowles, *Political Obligation: A Critical Introduction* (Routledge 2010) 4, 12.

[79] Mark C Murphy argues that 'surrender of judgment' equates to consent: see 'Surrender of Judgment and the Consent Theory of Political Obligation' 16 (1999) *Law and Philosophy* 115.

the second of the proposals above (gratitude).[80] Let us call this indebtedness: each person is indebted to political authority for all of the goods that flow from order and stability: peace, justice, security, safety, prosperity, economy. Each person's life is shaped by such goods, and flourishes only because such goods are set in place. Unlike the case of gratitude, one does not have a choice whether to be dependent (here and now) upon such goods, and hence one does not choose whether or not to be indebted to the authority that makes them possible: one simply is. This indebtedness obviously depends upon a political authority that is benign and which seeks to uphold the common good. One's indebtedness to political authority obviously wanes as political governance is perverted towards its own ends rather than those of the people. Precisely where this point lies is beyond the scope of the present argument and of this book, though aspects of the issue are touched upon in Chapter XI.

One cannot avoid being indebted to one's community and to the political authority that makes it possible. One's family life, the advantages and opportunities one has, the goods in which one participates, the very language one speaks: all of these depend upon a settled community under the power of governance. One cannot avoid being indebted to political authority. Now the reader might be surprised at the statement that those ranges of goods depend upon the power of governance: do such goods not exist in primitive communities prior to and independent of governmental authority? Certainly, governmental authority does not *establish* such goods, but neither are they prior to government nor fully independent of its agency. For, as we saw in Chapter VIII, there is no origin of political power, it is exercised in one form or another in every human society, and it thus helps to shape the goods upon which all people depend. To be clear, this does not mean that all of those ranges of goods are artificial products of positive action by political government. For (1) political government is itself natural, and (2) political government is not the origin of those goods, but merely cultivates a space in which those goods can grow and stabilize. No suspicion should therefore be held that the notion of obligation and that of indebtedness are the same, so that the one cannot explain or illuminate the other. To be sure, there are ranges of meaning in which the two are equivalent (to owe somebody money is to have an obligation to repay them); but this is not universally the case. One may be in someone's debt (say, for one's life having been saved when otherwise one would have drowned) without being under an obligation to that person. An author may owe some of his or her ideas to another person, without being under a reciprocal obligation to them (that is, aside from acknowledgment). One remains indebted to someone (say, for a kindness done at a difficult time) even if that person waives any obligation of reciprocity. Or one is cured by state-funded doctors, but not thereby obligated to

[80] Cf A John Simmons, *Moral Principles and Political Obligations* (Princeton University Press 1979) 185.

them. In the case of political authority, indebtedness *explains* obligation for our obligation(s) to political authority—keeping the peace, avoiding acts of harm or malice, reasonably cooperating with others, obeying the law, acting to sustain oneself and one's family—are grounded in the state's creation of conditions which make possible the entire edifice of civility to which one's obligations now contribute.

The indebtedness one has to political authority is not dissimilar from one's indebtedness to one's parents. Here again it is necessary to distinguish between indebtedness and mere gratitude: one may be entirely ungrateful to one's parents yet remain in their debt for all they have done for one. In other words, indebtedness is objective, whereas gratitude is merely subjective. Those philosophers who have conflated the two ideas entirely misunderstand the idea of indebtedness.[81] Nor ought we to think that there is any kind of parity or notion of equal return implied in the idea of indebtedness. Consider one's indebtedness to God as the Creator of one's life (with the cooperation of one's parents). One cannot ever hope to repay one's Creator in full for all benefits, including saving Grace, that are given to one. Analogically, one probably cannot adequately repay society for the benefits it brings: peace, stability, justice, and the rest. But this does not matter, for political authority does not exist for its own ends, but for that of its citizens. One's obligations to political authority are exactly those of upholding those basic values, something one cannot do alone but only in concert with others: in other words, conforming to core morality as defined in Section III.4.

For anyone unconvinced by the idea that political obligation lies in indebtedness, an alternative point of view is available.[82] Let us suppose that there is a natural duty on the part of each person to respect others. Such a duty would arise from the fact that each person is a separate locus of goods and forms of flourishing, no one person having naturally a greater or lesser claim to such goods and forms of flourishing than others. Now it is impossible to identify and quantify that respect without reference to a body of principles of behaviour which apply to every person and oneself. But such principles of behaviour mean nothing if not given force, application, and settled meaning by some authoritative source: such is apparent from Hart's treatment of the movement from a pre-legal into a legal world.[83] There is, to be clear, no definitive starting point at which obligation to political government arises. The 'step' into the legal world is not taken in one bound; and pre-legal societies (if one could so call them) likewise have structures of authority to which their members are in some way committed. But it remains that our civility, our debts to one another, are intelligible only in virtue of political structures (however primitive) which have no beginning. Thus we arrive by

[81] See e.g. Richard Price, *A Review of the Principal Questions in Morals* (OUP 1974), ch 7.

[82] See Alexander Douglas, *The Philosophy of Debt* (Routledge 2016) esp the link to Scholastic *debitum* 5–6.

[83] Hart, *CL* (n 38) 42, drawing upon a tradition stemming from Hobbes and Locke.

another route to the same conclusion, that obligation to political systems is an inherent part of human life.

Note however that such obligations are not reciprocal: they do not depend upon others behaving in accordance with their obligations.[84] If the majority of people were free-riders, this would not permit the minority to follow suit. Those obligations instead arise through practical reason's grasp of human goods and moral responsibilities, responsibilities which already involve sociability: see III.3.

## IX.6. THE TWO SENSES OF LEGAL OBLIGATION

To return briefly to the subject of legal obligation: In his discussion of legal obligation, Finnis draws a distinction between 'legal obligation in the moral sense' and 'legal obligation in the legal sense': for one can elect to obey the law because one understands that law is a central means of upholding the common good, and thus is part of one's unrestricted reasoning about matters that pertain to the common good; or one can regard law as a means of isolating certain norms from the free play of reason which would otherwise be without conclusion, definition or (probably) force.[85] Furthermore, Finnis argues, a breach of certain legal rules is less serious, from the moral point of view, than breach of others, but from a legal point of view each law is equal in terms of legal obligation to obey.[86] This is doubtful: whilst the law is enforced through the courts, and through committed though disinterested policing, the penalty imposed by the courts in relation to petty offences is much less than for that of serious criminal offences. This reflects the fact that a breach of the criminal law is more serious than that of a contractual breach, for example. Similarly, police powers as legislatively defined and as shaped by public policy considerations, are not concentrated on all criminal activities equally, but on priority areas, or even pragmatic directives in the face of insufficient manpower or resources of detection and investigation. Barring such pragmatic reasons (which also affect the courts: plea deals for reduced sentences, fines or community behaviour disorders being imposed instead of jail time due to prison overcrowding, etc) the ranking of offences reflects the moral harm done to the common good by different kinds of offences.

Now, Finnis proposes to differentiate legal and moral obligation to obey the law as follows.[87] Consider these three steps of a practical syllogism:

[84] Cf Hobbes, *Leviathan* XIII-XIV.

[85] See Finnis, *NLNR* (n 4) 314–20. The text does not re-state Finnis's distinction exactly, but is adapted to the accounts given above.

[86] Ibid, 318. See generally Christopher Wellman & A John Simmons, *Is There a Duty to Obey the Law?* (CUP 2005).

[87] For the following, which differs syntactically from Finnis's argument but in all other respects is identical with it, see Finnis, *NLNR* (n 4) 316–17.

A. We need for the sake of the common good to be law-abiding.
B. Where *x* is stipulated by law as obligatory, the only way to be law-abiding is to do *x*.
C. Therefore it is obligatory for us to do *x* where *x* has been stipulated by law as obligatory.

Principle A can be included in our ordinary moral reasoning, and as such will vary in force and applicability. But the invariant force of law is derived from Principle B with 'an interpretation of [Principle] A as an undiscussed postulate' which is isolated from the further demands of moral reasoning. Yet Finnis's argument is mysterious. We can assert from the perspective of moral reasoning that there are exceptions to Principle A, that is, that there are occasions on which the common good is served by *not* obeying the law. Who does this asserting? Any person with the moral insight and intelligence to understand thoroughly the needs of the common good. Such a person would still obviously believe Principle B. Who then provides an *interpretation* of Principle A as a postulate, not invoked, removed from further moral inspection? This can only be a legal official of some kind, for the moral reasoner who understands the needs of the common good understands that on certain occasions, Principle A is *false*. But since we are talking here about the obligation to obey the law, the relevant perspective is that of the citizen, not the official. There is, therefore, no distinctly *legal* obligation to obey the law, as I argued above in Section IX.3. Like the obligation to obey the law, Principle A is a *presumptive* moral principle, but one that is, as we have seen and shall see in Chapter XI, defeasible. Thus also, the first occurrence of the term 'obligatory' in Principle C must refer to moral obligation, not legal obligation. We can therefore reject Finnis's schema and the distinction it seeks to draw.

# X
# LAW AND LEGALITY

## X.1. SCOPE AND POINT

This chapter deals with law in the central sense, not with law in a primitive or disintegrating condition, nor with unjust systems of law. Such instances of law are deficient, though still recognizable (or cognizable) as legal orders, but they are so only to the extent that they resemble the central case. It is therefore necessary for us to gain an understanding of the features of law in the central sense. Some caution is required: when seeking to identify the 'central features' of law, are we seeking after the distinctive features of *modern* law (i.e. the law of a developed society), as opposed to, say, the distinctive features of feudal law? Or is it possible to identify features that are central to law as such? Can we rightly hope for a universal definition of law? What relationship has modern law to ancient law-codes such as the Code of Ur-Nammu (c. 2400 BC) or the Code of Hammurabi (c. 1754 BC)? Such codes bear distinct similarities to modern-day legal systems: they institute public rules for the guidance of human conduct *and* at the same time, by this token, for the guidance of officials of the state in governing human conduct. The precise form taken by such provisions does vary in important respects: the Ur-Nammu code takes the form of conditionals ('If one commits a murder, [then] that one must be killed' . . . .); that of Hammurabi, a *lex talionis* (Provision 196); modern legal systems, typically a series of definitions of kinds of human behaviour, associated with specific normative consequences (see e.g. s 8(1) *Theft Act* 1968 or Articles 221–224 French Penal Code). This association of human behaviour with normative consequences, particularly penalties, is a feature of all systems of law and they are therefore, in this sense, *public* systems, rather than systems of the private advantage of the law-giver.[1] This is so in a number of ways. For example, the definition of serious or capital offences (where defined) and the association of crimes with penalties is perfectly general, and is not restricted to occasions on which such conduct is directed to the law-giver. A legal system may conceivably be administered for the law-giver's private advantage, or of the law-giver's party, but such governance would be quite contrary to the general scope of the laws, which prohibit murders, sexual

[1] Though see Aquinas, *Summa Theologiae* (hereafter *ST*) I-II.90.2c; Aristotle, *Politics* IV.1.1289a.

*Natural Law and Modern Society.* Sean Coyle, Oxford University Press. © Sean Coyle 2023.
DOI: 10.1093/oso/9780192886996.003.0010

crimes, fraud, violent acts, etc. Despite surface differences in form, such laws are concerned principally with human behaviour as it affects relationships *between persons*, not only with such behaviour as it affects the law-giver's private interest. A system of rules that is only enforced insofar as it directly affects the law-giver is not in the proper sense a system of laws. As Hart observed, laws are public in another way also: it is impossible to administer a system of laws that consists in private instructions to individuals; they must be general as to persons, acts, places etc. And a legal system is public in that it is quite impossible, without general standards, to treat like cases alike and dissimilar cases differently (the most basic aspect of justice and of legal judgment).

Part of our understanding of human law and human legal systems is that they are amenable to corruption, just as all human beings are prone to corruption. But this should not divert us from recognition of the central case of law, for the use of law for evil or repressive ends (that is, the suppression of human talents and creative growth) is neither the statistically most prevalent nor the conceptually most powerful understanding of law. An understanding of law in terms of its potential for corruption is indeed required in order to explain the actual facts of experience, and such an explanation is an aspect of the concept's conceptual power. But such an explanation is not primary: we cannot extrapolate from the corrupt to the benevolent any more than we can extrapolate from the case of the diseased to the healthy. The latter in each case explains the former (as a lack of certain properties), but the former has not the conceptual apparatus to explain the latter. The repressive or totalitarian legal system cannot, of itself, explain what I am calling the *public* character of law, its efforts to uphold general rules to adjudicate between the legal interests of persons in virtue of *what* they are (subjects, citizens, members of a legal community, tortfeasors, criminals) rather than *who* they are. The public character of law can also be seen in the example given above, that of the criminalization of violence and murder. Modern-day legal systems virtually all specify a right of self-defence against serious assaults, a specification that makes no sense if extra-legal beatings are handed out by party thugs or other unofficial or quasi-official bodies. Restraint and suppression of criminality in all of its forms, the execution of legally effective documents and deeds, administration of property, etc, are required if the law-giver is to rule securely, but they are not entirely for the benefit of the law-giver. All such legal institutions can be poisoned, but the poison does not corrupt entirely the public aims of law. When the state places a person on trial for murder, it does so in order to prove that the accused did in fact commit a defined act, not because the act was one against the law-giver, but because of the interests, rights, and wellbeing of the people: rights and interests that are deemed to be worth upholding even if the benefit to the law-giver is exceedingly remote. You may say (with Hart): the law-giver can restructure the rules of court such that all and only dissidents are found guilty and punished, but this possibility, real as it is, represents an emaciation of the law, in which legal rights, rule according to law and the process of adjudication have all been eliminated. To quote Aquinas, the rulings of such 'courts' more greatly resemble naked force (*violentia*) than law in the proper sense.[2]

Such issues pertain to the external aspects of law (in Hart's sense); but of the internal aspect of law many things also might be said. For it is a precondition of obedience by the majority in community that the rules are seen to be obeyed by most; that those who flout the rules are, by and large, detected, apprehended, and punished for their violations; that public institutions, such as local councils, face sanctions if they act outside the scope of their lawful powers, and have their *ultra vires* acts reversed; and that legal rules governing private transactions are of a kind that encourage observance, operate fairly, deal justly and drive illegal dealings (e.g. concerning narcotics, criminal enterprises and the black economy with all its uncertainties) into the shadows. The 'internal aspect' of rules does not end with the rule: it ends with the general allegiance of the governed to the government, something that is morally owed by virtue of gaining key advantages from those rules (central human goods such as physical safety, the ability to trade on just terms etc), but which a government loses, forfeits, squanders away when it ceases to look after the interests of *all* in community. For that allegiance depends upon the continuing situation in which the guilty are punished, the wronged are given reparation, the criminal is not left in possession of their illegally obtained advantages, and public officials are scrutinized and all forms of corruption and cronyism stamped out. It is worth stating the point again: such examples are not theorized on the same plane as 'healthy' systems of law and governance; rather they concern something—some dimension of law or government—that is missing from the example. Obviously, no actual legal system is completely successful in detecting and punishing criminality, rooting out instances of corruption in the use of official power and so on. Does this matter? There is no clear line to be drawn: the point at which allegiance breaks down, and the law ceases to be effective, is an empirical matter not a theoretical one.

It is worth pointing out that we are entertaining above two different forms of legal injustice (to be explored fully in Chapter XI). First there is injustice through omission or lack of effectiveness. Second there is deliberate injustice, the systematic oppression of the people by its governing authorities. The second case, in particular, highlights the outer limits of the concept of law. Evil comes in many forms, but the worst is in the form of law, since here it wears the clothes of the good, the legitimate and the just. All evil is to be opposed and, firstly, held out to be what, contrary to appearances, it really is, and to be stripped of the robe of legitimacy. The acts of a tyrant (inasmuch as they are oppressive) are essentially *ultra vires* as

[2] Aquinas, *ST* (n 1) I-II.96.4c.

they are set against that care of the community that is central to governance (see Section XI.2).

Hart's exploration of the issue was fragmented: he famously wrote that it is 'quite vain to seek any more specific purpose which law as such serves beyond providing guides to human conduct and standards of criticism of such conduct'.[3] But, shortly thereafter, he averred that the law's purpose is in fact richer than this statement would imply: for it is not just any human conduct (including murderous or genocidal human conduct) that the law 'as such' assists and promotes, but specifically that which promotes, advances or guarantees *human survival* (see Section I.2).[4] But any sustained reflection upon the 'guidance' that legal systems across the world offer to human conduct displays a richer set of values than mere human survival even where the 'goods' sought after are e.g. communistical or, as Hart also observed, favour one social group at the expense of another.[5] In so saying, we are again speaking here of law in the central sense, as opposed to borderline instances of law such as law under the Nazi tyranny (see Section XI.7).

Hart's concept of law is based upon an understanding of a modern, well-functioning legal system. He describes law thus constituted as 'a union of primary and secondary rules'. But he is inconsistent in his treatment of normative orders that lack such features: he sometimes describes such a union as a 'step from the pre-legal into the legal world', but elsewhere suggests that a regime of primary rules represents a primitive but nevertheless *legal* form of social order.[6] The discussion is confused, because a socially recognized body of rules, even if merely carved on tablets of stone, must (insofar as they genuinely 'enjoin behaviour' and insofar as they are created by a rule *applier*) be associated with 'secondary', or as I shall say, 'institutional', rules which at least involve mechanisms for administration and application. My reason for referring to such rules as 'institutional rules' will become clear in the course of their description. Hart refers to three kinds of institutional rule: rules of change, rules of adjudication, and the rule—or rules—of recognition. Rules of change, as Hart describes them, facilitate changes of legal position brought about by either deliberate (as in contract law) or accidental (as in tort law) means. The rules governing offer and acceptance in contract law allow for the creation of primary rules (contractual obligations) and the justiciability of such rules. One speaks in this context of contract as an 'institution'; similarly rules of change which provide for changes of government or monarch are 'institutional' in character.

[3] HLA Hart, *The Concept of Law* (3rd edn OUP 2012, hereafter *CL*) 249.

[4] Hart, *CL* (n 3) 191.

[5] See Gavin Byrne, 'Taking the Minimum Content Seriously: Hart's Liberalism and Moral Values' 63 (2012) *Northern Ireland Legal Quarterly* 485–87.

[6] Hart, *CL* (n 3) 42; 3–4. Aquinas anticipates Hart in his discussion of the defects a legal order is intended to secure: Aquinas, *ST* (n 1) I-II.95.1 ad 2. See further Cristobal Orrego, 'Gains and Losses in Jurisprudence Since HLA Hart' 59 (2014) *American Journal of Jurisprudence* 111.

Rules of adjudication provide for the *institutions* of the court system and of their authority and duty to provide a determinate decision even where the law is uncertain. Adjudication at its heart involves deciding whether some party has kept within the relevant rules or operated outside the rules. This power is implied by the very nature of primary rules *as rules*, and not mere sources of advice or counsel, and casts doubt upon Hart's distinction between the 'pre-legal' and the 'legal' world. In place of Hart's conception of a 'rule of recognition' we might speak of a practice, or practices, of recognition. All legal orders are associated with recognized sources of law (statute, precedent, *la jurisprudence*, custom), but legal reasoning involves more than merely deducing consequences from those sources. For judges reason, when they reason well, according to justice, and 'justice' is not, on any conventional view, a source of law per se. Each judicial decision (when sound) advances justice within its own limited horizons: there is not one overarching project to which all decisions contribute, and thus not a single 'theory' by which the 'soundest conception' of law can be 'fitted' to the highest number of decisions.[7] One cannot know the full significance of one's decisions: such decisions contribute to an effort 'that goes beyond any goal or purpose which anyone could envisage or pursue'.[8] The 'local' reasons for decision in a particular case are as likely to turn upon specialized meanings, technical definitions, exclusions, or procedures (such as that of presenting evidence to the court) as they are to grand theories. By the same token, any submission of a dispute to legal resolution is primarily driven by the desire to do justice to the litigants,[9] and not to set out some general scheme of justice. Even in cases where some general principle or set of principles is set out for the first time, or where the case concerns some *cause celebre*, the statement of the court is generally cautious, laid out in a way that consciously understands that the fixed words of the judgment, the definition or principle, are not the final word but will be taken up in future cases, restated and reformulated as they are applied to particular sets of facts. In addition to justice, then, let us refer to the rules, principles, definitions and concepts as 'doctrine'.

What, exactly, then, is justice in the context of law? It is a 'demand': a substantive demand as opposed to various procedural demands placed upon a legal judgment, demands such as that the judge must, however much she or he sympathizes with the defendant, find for the claimant if that is what law and justice require. The law is thus constituted from established sources, demands and doctrines. It is institutional, that is, stable in form and substance, regular and undeflected by extraneous pressures, as opposed to ad hoc, temporary, or inconsistent. It is not simply a union

[7] See Ronald Dworkin, *Taking Rights Seriously* (Duckworth 1977) chs 2–7; Ronald Dworkin, *Justice in Robes* (Harvard University Press 2008) ch 2; Ronald Dworkin, *Justice for Hedgehogs* (Harvard University Press 2011) 180.

[8] John Finnis, *The Collected Essays of John Finnis* (OUP 2011, hereafter *CEJF*) I.14.213.

[9] See Nigel E Simmonds, *Law as a Moral Ideal* (OUP 2007).

of 'primary' and institutional ('secondary') rules, but also a pattern of formal and substantive demands that are central to the very character of law (see Section X.3).

The later career of Hart's jurisprudence is worth briefly mentioning for the light that it sheds on the notion of normativity. Shapiro believes that Hart's theory of rules is fundamentally mistaken because rules are 'abstract objects' as opposed to practices which are 'concrete events'.[10] Hence the one cannot be identified with the other. This in fact ejects the most important feature of Hart's theory of law in favour of the less important: practices are not 'events' but highly complex concatenations of events which taken together can be recognized as a single practice because of their overarching *point*. They can be so taken because the attitude of those subject to the practice is (what Hart calls) an *internal* attitude or point of view,[11] that is, an understanding of the law as normative. Kramer preserves the idea of the internal point of view (which he refers to as a 'general disposition' (in fact a series of general dispositions), but emphasizes that one who takes a critical and reflective attitude to some particular norm N may do so not because they regard it as morally worthy (normative) but out of self-interest 'or other factors'.[12] This appears to run together two separate judgments, which can be clarified through the example of lying: (1) I understand that lying is wrong but I will (at least on this occasion) allow self-interest to overcome what I morally ought to do; (2) I do not recognize that lying (at least on this occasion) is wrong, but perhaps believe that all morality is grounded in or indistinguishable from self-interest. In both cases, self-interest is victorious but in different ways (e.g. the presence of guilt in (1) but not in (2)). Both attitudes are possible, but to return to the legal example, the following seems scarcely intelligible: (3) I have no interest in discerning whether this or that particular law is morally worthy, I simply choose to obey or disobey it according to self-interest. For to adopt this point of view is not to regard oneself as bound by the law at all. It is, at any rate, a highly irregular (and not focal) attitude to law.

One of the most prevalent ways in which legal positivists resist natural law theory is by pointing to the conventionality of law (see Section X.2). But conventions are not imposed without reason: they are created or come about in order to secure some good. This 'good' is sometimes, of course, the good of the lawgiver rather than those to whom the law applies; but natural law theory reasonably points out that such laws are deficient or corrupted laws, which, when compared with other possible forms of government, seem to have more in common with force or violence, rule through fear or, perhaps, the internal and entirely deformed justice of a criminal organization.[13] Such norms possess only the most rudimentary

[10] See Scott Shapiro, *Legality* (Belknap Press 2011) 103.

[11] See MS Green, 'On Hart's Category Mistake' 19 (2013) *Legal Theory* 358. See also Brian Bix, 'HLA Hart and the Hermeneutic Turn in Legal Theory' 52 (1999) *SMU Law Review* 179 & 186–94; Scott Shapiro, 'Was Inclusive Positivism Founded on a Mistake?' 22 (2009) *Ratio Juris* 326.

[12] Matthew Kramer, *HLA Hart* (Polity 2018) 61–62; see also Jeffrey Kaplan, 'The Internal Point of View' 42 (2023) *Law & Philosophy* (forthcoming).

[13] See Aquinas, *ST* (n 1) I-II.96.4c; Augustine, *De Civitate Dei* IV.4.

connection with law (namely, enforcement, policing, court structures, etc) but are as remote from law as rampantly specious or circular arguments are from arguments. To make these comparisons (between unjust law and violence) we need both a theory of law and a theory of violence, particularly organized violence. This is true irrespective of whether a given theory seeks to dispute the connection or to assert it.

Violence can obviously be (1) physical, (2) psychological, (3) an attack on one's interests,[14] (4) a concerted violation of one's rights, (5) pressure to carry into action something that one does not want to do, and which one would resist if one could, or (6) pressure not to carry into action a project that one wishes to advance. This will perhaps serve as a rudimentary theory of violence. It would seem that a law can deploy violence in the form of (1), (5), and (6), for physical restraint, for the purposes of lawful arrest, or to give care to a person exhibiting extreme symptoms of mental illness. Those same interventions could of course be used unreasonably, unjustly; the level of extremity involved would then inform the closeness of that law to sheer violence, that is, to a law that has been hollowed out entirely of legality, a non-law. But it would appear that the deployment of a state's resources for the purposes of (2), (3), or (4) would always be unreasonable, non-law. They would more closely approximate to mob violence than to law in the focal sense. But what of a theory of 'law'? This is the subject of the present discussion.

It will prove useful to state a general definition of law at the outset of discussion, elements of which are to be examined and interrogated in later stages of this chapter. The definition is the following: law (or *a* law) is a set of reasonable directives, ordered towards the common good of the community, issued or otherwise applied by the person or body responsible for the wellbeing of that community. The definition is in essence that of Aquinas.[15] The remaining sections of this chapter will explore the various elements of this definition, as well as some of their consequences.

## X.2. COORDINATION AND CONVENTION

How does law emerge from, and how is it different from, the socio-political background of society? What is distinctive about it? There are two different kinds of answer to this question. The first is what we might call a formal explanation: the law is distinctive from other elements of the social-political machinery of state in its *form* and *methods*, that is, in its characteristic structures of positive law and its method

[14] For some analysis see Nicole Keenan, 'Theories of Violence' 12 (2020) *Philologia* 1. See also Susanne Karsedt & Manuel Eisner, 'Is a General Theory of Violence Possible?' 3 (2009) *International Journal of Computer Vision* 4, discussing Alasdair MacIntyre, *Against the Self-Images of the Age: Essays on Ideology and Philosophy* (Duckworth 1971) 260.

[15] See Aquinas, *ST* (n 1) I-II.90.4c.

of adjudication. This explanation conceives of law as an instrument of a particular kind. The second kind of explanation is a substantive one: it takes law to be a distinctive contribution to the *values* and *principles* deemed politically important by the community.[16] These different answers, as we shall see, are not entirely incompatible as an explanation of the law's distinctive contribution to society: it may be that the values and principles remain valuable only when delivered through particular forms and methods. But it is nevertheless pertinent to inquire into which of the two answers is primary, and which secondary.

One of the most important, and most prevalent, conceptions which takes the substantive view, is that of law as the solution to coordination problems.[17] The central example that is given of such a problem is that of motoring. There is no persuasive reason why traffic should drive on the left hand side of the road rather than the right (or vice versa). But a determination is necessary if the community is to avoid (1) frequent collisions between and damage to motor vehicles, (2) chaos on the roads preventing motorists and others from making progress in their journeys, and above all (3) constant injuries and deaths to pedestrians and road users alike. By coordinating action in this way, unacceptable costs are avoided and significant personal and economic benefits are secured. Another instructive example is that of tort law. It is inevitable that accidents will occur within a community in which people live in close proximity, and that every person will, at times, act negligently. Without a law of tort, specifically torts of negligence, one is left unsure how to respond to an accident that one has caused or suffered. How ought one to compensate the victim, if compensation is indeed recognized as being required? By some action (e.g. taking care of the victim) or monetary value (in which case how much)? Should the victim or the victim's family pursue a private act of punishment (an eye for an eye)? It is all unclear. Similarly, torts of nuisance coordinate the acts of property owners in such a way that they can live in proximity without endlessly escalating tensions arising out of incompatible users. Coordination problems are also classically confronted in the context of commons: some scheme of cooperation or at least coordination is necessary if degradation of the commons is to be avoided. Use of commons requires to be managed, coordinated, and limited, its value thus preserved. In the law of contract, the making and breaking of legal agreements (a defined subset of all agreements) requires to be regulated in such a way that both private and legal persons can enter into agreements with the same set of understandings: such coordination is a necessary foundation of the market in property, in economic entities (e.g. futures, indentures, shares) and in labour.

[16] Legal positivists such as Hart, Kelsen, and Shapiro appear to give the formal kind of explanation, whereas Dworkin and (perhaps) Finnis the substantive one.

[17] For some discussion see Andrei Marmor, *Social Conventions: From Language to Law* (Princeton University Press 2009) 155ff.

Coordination problems (on this view) extend into all areas of law and legal regulation: the education of children, management and use of natural resources, the use of force, forms and contents of communications, the reconciliation of aspects of justice with one another and with legal rights, public health and public order: all of these are coordination problems 'in the broad sense'.[18] Indeed, '[s]uch coordination ... needs to extend to essentially all the matters with which the law deals'.[19] In short, every person's actions and choices need to be coordinated with those of others: not in any Platonic conception whereby each person represents one cog in the giant wheel of state, and must align their conduct to the state's greater purposes (coordination does not imply commensuration), but in the sense that, but for the coordination, there would exist a free-for-all in which nobody's choices could be consistently voiced or pursued. Nor is coordination a response to human malfeasance: a society of angels would still require rules to coordinate their separate activities and to avoid one impeding another each in pursuit of their own ends.

But this treatment of law as a resolver (sometimes mere manager) of coordination problems does considerable violence to ordinary understandings of its role. Nor are such ordinary understandings linked to surface appearances; they seem to be deeply grounded in the law's character. The prohibitory norms of the criminal law, for example, are most immediately and best understood as an aspect of *justice* rather than coordination. They are direct derivations (*conclusiones*) from natural law precepts against unjustly harming, restricting, or defrauding the innocent; the punishments they mete out are not reckoned according to the most efficient way to coordinate the future acts of criminal and victim, but according to the injustice suffered by the victim, the mitigations that may be offered to the court's attention, and aggravating factors led by the prosecution. The centrality of punishment as a response to criminal activity, even in jurisdictions where rehabilitation is a significant aim, underlines the concern with justice over mere coordination: coordination that is actually a significant aim only for those agencies responsible for reinserting the criminal into the community *after* their punishment, and with diminishing the likelihood of recidivism. This aim is indeed itself qualified by the fact that (in virtually all jurisdictions) the recidivist will receive a *further* punishment if they are found to have violated the terms of their probation.[20] But it is not only the criminal law that fails to fit the theory that the central aim of law is to solve problems of co-ordination. The law of torts, for example, has the purpose of rebalancing injustices between persons by compensating for loss caused through negligence, nuisance, trespass, defamation, battery, and so forth. The level of compensation due is *not*

[18] John Finnis, *Natural Law & Natural Rights* (2nd edn OUP 2011, hereafter *NLNR*) 232. See also Gillian Hadfield & Barry Weingast, 'What is Law? A Coordination Account of the Characteristics of Legal Order' 4 (2012) *Journal of Legal Analysis* 1.

[19] Finnis, *NLNR* (n 18) 468.

[20] See e.g. Criminal Justice Act 2003 Schedule 8; US Constitution Amendment XIV.1; and poignantly in Victor Hugo, *Les Miserables* (1862); see Finnis, *CEJF* (n 8) IV.3.66.

determined according to what would be mutually acceptable to tortfeasors and victims, that is, to provide a compromise that would best assist the resumption of coordinated behaviour between the litigants: one might expect some such solution were the law's primary aim to resolve problems of coordination. Instead, the court decides the amount of compensation according to what, in *justice*, is *due* to the victim. Nor is the abstract aim of tort law to provide a pattern of rights and obligations that enables the coordination of individuals each pursuing distinct projects: it is justice. Coordination is, as it were, a secondary component of justice. Similarly with property law: its main aim is not to create a pattern of rights and obligations for the purpose of enabling coordination (people knowing when a particular use of land constitutes trespass; what rights of property are asserted by, or actually held by, others, and so on); its main aim has to be the establishment of rights of ownership, of enforcing such rights as they appear in contexts of distributive or commutative justice, and of thereby securing (recognition of) all those rights and incidents of ownership that are, as Aristotle pointed out, essential for any human flourishing. For in the absence of such rights, no giving or enjoying of anything is possible, for to give (one's time, resources, affections, attention) requires something of one's own that may thus be given.[21] Property and ownership, at least of some things, is a fundamental requirement of justice, and also of that great social good, peace. It is only through the existence of a system of property law (of whatever kind) that aspects of a person's life remain private and off limits to others and to society generally, *suum ius* in Grotius's terms, a key component of human flourishing. Again, coordination is a subsidiary *means*, and not an *end*, of legal regulation.

Of all areas of law that might seem most obviously concerned with coordination problems, it is the law of contract that comes most readily to mind. Is not contract law's primary purpose the formalization and stabilization of valuable promises, and thus to bring much-needed certainty and enforceability to market transactions that would otherwise be in chaos? This seductive line of reasoning should be resisted. As I have argued elsewhere, the primary purpose of the law of contract is to inject a minimum morality into the marketplace by enforcing valuable bargains (or awards of damages), defending the vulnerable against fraud or other immoral practices, ascribing penalties to free riders, clarifying the meaning of the various legal acts that are constituents of enforceable contracts (offer and acceptance, etc), and by tracing out the line between private promises that lie outside the law (i.e. are left to the morality of the promisor), and valuable bargains that are enforceable through the courts. In short, the law of contract seeks to determine and to render to persons what is owed or due to them in justice. It is true that a 'society of angels' would still require a law of contract, but the reason for this is not, or not merely, that of coordination, for angels of course wish to be just in their dealings, and thus

[21] See Aristotle, *Politics* II.3–6; also Finnis, *NLNR* (n 18) 144–47.

require an objective and specific (that is, specified) *quantum* of justice by reference to which to orientate and guide their dealings. It should also be observed that a society of angels would not require the *whole* of contract law, but only those parts that set out the formal requirements pertaining to the creation and dissolution of contracts, and the principle of *restitutio in integrum*. They would not require any of the enforcement mechanisms and provisions of contempt of court or much of the jurisprudence that deals with intractable disputes between litigants. For they would, *ex hypothesi*, wish to do justice in their relations, relying on the law only to specify what justice requires in a given instance. Again, a society of angels may need definitions of negligence, force, and fraud (even this is debatable), but not the elaborate legal machinery that lies behind such terms. Their needs are those of justice, not mechanisms of coordination.

The foregoing line of argument sought to show that a substantive account of the law's distinctiveness (its values and principles)—that of the character of legal justice—is superior to another (that of law as a response to coordination problems). But what of the other account of the law's distinctiveness: its forms and methods? Here the focus is upon legal reasoning: what is it that allows legal reasoning to be insulated (not entirely but substantially) from the broader ebb and flow of political discourse? Such insulation is of undeniable importance. Without it, law is indistinguishable from politics, and in particular from the constantly changing utilitarian calculus of interests. (The question of how and to what extent legal reasoning differs from that of ordinary morality is one I defer to Section X.5.)

There seem to be two possibilities: that legal reasoning differs in form from ordinary political reasoning, and that legal reasoning differs in its characteristic content. At a relatively abstract level, both possibilities contribute to the distinctive character of legal reasoning. For on the one hand, reasoning in law is channelled by a number of specialized argumentative forms: specifically, (1) reasoning from statutory laws or codes, as a matter of legal *interpretation*: interpretation that is itself highly specialized and carried out in accordance with sundry limitations upon what can count as an interpretation, and by reference to tested legal concepts; (2) reasoning from statute, as a matter of *application*, that is, of a general rule to a specific situation, which is again subject to constraints of form and substance; and (3) reasoning from precedent: the rule(s) of *stare decisis* and the practices of distinguishing, widening and reformulating legal rules in light of the facts of the unique case before the court: a practice that involves, but is not reducible to, a mode of analogical reasoning.[22] On the other hand, legal reasoning, given the above, is distinctive in that it is orientated around a limited number of highly technical concepts, definitions, distinctions, and principles. These range from legal definitions of

[22] Cf Grant Lamond, 'Do Precedents Create Rules?' 15 (2005) *Legal Theory* 1; also Katharina Stevens, 'Reasoning by Precedent: Between Rules and Analogies' 24 (2018) *Legal Theory* 216. See also Neil Duxbury, *Dicta and Dissent* (CUP 2021) 77–81.

substantive forms, such as contracts, torts, and crimes, to matters as diverse as legal standing, *nullum crimen sine lege*, *res iudicata*, and the grounds of appeal. Both of these aspects give legal reasoning its distinctive form; to which may be added a third: that legal reasoning is characteristically *self-referential*, that it continually refers to its own concepts, doctrines and precedents in pursuit of a just judgment. The formulation of the 'neighbour principle' is a clear example of this: rightly regarded as a landmark judgment, the novelty of the neighbour principle can be exaggerated, for it essentially involved recognition of a new ground of action in relation to negligence in product liability cases and an extension of the principle *res ipsa loquitur*. The new principle did not spring from nowhere, but emerged through the widening and narrowing of existing concepts, themselves highly technical, specifically those laid out in *Heaven v Pender* and *Le Lievre v Gould*.[23] The judgment is also partially shaped by the counter-allegations of Stevenson (e.g. that Mrs Donoghue was already of precarious health: a matter which would not have naturally arisen in the judgment if it had not been alleged), themselves grounded in legal authorities rather than being spun out of thin air. It would be wrong to conclude, as some have done, that legal reasoning is essentially analogical. Though such reasoning does involve the exploration of analogies and dis-analogies between cases, its main business is the estimation of the justice or injustice of legal principles as they apply to the present context of judgment: a mode of reasoning that is not primarily *interpretative* but rather *applicative*. It is the mode of reasoning that Aquinas calls *determinatio*, a mode of reasoning that can be misunderstood.

Aquinas's examples of *determinatio* are not entirely helpful. His first example is that of the architect designing a house: although the architect's creativity is constrained by the general form a house must take (it requires doors of a certain height and width, windows to let in light, division into different rooms, load-bearing walls, etc), s/he nevertheless enjoys a relatively wide creative freedom as to, for example, the design of window locks, door handles, the placing of the windows and precise pattern of interior rooms, use of colours, etc. Aquinas's second example is that of laws of homicide: the law that murders be punished is a direct expression (*conclusio*) of natural law, but the question of *how* the murderer should be punished (imprisonment, death, confiscation of property, withdrawal of voting rights, etc) is left undetermined by natural law and thus requires a creative decision (*determinatio*). The difficulty with both examples is that they tend to exaggerate the level of freedom and scope involved in the process of *determinatio*, a mistake originating in Aquinas's intellectual ancestors, as for example in Aristotle, who said that while natural justice is universal, conventional justice varies from place to place and fills in areas where the rule of natural justice is indifferent.[24] The archetypal example given is again that of motoring on the left rather than the right hand side of

[23] See *Donoghue v Stevenson* (1932) HL 31 at 45 per Lord Atkin.

[24] Aristotle, *Nicomachean Ethics* (hereafter *NE*) V.7.1134b.

the road (or vice versa): it is indeed a matter of complete indifference whether the rule prohibits driving on the right as opposed to the left, so long as a rule is in place. But this does not represent the activity of determination in the overwhelming majority of cases. For example, it is not an indifferent matter, or a matter of free choice, how to punish a murderer. Clearly, choice is available (prison, execution, confiscation of property or assets . . .), but the choices are not in any sense 'free', for they are determined according to the requirements of justice, specifically the need for the punishment to be proportional to the crime and to the common good. Thus an exceedingly short term of imprisonment is clearly contrary to the demands of justice as is, contrary to Aquinas's own views, execution. Criminals themselves would be more than satisfied with an overly short or otherwise tame sentence, but would presumably object to an overly harsh one. The process of setting a sentence, and the deliberations that form part of that process, are simply not 'free' in the manner that Aquinas's examples suggest. *Determinationes* must have the same character as the existing law, and thus legal reasoning gives a high status to its stock of technical definitions, meanings and body of interpretations and precedents, and a low priority to unstructured thinking.

There is not therefore a bright line to be drawn between laws based upon natural law precepts and laws based on convention. In the majority of cases of *determinatio*, the relevant standards are yet grounded in natural law and are not pure invention. Indeed, Aquinas amends his somewhat rash statement that *determinationes* 'have no other force than that of human law' [*ex sola lege humana vigorem habent*][25] by observing that certain laws *derive their force not from reason alone* [*non habeant vim obligandi ex sola ratione*], but (in the limiting case) from their having been legally created [*sed ex institutione*].[26] Now indeed among the laws that are not derived in any way from natural law (from right reason) but have their source in pure convention are those that are unreasonable, stifling of human talents and creativity, or serving evil or unjust ends. Such laws are neither *conclusiones* nor *determinationes*, the two principal modes of law-creation, and for this reason are not valid laws in the strict sense and have more in common with brutality (*violentia*).[27] This is especially true of judicial discretion (a phenomenon much discussed in jurisprudence); the majority of judgments handed down from the bench are either (1) straightforward inferences from morally sound legal rules (*conclusiones*) or else (2) reasonable *determinationes* insofar as they are just and legally sound pronouncements creatively applying laws and past decisions. In the latter case, judicial discretion ranges over a number of possibilities (more or less, depending upon the richness of the area of law in question), either supplying judgment where there is little legal specification in existing laws, or else deciding between competing values where the

25 Aquinas, *ST* (n 1) I-II.95.2c.
26 Ibid, I-II.104.1c; Aquinas, *Sent.* IV.15.3.2.1c.
27 Aquinas, *ST* (n 1) I-II.93.3 ad 2, I-II.93.3 ad 1; see above section X.1.

law supplies alternative possibilities for judgment. The scope of judicial discretion is indicated roughly by (2), and to (1) only to the extent that specific wording is given to general rules. Not to be overlooked are (3) judicial reasoning which proceeds from *determinationes* but ends in muddle, mistake, or injustice, and (4) judicial reasoning that proceeds from error and concludes in error: this is not, in the focal sense, judicial discretion at all: for that discretion is defined by law, and judges are not empowered by law to decide cases unjustly or erroneously: see Section X.5. But they retain some of the characteristics of laws in a watered-down way because and to the extent that they conform to the patterns of legal thought (of interpretation, application, and specialization) rather than straightforward military coercion. This contrast, between adherence to legal forms and direct military coercion, leads nicely onto a discussion of legality, or the rule of law.

## X.3. THE RULE OF LAW

A central part of the idea of law is that it enables people to enjoy goods that would not otherwise be attainable if law did not exist: such as social peace, forms of co-operation, stable expectations and whole ranges of goods that could not otherwise be obtained or enjoyed securely. But how, we might question, does law fulfil this function? In recent legal philosophy, emphasis has been placed upon the idea of legality, or the rule of law.[28] The rule of law in modern times has been associated with a set of theses identified by Lon Fuller and, after him, Joseph Raz. These theses bring into perspective the classical idea of 'the rule of law, not of men'.[29] Many of them were identified by Isidore, as reported by Aquinas. Here I offer a shorter though more comprehensive list of theses: taken together they comprise formal precepts of legality but, at the same time, *substantive* demands of justice.

(1) There must be norms: laws create and express norms; a norm is a genuine standard for directing behaviour and thus must not be: (i) contradictory either with itself or other norms; (ii) impossible to comply with; (iii) imprecise; (iv) transient; (v) retrospective i.e. applicable only to past behaviour not future; (vi); unpublished; (vii) administered in a way that is inconsistent with its apparent meaning; or (viii) non-general or non-generic in scope and application, as to act-descriptions and addressees. If any of (i)–(v) obtain, the 'norm' concerned is no norm *at all*; if any of (vi)–(viii) obtain, the

[28] See Paul Burgess, 'The Rule of Law: Beyond Contestedness' 8 (2017) *Jurisprudence* 480; John Tasioulas, 'The Rule of Law' in Tasioulas (ed) *Cambridge Companion to the Philosophy of Law* (CUP 2020) 117; Julian Sempill, 'The Rule of Law and the Rule of Men: History, Legacy, Obscurity' 12 (2020) *Hague J of the Rule of Law* 511.

[29] See Plato, *Laws* 715d.

'norm' concerned is only defectively a norm and may not be a sound guide to conscience.

(2) The legal norms must be applied in the same way to every person, without bias or prejudice.
(3) There must be opportunity for litigation; this should be extended to every citizen: justice must be available for all in society, not just the rich. There must be mechanisms that allow access to justice for the poor. There must be a caste of lawyers and officials to uphold the law; and legal advice must be potentially available to all.
(4) There must be clearly defined powers of law-making and law-applying.
(5) The independence of the judiciary must be observed and maintained.
(6) Legal authorities must legislate or otherwise extend legal regulation into all aspects of social life (including but not limited to criminal law, torts, contract, property, public and administrative law, rules of evidence and procedure, etc).

If any of (2)–(6) are lacking, a legal system is a highly defective legal system. The norms identified by (1) can take numerous forms, specifically those of right, duty, liberty, no-right, power, liability, immunity, and disability. Hart noted that his 'secondary rules', of change, adjudication, and recognition, are *power-conferring*, for a legal power is the power to change one's legal relationship to another, and adjudication is both a power to change the legal situation of the litigants, and a power to make a ruling, that is, to apply and state the law. The failures mentioned in (1)(i)–(viii) are never entirely eliminated even in a codified system of laws, but they point to qualities that all laws incline towards: for even a secret law seeps into public knowledge the more it is applied; inconsistencies between laws are gradually ironed out in adjudication; impossibilities become rationalized; aspects of laws that are subject to continual revision are minimized, and so on. These innate characteristics of law express the law's specific virtue, its 'inner morality', but are deemed by Fuller (and others) as distinct from, and independent of, the 'external' or substantive morality of the legal rules of any jurisdiction. Specifically, Fuller observes that the 'internal morality of law' captured by (1)(i)–(viii) (and which is not fully captured unless augmented by (2)–(6)), is neutral with respect to many ethical issues but is not neutral with respect to the concept of the human being as a responsible agent.[30] These ethical issues concern not only 'survival' (as in Hart's philosophy) but 'communication' (i.e. sociability).[31] But this exceedingly schematic view of the human being vastly underestimates the ethical issues that attach to the 'internal morality'. For if the human being is *a responsible agent* then he or

[30] Lon Fuller, *The Morality of Law* (Yale University Press 1964, hereafter *ML*) 162; see Nigel E Simmonds 'Freedom, Law and Naked Violence' 59 (2009) *Toronto Law Journal* 381.

[31] Fuller, *ML* (n 30) 185–86.

she must be understood as seeking and pursuing diverse human goods; hence a range of human goods come into view which—if it is the law's purpose to respect or (in some cases at least) to assist responsible agency—the law ought to protect, and to which it ought to facilitate pursuit. These goods go way beyond the needs for survival and sociability. Nor is the promotion of such goods exclusively concerned with the creation of legal powers: even restrictive or punitive laws presuppose or assist in defining possibilities for the pursuit of human goods. Thus, as Fuller observes, adultery (as a legal ground for divorce) requires first the legal definition of marriage, and the specification of the terms on which a marriage can be said to exist.[32] Likewise, trespass, theft, and fraud all require first the legal recognition of property rights, with the liberties, powers and immunities involved, at least some of which are essentially private.

The smoothing of inconsistencies between legal rules, the curing of vagueness or of impossibilities, is a step from non-law into law, for laws exist only when their terms are given a definite meaning, and a genuine norm is created only when compliance with it is possible(etc). There is nothing essentially mysterious about this process: a law (a valid legal norm) comes into existence at the precise point at which its previously vague terms are supplied with a definite meaning, or a command to do the impossible is rationalized into something possible, and so on. Here, then, is a prime example of judicial lawmaking: decisions are arrived at under the authority of rules of adjudication rather than (exclusively) of a (putative) rule of recognition. For although in terms of seniority, the legislative ranks higher than the other branches of government, including the courts, in terms of importance it is the courts that rank highest, because *every* aspect of the law runs through the prism of the courts, including the constitutionality of the legislative and executive branches.[33] It is adherence to legal *forms* that separates judicial lawmaking from the arbitrary and unregulated use of power that Aquinas equates with military rule.

Insufficient attention has been paid to the fact that Fuller referred to his 'desiderata' (roughly (1)(i)–(viii) above) as that without which law cannot *be* law, that is, that certain positive and ostensibly law-creating acts fail to create binding *laws* because they do not in fact conform to basic moral requirements.[34] As I have indicated above, this claim is rather too strong in relation to (1)(vi)–(viii). But it should be observed that the moral grounds Fuller identified for regarding ostensible legal

[32] Ibid, 204.

[33] See Aquinas, *ST* (n 1) I-II.95.2 ad 4. These features of judicial decision-making are considerably wider than the practice of 'judicial review', and thus, it seems to me, escape the criticisms in Jeremy Waldron, 'The Core of the Case Against Judicial Review' 115 (2006) *Yale Law Journal* 1346. For some criticisms of Waldron's view see Dimitrios Kyritsis, 'Representation and Waldron's Objection to Judicial Review' 26 (2006) *Oxford Journal of Legal Studies* 733 and Alexander Kaufman & Michael B Runnels, 'The Core of an Unqualified Case for Judicial Review: A Reply to Jeremy Waldron and Contemporary Critics' 82 (2016) *Brooklyn Law Review* 163.

[34] Though see David Luban, 'The Rule of Law and Human Dignity: Re-Examining Fuller's Canons' 2 (2010) *Hague Journal on the Rule of Law* 29.

acts as null ((1)(i)–(v)) or heavily qualified ((1)(vi)–(viii)) are somewhat more narrow than the totality of moral grounds of legal invalidity. For the thesis that laws rescue the human being from the blind play of chance is itself intimately connected with the realization that rescue from arbitrary forces and creation of purposeful opportunities is explicable as only one (though an important one) of many forms of human good: goods that are the central concern of the autonomy thus secured. This line of thinking also suggests that, whilst the law should expand to regulate all areas of social life (and some areas of private or family life), it must not render determinate every action or omission: the laws should make room for, and define, interstitial liberties within which human beings can make free decisions and choices to shape their own destinies. (This much was recognized, inter alia, by Aquinas.)[35] Indeed, many of the laws duly enacted in a tolerably just community (and not a few unjust ones) will be provisions to enable the free flow of personal, mercantile, and cultural relationships between persons. Without these anchor-points to a system of exchange (whether expressed legislatively or through case-law) there is nothing upon which to ground our judgments of justice.

Obviously, the desiderata listed in (1)–(6) above do not eliminate all injustice in law, or even every formal (procedural) injustice: a tax statute that levies duty on transactions that occurred years ago is unjust, but not actually retroactive in terms of (1)(v);[36] nevertheless it does not conform to the principle of allowing people to plan for the future without fear of laws that undo today steps taken yesterday. Fuller quite explicitly admits that formal justice is only one dimension of a broader problem of 'clarifying the directions of human effort essential to maintain any system of law', even a repressive one.[37] This characterization of 'the broader problem' indicates the necessity (in Fuller's mind) of pragmatism alongside that of justice: keeping a legal system in existence, even an unjust one, may be preferable to its utter destruction. Its 'directions of human effort', even if oppressive and in violation of substantive principles of justice, may yet be superior to a general disintegration of norms governing such efforts.[38] The examples used by Fuller himself illustrate the problem: a government quietly passes a law requiring an official stamp on a marriage certificate in order for couples to be legally married; the law is not observed but later comes to light. Meanwhile a great many couples have entered into married life, creating joint bank accounts, shared mortgages, producing children, claiming family state benefits, and so on. What ought to be the law's response? To undo such actions as can be undone, or retroactively grant the official marriage stamp?[39] The answer may seem logical and reasonable. But essentially the same reasoning permits us to think that a retrospective statute ordering

[35] Aquinas, *ST* (n 1) I-II.99.3c, I-II.105.2c, I-II.100.12 ad 3, 100.2c.
[36] See Fuller, *ML* (n 30) 59.
[37] Ibid, 4.
[38] As is clear from Aquinas, *ST* (n 1) I-II.96.4c.
[39] Fuller, *ML* (n 30) 53.

the liquidation of dissidents or undesirable groups can 'cure' acts of premeditated murder. Hence we must constantly understand the desiderata in the light of substantive and not merely formal justice; yet sometimes formal justice must take priority over immediate concerns of justice: a society that permits the cure of the marriage certificates demonstrates its willingness retroactively to alter legal rights and duties on grounds the scope of which is not clear. But the problem becomes clearer if we understand it as one, not between pragmatism and substantive justice, but of formal justice *as a dimension of substantive justice.*

This problem is an aspect of the rule of law ('not men'). To be ruled *by law* is to be ruled *through* law; it demands that 'men' (i.e. judges and ultimately the litigants and the rest of us) submit themselves to the legal norms such that their decisions are shaped by those norms and not their own preferences, even their own preferred views on justice. But rule through law also demands deference to the desiderata of the rule of law: *not* to apply hidden laws to unsuspecting litigants; *not* to apply an impossible duty to a defendant without seeking interpretatively to rationalize or minimize its (only *quasi*-legal) effects; *not* to shape one's decision according to norms that vary from established legal norms; and so on. Obvious as this may be, the conclusion is important: departure from any of these desiderata is a retreat from the principle of rule *through* law.

Having identified the necessary desiderata of the rule of law ((1)–(6)), it is now time to consider how they can be mobilized to defend the common good of community, that is, to understand their full 'meaning' within a *polis* or *rechtsstaat.* The main issue is one identified, but not successfully defended, by Fuller, and explored with greater success by his intellectual heirs: that of the extent to which a repressive political regime can benefit from adhering strictly to the rule of law in pursuit of its ends. This is a subject that has been extensively discussed in recent years, and thus discussion here can be brief. Departure from the rule of law is deeply damaging to the common good, and hence to the good of persons. Tyrannies are destructive of the common good either by reducing naturally diverse conceptions of the good life to one official ideological position, or by extorting monetary, labour, and intellectual capital from their citizens. In the latter case, one has a return to the Platonic conception of the ideal state from the *Republic* that was uprooted by Aristotle's critique. In the former, human efforts are not exploited but suppressed. In either case (as Finnis observes) a key goal of the state will be to increase its grip on power at the expense of the wellbeing of its citizens.[40] Aside from the most visible abuses (punishment without trial, excessive force against its own citizens, genocide, etc) such a regime would greatly profit from, and increase its grip on power by, closely controlling the court system; depriving citizens of the opportunity to litigate, particularly against officials of the system; enacting laws of ambiguous scope such that

[40] Finnis, *NLNR* (n 18) 274.

the state enjoys a wide discretion to proceed against its victims; giving such laws retroactive as well as prospective force; applying a different set of norms to citizens than that enshrined in legislation, thereby presenting a more reasonable, official face to the international community whilst ruthlessly pursuing its real aims in secret; and so on.

To those who point out that a reasonable regard for the desiderata is entirely compatible with evil or repressive governance (i.e. that the desiderata are theorems of efficiency in law-making) the answer must be: yes, the desiderata do indeed increase efficiency, for example in getting the state's message across to its citizens. But such gains in efficiency—for example by ensuring that laws are free of ambiguity—are as nothing compared with the efficacy of ambiguous laws, etc, in allowing repressive regimes to operate at will against their own citizens or some despised subset thereof. Thus, while both evil and benevolent regimes benefit from conforming to the rule of law, the rule of law is hardly serviceable for good and evil in equal measure.[41] Whilst the rule of law may smooth the path of evil in some respects, it forestalls it in many others. Indeed it is relatively little observed that departures from the rule of law embodied in (1)–(6) are precisely ways of *failing to make law*; hence a regime which departs from those desiderata is more accurately characterized as a government of will rather than a government of law, that is, in Aquinas's sense, creating something that more resembles military coercion than law.

Aside from the formal requirements of the rule of law there is a further principle, that those who are required to uphold and apply the law are accountable for their level of compliance with the norms (1)(v) & (vii)–(viii), and (2)–(6) that attach to them. Failure so to comply gives rise to different sanctions and effects in different kinds of legal order. In a civil law system, the rules of compliance are spelled out explicitly, and failure to comply is an obvious *ultra vires*; in a common law system, lower courts are subject to the authority of, and correction (and sometimes rebuke) by, higher courts, the compliance of the supreme court being assured by reference to constitutional rules (as in the United States) or (in the case of an unwritten constitution such as that of the United Kingdom), by the desire to avoid a constitutional crisis.

Thus, the desiderata (1)–(6) are only fully observed when they are observed by all legal officials (legislators, judiciary, local authorities, etc) and by non-official agents of the law, that is, lawyers through whom the law is also publicized (in advice to clients), argued (and thus reduced to logical, non-arbitrary, clear, possible rules) and represented in open court. The rule of law therefore depends not only upon the desiderata mentioned, but also upon the collective but also personal

41 See generally Nigel E Simmonds, 'Straightforwardly False: The Collapse of Kramer's Positivism' (2004) 63 *Cambridge Law Journal* 98–131; finally Nigel E Simmonds, 'Kramer's High Noon' 56 (2011) *American Journal of Jurisprudence* 135.

effort to uphold the law against caprice, indifference, malice, corruption, etc. If a tyrant overcomes or perverts the judicial application of law, so that principles of justice, fairness, impartiality, and rules and procedures of evidence etc no longer inform the relevant practices, then we reach a stage at which those processes are not *legal* processes.[42]

In sum, a community's approach to its central aims (creating social peace, enabling private and public transactions, compensating harms, deterring and punishing crime, determining ownership of property in land and in things, management of the economy ...) is shaped and limited by its procedural constraints and desiderata. Without such constraints, any one of those aims will threaten to become a form of political force quite out of character with rule through law.

## X.4. LAW AND MORALITY

Some lingering suspicion might be felt towards the end of the preceding section that to refer to the desiderata of legality (1)–(6) is to refer specifically to modern and sophisticated systems of law, and can hardly be predicated of primitive societies of long ago. To this it must be responded that we should be mindful of the warning given in Section X.1 that this chapter is concerned with a focal conception of law and not law in a diminished, corrupted, or primitive state. However, even with that focus in mind, some words should perhaps be said here of non-focal instances of law. Instances of primitive legal orders may indeed lack some of the features of legality associated with a modern legal system, most notably the absence of adjudicative organs. In this sense 'primitive' or pre-modern legal orders are extremely deficient legal orders; they typically possess practices of law *application* (perhaps with brutality), without which they would not resemble law at all. In the same sense, as previously mentioned, Hart characterizes the presence of secondary rules (of change, adjudication and recognition) as the step from the pre-legal into the legal world, yet he is happy to speak of a system of primary rules as one of primitive *law*. In either sense it may be best to classify pre-modern legal systems as analogically rather than literally, law: insofar as such a system altogether lacks one or more of the desiderata of legality, it is not properly a system of law, but insofar as the system has made progress towards an adequate fulfilment of some of the desiderata, it is analogous to law in the proper sense.

In what ways are pre-modern systems of law deficient rather than merely divergent? Their hypothesized lack of mature adjudicative organs is a deficit of *justice*.

[42] For a particularly important discussion see Kristen Rundle, *Forms Liberate* (Hart Publishing 2012) and Dan Priel, 'Reconstructing Fuller's Argument against Legal Positivism' (2013) 26 *Canadian Journal of Law & Jurisprudence* 399: Priel believes the two accounts to be opposing (413 n49) rather than complementary, though there is no argument for this.

Without them, and without a developed system of precedent, it is all but impossible to treat like cases alike. Hart's hypothesis of diffuse social pressure rather than legal enforcement likewise constitutes a lack of justice, which requires at least an organized body of specialized lawyers (counsel, advocate, judge, prosecutor . . .) who can interpret and apply the law with a high degree of uniformity. Finally, the lack of secondary rules of change (to vary one's legal position or another's) renders more difficult the distinction between civil wrongs (such as torts or breach of contract) and crimes.

In relation to corrupted legal orders, the most obvious and most frequently explored example is that of Nazi Germany (see Sections XI.7; X.1). Here we seem to have, in Hart's words, a legal order that has withdrawn its protection from some despised group within the community. More specifically, we appear to have a legal system that departs from the desiderata of legality in its treatment of racial minorities and 'undesirables' within its borders, but observes those desiderata, at least to some degree, in its treatment of 'ordinary' citizens. Is this not a system of *law* notwithstanding its failure to confine its actions to the rule of law? The extensive treatment that the issue has received elsewhere permits of a short and merely indicative discussion here. It is true that under the Nazi terror Germany in effect ceased to be a *rechtsstaat* and became a society ruled by prerogative, enforced by intimidation and fear, usually by non-legal officers of state such as the *Schutzstaffel*. Yet certain aspects of the law that existed prior to the tyranny were still visible: rules which related (in the *Bürgerliches Gesetzbuch*) to contracts, delictual liability, and so on. To ask whether Nazi Germany 'had law' in spite of its positive action to withhold aspects of the rule of law from large sections of the community, is misleading. Germany in fact had two systems of rule after 1933: one a continuation of rule through law, and one of arbitrary rule. Yet the rule through law became increasingly compromised as the reign of terror progressed: the independence of the judiciary was annihilated; avenues of litigation were cut off; any limitations on lawmaking authority were thrown off; to the extent that the German legal system became increasingly hollowed out: a semblance of law, a mere analogy.[43] (See Section XI.7.)

This classification is not merely a verbal one. The question of whether something is classifiable as 'law' is not semantic. Its meaning may, in an uninteresting sense, be said to be stipulative; but the stipulation is not arbitrary. In tying the notion of law to that of legality (principles 1–6) we are seeking to understand social and legal practices in light of their apparent point or purpose. Such a purpose is not technical but, in the case of law, ethical: to place the human being under the governance of

[43] One telling example is the trial of Werner Hollander in 1943. Convicted of having a relationship with an Aryan woman in contravention (though he did not know it) of the German race laws, he was sentenced to death despite the fact that such a 'crime' did not carry the death penalty. The judges massaged the legal rules to accomplish their end: see Raphael Gross, 'Guilt, Shame, Anger, Indignation: Nazi Laws and Nazi Morals' in Alan Steinweis & Robert Rachlin (eds) *The Law in Nazi Germany: Ideology, Opportunism and the Perversion of Justice* (Berghahn Books 2013).

rules that are accessible, clear, prospective, etc, and thus rescue him or her from the vicissitudes of chance and create conditions in which each person can pursue their freely chosen ends. This does not beg any questions: it remains open to the theorist to claim deficient legal practices as instances of legal systems, but they cannot reasonably maintain the ethical understanding of law as marginal, corrupt, deviant or in any way non-focal.

But this naturally leads us to consider the relationship between law and morality more widely. A thorough discussion of this subject requires an understanding of both component terms, 'morality' as well as 'law'. This is in part why a lengthy discussion of morality was provided in Chapters II and III. Here, a more limited account may be given, and most naturally appears in the response(s) to misunderstandings of morality in the work of legal positivists, mostly of Hart. Natural law precepts are appropriately law-like for they are intuitable in the form of *precepts*, the primary precept being the directive that the good is to be done and pursued and the bad avoided. A basic study of human needs and capacities discloses further precepts, in a sense based on the first, which correspond to fundamental human goods. But natural law also extends to moral standards that are not reducible to precepts, though they do give rise to precepts: the virtues.[44] Virtues transcend the law: it is not the function of law to ensure compliance with the full range of virtues,[45] nor to suppress all vices.[46] The first issue that requires discussion, however, is the one briefly touched upon in Section II.7: namely the persistent image that an unjust law is not truly law. This image is projected onto natural law theorists down to the present day: Timothy Macklem, for example, writes: 'Is an unjust law really law? For an idealist clearly not. Practices that do not succeed in living up to their moral inspiration are simply not cases of what they are supposed to be.'[47] Has any natural law theorist ever said this? Let us take Blackstone, whilst not a reputable natural law theorist, as the closest example: he does write that natural law, 'being coeval with mankind, and dictated by God himself, is of course superior in obligation to any other. It is binding over all the globe in all countries, and at all times: no human laws are of any validity, if contrary to this; and such of them as are valid derive all their force and all their authority, mediately or immediately, from this original.'[48] This is the passage that comes closest to the claim in Macklem's essay, and the one lampooned by John Austin in *The Province of Jurisprudence Determined.*[49] But Blackstone in fact immediately qualifies his statement, writing:

[44] See generally Aquinas, *ST* (n 1) II-II, in which discussion of the virtues implicates various precepts *associated with* each virtue.
[45] Ibid, I-II.96.3c.
[46] Ibid, I-II.96.2c, I-II.99.5 ad 1.
[47] Timothy Macklem, 'Law and Living Well' in John Tasioulas (ed) *The Cambridge Companion to the Philosophy of Law* (CUP 2020) 84.
[48] Blackstone, *Comm* I.41.
[49] John Austin, *The Province of Jurisprudence Determined* (Cambridge University Press 1995) 184–85.

> [N]o human laws *should be* suffered to contradict these. There are, it is true, a great number of indifferent points in which both the divine law and the natural leave a man at his own liberty, but which are found necessary, for the benefit of society, to be restrained within certain limits. And herein it is that human laws *have their greatest force and efficacy*; for, with regard to such points as are not indifferent, human laws are only declaratory of, and act in subordination to, the former.[50]

The italicized words indicate that Blackstone was at least dimly aware of the natural law tradition's insistence that unjust laws are obviously laws, Aquinas for example being much more interested in the question of whether such laws are binding in conscience. At the limit case, of a law enacted *ultra vires*, Aquinas states that such a law has more in common with political coercion than with true law,[51] but of course such a law would retain the technical realities of positive law, namely that one who breached it would be arrested, charged, and tried. Or again, Hart writes that according to the natural law theorist there are 'certain rules for the government of human conduct that can be seen by men endowed with reason as necessary to enable men to attain the specifically human optimum state or end (*finis*, *telos*) appointed for men by Nature or (in Christian doctrine) by God'.[52] Now it is perfectly true that natural law theorists (of the kind mentioned by Hart) speak of the highest end (*finis ultimus*), and identify that end with the soul's return (*reditus*) to God in the life to come. But those same writers also recognise the wide variety of ways of living and of pursuing many different ends in the present life: ends that may be virtuous (preferably) or unvirtuous, but irreducibly multiple and diverse. Elsewhere, Hart observes that natural law (theory) 'in all its protean guises' attempts to assert that all human laws are equally devoted to, and united in, their conception of aims 'higher than that of survival'.[53] Two things require to be said here. First, natural law theorists of course do not try to assert that all human laws are equally devoted to higher ends. The laws calculating the income tax rates are not 'equally' devoted to higher ends with those of the criminal law of assaults. Laws setting out penalties for drug-cheats in sport are not on the same level as laws establishing principles and remedies for negligence, and so on. Second, however, natural law theorists do claim that there are higher ends than mere survival on which reasonable persons would agree. Since I devoted some discussion to these issues (see Sections II.7(b) & II.9) suffice it here to say that laws promoting, protecting, or securing such 'higher' ends can claim to be derived from natural law.

50 Blackstone, *Comm* I.42 (emphasis added).
51 Aquinas, *ST* (n 1) I-II.90.1 ad 3; though they retain the generality that is a key feature of law.
52 HLA Hart, *Essays in Jurisprudence and Philosophy* (Clarendon 1984) 113.
53 Ibid, 80–81.

Hart's assumption that law embodies moral precepts is worth testing. In a different place, he observes that law may 'mirror' morality.[54] This statement encourages the image that the law stands in a one-to-one correspondence to certain moral precepts. But in fact substantive moral progress—that is, the securing, promoting, or protecting of human goods—is rarely achieved by one legal provision alone. Consider the Homicide Act 1967: the Act begins by dis-applying the condition of constructive malice; it states that: 'Where a person kills another in the course or furtherance of some other offence, the killing shall not amount to murder unless done with the same malice aforethought (express or implied) as is required for a killing to amount to murder when not done in the course or furtherance of another offence.'[55] It immediately follows: 'For the purposes of the foregoing sub-section, a killing done in the course or for the purpose of resisting an officer of justice, or of resisting or avoiding or preventing a lawful arrest, or of effecting or assisting an escape or rescue from legal custody, shall be treated as a killing in the course or furtherance of an offence.'[56] What is the moral norm described by these sections? Note that these two sections in fact cover a multitude of subjects, including not only malice but also resisting or preventing arrest, procuring an escape, etc. Furthermore, these two sections establish very little on their own in regard to the definition of murder, associated defences and mitigations, aggravations, and so on. Suffice it to say that laws tend to be complex and multifaceted, and that one cannot easily extract one rule from one provision, for even the basic rules of criminal law are spread over numerous statutes and statutory instruments, and judicial doctrines. There simply is no unique correspondence between laws and moral values, and indeed the statement that law 'mirrors' morality ignores the very many *determinationes* that grow up around the most basic rules, and that inform their operation. Rules (as we shall see) are essentially fragments of rights, in that they give fragmentary expression to rights the definition of which may encompass numerous statutes and judicial decisions. Furthermore, the common law is best understood not as a body of rules, but a body of reasons for decision. To this extent, the common law is not orientated towards law-making, and its mode of creativity in application is such that a novel 'rule' or principle cannot be spoken of as 'validly made'[57] (see Section X.6). Thus, it should not be presumed that propositions of law are capable of being neatly demarcated, or individuated, but gain their meaning from a potentially difficult and complex task of reading together a number of valid acts, the validity of which may in turn depend upon substantive as well as procedural considerations.[58]

[54] Ibid, 54.
[55] Homicide Act 1967, s 1(1).
[56] Ibid, s 1(2).
[57] See Maris Köpcke, *Legal Validity: The Fabric of Justice* (Hart Publishing 2019) 147–48.
[58] Ibid, 151–52.

We are focusing on the argument that an unjust law is no law at all (see further Section XI.5). This is problematic because there is seldom if ever any unique correspondence between individual laws and moral values. Now laws, according to the classical treatment given to jurisprudential matters, may offend morality in three possible ways: (i) by stemming from acts that are *ultra vires*, exceeding the authority of the lawmaker; (ii) by requiring the commission of an unjust act, or failing to prohibit such an act; and (iii) by failing to be proportionate to the common good. Only in the case of (i) is an unjust law 'no law at all'. In the case of (ii), an unjust law retains only the form of a law (its characteristically legal style of exposition and framing, and its association with stark realities of detection and punishment). Such a law is frequently not binding in conscience. In the case of (iii), an unjust law quite often retains the obligatory character of law in the conscience of the addressee, though within limits.[59]

But is there nothing more to natural law theory than this? No, for there are other theorems of legal positivism that natural law theory opposes. For instance there is the legal positivist claim that laws come about through speech-acts, specifically the use of a 'say-so' by which, for example, contracts are concluded or applications made.[60] By saying so, one changes one's legal relationship vis-à-vis others, and therefore also the legal position of those others: for example, altering the position of the litigants by making a determination or finding. But we should ask: are legal rules *so* because they have been (validly) *said*? Are there not some legal standards that are *so* prior to and independently of what has been *said*? Such is the claim of natural law theory. For there are certain matters that follow on from the most basic precepts of natural law, such as that criminality should be punished. (Indeed one can scarcely comprehend the idea of 'criminality' without the associations of blame and punishment—as opposed, say, to celebration and reward.) Positivists have directed criticism to natural law theory precisely on this point, that there appear to be certain norms 'awaiting discovery' prior to their formal acknowledgement. The real focus of this concern is with the idea that certain legal norms are already in existence, somehow already part of the law's established normative framework, in advance of their being announced in some 'valid act' (see discussion in Section X.6). But the 'somehow' here is redundant, for the relevant sense to be given to 'already in existence . . . in advance of their announcement' is that of the underived conclusion (*conclusio*) of known premises, given shape and definition with the minimum of creativity in a particular form of words that may have been otherwise expressed. Aggravating factors affecting basic crimes are a case in point: these are straightforwardly inferable from defined criminal acts, however a legal order chooses to express them (e.g. as a constituent part of a criminal act, or as pleadings introduced

[59] Aquinas, *ST* (n 1) I-II.96.4c, I-II.93.3 ad 2, I-II.95.2c, I-II.92.1 ad 4.

[60] Köpcke (n 57) 26, 37–48; see also Mark C Murphy, *Natural Law in Jurisprudence and Philosophy* (CUP 2006, hereafter *NLJP*) 25–59.

at the point of sentencing). It is also true that a body of jurisprudence can grow around an existing legal norm (a legislative rule or judicial determination), not as conclusions from existing premises but through creative linkages of ideas: ideas that are not latent within the existing provisions in any interesting sense, but which are extensions of those provisions, systematically in harmony with their aims and purposes, and necessary in order to give them their full effect in various situations. To say that such norms 'might have been otherwise' is perhaps to overplay the point; it is true that in the limiting cases such norms might take the law in this direction or that, but the majority of *determinationes* cannot be radically different than they are, and do not derive their force entirely from the act of positing.[61] For example, the formalities and protections surrounding the making of wills cannot be radically other than they are if they are to achieve the purpose of ensuring (i) that wills are not created by accident, (ii) that force and fraud have not been applied, and (iii) that bogus claims are discovered and excluded.

Again, let us briefly examine why the majority of laws are *determinationes* rather than pure inventions. Aquinas's statement that *determinatio* is required where natural law is silent is rather unhelpful, for the creative element of *determinatio* is nonetheless a kind of derivation from natural law principles. Now the laws are not created *ab initio*, but into a rich fabric of existing laws, the overwhelming majority of which give shape and substance to justice, whether by circumscribing legal powers, creating rights, or specifying penalties (etc). At the most basic level, such laws are (i) directed to the common good, and (ii) create or maintain elements of peace, justice, prosperity, and other human goods. To the extent that newly created laws are not disruptive, but form a coherent part of existing law, they make a contribution to those underlying aims of law, promoting peace, stability, whilst themselves taking shape against the background of those values. Take Aquinas's chosen example of punishment: it follows from natural law's primary precepts that wrongdoer requires punishment, but the natural law is silent on what that punishment should be.[62] This is not entirely accurate: natural law principles militate against a proposed sentence of community service in the case of a convicted murderer, or a sentence of death or torture in the case of a pickpocket. To some extent, the sentence is determined against a background of a scale of sentences more or less theorized as a matter of preexisting law. Other types of sentence presuppose existing principles of property law, both in the framing of the crime and various avenues of response in sentencing. Without labouring the point, most created laws are determined according to values of justice and human good enshrined in the law rather than purely positive laws: even road traffic laws foster the aims of peace, safety, and justice.

[61] Aquinas, *ST* (n 1) I-II.104.1c, I-II.99.3 ad 2: '[T]hese very determinations which are made by human law are said to be, not of natural, but of positive law.'

[62] Ibid, I-II.95.2c.

In his book on HLA Hart, Matthew Kramer writes that natural law theorists seek 'to show that law is an inherently moral phenomenon'.[63] Now the above discussion demonstrates that this is not the case: tyrannical legal systems that exist for the enrichment of the tyrant (for example) are not 'inherently moral'. Nor are iniquitous laws 'inherently moral'. But if the meaning of Kramer's statement is that law is inherently a *concern* of morality, then the statement is true, if relatively uninformative. What form does this 'concern' take? It goes beyond, for example, Hart's suggestion that there is no further specific point that law serves beyond providing guides to human conduct and standards of criticism of that conduct.[64] For there are a great many specific purposes that the law serves, including those legal rules (areas of law) that are inherently concerned with the treatment and distribution of *risk*, with the aftermath of *harm* whether intentional or accidental, and with the social and personal costs of forms of *deception* or *force*. These concerns provide the foundation on which the criminal law, law of torts, and law of contract are built. But they are merely indicative and schematic of the ways in which law is a concern of morality.

Recently, Murphy has sought to move natural law theory away from the idea that law and morality share a necessary connection, for he argues instead that law must be backed by decisive reasons for action.[65] This, he argues, is the meaning, somewhat cryptically stated, of *ST* I-II.90.1c, the relevant part of which is as follows:

> *lex* is derived from *ligare* [to bind], since it obligates one to act. Now the rule and measure of human acts is reason, which ... is the first principle of human acts. For it belongs to the reason to ordain things to their end, which is the primary principle in all matters of action ... Now whatever is the principle in any genus, is the measure and rule of that genus: for example, unity in the genus of numbers, and the first movement in the genus of movements. Thus it follows that law is something pertaining to reason.

But in order to accept Murthy's claim, two things must hold (1) the passage is obscurely worded, and (2) the passage contains Aquinas's doctrine on natural law. Yet neither holds. There is nothing obscure about Aquinas's doctrine, which simply draws attention to the fact that law (all law, from eternal law to unjust human laws) pertains to reason (i.e. is a work of reason). (Hence law is not merely 'backed by reasons' but is itself a form of reason.) And it is quite clear that Aquinas had many more things to say on the subject of law in general and natural law in particular than is stated in this passage: remarks that make clear that law is a kind of justice,

[63] Kramer (n 12) 148.

[64] Hart, *CL* (n 3) 249; but see ibid 99: the union of primary and secondary rules is insufficient and needs to be augmented with other elements.

[65] Murphy, *NLJP* (n 60) 1–2.

and unreasonable law is a kind of injustice;[66] and that law as such is expressive of and proportionate to human happiness (*beatitudo*) in general and the common good in particular.[67] Murphy's main thesis is that laws that are not backed by decisive reasons are 'defective as laws'. But surely this is the wrong way round: it is our judgment that a law is defective (insufficiently directed to the common good or to some aspect of human flourishing, or indeed opposed to them) that lead us to conclude that one does not have decisive reasons for action. This is what appears to drive Aquinas's relatively brief discussions of whether and when laws ought not to be complied with. So natural law theorists need not confine themselves to Murphy's narrow approach. Of course, Murphy might claim that only the narrow view survives philosophical scrutiny. Let the preceding sections of this chapter stand against such a claim: see also the long endnote to Section I.2.

Thus, the foregoing discussion has explored some of the 'connections between law and morality'. In fact, it could perhaps be said that legal reasoning is a specialized type of moral reasoning (a claim I explore in Section X.5). (As Gardner admits, every legal issue, no matter how abstrusely technical, is a moral issue, for its resolution invariably has morally important consequences for someone.)[68] It is worth underlining, however, that laws do not (and natural law theorists do not deny that laws do not) simply reproduce moral principles.[69] For again, legal language is tonally different from moral language; it employs and circles around a more limited array of concepts such as reasonableness, harm, foreseeability, bona fides, obligation, and so on. There is a high degree of formalization of such concepts: they do not have the same extension as their ordinary language counterparts but require to be interpreted against myriad statutory provisions and judicial precedents. Frequently, the meaning of individual laws is connected with that of other laws and legal principles, so that an especially high price is put upon coherence, not only between laws but also of present laws to the past, especially past judicial decisions. There is also an unusual focus on the future, particularly the future interpretation of legal rules: this can be seen particularly in the judicial desire to avoid 'slippery slopes' and 'opening the floodgates'. There is the need and tendency to announce legal rules through the prism of legal *rights*, and not merely what is morally *good* or *favourable* or *sound*. (Despite his injunction to 'take rights seriously', Dworkin does not appear to have comprehended this last point.) There is the emphasis on predictability. Finally, there is the need for law and legal discourse to be relatively autonomous with respect to other branches of government. But the principle behind the separation of powers can be taken further—that the concentration of legal power should not lie in a few hands but many hands and over time, for

[66] Aquinas, *ST* (n 1) II-II.57.1c & ad 1.

[67] Ibid, I-II.90.2c.

[68] John Gardner, *Law as a Leap of Faith* (OUP 2012) 161; see also Nigel E Simmonds, 'The Centrality of Jurisprudence' 64 (2019) *American Journal of Jurisprudence* 1.

[69] See e.g. John Finnis, *Aquinas: Moral, Political and Legal Theory* (OUP 1998) 266.

this reduces the possibility of tyranny (where all norms are set at once by a limited number of actors).[70]

## X.5. LEGAL REASON

How are such matters carried into effect? That is the general question with which this section is concerned. Legal reason or reasoning is frequently thought to be the topic of adjudication; but it is also the concern of lawmaking in the legislative mode. Unreason on the part of the lawmaker is, as we have already seen (Section X.3), a violation of the rule of law.[71] A complete understanding of legal reason must proceed from an insight into the principal purposes for which law is made and applied. They can be gathered from Aquinas's treatment of law, and apply in large measure to both legislative and judicial processes of reason: (i) to safeguard and promote the common good of the community;[72] (ii) to guide citizens to virtue through dictates of reason;[73] (iii) to guide and supplement the natural reason of ordinary persons;[74] (iv) to moderate the effect of natural laws in particular cases, that is, to employ casuistry in acknowledgement of the great variety of human circumstances;[75] (v) to educate the uneducated in their moral duties;[76] (vi) to exercise judgment about which transgressions to penalize.[77] To this list we may add: (vii) fairness to litigants, both in adjudication and in legislatively determined rules of procedure and evidence, etc; (viii) to offer public reasons for decisions affecting persons, especially litigants; and (ix) making clear the boundary between legal reasoning and private moral reasoning. Let us explore the mechanisms through which the law attains, or aspires to, these ends.

We might start with the legal positivist concept of a 'rule of recognition', the full implications of which do not seem to have been discussed. The term is scarcely applicable to the process of *law creation*, as opposed to *application*, for a law is either validly made or it never was a law at all. The term 'recognition' distinctly implies a process of reflecting, discovering, and/or judging norms that are *in some sense* already in existence prior to the present use that is being made of them.[78] This process

[70] Köpcke (n 57) 5–6.

[71] One that is also pointed out by Aquinas: see Aquinas, *ST* (n 1) I-II.90.1 ad 3.

[72] Ibid, I-II.90.2c: an aim which includes the temporal tranquility of the state, suppression and punishment of criminality, establishment of penalties for negligent harm, or for breaking solemn agreements, establishing at least minimum prosperity for all; see Section I.4.

[73] Aquinas, *ST* (n 1) I-II.92.1 ad 2.

[74] Ibid, I-II.91.2c.

[75] Ibid, I-II.95.2 ad 3, I-II.97.1 ad 1, I-II.105.2 ad 8.

[76] Ibid, I-II.100.11c.

[77] Ibid, I-II.101.3 ad 2.

[78] To the contrary, see Neil Duxbury, 'Custom as Law in English Law' 76 (2017) *Cambridge Law Journal* 337. See also the excellent essays in Amanda Perreau-Saussine & James Bernard Murphy, *The Nature of Customary Law* (CUP 2007).

is particularly in evidence on those occasions on which a court decides a case on the basis of a legal principle that has been given definite expression for the first time but which has been latent within the case-law prior to such expression. Such principles do not come 'out of nowhere'; their presence in legal doctrine has been *recognized*. This must be the case if a key premise of law, that litigants should receive the same decision from the judge in their case as from any other judge had that other judge in fact sat in their case, is to be satisfied.[79] Further, it is preferable to speak of 'practices of recognition' rather than a 'rule of recognition'. The phrase 'whatever the Queen- or King-in-Parliament enacts is law' (not, incidentally, in this form, a rule at all), Hart's suggestion for the rule of recognition for the system of English law, was never an adequate statement even of the sources of law, let alone a guide to how legal norms may be recognized through these sources. The process of 'recognition' is no simple one (were it so, there would be no need of extensive training of the judiciary, nor any reason why judges should be drawn from the ranks of experienced senior lawyers).[80] But further, why only practices of recognition? Why not also practices of judgment, interpretation, deduction, application, justification, and estimation: all of which are quite as germane as recognition in the judicial application of law? It is far from obvious that such practices in any way derive from a prior rule or practice of recognition; they are related but distinct elements of the process of applying law in codified as well as common law systems of law.

Judges may employ one, some, or all of these practices when applying 'the law' to the instant case: 'the law' being often not explicit but presupposed by bodies of law or legal principle, in harmony with other legal standards (whether or not directly relevant to the instant case) or contributing to the implicit point of legal values and principles that are in some measure already settled. Furthermore, the role of the judge is to provide a justification not only of the instant case but also the previously settled law, for what matters in contexts of adjudication is not whether some rule or principle has been 'laid down' but whether it continues to be received as sound in present cases.[81] References here to practices of interpretation or justification should not be taken as support for the theory of adjudication set out by Ronald Dworkin. Whilst he contends that the point of law is to discover the existence of a justifying relationship between past legal decisions and present practices of judgment, previously settled ('past') legal norms are not morally elastic forms in search of this or that justification; legal reasoning does not take the form of an effort to discover the most morally sound interpretation of legal norms (from amongst other,

[79] See Finnis, *CEJF* (n 8) I.14, 229.

[80] For some empirical testing of the extent to which the rule of recognition plays a part in actual legal thinking see David Howarth & SW Stark, 'HLA Hart's Secondary Rules: What do "Officials" Really Think?' 14 (2018) *International J of Law and Context* 61. For an American perspective see Matthew Adler & Kenneth Himma (eds), *The Rule of Recognition and the US Constitution* (OUP 2009), esp Jeremy Waldron, 'Who Needs Rules of Recognition?' 327.

[81] See Finnis, *CEJF* (n 8) IV.3, 129–30.

presumably less sound interpretations of those same norms), which 'fit' with the extant authorities. For the notion of 'fit' is itself presumably based upon an 'interpretation' of legal norms, an interpretation that is faithful to the textual form of the norms rather than the moral 'interpretations' that such norms can potentially bear. But the notion of 'interpretation', if not intimately associated with the other practices of legal reasoning (deduction, application, etc) can suggest that the meaning of settled legal norms is more fluid, less univocal, than it in fact is. Yet this should not be taken as agreement with Dworkin's other famous contention, that there is a single right answer available in every case. There is more than one way in which a present case can avoid injustice to the litigants, or create a bad precedent or poison legal principle.

There are certain basic principles in addition to the ones named above (i)–(ix) that a court needs to respect in the course of its deliberations. For example, there is the principle (quoted by Hart) that certain acts belong to the realm of private morality and immorality that ought not to become a concern for legal regulation.[82] Further abstract principles are readily identified: the need to avoid contradictions, avoiding fear or favour, providing clear grounds for decision, banishing passionate reasoning, etc. One can then descend to more specific requirements implied by those abstract aims: the aims of prevention, restitution, penalty, recognition (of contracts, marriages, valid exercises of power, etc); and to still more specific objectives: the application of an appropriate penalty to the defendant, the grant of a marriage licence, prevention of trespass or insider-dealing, etc. If such measures are to become a reality, there is a need for a body of judges, legislators, and officials who settle questions of the scope, meaning, interpretation, existence, application, and operation of the relevant doctrines, rules, and principles.[83] But such officials can legitimately be motivated by the need (or perceived need) of reforming the settled law. Here again, sets of skills are involved so that personal visions can be sidelined in favour of sound *legal* reasons for undertaking reform, and for reforming the law in this way rather than that. Thus statutes may be repealed or disapplied; new laws created which overwrite older provisions to improve or streamline the law, or to bring the law into line with technologies, public opinion, or social changes; codes may be rewritten; judicial authorities distinguished, widened, or overturned. All of these measures share something in common, or are premised upon a common presupposition: that the laws being created or applied are in harmony with areas of law considered to be just and reasonable.[84] Of course, such processes (particularly the legislative process) are capable of being hijacked for party political considerations, careerism, corruption for financial gain, etc. But that is not the *point* of them. Their point is the application of practical reason to social problems in the distinctive

[82] Wolfenden Report § 61.
[83] See Finnis, *NLNR* (n 18) 268.
[84] Finnis, *CEJF* (n 8) IV.3.102.

ways just mentioned. Seventeenth-century common lawyers marked this distinctiveness by distinguishing the 'artificial perfection of [legal] reason' with ordinary moral reason.[85]

How does the claim that the English common law embodies the 'artificial perfection of reason' sit alongside the idea that this same body of laws articulates or declares the natural law? Let us ponder for a moment the claimed artificiality. There are two respects in which the common law is artificial: (i) in that its characteristic processes of reasoning relies on precedents, general rules, and principles that are 'settled' in the sense that decisions were made justifying the resolution of innumerable cases to past litigants which therefore cannot be scrapped wholesale; and (ii) the reasoning of many minds is superior to that of one mind reasoning on the problems implicated by civil society. In the second sense, the common law is not vastly different from ordinary efforts of reasoning: no philosopher works entirely alone and without the input of other minds—Suarez and Grotius had their Aquinas; Aquinas himself had his Aristotle and his Augustine, amongst others. Natural law theories are the product of many minds, not one acting alone. In the first sense, there seems to be a formal difference: the legal determination of a problem typically restricts the moral interpretation of a problem to a set of more-or-less defined issues. Thus, the question of whether A owes B damages for breach of contract is restricted to concepts of offer and acceptance, consideration, foreseeability, and so forth; whether A is poor and B is rich enough to absorb the loss, or whether A is a good person and B bad, is not material. But those latter questions are of at best secondary relevance, the real question being whether A caused B to incur a loss. Furthermore, the artificiality of the common law is very often associated with *determinationes*, matters on which 'natural reason' must be supplemented by positive decision-making.[86] Such decision-making is in turn generally carried out with an eye to coherence with existing common law concepts, principles, and doctrines, reinforcing the sense of artificiality. Or, quite conceivably, the artificiality is due to a legal rule being a *lex iniusta*, a posited rule in opposition to natural reason.[87] In sum, the 'artificiality' of the common law is not incompatible with its declaratory character.

Similarly, legal reason's declaratory function must be reconciled with its creative character. We may for present purposes distinguish two modes of creativity: (1) the creativity involved in reconciling apparently or genuinely conflicting principles; (2) the creativity of extending principles where lacunae exist. Both legislative and judicial authorities engage in these enterprises, but it will be instructive to confine discussion to judicial reasoning. In regard to the first mode, it must be remembered

[85] See *Bonham's Case* [1610] 8 Co Rep 107a.

[86] Thus for example, Hohfeld's analysis sets out the minimum consequences for holding an entitlement. Any further 'consequences' (e.g. an entitlement of A against B resulting in some form of entitlement to C) can only be brought about through positive law: *determinatio*.

[87] Though still a part of legal reason: Aquinas, *ST* (n 1) II-II.57.1 ad 1.

that the domain of legal reason is not, and cannot be, completely self-consistent, given the unusually high degree of specificity involved in legal reason (versus ordinary moral reasoning) across a wide range of subjects and issues. It is obvious that ordinary persons who utter two contradictory or inconsistent sentences might be called upon to utter a third sentence with which to resolve the inconsistency. This third sentence will not be composed entirely out of new elements, though it will contain some; one would also expect, if it be a genuine attempt, to draw upon elements, of one or both original sentences. The third sentence will be, perforce, *new*, but composed of old elements. So it is with judicial creativity with regard to mode (1). For example, the courts may in certain circumstances translate the principles surrounding latent defects in contractual provisions into an extension of the doctrine of impossibility, to refer not only to intervening acts and circumstances (frustration) but to the parties' mutual lack of insight into the nature of the obligations they are creating. Such a doctrine could equally be brought under the auspices of an extended doctrine of common mistake (though without some of the onerous requirements of that doctrine); which route is chosen will depend upon whether the court treats the attendant risks as requiring to be distributed across both parties to the contract, or substantially borne by one of them. In regard to mode (2), Hart provides the following example: 'In every legal system, there will always be certain unforeseen cases, unregulated by the law; that is, cases in which no decision either way is dictated by the clearly settled law and, consequently, the law is partly indeterminate or incomplete.'[88] Hart here provides an example in contradistinction to the mode in which there is indeterminacy because established lines of authority conflict, requiring an authoritative resolution. Presumably such a case must be one in which the defendant is arguing that there simply is no law in point to convict him, and the state or claimant is seeking some extension or novel application of existing rules. But in such a case, 'indeterminacy' is merely an indicator that there is more than one way to do good, to respect and uphold the common good by resolving the case in one way rather than another, even if supported by arguments that are not conclusive. At the same time of course, the courts are aware that creativity must not assume more freedom than the particular point of law gives to it. Sometimes judges use their position as an opportunity to rue the lack of legislative intervention on a particular subject and decry the necessity of finding for a party who ought to be held to account and against an injured party who ought to be compensated.

In some moods, Hart was aware that certain legal rules are 'not brought into being by *anything analogous* to explicit prescription',[89] and that the law 'must contain rules concerning the basic conditions of social life ... if fundamental human

[88] HLA Hart, 'The New Challenge to Legal Positivism' [1979] 36 (2016) *Oxford Journal of Legal Studies* 462.

[89] Hart, *CL* (n 3) 79.

needs are to be satisfied'.[90] He also admitted that the very use of rules provides a minimum of formal justice—treat like cases alike—in legal reasoning (though not the reverse principle—treat different cases differently).[91] This minimum of morality in the form of legal reasoning, underestimating though it does the essentially ethical character of legal reasoning, is not deemed by some modern positivists to be a necessary feature of all legal reasoning. John Gardner has stated the thesis that the validity of a law can depend upon its content but not the 'merits' of its content.[92] It is difficult to make sense of this. A law singled out and individuated would *ipso facto* stand or fall on its own merits; its 'content', thus denuded of its merits, would be quite incapable of being justified in application, and the norm would be equally incapable of being 'recognized' on its content alone (aside from the merits of its content). It would be, precisely, a *norm*, not a mere piece of content, such as the content of a novel, requiring no justification for its existence. Understood in its relationship to other laws, it would require at least the merit of being interpretable in the light of those other laws; if at variance with them, it would require reasons why or why not to be followed or applied: decisions that cannot be made by reference to 'content' alone, shorn of its intrinsic justifications. One could, for example, detach the rule that two witnesses are required to formalize a will from its justifications or 'merits'. Its validity as a rule can be said to depend entirely upon its having been instituted by statute. Denuded of 'merit', it would be quite unclear whether the provision were intended to reduce force and fraud, or simply place obstacles in the way of creating wills, perhaps where the property of intestates defaults to the state. But this cannot be the kind of rule Gardner has in mind, for this rule's validity does not depend on its content, but on its source. It remains completely unclear how a legal rule could be 'validated' by reference to its content alone, without any sense of its purpose or 'merits'. Hart himself seems aware of this: in a famous essay he wrote: 'In the case of legal rules the criteria of relevance and closeness of resemblance depend on many complex factors running through the legal system and on the aims or purpose which might be attributed to the rule.' He immediately continues: 'To characterise these would be to characterise whatever is specific in or peculiar to legal reasoning.'[93]

It is to be hoped that the above discussion casts at least a few rays of light on that subject, that is, of legal reason's peculiarity and relationship to moral reason: a relationship that is not 1:1. It explores in some measure how the particular laws of particular societies are related to the permanent principles of natural law.[94] The outcome of such reasoning is not a mere ratification of moral reason, but more akin

[90] HLA Hart, *Essays in Jurisprudence & Philosophy* (OUP 1984, hereafter *EJP*) 112–13.

[91] See John Gardner, *Law as a Leap of Faith* (OUP 2011) 251–53; also David Dyzenhaus, 'The Genealogy of Legal Positivism' 24 (2004) *Oxford Journal of Legal Studies* 41.

[92] Gardner (n 91) 30–31.

[93] Hart, *EJP* (n 90) 127.

[94] See Finnis, *NLNR* (n 18) 281.

to a partnership between legal and moral reason in arriving at a just result. This is the correct way to interpret Aquinas's statement that 'all human laws that are laid down have the character of laws just to the extent that they are derived from natural law'.[95]

Despite having focused on judicial reasoning, it should be emphasized that the application of law pertains not just to litigation but also to implementing laws by local authorities in pursuance of national legislation, ensuring consistency of state law with federal law, etc. This raises the issue of whether, among these complex processes, there are general principles visible to analysis. Section X.6 considers one such general principle.

## X.6. LEGAL VALIDITY

The foregoing discussion made use of a concept that has until recently been little understood by legal philosophers: that of 'legal validity'.[96] The notion of validity is not to be found in the classic treatments of law found in Aquinas, Suarez, and Grotius, though they do, of course, contain the concept(s) of 'positive law'. But one does encounter the notion in later accounts of natural law, for example in this classic passage from Blackstone: '[N]o human laws are of any validity, if contrary to [the natural law]; such of them as are valid derive all their force and all their authority, mediately or immediately, from this original.'[97] Blackstone's statement would have been regarded as at best an exaggeration by his intellectual ancestors, as their sensitive discussions of matters such as unjust laws and *ultra vires* acts attest. But of note in Blackstone's passage is the new and specific technical meaning given to the notion of 'validity': for a rule to be 'valid' means that it 'exists', 'is recognised', 'forms part of', 'belongs to' a certain legal order the *criteria of validity* of which the rule in question satisfies. This usage is rather curious. Widely used by legal philosophers, it is not a visible part of lawyers' or judges' or legislators' discourse, and plays no discernible role in legal reasoning. When lawyers use the term 'valid', they generally have in mind the conformity of some formal document or act to legally specified canons, guidelines, or formalities, the fulfilment of which give official recognition to that document's or act's legal operativeness, generally for a fixed period of time. One can therefore refer to legally valid passports, marriage certificates, licences, contracts, uses of local governmental power, or even validly enacted statutes, codes, or constitutional amendments,[98] but such uses of the term

95 Aquinas, *ST* (n 1) I-II.95.2c. The key term is 'derived': to achieve justice not only must the laws be just, but also their application/institution—the avoidance of show-trials, biases, or vested interests; due consideration to property rights in decisions of eminent domain; etc.

96 See Köpcke (n 57); see also Kenneth Einar Himma, *Morality and the Nature of Law* (OUP 2019) 61–79.

97 Blackstone, *Comm* I.41.

98 But see Köpcke (n 57) 1.

'validity' are not the same as the notion of Blackstone and later legal philosophers. For (in the lawyer's sense) it is not a measure of the document's or act's *belonging* to a legal system that is in question but its *operativeness*. There is only a tenuous analogy between the notions of 'operativeness' and 'belonging' (perhaps most visible in the case of a valid *membership* of some organization), which does not hold in the case of most of the forms and actions we ordinarily refer to as 'valid'.

Thus, the lawyers' sense of 'validity' and that of legal philosophers do not match up. The latter's extension of validity to the *existence* of legal rules departs in significant ways from lawyers' ordinary usage.[99] This (philosophers') wider notion of validity creates confusion, and the confusion is enhanced by the search for a single or ultimate validating mechanism for resolving questions of the legal validity of rules: something that is presupposed by the wider notion itself. But it is not clear why an ultimate foundation—a rule of recognition or *grundnorm*—should be thought necessary. In common law jurisdictions, for example, there is (i) a doctrine of sources of law; (ii) an established hierarchy of sources; and (iii) a constitution: none of these need be termed the 'ultimate' validating authority; a working relationship between them is sufficient for all practical purposes. Similarly, an enumeration of the sources of law does not stand in need of being elevated to the status of a '*grundnorm*'; there only needs to be a high degree of practical consensus on such sources, even if not all questions are settled about their nature and importance (e.g. unclarity about how, or when, customs become laws). An illustration of the difficulties presented by the legal theorist's sense of 'validity' can be found in Finnis's replication of the positivists' notion in the language of Aquinas. The passage is worth quoting in full:

> The legal validity (in the focal, moral sense of 'legal validity') of positive law is derived from its rational connection with (i.e. derivation from) natural law, and this connection holds good, normally, if and only if (i) the law originates in a way which is legally valid (in the specially restricted, purely legal sense of 'legal validity') and (ii) the law is not materially unjust either in its content or in relevant circumstances of its positing.[100]

By way of clarification, the focal sense of 'legal validity' is later termed by Finnis as 'morally predicated legal validity', and the 'specially restricted' sense as 'intra-systemic' legal validity.[101] The implication of the latter version of the distinction is merely hinted at in the former: that the moral sense of legal validity is somehow 'extra-systemic', that is, outside the body of norms of which law is comprised. In

[99] Ibid, 59: a say-so will not be *valid* (cf existent) unless it conforms to legal procedures.
[100] Finnis, *NLNR* (n 18) 27; the Thomist authority supplied is *ST* (n 1) I-II.96.4c.
[101] John Finnis, 'Natural Law Theory: Its Past and Its Present' 57 (2012) *American Journal of Jurisprudence* 100.

the former version, we must therefore assume that (ii) (in Finnis's account) points to an extra-legal standard. Now it must also be assumed that the extra-legal, moral standards are sufficiently law-like in form so that the 'rational connection' or 'derivation' can be made. This does not mean that the moral standards are framed in the language of, and employing the conceptual devices of, written law; but they must be translatable: 'killing is wrong/forbidden/evil' into 'it is/shall be an offence/crime willingly to take the life of another human being, except in the following cases ... and with the minimum punishment of ...'. This appears to be the kind of 'rational connection' Aquinas has in mind. But notice that this translatability of moral norms to legal norms has nothing essentially to do with the notion of 'validity' *in the legal philosophers' sense*: 'it is' or 'it shall be [an offence]' is an operative clause, not a validating one, for the relevant notion of validity 'in the specially restricted, purely legal sense' pertains to the traceability of a legal rule to its source. Legal validity, as understood by legal philosophers, even by Finnis, is concerned with 'intra-systemic existence', that is, by (i) above.[102] And (i) above is treated by Finnis as distinct from (ii), so that (ii) represents an *additional* normative requirement distinct from the *lawyers'* ('purely legal') understanding of legal validity. When these connections are spelled out it becomes sufficiently clear that the legal theorist's conception of legal validity is a potential source of confusion.

Now lawyers have a 'purely legal' notion of legal validity, as the foregoing discussion illustrated. It is a notion of operativeness. But this notion is itself morally significant in that it creates and defends forms of human wellbeing which otherwise would not sufficiently appear, and is key to the law's ability to bring about justice.[103] It does so through what Maris Köpcke terms 'specific convergence', the convergent conduct of many persons following specific patterns to bring about some goal of public welfare: patterns of conduct that may be private (the returning of items borrowed on deposit), or public (every person's duty not physically to assault another person).[104] Refraining from maliciously injuring another person is specifically apt to the goal of human wellbeing because it is (i) effective, (ii) easily achieved, and (iii) there are no feasible alternatives, and is therefore due. Furthermore it remains due where there is a context of other acts that serve to reinforce the goal of bodily soundness, such as clean air and water, adequate food, nutrition, etc.[105] But from a Thomistic point of view this is inaccurate: the natural law duty not to harm another person is not 'reinforced' by any further values but simply that of the wellbeing of the person concerned and, by extension, of all persons. It does not depend on there being adequate food to go round, nor on any environmental factors. The duty

[102] See e.g. Michelle Dempsey, 'On Finnis's Way In' 57 (2012) *Villanova Law Review* 827; John Finnis, 'Response' 57 (2012) *Villanova Law Review* 925, 927.

[103] Köpcke (n 57) 4, 11. (Köpcke's use of validity is much closer to the legal philosopher's notion but provides a richly enhanced account of its legal significance.)

[104] Ibid, 69; see also Murphy, *NLJP* (n 60) 32.

[105] Köpcke (n 57) 71–73.

would remain due to each person even if there were squabbles over scarce food: I cannot kill or otherwise incapacitate my neighbour so that I may live. Indeed, the duty would remain operative even if the civic authorities ended the criminal prohibition on murder and created conditions for a free-for-all.

In the case of natural laws, to say that a natural law obligation exists is to say that it is operative; in the case of positive laws, to say that an obligation or rule exists is not necessarily to say that it is operative. For example, a will might contain clauses to the effect that certain other clauses of the will (which will convey property from the deceased's estate to some identifiable beneficiary) are not to enter operation until the beneficiary has obtained the age of twenty-one. One might conclude that all that is legally valid is created by an exercise of what Hart called secondary rules of change: power-conferring rules (including, for these purposes, rules of adjudication which empower judges to change the legal position of litigants).[106] But not all changes of legal relations are the result of an exercise of power, for in a perfectly straightforward sense A's exercise of a right renders operative B's duty (a duty B has prior to the *exercise* of the right), and C's immunity renders inoperative D's otherwise operative power, a power which, but for the immunity, would render operative a standing liability in C. We should not, however, draw the conclusion that all valid legal rules are created, instituted, or made. Some legal rules are instituted in this way: by saying the relevant form of words, one makes it so—making an application, concluding a contract, and so on.[107] Such rules are given existence and operation by a certain form of words: a speech-act. Such speech-acts do not generally act on their own, but draw their significance from an array of already-operative rules, principles, and procedures. But as mentioned in Section X.4, not *every* legal rule is *so* because it has been *said*. Some legal rules are *so* prior to their having been *said*. This warrants some further discussion.

Both natural laws and legal customs fall into this bracket. Natural laws are laws prior to being said, are laws even in the face of vigorous opposition and counter-speech, and are laws even if never spoken. Legal customs are laws prior to being spoken, can survive a certain degree of counter-speech, but are not laws if never spoken. Jurists from Cicero down to Grotius and other early-modern philosophers employed the concept of *ius commune* and *ius gentium* to describe laws that were common to different peoples and thus more akin to natural law than to purely positive law (see Section XII.2). But they described those systems of law quite without the idea of 'validity' in the modern legal philosophers' sense. Aquinas, for example, does not (to my knowledge) use the term *validitas* in connection with positive law at all, preferring to say that positive laws have been *determined*. Suarez does employ the term, along with variants, but predominantly in the context of the validity (operability) of certain laws and connected with their *value* (*valor*).[108]

106 Ibid, 14.
107 Ibid, 29.
108 See Maris Köpcke, *A Short History of Legal Validity and Invalidity* (Intersentia 2019) 101.

This connection of validity with 'value' remains visible in modern contexts. In the examples employed earlier in this Section, the 'validity' of rules (their having been brought into operation) is in some way connected with their content: that is to say, they are valuable only because they are related to the content of other rules. For although it is possible to create contractual relations on a wide array of subjects, and establishing many forms of duty, it is not open to contracting parties to contract in pursuance of, for example, a criminal enterprise; nor is it open to either contractual party to create terms that are fraudulent in intent. Thus the substance of what we might call 'framing laws'—laws not immediately connected with contracts but informing their creation and operability—variously guide and constrain the substance of contractual obligations. The 'legal validity' of certain laws depends upon their rational connection to other laws. Hence, 'the [positivist] sources thesis downplays the relevance of content in identifying law'; in particular Hart and Gardner obscure the extent to which propositions of law (norms) are incapable of being neatly demarcated (individuated) to enable them to be determined by their source, but derive their meaning from the potentially complex process of reading together a number of valid acts the validity of which may depend for *their* validity on their substance.[109] Classical and early-modern accounts of law were not impeded by the absence of an equivalent of the sources thesis. The lawyerly notion of 'validity' is hence separable from that troublesome thesis.

One further issue should be mentioned. The various primary and secondary rules that validate, say, particular contractual obligations, and which we might call 'validating laws' (of wills, applications, offices ...) are at the same time capable of being theorized as *invalidating* laws: the same provisions which state the terms on which contractual relations are valid also operate to render such relations invalid, where the parties have failed to conform to the requirements of the rules. The rule requiring two witnesses to a will state the terms on which a will is validly executed, but also state the terms on which it is invalid. This property of valid legal norms is quite distinct from anything in the legal philosophers' usage. It is in something like the lawyers' usage that Finnis writes that the purpose of the law is to grant validity to all other normative arrangements affecting members of the community.[110] This flexibility of the notion of validity (its serviceability for operationalizing contracts, delicts, appointments, distributions, benefactions, criminal punishments) renders it a powerful tool for lawyers, but a dangerous one in the hands of legal philosophers.

109 Köpcke (n 57) 147–48.
110 Finnis, *NLNR* (n 18) 260.

## X.7. NECESSARY CONNECTIONS

The preceding discussion enables us to pose the question of the law's positivity in more precise terms: '[b]y law's positivity [is meant] the fact that the legal positions persons are in at any point are determined by the legal meaning of valid acts rather than by moral considerations that are not part of the legal meaning of valid acts.'[111] The question is therefore how are we to determine whether a particular moral principle is or is not part of the legal meaning of valid acts. If morality is *sometimes* a part of the meaning of legally valid acts, how does one tell when that moral principle ends and the morality that is not a part of that legal meaning begins? Does this denote a *necessary connection* between law and morality?

To assert that there are (or are not) 'connections' between law and morality is to speak too imprecisely.[112] Rather there are many ways in which law and morality *coincide*, in which law *gives effect to* moral values, in which the law *has moral aims*, *is derived from* general precepts of natural law, in which the law intervenes in otherwise private moral choices and decisions, and in which morality *is a source of* positive law. There are many such intimate modes of relationship. The law is necessarily *a moral enterprise*, for example, in that whatever is not prohibited is a matter of liberty.[113] It did not occur to natural law theorists, for example, to frame the question in terms of the law's 'connection(s)' to morality. They were far more concerned with a matter little discussed by modern legal philosophers: the mode by which the law is *communicated* to us. Aquinas therefore observed that laws are a species of 'rational norm'; for people's desires, appetites, and emotions are more variable than reason, making them unsuitable for the communication of norms. Reason itself, of course, is not entirely without variation, so that as Hart observed, legal language (whether contained in statute or in judicial decisions) is 'open-textured': capable, more or less, of varied interpretation. But reason is the primary mode by which norms of any kind are communicated, and in the two primary modes of law-creation, *determinatio* and *conclusio*, there is derivation rather than connection of morality to law. Similarly, there is no thesis of 'connection' in the common law theory of custom: that a custom has the status of law because it has existed from time immemorial, and would not have continued in this way if it had been somehow contrary to reason.[114] But the 'connection' thesis is resilient, and has advocates beyond legal positivism. Dworkin, perhaps surprisingly, is such an advocate, because, for him, 'interpretation is not ... an activity that we routinely

[111] Köpcke (n 57) 124.

[112] For a recent account see Tony Honore, 'The Necessary Connection Between Law and Morality' 22 (2002) *Oxford Journal of Legal Studies* 489; Robert Alexy, 'On the Thesis of a Necessary Connection Between Law and Morality: Bulygin's Critique' 13 (2000) *Ratio Juris* 138.

[113] For an explanation of the moral significance of liberty see e.g. Nigel E Simmonds, 'Straightforwardly False: The Collapse of Kramer's Positivism' 63 (2004) *Cambridge Law Journal* 124.

[114] Neil Duxbury, 'Custom as Law in English Law' 76 (2017) *Cambridge Law Journal* 350.

engage in: it is characterised by the adoption of a special "interpretive attitude" which (by a move of detachment from our ordinary immersion in understood meanings and familiar practices) seems to render that which was formerly agreed newly problematic'.[115] It requires, that is, a connection between our ordinary interpretations and the deliverances of a heightened 'interpretative attitude.' It is easy, when thinking in terms of connections, to slip into the habit of speaking of legal 'rules'. But legal norms are of various kinds: rules, principles, powers, immunities, rights, disabilities, liberties, obligations, discretions, rulings—and it should be remembered that, at least in common law jurisdictions, the ability to isolate the *ratio decidendi* from the general judgment of a case is often immensely difficult, and can hardly be reduced to a rule without an understanding of the values it upholds. But let us broaden out the discussion from the narrow focus on 'connections'.

Consider the following argument: 'law' implies not only that like cases be treated alike, but implies also that there is some authority behind it. But the notion of authority should be guided by the central, focal instance of peaceful, just governance for the common good. Hence the *idea* of 'law' is necessarily connected to the common good. The argument is not successful, of course, for even a just and wise authority may implement unjust laws by error or mistake (e.g. about consequences or the actual character of human interests), or even, perhaps on occasion, by design: it is important to remember that the law also serves values other than justice, such as expediency, efficiency, and policy for example. In most ordinary circumstances, the value of justice ought to prevail over these others; but circumstances might tempt even a just authority to resolve a social problem by reference to values other than justice. An example might be eminent domain: the stripping of a private person of their lawful property rights (with or without compensation) in order to allow some major capital building project to proceed; subjecting persons to the dislocation and stress of moving one's dwelling, other than by choice—any conscientious protest made by the homeowner (or even the affected community) is likely to be a protest against the inevitable. In such cases, there is little to do except swallow the injustice and comply with the law.[116] Similarly, contracts of insurance often contain a provision to the effect that '...if the motor vehicle legally belonging to the first party [the insured] is unlawfully taken by parties unknown, such that the first party is unable to recover the vehicle within six weeks of the theft, then liability for the claim shall rest on the first party and any accrued no-claims discount will be lost.' The contractual term, although legal, is fundamentally unjust; yet it cannot be conscientiously resisted, one can only submit.

[115] Nigel E Simmonds, 'Between Positivism and Idealism' 50 (1991) *Cambridge Law Journal* 325; cf Kramer (n 12) 148ff.

[116] That is, if one wishes to avoid a lengthy and expensive appeals process in domestic or international courts.

But the argument is not entirely unsuccessful, either. One of the key ways in which a ruling authority, benevolent or otherwise, contributes to the common good (when governing through law) is by bringing specificity, definition, precision, and therefore predictability to human interactions,[117] each a dimension necessary for the moral goodness of the law (see Section X.3). For clearly, benevolent rule cannot take place unless these elements be present in its laws. But each of these elements betrays a relationship (not connection!) of law and morality, for in specifying the norm, the meaning, purpose and value of the norm are made definite; definition in turn provides a canonical guide to the meaning of the norm and ensures, up to a point, its permanence; precision establishes the boundary between obligation and non-obligation; and predictability is essential for freedom and is a moral foundation for life.

Finally, let us briefly consider and correct some impressions of the relationship of law and morality in the writings of Hart. In his *Essays in Jurisprudence and Philosophy*, Hart observes that nothing is a rule of law simply because it is morally good.[118] But who would assert otherwise? It is 'morally good' to visit one's sick relative in hospital, but no natural law theorist would suggest that this is, therefore, a rule of law. Further, as Aquinas makes perfectly clear, there are certain moral virtues—the practice of which is certainly 'morally good'—which the law specifically *does not* enforce on its citizens. Hart also identifies as a liberal position on law that 'law is not morality; do not let it supplant morality'.[119] But again, it is doubtful whether any natural law theorist would suggest otherwise. They, as much as any positivist, wish to point out the existence of certain *laws* that are unjust, and would regard with horror the claim that the law is always morally good. They would do so, because of their overarching aim (in discussions of 'human law') to calibrate with great sensitivity the extent of a person's duty in conscience to obey unjust laws.[120] Again, Hart argues that to equate law 'as it is' with law 'as it ought to be' is to suggest that all legal questions are penumbral ones.[121] Yet once again, natural law theorists do not make any such assertion. First of all, they do not make the assertion that law is to be identified with its ideal moral state. Secondly they would not wish to push all 'legal questions' (presumably questions about the substance of legal rules) into the penumbra; rather, they would wish to assert that there are indeed clearly identifiable legal norms—natural laws (*conclusiones*) —that are clear and firm enough

[117] Finnis, *NLNR* (n 18) 268.

[118] Hart, *EJP* (n 90) 55.

[119] Ibid, 75.

[120] See Murphy, *NLJP* (n 60) 32: The function of law is to create order, and specifically to achieve this through the provision of rules and standards with which agents have decisive reasons to comply (cf obligations of conscience). Decisiveness must give way to variability (calibration) for the moral priority of specific laws depends partly upon the moral priority of all laws: there may be cases in which the moral priority of the system of laws as a whole entail the moral priority of unjust laws that would otherwise not be binding in conscience.

[121] Hart, *EJP* (n 90) 72.

and not 'penumbral' in anything like Hart's sense; and they would equally want to point to clear and unambiguous legal obligations that do not correspond to moral obligations, or in some cases act against moral obligations (and thus to be resisted). Thus, Aquinas observes that the first duty of the ruling authority is to the common good, and only secondarily to the order of justice and virtue 'by which the common good is protected and maintained'.[122] Therefore, 'a prudent lawmaker ought to suffer minor sins so that greater ones may be avoided'.[123]

So much for the focal, central meaning of law, which the present chapter seeks to elucidate. The present discussion can be concluded by summarizing the basic modes of intention. In doing so, it will be useful to quote from Finnis, who says the following: 'The tradition of "natural law" theorizing is not characterised by any particular answer to the questions: 'Is every "settled" legal rule and legal solution settled by appeal exclusively to "positive" sources such as statute, precedent and custom? Or is the "correctness" of some judicial decisions determinable only by appeal to some "moral" ("extra-legal") norm?'[124] He continues:

> The concern of the tradition ... has been to show that the act of 'positing' law (whether judicially or legislatively or otherwise) is an act which can and should be guided by 'moral' principles and rules; that those moral norms are a matter of objective reasonableness, not of whim, convention or mere 'decision'; and that those same moral norms justify (a) the very institution of positive law, (b) the main institutions, techniques and modalities within that institution (e.g. separation of powers); and (c) the main institutions regulated and sustained by law (e.g. government, contract, property, marriage, and criminal liability). What truly characterises the tradition is that it is not content merely to observe the historical and sociological fact that 'morality' thus affects 'law', but instead seeks to determine what the requirements of practical reasonableness really are [ ... ].'[125]

Quite why Finnis takes such a diluted approach is somewhat unclear. For the present chapter has argued that (i) there are indeed types of law (*ultra vires* laws) that are *not law at all*; (ii) that the law of a community is partly composed of natural laws: laws which, if breached or unenforced represent a significant deficit of justice within that community and an *error* of legal reasoning; (iii) that natural law and conventional standards come together in legal reasoning to determine the existence and content of laws, especially judicially; and thus that (iv) natural law theory is indeed characterized by a particular (and negative) answer to the questions whether every 'settled' legal norm is settled exclusively by appeal to positive legal

[122] Aquinas, *ST* (n 1) I-II.100.8c.
[123] Ibid, I-II.101.3 ad 2.
[124] Finnis, *NLNR* (n 18) 290.
[125] Ibid.

sources, and whether 'moral' norms are 'extra-legal' norms. The 'rational basis' for the activities of governing, legislating, judging, and obeying the law are therefore much richer than a determination of the requirements of practical reasonableness.

Lastly, a word about Murphy's 'natural law thesis'. Murphy distinguishes the 'strong' natural law thesis (that an unjust law is not a law at all) from the 'weak natural law thesis', that an unjust law remains a law, but is 'defective precisely as law'.[126] Murphy leaves undiscussed the issue of what remains law-like in a defective law: on what basis is it still describable as a law?[127] But the issue, and the silence, are genuine problems. One may point, as I have done, to the institutional realities that remain even in a hollowed-out immoral law: realities of policing, detection, trial, and punishment. But these features, important as they are, do not explain why the unjust law remains *law*, for those realities are more-or-less peripheral to the central concept of a law, namely that it constitutes a *norm*, that is, as something that is to be done or obeyed. How can it be the case that one conscientiously ought to do what one ought not otherwise to do? Let us suppose that such a law forms part of a legal system that is otherwise just and fair. In setting up the problem in these terms we are making some assumptions about the substance of the defective law, namely that it does *not* require the performance of an unjust act, one harmful to others or to their interests, and that it is not egregiously unjust but only mildly so. For in other cases, one must indeed disobey the law and take the consequences: see Section X.3. But in those cases in which the unjust law does not require an unjust act, one's compliance with the law is explainable not as direct obedience to that law (i.e. in isolation), but to one's commitment to the system as a whole insofar as it is an (imperfect) instrument for the common good. This is the case, for example, where a change in the law to reduce a higher rate of taxation on the most wealthy is made in the face of benefit cuts to the least well-off, materially worsening their position. One cannot practically refuse the reduction in taxation if one qualifies for it, but one cannot be satisfactorily explained as 'obeying' it either. Those officials charged with implementing and overseeing the tax and welfare regimes might be said to obey the unfair tax law, but they apply it as part of their overall obedience to their office, in all of its facets, and are, as it were, discharging their office without corruption, inconsistency, partiality, or favour. Quite conceivably, they may do so without a definite knowledge that the law is unjust. They, like we, obey an entire system of norms, and we do so without an exact or uncontroversial knowledge of how to perfect it. But one cannot progress from the present situation to a more perfect one by refusal to apply unjust laws of this kind. To obtain a flawless diamond, it must be cut from one that is impure: refinement presupposes an initial situation that contains the possibility of transforming imperfections, not a mere abstract possibility.

[126] Murphy, *NLJP* (n 60) 9–10.

[127] See Geoffrey Callaghan, 'Defective but Still Law: A Critique of Mark Murphy's Weak Natural Law Thesis' XXVI (2015) *Canadian Journal of Law and Jurisprudence* 219–20.

The answer to the problem is therefore that legal norms are *only relatively norms*, that is, are never absolute but always subject to one's conscientious judgment of what to do, or how to act. Even morally just laws are relative *as laws* to the natural laws they attempt verbally to capture. And the system of laws as a whole is binding in conscience to the extent that it secures the common good. Obviously, one is not free, either legally or morally, to pick and choose among laws, nor lightly to decry the legal order as inferior to one's own judgment. The idea of binding-in-conscience is explored a little further in the following Chapter XI, as part of a general discussion of unjust law.

# XI
# UNJUST LAW AND UNJUST LAWS

## XI.1. FRAMING THE ENQUIRY

The concept of 'unjust law' has been broached at numerous points during the preceding discussion, a discussion that has taken us from initial arguments about the nature of natural law and natural law theory, through discussions of justice, obligation, and rights, to a long discussion of law itself. But the reader is owed some systematic explanation of unjust law, to round out the arguments, concepts, ideas, and doctrines encountered in those earlier chapters. So, just as the preceding chapter focused attention on the central case of law, in this chapter the focus will be on law in a diminished, peripheral sense. The idea of a diminished or peripheral manifestation of law can easily be misunderstood, for it is not intended to deny any of the sharp realities of law in the context of everyday life. Rather, it is diminished or peripheral in the sense of being *dependent upon*, or (hence) *secondary to*, law in the primary, focal sense: that is, law ordered towards the common good of the community, proportionate to that end, just in terms of its substance and methods, and conforming to the ideal of 'the rule of law not men' (see Section X.3). The present chapter is premised upon the contingency that readers, already familiar with the tenets of natural law theory's treatment of unjust law, scattered though they are throughout the preceding chapters, may reasonably wish to know more about what Aquinas and other scholastic philosophers said on the subject, and the terms on which it remains necessary to affirm them. In doing so, it is important to distinguish between two topics: unjust *law* (that is, unjust systems of law) and unjust *laws* (that is, individual laws that are unjust, either in the context of a legal order that is devoted to unjust ends as a whole, or one that is broadly just). In drawing this distinction, we are confronting the two purposes for which these doctrines were disseminated: the first being advice to princes (lawmakers and administrators), and the second being to inform the conscience of the law's subjects.

The doctrine of *lex iniusta non est lex*, which appears only sporadically in the primary natural law theory texts, is firmly concerned with the second of these purposes: guidance of conscience. This in itself ought to dispel the impression, reinforced by many *secondary* texts, that this doctrine is all the scholastic writers and Aquinas had to say on the matter of unjust law. In fact they had a great deal more to say than this. However, the following discussion must be read with care, for it can overplay the significance of the doctrine, which Finnis says represents only a

*Natural Law and Modern Society*. Sean Coyle, Oxford University Press. © Sean Coyle 2023.
DOI: 10.1093/oso/9780192886996.003.0011

subordinate theorem of natural law theory. Subordinate perhaps (see Section XI.2), but here we give the doctrine a maximal rather than a minimal interpretation.

In framing this enquiry another proviso should be borne in mind: that of our detachment from serious forms of injustice. Modern Western societies have benefitted, by and large, from protracted periods of social peace, political stability and just laws. Even the stark memory of two World Wars is beginning to fade into the past, aided by the fact that unjust law was confined geographically and politically to the enemy powers. Those corrupt legal orders were long ago replaced with broadly just legal systems (with the exception of the former Soviet Union). It is therefore easy to take an armchair view of seriously unjust legal orders, so it is necessary imaginatively to consider the abuses faced by subjects of unjust law. The position of the Jewish people, and others, during the Nazi tyranny, provides a poignant illustration: contracts no longer enforceable; confiscation of property and freezing of bank assets, leading to a black market in essential goods based on hidden wealth such as watches and jewellery; crimes against Jews going unpunished; being uprooted and relocated into ghettos where there is insufficient accommodation; education outlawed; being brutalized or living under the threat of brutality; navigating the fallout from competition between semi-formal organizations such as the SS and Gestapo; being increasingly subject to scrutiny for the purpose of being detected in some technical breach of regulations that apply to Jews and others in particular; being singled out for arbitrary punishment or liquidation; dealing with the shifting character of social institutions moving (for example) from executive to policy-making; outlawing professions in favour of manual labour; and so on.[1] These purportedly *legal* developments resemble, as Aquinas says, more military violence than law. To confront these abuses directly exposes the weakness of the glib assertion that 'unjust law is law' (see Section XI.3). Some unjust laws are plainly laws, some repressive legal orders plainly legal orders (see Section XI.2). But it is equally plain that certain laws are not truly laws, that is, are not what they purport to be, and some systems of governance are not legal systems. In Chapter X, I pointed to a clear reason why some laws are not genuine laws: where the lawmaker acted *ultra vires* in its creation. But that discussion left unsaid the reasons for which an authority can be said to have acted *ultra vires*. Clearly, a legislature or court acting in breach of constitutional norms does not create or validly apply a legal norm. Or, a lawmaking or law-applying body can be acting *ultra vires* where it acts in contravention of the very norms of legality itself: desiderata (1)–(6) (Section X.3). But more generally, an authority that acts in such a way to contravene the very norms of *authority* will enact measures that are not truly laws.

To a certain extent, a legal order is determined by the presence of certain social facts, such as 'acceptance' by legal officials (as Hart says), yet also, and necessarily,

[1] For some context see the entry 'Anti-Semitic Legislation 1933–39' Holocaust Encyclopedia, United States Holocaust Memorial Museum, retrieved October 2022.

the presence of a body of professionals who are trained to interpret the laws, such that their several interpretations are broadly consistent, further objectives are also largely agreed upon, and such as to provide resources to enable litigation, application, and enforcement. Moreover, however, an authority will be acting *intra vires* only where it confines its lawmaking activities for the common good of the community. Since I have earlier dwelt upon the issue of political and legal authority (see Section VIII.3) it is permissible not to repeat those arguments here in any depth. Save to say that there are two possible views of the purpose of law: either (1) law exists to promote the common good of the community, or (2) law exists for the benefit of the ruler at the expense of legal subjects. But (2) does not produce the contrast it implies, because any system of rules, no matter how repressive, creates interstitial liberties within which those subject human beings can to a certain extent order their affairs for their own benefit and not that of the ruler.[2] Even a highly repressive regime creates (and not merely allows for) opportunities for human flourishing, that is, promotes—albeit in a limited way—the common good of the community. This in no way blunts the observation above that the Nazi terror completely undermined ordinary life for Germany's Jews; for the regime(s) to which those Jews were subject did not create any of the stable expectations and consistency of governance with which genuine legal order is associated, even when highly repressive.

Our detachment from serious forms of injustice colours our attitudes towards the plight of the law's victims. Hart famously said that a legal system can withdraw its protections and its system of mutual forbearances from a victimized group within the society, though they remain in place for the majority.[3] He intended by this statement to suggest that what he called the 'wider view' of law is preferable in analytical power to the 'narrow view'. But his own example betrays him: by withdrawing the law's protections from the hated group, a tyrant places them in a space without law, a space of arbitrary governance, of non-law. You may say: the tyrant removes such people from the law's *protections* but not its *punitive* mechanisms. But this ignores the fact that it is precisely the law's protections that help to define the citizen's liability to punishment, for example by the criminal law's definition of offences and the defences that qualify or excuse them. To that extent, the legal protections offered by the law—including but not limited to the general protection from punishment outside of the context of defined crimes and legally defined defences—define when and how a person is liable to be punished under the law. One does not, for example, usually regard normal contracting relationships

[2] See Nigel E Simmonds, 'Straightforwardly False: The Collapse of Kramer's Positivism' 63 (2004) *Cambridge Law Journal* 98–131; see NP Swartz, 'Thomas Aquinas on Law, Tyranny and Resistance' 30 (2010) *Acta Theologica* 145; Mark C Murphy, 'Hobbes (and Austin, and Aquinas) on Law as Command of the Sovereign' in AP Martinich & Kinch Hoekstra (eds) *The Oxford Handbook on Hobbes* (OUP 2013) 339.

[3] HLA Hart, *The Concept of Law* (3rd edn OUP 2012, hereafter *CL*) 201.

as involving 'punishment'.[4] But as protections are withdrawn, punitive mechanisms fill the gap so that, for instance, it becomes an offence for Jews to enter into contractual relations with non-Jews, or even to possess the requisite ranges of goods and currency. Law is a tremendously blunt instrument for outlawing, in non-retrospective terms, the numerous ingenious workarounds by which people, in desperate times, seek to subvert such legal measures. The options for the tyrant or the tyrant's regime, are either (a) to punish such acts extra-legally, that is, outside the official legal system, or (b) to issue an astonishingly general mandate granting powers of punishment to officials of the state to use against the hated population without the need for emergency legislation to prohibit the given act. Case (b), just as much as (a), hands over the population to arbitrary (i.e. non-legal) government.

I will have more to say on this matter below (Section XI.7). For the moment, it is appropriate in terms of framing the enquiry, to remove two sources of potential confusion in relation to the doctrine *lex iniusta non est lex*. The first is Blackstone's statement in the Prologue to his *Commentaries on the Law of England*: 'This law of nature, being coeval with mankind, and dictated by God Himself, is of course superior in obligation to any other. It is binding over all the globe in all countries, and at all times: no human laws are of any validity, if contrary to this; and such of them as are valid derive all their force and all their authority, mediately or immediately, from this original.'[5] This formulation deviates from the classical in a number of respects, not least its mention of 'validity' and 'valid law'. The first point of note is that the passage is a (rather crude) summary, rather than the careful statement of a philosophy; the second is that the statement that 'no human laws are of any validity if contrary to [the natural law]' must be read in the light of a slightly later passage, where Blackstone says:

> [N]o human laws *should be* suffered to contradict [the laws of nature]. There are, it is true, a great number of indifferent points in which both the divine law and the natural leave a man at his own liberty, *but which are found necessary, for the benefit of society*, to be restrained within certain limits. And herein it is that human laws have their greatest force and efficacy; for, with regard to such points as are not indifferent, human laws are only declaratory of, and act in subordination to, the former.[6]

The italicized words indicate the gap between the two quoted passages. This second passage clearly envisages the possibility of unjust *laws*, and that laws which may be 'necessary for the benefit of society' which may deprive human beings of aspects of

[4] See e.g. *Addis v Gramophone Co Ltd* [1909] AC 488: punitive damages are not available under contract law.

[5] Blackstone, *Comm* I.41.

[6] Ibid, I.42.

their liberty, and which would otherwise be unjust, may nevertheless form part of the positive law: for example, quarantining significant sections of the population to decrease the spread of disease, or enacting a provision to suspend general elections during periods of war.

The second source of potential confusion derives from Martin Luther King's *letter from a Birmingham jail*. In that document Luther King memorably wrote that:

> [T]there are two types of laws: there are just laws, and there are unjust laws. I would agree with St. Augustine that 'An unjust law is no law at all.' Now, what is the difference between the two? How does one determine when a law is just or unjust? A just law is a man-made code that squares with the moral law, or the law of God. An unjust law is a code that is out of harmony with the moral law. To put it in the terms of St. Thomas Aquinas, an unjust law is a human law that is not rooted in eternal and natural law.[7]

Here, Luther King misquotes St Augustine, the exact quotation featuring in the discussion of Aquinas below (see Section XI.2). Nor is he correct to say that the proposition 'an unjust law is a human law that is not rooted in eternal and natural law' comes from Aquinas. For there are many laws that, according to Aquinas, are grounded in positive law alone, deriving all of their force from their having been laid down by earthly authority.[8] The context of these assertions gives some clue to their intent: for they take place within a context of the question, when ought human laws to be disobeyed? The document is not an academic tract, but a political instrument. The political system is, not for better but for worse, a forum not designed for nuanced understandings and distinctions, but memorable phrases and pithy slogans. The *Letter* is thus not a reliable source of natural law thinking.

Readers may therefore want some account of what Aquinas and other scholastics said about these matters, and Sections XI.2 (on Aquinas) and XI.3 (on Suarez) examine these writers in a more systematic way than hitherto has been given in this book, specifically on the subject of unjust *laws*. I defer a discussion of unjust *law* until Section XI.7. The intervening sections touch upon Hart's and Finnis's account of unjust laws. The discussion will aim to distil what is true, valuable and sound in these theories, that is, what is of continuing importance and significance for our times.

[7] Martin Luther King, *Letter from a Birmingham jail*; paragraph break suppressed.

[8] Aquinas, *Summa Theologiae* (hereafter *ST*) I-II.95.2c.

## XI.2. AQUINAS ON UNJUST LAW

The Latin phrase '*lex iniusta non est lex*' does not appear in Aquinas's work, but it is worth considering its translation due to its similarity to phrases Aquinas *does* use: for Aquinas twice quotes, in support of arguments he is making, St Augustine's phrase '*lex mihi esse non videtur, quae iusta non fuerit*'.[9] The most widely available translation, the Dominican translation, of Aquinas's *Summa Theologiae* translates Augustine's phrase as follows: 'a law that is not just, seems to be no law at all.' This would appear to be the source of Hart's characterization, in the ninth chapter of *The Concept of Law*, of natural law theory as the thesis that 'an unjust law is no law at all'. But this is not what either phrase actually says. '*Lex iniusta non est lex*' simply says 'An unjust law is not law'; neither Aquinas nor any other natural law theorist holds that such laws are not laws *at all*, that is, in any event, for any purpose.[10] Similarly, Augustine's phrase, when quoted correctly, states that 'For me, a law that is unjust does not conform to the appearance of [literally: does not appear to be], law.' Augustine's formulation is one of a sequence of propositions that, together, spell out the context of the remark just stated, demonstrating the untenability of any translation that adds the key words 'at all' onto the sentence as it is written. For Augustine says: '*Non ergo lex iusta est, quae dat potestatem vel viatori, ut latronem, ne ab eo ipse occidatur, occidat, vel cuipiam viro aut feminae, ut violenter sibi stupratorem inruentem ante inlatum stuprum, si possit, interimat. Nam militi etiam iubetur lege, ut hostem necet, a qua caede si temperaverit, ab imperatore poenas luit. Num istas leges iniustas vel potius nullas dicere audebimus? Lex mihi*', that is, 'Law is not just that allows a traveller to kill a robber, nor any attacker to be killed by a man or woman, if possible, prior to the assault taking place. Neither is law [just] which requires a soldier to kill an enemy, or, if he refuses, to be punished by the military commander. Now are these laws to be called unjust, or more, not laws?'[11] The question for Augustine is therefore not whether 'unjust law is not law', but (as the context makes clear) whether *these laws* are laws, and one cannot gain from this passage anything more than that Augustine regards these particular laws as non-laws, and (by implication) that *some* unjust laws are not laws. The question does not arise in any wider context, and it is thus reasonable to surmise that the judgment (that unjust laws are—sometimes—not laws) is confined to its stated cases, so far as Augustine is concerned. Interpreters of this passage have entirely failed to note Augustine's contrast, 'unjust laws *or more, not laws*'.

Aquinas's use of the above phrase nevertheless warrants some further investigation, for he quotes the phrase without mention of the context set out above. One

[9] Augustine, *De Libero Arbitrium* I.5.11.33.

[10] Murphy repeats the formula: an unjust law is 'no law at all': Mark C Murphy, *Natural Law in Jurisprudence & Philosophy* (CUP 2006, hereafter *NLJP*) 10.

[11] Ibid. For a recent case in point see Philip Soper, 'In Defence of Classical Natural Law Theory: Why Unjust Law is No Law at All' 20 (2007) *Canadian Journal of Law & Jurisprudence* 201.

may reasonably assume therefore that he intended it to have a greater range of application. To demonstrate that he is serious about it, Aquinas quotes the phrase twice: 'an unjust law does not conform to the appearance of law'.[12] Furthermore, he silently removes Augustine's qualification, '*to me* an unjust law ... ', indicating that it is stated as an objective, rather than subjective, truth. For these reasons, Aquinas's use of the phrase is more expansive than that of Augustine. Finnis states that the idea '*lex iniusta non est lex*' is never more than a 'subordinate theorem' of natural law theory.[13] But this does not seem to be the case. It is quoted at the outset of Aquinas's response in *ST* I-II.95.2c, and is the focus of two Articles. If it is said that the 'theorem' is 'subordinate' to *ST* I-II.94.2c, Aquinas's explanation of the basis on which natural laws can be derived from practical reason, because it depends upon the latter treatment as a theorem of natural *law*, then any and every theorem of natural law other than that in *ST* I-II.94.2c is 'subordinate'. There is indeed no harm in admitting that the unjust law 'theorem' is in this way logically subordinate to a prior theorem. But the theorem is *not* subordinate in the sense of being of less significance. For it sets out a framework for understanding the nature and power of human law, one of the central topics of the *Summa*'s 'treatise on law', and of Western politics more generally. I say that it establishes a 'framework' for understanding human law, because it requires to be understood in the light of other principles concerning the relationship of natural law to human law. I have emphasized the importance of Aquinas's theorem, as a general statement of natural law's relationship to positive law, but it is now time to examine its implications in detail.

The starting point for the investigation is the realization that the second occurrence of the term 'law' in the phrase 'an unjust law is not a law' possesses a silent adjective: *lex iniusta* [is not] *lex simpliciter* or *lex moralis*. It is not law 'without qualification' or 'law that is moral, normal'. Unjust law is law only in a qualified sense. Aquinas proceeds to spell out the relevant qualifications which are, at the same time, both judgments of and limitations upon practical reason: judgments because they specify the structures of norms that compose our practical understandings and deliberations, and limitations because the same structures of norms set out what it is necessary or permissible to will, and not to will. In exactly the same sense, Aquinas employs the same framing concept in his discussion of justice: '*iniustum iudicum, iudicum non est*', an unjust judgment is not a judgment.[14] The scholastic strategy will be misunderstood if the second term is understood as *literally* or *categorically* not an instance of the first term. An unjust judgment belongs to the same category as just judgments, but is qualified, a *mis*-judgment. It may well enter into one's deliberations, but one's deliberations *ought not* to be shaped by a

[12] Aquinas, *ST* (n 8) I-II.95.2c, I-II.96.4c.

[13] John Finnis, *Natural Law & Natural Rights* (2nd edn OUP 2011, hereafter *NLNR*) 351.

[14] Aquinas, *ST* (n 8) II-II.70.4 ad 2.

misjudgment. Or again, the formulation appears in Aquinas's discussion of the virtues at *ST* I-II.60.5c: '*puta quod aliquid sit bonum absolute, et aliquid bonum cum aliqua arduitate*' ('for example, [between] that which is good absolutely speaking, and that which is good yet difficult to obtain'). With this in mind, let us begin by considering the ways in which human law, that is, positive law, can be laid down by an *ultra vires* act of an authority and is, indeed, not law *at all*, howsoever it masquerades as law, unlike the way a misjudgment is not properly (but still is in some sense) a kind of judgment, that is, not a right arrangement of thoughts leading from valid premises to a valid conclusion, but a deflection of the mind away from that proper arrangement. This is no doubt what Aquinas has in mind when he says that, just as a law is a kind of rational precept, an expression of the will of an acknowledged lawgiver lacks the character of law to the extent that it is not in accord with proper reason.[15] In the same way, it is an element in the definition of law that it is aimed at the common good, hence to the extent that a law is deflected away from the common good, it lacks the true character of law.[16] Does this latter proposition hold up to scrutiny? Many legal positivists might argue that law may serve good or bad ends: it may uphold the common good, or it may detract from the common good in favour of, for example, the enrichment of the ruler. If that suggestion is made, then it should be pointed out that the preceding chapters provided two independent sources of argument that supreme legal authority is naturally limited to operate for the common good, and for the benefit of human agency (Sections VIII.2 and X.3). Thus we can argue as follows: a law that is deeply contrary to the common good is indeed *ultra vires*, outwith the legitimate competence in lawmaking, and thus, in itself, non-law. However, where we are dealing with unjust *laws* which belong to an essentially just legal order, taking their place alongside just laws, such unjust laws gain a veneer of legality, and *perhaps* ought to be obeyed and recognized, for the sake of the integrity of the legal system. This is not a stable situation: the *ultra vires* law will require to be interpreted in the context of other laws of a reasonably just character, so that its injustice, though not disappearing altogether, may become diminished with successive applications, a process similar to that which led, for example, to the protection of rights of actual occupiers of land under the Land Registration Act 2002 Schedule 3. Is there any intellectual impropriety in treating as enforceable legal measures that are characterized (by the legal theorist) as *ultra vires* and hence non-law? No, for judges are not infrequently accused of lawmaking in novel cases: that is, of taking a principle or rule that is non-law and applying it as law to the litigants. But more importantly, it is the role of the courts to disapply principles or rules that are enacted *ultra vires* and hence (often) unconstitutional. By electing to enforce such rules, the courts are (1) complicit in injustice, (2) *failing*

15 Ibid, I-II.90.1 ad 3.
16 Ibid, I-II.90.2c.

in their duty of justice, and (3) giving certain legal realities to rules that, as a legislated principle, they did not possess.

It might be said that the above doctrine, stemming from Aquinas, extends the doctrine of *ultra vires* beyond the narrow confines established by existing legal categories. In United Kingdom, the doctrine is associated principally with company law, where legal actors act beyond the scope of powers conferred on them (such as powers of contract), and constitutional law, where it applies both statutorily and judicially, but most frequently occurs in relation to delegated powers of legislation. To this argument it may be replied that in relation to the exercise of statutory or judicial powers, rules or principles that are very seriously against the common good of the community are not simply *ultra vires* in the consciences of persons as opposed to reality, but rationally break the bond of obedience between subject and sovereign. Just as ordinary *ultra vires* acts enjoy a demonstrable measure of legal effect until a correcting *intra vires* act takes place, so the *ultra vires* acts of a legislator or court may be applied as law for a time. Moreover, in referring to such acts we are not pointing to unjust laws that are contrary to the good of persons within the community, and *thus* against the common good, but to acts of legislation that are seriously and directly destructive of the common good and of cultural capital. Thus a system of taxation that is moderately unequal, the revenue from which is put back into public projects and welfare programmes, is unjust without being *ultra vires*, whereas a hugely burdensome system of taxation of which the revenue is absorbed by the sovereign (or some specific social class) is indeed *ultra vires*: seriously and deliberately unjust.

To these doctrines, Aquinas adds a number of arguments. In these arguments, we move away from the idea that 'an unjust law is not a law', towards a more complex position. First of all we have the doctrine already mentioned, that human law has the reality of law to the extent that it conforms to right reason; but now the doctrine is deliberately linked with eternal law, for a measure conforms to right reason just insofar as it *derives* from eternal law. I italicize the word 'derives', for Aquinas is clear about where ultimately the binding force of human law originates: not with terrestrial authorities.[17] He then argues that a law is just, insofar as it derives from an eternal, not human, source, and that it possesses the quality of law only to the extent that it conforms to reason, possessing the quality of mere force (*violentiae*) to the extent that it does not. And yet, he then says, even an unjust law retains a superficial similarity (*similitudine*) to a law, to the extent that it has been laid down by a powerful authority, since all such authority derives from eternal law. Secondly, Aquinas observes that the law of an oppressive or immoral ruler, though unjust, still provides a norm that ought to shape the subject's deliberations (that is, ought to be obeyed) because a key benefit of rule through law (that it exhorts and

[17] Ibid, I-II.93.3 ad 2.

ensures that a person will be good) continues to apply in the case of unjust law, but in a reduced and mutilated sense: it makes the citizen good, not absolutely, but only relative to the norms and aims of the immoral governor.[18] For so long as the rule of law exists, it creates opportunities for citizens to act with moral probity towards one another, opportunities that would be quickly eliminated if such rule were replaced with anarchy.

Of course, all earthly lawgivers are capable of enacting norms against the natural law, due to the perversion of human reason. This can occur in large ways, such as the putative fact that the German peoples of Julius Caesar's time did not understand that theft is wrong,[19] or in smaller ways, either because (i) lawgivers have to make judgments about the future and in general terms, and may fail to anticipate matters of detail, or (ii) they are as subject as anyone to hatreds, prejudices or *idees fixes*, which pervert their judgments.[20] It is important to understand that the phrase 'unjust law' does not denote one single idea, but a range of more-or-less seriously wrong enactments/judgments. Aquinas states that the degree of binding character of law depends upon the *extent* of its justice, and that consequently 'every [human] law has the character of a law just to the extent that it derives from the natural law' and so, in the limiting case, 'if such a law is set against the natural law, it is no longer a law but a corruption of law'.[21] In broader terms, then, a law can be unjust in two ways, either its end or purpose is immoral (as when a ruler diverts resources away from the common good and instead to him/herself), or because the legislative act goes beyond the limit of the lawgiver's moral authority (as when the ruler imposes unequal burdens, financial or otherwise, that are nevertheless intended for the common good).[22] It is at this point that Aquinas states that such unjust laws are *prima facie* not binding in conscience, yet indeed may, for the benefit of social peace and stability, still require obedience even if one must give up one's right.[23]

The main thrust of Aquinas's discussion is the issue of conscience. Its intention is to aid the Christian subject in navigating the various conflicting pressures that may be brought to bear upon the ordinary citizen. For the entire discussion of law and non-law can be translated into a concern with 'binding in conscience' and 'not binding in conscience'. For example, Aquinas observes that because human rulers are fallible, they may end up creating rules for the general welfare that are burdensome to some.[24] In such cases, it would be immoral and thus against conscience to

[18] Ibid, I-II.92.1c. Elsewhere, Aquinas states his opinion that tyranny (in the worst sense) has no corresponding law: ibid, I-II.95.4c.
[19] Ibid, I-II.94.4c.
[20] Ibid, I-II.95.1 ad 2, I-II.94.6 ad 3.
[21] Ibid, I-II.95.2c, I-II.96.6c.
[22] Ibid, I-II.96.4c.
[23] Finnis, *NLNR* (n 13) 361 refers to this as a 'collateral obligation'. See Cajetan Cuddy OP, 'Thomas Aquinas on Conscience' in Jeffrey B Hammond & Helen Alvare (eds) *Christianity and the Laws of Conscience* (CUP 2021) 112.
[24] Aquinas, *ST* (n 8) I-II.96.6c.

disobey the rule; one should absorb the loss. Yet the question of when one ought to obey or disobey the law is not given by Aquinas the detailed treatment it deserves. Perhaps a very general guide should be this: an unjust law should be disobeyed if (i) it violates the rule of law; (ii) it is seriously contrary to the common good; (iii) it requires the performance of an immoral act or injustice;[25] (iv) it disrupts the internal tranquillity of the community; but must be obeyed if (i) it affects one's own rights but not those of others, perhaps including one's family and friends; (ii) the injustice can be borne without significant loss; (iii) it affects the common good in a relatively minor way and the goods at stake are less important than the maintenance of social peace and good order. All of this is subject to a maxim to which Aquinas gives expression in the same Article: that the law should not be left for individuals to determine or interpret, or to select which rules to obey and which to disobey: such a situation would plunge a community headlong into anarchy and violence. One therefore has an overriding duty of conscience to obey the law, that is, a presumption that given laws ought to be obeyed except in the relatively narrow circumstances listed above.

Thus much for the doctrine that 'an unjust law is not a law'. But to the long discussion of that doctrine above, must be added some more minor ways in which law can be said to be unjust (yet binding in conscience). First there is Aquinas's assertion that the 'sentence' (or any judicial judgment) of a court represents the law (*ius*) 'even if unjust'.[26] Such a sentence is law unless and until overturned by the action of a higher court. Furthermore, the law may be said to be unjust in that it does not suppress all vices, but all and only those that are (a) seriously wrong and (b) can easily be avoided by most people.[27] For example, the law prohibits grave acts of dishonesty (fraud, misrepresentation, false advertising, embezzlement, breach of trust) but does not step in to punish ordinary instances of minor dishonesty, such as ingratiating oneself to potential acquaintances (not one's employer) by falsely boasting about qualifications. And the law is mildly unjust in that it does not demand the performance of all the virtues, but leaves some unenforced in order that the people do not become discouraged and abandon more fundamental standards of conduct.[28]

Such is Aquinas's discussion of unjust laws. I defer an examination of his treatment of unjust *law* until Section XI.7. But the reader may wish to know what the later scholastic natural lawyers said about these subjects, so there follows an account of Suarez's treatment of the subject.

[25] See Ibid, II-II.57.2 ad 2: a law legalizing rape, theft, or the like is contrary to justice and (Finnis adds, though Aquinas does not, 'morally void and of no effect'). But even less extreme injustices to one's neighbour count as immoral acts that should not be done.

[26] Ibid, II-II.57.1 ad 1.

[27] Ibid, I-II.96.2c.

[28] Ibid, I-II.96.2 ad 2, I-II.96.3c.

## XI.3. SUAREZ ON UNJUST LAW

Suarez's discussion requires a small amount of rational reconstruction. Its founding principle is that law is made for the governance of some community, and is thus instituted for the good of that community.[29] That is to say, law is made *for* the community and not *against* it. It is *for* the community, in a generic sense, because it deals with matters that are common, or with the good of individuals insofar as such individual goods are conducive to the common good, because the good of individuals is part of that common good.[30] One who is sufficiently interested and motivated to fashion laws and see them disseminated, policed, obeyed, can be assumed to have in mind the care of that community. This position is not naive. A tyrant out for personal gain will certainly enact measures for the extortion of the community, such as levies of taxation or tribute, but (a) will not spend much time trying to calculate what is 'owed' by each person, or in creating general rules to govern contributions; s/he will just exact the greatest amount possible without utterly exhausting the source; and (b) will not be motivated to enact a carefully calibrated scheme of what Hart calls 'mutual forbearances', that is, spreading the law's governance into all areas of human life and endeavour. Such a tyrant would stand to gain nothing by scrupulously refraining from extra-legal violence and punishment; the real but relatively modest gains in efficiency associated with the rule of law would not offset the advantage (to the tyrant) of arbitrary rule. But Suarez, every bit as much as Aquinas, understands that there are unjust *laws*, for he states that 'law *can be* moderated by equity and the requirements of the good'.[31] This obviously leaves open the live possibility that there can be laws that flout equity and the good. Further, Suarez makes specific reference to 'just law',[32] which implies that there are unjust *laws* and not mere injustices. And, finally, Suarez states that for human law to be righteous, it must conform to eternal law (*omnes leges sint effectus legis aeternae*):[33] thus he clearly supposes that unrighteous laws are also possible.

Like Aquinas, Suarez is most interested in the question of conscience. All just laws are binding in conscience, but even a law that is created through hatred, but which is actually conducive to the common good, is a valid law and therefore requires obedience.[34] Unlike Aquinas, therefore, Suarez is willing to admit that a legal rule or principle with an unjust *purpose* can be binding in conscience in the narrow circumstances that it does no evil. These judgments must be finely calibrated: Suarez observes that jurists typically regard as unjust a law that is articulated

[29] Francisco Suarez, *De Legibus* (hereafter *DL*) I.2.4.

[30] Ibid, I.2.7–8.

[31] Ibid, I.2.9–10. See also Tobias Schaffner, 'Is Francisco Suarez a Natural Law Ethicist?' In Danae Simmermacher et al (eds) *The Concept of Law in the Moral and Political Thought of the School of Salamanca* (Brill 2016) 150.

[32] Suarez, *DL* (n 29) I.2.4.

[33] Ibid, II.4.8.

[34] Ibid, I.7.9.

in general terms but with the object of injuring a specific person. But he is willing to recognise the validity of such a law, even if the intention behind the law was to cause the injury, and the injury was not merely a side-effect of some benevolent legislation: only on the condition that the benevolent consequences are secured; for the evil intention does not affect the justice of the parts of the law that bring about the benevolent ends.

Suarez is more cautious than later writers in the natural law tradition (and perhaps even Aquinas) on the subject of unjust law. He states:

> A human lawgiver does not have (as God has) a perfect will, and so, acting of himself alone [that is, without God's guidance] and in relation to the action demanded, may occasionally command actions that are unjust, and the truth of this is manifest; but the lawgiver does not have the power to obligate by reference to unjust laws and thus, even if s/he commands that which is unjust, that command is not law *to the extent that* it lacks the power or validity that is required for imposing a binding obligation.[35]

Thus, he states, when Augustine writes that 'to me, a law that is unjust does not conform to the appearance of law', this is to be taken as being confined to the commanding of an action that is contrary to divine law. Suarez takes the argument further: injustice arising from the subject-matter of the law is to be distinguished from injustice arising from its mode (i.e. from its very character as law as opposed to some other source of norms). Venturing again beyond Aquinas, Suarez states that, in the case of subject matter, it is in no circumstances permissible to obey an unjust law, even for the purposes of avoiding 'any injury or outcry'. For it can never be morally right to perpetrate a wrong for the sake of any end whatever.[36] But in the second case (that of mode), although the unjust law is not binding in itself, the subject may elect to obey the law, so long as in doing so s/he does not cooperate in any further injustice arising from that law, for it is always possible to renounce one's own right. And it is in this context that Aquinas's dictum holds good, that is, that one may be obliged to obey an unjust law for the sake of avoiding outcry (*scandalum*), for (presumably) the character of law *as* law has a value beyond its subject matter. Nevertheless, in this passage, Suarez appears to be articulating a position implicit in, but unexplored by, Aquinas: that one ought to obey unjust laws where the injury or injustice is towards oneself, but to disobey laws that perpetrate injustice on others, especially if in obeying the law one oneself commits an immoral act. Insofar as this is the case, Suarez is on sound ground. But he is mistaken in his claim that substantive legal injustice must never be complied with for any reason. A tax regime that levies a charge that will propel a family into penury

[35] Ibid, I.9.4.
[36] Ibid, I.9.20.

is unjust. But if the alternative to obedience is the levy of an even larger fine which would leave the family absolutely destitute, the head of the family ought to pay the tax, and thus 'cooperate' with the unjust law. At all events, Suarez states that there is a presumption that one ought to obey in doubtful cases of injustice, as opposed to clear cases.

Human laws, as noted above, derive their force (*effectus*) from the eternal law. And to the extent that human laws give expression to the norms of eternal law, such human laws are binding in conscience for a twofold reason: (i) because of the moral need for the human being to conform to eternal law, but also (ii) because of the power of the earthly ruler (an independent source of conscience-binding obligations), since even when *not* giving expression to eternal law, the eternal law demands obedience to civil powers.[37] This position, as has been seen (Section VIII.4), conforms to the doctrine that the people of a state ought to conform to the laws of at least just rulers, at least insofar as their legal systems conform largely to natural law. Insofar as the laws of the state are reasonably just, and do not require the commission of unjust acts, those administering the system and exercising political authority for the common good can be said to be exercising their power 'from God' Even an unjust ruler holds their power from God in this way, for unjust laws are preferable to anarchy. This prompts Suarez to state that whereas the 'law' of a person's conscience has no binding effect except inasmuch as it is a manifestation of Divine reason, in the case of human [positive] law, the obligation is not immediately derived from Divine reason but rather immediately from the ruler; yet the full extent of our obligation emanates from eternal law. But the tyrant, whose laws are not only unjust but also fail to conform to the proper character of laws, has no connection with Divine authority: as Aquinas hyperbolically says, tyranny is utterly incompatible with rule according to law.

Suarez, as much as Aquinas, holds that many human positive laws are expressions of natural law. Natural law binds in conscience because (i) it is the law of God, (ii) concerns serious matters, and (iii) is necessary for human happiness(*feli citatem*).[38] But human laws that are not directly derived from natural laws remain binding on the consciences of subjects: Suarez states that some conscientious obligations arise not from natural law but from positive law.[39] Suarez is not as clear about this as is desirable. For he then launches into a discussion of *determinatio*: 'although the civil law is not derived from natural law speculatively, but by means of *determinatio*, through the will of the human authorities (*principis*), its obligations derive from the natural law *per se*; but some obligations either to perform or not to perform some act may be imposed by human law immediately and are

[37] Ibid, II.4.8: [*In lege autem humana obligatio non est immediate a Deo, quia prout est in subditis, immediate respicit voluntatem principis* ...].
[38] Ibid, II.9.2.
[39] Ibid, II.9.8.

related to natural law more remotely'.[40] What are we to make of this remarkable passage? Suarez appears to be suggesting that the human sovereign mediates between the subject and the natural law in two ways: through *determinatio*, the semi-creative process of concretizing the universal precepts of natural law to specific situations, and the creation of laws (*obligationes*) that are more or less purely positive (i.e. human, conventional) in origin and effect. Extracting the analysis of this passage, Suarez seems to have in mind four distinctions between different sources of laws that are binding in conscience: (1) laws that bind in conscience because they are directly derived from natural law precepts (*conclusiones*); (2) laws that bind in conscience because they are concretizations from natural law precepts (*determinationes*); (3) laws that are binding in conscience because they are either just or neutral, and belong to a legal system that is broadly just, even though possessing no connection to natural law precepts; and (4) laws that are binding in conscience even though unjust, because they belong to a legal system that is broadly just. To these we can add (5) laws that are seriously unjust and therefore not binding in conscience even if they belong to a legal system that is broadly just; and (6) laws that are not binding because they belong to a system of governance that is tyrannical or otherwise deeply opposed to the common good.

Suarez elsewhere states that human law cannot derogate from natural law: that it is impossible for human authorities (including the Pope) to make an enactment that is contrary to natural law.[41] The appearance of contradiction between this statement and the others preceding can easily be assuaged by the realization that the 'impossibility' mentioned is not factual impossibility but moral impossibility. But it is not ungrounded in fact, for Suarez observes that the natural law is made for the human person with the nature he or she has; therefore any human law that seeks to negate, pervert, or controvert that nature can be of no (moral) effect. In this sense, too, natural law is the foundation of human law. The scope of this doctrine, similar in fact to Hart's 'minimum content of natural law' (see Section XI.4), is potentially very wide. For any penetrating insight into human nature discloses not only the need for the avoidance of criminal harms, but also the deep requirement of norms of contracting as a foundation for sociability, the need for carefulness in one's daily activities so as to avoid indiscriminate harms, and the whole range of social goods such as peace, security, the opportunity to exercise one's talents, and so on (see Section I.6, III.4, IV.5).

In the *De Legibus*, therefore, Suarez amplifies Aquinas's treatment of unjust law, disagreeing in a few matters of detail. But the natural law tradition was remarkably consistent on these questions, right up until modern times. Both modern works of natural law theory and positivist tracts blunted the theory of unjust laws, so that progress in the subject of law took a backward step. Thus, D'Entreves writes that

40 Ibid, II.9.12.
41 Ibid, II.14.8.

'The problem [of law and morality] is no longer one of form or of structure. It is a problem of content. The content of law is a moral one. Law is not only a measure of action. It is a pronouncement on its value. Law is an indication of what is good and evil. In turn, good and evil are the conditions of legal obligation.'[42] Though he writes further on that 'The association of morals and law does not rule out the possibility of a demarcation between them', nevertheless here is a good source for Hart's criticisms of natural law theory on the matter of unjust law: that the theorist who blends law and morality in this way deprives himself or herself of the analytical clarity that comes with the realization that a law that is unjust is nevertheless a (valid) law, and likely to be applied and enforced, and with the normative concern to examine realistic opportunities for addressing, resisting, mitigating, or minimizing the injustice. Thus, natural law theory experienced a reduction after the late scholastic period to a series of wild and improbable dogmas that were easy prey to legal positivists like Austin and Bentham, and to moral sceptics like Hume. It is not necessary to trace the course of those ideas. Instead, it will be necessary to examine Hart's and Finnis's understandings of the relationship of just to unjust law, for by doing so we gain a stronger impression of truth and error in current thinking. There are many other natural law theorists to whom the title 'modern thinker' could of course be applied, but the two figures mentioned have the distinction of being representative of late twentieth-century legal thinking, and whose influence on current thinking has been considerable. In Section XI.4 we can briefly expand on the treatment given to Hart's natural law theory in Section I.2.

## XI.4. MODERN VIEWS ON UNJUST LAW: HART

Hart's consideration of natural law theory is shaped by the defects of his sources. He seems to have read Aquinas only in translation, and thus amplifies the licence with which Aquinas's translators have interpreted the text (as stated above the Dominican version of the text wrongly translates Q 95.2 of Aquinas's *Summa* as stating that unjust law is no law 'at all': see XI.2). In the long endnote to p.185 in *The Concept of Law*, Hart cites D'Entreves as his source for Aquinas, and the famous, but flawed, 1925 translation of Grotius's *De Iure Belli ac Pacis*. The endnote articulates the need to gain familiarity with the primary sources on natural law, but Hart would appear to have experienced those sources only at second hand.[43] He appears to treat natural law theory as one single univocal tradition, variously drawing upon the ideas of Plato, Aristotle, Aquinas, Montesquieu, and Blackstone, apparently without an appreciation of the differences, large or small, between their doctrines and approach. His first characterization of natural law theory occurs not

[42] Alexander D'Entreves, *Natural Law* (3rd edn Transaction Publishers 1994) ch 6.
[43] See Hart, *CL* (n 3) 302.

in his ninth chapter, but the eighth, on the subject of justice. Natural law theorists, he contends, believe (1) that there are principles of true morality or justice, discoverable by human reason without the aid of revelation even though they are of divine origin, and (2) that 'man-made laws which conflict with these principles are not valid law, *Lex iniusta non est lex*'.[44] The first is misleading: the 'Thomist' natural law theorists to whom Hart specifically refers would not express matters this way: this formulation tends to imply that the work of reason is carried on by itself, formulating principles at least initially in the abstract before applying them to the sub lunar world; whereas Aquinas himself, and his late scholastic followers, regard the work of reason as taking place in tandem with an account of the natural properties of the human being. The second contention is, simply, wrong (see XI.2). Hart's professed attitude to natural law is also to be found in his contention that it is not clarifying of our deliberations to say 'this is *in no sense* law' than to say 'this is law, but it is too iniquitous to obey or comply'.[45] But natural law theorists would not claim that unjust law is 'in no sense' law, but they would agree that (being law only in a qualified sense) it would be unjust to obey.

Hart is more disturbed by the supposed metaphysical implications of natural law theory than the thesis that an unjust law is not a law.[46] Such 'monstrosities' are 'somewhat comic'[47] and 'too metaphysical for modern minds'.[48] Such is Hart's hostility to natural law metaphysics (at least as he sees it) that he rejects virtually every element of natural law thinking. Hart's statement that there is a core of good sense to natural law theory in a 'minimal' version belies the true extent of his rejection of natural law doctrines. For all he is prepared to allow is that the 'modest aim' of survival contains 'the central indisputable element which gives good empirical sense *to the terminology* of Natural Law'.[49] Hart's interpreters have uniformly ignored the implications of the italicized words: what Hart retains of natural law theory, in his 'minimal content', is not any set of substantive doctrines, but a mere terminology which *may* be associated with the doctrines that he derives from Hobbes, but which 'empirical good sense' ought to see past or otherwise overcome.[50] Nevertheless, Hart does point to certain connections between law and morality with which

44 Ibid, 156. See also HLA Hart, 'Positivism and the Separation of Law and Morals' 71 (1958) *Harvard L Rev* 594.

45 Hart, *CL* (n 3) 210 (emphasis added).

46 See e.g. 'The Problems of the Philosophy of Law' in HLA Hart, *Essays in Jurisprudence and Philosophy* (Clarendon 1984) 111 & 113; Hart, *CL* (n 3) 188–91.

47 Hart, *CL* (n 3) 190.

48 Ibid, 192.

49 Ibid, 191.

50 This is overlooked for example by Cristobal Orrego: see 'Hart's Understanding of Classical Natural Law Theory' 24 (2004) *Oxford Journal of Legal Studies* 287. Hart's other source for natural law thinking seems to have been Michel Villey's *Lecons d'Histoire de la Philosophies du Droit* (1957): see Finnis, *NLNR* (n 13) 415. See also Nicola Lacey, 'HLA Hart's Rule of Law: the Limits of Philosophy in Historical Perspective' 36 (2007) *Quaderni Fiorentini* 1203; Petar Popovic, 'Hart on the Role of Justice in the Concept of Law: Some Further Remarks' 12 (2022) *Jurisprudence*; John Gardner, 'Hart on Legality, Justice and Morality' 1 (2010) *Jurisprudence* 253.

natural law theorists would agree. For Hart, even the formal features of law have a connection to morality or justice: for instance, the very fact of *following* a rule involves applying it without prejudice, interest, or caprice,[51] and thus involves basic requirements of justice. For implicit in the very idea of 'following a rule' is that like cases be treated alike (though admittedly not necessarily, as Hart supposes, that different cases be treated differently). But he also stressed that judgments of 'like cases' are relative to the moralities of different societies, and are thus open to the criticism of external observers from the perspective of *their* morality.[52] The point that the conventional rules (*mores*) of a given society may find certain likenesses or unlikenesses between persons on the basis of arbitrary considerations such as racial characteristics, gender, or social position, is empirically true and important to keep in mind. But Hart does not fully articulate the proposition that such judgments are *immoral*; and that the ultimate reason for respecting or trusting the judgment of the external observer in preference to that conventional morality, is not that such a judgment is simply one more conventional perspective, but that it is *morally sound*: not, or not merely, reflective of any particular society's conventional *mores*. The clash between one conventional system of *mores* and another, as such, can only ever be a question of fact. Hart, however, was not consistently a positivist with regard to the question of *quid iuris*. Where a community's legal order is taken over by an invader, he observed, the question of when the extant legal system ceases to exist is *not* a question entirely of fact; more significantly, once the lawful government is restored, the question of what was and was not law during the interruption 'may not be one of fact'.[53] Thus Hart appears to make room for the fact that a *practical*, and not merely *empirical*, judgment is required in order to comprehend the legal status of norms during the reign of an unjust ruler. Hart does not seem to be saying that (a system of) unjust *law* can be called into question in this way, but—perhaps—the status of unjust *laws* as laws may be determined according to standards of practical reason rather than empirical judgment.

But not all unjust laws are non-laws (see Section XI.5). For the same practical judgment, Hart observes, can discern cases in which justice is traded off against some other value, such as the security of the community. Thus, an exemplary sentence given to a convicted criminal, in excess of what is just *pour décourager les autres*, makes such a tradeoff. Two points must be separated here. In the first place, it might be said that even if criminals knowingly run the risk of a higher sentence, occurring from time to time, and thus make their choices in light of that knowledge, the tariff is *unjust*, although still a law, and precisely insofar as it is an unjust law, it will normally constitute a ground of appeal. In the second place, there are indeed times when it is necessary for a state to 'trade off' justice against other

51 Hart, *CL* (n 3) 161.
52 Ibid, 163.
53 Ibid, 118–19.

values, as when the state deprives landowners of their property without compensation in times of war, for the purpose of temporarily converting private land into army barracks or field hospitals. Or again, food production may cease to be run for profit in conditions of famine, and food and other resources rationed. Here perhaps we are not dealing with an unjust law, for in this instance there is no sacrifice of justice against the other value; the question of what is just depends in part on the prevailing conditions: the 'circumstances of justice' are not fixed but can shift in times of national emergency. Private assets, including land, may be required by an overriding public interest, such that their redistribution is not, in those exceptional circumstances, unjust. Clearly this doctrine is capable of being abused; but again the distinction between governmental acts that are 'just in the circumstances' and those that constitute unjust redistributions can only be delineated by a practical—and not an empirical judgment.

In a telling remark, Hart observes that the issue of the connection of law to morality only emerges where social morality has reached the stage where it is distinguishable from law.[54] But the history of the Western world demonstrates precisely the opposite of this idea of social development. The law of the earliest societies, through to Ancient Rome, derived from religion and morality, and the intricate system of Christian morality was firmly in place long before the English common law or European *ius commune* reached any stage of sophistication. The remark reveals Hart's prejudice, that morality is indeed merely a social phenomenon (like law), expressive not of timeless moral truths but only of prevailing social attitudes. Indeed he thinks that such prevailing attitudes are shaped by understandings, or misunderstandings, of human nature and its predicament, but he regards that nature, and hence that predicament, as contingent. Hart has, of course, no evidence for this proposition; but even in the light of this assumed contingency, he is willing to agree that there is a fundamental connection between the content of laws and this human nature.

But while Hart agrees that there may be many points of connection between law and morality, he nevertheless identifies the 'illicit' proposition that law *must* exhibit a certain conformity to justice or morality.[55] It would be easy to regard this statement as a further instance of Hart's rejection of natural law and natural law theory. Yet in fact (a) this statement comes *before* those examined above in which Hart perceives the need for a practical judgment, and (b) this statement is merely pointing to the logical invalidity of moving from the descriptive premise, stated immediately before, that law *does* coincide with morality at many points, to the modal conclusion that law *ought to* or *must* conform to morality. Such an observation is incontestable, but the statement that such a conclusion does not follow logically from that particular premise must be distinguished from the claim that

[54] Ibid, 171–72.
[55] Ibid, 185.

the conclusion is false. This is further evidence that the positivist framework of Hart's thinking can barely contain the natural law assumptions he is at such pains to avoid.

The implications of Hart's theory for the subject of unjust law can be explored further in relation to his notion of a 'minimum content of natural law'. The reader will remember that Hart is merely concerned with the *terminology* of natural law theory and not, despite appearances, its substance; and that the substantial propositions that he derives from Hobbes are more clearly understood if that terminology is renounced. The pattern of Hart's argument is as follows: (1) without such a content, laws and morals could not forward the minimal purpose of survival which human beings have in associating together; and (2) in the absence of this content human beings would have no reason for obeying voluntarily any rules, and without such cooperation there is no prospect of enforcing the rules against recalcitrants.[56] His examination of truths ('truisms') about human nature exhibits a concern with both of these elements. Thus Hart's central concern is with the establishment of a 'system of mutual forbearances': a generalized feature of legal systems which includes suppression of criminality and violence, laws on contracts and torts, and the mutual recognition of private property. Most telling, however, are the truths for the sake of which such a system is necessary: vulnerability, approximate equality of physical and mental capacities, limited altruism, limited resources, and limited understanding and strength of will. For positive laws that transgress these limitations are inherently unjust. Thus a legal system that did not take account of human vulnerability, for example by failing to enact laws prohibiting the use of violence, intimidation, extortion, etc, would be doing a profound injustice to its subjects. Likewise, a system that failed to recognize approximate equality would quickly become embroiled in distributive injustices, as in Aristotle's time there was the doctrine of 'natural slaves'. A system that exaggerated the level of altruism of human beings would unjustly fail to create laws of, for example, contract, and tort, or of crime; and similarly a legal order that supposed there to be unlimited resources would fail to create laws to alleviate poverty, wage slavery, fraud, and would be fiscally irresponsible with public money and management of the economy (which in circumstances of unlimited resources would cease to be relevant). Finally, a legal system that took no account of limited strength of understanding and will would create potential burdens and obligations on persons that would be impossible to perform. All the laws lately mentioned, therefore, are unjust laws. For Hart, then, a legal order that did not shape its laws around these truths of human nature would be an unjust legal order to such an extent that 'men, as they are, would have no

[56] Ibid, 193.

reason for obeying voluntarily any rules.'[57] That is, in the language of natural law theory, such rules would no longer be binding in conscience.

## XI.5. MODERN VIEWS ON UNJUST LAW: FINNIS

The later career of the concept of unjust law has been predominantly shaped by responses to Hart. In particular, it was necessary to correct Hart's reduction of the essentially practical nature of juristic thought to the notion of the 'internal standpoint'. From that standpoint it is possible to adopt a number of more-or-less related *attitudes* (a concept already practical in nature) ranging from the fully committed law-abiding citizen to the stark immoralist who conforms to the law only if and when that conformity is advantageous. Finnis, therefore, recalled attention to the fact that these possible standpoints are not all equal; the attitude of the law-abiding citizen being primary and the others intelligible as attitudes *to law* only to the extent of their relation with the primary, focal case.[58] This reminder, as with Finnis's main analytical framework for discussing obedience to unjust law, is not presented in terms of conscience. For, he states, one might obey an unjust law (i) to escape the sanction attached to disobedience; (ii) out of legal obligation 'in the legal (intra-systemic) sense' whereby the practical judgment that one ought to obey the law is insulated from the rest of practical reason; (iii) legal obligation in the moral sense: the presumptive duty to obey the laws imposed on one by legal obligation in the preceding sense; (iv) moral obligation deriving not from the law but from a collateral source i.e. to avoid scandal or disturbance in the community, or the depletion of any other communal goods.[59] The relevance of (ii) is debatable: in relation to it, Finnis offers the following justification: 'In my [previous] discussion I emphasized the way in which the enterprise of exercising authority through law proceeds by positing a system of rules/which derive their authority not from the intrinsic appropriateness of their content but from the fact of stipulation in accordance with rules of stipulation.'[60] I have interposed an oblique stroke ('/') in the quoted sentence to simplify matters as follows: the partial sentence before the oblique is true, but the part after is false. For the authority of rules is at least dependent on the authority of the person or body that posits them: otherwise they are *ultra vires*, not properly law at all: see Section XI.2. And to be a lawgiver in the full ('focal'), and not merely *de facto*, sense, laws must be created and promulgated according to (and proportionate with) the common good of the community.[61] This proportionality

[57] Ibid. See also Bruce Frohnen, 'The Irreducible, Minimal Morality of Law: Reconsidering the Positivist/Natural Law Divide in Light of Legal Purpose and the Rule of Law' 58 (2014) *Saint Louis University Law Journal* 467.
[58] See Finnis, *NLNR* (n 13) 11–18.
[59] Ibid, 354.
[60] Ibid, 355.
[61] See Aquinas, *ST* (n 8) I-II.90.4c.

and directiveness to the common good is the true source of the obligatory quality even of unjust laws. Without this, (iii) makes no apparent sense: a moral obligation to obey *merely* positive law, out of its sheer positivity. What could be the moral motive for such obedience except for (iv), the maintenance in place of a system of governance for the sake of social peace and order, or (i), escaping some sanction? Accordingly, (iii) should be reworked as: the presumptive obligation to obey the laws imposed on one due to their contribution to the common good.

Finnis rightly points out that *legal* thought allows the system of laws to be permeated by principles of practical reason that 'derive their authority from their appropriateness (in justice and for the common good), and not, or not merely, from their origin in some past act of stipulation',[62] such that unjust laws may become inapplicable. These reasonable principles are hidden in English law, but can be glimpsed in, for example, the 'Golden rule' of statutory interpretation (that statutes should be interpreted in a way that avoids absurdity or injustice), and in decisions of a supreme court deciding that a norm is to be wholly or partially abandoned, even if well-established.[63] At the same time, the justice of legal rules is not due to supervenient principles of morality determining the reasonableness of positive rules; for the positive laws themselves not infrequently embody principles of justice and morality: the neighbour principle; the duty of care owed by a hospital to its patients; the criminal penalty for fraud; the recognition of property rights on the Land Register: all of these norms are just in themselves and not dependent for their moral force on interpretations according to the golden rule, or supreme court litigation. This is not to deny, of course, that principles of the kind Finnis is discussing do exist and operate in the ways he mentions. Finnis says that people who deny that principles of this kind have a place in law are actually making a constitutional claim to the effect that law application and law creation should be left to the legislature, whereas those who seek to maximize the pervasiveness of those principles typically take the contrary view. This last claim is debatable: those who say that the common law consists not of a system of rules but a body of reasons for decision that are essentially derivations from natural law need make no claim to the effect that law-making and law-creation should be left to the courts. Indeed it should also be recognized that many statutory laws derive from natural law precepts: there need be no bias towards the courts.

Of course litigating parties may go to court in order to test the justice (and at the same time validity) of a legal argument, though Finnis states that once all the arguments have been heard at the highest level, and the courts *still* regard a provision as applicable, then there is little use in continuing to regard it as non-law. And indeed this must be the case if, with Aquinas, we are to say that certain unjust laws *are laws* and may even be binding in conscience.

[62] Finnis, *NLNR* (n 13) 356.
[63] Ibid.

Indeed there is a further reason to obey laws that we suspect are unjust: it is often extremely difficult to calculate the justice of relative burdens, duties, and arguments (particularly when one is a judge in one's own cause). It will in general then be *morally* best to obey a law that one thinks *might* be unjust, but is not starkly unjust, rather than trying to calculate the justice/injustice for oneself. This thesis is distinct from that of Murphy, who argues that laws must be 'backed by decisive reasons for action'.[64] For one's reason for obeying the law, even when unjust, is simply that the law is in general a guide to justice: this assumption is the central case of one's critical and reflective attitude towards the law; all other responses to law are parasitic upon this attitude. Even the prudent criminal obeys many of the laws of a community, in relation to the law of real property, for example, or of contract in many situations. Murphy's argument raises the question of where are these 'decisive' reasons from: are they political reasons, or legal reasons, or ethical reasons? It would seem that they are not ethical reasons, because a key purpose of law is to rescue the community from never-ending and intractable moral argument. It would neither seem that such reasons are political reasons, for the notion of 'unjust law' cannot be reduced to questions of expediency, nor can a legal system be reduced to a political system. But if we consider the remaining proposition, that the decisive reasons are a form of *legal* reason, what kind of reason are they, and how are questions of the justice or injustice of laws linked to or informed by other sources of legal reason? Various answers are available, of which I will touch upon two. According to the first, the law itself is informed by a coherent ethical (or political) system of value such that unjust laws are to be treated as 'mistakes', to be given minimal interpretation and excluded from the main flow of legal reasoning.[65] The difficulties with such an approach are well known and do not require extensive rehearsal. For present purposes suffice it to note that an ethical-legal system that is subject to continual reinvention through the parameters of 'fit' and 'soundness' never arrives at truly 'decisive' reasons for action but only morally weighty ones, and the initial statement was not that law must be backed by weighty reasons for action. Secondly, there is the classical common law position, that the common law represents an 'artificial perfection of reason', the product of many sound minds which exceeds the brilliance of any one mind working alone. This is more promising than the first alternative for one might be said to have decisive reasons for acting in accord with principles that have evolved over time in the hands of experts. But it applies only to common law reasoning, and does not explain how individuals have decisive reasons to act on statutory or codified systems of law. I myself do not think that the 'decisive reasons' approach is very fruitful as an explanation

[64] See Mark C Murphy, 'Natural Law Theory', in M Golding & W Edmundson (eds) *The Blackwell Guide to the Philosophy of Law and Legal Theory* (Blackwell 2005) 15.

[65] See classically Ronald Dworkin, *Law's Empire* (Fontana 1986) chs 6–7; most recently Ronald Dworkin, *Justice for Hedgehogs* (Harvard University Press 2010) 123ff.

of why we should obey unjust laws. I think the answer is much more straightforward: we obey unjust laws in order to avoid greater injustice, yielding our rights, avoiding scandal or disorder, not cynically opting to obey only those laws that are in our interests; also, less focally: feelings of powerlessness, fear of consequences, calculations of long term self-interest, etc. When we disobey unjust laws, it should be because they are seriously at odds with what is morally right or necessary. Such laws are hollowed out by injustice and immorality, they are scarcely laws, but laws in a sense.

I made the case above that unjust laws come about due to the *ultra vires* actions of the institution that creates them. For political power is held on the basis of its directness and proportionality to the common good; norms created for purposes which contravene this duty are in principle unjust, for no political institution has the authority to create unjust laws.[66] In this sense all unjust laws are the product of *ultra vires* acts. This is not to suggest that unjust laws stem from purely institutional ('procedural') concerns; rather it is possible to point to an act as *ultra vires* because it is substantively unjust. But there may be many laws, particularly in common law jurisdictions, which we may term 'legacy laws': laws or principles latent within the existing law the injustice of which only comes to light at a later date when tested in adjudication. Such legacy laws are not directly the product of authority—more that of authoritative interpretation. Courts do not exceed their authority in deciding such cases.[67] Laws of this kind are not *non-laws*, where they are the incontrovertible conclusion of legal reasoning, but they are defective (possibly highly defective) laws, the scope of which should be progressively narrowed as far as possible through juridical reasoning in cases to which they incontrovertibly apply. For courts are institutionally bound to suppose that legislative acts and all forms of law have as their point equity and the promotion of common good: a realization that appears even in the work of the positivist Hobbes.[68] To be clear: instances of unjust

[66] Cf Murphy, *NLJP* (n 10) 54: norms are not unjust merely because the lawgiver lacks authority. (But the argument here is not based on any idea of *mere* lack of authority, but that a lawgiver acts *ultra vires* when creating an unjust or immoral law because they lack the necessary authority to act in violation of the common good.) Murphy further argues that it makes no sense to say that a norm can be partly law or law by degrees; it can only be defective as a law: 'Two Unhappy Dilemmas for Natural Law Jurisprudence' 136. (But it makes perfect sense to say that a law that has been severed from the common good of the community, which is at odds with human flourishing and normal human development, possesses only some of the features of law in the proper, fullest sense, and is therefore only *partially* a law.) Murphy offers no greater precision: the more or less just and reasonable the law, the more or less reason there is to obey it: see George Duke, 'Finnis on the Authority of Law and the Common Good' 19 (2013) *Legal Theory* 50. See also Jonathan Crowe, *Natural Law and the Nature of Law* (CUP 2019, hereafter *NLNL*) 147.

[67] As Aquinas plainly states: *ST* (n 8) II-II.57.1 ad 1.

[68] See Thomas Hobbes, *Dialogue Between a Philosopher and a Student, of the Common Laws of England* [1681]. Scott Shapiro states that: 'Unjust systems [of law] have all the properties that make legal systems the things that they are, but they do not do what things of this sort are supposed to do' (*Legality* (Belknap Press 2013) 391–92). But unjust systems do not have *all the properties* that make legal systems what they are, for they lack justice and proportionality: and what a legal system *is*, cannot be understood apart from its purpose, just as a chair cannot be understood without understanding its purpose, or any

laws are not *determinationes*; for a *determinatio* is precisely a creative derivation from natural law of a principle where the natural law itself is open-textured. Unjust laws are not derived from natural law but constitute pure positive laws, laws the content of which derives entirely from perceived human desires, albeit disordered desires. But to the extent that unjust laws are at least partially reasonable, they aim at some human good that is in accordance with natural law, either improperly derived or containing an admixture of unreasonable desires.

## XI.6. MURPHY ON UNJUST LAWS

We have had occasion to discuss Murphy's position on unjust laws in Section I.6. It may be recalled that for Murphy, an unjust law is one that is not 'backed by decisive reasons for action'. I earlier commented that in most situations the reverse is true: a law that is (deemed to be) unjust—or defective—invites the judgment that it is not attended by decisive (of even merely strong) reasons for action. Murphy's main contention is that an unjust law is semantically like a 'glass diamond': the adjective 'glass' does not always destroy the noun (a glass table is a table) so that there can be unjust *laws*.[69] But certain adjectives such as 'false' cannot any longer merely qualify the noun, but they take away the noun's reference: a false law is not a law, even in a restricted sense. This tends to suggest that 'unjust' is a portmanteau term, for it sometimes merely qualifies the noun 'law' or 'a law', but in other cases eliminates it. One can ask: is the judgment (qualification vs destruction) a matter of the *degree* of injustice, or of the *kind* of injustice involved? Murphy, like Aquinas, does not say.[70] But the answer is likely to be that our judgment will be shaped by our reasons for raising the question: either from an intellectual point of view, or the practical point of view of the person having to decide whether a certain law is binding in conscience, whether it is to be obeyed even if unjust, or whether it must not be obeyed in any circumstance. Clearly, questions of the intensity of an injustice will be extremely problematic: injustices are to some extent incommensurable, and any injustice is an injustice just as any lie is a lie. But it must be remembered that there is always a significant cost to disobeying the law, namely the common goods of peace and stability. It would seem reasonable that such a significant cost should not be incurred over a relatively trivial injustice. This invites many problems, including the question of how one navigates the relative pressures of state power and moral value. If one is lucky enough to live in a broadly just society, then the *spoudaios*,

physical object, or human being, or even mathematical equation. Further on Hobbes and unjust law see David Dyzenhaus, *The Long Arc of Legality* (CUP 2022) 88.

[69] Murphy, *NLJP* (n 10) 13–14.
[70] Ibid, 35–40.

the person of seriousness who wishes to act morally, will have a scale of values that broadly conforms with that of the law. She or he, as Aristotle observes, will not require the law to make her or him virtuous, but they will require the law's judgment on, for example, the extent and computation of damages due to someone they have inadvertently injured, or how to comply with laws relating to income tax. Confronted with an example of the law's injustice, such a person is likely to recognize that the law's sufficient conformity to justice and its general orientation towards the common good requires one (as Aquinas says) to yield their right (perhaps after pursuing it in the courts and not on the street) and absorb the injustice. This is not only because the common good is much more important than anyone's individual entitlements, but also because in breaking the law we are taking the law into our own hands, adjudicating in our own cause, eroding the line between justice and self-interest.

But (as neither Murphy nor Aquinas makes clear) one must always resist a legal obligation to harm another person, or their interests, by committing an injustice or performing an immoral act. This suggests that it is not in fact the relative seriousness of the injustice that matters, but the kind of injustice. This perhaps explains why the needle moves towards resistance to the law when the law is deflected away from the common good, and even, in some cases, rebellion.[71] This way of putting the point is not without danger. For in a very important sense, there can *be* no common good without law (Hobbes was correct about this up to a point), for a genuinely *common* good is one that requires a certain amount of organization, mutual understanding as to the social rules one should follow to preserve peace, etc, and avenues of response that are open when hostilities are ignited between persons. But a legal order that is really a perversion of legal order reverses the polarity of moral good, such that an act of disobedience to the law in such circumstances constitutes a refusal to become involved in an activity that directly harms other persons or their interests. By *breaking* the law, one *favours* the common good of the community, refusing to become involved in practices designed to suppress it (unless, as Aquinas says, one's attempted rebellion causes the tyrant to rage all the more).

Let us put on one side these issues. Murphy explains that 'unjust' as a descriptor of 'law' is an *alienans*, 'a certain sort of attributive adjective':[72] non-comparable, distinguishing, modifying. Thus the adjective 'rubber' is not an alienans when applied to 'band', but is such when applied to 'duck', for a rubber duck is not a duck. According to Murphy's preferred thesis, for something to count as a defective instance of some X, it must be that something central to the life or functioning of X is flawed or missing: unpleasing feather-patterns on a young duck make it an ugly

[71] See George Duke, 'The Weak Natural Law Thesis and the Common Good' 35 (2016) *Law & Philosophy* 490.
[72] Murphy, *NLJP* (n 10) 13.

duckling, not a non-duckling; whereas lack of flight-feathers, ability to swim, and to reproduce, would invite the judgment that the creature is not a duck.[73] In each case, however, we are basing our judgment as to what is *not* X, or *deficiently* X, on the functioning of a normal instance of X. This brings us nearly back to the *pros hen* ('in relation to the one') theory from which Murphy seeks to depart. For that theory is perfectly capable of distinguishing between a *defective* version of X and a *deviant* version of X. Both are characterized by the different ways in which they fail to embody all of the features of X, including the usages and purposes surrounding X.[74] A particular statutory provision on quantum of damages in tort may, through lack of foresight (or lack of skill in draftsmanship) be in some degree of contention with other laws on that subject, and therefore count as a *deviant* but not *defective* law. But a law that deprives an innocent party of their interests is a *defective* law. The two examples are distinguished because the first is not a deficit of any demand of justice or common good; its deviance is merely technical; the second is clearly a deficit of justice, irrespective of the question of obedience.

Notice four levels of inquiry: (1) there are laws that are merely deviant rather than defective; (2) there are laws that are deficient because they lack certain properties that laws ordinarily possess; (3) there are laws the deficiency of which is due to a moral defect or defect of justice; (4) there are laws which, in virtue of their deficiency, are not laws at all. This inquiry is prior to any discussion of whether certain laws are to be obeyed or disobeyed, and of the complexities surrounding the issue of norms that exist as part of a system of laws that is broadly just, and those in a system perverted away from the common good of the community. These alternatives can be compatible with two different ways of measuring the deficiency: (i) sufficiency argument: this law or legal system is sufficiently rational/just to be described as a law or legal system; (ii) proportionality argument: whether this law or legal system is describable as law depends on its exhibiting a greater degree of rationality/justice than irrationality/injustice. I employ the disjunction here because Murphy prefers the question of the law's rationality to the relationship between law and morality.[75]

[73] Ibid, 12 (I have adapted the examples slightly).

[74] Note that even a glass diamond is a false *diamond* (and not a false horse, or building, or tree).

[75] See Crowe, *NLNL* (n 66) 147: thus a law may be morally defective yet sufficiently rational, or sufficiently moral but insufficiently rational. But morality is an aspect of rationality. Thus the two alternatives here must relate to laws that, for example, are unjust (and in that sense irrational) but clearly expressed and with clear penalties for transgression, not asking the impossible, etc, and thus with a measure of rationality. Or a law that is morally just (and in that sense rational) but in other respects irrational. This second possibility is hard to imagine, for all of the ways in which a law may suffer a detriment of rationality would tend to bring about a detriment of morality also. This is the lesson of Fuller's desiderata of legality (see Section X.3). A law that is unclear does not express a moral rule at all, it expresses no rule. A law that asks the impossible or is at cross-purposes likewise does not express a moral proposition. And so on.

## XI.7. GERMAN LAW 1933–1945

The judgment that certain laws within a moderately just legal order are *non-laws*, in virtue of their injustice, creates moderately difficult questions; questions that are nevertheless solvable by reference to the foregoing arguments. But the question of whether unjust *systems* of law retain the quality of being a legal system, is a more difficult question. For, in the case of an unjust law that is not binding in conscience, one does not undermine the entire system of governance by one's act of disobedience to that law (though the regime may fine or imprison you, or render some other form of punishment). Even a concerted campaign of disobedience to an unpopular law does not overly threaten to overturn a legal order, even if it leads as Aquinas says to civic disturbance: a serious but time-limited confrontation between state and citizen. Such situations demand a clear and sober judgment that *this law* is too iniquitous to be obeyed, even if that disobedience would produce negative and unwanted, but nonetheless foreseeable, consequences. The judgment that *this legal system* fails to retain its character as law is vastly more serious, given its much more serious consequences. (Thus Hobbes calculates that even a profoundly authoritarian state is preferable to lawlessness.) It is more serious also in the fact that the evil confronted is much greater: an unjust legal system is characterized as such not merely for its unjust *laws*, but also the guiding purpose behind them. Unjust systems of law do not become so *per accidens*. I have already remarked (Section XI.1) that armchair philosophizing is to be avoided: that those who have experienced only just and stable legal order must make a genuine effort to enter into the mindset of those who are victims of, and those who orchestrate, a deliberate policy of unjust law. This is not a comfortable exercise but it is a necessary one. It is easy to rationalize, from a distance of decades, the questionable legality of the proceedings of the Nuremberg military tribunal in relation to the trial of the major Nazi war criminals. But to allow those men to go free, without being convicted of any crime, would have been unthinkable from the standpoint of justice, the law's primary virtue. The difficulty is not that the officers were tried and found guilty (they violated comprehensively the natural law that is a part of all law and all legal systems, however mutilated they become); rather, it is the reality of 'victor's justice': was the bombing of Dresden by the Allies a war crime, targeting the civilian population?[76] Were the bombings by American forces of Hiroshima and Nagasaki crimes against humanity? These actions have been the subject of academic and political debate since 1945, but they were not added to the roster of charges to be settled by the tribunal.

In terms of just war theory, at the conclusion of fighting, both the victorious powers and the vanquished powers, ought to seek (1) the re-establishment of peace,

[76] See e.g. Sinclair McKay, *Dresden: The Fire and the Darkness* (Viking 2020).

and (2) a process of healing damaged relations between nations. From the perspective of natural law theory, nations must refrain from using force once peace has been concluded, including the extortion of concessions from the losing powers. It is sound ethics that the warring nations ought to work together to construct the architecture of peace, that is, the creation of a framework for peace treaties, economic reconstruction, repatriation of prisoners of war, and the rebuilding of trust. Lying, including the destruction of documentary evidence of (the extent of) criminality, or about one's peaceful intentions, is inimical to peace. Lying is indeed contrary to law: the Nazi state for the longest time kept up the pretence that the relocation of Jews was not to death camps but merely elsewhere, so that hope was given to Jewish families that they would not be broken up, that once they had been moved the German state would leave them alone, that daily life could continue. To lie systematically to the civilian population is the opposite of treating them as autonomous subjects capable of making their own way in life within the parameters set by the law. In being lied to, the Jews could no longer depend upon their current range of choices being protected rather than prohibited by law: for example, the right to self-defence against assault from German citizens, or to enter into enforceable contracts, to possess land, and so on. Official lies take away not only choices but the entire ability to trust in legal order as a source of certainty, stability, rights, and freedoms. It essentially removes the domain of permissibility from ordinary life.

The foundation of these lies was partly substantial, but also partly institutional. Ernst Fraenkel wrote, notably, of the 'dual state':[77] on the one hand, a normative state (in my terms, a 'government of law'), and a prerogative state (in my terms, a 'government of will'). That is, a legal system that enacts and enforces rules, in distinction from a 'system' of government based on arbitrary whim. Fraenkel's contention was that the two systems ran in parallel in Nazi Germany, all citizens (including Jews) being governed by certain laws, but Jews being for the most part governed by will rather than law. In fact the picture was more complicated than this dichotomy suggests. For although there were senses in which the Jews were subject to a 'system' of government by will (e.g. the systematic rounding up and destroying of Jewish persons and looting of their property) they were for the most part 'governed' by various official bodies, such as the Gestapo and the SS, each of which operated semi-autonomously so as to make almost impossible doing or refraining from the 'right action' at the right time and place. But Fraenkel's picture is nonetheless correct in suggesting that two very different regimes of governance were in place at the same time: or, as Hart would say, that it is possible for the law to extend the benefits of the system of forbearances to some in society, but withdrawing them from a particular class of person in that society. What Hart seems not to perceive is

[77] Ernst Fraenkel, *The Dual State* (OUP 2017).

that such a system of laws (limited as it is in application), even if largely just, would be, *as a whole*, entirely *unjust* due to its otherwise just provisions actually perpetrating injustice: for such provisions would carry the general, if not specific, instruction to the courts to disapply the provisions from the hated group, and any such provision would therefore express a norm that is unjust. Related to this is the category employed under Nazi rule of the 'political crime', that is, (i) a crime not related to conduct or omission but rather to being part of a constituent group (one might also refer to this as an ontological crime: a crime of being not of doing), or (ii) of holding property,[78] (iii) of kissing a person outwith the hated group, and so on.

Despite the Nazi political programme which saw the Jews as non-persons, 'by relying upon [their] capacity for rationality and self-directed agency in order to give effect to the policy goals of their laws, the Nazis necessarily recognized and relied upon the essential humanity of the Jewish legal subject even while their purpose was to secure the dehumanization of that same subject'.[79] Thus the Reich Citizenship Law of 1935 stripped Jews of their German citizenship and thereby of the protections under German law,[80] a law that could only be applied if Jewish persons were of such a degree of humanity that they could understand and act on its terms. To this extent the law was paradoxical. But the clear commands issued in §§ 1–2 of the Law are then, characteristically, undermined by § 3, which states that 'The Reich Minister of the Interior in conjunction with the Deputy of the Fuhrer will issue the necessary legal and administrative decrees for carrying out and supplementing this law.' For the 'necessary decrees' are left in complete doubt; the relation of executing the law ('carrying out') with legislating ('supplementing') rendered wholly unclear. With one stroke Jewish persons in Germany were removed from all the legal protections citizens enjoy.

But a significant step in treating Jewish persons arbitrarily was what might be called the 'progressive injustice' of Nazi law: the means by which Jews were given the false confidence that, for example, the creation of the ghettos would mark an end to discrimination, and that the Nazi government would thereafter leave them unmolested. Such hopes turned out to be mere smoke, as the full extent of legal protections that were hitherto taken for granted by Jews (as German citizens) were gradually removed. One of the most intimate choices was removed by the Law for the Protection of German Blood and Honour in 1935: the right for a Jew to marry or have extra-marital relations with a non-Jew; all existing 'mixed marriages' were void.[81] Personal, as well as economic, life was thus subject to regulation: a move condemned centuries before by Aquinas.[82]

[78] See 1937 Decree on the Confiscation of Jewish Property, which regulates the transfer of assets from Jews to non-Jews in Germany.

[79] Kristen Rundle, 'The Impossibility of an Exterminatory Legality' (2009) 59 *Toronto LJ* 67.

[80] See Reich Citizenship Law §1.1 & § 2.3.

[81] Law for the Protection of German Blood and Honour 1935 §§ 1 & 2.

[82] Aquinas, *ST* (n 8) I-II.96.2c.

It will not have escaped the reader's notice that measures discussed so far are *legal* measures, duly enacted by the state. Clearly such laws are unjust laws, and as such not binding upon the conscience of those to whom it is addressed. But neither, for the most part, do they involve any requirement to commit an unjust act. In consequence, and given the consequences to self and family for non-obedience, it was reasonable (in this highly qualified sense) to obey such unjust laws. Many such laws, however, did not require obedience as such from their intended subjects, for it was impossible to disobey. Thus for example, the looting of Jewish assets by the German authorities, made legal by the October law of 1937, neither proscribed nor prescribed any act on the part of Jewish people.[83] It may be objected that such laws, and the earlier laws on citizenship, which of their nature did not require action on the part of their intended subjects, were in fact directed to the actions of state officials responsible for overseeing their implementation.[84] A clear example of this is the April 1937 Decree removing all Jewish children from the education system.[85] In fact by 1938, the German authorities had significantly increased the legal persecution of Jews within its territory, systematically expelling them from economic life and rendering them unable to generate any income. There is much truth in the suggestion that these laws were directed to authorities, rather than the people to which they were ostensibly applied. Natural law on the matter is clear: one should, to the extent possible, refuse to be complicit in an unjust law, and must absolutely refrain from applying it in such a way as to create an injustice to its subjects.

It might be argued: a 'good' German official may do more good by applying the law in the most minimal way possible, with the least amount of injustice as can be managed, rather than refusing or resigning, leaving open the probability that his or her replacement will apply the law fully and without mercy. Such an official, it may be concluded, is morally bound to remain in office and carry on the 'good' work of giving minimal expression to the law. The argument is false. It is reminiscent of the argument that, faced with voting on a Bill that outlaws abortions beyond the twelfth week, which if defeated would retain in place an existing Act which allows abortions up to the twenty-eighth week, a legislator ought to vote in favour of the Bill *not* because it continues to permit abortions up to the twelfth week, but because it reduces the overall number of abortions.[86] For such a legislator, so long as she or he is widely known as an opponent of abortion, can be construed as using his or her vote to vote *against* the more permissive statute, and not *for* the legality of abortions within the first twelve weeks. One is voting for a restrictive, not a permissive, Act. The argument is not wholly sound (see endnote to Section IX.5), but the

[83] By contrast the Decree of April 1937 required Jewish persons to disclose any property holdings in excess of 5000 Reichsmarks.

[84] See Rundle (n 79) 108.

[85] This completed the work begun by the 1933 Law against Overcrowding in Schools and Universities, exactly five years earlier.

[86] See John Finnis, *Collected Essays of John Finnis* (OUP 2011) IV.22.

analogy is in any case dubious. The argument is claimed to be sound on the ground that the *purpose* of the Bill is to reduce the number of legal abortions, and one may vote with that in mind: one is choosing the lesser of two evils (against the larger evil of leaving the existing code or statute in place, versus the lesser evil of restricting some, but not all, abortions). One should not restrict oneself to actions that require total moral purity, or nothing good would get done. The argument is dubious because one is still *voting for* an evil, that is, for any number of abortions to go ahead legally. But the position of the good German is not analogous to this case. In the first place, the good German official would need to conceal, rather than make generally known, his or her aversion to the Nazi laws he or she is charged with applying. But more importantly, the German is not applying a narrower rather than a wider statute; he or she is applying, maximally or minimally, precisely the set of unjust norms that are in contravention of natural law. Thus even the good German is complicit in the crimes of the German state: complicit in the law depriving Jews of their property and livelihoods, and complicit in the deaths of many thousands of German Jews, even if seeking to save, through their involvement, thousands more.

But once the German state apparatus reorientated itself towards the extinction of all German Jews, there was not unjust law but no law: for the fate of Jewish nationals no longer hinged upon directives given to those subject to them, but direct action against the Jewish population through non-juridical institutions such as the SS and those in charge of the concentration camps. Not without reason, the Nazi authorities wished to keep this aspect of their programme hidden from external, as well as internal, eyes. If the fate of Jewish nationals in the concentration camps had been governed according to law, many fewer would perhaps have gone to their deaths, and would not have been subject to the most unimaginable persecutions. It is instructive that the career of one of the worst absolute tyrants of the Nazi regime, Amon Goeth, was brought to a close in late 1944 not due to his extreme mistreatment of inmates at the Plaszow camp, but due to embezzling Jewish wealth that by law belonged to the Nazi state. But the Nazi state was far from proceeding by law in the later stages of its tyranny, and this is perhaps necessarily the case, for (as Hart himself said) the '[human] concern' at the heart of law 'is with social arrangement for continued existence'[87] and here is a connection with morality even if 'law has no other necessary connection to anything of moral value.'[88] Matters can be put another way: the mode of governance in relation to German Jews, especially after 1939, was nihilistic in intent: at the camps, and in the ghettos, there was nothing that could not be done to Jewish persons, families, and children. They could be arbitrarily, and without committing any defined crime, beaten, starved, shot, experimented upon, used as mere fodder and as hard labour, and demeaned in every way. This form of nihilism, then, is antithetical to law and legal governance. It gives

[87] Hart, *CL* (n 3) 192.
[88] Rundle (n 79) 123.

rein to the worst form of injustice: for the source of injustice is not only (a) that wrong has been done to a person, but also (b) that that wrong may never be able to be undone.

There are thus many reasons why Nazi 'laws', especially after 1939 were not merely unjust, but not law in any sense: the state proceeded against the Jews through non-juridical institutions such as the SS and camp commandants, and the extermination programme itself was not translated into any set of laws; the laws passed against the Jews were essentially *ultra vires*, for (1) they controverted the basic principle of authority that laws are required for the common good of the *whole* community (see Section VIII.4) and (2) they undermined the most basic principle of justice: treating like cases (Jew and *Reichs*-citizen) alike; and the laws on the books did not reflect the 'laws' that were actually being enforced by members of the Gestapo and SS. By complying with such laws as they were given (even though clearly not binding in conscience), the Jews not only did as prudence dictates, but also conformed to natural law: for Aquinas observes that when confronted with tyranny, one should rebel only if there is a realistic prospect of victory; or else the tyrant may become more enraged and determined.[89] In the circumstances in which the Jews found themselves, they had not the numbers, organization nor favourable opportunity to form themselves into a militia capable of challenging the Nazi state. They did the only thing that they could do: obey the laws, even as those laws led to the slaughterhouse.

This concludes this extended treatment of the subject of unjust law: laws that are moderately unjust in a moderately just legal system (which should normally be obeyed); laws that are moderately unjust in a moderately unjust legal system (binding in conscience though only in restricted circumstances); laws that are moderately unjust in a severely unjust legal system (probably binding in conscience);[90] laws that are extremely unjust in a severely unjust legal system (not to be obeyed except (i) under duress and (ii) not requiring performance of an immoral act); laws that are so unjust that they ought in no circumstances to be obeyed (laws completely antithetical to the common good or which require performance of an immoral act); and laws that are non-laws because they are *ultra vires*. As should be clear, natural law theory's treatment of the subject of unjust law is nuanced and not limited to the (itself limited) doctrine that an unjust law is not law. But there is some truth in that doctrine, and natural law theorists should not feel inhibited from relying upon it.

[89] Aquinas, *De Regno* 44.

[90] Ibid, 46: The majority of tyrannies should be borne with, and uprising generally is not in accordance with apostolic tradition, for St Peter says that rulers ought (in normal circumstances) to be obeyed, not only the good and the gentle but also the aggressive.

# XII
# INTERNATIONAL COMMUNITY, INTERNATIONAL LAW

## XII.1. INTERNATIONAL LAW AND ITS THEORY

This chapter concerns the law of the international community, but also, in part, its theory. Historians of international law typically point to four periods in the development of international law: (1) the *ius gentium* (law of peoples) stretching from Rome's imperial relations with its colonies to the eighteenth century;[1] (2) the extension of international law to other subject matters such as warfare, division of the seabed, etc, in the writings of Grotius; (3) the emergence of the 'nation state' as the subject of international law, with emphasis placed upon state practice and sovereignty, in the work of Vattel (but in fact begun at least a century earlier in Pufendorf's treatise *De Iure Naturae et Gentium* (The Law of Nature and Nations) in 1672.); and (4) modern international law's focus on actors other than the nation state, such as international corporations, institutions, and other non-state actors.[2] Each of these divisions can be challenged: the *ius gentium* was not stagnant for the better part of two millennia, but underwent significant change; the innovations introduced by Grotius, Pufendorf and Vattel did not replace that idea but gave it a central place in their major works, as is clear from the title of Pufendorf's treatise just mentioned; the notion of the 'state' is indeed a modern one, but it did not announce itself, fully realised, in Vattel's work, without antecedents; the question of non-state actors is reducible to the question of the character and identification of truly law-creating bodies in international law. Despite the so-called fragmentation of international law in recent decades (which has brought about only a limited fracturing of international law's underpinning realities), the focus of the present chapter will be upon the state, for it is the state that is principally responsible for the

[1] See Cicero, *Republic*, Book III.

[2] See Vattel, *Law of Nations* Preliminaries § 3: the primary purpose of the law of nations is to describe the rights and obligations of states. See e.g. A Kleczkowska, 'Armed Non-State Actors and Customary International Law' in James Summers & Alex Gough (eds) *Non-State Actors and International Obligations* (Brill 2018) 60; Vladyslav Lanovoy, 'The Use of Force by Non-State Actors and the Limits of Attribution of Conduct' 28 (2017) *European Journal of International Law* 563. For some modern introductions to theory of international law see Robert Kolb, *Theory of International Law* (Hart Publishing 2019); Anne Orford, Florian Hoffmann, & Martin Clark (eds) *Oxford Handbook of the Philosophy of International Law* (OUP 2016) esp chs 4, 19.

*Natural Law and Modern Society*. Sean Coyle, Oxford University Press. © Sean Coyle 2023.
DOI: 10.1093/oso/9780192886996.003.0012

common good of the people, and is a crucial unit in discussions of subsidiarity (see Section XII.4).

During the course of the twentieth century, international law writers focused increasingly on state practice as the principal or only source of international legal obligations. In the twenty-first, writers have increasingly sought to recognise obligations that are peremptory in character and which derive from other sources than state practice. In particular, such writers have made extensive use of the concept of *ius cogens*, norms that do not emerge from customary practice in the normal sense but are of compelling character. The concept of *ius cogens* does not appear explicitly in the list of sources set out in Article 38(1) of the Statute of the International Court of Justice, but it does appear in the Vienna Convention on the Law of Treaties 1969 Article 53, which states that a treaty is void if in conflict with a peremptory norm of international law. But, as with treaty-making, custom and other sources listed by the ICJ Statute, *ius cogens* is in fact also a facet of state practice. For who identifies or recognises, or abides by such norms except the international community of states? As the International Law Commission states: 'A peremptory norm of general international law (*ius cogens*) is a norm accepted and recognized by the international community of States as a whole as a norm from which no derogation is permitted and which can be modified only by a subsequent norm of general international law having the same character.'[3] By placing such emphasis on *ius cogens*, a facet of state practice, international law scholars and practitioners have overlooked a much surer basis of international legal obligations: natural law. For natural law does not end with the human community of the nation state, but extends to the governance of relations between states, for the benefit of the human community of the whole world. This is so because it is obvious that, if the primary duty of the state is to procure the flourishing of its citizens, this duty must extend to efforts to reduce the danger of a lawless international community, indeed efforts of a particular and quantifiable kind (see especially Section XII.5-6 below).

My main contention, then, in this Chapter is as follows: that international law consists of two distinguishable elements: (a) *humanly created laws and norms*, including peremptory norms, and (b) *natural law*. This division is discussed and is reflected in the structure of this Chapter. It suggests that international law should be understood theologically as well as philosophically; indeed there is no clear line between the two.

In speaking of the theory of international law, it is important to distinguish two questions: (1) the reality of international law; and (2) its legitimacy. The second of these questions will be taken up below, particularly in Sections XII.5 and XII.6. The first question is considered here. The reality, or realities, of international law have been disputed by philosophers and legal theorists throughout the modern

[3] Report of the International Law Commission, 71st Session 2019, V.1 Conclusion 2.

period in history, to a much greater extent than the features of municipal law. It is worth discussing some of these accounts of international law before addressing the substantive content and justice of international legal rules and mechanisms. As is well known, Jeremy Bentham coined the term 'international law', which he took to be 'law' on the basis of its being sufficiently analogous to municipal law.[4] But later writers did not follow Bentham in this supposition. Thus Hart, Bentham's critic and expositor, pinpointed the key issue as being, not similarity, but the compatibility of state sovereignty with binding rules of international law. But this opposition itself rests upon a concept of 'sovereignty' that is contestable and distinctly Benthamite, that of a sovereign power that is (1) the source of all law, and (2) 'above' the law.[5] But these are provably false even in municipal law: as Hart goes on to say, the idea that states are incapable of limitation except by themselves (i.e. are auto-limiting) is untrue of modern societies in which the rule of law is developed and respected, and the concept of sovereignty is not fixed prior to the law, for in order to know the extent of sovereign powers, we must first know what the rules are.[6] Further, if states are deemed (against fact) to be auto-limiting, i.e. self-binding, then from where do the relevant ranges of norms of promise and agreement come? Such norms provide the structure of the practice that makes intelligible and possible the notion of self-binding.[7] Though sometimes derided by international law theorists as portraying international law as a form of primitive law, Hart is actually open to acknowledging the legal character of international law despite not fully conforming to his 'concept' of law as a union of primary and secondary rules. International law is far more complex and sophisticated than a simple order of primary rules;[8] and a search for a grounding rule or rule of recognition is as useless and unnecessary as is the search for a grounding rule of etiquette: the absence of such a rule makes little difference to the normativity of the relevant ranges of norms.[9] But this raises a question not confronted or apparently anticipated by Hart: if the secondary rules of recognition, adjudication and change are intended to cure the problems of a domestic society of primary rules, what are the defects, and what are the mechanisms that overcome them, in relation to international law?

In order to pursue this question, it must be remembered that the defects of a domestic society of primary rules are defects of *justice*. This is also true of international society. Just as Hart explores in more detail the basic *needs* of a society,

[4] Jeremy Bentham, *Principles and Morals of Legislation* in JH Burns & HLA Hart (eds) *The Collected Works of Jeremy Bentham* (OUP 1970) XVII.25 n 1.

[5] HLA Hart, *The Concept of Law* (3rd edn OUP 2012, hereafter *CL*) 221. See also David Lefkowitz, 'What Makes a Social Order Primitive? In Defense of Hart's Take on International Law' 23 (2017) *Legal Theory* 258; Jeremy Waldron, 'International Law: "A Relatively Small and Unimportant" Part of Jurisprudence?' 13-56 (2013) *NYU Public Law & Legal Theory Research Series* 209.

[6] Hart, *CL* (n 5) 223.

[7] Ibid, 224–25.

[8] Ibid, 227; see Giovanni Bisogni, 'The Question to be Faced is One of Fact: HLA Hart's Legal Theory Through His View of International Law' 34 (2021) *Canadian Journal of Law & Jurisprudence* 283.

[9] Hart, *CL* (n 5) 234.

which justice supplies, so we must trace out those of international society. Hart expresses such needs in the form of corollaries of 'truisms' about human living in society; so those of international society consist of corollaries of truisms about human living in international society, which is currently, although not necessarily, organised on the basis of interactions between *states*. Of these, six are worth exploring here:

(1) States are not approximately equal to one another. Hence there is a need for rules and mechanisms (such as courts) which avoid small states becoming targets of the large and powerful, or which avoid the voices of small states from being drowned out by larger nations in international discourse.
(2) States are not on the whole aggressive, but neither are they entirely without imperialising ambitions regarding smaller or less 'developed' states. There is thus the need for precepts which reflect the fact that states territorially expand and contract, but which regard invasion as an act incompatible with sovereignty.
(3) States envy the resources of other states and have limited patience in refraining from them. If there were a lack of any structure or system of norms to restrain states in this regard, there would be a free-for-all the consequence of which would be that the plunderer would become the next target of lustful eyes.
(4) States which seek to flourish must engage in international trade and commerce. There is therefore a need for a system of international laws that prevent or penalise fraud, extortion, piracy, faithlessness in bargaining, etc.
(5) States are made up of countless persons, the basic humanity and dignity of whom all persons are aware. Thus states have limited patience in tolerating abuses of a foreign people by its state, and limited will to refrain from intervening militarily or economically to alleviate the condition of an oppressed people. Hence there is a need for a framework of rules of engagement of one state in the internal affairs of another, in the name of humanity, and the establishment of international bodies, the task of which is to decide when such intervention is permissible or necessary.
(6) States wish to enjoy the fruits of their industries, promote the interests of their citizens and store up economic and public capital. Therefore, states require for their flourishing protracted periods of peace, and a set of laws that define and protect 'peace', and which give peace some structure.

There is, of course, some overlap between the needs identified in these 'truisms', as there is in Hart's original scheme (a 'system of mutual forbearances'). But they reflect that the international arena is far more dangerous than the internal society of a state, given the sheer scale and resources of its subjects. Nor is it entirely clear how relevant international bodies should be constituted, and what manner of decision-making processes should be set in place: ought, for example, unanimity or majority decision-making apply; secret voting or publicised decision? Ought there to be a threshold of entry: states sufficiently 'developed', liberal, democratic? Ought smaller or less developed states have as great a voice as larger, more developed ones; or ought larger states to have a greater influence on decision-making procedures akin to an 'electoral college' system? Ought purely commercial interests be represented? On the level of substantive issues, the truisms leave open a wide range of issues on which there may be profound disagreement, such as on economic issues: ought there to be a free international market in goods, services and resources, or should equalisation of wealth be a key demand? Setting aside such doubts, each of the needs identified by the truisms, is a demand of justice. Hence justice (as well as peace) is a basic value of the international community.[10]

One aspect of justice is worth exploring. The enforcement of international laws against states that do not comply with their obligations will never gain unanimous support even in the international organisations created for the purpose. Inevitably, the enforcement of international laws will at least in some, potentially many, cases, be carried out by the military forces of certain nations (or those of organisations such as the United Nations, funded by certain nations). It is then a requirement of justice that those certain nations, when in breach of international law, must themselves acknowledge their wrongdoing, immediately cease the wrongful action, and submit to the relevant penalties. Failure to do so divests those states of any credibility, moral authority or (likely) allies when challenging similar wrongful state practice in the future. The UK Government's inclusion of a clause in its Internal Markets Bill, which created legal powers in contravention of the (European Union) Withdrawal Agreement in 2020, is a case in point: if a state government regards itself as free to breach international law in (what it perceives to be) the national interest, then it is not in any position to call into question any other state's actions in contravention of international law, of at least similar levels of seriousness; furthermore such actions erode the legal understandings on which the interests of all nations rest, and are thus particularly irresponsible.

All of this raises the more basic question of why states should consider themselves bound to follow international law at all? Obviously, not all states obey international law out of respect for justice. There may be many reasons why such states obey, just as there is a variety of different reasons for citizens to obey their governments, as Hart pointed out. But just as in domestic law that variety of positions is relative to a 'focal' position; in international law the reason for obedience to international laws is (focally) the sheer reasonableness of those laws and the

[10] See Sean Coyle, 'Natural Law in Aquinas and Grotius—An Ethics for Our Times?' 97 (2016) *New Blackfriars* 592ff; Dante Fedele, '*Ius gentium*: The Metamorphoses of a Legal Concept (Ancient Rome to Early Modern Europe)' in Edward Cavanagh (ed) *Empire and Legal Thought: Ideas and Institutions from Antiquity to Modernity* (Brill 2020) 213.

benefits that flow from obedience to them. For as Aquinas never tires of pointing out, law is fundamentally an ordinance of *reason*, not of *will*.[11] It is from incomplete or deficient attention to these facts that much of (imperfect) compliance with international law derives: principally the calculation of how to secure the benefits whilst avoiding perceived costs, or vastly inflated pride in one's nation such as to render all international laws as threats to the safety of the nation or to the position of the ruler. Thus, a sizeable number of the world's states fail to identify the inherent reasonableness of international laws. But even the hardened sceptic about international law, who believes that nations are bound only to their self-interest, and denying the reality of peremptory norms, can surely grasp the opportunity presented by new frameworks of thinking about international law, including such norms? That at least is the invitation extended by the remainder of the chapter.

## XII.2. *IUS GENTIUM*

From around the beginning of the sixteenth century, writers on ethics, theology and politics drew a distinction between the law of peoples or of nations [*ius gentium*], on the one hand, and the law of nature, or the 'necessary law of nations', on the other. Sharing a common core of belief, writers in the tradition were nevertheless divided over the precise lines of the distinction. The chief difficulty, out of many, related to the concept of *ius gentium* itself. For since the Roman period, discussions of the *ius gentium* had variously emphasised its positive law character, for it simply represented what was agreed between numerous distinct peoples, and its natural law character, for such agreement reflected dictates of reason, the rationality of the relevant norms and doctrines being the explanation for the possibility of agreement among so many nations. Thus for example, we find Grotius employing the concept of *ius gentium* in his search for *a posteriori* evidence of natural law.[12] This dual-faced character of *ius gentium* was undoubtedly useful in providing a stock of moral principles and a common language in which to argue about them. We encounter similar treatments of the subject in the present era: for example, Tasioulas and Besson state that international norms are distinct from moral norms because the former are (a) *often* morally indifferent and (b) changeable by states.[13] The emphasised word suggests that in fact some international norms are moral norms; as to changeability, states have the power to decriminalise or altogether do away with internal laws prohibiting fraud, but that does absolutely nothing to change the morality of those norms. The same kind of objection can be found in

[11] e.g. Aquinas, *Summa Theologiae* (hereafter *ST*) I-II.90.1c.

[12] Grotius, *De Iure Belli ac Pacis* (hereafter *DIBP*) Proleg XL–XLII.

[13] See Samantha Besson & John Tasioulas, *The Philosophy of International Law* (OUP 2010, hereafter *TPIL*) 10. Emphasis added.

the eighteenth century where we see glimpses of the idea that states are brought together by commerce rather than by sociability, i.e. by the minimum morality of the market, not the higher norms of natural law. These issues will be discussed further below, the emphasis for the moment lying on the shifting perspectives on the *ius gentium*.[14]

It will be worthwhile to trace a little the career of the *ius gentium* as it appeared to late scholastic, early modern and eighteenth century treatise writers. The aforementioned duality of *ius gentium* displayed a shifting understanding, or unclarity, among writers in the natural law tradition. There was in consequence no consistency as to how the boundary between the *ius gentium* and the natural law was drawn. Thus Vattel was led to argue that the primary purpose of the *ius gentium* is to describe the rights and obligations of states, but went on to observe that 'the *necessary* law of nations' is that part of the *ius gentium* that derives immediately from the natural law.'[15] This resembles the case of secondary precepts of natural law discussed by Aquinas, which follow on closely from the primary and self-evident principles, and about which there is a certain variability of reason, if not actual choice. Grotius gives a useful example: he holds that it is by custom rather than precept that ambassadors be admitted, but the *ius gentium* forbids their expulsion without grave reason.[16] Further, the *ius gentium* provides that whilst ambassadors possess immunity in the host state, crimes ought not to go unpunished (as a matter of natural law), and hence if an ambassador commits a serious crime whilst in the host state, they should (as a matter of *ius gentium*) be deported and punished in their home state.[17] This aspect of *ius gentium* is described as 'volitional' by Grotius, in contradistinction to Vattel's 'necessary' *ius gentium*. But Grotius's own writings display a certain confusion concerning this concept, for whilst he is eager to emphasise the 'natural' quality of at least some laws of the nations, elsewhere he seems to suggest that the whole of *ius gentium* is volitional in character: 'What the common consent of all human kind has shown to be the will of all persons, that is law.'[18]

Contrast this with Suarez, who holds to the medieval consensus that the *ius gentium* is an intermediate kind of law situated some way between natural law and positive law, but 'more proximate in character to natural law.'[19] Shortly thereafter he clarifies his meaning: the *ius gentium* is the natural law 'poured into' the civil

[14] Throughout this section I will use the term *ius gentium*, where some of the writers to be considered use the vernacular 'law of nations', so as to emphasize that they are talking of the same object of thought and to keep that object steadily in view.

[15] Vattel (n 2) Proleg §§ 3 & 7.

[16] See Grotius, *DIBP* (n 12) II.18.1.

[17] Ibid, II.18.2.

[18] Grotius, *De Iure Praedae* Proleg, Rule II. See James Crawford, *Brownlie's Principles of Public International Law* 9th edn (OUP 2019) 3–17; Michael Scharf, 'Hugo Grotius and the Concept of Grotian Moments in International Law' 54 (2022) *Case Western Reserve J of International Law* 17.

[19] Suarez, *De Legibus* (hereafter *DL*) II.17.1.

law reflecting the common usage of humankind; but then he proceeds to say that it is the unconstrained and willing assent of humankind *or the greater part thereof*, such that one cannot say that its norms were written on the hearts of all human beings, and are therefore not equivalent to natural law.[20] But the *ius gentium* is not equivalent with civil law because it represents the customary usage of not only a few states, but the common consensus of the majority of states, and is unwritten.[21] Suarez states, with some consistency, that there are thus two kinds of *ius gentium* [*duplex modus*], the secondary kind of which does not relate to every person and is not 'written on the heart' of all persons.[22] But in other passages he implies that *ius gentium* is one distinct kind of law, which is neither natural law nor positive law [*ius civile*], for it is not the dictate of a legislator.[23] Elsewhere he gives an alternative explanation of this singular form of *ius gentium*: it is only considered as *ius civile* in an analogical sense, and likewise only analogically natural law, because it tolerates certain evils in which all or the majority of states participate, which are in contravention of natural law[24] (for example, use of deception in warfare). At the same time, positive law in the strict sense is 'most unlike the character of *ius gentium*'.[25] These seemingly confusing passages illustrate the difficulty post-medieval writers experienced in seeking to pin down the meaning of *ius gentium* as a middle way between natural law and positive law. But they also demonstrate the willingness of such writers to recognise what we would now call 'international law' as a genuine and distinct form of law, different in character from both natural law and positive state law, though at least analogous to both. An earlier passage of Suarez represents this most clearly:

> Although a sovereign state, or kingdom, or commonwealth may be a perfect community in itself, . . . nevertheless each state can be viewed in a certain sense and in relation to the human species, or as a member of international society; for such states when standing apart are never so self-sufficing that they do not stand in need of mutual assistance, association or intercourse, sometimes for greater welfare or advantage, and at other times for the sake of moral necessity or need . . . In consequence such communities stand in need of some system of laws by which they may be directed and properly ordered toward such intercourse and association. Yet although such guidance is to a greater extent provided by natural reason, it is not sufficiently provided and in a direct manner in regard to all matters, and so it was possible for certain specific rules of law to be introduced into the practice of such nations. This was more greatly possible because the matters

[20] Ibid, II.17.2 & 8; see also David Hume, *Treatise of Human Nature* III.2.2.
[21] Suarez, *DL* (n 19) II.19.6.
[22] Ibid, II.19.10.
[23] Ibid, II.20.1.
[24] Ibid, II.20.3.
[25] Ibid, III.Proem.2.

> comprising such laws are [relatively] few, very closely related to natural law, from which they are very easily deduced.[26]

Can we, though, do no better than this? Let us attempt to cut through the confusion by stating that *ius gentium* (the law of peoples or of nations, or general international law) is a matter of state practice and thus of international *positive* law. But, like all facets of state practice (treaties, agreements, accords, customs, rulings, peremptory norms), general international law *may* give expression to precepts of natural law (norms that are binding whether or not they are matters of state practice), but may equally diverge from such norms, or may as a matter of *determinatio* supplement the natural law by adding detail and specificity to general principles.

Insofar as the *ius gentium* is rational or reasonable in character (and thus in accord with natural law), Suarez considers that it can never be entirely abolished. Living in an age of nuclear weapons, where peace is preserved not by disarmament but by the principle of mutually assured destruction, this may seem to be a fragile, if not a false, hope. Yet it can also be regarded as another instance of Aristotle's principle, that falsehoods conflict whereas truth harmonises. Thus the *ius gentium* can never be entirely obliterated because truth can never be obliterated: state practice will never lose every last vestige of civility, though the potential for depravity is very great. It will never utterly fragment so that there is no consistency and coherence. The practice of states (and some non-state actors) as moral communities will always give expression to some truths of natural law. But state practice is often a matter of compromise and negotiation, not a search for truth. Suarez therefore remarks that the *ius gentium* does not emerge from natural reason alone, for it concerns not human beings as such, but (1) human beings in community and (2) the processes whereby those communities are formed.[27] But is there a general problem with state practice? It would appear so: for it is true that wealthy, technologically advanced states can afford to engage in a wider set of practices at the international level, than developing nations. Developing or emerging states have little choice but to engage with paradigms and systems created by wealthy, developed nations, such as the WTO regime. Such norms are reflective of a particular time and place. But the question of provenance is misdirected: even if all states agreed upon a practice, this would not confirm that the relevant practice was morally righteous.[28] It is the reasonableness of such norms and systems that matters but also, crucially, the willingness of wealthy, developed states to subject themselves to such systems by, for example, regarding themselves as bound by an adverse ruling of an international tribunal. Writers as far back as the eighteenth century perceived that such a requirement is a necessary feature of the *ius gentium*, though less clearly: Locke,

[26] Ibid, II.19.9.
[27] Ibid, II.18.3.
[28] Tasioulas in Besson & Tasioulas, *TPIL* (n 13) 105–106.

for example, stated that the *ius gentium* is in vain if there is no centralized organ to punish states in transgression.[29] This statement is correct to the extent that some non-state body, fully independent from nation states, must be entrusted with adjudicating between competing claims, or even competing interpretations of international law, on the part of states, lest the *ius gentium* lies in a primitive condition. But Locke's statement is incorrect in assuming that such a body must resemble municipal courts in their 'centrality', i.e. compulsory jurisdiction. International law would be much impoverished if it had to await that condition, though increasingly international courts and tribunals have *de facto* compulsory jurisdiction insofar as states that wish to enjoy the benefits of a system must submit themselves to adjudicative mechanisms associated with that system. This is not true compulsory jurisdiction, so long as states can choose to withdraw from the system. Furthermore, unlike the judicial organs of many countries, international courts and tribunals lend themselves to being suspected of being vulnerable to bribery, political pressure, secret diplomacy, etc. Of course, peremptory norms (e.g. against slavery, genocide or torture) entail that states are not fully able to vary or modify the extent of their obligations under international law.[30] But such norms (a) emanate from a source that is defined, amid contention, through state practice, and (b) are substantively defined through state practices of interpretation and assertion.

The *ius gentium* therefore is best understood as positive law which encapsulates natural law precepts, either wholly or in part. But it is positive law only in an analogous sense when compared with domestic state law. For domestic positive law emanates (in part) from a legislature; it does not form part of a chorus of proposals or interpretations from which a law, in part a compromise between opposing practices, eventually emerges, but which is never fully finished emerging.

A word ought to be said about *opinio iuris*: it is odd that international lawyers have not paid more attention to Finnis's subtle account of *opinio iuris* in *Natural Law and Natural Rights* (see Section VIII.3).[31] But for present purposes it can be said that *opinio iuris* involves a widespread conviction amongst states that a certain emergent norm is alternatively (i) reasonable and ought to be followed; (ii) reasonable and permissible; (iii) unreasonable but the best that can be arrived at in the circumstances and better than other real possibilities (and in that reduced sense 'reasonable'); or (iv) unreasonable but preferable to lawlessness (and in that very reduced sense 'reasonable'). For states are not in the usual sense *choosing* norms but recognizing a collective practice, though the recognition brings the norm more concretely into effect. To be clear, this is not a suggestion that possibilities (iii) and (iv) ought to form a basis of lawmaking, but that they describe the practice of *opinio iuris* as it actually exists.

29 John Locke, *Second Treatise on Government* § 7.

30 See David Lefkowitz, *Philosophy and International Law* (CUP 2020), 55.

31 John Finnis, *Natural Law and Natural Rights* (2nd edn OUP 2011, hereafter *NLNR*) 238–44.

## XII.3. NATURAL INTERNATIONAL LAW

International law is comprised of positive law (state practice) and natural law (see Section XII.1).[32] The positive law emanates from the sources of international law enumerated within Article 38 of the Statute of the International Court of Justice, namely, conventions between states, custom, general principles of law (the primary sources) and (subsidiary sources:) judicial decisions and teachings of renowned publicists. But all of these sources of course depend upon recognition by states which incorporate them into their practice, for one reason or another. We can therefore ask: what are the ultimate sources of this practice? The answer is likely to lie in a range of attitudes: unilateral advantage; security; compulsion; lack of reasonable alternatives; political reasoning; policy; *opinio iuris*; conscience. Of this incomplete list, the latter two items are (sometimes) expressive of natural law precepts. It was clear to the medieval and late-scholastic philosophers that natural law is an important source of the *ius gentium*. For in any arena in which there is a need for political ordering, and where ethics is of paramount importance (not always in the minds of the actors), human practices must be understood not only in terms of their motivations (that is, at the level of history), but in terms of their deeper significance (as good, bad, right, wrong, politic, impolitic, contrary to or in harmony with essential human needs ... ). It is thus surprising to find a modern scholar of international law stating that, by the nineteenth century, 'natural law was dead beyond resurrection.'[33] Indeed: 'The idea of natural law is a paradox, a *nomos* which is rooted in *physis*.'[34] The first of these sentences is perplexing: the reference is to 'natural law' rather than 'natural law theory'; the latter is clearly far from dead, but the former either exists or it does not exist; it cannot be that there are permanent moral truths at one time but no longer at another. Whether there are or there are not, the reader may form an opinion based on the material in previous chapters of this book, or other books. The second sentence is a misconception: natural law, and ethics in general, concern questions not about what there is, or what is the case, but of how one should act, or refrain from action. It concerns, in other words, practical rather than speculative questions. It is true that such practical questions are asked, and answered as they are, due to facts about human needs (as are any political/ethical questions, including Allott's own), but the claim that natural law theories are guilty of paradoxical violations of the fact-value distinction is simply false. It should further be stated that the nation state is not the last horizon of ethical

[32] See Grotius, *DIBP* (n 12) Proleg § 39; see also Anthony D'Amato, 'Is International Law Part of Natural Law?' 8 (1989) *Vera Lex* 8.

[33] Philip Allott, *Health of Nations* (CUP 2002, hereafter HN) 14.46.416. See James Crawford et al, 'Review Essay Symposium: Philip Allott's *Eunomia* and *The Health of Nations Thinking Another World*: This Cannot Be How the World Was Meant to Be' 16 (2005) *European Journal of International Law* 255.

[34] Allott, *HN* (n 33) 12.52.364; see also 14.39.411.

thought: there is only one natural law, and it encompasses the whole of human life, including international life. In consequence, the central question for the natural law theorist is not, whether international law is truly law, but whether, is this or that provision of international law *not* law owing to its disharmony with natural law?

The latter remark should be contextualized.[35] As with many instances of domestic laws, disharmony with natural law does not necessarily lead to the judgment that a certain provision is 'not law', for its ongoing reception by the majority of citizens provides one powerful reality of law that abides. Only in extreme circumstances are we entitled to the judgment that some 'validly enacted' norm is not law. Similarly in the international community, many of the provisions, treaty articles, customs, usages and rulings of international courts and tribunals, may be less than just; but they should continue to be recognized as 'law' for (as with the rules of domestic law) they provide stability and peace for the international community, and restrain states from even worse abuses. This is not to suggest that such provisions be condoned (for the strongest representations should be made to the relevant organs to repair the injustices); merely that they be temporarily borne with, since anarchy in the international realm is a far more realistic prospect than is the case in domestic society. State practice and treaty-making are subordinate to the natural law, but they have a vital role to play in giving shape and expression to norms of natural law as they play out in numerous contexts. Thus the function of state practice is twofold: (i) to act in accordance with the natural law of the international community, and (ii) to seek lawful solutions to problems of international relations, that is, to flood the international arena with law.[36] One cause of friction in the international community, arising from (ii), is that an element of serendipity or benevolent political circumstances are often required in order to perceive the truth of certain moral propositions.[37] Both Rawls and Fukuyama point to liberal and democratic political orders as in some sense optimal states or as morally enlightened.[38] This is an obvious source of friction in the international community for it is often mistaken for cultural imperialism. This is especially the case when international natural law is grounded in self-preservation: for the modes and means by which a large, technically advanced state can defend its interests, interests extending to the preservation of certain international regimes (such as free-trade agreements or military zones) will far exceed those of smaller or less well-developed states. Vattel follows Aquinas in suggesting that, in view of their

[35] For a different, predominantly historical, contextualization, see Stephen Hall, 'The Persistent Spectre: Natural Law, International Order and the Limits of Legal Positivism' 12 (2001) *European Journal of International Law* 269; another alternative: Martti Koskenniemi, 'Empire and International Law: The Real Spanish Contribution' 61 (2011) *University of Toronto LJ* 1.

[36] Grotius, *De Iure Pradae Commentarius* (hereafter DIPC) Proleg Rule XII: 'No state or citizen may seek to enforce his own right against another state or citizen thereof, except by judicial procedure.'

[37] See Besson & Tasioulas, *TPIL* (n 13) 15.

[38] John Rawls, *The Law of Peoples* (Harvard University Press 1999) I.5–6; Francis Fukuyama, *The End of History and the Last Man* (Penguin 1992).

disproportionate power, larger, more developed states may need morally to forgo their rights in the name of international peace:

> It is therefore necessary, on many occasions, that nations should suffer certain things to be done, though in their own nature unjust and condemnable; because they cannot oppose them by open force, without violating the liberty of some particular state, and destroying the foundations of their natural society. And since they are bound to cultivate that society, it is of course presumed that all nations have consented to the principle we have just established.[39]

It should be observed that the concept of international natural law does not depend, any more than natural domestic law, on an imagined 'natural condition'. Grotius, for example, mentions the term 'state of nature' [*status naturae*] only twice in his lengthy *De Iure Belli ac Pacis*.[40] Other natural law writers do not use the term at all. The idea that there is or could have been a pre-societal state, a lawless realm, is no more true of the international realm than of the domestic: states at war have always concluded treaties of peace, or acknowledged solemn vows as binding; the international community has always recognized the boundaries that divide states (or peoples, or city-states, or empires), or else history could not have recorded warfare between such states, or peoples... This is an instance of the general principle that there is no origin of power within any community, and political power (the use of power self-consciously for ends other than pure self-interest) is without any defined beginning: see Section VIII.1. In all events, the idea of a 'natural condition' plays no operative part in the theories we are presently discussing, and the theory of international natural law can proceed quite without it.

If international natural law does not require an origin as such, then neither does it require an ideal end-point. Such end-points have been proposed by numerous writers: Rawls observes that Christian natural law and the law of peoples (in Rawls's specialized use of that phrase) '... are similar in that both imply that universal peace among nations is possible';[41] Kant in his First and Second Articles of Peace, in his essay on *Perpetual Peace* envisages a society of nations based on the transformation of the present order into one in which all states are of republican constitution, and formed into a federation of free states. But such a transformation cannot be achieved, in one step, without severe injustice to the lawful interests of states and non-state actors whose interests are bound up with various kinds of political and social capital and past economic activity. Not every aspect of Kant's essay is flawed in this way, for among his Articles of Peace are provisions relating to the

39 Vattel (n 2) Proleg § 21.

40 Grotius, *DIBP* (n 12) II.5.15.2, III.7.1.1; see also Kant, *Perpetual Peace* (Second Definitive Article of Peace).

41 Rawls (n 38) 14.6.

use of spies and agents in warfare, practices that he correctly regards as incompatible with the search for *perpetual* peace: these must be forsworn in their entirety and by every person, and (we can add) unilaterally, for it is no justification to use such methods to say that all other states employ them, any more than we could state that states are justified in targeting innocent populations since all others do so. Given the current state of the international community, then, the main function of international natural law resembles more the management of a predicament, rather than (first and foremost) the realization of a well-understood end-state. It thus incorporates immanent moral demands such as that states seek redress through international courts rather than by war, and pursue economic and trade goals without force or fraud, and with an eye to justice towards less developed states (e.g. to end the purchase of natural resources or manufactured goods at artificially low prices): see Section XII.7. Thus Pope John Paul II urged all persons to be responsible builders of earthly society, but they must do so by interpreting events, with the aid of the Holy Spirit, as they unfold in the course of history.[42]

The proposition that natural law resembles the management of a predicament does not exclude the need for (gradual) transformation of the international community; but it recognizes that law is presently intertwined with injustice, and has been so throughout recorded history. Despite this, it remains a moral obligation of all states (indeed all persons) to strive after peace.[43] There is good reason, however, to be optimistic about the state of the world, from which many injustices will disappear. For to affirm that all persons are capable of discerning right from wrong, whether or not they accept the Lordship of Christ, does not entail that there can be any natural reason unaided, outside of Christ's salvific love. We can accordingly be confident that our sincere efforts to bring about a better world are not entirely condemned to be missteps, mistakes and injustices. The human being is a creature of God, not of damnation.[44] The end of all law is God, and there is no aspect of human political community that is unrelated to the history of redemption; *all* of human history (even its darker periods) is on a path towards final judgment.[45] Likewise, Rawls rejects both Sherman's famous phrase that 'war is hell' (and thus without any limits), and the notion that we are all so guilty that none of us can cast blame, or in turn be blamed:[46] down that dark path to moral nihilism we should not go.

In contrast to Kant's fully free republican states, it will likely prove necessary to impose an international legal system on the recalcitrant. But again, this will only prove successful (if it does prove successful) if the imposing states also abide by its terms, and do not employ force or stratagems to evade their obligations. Further,

[42] Encyclical of Pope John Paul II, 30 December 1987 *Sollicitudo rei socialis* § 1.

[43] See Esther Reed, *A Theology for International Law* (T&T Clark 2013) 2; see also Genesis 9:5; Psalms 10:18, 33:5, 106:3; Isaiah 1:17, 28:17.

[44] Ibid, 27.

[45] Ibid, 41.

[46] Rawls (n 38) 14.6.

such efforts of imposition must only come (1) after every political and diplomatic effort has been made to accommodate recalcitrant states to its terms, and (2) if greater evils of warfare are avoided. Recalcitrant states should not in any circumstances be regarded as colonies, principalities or vassal states to the powerful: states as such are instruments of Divine peace and justice, and thus should not be extinguished, overthrown or compromised by the strong, for they are an essential source of the common good of their communities (see Section XII.7).[47] Above all, international natural law demands the love of neighbours and of enemies: dimensions of which include benevolence of motives, duties of assistance at need, rebuke in the face of evils and war, as a last resort, to redress injustices and suppress the will of the headstrong (see Section XII.6). If the theological dimension of international law is removed, leaving behind it only state practice, the result would be an entirely conventional set of practices with no *a priori* limits (in which 'each society has its own morality'),[48] the likely outcome of which would be either a Social Darwinist position (which as previously observed is a natural law theory in all but name: see Section II.5), or a pure Darwinist position which would consume the world in war.

The concept of international natural law has been widely misunderstood, when it has been remarked at all, and it is worth correcting one instance because it highlights some essential features of international natural law. Allott's understanding of international natural law forms a paradox. There are (he avers) two 'versions' of natural law theory: (i) a universalizing one in which all things, including international law, are governed by universal laws; and (i) a particularizing one proceeding from general judgments of reason to the specific content of rules.[49] But in fact there is only one 'version' of natural law theory at work here: in relation to (i) Allott has in mind the process of *conclusio* (the derivation of general principles from absolutely first principles of natural law), and in relation to (ii) he has in mind the process of *determinatio*, the process whereby general principles are concretized with a certain degree of creativity and conventionality into rules that, although reasonable, could have been settled on other terms. This second process is chiefly the one at work in the field of international law, for states must clarify the nature of the international community in the making of it; and international society is developing at a much quicker pace than established domestic societies.[50] As Suarez observes, natural law is a single law that binds for all times and in respect of every condition of human nature.[51] This latter phrase indicates the reach of natural law, from the situation of the citizen in a domestic society to states (of citizens) in international society. And

[47] See Revelation 21:24.

[48] Philip Allott, *Eunomia* (OUP 1990) 6.59.107.

[49] Ibid, 11.24.327. For another theory seeking to place natural law and thaw law of nations on different trajectories see Jeremy Waldron, 'Foreign Law and the Modern *Ius Gentium*' in Mads Andenas & Duncan Fairgrieve (eds) *Courts and Comparative Law* (OUP 2015) 539–44.

[50] Grotius, *DIBP* (n 12) II.15.6.

[51] Suarez, *DL* (n 19) II.7.9.

just as citizens have certain basic natural rights (e.g. not to be assaulted, or to be assisted at need), states also conform to lines that must not be transgressed by any other state. As Vattel writes:

> Since then a nation is obliged to preserve itself, it has a right to every thing necessary for its preservation. For the Law of Nature gives us a right to every thing, without which we cannot fulfil our obligation; otherwise it would oblige us to do impossibilities, or rather would contradict itself in prescribing us a duty, and at the same time debarring us of the only means of fulfilling it . . . [52]

The reader may have noticed that throughout this discussion of international natural law no mention has been made of human rights. This is for two reasons: (1) human rights are expressions of state practice and thus of positive law (see Section VI.3); and (2) such rights are conceived as applying to every person 'in virtue of their humanity': but this should be contrasted with the ultimate grounds of *natural* rights, which hold by reason of the human creature's essential likeness to God, and not simply their human nature.[53]

Thus we can say that natural law is the missing source in Article 38 of the Statute of the International Court of Justice, the source from which all international law norms derive (insofar as they are just and in conformity with reason), through the processes of *conclusio* and *determinatio*. If states create law or custom that is in fundamental opposition to natural law, such law is not binding on the international community and may, or may not, be lawfully resisted by the states to which it has been applied. No amount of customary practice can render an immoral norm licit in this sense. This is the case in relation, particularly, to norms that are (a) extremely unjust, or (b) malevolent in intent. Unjust norms that are neither of these alternatives may require to be complied with for the sake of international peace and in the absence of better alternatives.

## XII.4. THE IMPORTANCE OF STATES

The concept of the 'nation state' is of relatively recent origin, but its ascendance has been lamented by many international lawyers, who perceive its associated doctrines (e.g. of sovereignty) as damaging to human interests at a global level, and who question its modern-day importance. Thus, Paulus claims that, although nation states remain the primary law-makers of international law, it is increasingly

[52] Vattel (n 2) I.2.18; see also I.2.23: 'a nation has a right to every thing without which it cannot attain the perfection of the members and of the state, or prevent and repel whatever is contrary to this double perfection.'

[53] Cf Pufendorf, *De Iure Naturae et Gentium* (hereafter *DINEG*) VII.1.7: the basis of society is the desire to be safe from others.

individuals and other non-state actors who shape international legal norms; the recognition of the nation state was only ever a device for promoting the wellbeing of individual citizens.[54] Likewise, Reed states that the dangers presently facing the world cannot be faced by early modern models of tolerance and power-balancing between states.[55] Allott, in a long argument against the idea of 'states' observes that the concept of 'nation' does not fit with the idea of 'state', for the former is definable by language, culture, race, birthplace etc, all of which may be present in a state alongside other 'nations', or may extend beyond the borders of one state into the territory of its neighbour.[56] Finally, Rawls laments that 'the typical view of international relations ... has not been transcended in modern times, when world politics is still marked by the struggles of states for power, prestige, and wealth in a condition of global anarchy.'[57] In contradistinction to these views, the arguments about to be put forward will explain the ongoing importance of states, their primary duties towards their citizens in international law, and their central features.

First the necessity of states: this does not mean either that the political form 'state' is the necessary development from the *polis*, city-state or people, or that the state is the permanent or final political form that is the focus of international relations. It means rather that there is an ever-present need for an intermediating institution in international affairs that stands between international law-making (or -breaking) organs, structures or agents, on the one hand, and the citizens of the state, on the other. For all of the reasons enumerated by Aristotle, a state (or *polis*) is an inescapably important means of protecting its citizens from harm: namely, by its internal organization of power and force, management of the market, punishment of criminality, recognition and enforcement of legal bargains, and (of particular importance in international affairs) its defence of the people from external enemies.[58] But as the international realm grows politically more complex, and legally more mature and sophisticated, the state increasingly takes on the role as an intermediate organ that stands between the people and the rulings of international courts and tribunals, actions of other states, and the activities of multinational corporations, just as organisations such as workers' unions stand between the individual citizen and the government of the state. Without this essential political form, contracts with foreign corporations, suppliers or service-providers for national infrastructure projects would be practically impossible. Markets, particularly the international markets, would become impossibly unstable. National projects, such as providing food for all, would be rendered difficult. The capacity of peoples or nations to create and advance international law would be fatally

54 Andreas Paulus in Besson & Tasioulas, *TPIL* (n 13) 216.
55 Reed (n 43) 4.
56 Allott (n 48) 12.56.200, 13.50.224, 13.104.242.
57 Rawls (n 38) 2.3.
58 See Aristotle, *Politics* I.2.

compromised. International borders would be eroded and thrown into doubt.[59] In fact the elimination of the 'state' from international affairs would create precisely the kind of global anarchy that Rawls quite without reason thinks is the present condition of international society. The notions of 'nations' or 'peoples', useful perhaps in certain contexts, represent the past rather than the future of international affairs: even though the 'state' does not represent the ideal political form for organizing international society and its law, its potential is significant; it is not to the past that one should look for a solution, for (it should be remembered) every political form (nation, people, ...) has its ideal form.

Writers of the eighteenth century saw clearly the advantages of the nation state: Vattel observed that the first duty of the state is to provide necessities for its people;[60] the second is to procure happiness for the people;[61] and the third is to fortify the nation again external attacks.[62] This classic statement of the responsibilities of and reasons for nation states continues to offer a sound justification for their existence. This is despite the historical and current state of international affairs, which for the past two hundred years have been the affairs of *states*. A poignantly optimistic argument is put forward by Vattel:

> Europe forms a political system, an integral body, closely connected by the relations and different interests of the nations inhabiting this part of the world. It is not, as formerly, a confused heap of detached pieces, each of which thought herself very little concerned in the fate of the others, and seldom regarded things which did not immediately concern her. The continual attention of sovereigns to every occurrence, the constant residence of ministers, and the perpetual negotiations, make of modern Europe a kind of republic, of which the members—each independent, but all linked together by the ties of common interest—unite for the maintenance of order and liberty.[63]

Vattel's argument was tragically premature; he did not live to see the devastation of two World Wars during which all European nations lost time and opportunity for development, and were set back culturally. The ambivalent position of nation states, which are distinctly non-ideal but necessary political forms, is captured in the following argument of Pufendorf's: states exist for the peace and safety of the world's peoples; in so doing, civil states implement the law of nature, but it is difficult at any point in time to say whether this particular array of states at this particular point in time are fulfilling God's Will.[64] For while the lands were divided up

[59] Cf Allott (n 48) 13.50.244: a nation exists as an ethnic, cultural, or linguistic group not formed under institutions of government.
[60] Vattel (n 2) VI.
[61] Ibid, XI.
[62] Ibid, XIV.
[63] Ibid, III.3.47.
[64] Pufendorf, *DINEG* (n 53) VII.3.2.

by God's people, it remains true that the available land on earth is fixed and does not change over time, whereas the borders of states are constantly being redefined and redrawn.[65] Of course a defence of the nation state cannot be historical; it must be normative. The principal outlines of such a justification are outlined in the second paragraph of this Section. But one may add to them. A key premise is that, just as the individual is incomplete in itself, and requires society for completion: indeed for life, basic necessities, avenues of reasonable labour, healthcare, civility; so the state (the *first*) society that [seems to be] perfect (complete in itself)[66] is itself revealed to be incomplete, and dependent for its wellbeing upon international society under international law.[67]

Such are the arguments against the modern view that international society is the society of all humanity, and its laws the laws of all peoples. The argument can be summed up thus: human beings (individuals) may be the ultimate subjects of international law; but they are not its *primary* subjects. International law is a form of governance, in which individuals are represented (well or badly) by their governments. It is therefore the states run by those governments that require most to be regulated: in their economic activity (which is not individual or even collective activity), military activity, treaty-making activity, law-making activity, advocacy before international tribunals, etc. The state's mediating activity is an element of the principle of subsidiarity: (a) individuals benefit—culturally, socially, economically—from international law-making and diplomacy, (though most never realise it) which they cannot themselves bring about. These benefits range from vast infrastructure improvements to the cost of oranges. A swift history lesson illustrates the point: consider Henry VI's inability to settle upon or advance coherent policies due to his dependence on courtiers, their control of the royal purse, and their diverging interests. Where political power is not concentrated in a well-defined entity (as with the state rather than the *estates* of the medieval period) the ability to conclude stable political alliances, economic reform, advance the interests of citizens, etc are hopelessly diminished. Like Rawls, Allott argues that there should be continuity between the law and legal ordering of domestic society and that of the international relations between nations, that is (in effect) against the principle of subsidiarity.[68] But he obscures the fact that (whatever its imperfections) the nation state is a highly successful unit for directing effort towards and providing focus for a range of goods, services, cultural exchange, economic relationships and so on. And he ignores the fact (b) that states are more proximate to their citizens and can more carefully and context-sensitively create spaces in which individuals and families can be left to flourish on their own terms,

[65] Ibid, I.1.6.

[66] See *Politics* I.1.

[67] See again Suarez, *DL* (n 19) II.19.9; also Allott (n 48) 12.13.347–12.19.349.

[68] Allott, *HN* (n 33) 10.209 Proem.

without (i) interference or (ii) neglect. Thus the argument that international society is first and foremost the society of all humanity, unnecessarily aggregates the subjects of that hypothetical society: for we need to take account of the wide variety of ways of living across the world; states rather than 'peoples' (i.e. 'the actors in the Society of Peoples, *just as citizens are the actors in domestic society*') are the most appropriate way of advancing the interests and wellbeing of those people.[69]

The principle of subsidiarity, as well as the arguments above, form part of the justification of the nation state. Such a justification is specifically a justification of the power that states have and use. It is, to repeat, a justification that must be normative, not historical. In fact there is no historical origin of the power of states, just as there is no historical origin of political power within domestic societies: power is always present in human societies, whether acknowledged or not for what it is, and however diffuse and disorganized. The *purpose* of such power is to procure key benefits for the population, to rule wherever possible through law, and thus to ensure all of the advantages of the rule of law (see Section X.3). Such would be the aim of all states that Rawls labels 'democratic' or 'decent'. Uses of power for repressive ends, or to maintain a dictator in power, are not focal instances of power, and resemble, as Aquinas says, military force rather than civil power.[70] Such states are of the kind Rawls labels 'outlaw states'. Power in the focal sense is naturally limited by its orientation towards the common good of the community. Such power cannot be legitimately wielded in order to gain foreign territories or realise imperial ambitions; it cannot be employed in order to subjugate the population for the purposes of extracting wealth or hard labour, or for depriving them of any say in the internal politics of the state. 'Power' of this kind is recognizable as a (diminished) form of political power in virtue of its relationship to focal instances. States draw their legitimacy from their representation of human beings in the international community, and by upholding that community. Thus we may say that state power in international law depends upon the extent of its justice.[71]

Theologically, the use of state power in international relations is connected to God's saving power insofar as such power confirms international law. But the idea that theology 'cannot recommend policy, it can only point to wrongs'[72] is mistaken. Some policies clearly can be recommended by theology: such as a policy of pursuing peace in all possible circumstances, and of going to war only for a just cause, and only when all other avenues have been exhausted. Other policies also come to mind: coming together with other states in relief efforts where there is famine or natural disaster; entering into friendly dialogue and trading agreements with other nations; and creating international institutions to which states may

[69] Cf Allott (n 48) 7.5.118: 'there is one humanity ... one society'. See also Philip Allott, *Eutopia* (Edward Elgar 2016) 11–29.

[70] Aquinas, *ST* (n 11) I-II.96.4c.

[71] Cf Allen Buchanan in Besson & Tasioulas, *TPIL* (n 13) 80–81.

[72] Reed (n 43) 36.

submit grievances and legal proceedings in order to bring difficulties to a peaceful close. But not all such policies: Drietzel observes that Pufendorf did not hesitate to suggest that states use commerce to strangle other states or cancel treaties if this would aid the *salus populi*.[73] The phenomenon of 'statecraft' is distinct from the policy-making in which states ought to engage for the benefit of (a) their peoples, and (b) the international community either in whole or part. Enlightened states realise that what strengthens and benefits international society under law also benefits their peoples, who benefit from peace, trade agreements etc. A purely non-theological vision of international society under law would have to fall back on the idea of human rights. If we are not God's children, what is the basis for the thought that we possess certain rights 'in virtue of our humanity'? But there are additional doubts: Raz states that human rights are universal only in a temporal sense: certain human rights depend upon particular social or political institutions that did not exist until recently.[74] Thus a society that does not educate its population is not to be censured if it simply lacks the infrastructure and knowledge to do so.[75] But the answer to this is that, indeed, such rights depend upon given circumstances, for they are *positive* rights (see Section VI.3). But such persons would clearly possess a *natural* right to be educated even in situations where that right cannot be actualized: it would be perverse to say that such persons are deprived of a right which they have in virtue of being the kind of being that they are. The current suggestion is not that the idea of human rights ought to be dispensed with wholesale, for the Universal Declaration on Human Rights is one of the central institutions in current international relations that commands the respect of states. It is perhaps the strongest reminder to states that their sovereignty is not absolute.

While there is no need to assume that forms of governance in international law should entirely resemble those of domestic legal order (e.g. kingship, oligarchy, plutocracy, democracy), there is yet a need to think about the ideal ordering of international law and its promotion of the common good. Even in its imperfect and (if compared with domestic society) underdeveloped condition, international law secures a range of benefits that are not available to states or groups of states alone:[76] the most obvious benefits include reducing the inherent danger of the international realm through its rules and tribunals, stabilizing the trading systems and striving for international peace, all in cases where unanimity cannot be expected. The presence of international institutions offer some of the same political benefits as domestic systems of law in the national sphere: such as correcting the view of the subject(s) in regard to a mistaken view of justice, through international treaty negotiations, or in making clear to a state that its circumstances

[73] See Besson & Tasioulas, *TPIL* (n 13) 47.
[74] Raz in Besson & Tasioulas, *TPIL* (n 13)333.
[75] Ibid, 334.
[76] Besson & Tasioulas, *TPIL* (n 13) 4.

are not exceptional.[77] Furthermore, by operating within the international legal system, states are reminded that, regardless of actual size, there is equality before the law: most especially before international courts and tribunals. Increasingly, states are subject to compulsory jurisdiction of international administrative institutions through membership of (for example) the WTO treaty, the Convention on the law of the sea, and the Statute of the International Criminal Court: states that do not conform to their obligations under such systems are faced with expulsion or exclusion from the benefits of the regime.[78] And operating within the international legal order entails that states must give reasons for their actions in public, and must as part of those reasons make reference to operative international legal norms. This is especially true of so-called peremptory norms, in terms of which states do not possess the power to vary or modify the extent of their obligations.[79] It should be clear therefore that international law does not encroach on the self-determination of states, for states were never unlimited in that sense.

## XII.5. THE OBLIGATIONS OF STATES: PEACE

The central question concerning the nature of states' obligations to peace is whether they can morally accede to a norm or norms of international law, which (in those states' solemn opinion) is or are unjust, on the basis that a failure to subscribe to the values and terms thereof will bring about greater injustice. For on the one hand, is the principle that one must never engage in evil that good may come, and on the other, that one must avoid the merest scrupulosity which would prevent any progress being made whatever to the international society and to international relations. The question is highly relevant to the aims of international peace, because of the dangers of lawlessness and the threat that injustice holds for peace. To resolve this question, recourse must be had to a casuistry. All rules of international law restrain the alternative of anarchy or lawlessness. The demerits of anarchy in the international realm are clear enough. Rules therefore that introduce a measure of governance into international society, whilst leaving in place a measure of lawlessness, are imperfect (unjust), but states can legitimately accede to such rules as (a) improving the situation of international society, and (b) not *introducing* additional evils. But states may *not* accede to norms proposed by other international actors that introduce injustices that did not exist before, though every effort should be made to give effect to those aspects of an unjust norm that improve international society without the injustice.[80] Thus it may be the case that a treaty is proposed

[77] See Lefkowitz (n 30) 108.

[78] Ibid, 94.

[79] Ibid, 55.

[80] For a domestic example regarding abortion statutes see Finnis, 'Just votes for unjust laws' in John Finnis, *The Collected Essays of John Finnis* (OUP 2011) IV.22.

to regulate trade in essential services that is likely to increase reliance of developing nations on incentives and loans on unjust terms. Such a rule may have a positive effect on international society in introducing regulation into an arena of international affairs that was either unsatisfactory or without clear law. But a state should not accede to such a treaty, however beneficial it would be to its domestic economy or to the state government's prospects of re-election. Every state's obligation to seek and defend peace must be given high (though not absolute) priority over other aims, for international peace is of benefit to all, and international war is to the detriment of all.

It should not be forgotten that justice is a prerequisite of any lasting peace, thus the aims of international peace and justice go hand in hand. (A discussion of justice in international law will be deferred to Section XII.7). However it is worth mentioning that sometimes (rarely) it is necessary to put justice above the aims of peace: there can be just wars (see Section XII.6). Some discussion is appropriate here of Kant's articles of perpetual peace. Kant is correct to say that the aim of international community is not the pursuit of mere temporary peaces between various nations, but that of peace in perpetuity. Roughly reconstructed, the articles are that: (1) states must *intend* lasting peace with other nations, without secret intention to resort to future war; (2) states are not the subject of trade or barter; they do not have economic value; (3) defensive weapons, instruments of war and military personnel must eventually be abolished; (4) no foreign economic aid should be used for the purposes of enabling a state to wage war; (5) states must not intervene in the internal affairs of other states using military force; (6) no state shall use stratagems of war (such as assassins and secret agents) that render mutual trust in a future peace impossible.[81] To these propositions can be added the following: that states have a right and duty of self-preservation, and this can be pursued, not by war, but only by *peace* with all states. And further: errors of religion are not to be punished by human efforts, nor those who reject the Christian religion; it was no part of Christ's teaching that people be brought to true religion by violent acts or punishment in this life.[82] Yet the majority of natural law philosophers recognise that war is sometimes a necessary path to peace: 'The sole object of a just war is peace, including the removal of menaces to peace.'[83] Even Kant comprehends that warfare must continue in the international realm for the time being, until such times as all states can be manoeuvred into a position of peace with one another. In consequence, we may say that the *primary* duty of states is to seek and preserve peace, and the *secondary* duty is to conduct war, where unavoidable, for just ends, and to confine military activities to securing that end, and nothing further (e.g. plunder, 'regime change', economic warfare etc).

[81] Kant (n 40) 344–347; see also Vattel (n 2) II.4.54.
[82] Grotius, *DIBP* (n 12) II.20.47–48.
[83] Grotius, *DIPC* (n 36) IX.7.1; see also Grotius, *DIBP* (n 12) I.1.1: 'war is undertaken to secure peace'.

However, political theorists and jurists fatally underestimate the fallen condition of humanity, implicit in their optimism concerning the future of international law and international relations. They implicitly affirm a final solution to humankind's predicament (e.g. Kant's 'cosmopolitanism', Allott's 'eutopia'), but no such solution exists. The exercise of right and law to improve the condition of some individual, state or nation almost invariably takes the form of an exercise of a power that impedes, or is contrary to the interests of, other individuals, states or nations. A lucrative trillion dollar contract for services is concluded by one state contrary to another. Arms are sold to one state to the detriment of another state. Supplies of an essential drug are stockpiled by a small group of states against a pandemic, or else are sold to developing nations at interest. One state annexes a smaller state which contains a sizeable minority who ethnically belong to the annexing state, but a large population who do not. Developed nations exploit the environment to the detriment of every human being. One could cite further examples. There is no end point to political action; there is no political formula that will unlock 'perpetual peace'. No such peace is available in this life, only God's peace in the next.[84] But the efforts that states make to generate a just and peaceful international society are not all in vain. The primary and secondary duties of states redound to the benefit of all humankind, and are in-keeping with God's divine plan. The absence of a true common good in the circumstances of the present or foreseeable future is a reminder that states must not relax their efforts to achieve justice in the international realm. State governments must remember the words of Pope Paul VI: 'Development [is] the new name for peace.'[85]

The foregoing argument raises a further issue. Its implication is that the international common good has no definite shape, but only temporary configurations. Many aspects of the present state of the world are decidedly unjust and clearly not steps towards perpetual peace (and justice). The situation in which the world's richest nations become richer at the expense of the poor is not the march of progress (see Section XII.7).[86] But there are in fact many features of current international society that demonstrate some progress towards a global common good.[87] For instance, international borders in most of the world are relatively settled and not the object of contestation. Furthermore, the creation of international legal institutions has played an important part in securing international peace. They are

[84] Cf Reed (n 42) 310; see Isaiah 9:6–7.

[85] Encyclical of Pope Paul VI, 1967 *Populorum progressio* § 76.

[86] Ibid, § 8.

[87] See Encyclical *Solicitudo rei socialis* § 6; see also Liam Murphy, 'Law Beyond the State: Some Philosophical Questions' 28 (2017) *European Journal of International Law* 203; Kostiantyn Gorobets, 'The International Rule of Law and the Idea of Normative Authority' 12 (2020) *Hague J on the Rule of Law* 227; Noora Arajarvi, 'The Core Requirements of the International Rule of Law in the Practice of States' 13 (2021) *Hague J on the Rule of Law* 173 (warning that purely abstract norms lack effectiveness; whether the reader agrees with this depends upon his or her response to the treatment of natural law first principles earlier in this book).

an aspect of the general obligation of legal subjects to seek first a legal solution to a problem of contention, through the appropriate legal channels, rather than resorting immediately to violence, to accept the verdict of the court or tribunal as settling the matter, and to refrain from nullifying an adverse judgment by proceeding to violate its terms through unsanctioned military action.[88] The Nuremberg Trials are a case in point: the guilt of the major war criminals was established judicially (based on natural law)[89] rather than by summary execution; some defendants were reportedly surprised at how well and fairly they were treated.[90] But the trials were fatally flawed due to the refusal to extend criminal responsibility to Allied nations in respect of the mass bombings of Hiroshima, Nagasaki and Dresden. Finally, there is a growing awareness that the common good of the state is not one isolated property but part of the good of others, that is, part of the common good and flourishing of all nations.[91]

This latter point is reflected in some fundamental features of international law. For as Christiano has observed, if international law is a voluntary association, then certain laws will be: (1) structural prerequisites, such as *pacta sunt servanda*; (2) required for the stability of the international legal system, for example peace treaties concluded with defeated states; and (3) express certain limits to that voluntary association, such as peremptory norms against slavery, genocide, torture, etc.[92] To which may be added: (4) that for a system of promise and contract to exist, most if not all must regard the relevant rules as binding upon them regardless of choice and of the preferences of other actors.[93] But it is necessary to remind state governments of a fact that has been obscured since the beginning of the eighteenth century: namely that international society is underpinned not by commerce, but by sociability; that is, not by the minimum morality of the market, but the higher norms of natural law. Thus, Gentili pointed out that the moral system of Justinian's *Digest* is not peculiar to the Roman polity, but extends to all nations.

One key way in which international society differs from domestic society is its reliance on diplomacy to diffuse tensions, create opportunities for peace and (through embassies) curate relationships with foreign powers. Many natural law philosophers elevate the efforts of ambassadors and diplomats, elsewhere dismissed as 'infantile'[94] as a necessary aspect of international relations. Hence Grotius observes that the office of ambassador should be protected to the extent

[88] See Grotius, *DIPC* (n 36) Proleg Rule XII: 'No state or citizen can seek to enforce his own right against another state or citizen ... except by judicial procedure.'

[89] That is, upon the extreme unreasonableness of the criminal acts (which were *mala in se*) and the reasonable approach to, and institutions of, trial and punishment.

[90] See David Luban in Besson & Tasioulas, *TPIL* (n 13) 580.

[91] Rawls (n 38) 12.2.

[92] Christiano in Besson & Tasioulas, *TPIL* (n 5) 122–23.

[93] Hart, *CL* (n 5) 225.

[94] See Allott (n 48) 15.25–26.270. See also Philip Allott, 'Beyond War and Diplomacy: A Giant Step for Mankind' 60 (2018) *German Yearbook of International Law* 269.

of (a) not being tried for small crimes in the host state, and (b) facing expulsion from the host state, rather than trial, to be punished at the will of the home state.[95] The importance of diplomacy is underscored by the fact that adjudication is frequently the last forum of dispute resolution in international society.[96] Diplomacy is often the main instrument by which tensions are reduced between states, and of ensuring the smooth operation of the relevant international laws. It can reduce tensions either completely or to a level at which international litigation is possible. But there is a dark side to diplomacy: it is carried on behind closed doors, the public that is being served does not know on what terms bargains have been concluded, pacts made, deals done, it may be decades later that information is released and a full account of the negotiations almost never appears. Diplomacy is an imperfect but necessary means of creating and maintaining peace between nations.

## XII.6. THE OBLIGATIONS OF STATES: WAR

Warfare in the public international realm is much more hazardous, its outcome much more uncertain, and its long-term effects much more difficult to calculate, than personal violence between private citizens.[97] Thus the rules and doctrines that have emerged to control it are rather unlike the laws that pertain to the use of violence in the private realm. In treating of the obligations of states in relation to war, we are speaking of a state's natural law obligations, and thus secondarily of the *ius gentium* or international law. The natural law tradition has been impressively consistent in its treatment of war. Even Hobbes places limits upon the kind of warfare that is allowed in the 'natural condition': only that which is deemed (however subjectively) to be necessary for preservation of one's being is permitted: a question of proportionality. There are just, as well as unjust, reasons for war.[98] But the most textured treatment of natural law's application to armed conflict is found in the work of Grotius. According to Richard Tuck's interpretation, Grotius's natural law theory is based only on self-preservation and leads to a shallow and impoverished corpus of rights and duties.[99] But this is simply not the case, for it should be remembered that Grotius names his treatise 'Of the law of war and peace': it is not intended as a treatise on natural law as such, nor does Grotius limit his account of war to the narrow self-interest of states. He begins, in fact, by observing that Aristotle's

[95] Grotius, *DIBP* (n 12) II.18.2.

[96] See Paulus in Besson & Tasioulas, *TPIL* (n 13) 207.

[97] It would be foolish indeed to attempt to say everything about this subject that deserves to be said. Instead, I offer some reflections centred largely around the contributions of Grotius, Aquinas, and Vattel.

[98] See *Leviathan* XIII-XIV; see also Christopher Greenwood, 'The Concept of War in Modern International Law' 36 (1987) *International & Comparative Law Quarterly* 283.

[99] Richard Tuck, *The Rights of War and Peace* (OUP 2002) 6. See also Randall Lesaffer, 'Grotius on the Use of Force: Perfect, Imperfect and Civil Wars' 41 (2020) *Grotiana* 255.

warning (that we should not expect more certainty in a subject than is in keeping with its nature); this serves as a reminder that there will be many cases in which it is difficult to discern whether the cause of a particular war is just.[100] There can be doubt on both sides.[101] Yet there is, as the tradition unanimously maintains, such as thing as a just war.[102] The ambiguity of war is reflected in the natural law precepts; for God's initial division of the lands between the twelve tribes indicates that national borders are beneficial and good, yet they are also an aspect of His wrath, for they are temporary and subject to violent contestation.[103] Moreover, the judgment that the enemy is not on God's 'side' is often not secure, for it violates the charitable love of enemies[104] which may include punishment for wrongdoing, but which also involves the sincere will to help them rejoin the international community on just terms. So-called 'holy wars' should be avoided in favour of peaceful dialogue between religions: there is no basis in natural law for aggressive holy wars.[105] The rulers of aggressor states who engage in such wars cannot enter the Kingdom of Heaven until they have fully repented.[106]

There are, in the classical tradition, two stages to the commencement of war: there is the warning [*dentuntio*], followed by the declaration of hostilities [*indictio*].[107] War must be declared in order to be lawful;[108] war cannot be commenced at the same time as the declaration.[109] Every just war must have its origin in one of four causes: (1) self-defence; (2) defence of property (i.e. the stock of human goods); (3) recovery of debt whether contractual or arising from another source; (4) any injury, whether by word or deed, arising from an unjust intent.[110] To this we can add that the end of all war is peace; but ought to be a *just* peace. Thus a war will not be morally justified unless (i) its aims and (ii) its means are just. Thus (iii) wars may be justly entered into only in defence of a people, and (iv) the means used must be proportionate to that end. From these four causes there derive basic duties of states in relation to war. These are discussed below. But it is necessary to interject here that it has been argued by McMahon that the rights and responsibilities of warring states are asymmetric, such that just combatants may lawfully attack unjust combatants, but that unjust combatants cannot lawfully attack just

[100] Grotius, *DIBP* (n 12) II.23.1. For the classic view on just war theory see Michael Waltzer, *Just & Unjust Wars* (5th edn, Basic Books 2015) 3–111 & 329–45.
[101] Ibid, II.25.5.
[102] See e.g. Grotius, *DIPC* (n 36) III.1.1.
[103] Reed (n 43) 238.
[104] Ibid, 165–67.
[105] See Aquinas, *ST* (n 11) II-II.10.8 ad 3.
[106] Grotius, *DIBP* (n 12) III.2.3.
[107] Grotius, *DIPC* (n 36) VIII.7.2.
[108] Grotius, *DIBP* (n 12) III.3.5.
[109] Ibid, III.3.13.
[110] Grotius, *DIPC* (n 36) VI.7.1; Grotius, *DIBP* (n 12) II.1.2.

combatants.[111] This is a confusion: for without unjust combatants there cannot be just *combatants*; if the former cannot lawfully attack the latter, then (presumably) the unjust combatants would be in a purely defensive posture, and not open to attack by just combatants at all. Even if it is true that an aggressor state cannot lawfully attack an innocent state, this asymmetry does not affect the combatants of either state, whose military training would exclude questions of responsibility of states. This does not, however, imply that soldiers of an aggressor state should not reasonably lay down their arms due to the extreme injustice of the aims for which they fight.

In modern international law, two conditions govern the resort to war: (1) that the war is one of self-defence in the face of aggression, and (2) that it proceeds with the UN Security Council's agreement. The combined force of these requirements is to avoid states going to war purely on their own interpretation of events, and to seek an independent (or at least neutral) perspective of the justice of the proposed action. The need for these two conditions can be explained in classical terms as that the justice or injustice of a proposed war is not a subjective, but an objective, matter: or in still other classical terms, that no war can be just on both sides.[112] Indeed Grotius's enumeration of reasons that are inadequate to justify war is the occasion of a remark that states need to be aware that the justice of their intentions may only be apparent and not real.[113] Among the aims of war cannot be: the desire to diminish the power of a neighbour or reduce an unused threat;[114] sheer advantage;[115] disappointment in procuring an alliance; desire for richer lands; discovery of precious materials on another's territory; desire to rule over another people, even if for their good; desire for a universal empire of the Church; the desire to fulfil a prophecy.[116] If a war is objectively just, but carried on in the belief that it is unjust, then the war is contrary to natural law.[117] A just war that involves mercenaries is thereby rendered unjust.[118]

None of the above remarks on just wars entail the conclusion that war is somehow, or in some way, 'natural'.[119] It is, in the terms of classical natural law

[111] See Besson & Tasioulas, *TPIL* (n 13) 159. This would seem to confuse the foundational principles of International Humanitarian Law (i.e. the *ius ad bellum*) which seek to protect *non-combatants* and which merely limit the methods of warfare used in relation to combatants.

[112] Grotius, *DIPC* (n 36) VI.7.2; Vattel (n 2) III.3.39. But see Ian Hunter, 'Law, War & Casuistry in Vattel's *Ius Gentium*' 28 (2011) *Parergon* 87; Stephen Neff, 'Vattel and the Laws of War: A Tale of Three Circles' in Vincent Chetail & Peter Haggenmacher, *Vattel's International Law from a XXI Century Perspective* (Brill 2011) 317.

[113] Grotius, *DIBP* (n 12) II.22.3.

[114] Ibid, II.1.17; cf Vattel (n 2) III.1.5: 'We attack a nation with a view either to obtain something to which we lay claim, to punish her for an injury she has done us, or to prevent one which she is preparing to do, and thus avert a danger with which she seems to threaten us.'

[115] Vattel (n 2) III.3.33.

[116] Grotius, *DIBP* (n 12) II.22.5.

[117] Ibid, II.23.2.

[118] Ibid, II.25.9.

[119] See Allott (n 48) 15.10.264.

theory, a 'privation', and therefore a falling away from what is natural, namely, the natural goods of peace and sociability. But this does not of course mean that warfare will come to an end at some point in history: human preferences for evil over good will not cease, though they continue to be unreasonable. The unnaturalness of warfare underpins the position of conscientious objectors, who should not be pressed into action with the usual duty of a people to defend the homeland, but should be found productive but non-military work.[120] Further, no unnatural (that is, unreasonable) act may enter into the conduct of warfare: thus there are certain acts which, according to Aristotle and his successors, can never be done rightly or with a right will: these involve the use of deception (disinformation, espionage), though it is permissible negatively to withhold the truth from the enemy;[121] or the use of rape as a weapon of war;[122] or the killing of prisoners of war to pressure an enemy into conceding. But the natural law philosophers we have been examining could not have foreseen the technological means by which dictators can in modern times oppress their peoples. This explains their attitude, not wholly incorrect or inappropriate in the conditions of modernity, that one state may not lawfully interfere in the internal affairs of another state. The doctrine is clearly expressed in the work of Vattel: 'It is an evident consequence of the liberty and independence of nations, that all have a right to be governed as they think proper, and that no state has the smallest right to interfere in the government of another. Of all the rights that can belong to a nation, sovereignty is, doubtless, the most precious, and that which other nations ought the most scrupulously to respect, if they would not do her an injury . . .'[123]

These statements should be viewed as exaggerations, or at the least require to be interpreted in the light of qualifying statements. Natural law clearly encompasses a right to intervene to free a population from the grip of a dictator, just as it is legitimate for one individual to defend another from someone committing an assault. Thus Grotius remarks that it is permissible (even obligatory?) to go to war with another state for the sake of its people.[124] This may seem to contradict the proposition above that one cannot fight even for the good of another people; but the explanation for this remark is that intervention seems to be limited to those peoples with whom one has some kinship, and does not involve the desire to govern. In modern times, international lawyers have been more open to humanitarian intervention: Franck argues that humanitarian intervention is permissible if substantially more lives are saved than lost through the military action.[125] Such a

[120] Grotius, *DIBP* (n 12) II.26.5.

[121] Ibid, III.1.6–9; cf Pufendorf, *On the Whole Duty of Man and Citizen According to the Law of Nature* II.16.

[122] Grotius, *DIBP* (n 12) III.4.19. This is difficult to square with Grotius's own remarks that it is permissible to firebomb the property or vessels of the warring state even if women and children (i.e. noncombatants) are on board: see III.1.2–4.

[123] Vattel (n 2) II.4.54.

[124] Grotius, *DIBP* (n 12) II.25.6.

[125] See Thomas Franck, 'Legality and Legitimacy in Humanitarian Intervention' 47 (2006) *Nomos* 143.

utilitarian perspective cannot be endorsed: either the oppressed population has a *right* to be relieved, or they do not. There is some considerable inconsistency in the international community's approach to humanitarian intervention, making any emergent norm difficult to classify or pin down. Certainly, the doctrine cannot be taken seriously so long as it is applied only to strategically important nations, and is unused in the context of other, equally pressing populations such as the Kurdish minority in Turkey.[126] In general, the use of military force to bring about an end to oppression ought to be carried out under the auspices of international institutions, such as the United Nations, but in any event should be pursued so as (1) to relieve the oppressed population, and (2) to bring the oppressor government into line with natural law, i.e. to ensure that the population remains emancipated. This can involve the removal of a dictator, so long as the intention is to bring about the least change possible to fulfil aims (1) and (2). That is, the force used must be *proportionate* to the end. Furthermore, the force must be used strictly for the ends in (1) and (2), not for further political reasons: in other words, the action must be in good faith, for (as Grotius observes) good faith is the foundation of the entire international community.[127]

The duties and rights of a state to enter into warfare might therefore be summarized as follows: (i) states have the right and duty to defend their populations and common good against external aggression, unless the situation is hopeless and war would more greatly harm the people;[128] (ii) states have a right to restrain evils, i.e. hostile acts that leave a state no room except to go to war;[129] (iii) states have a right and duty to intervene in the domestic affairs of another state in order to save the population from the oppression of a tyrant, or to prevent or bring to a halt a genocide or an attempt to suppress a culture or religion among the people; (iv) states have a duty to limit lethal actions to the minimum required to bring about victory; (v) they have a duty to care adequately for prisoners of war, and to avoid use of torture; (vi) states have a duty to consult with other nations or with international institutions before initiating actions, unless the defence of the realm is immediately under threat; (vi) the right of states to go to war is limited to bringing about the termination of the threat to their common good, having secured which it is necessary to seek peace; (vii) any action must be proportionate to the aim of securing victory (i.e. bringing about peace); (viii) there is a standing obligation to seek and maintain peace with other states; (ix) no state action may breach international law in order to obtain victory, nor contravene the natural law.

This swift account of the rights and obligations of states regarding war spans both the *ius ad bellum* and the *ius in bello*. That lawyer's distinction is not very

[126] See Danilo Zolo in Besson & Tasioulas, *TPIL* (n 13) 561.
[127] Grotius, *DIBP* (n 12) III.25.1.
[128] Aquinas, *ST* (n 11) II-II.40.1 ad 2.
[129] Ibid, II-II.83.8.

helpful for as Grotius observes, a state's willingness to use unjust means in war nullifies the justice of its decision to go to war, i.e. renders that decision unjust.[130] For simplicity the account given above ignores large questions such as secession, war crimes, punishment of states, and the *ius post bellum*. Those issues too derive much of their force from natural law, which is a source of international law, but by way of *determinatio*. Thus for example, natural law requires the punishment of war crimes and crimes against humanity, but does not state (1) how those guilty of such crimes are to be punished and (2) through what mechanisms. Current international institutional arrangements for the prosecution of war crimes could justly have been different. Indeed, there are obvious injustices to the way in which such institutions currently operate: they operate in contravention of the natural law demand that all states are equal and equally under the law.

## XII.7. JUSTICE IN THE INTERNATIONAL COMMUNITY

The world's states are not equal, either in size or wealth. This in itself is not a problem of justice. It is not a source of obligation for more developed states. The technological development and political circumstances which permitted the world's wealthiest countries to bring to their citizens many benefits of good living, insofar as they are not produced by exploitation of less developed or affluent nations, are not of themselves an injustice towards less developed states. But all persons, whatever the country of their birth, have certain basic natural rights: to life, education, health care, at least minimum prosperity, and so on (see Section V.5). The central question of international justice is: who owes duties to supply these basic needs, and on what basis? To meet these needs would necessitate a significant shift of wealth, services, intellectual property and workers to developing nations. It is impossible morally to sustain assent to the current state of disparity in wealth in international society. Hence the issue that must be faced is the extent to which affluent, developed states owe obligations of economic assistance to less developed states. The term 'state' in this context is appropriate, for only at the level of domestic government can concerted action against poverty take place; however, the term can mislead for the costs of the diversion of goods, services, technical expertise, and so on are ultimately borne by individual citizens of those states, most often through progressive taxation or unavailability of certain goods. This is entirely in keeping with the demands that justice places on each person (see below).

It is not difficult to point to severe economic injustices in the international community. Thomas Pogge states that the current rules of trade allow the rulers of developing nations to enter into economic relationships of a most exploitative

[130] Grotius, *DIBP* (n 12) II.23.2 (see above); Aquinas's position is similar: see John Finnis, *Aquinas: Moral, Political, and Legal Theory* (OUP 1998) 285n .

kind: economic activity centres upon which state has the cheapest and most hardworking workforce (e.g. slave labour, child workers).[131] Such countries are ruled by autocrats whose focus is not on improving the situation of the poverty-stricken, but on maintaining their own grip on power:[132] forms of corruption in which affluent states have little interest. Ethical consumerism is still in its infancy. Thus the entire structure of international relations has been created by affluent nations, often in contravention of natural laws of justice and fairness.[133] The question of justice posed above is therefore more complex that perhaps first appears. For Aristotle's principle, in modern times encapsulated by the principle of subsidiarity, requires that moral responsibility rests first and foremost on those close to home, i.e. one's neighbours, rather than any generalised principle which unreasonably attempts to promote the good of everyone. Thus states must first take action against poverty, hunger and homelessness internally, before looking further afield. It is also true that Christ was asked 'Who is my neighbour?'[134] His answer, in parable, is that everyone is my neighbour. Similarly, Aquinas asks the question: ought I to love my fellow nationals more than the inhabitants of other nations far away? In response he observes that though I have many reasons to love fellow nationals (such as linguistic community, proximity, shared values and culture), it is possible to love others for no other reason than charity itself.[135] Hence our obligations in charity (love) do extend to others in remote parts of the globe, and indeed affluent states do provide aid to developing nations, though in insufficient quantities, and in parallel with the very practices (such as lending at interest) which maintain those nations in poverty.

It is reasonable for (and unreasonable not for) developed states to donate their surplus wealth to developing nations: not only monetary wealth but social, academic and technological capital. Too often, surplus wealth is diverted into other areas such as weapons, weapons that are 'needed' because of the general level of technological prowess of other developed nations. But there is nothing wrong as such with disparities in levels of wealth: a quite general movement of goods and capital to developing nations, in order to achieve economic parity, would result in fewer arts, less scope for scientific innovation, impoverished cultural life, lower healthcare provision, and so on.[136] A levelling-down of the international community is not to anyone's long-term advantage. There are other matters to consider, such as a state's inward investment in green energy or rapid transit, which are of benefit to all nations and future generations. These projects can to some extent take priority in a state's spending plans. Vattel expresses this idea in his 'first law' of state

[131] Thomas Pogge in Besson & Tasioulas, *TPIL* (n 13) 428.
[132] Ibid.
[133] Ibid, 417.
[134] Luke 10:29.
[135] Aquinas, *ST* (n 11) II-II.26.7c.
[136] For the basic principle see Finnis, *NLNR* (n 31) 174.

responsibility under natural law: 'The first general law that we discover in the very object of the society of nations, is that each individual nation is bound to contribute every thing in her power to the happiness and perfection of all the others ... But the duties that we owe to ourselves being unquestionably paramount to those we owe to others—a nation owes herself in the first instance, and in preference to all other nations, to do every thing she can to promote her own happiness and perfection.'[137]

The idea that, in the words of a prominent international lawyer, there is no substance to the idea of justice, is therefore incorrect.[138] For example, states must strive to enable free and fair exchange, under norms of fairness and reasonable profit: a black market in goods is to no one's benefit. Similarly, the international community must suppress black markets in harmful products such as drugs or weapons, which cause untold misery on a global scale. If affluent states are serious in their rhetoric of human rights held by every person 'solely in virtue of their humanity', then they have an obligation in justice to provide some assistance in bringing those in poverty or oppression into possession of those rights. Fundamentally, as Suarez observes, in order to be just, the law must be orientated towards the common good.[139]

There is such a thing as the global common good. It is the flourishing of the international community, ultimately of persons. Such a condition does not come about on its own, but requires the coordinated actions of states. State governments therefore have duties that are outward facing as well as inward facing. From the particular goods of persons to the grand affairs of international society, all is under the governance of natural law.

*Salve, Regina, Mater misericordiæ,*
*vita, dulcedo, et spes nostra, salve.*
*Ad te clamamus exsules filii Hevæ,*
*Ad te suspiramus, gementes et flentes*
*in hac lacrimarum valle.*
*Eia, ergo, advocata nostra, illos tuos*
*misericordes oculos ad nos converte;*
*Et Jesum, benedictum fructum ventris tui,*
*nobis post hoc exsilium ostende.*
*O clemens, O pia, O dulcis Virgo Maria.*
*Ora pro nobis, sancta Dei Genitrix,*
*Ut digni efficiamur promissionibus Christi.*

[137] Vattel (n 2) Proleg §§ 13–14.
[138] Allott (n 48) 5.41.82.
[139] Suarez, *DL* (n 19) I.4.3; 'it would be against every canon of rectitude for the common good to be subordinated to the private good in any community' (ibid, I.7.4).

# Notes

## CHAPTER I

### I.1.

*Natural law does not encompass the whole of ethics*: This directly opposes Finnis, *Natural Law & Natural Rights* (2nd edn OUP 2011), 437; see also 18, 23, 251, 280, 374. It receives confirmation in (for instance) Aquinas's treatment of infused vs natural virtues in the context of the theological virtue of charity, *ST* I-II.63.1-4. Also see Grotius, *De Iure Belli ac Pacis* I.2.5(1): 'matters that pertain to a domain outside the law of nature, and do not properly belong to it, can be the subject of prohibition or command by the divine law', i.e. as a matter of God's free will in creating moral demands outside the domain of natural law. (For an equivalent passage in Aquinas see e.g. *ST* II-II.57.2 ad 3, II-II.57.3).

*Conversational interpretation versus interpretation of a social practice*: See Dworkin, *Law's Empire* (Fontana 1986), 54–55. The point in the text holds true even when the practice is considered 'in its best light' or so as to make it 'the best example of its genre': for the question is then by reference to whose ideal or which set of values is the interpreter considering the practice? It should be noted that Finnis also acknowledges the possibility of neutral, value-free descriptions in 'descriptive social science' (see *NLNR* 426–28).

*Practical philosophy*: Aristotle, *Nicomachean Ethics* II.2.1103b; Aquinas, *Eth*, II.2.256. See also Aristotle, *De Anima* III.2.432b–33a: contemplation of an object (as to be pursued or avoided) does not invariably invoke action. Finnis states the case for the evaluative basis of legal concepts, but does not appear to recognize the practical starting point of legal philosophy, which he regards (like his opponents) as a social science: *NLNR* 3–4, 18–20, 426–28.

*Practical point of view and the principal case*: It may be, also, that participants (willing or otherwise) in a legal order like that of the Nazis could go so far as misidentifying the peripheral case as the central, and regard characteristics intrinsic to the central case, such as moral goodness, as peripheral. The unreasonableness of any such view is demonstrated by a precept to be discussed later, namely that of Aquinas at *Summa Theologiae* I-II.94.2c, 'The good is to be done and pursued, and the bad is to be avoided.' The immediate force of this precept extends over the broadest range, since every person manifests it in every practical choice and decision (see Section II.3), but in the principal meaning or central case of the precept 'good' refers to moral good, and 'bad' to moral badness. The practical question that identifies the principal case of law, is therefore of pursuing human good in the proper sense of that term, unrestrictedly and without relativity to ideological commitments or the private ends of some person or group.

*A theory of law cannot achieve generality, unless it perceives this point (and the point of similar efforts in varied times and circumstances) as an instance of the effort to pursue and secure certain human goods*: The reader might ask, why not begin with governance, or with the tyrannical desire to enrich the ruler at the expense of his subjects? The answer must be that (1) governance is not an end in itself, but a goal-directed activity that can only be understood in terms of securing (human) goods of one sort or another; and (2) the tyrant is still using law to pursue goods, but in a highly immoral way by securing goods for himself at the expense of others.

*Aquinas on tyranny*: The objection (that tyrannical laws are not aimed at making citizens good) is due to Aristotle (*Politics* III.6); Aquinas disagrees, not by opposing the idea that laws seek to make citizens good, but by casting doubt on the legality of tyrannical 'laws', which will become in some cases merely a corruption of law: *ST* I-II.92.1 ad 4.

*The scholastic method and truth*: See e.g. Tobias Schaffner, 'The Eudaemonist Ethics of Hugo Grotius (1583–1645): Modern Moral Philosophy for the Twenty-First Century?' (2016) 6 *Jurisprudence*. This is not to claim that all writers of significance within the natural law tradition practised this method in their work against perceived enemies. See for example Cardinal Newman's sharp ripostes in his *Apologia pro vita sua*, 73.

## I.2.

*Aristotle and Plato on the greatest good*: For an instructive comparison, see R Kraut (ed) *Plato's Republic: Critical Essays* (Rowman & Littlefield 1997), 218–19n.

*Aristotle and the idea of a thing's optimal condition*: See Aristotle, *Politics* I.2.

*Murphy and Kant on happiness*: Both of these positions seem to me to be a mistake. In the case of Murphy, to say that happiness is a distinct aim might seem to be in line with Aquinas's remarks on *beatitudo*, but this ignores the fact of Aquinas's many remarks about the love that accompanies pursuit and realization of human goods, and the rest that one finds in that realization (contrary to Hobbes's vision of the mind as always restless and in motion). On the one hand, happiness aside from pursuit/realization of human goods seems scarcely intelligible; and pursuit/realization without happiness is inexplicable. As I read Murphy, he would affirm the first but deny the second. In relation to the first, Murphy's worry is that happiness reduces to the goodness of human goods (and their choice-worthiness): *Natural Law & Practical Rationality* (CUP 2001) 134. He also denies the contrary viewpoint, that the goodness of human goods is entirely explained by their contribution to happiness (which denies their choice-worthiness). Murphy's concern seems misplaced: he appears to forget that in his own catalogue of goods there is 'excellence in agency', the structuring of one's whole life, the organization of the totality of human goods so as to live a happy and worthwhile life (cf Finnis's practical reasonableness). The problem is reminiscent of Aristotle's dilemma as to whether the happy life is something that can be said to exist only at the end of life rather than during its whole course. The dilemma is easily resolved, for happiness at time *Tn* depends upon happiness at *T1* + *T2* … In other words, one cannot be said to have lived a happy life unless the human goods one has chosen over the course of that life are themselves promotive of happiness. In the case of Kant, the summation of all desires might lead to 'happiness' in the sense of delight, but not the *eudaemonia* of Aristotle, except in case one defines 'desire' as incorporating a rational measure of what is delightful (e.g. delight in knowledge, friendship, etc).

*Kelsen on legal personhood and human existence*: See the discussion in Finnis, *Collected Essays of John Finnis* (OUP 2011) II.1, 24–27, along with further references to Kelsen. Finnis's worry demonstrates that he regards Kelsen as an anti-eudaemonist. He sees not one ounce of truth in Kelsen's position: he regards Kelsen's position only as a source of errors, not a potential source of truths that may be extracted.

*Kelsen and Kant on moral duty*: Modern Kantians such as John Rawls seem to have offered definitive evidence that the right is prior in thought to questions of goodness or the good. But this conclusion falls away the minute we reflect that the conditions of the 'original position' itself are concerned with the good of peace over the ills of all-out war; of stability and social structure (institutions) over anarchy, and of human beings as worth the effort of deliberating about complex social questions, rather than abandoning each person to live by their own wits.

*A calculus of interests aggregates units of utility*: The other great objection to the utilitarian calculus is that it regards pain as unremittingly negative, to be minimized or avoided. It is to be put into the balance against pleasure, synonymous with that which is 'good'. But pain too can often be good: it can alert a person or medical professional to an otherwise symptomless disease, pain in any event prevents the injured limb from further injury (one cannot run on a sprained ankle), and it is instructive of activities that are hazardous or unwise or otherwise not to be done: 'the burnt hand teaches best'.

*Finnis on concept-formation and focal meaning*: Finnis's position has been attacked by a number of theorists, of which I select only one for present purposes: Mark C Murphy. See in particular 'Defect and Deviance in Natural Law Jurisprudence' in John Keown & Robert George (eds) *Reason, Morality and Law: The Philosophy of John Finnis* (OUP 2013) 45. Murphy's starting point is Aquinas's statement that 'law is a dictate of reason': *ST* I-II.90.1c (I use Murphy's translation throughout). From this, Murphy gathers that law is backed by decisive reasons for compliance. It is highly debatable whether Aquinas can be interpreted in this way, for he is especially clear that conformity to law is a matter of habit/disposition (*habitus*): *ST* I-II.90.1 ad 2. Like Aristotle, Aquinas seems to believe that many persons conform to the law *not* because their minds come to agreement with the rational standard, but because they are oppressed by possible sanctions for disobedience (see *NE* II.1.1103b.) Nevertheless, Murphy's summary has some appeal. There are rational standards that do not create decisive reasons for compliance (school rules fall into this category), and there are laws which fail to create rational standards (e.g. immoral laws). But something that is *both* a law and a rational standard may be considered as being backed by decisive reasons for compliance. (Actually, the phrase 'backed by' decisive reasons is rather curious: is it not simpler and truer to say that laws *are* decisive reasons for action? If this were not the case, what exactly provides the backing? On this point Murphy's otherwise careful argument peters out: the elusive 'backing' may come from a 'norm that [carries] overwhelming weight, or through the norm's making precise what is already a mandatory but vague moral rule, or through the norm's giving protected reasons, *or whatever*') (46). Excuse the following lengthy quotation: 'One might claim that law is a dictate of reason in this sense: there is necessity, in that to the kind essentially belong these non-defectiveness conditions, so that *x* cannot be a law and fail to be a dictate of reason without thereby being defective as law. If one brings into being some norm or rule that is, though lacking in adequate reasons for compliance, non-defective, then what one has brought into existence is not a law' (ibid). Finnis believes (as do I) that some laws are so deficient or unjust that they are not laws at all (47): see Chapter X.3, XI.2. Finnis, as Murphy observes, holds the view that (1) unjust laws are defective *precisely as laws* (*NLNR* 24), and (2) that certain laws are so radically defective that from certain viewpoints or purposes they are non-laws. He then suggests that some of these perspectives are privileged and primary, whereas others are secondary or in a reduced sense. (This is a straightforward application of Aristotle's doctrine that one should take one's understandings of the practical life from the *phronimos*, rather than bandits or those of lax morals.) Murphy attributes to Finnis the view that an instance of law with which one does not have decisive reasons to comply is defective precisely as law (49). But this view does not 'immediately follow' from the point about selection of viewpoint; Finnis's interest is rather in the selection of concepts involved in the construction that viewpoint (*NLNR* 15–16). Murphy objects that the point of view of those who create a legal system may differ in important ways from that of those who maintain it in place. Two responses are in order: (1) Legal orders arise and decline in the world in many different contexts and under different pressures and needs; how is one to determine a set of ideas ('viewpoints') common to them all? (2) If such a determination were possible, would one not expect the same viewpoints and needs that attended the creation of the system to inform its ongoing reception? Regardless, Murphy's central claim is that instances of law that are non-central are not immediately theorizable as deficient but merely deviant (50). By way of illustration, it follows from the laws of nature that turtles are slow; if a given turtle is fast this does not render it a defective turtle (merely deviant) but if it lacks a shell, which is the reason for its relative speed, then it is defective as a turtle. Thus a thing is defective if it lacks some property that is 'internal' to the thing in question (52). Murphy states numerous times that, on this view, if a law fails to be a dictate of reason, it is merely deviant rather than defective. But this claim is asserted without being fully examined; it proceeds by example. The central example given is that of a society of unreasonable people who can be guaranteed to under-perform their legal obligations. In this situation a legal system that exceeds what is reasonable is not defective as law, for it simply aims at getting the people to do what is reasonable (53). Two replies can be made: (1) The example is ludicrous, and such hypothetical counter-examples tell us very little about the real world conditions in which legal systems operate; (2) It is far from clear that such laws would be merely deviant and not defective, for the laws are precisely *unjust laws*, and are not rendered just by pointing to salutary effects (in this case, because people will not fully apply them to themselves). Murphy (following Alexy) believes that to be non-deficient, law must be sufficiently good, and the sufficiency lies in its being sufficiently in line with reason to be capable of being backed by decisive reasons (56). This appeals not to justice as the standard for determining deficiency, but to the nature of the illocutionary acts implied in its use: testifying presupposes giving sufficient reasons for believing the truth of what is being said; non-defective advice gives a person good reason to comply with it; non-defective assertion gives the listener good reason to believe what is relayed, etc. And (for Alexy), a constitutional commitment presupposes the justice of the scheme to which commitment is being made. Murphy takes the speech-acts involved in law (commanding, committing, permitting, promising, threatening) to imply that there are, or can be brought about, reasons to comply of the required strength (56). To be defective is to fail to live up to the standards implied by those practices. Further, Murphy contends that a law must exist as law in order to be defective (or non-defective) as law (59). Now a legal norm is created with some measure or absence of justice; the justice or injustice is not superimposed on the law at some later stage (e.g. through its reception by jurists) and is not explanatorily posterior to its positing. For there are some norms that were either (1) created through defective or *ultra vires* procedures or (2) so unjust that they do not exist as *laws*; but others that are laws despite injustice, yet the injustice forms part of the explanation of the extent to which it is a law (for example, by narrowing its scope through interpretation, distinguishing precedents that have formed around it, preferring certain justifications based on other grounds, etc and thus defining its shape). Murphy ends by suggesting that to defend natural law jurisprudence is to defend the claim that the law's normative non-defectiveness conditions explain its existence-conditions (60). See also Geoffrey Callaghan 'Defective but Still Law: A Critique of Mark Murphy's Weak Natural Law Jurisprudence' 26 *CJLJ* 219. Finnis's central argument I think is sound: that for non-univocal concepts, 'their different meanings can be associated with a core concept, and this association can be realized in different ways' (Veronica Rodriguez-Blanco, 'Is Finnis Wrong?' 13 (2007) *Legal Theory* 269). For an excellent account (upon which Finnis's is partly based) see WW Fortenbaugh, 'Aristotle's Analysis of Friendship: Function and Analogy, Resemblance and Focal Meaning' 20 (1975) *Phronesis* 52–56.

## I.3.

*Theoretically orientated practical inquiry*: It should be noted that both Aristotle and (more explicitly) Aquinas regard the inquiry into the truth alone of, for example, virtue, without the corresponding effort to become virtuous, as empty and vain: Aquinas, *Eth* II.2.256.

*Hart on theoretical power and practical purpose*: The key passage is at *CL*, 209: 'If we are to make a reasoned choice between these concepts, it must be because one is superior to the other in the way in which it will assist our theoretical inquiries, or advance and clarify our moral deliberations, or both.' Alexander Somek displays a lack of patience with both theories, suggesting that both legal positivism and natural law theory have 'run their course' and that the latter is 'embarrassing': see *The Legal Relation: Legal Theory After Legal Positivism* (CUP 2017) 6–7. But I do not detect the embarrassment in the subordination of speculative knowledge to practical knowledge *when reasoning ethically*, any more than does Aristotle in Book Two, Chapter 1 of the *Nicomachean Ethics*: the primacy of the life of contemplation *includes* practical reasoning for one of the essential topics of contemplation for any reasonable person is the truth of ethics. Somek suggests in several places that legal positivism has sometimes sought to incorporate elements of natural law theory into its doctrines (see *The Legal Relation* xi), a development he deplores because of the naivety of the idea of uniquely correct answers in hard cases. Fortunately, natural law theory proposes no such thing. But Somek does say that legal positivism cannot begin and end with the concept of legal validity, but must instead be concerned with soberly chosen methods of interpretation which permit inferences of validity to occur (ibid, 24).

*The law serves real or apparent goods*: The apparent goods in question are pointed out by Hart, *CL* 200, but he does not relate them to the genuine forms of goodness of which they are a corruption. By contrast, Thomist philosophers were well aware that unjust law must be understood by reference to the apparent goods at which it aims.

*Speculative/descriptive v practical ends*: Note the remark of Aquinas, *ST* I.79.11c & ad 2, that the distinction between speculative and practical ends does not suppose an absolute distinction in intellectual processes; for the intellect first apprehends an object before directing it to consideration of truth, or to operation; yet the mind reasoning practically first apprehends an object as true, before directing it to operation. See also Aristotle, *De Anima* III.9–10; Aquinas, *De An* III.10.15.823–26. Note also the warning in the text, that practical *philosophy* is 'directed to operation' only in a more indirect sense. It does not directly resemble the agent-specific point of view that asks, 'What should I do?', but it is at the same time not merely clarificatory, for it is directed to proposals about how citizens and officials should act, or in many cases, continue to act. (See also the wider definition of the subject of practical philosophy in Aquinas, *Eth* I.1.3 as 'human action directed to an end'.)

## I.4.

*Gardner on legal norms*: Much more can be said on this subject, but I will confine discussion to one or two aspects. The first is Gardner's claim that LP* captures the theories of the majority of legal positivists past and present. But this is open to question. Hobbes, for example, is more focused on the issue of the law's conventionality, not with the question of 'merits': see *Leviathan* XIX–XXI. The question Gardner asks is relevant really only to modern legal positivists and was an invention of the nineteenth century. Second, the search for legal answers in judicial reasoning is often or even largely a matter of a *search* for norms or 'merits' when judges look to define what is reasonable in the circumstances. These deliberations may involve complex and subtle ideas and arguments, but they are not ideas and arguments that begin with the deliberator; they form the latest expression of legal justice that extends back through a considerable period of time. One only needs to bring to mind much of the content of Tort law or Criminal law, much of which would be recognizable to a law practitioner of the late eighteenth century, in spite of new developments. It is ironic that positivists, who place so much emphasis on legal sources, largely lack much interest in the actual sources of law, beyond the meagre formulation of 'the Queen in Parliament': see Chapter X below.

*The concept of immoral law can only be imagined by reference to that of good law*: Further to this, Gardner states that law that is presumptively moral is defeasibly binding whether or not it is actually immoral: *Law as a Leap of Faith* (OUP 2012) 167. Here Gardner touches upon a question that is left in an unsuitable position by Thomas Aquinas, the general outlines of which are fairly well-known: (1) just law is always to be obeyed unless this would by mischance pervert the common good; (2) unjust law is to be disobeyed at whatever personal cost, unless to do so would further undermine the common good, and obedience would largely preserve it. Aquinas's position hints also at a distinction between the seriously unjust and the only mildly unjust, the implications of which are unclear. But if such a position is indeed implied by (2), we must ask: does this imply a calculation of harm done vs benefit secured (proportionalism), does it imply the existence of some threshold of harm, or does it simply estimate the damage done to a range of basic human goods or the common good? These are questions I do not propose to go into here. But it might be supposed more generally that the law is merely an instrument which can serve good or bad ends. It has been forcefully argued that this is not the case: see NE Simmonds, 'Freedom, Law and Naked Violence' 59 (2009) *University of Toronto LJ* 381. For although law can serve substantively unjust ends, its institutional structure and inner mechanisms cannot be distorted into assisting evil except in superficial ways, such as clarifying the will and intent of the ruler. Law conceived as such a structure ('the rule of law') intrinsically inclines to the ends of good and freedom. The law serves the ends of freedom in both positive and negative senses: negatively by creating interstitial liberties in which each person enjoys a measure of freedom from the will of others and of the state, positively by providing opportunities for individuals to become involved in the lawmaking and law-applying aspects of governance. The law serves the good by fostering goods as social capital, by allowing each person reasonable scope to formulate and pursue their conception of the good life, and by building infrastructure, hospitals, schools, universities, and so on. But even if we denied all of this and return to Gardner's presumptive claim that evil regimes use the law not for good but for bad, this would not confirm the view that law serves the good only sometimes. For as Aquinas makes clear (*ST* I-II.92.1c) even in the case of an evil regime, the law makes the citizens 'good' though only according to that regime's measure of 'good'.

## I.5.

*Whether it is right in the circumstances to pursue knowledge*: See for example *ST* II-II.116–17, which distinguishes the properly virtuous desire for knowledge (*studiositas*) with an inordinate desire for the satisfaction of one's inquisitiveness (*curiositas*). Cf. Finnis, *NLNR* 60, in which the 'good' of knowledge extends to a greater or lesser degree to all instantiations including discovering the truth of 'some gossipy rumour'.

## I.6.

*Natural Law's permanence and timelessness*: Some writers, sympathetic to natural law theory, have pondered whether natural laws are truly timeless and might not have applied to Neanderthals. And this is taken to be an objection to the idea of timeless norms or rights. See John Tasioulas, 'Taking Rights out of Human Rights' 120 (2010) *Ethics* 671; also RN Fasel, 'Simply in virtue of being human'? A critical appraisal of a human rights commonplace', 9 (2018) *Jurisprudence* 461. The same line of reasoning also applies to the argument that there is one best form of human life. But there is a clear sense in which the best, most flourishing life for a human being is also the best, most flourishing life for a Neanderthal (or any proto-human creature), even if that form of life is unavailable to the latter. For if (let us say) knowledge is a good, then it is good for any creature with the capacity for true knowledge, and to understand true answers to questions, and true implications from true premises (i.e. truth-preserving modes of inference). This is as much the case with the production of primitive tools as it is with knowledge of Greek poetry or calculus.

*MacIntyre as a non-relativist*: As Emile Perreau-Saussine illuminatingly mentions, MacIntyre was influenced by the later Wittgenstein's 'private language' argument: that there are no innate ideas or concepts except through an acquired language, and that rationality must be understood by reference to an established language: see *Alasdair MacIntyre: An Intellectual Biography* (University of Notre Dame Press 2022) 48. The majority of natural law theorists, including Aquinas, would agree that there are no innate ideas: a position they learned from Aristotle. But they would nevertheless believe that reason as such transcends particular languages, and is available to all languages, for there are rational standards that are independent of all languages: God's reason. It is true that human beings have no direct access to the eternal law, but they nevertheless have natural reason which is a 'participation of eternal law in rational creatures': *ST* I-II.91.2c. See Alasdair MacIntyre 'Natural Law as Subversive: The Case of Aquinas' 26 (1996) *Journal of Medieval and Early Modern Studies* 61. MacIntyre's union of reason and tradition (he does not oppose the one to the other) is thus unanchored and free floating. His question Nietzsche or Aristotle? Is answered without any final option for a framework in which deliverances of reason transcend the horizons of tradition.

*Forms of marriage*: Some modern writers such as Robert George have rejected the view that marriage amounts to sexual and romantic companionship, but insist that marriage means fundamental openness to children: see R George et al, *What is Marriage?* (Encounter Books 2020). I suggest instead that marriage is founded upon the solemn binding promises of the spouses (promises of fidelity, support, companionship come what may), made before God and dissolvable only by death. Such promises definitely include mutual promises of assistance with raising children *if they come*, but are not centred upon the openness to children on the part of the spouses. For example, the woman may have been medically advised not to have children, in which case the spouses may use permissible forms of contraception such as the rhythm method.

*Aristotle v Nietzsche*: MacIntyre makes some interesting points: that practical reason is both individual and social in nature, for it shapes the understanding of every person of one another's actions; and that reasoning as conceived by modern liberals is almost entirely concerned with satisfaction of preferences rather than the common good: see Sante Maletta 'MacIntyre and the Subversion of Natural Law' in Paul Blackledge & Kelvin Knight (eds) *Virtue and Politics* (Notre Dame Press 2011) 182–83. But as before, these criticisms of liberalism presuppose an independent and critical standpoint that is superior to liberalism. It could be that MacIntyre believes that the human condition is a predicament, on the road to nowhere and with no 'end of history' in view. A natural law theorist could subscribe to such a belief but with the following two important caveats: (1) there is a supernatural order to which human beings are summoned which is partially revealed to us through Divine law and natural law, which is unchanging and culture-independent, and (2) an aspect of that supernatural order is present and active within human affairs through the actions and forbearances of the community of believers in that supernatural order. It should also be noted that MacIntyre underplays a vitally important aspect of human ethics: grace, as a well as the existence and nature of *synderesis*, which securely puts human beings in touch with the natural law's most fundamental precepts. It could also be possible to make a postmodern interpretation of MacIntyre, as being engaged in clearing away the rubble of existing philosophies of ethics, in order to provide a starting point for a new ethics. Such an interpretation would inevitably fall prey to the criticism that any such effort would likewise destroy the ground upon which the postmodern theorist themselves stands. MacIntyre's theory appears to imply the more sophisticated position mentioned above.

## CHAPTER II

### II.1.

*Render intelligible the goodness or badness of ends*: This is contrary to Finnis (*NLNR* ch III), who regards 'basic goods' as pre-moral: see Section II.5.

*Moral ideas*: To a society which has long since renounced an interest in metaphysics, there may appear to be little to distinguish the apprehension of a moral *claim* from the holding of a moral *idea*, or an attachment to a moral *ideal* or *ideology*. Even the term 'moral discourse' has certain suggestive connotations of subjectivity. Here, the primitive notion seems to be that of idea, so that 'claim' (even when understood nominatively rather than verbally) does not entirely escape from active associations, in this case the *act* of cognition in 'arriving at' or 'formulating' an idea. Here, however, I use 'claim' in its objective sense as the primitive term in relation to which ideas (perfect or imperfect) can be formed. See also John Finnis, 'Law and What I Truly Should Decide', 48 (2003) *Am J Jurisprudence* 112, where 'claim' is distinguished from both the 'logic' and 'experience' of moral belief.

*Morality of aspiration v morality of duty*: Certainly the instruments through which human rights are promulgated have something of this aspirational character: the 1789 *Declaration of the Rights of Man and Citizen* articulates principles which 'tend toward maintaining the constitution and the general welfare' [preamble]; the *Universal Declaration of Human*

*Rights* 1948 refers in its preamble to matters that it is 'essential to promote', and understands the proclamation as 'a common standard of achievement'. It may indeed seem as if, after 1789, the rights of 'man' had been replaced by the rights of the citizen, i.e. had become by nature 'political' rights. Accordingly, human rights appear as the embodiment of a remarkable crystallization of political will or mood, a dominant ideology to challenge the narrower parochial ideologies of national governments: see e.g. Pierre Manent, *A World Beyond Politics?* Trans. M LePain (Princeton University Press 2006), 98–99. A closer familiarity with the history and substance of such documents dispels such an easy explanation, however. The declared norms of 1789 were no mere principles, but a 'solemn declaration [of] the natural, inalienable and sacred rights of man'; those of 1948 concerned rights again already existent and operative, whether or not actually protected by the rule of law. There is thus an important sense in which duties, understood as present demands of justice, stand in contrast to aspirational ideals. The drafters of such documents took themselves to be officially recognizing and recording, at a constitutional level, rights which are not fundamentally political in nature, but have their foundation in 'nature'. This claim is capable of being severely misunderstood. It is of the first importance to understand that the 'natural rights' upon which the scholastic and early-modern philosophers wrote owe their intelligibility to the workings of practical reason, and the central question concerns the identification of a mode of practical deliberation (that is, concerning goods and ends) which is not in any sense the instrument or incident of an ideology.

*'Ethics' and 'morality'*: 'Ethics' is the Greek term for practical reasoning directed toward the contemplation of ends (and goods). 'Morality' finds its root in the Latin *mos*, or 'custom'. The extension of both these terms is wider in the Greek and Latin discourses than it is today (see Section II.3), and the difference in terminology is mostly regarded as stylistic, or as a means of distinguishing between Greek and Latin ideas. To that extent, some writers have tended to associate 'ethics' with what is now called 'virtue ethics', and have employed the term with this more restrictive reference, whereas 'morality' is understood and used to refer to moral theories of a more deontological character. Throughout this book, the discussion supposes no such division. I treat 'ethics' and 'morality' as basically equivalent terms, though I tend to use 'ethics' to signify the subject of reflection, and 'morality' as the content of the precepts which are disclosed as a result of that reflection. Nothing in the discussion turns on this terminological preference.

*Historical extension of moral precepts*: The distinction is noted by Saint Augustine (Epistle 91, § 4), who complains that justice has been 'rather investigated or described by [the wise] in private discussions, than established in reality by them in public measures'. Much of Book XIX of *De Civitate Dei* is likewise given over to a consideration of the extent to which true justice has been (or is capable of being) implemented on the level of concrete political institutions, as opposed to some corruption of justice.

*An inquiry into ethics and natural law is an investigation neither of ideology nor of the history of moral standpoints*: Another somewhat similar perspective is that of Jean Porter, who argues that moral philosophy requires a kind of rhetoric. But this relativizing of ethics to various 'audiences' was decisively debunked by Plato in the *Gorgias*. For rhetoric's tendency to falsity over truth is well-documented: in extracting starting points from what one's audience accepts or believes there is simply no reason to assume that these will be *sound* starting points, indeed quite the reverse. This is true even of very sophisticated types of rhetoric such as the devices of the original position and reflective equilibrium in Rawls's theory of justice. On archetypes, see NE Simmonds, *Law as a Moral Idea* (Oxford University Press 2007).

## II.2.

*Ethics is inherently complex*: *EN* I.3.1094b.14–24: 'Now our treatment of this science will be adequate, if it achieves that amount of precision which belongs to its subject matter. The same exactness must not be expected in all departments of philosophy alike, any more than in all the products of the arts and crafts. The subjects studied by political science are Moral Nobility and Justice; but these conceptions involve much difference of opinion and uncertainty, so that they are sometimes believed to be mere conventions and to have no real existence in the nature of things. And a similar uncertainty surrounds the conception of the Good, because it frequently occurs that good things have harmful consequences: people have before now been ruined by wealth, and in other cases courage has cost men their lives. We must therefore be content if, in dealing with subjects and starting from premises thus uncertain, we succeed in presenting a broad outline of the truth: when our subjects and our premises are merely generalities, it is enough if we arrive at generally valid conclusions ... for it is the mark of an educated mind to expect that amount of exactness in each kind which the nature of the particular subject admits.' See also V.7.1134b.27–34. Unhelpfully, Aristotle characterizes his enquiry in the *Ethics* as 'political' [*politike*]: I.2.1094b.10–11, but this should be read in light of 1141b.23–33, where 'political science' is clarified as one part of an enquiry into ends that is undertaken through the operations of prudence [*phronesis*], which 'truly belongs to all kinds'.

*Apprehension of goods requires experience of inclinations*: Here the experience may not be direct. If we think of curiosity, the name for a felt inclination that everyone experiences directly (even if only the desire to find out what happens in the next episode of a television programme), it becomes tempting to say that anyone who has experienced curiosity *thereby* perceives knowledge as (self-evidently) good. But this hardly holds true for all of the inclinations that Aquinas mentions, for example, the natural inclination to beget and raise children. One need not experience it to know its goodness; indeed one may never experience any such inclination, even to the extent of (immorally) aborting the foetus in one's womb. But persons in this condition can nevertheless still regard the good of children as a true good. How? Through reflecting on the fact that this good is a *human* good, one self-evidently enjoyed and promoted by almost all human beings, and by grasping the desire (in others) for children is an entirely rational end to pursue. It is not, like some perceived goods (such as incest) blatantly pathological. Thus all persons can experience the good of child-rearing if only at second-hand.

*That which is conveniens to human nature*: Murphy resorts to the theory of indexical vs non-indexical statements in order to suggest that while there are no direct lines of implication running between statements that human nature is such-and-such, on the one hand, and statements that such and such is a human good suitable for beings with a nature like ours, on the other, they nevertheless are closely (non-inferentially) related: see *NLPR* 18–19. The resultant position Murphy calls 'the real identity thesis': that (a) there is a set of truths capable of apprehension by the theoretical reason that (i) affirms the existence of something (not merely some *concept*) called 'human flourishing', and (ii) articulates the various types of human flourishing that there are, and that (b) strong grounds exist for affirming that any state of affairs correctly marked out by theoretical reason as '*x* is an aspect of human flourishing' would be correctly grasped by practical reason as '*x* is a good worth having/pursuing' and vice versa. But teleology is not grasped only by practical reason for we can make judgments about the teleology of other species: *NLPR* 29–30. Murphy points to Aquinas *ST* I.5.1c: 'Goodness and being are really the same, and differ only in idea': *NLPR* 44. But Aquinas's grounds are different: on his view, actuality (*ens*) is coterminous with perfection, and one desires that which is perfect. Murphy could have quoted from the very next article, in which Aquinas affirms that being (actuality) is prior to good, which he reaffirms in I-II.94.2c (the absolutely first thing that a person apprehends is *being*, whereas the first thing to fall before the intellect *when reasoning practically* is *good*). But there is clearly two-way traffic here, for Dudley Knowles points out that because we know that making and keeping friends is an important aspect of human flourishing, we would evaluate brain-states that inhibit that ability to be malfunctionings rather than peculiarities: Knowles 'Review of Murphy, *NLPR*' 112 (2003) *Mind* 555–56. This seems to me to be entirely compatible with Aquinas's teaching in the Articles just cited. It appears to contradict Finnis's view that one *always* proceeds (at least as a matter of deep logic) from understood goods to proclivities of 'nature'. For without the judgment that certain things are genuinely good, what reason is there to regard human nature as good, benevolent, politic as opposed to unremittingly evil? (Finnis, as Murphy observes, admits the following: 'But . . . the basic forms of good are opportunities of *being*; the more fully one participates in them the more one is what one can be. And for this state of being fully what one can be, Aristotle appropriated the word *physis*, which was translated into Latin as *natura*': *NLNR* 103). None of this undermines the thesis that conceptions of human flourishing are essentially practical, for the grasp of *being* (that something *is* in conformity with human nature) is radically incomplete unless accompanied by the judgment that it is *good*, ought to be pursued, or attained. Friendship is something that is in conformity with human nature (I feel lonely and incomplete in periods of solitude, happy when I am with friends; I can process these feelings without explicitly invoking notions of friendship), but there are times when it would not be in accordance with my flourishing to socialize with friends: if, for example, such socializing would take the place of studying for the sake of my intellectual development, or led me to neglect my religious observances. Thus my processing of feelings (or reading Aristotle) may initially lead me to formulate the idea that friendship is in accord with my nature, but it is only once I reflect practically that I comprehend that it is truly *good*, not merely pleasurable or a distraction from unpleasantries.

*Real and false goods*: For a fuller discussion see Section II.4. The relevant distinction is outlined by Suarez in *Disputationes Metaphysicae* X.2.1: apparent good is to be understood as an *ens rationis* (existing only in the mind, and thus possessing a kind of being, but having no existence in reality, and thus no real being). See *DM* LIV for Suarez's detailed treatment of the *entibus rationis*. See also *Nicomachean Ethics* III.4.

*Coherence between goods as evidence of their probity*: This is the forerunner to the strategy Aristotle proposes at *NE* I.8.1098b: that all data harmonize with the truth, whereas they will readily and multiply clash with falsity.

## II.3.

*The difference between practical and speculative reasoning*: see *ST* I.79.11: 'Where a thing falls under the apprehension of the intellect, it is accidental whether or not it is directed to action (*opus*); and accordingly it is possible to differentiate between the intellect as it operates speculatively and as it operates practically. For speculative intellection is directed to what it apprehends not as toward action, but only toward consideration of truth. Practical intellection by contrast directs what it apprehends toward action.' See also *Summa Contra Gentiles* III.10; *ST* I.16.4, I.79.11 ad 2, I-II.9.1, I-II.17.1, & I-II.19.3 ad 2. Aquinas here seems to suggest that 'speculative intellect' has a wider reference than the traditional Aristotelian category of 'speculative' (i.e. 'theoretical') reason: an assumption backed up by his comment on Aristotle in *Eth* VI.2.1131, where he suggests that Aristotle's remark (*EN* VI.2.1139a.29-35) 'gives rise to some doubt', for the very rectitude of appetite by which the practical intellect determines its truth is itself determined by right reason (*rationi verae*), thus resulting in apparent circularity. Aquinas attempts (not altogether successfully) to resolve this circularity by arguing that it is only the means ({*ea*} *quae sunt ad finem*) which can be investigated by reason, whereas ends (the proper measure of truth for the practical intellect) are determined 'by nature'. Read in conjunction with what he has to say about the first principles of practical reason (principally in *ST* I-II.94.2), this seems to indicate that the reference to 'nature' here is again not to be understood as an invitation to observe human inclinations 'from the outside' (as GK Chesterton once put it) but to experience them, as it were, 'from within'. Hence Aquinas regards 'natural inclinations' as falling within the grasp of the practical intellect as self-knowable (*per se nota*) and indemonstrable (*indemonstrabile*) terms (id). For some further reflections on the issues raised in the text, see Martin Rhonheimer, 'Practical Reason, Human Nature, and the Epistemology of Ethics' 57 (2012) *Villanova LR* 873–87; Finnis, *NLNR* 34. Notice also Aristotle's remark that the blessed person will spend the majority of their time engaged in 'action *and contemplation* in accordance with virtue': *EN* I.10.1100b, my emphasis.

*The order of precepts follows the order of inclinations*: Aquinas is careful to say that both human beings and other animals possess natural inclinations, but humans also have reason. It is through reason that humans participate in eternal law, a mode of participation called 'natural law'. But the two sources, inclination and reason, are linked, because the order of inclinations is reflected in the order of precepts. Yet the ordering of inclinations is law 'only by a kind of similitude': *ST* I-II.91.2 ad 3. For two (in my view) erroneous accounts of Aquinas and eternal law, see Anthony Lisska, *Aquinas's Theory of Natural Law: An Analytical Reconstruction* (Clarendon 1996) esp chs 4 &5; Christopher Martin, *The Philosophy of Thomas Aquinas* (Routledge 1998).

## II.4.

*Aquinas on misapplication of first principles*: At numerous points, Aquinas states that no one errs regarding the first practical principles (e.g. *ST* I.79.12 ad 3, I-II.8.1c & 100.11c; *Sent* II.39.3.1 ad 1) but can go astray in the movement from the principles to conclusions (e.g. *De Mal* 7.5 ad 6; *Sent* [loc cit], *Ver* 16.2c & ad 1 & 6; *ST* I-II.72.5c, II-II.156.3 ad 1 & 3). On some of these occasions, Aquinas comes close to suggesting that error regarding first principles is, after all, a possibility; but this is to be understood as a kind of perversion of one's basic intellections: one may come to deny the first principles as falsehoods, even basing one's life around their denial, due to a dedicated pursuit of bad ends, but one's deeper understanding cannot be entirely annihilated, and will perpetually stand in criticism of one's actions: *Sent* II.39.3.1c; thus in making such denials one is really lying to oneself: *Eth* VI.10.18. This is not a mere stipulation on Aquinas's part. It represents the underlying belief, clearly articulated in the twentieth century by Lon Fuller, that 'when men are compelled to explain and justify their decisions, the effect will be to pull those decisions toward goodness, by whatever standards of ultimate goodness there are': Fuller, 'Positivism and Fidelity to Law: A Reply to Professor Hart' 71 *Harvard L Rev* (1958), 636. Fuller's belief that coherence and goodness are more closely and fully related than coherence and evil is the premise upon which all moral assumptions rest: for insofar as morality falls under the scope of *reason*, it follows that the existence of definitive reasons for action (i.e. not exclusionary but all-things-considered) are capable of being relentlessly and soberly advanced against supposed justifications for immoral action: justifications which must eventually be exposed as dishonest, pragmatically self-serving, incoherent, or contradictory.

*Types of goods*: The key text is Aristotle, *NE* I.9-11, which discusses the form of the happy life. Aristotle repudiates the Socratic argument (in *Euthydemus* 279c.9-d.9) that honour or virtue alone is sufficient for happiness, even in the absence of favourable external conditions. Against this, Aristotle insists that although the good is 'something of one's own' (I.5.1095b.25), nevertheless 'when one is suffering terribly or experiencing the greatest misfortunes ... no one could call a person living this kind of life happy' (I.5.1096a.1-2). Thus a certain level of material prosperity is required for the happy life (I.8.1099a.31; cf. X.8.1179a.1-14). At the same time, the happy (i.e. truly and finally *good*) life is not at the mercy of external goods, but is under the control and guidance of the virtues, as they direct the agent regarding the use of such goods: I.10.1100b.8-11. Suarez (*DM* X.2.33) similarly distinguishes between goods of the body (*bona corporis*), of the soul (*bona animae*), and extrinsic goods (*bona extrinseca*); thus in distinguishing between nutritive substances and their consumption by the agent, we are distinguishing between a *bonum extrinsecum* and a *bonum corporis*. Over-consumption is always going to be a matter of moral wrongness, insofar as it lies within the free actions of the agent; whereas under-consumption may be attributable to the moral wrong of deliberate starvation (e.g. hunger strike), or to a lack of *bona extrinseca* where there has been no failure of virtue. (To this one might add medical conditions, either physical or mental, which might produce under-consumption, which are certainly human *bads* though not necessarily moral wrongs.)

*The distinction between natural and moral good*: Suarez observes that the distinction of natural and moral good pertains to the distinction between (i) the agreeability of certain things with nature, and (ii) the specific conformity of something with *rational* nature, which in virtue of being 'free' (not acting from necessity or unconsciously) is itself moral in nature: *DM* X.2.30. But therefore in a more general sense, the distinction between moral and natural good applies more generally to the categories of useful and pleasurable good *as they are pursued by man*, for 'when pursued without nobility [such goods] cannot be understood as good without qualification, both in depriving man of a greater good and because it does not lead to the unqualified good of man, which (as St Thomas said) is to live according to reason. In this sense, the Fathers often taught that nothing is good except virtue' (*DM* X.2.29). See also *De Legibus* II.1.5: 'Therefore as regards the objects of human actions, benefit to nature alone is not sufficient for the rightness of action.' Finnis (*NLNR* 76) creates the impression that Suarez is misled over the character of the *bonum honestum*, for in drawing the distinction between natural and moral good *within* the category of *honestum* Suarez fails to grasp that certain *honesta* are non-moral goods. But Suarez's point in bringing these terms together under the umbrella of the *honestum* is to indicate that, for Aquinas and earlier writers in and around the Aristotelian tradition, *bonum honestum* is correctly understood as 'virtuous good', not simply 'good in itself' (*in se bonum*), for it pertains to Aristotle's use of the Greek *kalon* (fineness, nobility, uprightness, honourability). See Irwin, *The Development of Ethics* (OUP 2007) II.438, 33. Finnis's understanding ('A *bonum honestum* is simply a good that is worthwhile having or doing or effecting for its own sake, and not just for the sake of any utility it may have as a means to some other good, nor just for the pleasure it may afford.') does not reflect Aquinas's usage: see e.g. his reliance on St Ambrose, *De Officiis* I.9.27: 'nothing is fitting or right (*honestum*) unless it is directed toward future goods more than to present ones; and furthermore nothing is useful unless it directs us to the grace of everlasting life, and not to the enjoyment of the present'; *ST* I-II.34.2 ad 1 & I-II.39.2 (the root of *honestum* is rectitude of reason and will); I-II.39.2 a 3 (*honestum* is praiseworthy and meritorious in character; referring to the discussion of moral good at I-II.21.2); II-II.102.2, 106.1 & 114.2 (*honestum* as an occasion of duty (*debitum*)); II-II.110.2 (the *honestum* is to be preferred even at the cost of one's bodily life). For the treatment of *honestum* in Aquinas's sources, see Marcia Colish, *The Stoic Tradition* vol 2 (Brill, 1990), esp ch IV; on the *honestum* in Aquinas and his interpretation of Aristotle, see Irwin, *DE* I.116, 180, & 332–34.

*Real v apparent good*: See also Aristotle, *Meta* XII.7.1072a.

*Reference to moral good in the primary precept*: This is why Aquinas regards the primary precepts as a first stage, or kind of beginning for moral thinking (*inchoatio*), which implant in human beings ideas and inclinations of virtue (*seminalia virtutum*): see *De Virt* 1.8c; *Ver* 14.2; *ST* I-II.51.1.

*The human being as a body-and-soul organism*: See encyclical of St John Paul II, *Veritatis Splendor* §49: 'A doctrine which dissociates the moral act from the bodily dimensions of its exercise is contrary to the teaching of Scripture and Tradition. Such a doctrine revives, in new forms, certain ancient errors which have always been opposed by the Church.'

## II.5.

*Good is to be done and pursued*: This precept is not a mere 'rule of rationality', for the reference to 'good' should be understood in the primary, that is, focal sense: it is only because we are capable of comprehending genuine or true goods that we can extend that notion to things not good in themselves but possessing the surface appearance of good. This distinction or capacity of discerning the difference between real and false goods is central to our moral life.

*Those who assert that the primary precept of natural law is non-moral*: See e.g. Finnis *NLNR* chs II-III; Martin Rhonheimer 'Sins Against Justice' in Stephen Pope (ed) *The Ethics of Aquinas* (Georgetown University Press, 2002) 299 n13. Jonathan Crowe is of the view that the debate has moved on since Finnis's work, and is no longer at the cutting-edge. This seems to me premature, and I am unsure whether Crowe's work represents a move in the right direction: see Chapter I; see also Jonathan Crowe, 'Natural Law Beyond Finnis' 2 (2011) *Jurisprudence* 308.

*Goods are valued simultaneously (i) for themselves and (ii) as constituents of eudaemonia*: In the wicked person, individual actions (such as stealing from another) are related to overarching ends of life purely instrumentally (e.g. for the sake of enrichment). In the virtuous person, the individual goods relate to *eudaemonia* intrinsically: for virtues such as constancy require the perspective of a whole life (see Alasdair MacIntryre, *After Virtue* 203): *eudaemonia* is present not just as a cumulative end of life but also (potentially) throughout life. Thus for Aristotle one's *telos* is not something pursued and attained at some future point, but is constituted by a certain *kind* of life (ibid, 175).

*Aquinas on good and evil*: MacIntyre wrongly suggests that it is possible to distinguish between (i) a positive act of evil and (ii) a mere falling short of what is good: *AV* 152. The distinction is set against the entire tradition of Christian theology and philosophy, which asserts that evil is not a positive thing but always a privation, both in ethics and in other aspects of life (e.g. illness is not a positive thing but the absence of healthy functioning).

## II.7.

*The natural law thesis*: Murphy actually distinguishes three versions of the thesis: the 'strong' thesis (a norm's legal validity is partly constituted by its being backed by decisive reasons for compliance), the 'weak' thesis (adopted by both Murphy and Crowe: a norm's non-legal defectiveness is partly constituted by decisive reasons for compliance), and the 'moral' thesis (a norm's authoritativeness is partly constituted by being backed by decisive reasons for compliance). Murphy dismisses the 'moral' reading as uninteresting (*NLJP* 2), says that the 'strong' reading can deflect many of the arguments levelled against it, but endorses the 'weak' thesis because the arguments raised against natural law jurisprudence do not raise even prima facie suspicions against it (ibid, 3). As I state in the main text, I am opposed to accounts of natural law that centre upon legal validity, not least because law practitioners hardly use the term in their working lives (see Section X.6). But ignoring that concern, we may make the following observations. The 'strong' version of the thesis seems the one devoid of interest: translating into Hartian or Razian language, it simply states that laws must be 'accepted by' or have 'exclusionary reasons for' those to whom it is directed. The 'weak' version requires an explanation of the term 'legal defectiveness', which would inter alia involve the common good, to be discussed in Chapter V: see for a different argument concerning the common good, as 'the principal normative reason in the public domain' (George Duke, 'The Weak Natural Law Thesis and the Common Good' 35 (2016) *Law and Philosophy* 485). The 'moral' version speaks of 'legal authority' rather than of 'law' per se. Murphy unfolds it further: according to the moral reading, 'all a natural law theorist wants to do in affirming a connection between law and reasons is to issue a dramatic reminder that adherence to some laws would constitute such a departure from reasonableness that there could not be adequate reason to obey them': Murphy, *Natural Law in Jurisprudence & Politics* (CUP 2006) 9. The effect of this thesis is (Murphy says) to '[transform] that thesis from a claim belonging to analytical jurisprudence into a claim belonging to moral philosophy' (ibid). The rigidity of that division is open to question: to assert it is to concede already a good deal of ground to the positivist. Many legal philosophers ('anti-positivists') dispute it. The present book, for example, begins with chapters on ethics, but strives to be relevant to concerns of at least academic legal philosophers.

*Reasons for the doctrine of natural law*: An additional reason to those suggested in the text, based on a hint by Aquinas (*ST* I-II.94.3), is that natural law explains how human beings are able to act morally through their own reason, without achieving the perfection of virtue to which Christian believers are called (e.g. through *caritas*).

*Murphy and Aquinas*: Murphy suggests that Aquinas's treatment of natural law is situated in a discussion of the nature of law: see Murphy, *NLJP* 10. This is untenable as an interpretation of Aquinas: Aquinas's central Articles on the natural law are to be found in I-II.94.1-1-6, and deal with, in order: whether natural law is a species of habit; whether there are many natural law precepts; whether natural law requires the practice of all the virtues; whether it is the same for all persons; whether natural law can be changed; whether it can be altogether abolished from the heart. None of these Articles is directed to a discussion of the nature of law. Furthermore, the other main *Questio* dealing with natural law (alongside human law, divine law and eternal law), I-II.96, is concerned largely with the relationship between those types of law, for example with the issue of whether positive law should proscribe all vices and require all virtues: I-II.96.2-3, and see also I-II.95.2c, dealing with the question of whether every positive human law is derived from the natural law. None of these Articles is concerned with the nature of law as such. Murphy further argues that what he calls 'natural law jurisprudence' and 'natural law political theory' are independent of a theory of 'natural law practical rationality': ibid, 4: For although these theories have connections to reasons and the common good, 'they make no claims about the specific character of those reasons of the common good'. Aside from the unwisdom of banishing parts of natural law theory to separate (even if related) disciplines, there is simply no reason for the assertion that these aspects of natural law theory are unrelated to a theory of practical reason or the common good. Both political and legal theory intrinsically make judgments about the common good: insofar as the law consists of general standards that apply to all citizens rather than a lone individual or group, there are questions, assumptions, and specifications of the common good, or in the case of unjust law, questions, assumptions, and specifications of what has failed to produce a common good. And both disciplines are concerned with identifying, in both general and concrete situations, with the specific content of practical reason, whether with reasonableness or unreasonableness.

## II.8.

*Rhonheimer on natural law as a work of reason*: But Rhonheimer goes too far in asserting that (therefore) natural law is an order of reason, not of nature: 'Natural Law as a Work of Reason' (2010) *American Journal of Jurisprudence* 50. This is close to Finnis's position. However, the 'order of reason' is one that is only applicable to rational *creatures* (*ST* I-II.94.2c), and therefore much must be known about the creature (organism) before one can be confident about the order of reason that pertains to it. For how can one know anything about the good unless one knows at least something of the world? (Aquinas agrees: see *ST* I.79.11 ad 2: the practical intellect knows truth just as the speculative intellect, but directs that truth to action). I should make it clear that this position does not endorse MacIntyre's thesis that natural law is changeable with changes in human nature, for there are no fundamental changes: the essence of humanity today is precisely what it was in the Age of Pericles. But it does coincide with *Veritatis Splendor* § 55, which is congenial to my thesis, not Rhonheimer's, for the 'light' of natural reason to which Aquinas continually refers cannot be grasped as an illuminator without a *source* of light. The forms of human goodness, the order of which natural reason grasps, were first created by the Source of light.

## II.9.

*Natural law's secular character reaches back at least as far as St Augustine*: MacIntyre's observation that it was only in the period 1630–1850 that morality became detached from theology is rather absurd. Certainly Aquinas treats moral questions as having a purchase on the human mind quite independently of theological investigations; even Aristotle's ethics are essentially secular.

*Synderesis*: It is an apparent difficulty that Aquinas recalls the example of 'Germanic tribes' whose morals were so corrupted that they did not regard theft as morally wrong. Despite Aquinas's Dominican translators opting to translate *laotra* as 'theft', Aquinas in fact draws a distinction between theft and forms of robbery at I-II.66.1-3. His use of the term is thus rather narrower than it seems; but more importantly, Aquinas is not seeking to draw upon a live example, but merely the content of a report by Julius Caesar. The example (thus essentially hypothetical) is intended to illuminate a particular question (see *ST* I-II.94.4c) but is not intended as a rival concept to what is elsewhere said about *synderesis*.

*The counterfactual hypothesis of God's inexistence*: Earlier sources relying on the same counterfactual include Vasquez, *In Primam Secundae* 97.1; Gregory of Rimini, 2 *Sent* 34.1 ad 2; Biel, 2 *Sent* 35.1.e21-25; Suarez, *De Leg* II.6.3. There is no indication in any of the medieval sources that the hypothesis was a novelty in argument in understanding the natural law.

*Lex indicitativa vs Lex praeceptiva*: The distinction is invoked for example by Suarez, *DL* II.6.3 & 6.10, identifying the *lex indicans* with natural goodness and badness, and takes the distinction to represent Aquinas's view (II.6.5). See also Biel, 2 *Sent* 35.1c-e.

*Vasquez and Finnis on natural law*: Vasquez's reasoning in objecting to the term *lex* seems to be that the natural law is not promulgated (in depending neither upon election nor a written text). He is however prepared to apply another synonym of law to it: *ius*. Finnis's standpoint is different, in that his remarks follow (at least, so the reader is led to suppose) from his remarks on focal meaning: to hold one conception of law in mind as the central case is to regard other uses as analogous to that case; but the choice of central case depends upon one's purposes in undertaking the inquiry. But his objections are also substantive, as the discussion of Suarez (*NLNR* II.6) makes clear. Oddly, Finnis regards Vasquez as siding with Suarez in adopting a voluntarist perspective on natural law, though Suarez himself presents Vasquez as the clearest example of the *strongest* form of rationalism that he wishes to challenge (*De Leg* II.5.1). Suarez's understanding of Vasquez's position is the correct one: Vasquez's thesis about natural goodness and badness (not divine will) as the foundation of natural law is so strong that it leads him to say that, although danger of death does not excuse lying (even venial lying), because there are no dispensations from natural law (i.e. as natural, rather than a command that could be rescinded), nevertheless circumstances may remove some element of natural law: *In Primam Secundae* 161.2.13, 179.15, 97.3. (This last might be the passage that leads Finnis to attribute to Vasquez a crude rationalism—'follow nature'—'eked out by voluntarism': *NLNR* II.6, 47–49, for it characterizes moral badness as opposition to rational nature. If this is so, Finnis ignores the rest of the passage, in which Vasquez is at pains to point out that 'some things are bad from themselves to such a degree [that] they have this character from their own nature, and not by the will of God in prohibiting, or His judgment in judging'). For Suarez's position on God's will, see *De Bon* VII.1; XI.2.

## CHAPTER III

### III.1.

*Aristotle's principle that the truth harmonizes with all data*: For another instance of this principle, see Wittgenstein, *On Certainty* (Blackwell 1975) §§ 142 & 274, which discusses the mutual or interdependent support within a system of propositions.

*Questions of human good immediately give expression to fundamental questions of interpersonal morality*: We can extrapolate the following series of propositions: (1) I can recognize human goods that are good for me; (2) if there are other beings like me, in terms of mental and physical power, then such goods will also be good for them; (3) there are no special reasons why one person, including myself, should have greater entitlement or prior claim on those goods, and so with others; (4) if the array of goods is not to be destroyed or depleted, some structure of participation in those goods must be created or discovered;

(5) such goods must be defended against the ploys of the wicked; (6) participation in such goods must be conditional on individual and collective efforts to defend and enrich the stock of those goods (avoidance of free-riding); (7) such goods must be made available to those who, for good reason, cannot otherwise participate in them, or are unable to protect and enrich them.

## III.2.

*There is no need to produce an exhaustive list of primary human goods*: The account in the main text does not begin with any such listing. I remain sceptical that the seemingly infinite array of possible or potential goods can admit of reduction to a finite list. The most famous such listing is that of Finnis: knowledge, life, play, aesthetic experience, sociability, practical reasonableness, and religion: see *NLNR* Chapter II. Subsequent lists borrow more or less heavily from this list. Thus Murphy submits: life, knowledge, aesthetic experience, excellence in play and work, excellence in agency, inner peace, friendship and community, religion, happiness (*NLPR* 100–35). Crowe proposes: life, health, pleasure, friendship, play, appreciation, understanding, meaning, and reasonableness (*NLNL* Chapter II). But it is not difficult to regard the members of such lists as, to quote Finnis, aspects or ways of pursuing one or more of his basic goods, or else reducible straightforwardly to such goods. Thus for example understanding, meaning and reasonableness can all be reduced to practical reasonableness as Finnis originally conceived it. Happiness is an aspect of pursuit and attainment of all the other goods in accordance with due prudence. Others are imposters: 'pleasure' is not a good in itself (except, Aristotle says in book I of the *Ethics*, perhaps for the coarse people) and should not be the target of any action, but a consequence of fulfilment in genuine goods. If pleasure truly were the aim of some actions, we would find difficulty in explaining why, for example, promiscuous sex is an evil/bad, or why we should not engage in pleasure at the expense (or mere opportunity cost) of participating in other goods. The inclusion of 'happiness' is also curious: Aristotle and Aquinas both regard it as the highest good, but it fits in Finnis's scheme into 'religion': the ultimate satisfaction that comes from a life lived well according to the other goods, and a good death not feared. Furthermore, there would appear to be some forms of good that are not present on any list: Murphy talks of 'excellence in play and in work' (echoed by Finnis in later versions of his list), but the emphasis here is on the worker's fulfilment through the act of labour; it does not include the good of work as a means of service to another. Being of use to others, to assist them in attaining *their* end, is itself a primary human good.

*A person aiming for some good X cannot consistently deny the goodness of the goods presupposed by X*: Note that this is a reference to *goods* presupposed by X. Evils brought about by or involved in pursuit of *X* (such as lying) are obviously not consistently intelligible as goods.

*Hart's treatment of human existence*: In light of this, Hart is a moral nihilist. His refusal to regard life/survival as an 'objective' aim for human beings, and in light of his willingness to lose concepts and structures of thought, and practice, Hart cannot then prevent a scorched-earth approach to morality and almost any other dimension of human life.

*Effects of original sin*: One could perhaps also draw attention to Aquinas's remark that doubts and misinterpretations of natural law creep in the more one descends from abstract principles to concrete particulars: see *ST* I-II.94.4c. For the Fall is an impediment to perfect knowledge.

*Social Darwinists and survival of the fittest*: see e.g. J Fiske, *Darwinism and Other Essays* [1879]; also Peter Dickens, *Social Darwinism* (Open University Press 2000).

*Custodianship of one's life is a perfection of the person*: See *ST* I-II.3.2 ad 1: life merely in itself is not a perfection nor a moral good; it is only when life is considered as an operation, or series of operative attempts to attain higher goods, whether through action or contemplation, that it has the status of a moral good, and hence is an element in a person's perfection. See also II-II.47.6c & ad 3. Re the point in the text on the relationship of potentiality to actuality, see *ST* I-II.55.3 and (on morality) I-II.58.1.

*The ordering of reason as a primary good*: See *ST* I-II.94.3c; also I-II.57.5 ad 1.

*Perfectibility as a determinant of true human good:* See esp *ST* I.5.1c, where Aquinas remarks that desire or appetite is explained by perfection (and not vice-versa); also I.5.3c & I.6.3c & ad 3.

*Natural human goods (natural appetites) are insufficient for ultimate beatitude*: See e.g. I.19.1c.

*Reflective equilibrium*: There is a tacit link here to the question of incommensurability. Finnis's standpoint, that basic goods are incommensurable, is challenged inter alia by Crowe, who argues that goods, if they cannot be commensurated, can nevertheless be *compared*. He offers numerous examples: to punch a person five times is worse than punching them once; to kill one person is worse than spreading malicious rumours about five people: *NLNL* 68–70. We can set up such examples as much as we like, but it is not clear what we learn from them, except perhaps the seductiveness, even among natural law theorists, of utilitarian thinking. For what is being 'compared' in the first example is the cardinality of the numbers 1–5, not the intensity of the wrongness of the act of murder. Nor is this to state that the act of killing one person is equally wrong as murdering five: for this, too, is an attempt at commensuration. If the image of cardinality must be maintained, one should view the matter as one of seeking to quantify two infinite numbers (for all life is infinitely precious). Similarly, in denying that the evil of the act of murder is commensurably greater than that of spreading malicious rumours, we are not making the (commensurable) judgment that the wrongfulness of murder is equal to the wrongfulness of spreading the rumours. To put the point in the language of the Catholic Church: the gravity of one mortal sin compared with another is not something human beings can determine: both involve a rift in one's relationship to God, and to this extent one mortal sin is equally serious as any other. The Decalogue, for example, states murder, covetousness, theft, and lying as things that *thou shalt not* do, but indicates no permanent hierarchy among them. Crowe also gives an example similar in terms to the classic 'trolley problem': intervening in situation A saves nine people whereas it causes harm to one person. But this involves a reasonably well-known analysis of intention, cause, and side-effect: by pulling a lever with the intent of saving A, with a foreseeable but unwanted consequence of causing harm to B, I act reasonably and morally. Indeed depending on the circumstances, it may be immoral not to pull the lever. Crowe's second example is related but slightly different: a road builder is causally responsible for the deaths of all those who (foreseeably) die while constructing the road (*NLNL* 74). But there is no causal link between the supervisor and the deaths, so long as he or she properly discharges their responsibilities as supervisors, for example by ensuring an environment that is as safe as possible, creating and implementing a health and safety plan, and taking all reasonable steps to avoid injuries and fatalities. The account of moral judgment this implies is a matter I do not propose to go into at this point, but I refer the reader to Finnis's discussion in *Fundamentals of Ethics* (OUP 1984) (without implying full agreement: I set out my own theory in Sections III.4–III.6).

*Crowe on inclinations and reflexes*: Crowe actually employs a third concept: that of instincts (innate, revisable). But this does not modify the essentials of my argument. It is simply a logical possibility in the unfortunate terms in which Crowe has chosen to shape his discussion.

## III.3.

*Mutual laying aside of right in Hobbes*: see *Leviathan* 14: 'The right of nature, which writers commonly call *ius naturale*, is the liberty that each man has to make his own decisions about how to use his own power for the preservation of his own nature—i.e. his own life—and consequently the liberty of doing anything that he thinks is the aptest means to that end.'

*Reciprocity is not the foundation of morality*: Aquinas too believes that self-love is the foundation of morality. See for example *ST* II-II.26.4c. But NB his statement at II-II.26.4 ad 3: 'The common good is always more lovable to each person than his private good, just as the good of the whole is more lovable to the part, than the part's own partial good.' *ST* II-II.26.5 is also suggestive but is ambiguous regarding this issue: we ought to love our neighbour more than our own body. See also Matthew 28:37–39.

## III.4.

*The death penalty as a reasonable determination of natural law*: Even Aquinas himself was led into error in this regard: see *ST* II-II.25.6 ad 2, II-II.64.2c. For some discussion see Finnis, *Aquinas* 279–84.

*No principle reduces to any other*: There is thus no 'master principle of morality' which is a source of the rationality of the other principles. These are not secondary precepts relatable to some higher principle. Cf Finnis, *CEJF* I.13, 210. But it should be observed that Principles (a) and (d)–(g) express norms of justice, though they go beyond those norms in the ways specified in the text; and Principles (b) and (c) express requirements of the common good.

# CHAPTER IV

## IV.1.

*Distinction between general and particular justice*: The distinction is discussed by Aristotle at *NE* v.12.1134b. This introduces some confusion as here legal justice denotes positive law as opposed to natural justice which 'has the same force everywhere'.

*The distinction between justice as a virtue, and justice as a series of principles that establish what ought to be done*: See the comment in the Catechism of the Catholic Church 1888, that the outward transformation of relationships and institutions depends upon an inner transformation of the soul.

*Justice is an other-regarding virtue*: See for example *In Eth* V.12.1106-07 (justice metaphorically considers the relationship of parts to other parts within a person, but never the whole person to the whole person). See also V.1.885-86; *ST* I-II.56.6.

*Punishment is a case of determinatio*: Within reason, it would obviously be wrong to punish a murderer with, say, a day in prison or a small fine. It seems clear, too, that punishment of any crime with execution is unreasonable. These examples show that there is at least *some* natural relationship between crime and punishment; and they also help to emphasize that acts of *determinatio* are not completely 'free' choices, unobstructed and uninformed by reason.

## IV.3.

*The state's obligations*: Crowe applies Justinian's maxim (to each their due) as encompassing the whole of the state: how to render to everyone in the community their due (see Jonathan Crowe, 'The Idea of Small Justice' 34 (2021) *Ratio Juris* 224). On first glance this appears a perfectly agreeable statement: surely *all* should receive their due. But the question *how* to bring about this state of affairs suggests that there is, or could be, a mechanism by which to produce this happy state of affairs. This mechanism cannot be the *law*, for the law does its best with limited and imperfect materials. But neither can it be the *state*, for no amount of political power can achieve justice for everyone. It is highly doubtful whether there is such a condition as total justice, justice for the whole society at every level and for every last one. Human free will prevents such a condition arising or enduring. The law, and the state, do not bring about total justice, they merely manage a predicament, 'the human condition', which does not admit of final solutions in this life. Despite this, Crowe is definitely right to foreswear the modern (Rawlsian) focus on social institutions as the components of social justice, and to focus instead upon justice in interpersonal relations: he calls this 'small justice'. But he adopts the Rawlsian concentration on distributive justice as the primary kind of justice, with commutative justice being reduced to the idea of 'corrective justice'.

*Difficulty of the difference principle*: Another problem is highlighted by Dennis Klimchuk (2003) 23 *Oxford Journal of Legal Studies* 53, who observes that 'It requires us to think of the objects of distribution as forming a fixed pool of goods, and of each citizen's holdings as consisting of her portion of such goods. This is true, for example, of political offices granted by appointment, Aristotle's paradigm example of justice in distribution. But the model does not hold for the distribution of material resources in a liberal democratic society. Such resources do not form a fixed pool. And no plausible account of distributive justice envisions a micro-managerial agency empowered to ensure that each citizen at any given moment has all and only her share of society's material resources.' See also Michael Walzer, *Spheres of Justice* (Basic Books 1983) 8: 'There is no single set of primary or basic goods conceivable across all moral and material worlds—or, any such set would have to be conceived in terms so abstract that they would be of little use in thinking about particular distributions.'

*The state's responsibilities in commutative justice*: It might be thought that in addition to the goods mentioned there should be full employment. But at least in a free market society, it is outside the sphere of the state's competence to control the number and type of jobs available, or indeed the number and skills of individuals available for work. Nevertheless it *is* an aspect of the state's duties in justice to *strive* for full employment, for example through economic growth.

*On the relationship between commutative and distributive justice*: For some discussion see Stephen Perry, 'On the Relationship Between Corrective and Distributive Justice' in Jeremy Horder (ed) *Oxford Essays in Jurisprudence Fourth Series* (OUP 2000) ch 12.

*Crowe on law's effectiveness*: The notion that people would continue to observe the law after a total collapse of the state (or at least its enforcement powers) is not entirely wrong, for civilized people do not become uncivilized overnight, and would doubtless continue to observe the same forms (such as contracting) at least for a while. But in a very real and pressing sense, legal observance would immediately cease for there is technically no law for them to obey. Furthermore, sufficiently many would be likely to employ legal forms for their temporary advantage: lulling unsuspecting dupes into entering contracts the contractor has no intention of honouring. These claims are of course untested, but they broadly conform to what we know of human psychology: see for example R Greene, *The Laws of Human Nature* (Profile Books 2019) chs 9–11 and ch 16; Richard Kraut, *The Quality of Life: Aristotle Revised* (OUP 2018) 76–77. See also GA Cohen, *Rescuing Justice and Equality* (Harvard University Press 2008) ch 3.

## IV.4.

*Virtue and the act of restitution*: As Aquinas makes clear (*In Eth* V.12.1018), the precept that one ought not unjustly to injure someone is among the primary precepts of natural law, which are grasped immediately (*per se nota*).

*Rawls on justice*: Most accounts of Rawls's *Theory of Justice* (revised edn Belknap Press 1999) tend to assume that the devices of the original position and the veil of ignorance form one single theoretical package. But it is interesting to speculate about the veil without the assumption of the original position: that the parties behind the veil are tasked not with the construction of a society *ab inito*, but reconstructing their own, established society to align it more towards justice. The parties would then obviously have knowledge of their own society, and perhaps a more vivid sense of human shortcomings, but all other respects, the parties would be deprived of knowledge for example of their gender, health status, conception of the good life. Would they find the task harder, or easier? Is it better, in order to advance, to raise existing structures to the ground, or to make incremental changes to existing institutions? I suspect that the parties behind the veil would experience the greatest of difficulties in improving social structures on a grand scale, for making adjustments to one aspect of a given social function would create destructive interference or instability in others, not least in allocations of public money. One can also speculate on how things would change about the parties' deliberations in the face of variations in the opacity of the veil of ignorance. Rawls already admits 'general knowledge' of matters such as scientific fact, of limited altruism, basic economics and other matters necessary to the deliberations of the parties. But this assumption is hugely significant, for it entails a judgment of what is essential knowledge for social-building. Thus, lightening the veil a little, we might say that the parties require a knowledge of the economic and political history of their society, and thus perhaps of monetary policy, supply-side economics, extent of government borrowing, national debt ... Aware of their own society's history—a history, for these purposes, one of injustices—they would need to confront its politics, its demands for and against affirmative action and the scale of redistribution necessary to redress past and present wrongs. Such an approach would rescue Rawls's method from the admitted charge of idealism, but it would render the task facing the parties vastly more difficult and subject to miscarrying. For some discussion see Jeppe von Platz, 'The Veil of Ignorance in Rawlsian Theory' (2017) *SAGE Encyclopaedia of Political Behaviour* 889.

*Justice is not a state of affairs but a property of actions*: See for example *NLNR* 175. But Aquinas at *ST* II-II.57.1 makes it clear that one can speak of individuals *rights* (*iura*) only because they are connected to what is *just* (*iustum*), indeed representing what is owed or due to an individual as an aspect of that just *situation*. GA Cohen too says that 'fundamental principles, that is, principles that are not derived from other principles, do not rest on factual grounds.' See Cohen, *Rescuing Justice and Equality* (Harvard University Press 2008) 278.

*Justice does not seek to unravel dealings back to the beginning*: There are, to be sure, differential although related conceptions of justice we might invoke here. These are non-focal interpretations of justice, though they can have very real effects. Consider, for example, the tearing down of a public monument to a (long deceased) civic personage whose wealth and importance were founded on money earned from the slave trade, and which is regarded popularly as a victory for justice, or the preservation in existence of public buildings of architectural merit the building of which was financed through that same money of that same personage. In relation to the second example, the preservation is likely to be justified (made just?) by reference to the loss of public amenity and economic cost of their destruction.

*The right of a person to take that which is another's in case of desperate need*: Presumably this right loses much of its force in a society with an established safety-net in the form of homeless shelters, free medical care, housing, and other benefits for the unemployed, etc.

*Purpose of public goods not redistributive*: If we broaden out to consider other taxes, such as value-added tax, the list of public goods grows more extensive: such as '[correction of] mispricing of goods in a free market; to create ancillary incentives or disincentives for consumers' and so forth: See AP Simester & Winnie Chan, 'On Tax and Justice' (2003) 23 *Oxford Journal of Legal Studies* 714.

*The function of justice is not self-constitution*: This is not to say that justice does not benefit its practitioners; as Plato twice observes (in the *Republic* and the *Gorgias*), it is preferable for a person to suffer injustice than to commit it. This does not of course mean that particular persons will prefer to avoid doing injustice, but it embodies the idea, argued for passionately and at length in Aristotle's *Ethics*, that the life of the morally good person is happier (more deeply fulfilling) than that of the wicked person, even if the wicked person readily finds ways to quiet their conscience. Typically, for example, the unjust or untrustworthy person is less likely to experience the full good of friendship as it is realized in the life of the worthy. Nor will they participate fully in the life of reason, as an honest person does.

## IV.5.

*The functioning of contract law under the difference principle*: For an interesting discussion, see Samuel Scheffler, 'Distributive Justice, the Basic Structure and the Place of Private Law' 35 (2015) *Oxford Journal of Legal Studies* 213. I do not think the author's 'weak distribution' theory escapes the criticisms I advance in the main text.

*Family as part of the basic structure*: Sen (*The Idea of Justice*, Penguin 2010 145–46) raises the possibility that if the family is to be counted within the basic structure, and thus subject to the norms of justice appropriate to that structure, then it might well affect such questions as who is to be born: depending, *inter alia*, on the presence or absence of a one-child policy.

*Are citizens owed a particular form of government?*: Though the Christian message does not relate to any particular form of government over others, Aquinas (following Aristotle) has no hesitation in naming monarchy as the best form: *In Eth* VIII.10.1674; *De Reg* I.10.68 & Prooemium. That he should do so should come as little surprise, for God the Father is King above all, Christ is King of Kings, and Aquinas can draw also on the examples of King David, Solomon, etc; that earthly polities should follow these forms of governance would have seemed obvious enough to a medieval writer.

*Provision of basic needs*: In most modern societies with a welfare safety-net, the natural right to minimum prosperity, that is, to goods necessary for survival, probably no longer permits the taking of another's property (a right affirmed in both ancient and medieval natural law writings) but becomes a right to state benefits, including homeless shelters, subsistence benefits, and so on. If this is true, state laws which punish thefts in such circumstances need not be contrary to natural law.

## CHAPTER V

### V.1.

*The common good that is invariant between states*: For see Aristotle *Politics* III.1: 'The goodness or badness, justice or injustice, of laws varies of necessity with the constitutions of states. This, however, is clear, that the laws must be adapted to the constitutions.'

*The common good that is specific to each state*: Examples may include the provision of education, the distribution of offices of power such as posts in local authorities, and affordable housing.

*Matters which enhance the lives of all the community, including the billionaire*: See Aquinas, *In Eth* VIII.1.1541: There is the commonality that all human beings share in virtue of their shared nature, and there is the more specific commonality they share as members of the same political union, with shared customs and social life.

*The common good should not be understood as merely instrumental*: Finnis acknowledges in his Postscript to *NLNR* that his account of the common good in that work seems to be instrumental: *NLNR* 459. But see also *Aquinas* 239. Crowe argues for a position that includes both the 'aggregative' and 'instrumental' theses, but it is unclear how such a position could maintain coherence, if the former term is defined as 'nothing other than' the view that the common good is an aggregation of the goods of all members of the community: *NLNL* 89.

*The common good is not static*: See e.g. *Gaudium et spes* § 26: the definition of the common good (as a sum of conditions for the flourishing of individuals and groups) is not a permanent formulation but an attempt to articulate 'the signs of the times'.

*It is not the purpose of public officials to bring about some specific state of affairs*: From a similar premise, Adrian Vermeule argues that the common good is a *justification* for state action, and does not prescribe any particular set of social institutions: see *Common Law Constitutionalism* 8–9. But at the widest level, the common good is not a justification (though its object must be justifiable) but an admittedly complex set of circumstances. There are institutions that are central to raising or protecting more complex common goods: Hart famously identified the pre-legal society as one subject to many sources of impoverishment. Thus the common good does require judicial institutions and legislative organs; it requires respect for rights and the privacy of individual lives and a regulated economy. It requires access to health care and education, and the openness to allow every member of the community to exercise their talents in the marketplace. The specific shape of these institutions will certainly differ across different societies, but their presence is part of the common good. Where they are lacking, suppressed or damaged, the common good is impoverished. Thus the common good can be identified as the object of the governor's attempt to marry the basic principles of natural law with the specific array of concrete social problems, in a potential and inventive variety of ways, in light of the needs mentioned above.

*Moral action is not rationally arrived at by counting votes*: Here it may be useful to remember that the common good is not, like the greater good, simply a matter of what the majority agrees upon. We do not for example want to favour the views of racists in the community even at the cost of social peace. But we want policies and ideas of the common good that we can explain and defend to racists and others, in principle if not in fact.

## V.2.

*Relationship of individual good to common good*: See Jonathan Crowe, *Natural Law & the Nature of Law* (CUP 2019) 70, where he discusses what he calls the distinctive good conception of common good, against Finnis's conception: Finnis pares down the notion of common good to principles of anti-paternalism and subsidiarity, but in such a case what is truly valued is once again the individual's good, not the common good as something distinctive. He cites Aquinas's proposition that the common good is composed of peace and justice (*ST* I-II.96.3); and justice is the proper relationship of persons to persons in which equality is preserved (*ST* II-II.57.1): see *NLNL* 73. I wonder if this is fair to Finnis for whom the common good is not merely that dyad of principles but 'an ensemble of conditions' that make individual lives richer, more just and at peace. That ensemble of conditions may thus include 'distinctive' goods such as justice and peace, but cannot include goods that have no bearing or basis in the good of individuals, for otherwise those 'common goods' would become burdensome without benefit: somebody's gain, or no one's. Crowe also observes (*NLNL* 75) that Aquinas's account is not merely individualistic, but concerns the good of families and community. He cites variously: *ST* I-II.19.10, II-II.26.3, II-II.26.4 ad 3, II-II.31.3 ad 2, & II-II.47.10. It is not clear that these passages have the import that Crowe suggests. What Aquinas says in I-II.19.10 is that it is perfectly possible for the wills of individuals to will opposing things that are nevertheless both connected to a common good, the example he gives being that it is the good of the community that a thief be executed, whereas the family of the thief desires his life, something in itself good: hence the common good of families is sometimes distinct from the common good of the community. *ST* II-II.26.3 states that individuals can admit harms to themselves or their property for the sake of the common good. But they do so not because the common good is distinct from their own good, but because it makes sense to them to act for the sake of common goods which would otherwise be diminished, through love of cherished family members, castes, one's country. *ST* II-II.26.4 ad 3 states that love of common good is greater in the individual than love of their personal good. There may be many reasons for this: for example, that if the common good is not tended or at least respected, no personal good can be realised; we do not act indiscriminately to get what we want, but respect the common goods of peace, justice, and honour. It is with this meaning that Aquinas (quoting Augustine) says that the common good is greater than the individual good. *ST* II-II.31.3 ad 2 repeats the proposition that the common good is more vital than the good of particular members of the community, but the example he gives is that the soldier, contributing to the defence of the whole community, may and should legitimately act, in that moment, for the sake of a comrade on the frontline, than for that of a blood relative. But again the soldier in upholding the common good, may simply be upholding the 'ensemble of conditions' listed by Finnis, not something distinct and beyond them. *ST* II-II.47.10 observes that the common good is greater than the individual's own good. This is in reply to a passage in Aristotle in which he states (more or less in common with Plato) that sometimes some people seem to act for their own sake rather than that of the community. These passages respond to the sceptical line of argument that it is better to commit an injustice rather than undergo it. Aquinas points out that such individuals act in opposition to charity, and fail to see what others see very clearly: that '[t]he one who seeks the good of the multitude consequently seeks his own good, for: the individual good is impossible without the common good of the family, state, or kingdom'.

*Conflicts between individual and common good*: A further, perhaps more problematic, example would be the state's attempt to frustrate the actions of jihadists within its territory: one might be tempted to argue that such efforts are to the good of the would-be jihadist (they are prevented from taking innocent human life), which is true; however the real aim remains the peace and security of the community and upholding its moral order, a community and moral order that the jihadist regards as utterly corrupt and opposite to the true realities of life. There is an aspect of private good in *carrying out one's intentions* (even one's harmful intentions), and it is this which, being suppressed by external forces, represents a conflict between the good of a wicked individual and the common good.

*It is necessary to resort to casuistry*: Casuistry is held in low regard, akin to hair-splitting. But it can also be a useful and powerful means of deciding what to do in cases of moral perplexity: see Albert Jonsen & Stephen Toulmin, *The Abuse of Casuistry* (University of California Press 1990). See also Aquinas, *ST* I-II.94.4c:

> Now the train of reason proceeds from the general to the particular . . . Speculative reason, however, is different in this respect from practical reason. Because speculative reason mainly concerns what is necessary, and such things cannot be otherwise than they are, its particular conclusions, akin to general principles, contain the truth without fail. On the other hand, practical reason is concerned with what is contingent, which includes human actions. Hence even though the general principles contain a kind of necessity, the more we descend to particular matters, the more frequently we discover exceptions . . . [Thus] in matters relating to action, truth or rectitude is not the same for all persons in questions of detail, except at the level of general principles; and even where rectitude is the same in questions of detail, it is not equally known to every person.

*Human beings also require the more specific form of communality that they share as members of the same political union*: See *NE* IX.9.1170b; living together for humans is to share thoughts and words, not merely grazing in the same place like cattle. Human society is a matter of minds in relation not bodies in proximity: see Michael Oakeshott, *Religion, Politics and the Moral Life* (Yale University Press 1993), 50. See also Aristotle, *Pol* III.5.1280b.

## V.3.

*Guidance toward heavenly beatitude is the function of divine law, not human law*: Aquinas says 'human law', not 'positive law' here, presumably because the final end is neither the subject of positive law *nor* human law understood as the mouthpiece or declaration of natural law, that is, not only to those laws whose authority derive entirely or substantively from the fact that they have been posited by the governing authority.

*Principle of subsidiarity*: Using a different terminology, Yves Simon articulates the principle in substance in the following passage: 'The common good itself requires the principle of autonomy as well as the principle of authority. The former asserts that: "Wherever a task can be satisfactorily achieved by the initiative of the individual or that of smaller social units, the fulfilment of that task must be left to the initiative of the individual or to that of small social units." The latter asserts that: "Wherever the welfare of the community requires common action, the unity of that common action must be assured by the higher organs of that community"'. (Yves Simon, *The Nature and Functions of Authority* (Marquette University Press 1940) 47.

*Real world judgments about the scope of state action*: To the parameters mentioned in the main text should be added provisions of international law, both customary and treaty-based.

## V.4.

*Friendship is above all else a common good*: But the prioritization of friends over strangers, family members over neighbours, etc. should not be equated with the corrupt advancement of the interests of members of a cult, or of, for example, Freemasons. For the promotion of such interests is contrary to the common good rather than an aspect of it; it is *contra* society to advance the interests of fellow criminals in a criminal organization, whereas the advancement of the interests of fellow professionals in a professional organization, or of workers in a workers' union is not inherently contrary to the common good.

*Punishment is for the good of the criminal as well as of society*: But note also Fuller's observation that were rehabilitation the sole purpose of criminal law, 'all concern about due process and a clear definition of what is criminal may be lost' (Fuller, *The Morality of Law* 165).

## V.5.

*Tribes of any great size become immobile*: The exception to this general rule is that of the Israelites, having been led out of Egypt by Moses and forced into a nomadic existence for forty years. The difference is perhaps that the fortunes of the Israelites and their ability to endure a desert existence for so long relied upon Divine protection, most visible in the manna from heaven.

### V.6.

*There is nothing wrong with stockpiling deadly weapons to be used as a deterrent against similar weapons possessed by hostile nations*: One must distinguish deterrent use from actual use. Weapons of mass destruction which will have catastrophic effects on the civilian populations of warring states cannot be used with a morally correct will, for one knows that they are indiscriminate and their purpose is precisely to inspire terror. Thus such weapons are among those that cannot be stockpiled.

## CHAPTER VI

### VI.1.

*Objective v subjective right*: See Thomas Mautner, 'How Rights Became "Subjective"' (2013) 26 *Ratio Juris* 111–32. On the question of antiquity of rights, see also Miller, *Nature, Justice and Rights in Aristotle's Politics* (OUP 1997) esp 97–108 on whether the Greek *dikaion* can be translated as 'right' without anachronism.

*Suarez on Aquinas's concept of 'right'*: See Finnis, *NLNR* 207. Finnis states that Suarez mentions Aquinas's central concept of right only vaguely, and takes as his own central concept one that is entirely absent from Aquinas. But this seems to me a misreading. As stated in the text, Suarez certainly extends Aquinas's meaning, but does so consistently with Aquinas's views and aims. The effect is one of teasing out, not abandoning. Finnis in later work came to reject the notion that a significant watershed divides Aquinas and the medieval writers, on the one hand, from post-medieval or early-modern conceptions of rights, on the other; but he does not use the opportunity to revise his assessment of the relationship between Aquinas and Suarez in the original text of the book: see *NLNR* 465–66.

*It is necessary to distinguish between private sins (failures of virtue in general) and social sins, which pertain to one's relationship with others, in which rights, and not virtues broadly defined, are in issue*: But see Aristotle's discussion of justice as general virtue as impinging on the interests of another.

*A benevolent community without rights*: Would such a society be truly benevolent? Some doctrines and rules at least would need to be put in place, even if respect for rights were not the underpinning consideration. Perhaps a 'benevolent dictator' could impose such a system. But the idea of a benevolent dictator is a political myth: no dictator could remain neutral between, or resolve all differences between, social groups in tension with one another (for example, conservatives and progressives). Any attempted compromise between rival belief systems would inevitably anger both sides, who would therefore not judge the dictator to be benevolent. And what dictator in history has not claimed to be benevolent?

*There is nothing preventing a reference to a class of persons*: Even in the case of rights against (or indeed in favour of) a given individual, A, the relevant legal doctrine, instrument, or rule must perforce *define* A, as being such-and-such a person of certain name, locality, national insurance number, tax number, and so on. Here, identifying characteristics are designed to identify the one and only member of a unit class, $\{A\}$; the principle is no different from that of identifying multiple members of a larger class.

## VI.2.

*Hohfeldian 'right' is itself a specialized form of power*: Note also that not all powers are advantageous to the holder. If I cause you an accident due to my negligent conduct, I can be said to have exercised a legal power which changes our legal relationship to one in which you can potentially sue me for damages. The laws of tort may be said to create an ever-present liability of all people to a change in their legal relations to others should they act in ways contrary to the standards in question.

*The right not to be defrauded*: This is not a non-Hohfeldian right, in spite of the non-Hohfeldian terminology employed here for convenience, but a right against certain types of interference (in the person's legal estate or other dealings) as opposed to the legitimate forms of 'interference'/intervention provided for under the trust or other instrument. Such legitimate interventions are also informed by the person's right to *assistance* by the trustee or fiduciary in administering the estate and/or investments.

*Balancing of interests*: Gregoire Webber's version of the interest theory (*The Negotiable Constitution* CUP 2009 ch 4) might seem to overcome this problem because in it interests are balanced and weighed as part of the specification of a right rather than its application. But when can this prior balancing take place? Only at the point of adjudication. And why in any case should such antecedent specification be thought conclusive? No common law principle is immune from revision.

*The will and interest theories*: Are other ways of regimenting thought about rights possible? Certainly. What we might term an 'object' theory of rights characterizes the ordinary lawyer's way of referring to 'rights *to*' objects, such as property. But such a non-Hohfeldian way of speaking brings with it all of the disadvantages and false implications that the Hohfeldian analysis was intended to avoid. Alternatively, one might adopt a 'value' theory of rights in which rights are said to protect important values (rather than interests or choices). Such rights would not extend to the protection of all values (e.g. chastity) but only to values that are of civic importance. Such 'civic values' might include: protection from criminal harm, enforceability of certain promises, compensation for tortious wrongs, and so on. This value theory of rights might draw support from Aristotle's view that the life of virtue is the most suitable life for human beings, but its disadvantage is that (a) it does not reflect to any great extent the ordinary usage of lawyers or anyone else, and (b) on any ordinary conception of rights, what is protected is (some concrete attribute of) the person, and not an abstract value that transcends the person.

*Neither the will theory nor the interest theory consistently reflect ordinary usage*: In a recent essay Mark McBride opens with the following statement: 'So the challenge for interest theorists is to respect the core of the interest theory while delimiting the set of right-holders in a principled manner' ('Preserving the Interest Theory of Rights' 26 (2020) *Legal Theory* 3). This is untrue. It is not the task of interest theorists to preserve the interest theory, just as it is not the case for will theorists to preserve the will theory. This would be anti-philosophical; the aim should surely be to uncover the truth about the subject-matter of one's investigations, not turning the subject into a partisan issue. Elsewhere, McBride advocates for a hybrid theory of rights (the 'tracking theory'), deriving in part from Nozick's epistemology: see for example Mark McBride, 'The Tracking Theory of Claim Rights' (2021) *Analytic Philosophy* 1. My discussion need not enter into the intricate details of McBride's theory, other than to observe that it seems entirely too complicated an explanation to have any claim to represent the deep logic of rights-talk.

## VI.3.

*There are strictly speaking no rights of son against father*: See inter alia *Quod* I.11.5.1[53] (children are owed (*debet*) the benefits of a good upbringing). Note the absence of language of rights.

*A society without a sense of rights*: Is such a society even possible? Any society that has institutions (however primitive) of judgment, adjudication, or public decision, if it aspires to consistency in judgment, adjudication, or decision, will effectively create rights, that is, the right of the claimant to the same decision that was reached in previous exactly analogous cases. A body of doctrines or rules would inevitably grow up around decision-making (at least where the reasoning is made public), and the consistent application of those doctrines (or rules, or principles) would create de facto rights.

## VI.5.

*Killing of the innocent for military advantage*: It is necessary to distinguish between military attacks or operations that deliberately target the civilian population, for the purposes of inducing terror or for sapping the will of the enemy, and attacks on military targets in which it is possible, or even probable or accepted, that civilians will be killed due to their proximity to the target. The former, deliberate targeting, is wholly immoral and a violation of natural law; the latter may sometimes be justifiable, provided that some or all of the following matters are taken into account: (1) the attempt to minimize civilian casualties, (2) that the killing of civilians is truly an unwanted side-effect of the military operation and not a means to a desired end, (3) that the parameters of the operation are well-defined, and (4) sufficient warning be given to allow the civilian population to evacuate.

# CHAPTER VII

## VII.1.

*Mysteries of the Holy Trinity*: In none of the recorded and attested manifestations of the Blessed Mother nor any other direct revelation has the doctrine of the Trinity been deplored or stated to be a blasphemy. At Lourdes, the Blessed Mother made the Sign of the Cross, and also spoke at some length about the Holy Trinity and Her relation to the Holy Trinity at Tre Fontane, saying 'I am She who is related to the Divine Trinity'. For Aquinas's views, see the first few sections of his *Commentary on the Gospel of John.* (For his examination of Plato and Aristotle on this question see this *Commentary* I.1.65.)

*Scientists improperly speak of times before the existence of space-time*: This was so from the very inception of the universal expansion (Big Bang) theory: see Georges Lemaitre, 'The Beginning of the World from the Point of View of Quantum Theory' (1931) 127 *Nature* 706.

*Scientific theory of the origins of the universe is just as easy or difficult to believe as a theological one*: Hawking, for example, argues that in the quantum vacuum state that precedes the Big Bang, subatomic particles will come into existence spontaneously.

## VII.2.

*Theories of events prior to the Big Bang*: It is sometimes argued that the universe began due to the effects of a dense field of quantum energy, perhaps a singularity. But many scientists agree in denying that talk of time or place can make sense outside the confines of space-time. Effects imply changes of state; but changes imply passage of time, just as existence, even of a singularity, implies space. Even ignoring such questions, the presence of a dense quantum field answers none of the questions with which this chapter is concerned. For what brought the quantum field into existence? Or, if we suppose that it existed backwards to infinity, what sustains that field in existence, and what brings about the change? Why did the change occur at that particular point rather than another?

*Idea of First Mover*: For the idea that God is not simply the means by which things are initially brought into existence but that they also subsist through His will, see Aquinas's *Commentary on the Gospel of Saint John* I.86.

*Talk of God is analogical*: Aquinas observes that 'Some truths about God exceed our faculty of reason, such as that God is both Three and One. But there are some truths [about God] to which natural reason can extend, such as that God exists, that He is One, and so on. Indeed, such truths have been the subject of philosophical demonstration, aided by the light of natural reason': *SCG* I.3.2.

## VII.3.

*The second argument investigates agency*: Suarez observes that there are in fact two kinds of objects. There are first the objects that occur naturally which are the descendants of physical material that God originally brought into existence and now sustains in existence. But the other kind of objects are those which in addition result from God's direct agency supervening on natural physical processes. Suarez calls these 'mixed objects' and they include any object (being) that possesses a soul: the parents of a child are the source of the genetic material that develops into the child's bodily life, but it is God who creates the soul: *Disputationes Metaphysicae* XXIX.2.13. It is a comforting thought, not remarked by Suarez, that God so loves the world, despite its troubles, that He is at any given moment bringing new souls into the world. (See John 3:16).

*Raz on authority*: The influence of philosophical anarchism is evident in Raz's example of a car being driven slowly through a red light at 04:00 in a deserted street. Ought one to obey the law in this instance, given that the harms that the law seeks to prevent are effectively absent from the scene? There are two aspects to this, similar to each other: (1) if, engaged in this action, you are unfortunate enough to be stopped by a passing police car, then you run the risk of a fine and penalties. In this respect, the putative driver is in no different position than one who runs the red light at 19:00 with other traffic around, except that the odds are stacked rather differently and the risk is greater; (2) at 04:00, the chance of running into a young child who has somehow escaped the house and run out into the road, is of course much lower than at 19:00, but it is not nothing. Accordingly, if your running the red light causes you to hit the child, you would face the same penalties whether at 04:00 or 19:00: the level of risk is proportionately smaller but it is not different in kind.

## VII.4.

*Though '2 + 2 = 5' could never have been true, the proposition '2 + 2 = 4' is valid only because existence itself exists*: Of potential interest here is the debate in the philosophy of mathematics between 'intuitionists' (who believe that mathematics is composed ultimately of human conventions or is drawn ultimately from material facts) and 'realists' or 'Platonists' (who hold that mathematics is fundamentally independent of the truth of material facts, and is composed of necessary abstract objects: see for example: B Hale, *Abstract Objects* (Blackwell 1987); Michael Dummett, *Elements of Intuitionism* (Clarendon 1990) and Dummett, *Frege: Philosophy of Mathematics* (Duckworth 1995).

*The primary term must be a being because it imparts consciousness*: This might seem to employ a fallacy, since life begins with the mingling of amino acids which themselves do not exhibit consciousness. But although brain chemistry undoubtedly has an effect on cognition, and thoughts correlate with electro-chemical impulses in the brain of intelligent creatures, the electro-chemical processes do not *explain* thought and intelligence. Such processes may well *accompany* efforts of thought, including the direction of thought to one object rather than another, or a decision, or success in following a logical argument, or a change of mind on some issue, but they can scarcely be said to be the *cause* of those phenomena. In general, intelligent causes cannot be reduced to unintelligent causes.

## VII.5.

*Argument from design*: In contrast to Aquinas, Suarez offers an intricate argument from design, roughly that nature consists of intelligible processes and this requires an intelligence behind them: *DM* XXIX.2.18–25. But his motive in doing so is not to demonstrate the existence of God, but instead to offer evidence for the proposition that there is only one God and not many, else nature would disclose many intelligences where in fact we find unity.

## VII.6.

*Elimination of moral evil entails the elimination of free will*: Some atheist philosophers dispute this (e.g. JL Mackie) and argue that a perfectly good God could create a world of free will in which people only ever chose the good. For an argument that this is impossible (if not incoherent) see Alvin Plantinga, *The Nature of Necessary* (OUP 1974).

*The argument is not one of intelligent design*: See also a different perspective on the argument in Aquinas's *Commentary on the Gospel of Saint John* (Prologue § 3).

## VII.8.

*The problem of the missing census*: There is some controversy about the date of the census mentioned in the Gospel of St Luke, with most commentators agreeing that it actually occurred in 6AD, and that Luke made an error. This is a reference to the census of Quirinius, the most likely candidate for the census mentioned in Luke. Additionally, it should be noted that the city of Bethlehem alluded to in Luke is not the famous Bethlehem near Jerusalem but Bethlehem in Galilee, a short distance from Nazareth. This last conjecture resolves another potential difficulty. It has been argued that the census could not have expected people to leave their lands and employment in order to register at the town of their birth: flocks would go untended, the entire economy would come to a halt, etc. But the conjecture of Bethlehem in Galilee makes more sense of this problem as (i) the mass movement that would have to have previously occurred if people would need to travel great distances to their homelands in a largely agrarian economy, would be scarcely possible, and (ii) if registration did require such movement back to one's homelands, the distances involved would be short.

*Authenticity of the prophesies concerning Jesus*: Here one could mention the facts later in this section relating to the authenticity of the teachings and records of the saints of the Early Church: those writers had nothing to gain, and everything to lose, by disseminating such teachings. They, and the resurrected Lord, despise lying: 'rather that the sun and moon fall from the sky than that one person utters one lie'. For the devil is precisely the father of lies.

# CHAPTER VIII

## VIII.1.

*The authority of law is the authority of past legal decisions and customs*: But also of present decisions and customs, for they have the quality, or at least semblance, of morality, that is, of moral norms that are judged not on their history but their rectitude or their value in upholding or advancing the common good.

*Hobbes and Locke seek to provide an origin of power in society*: But note that Hobbes, at least, characterizes political power as deriving from the exercise of a prior power, on behalf of all persons, to give up their previous power to determine for themselves the relevant form of action: *Leviathan* XIII & XIV.

*Authority is the socially recognized power to create and enforce laws*: This is *not* the suggestion made by Raz (*Authority of Law* 19) that power over others is authority over them. For as is suggested in the main text, human beings possess various kinds of power (such as the power to set high prices in times of high demand) that are not instances of authority in any sense.

*Possession of moral authority cannot be traced to any original transaction or originary act, but must derive from a set of moral norms that become apparent only after authority has been established*: This proposition must be reconciled with the one above, that moral authority is posterior to legal and political authority. The situation admits of further complexity: one should say that moral norms are *recognized* or *identified* prior to the fact of political or legal authority, but plainly the political and legal arrangements of a state, or proto-arrangements, are themselves either moral or immoral in themselves, prior to their being identified.

## VIII.2.

*Need for coordination is a secondary matter*: To be sure, Finnis does not suggest that authority exists to solve coordination problems in any straightforward way and without context. As Aiyar remarks, 'his claim is not just that law co-ordinates in particular cases but that it can encompass the entire range of human goods, aspirations and transactions and co-ordinate them not just for the sake of co-ordination but in a fair way, consistent with the requirements of self-direction, friendship and of accommodating the incommensurability of human goods—each being aspects of the common good.': S Aiyar, 'The Problem of Law's Authority: John Finnis and Jospeh Raz on Legal Obligation' 19 (2000) *Law and Philosophy* 485.

*Crowe on coordination problems*: Crowe is correct to reject the coordination account of authority, but his reasons for doing so are problematic. For he argues that the point of the law's coordination of activities is to prevent a situation in which people are free to pick and choose the laws they wish to obey, and argues that in practice people do pick and choose: he gives the example of a road with a lower speed limit than the traffic actually travels; in such a case (he argues) it is safer to travel at the higher speed. There appear to be two responses to this: (1) the point is not whether people do choose to disobey particular laws—whether they act in contravention of the law—but whether they are *free* to pick and choose; (2) the example given is strange: driving at the higher speed is a criminal act, one that is presumably more dangerous given the road conditions than driving at the correct speed; there may be a greater risk of accidents at the higher speeds, or greater harm than if an accident occurred at the lower speed. Consequently, the act of picking and choosing, on this example, is not a matter of indifference.

*Raz on authority*: See *Morality of Freedom* (Clarendon 1988) 70–103. Raz's claim that the moral basis of authority lies in authority's improvement of one's conformity to reason is doubted by Jean Porter: see *Ministers of the Law* (Eerdmans 2010) 38. But there are some good reasons for accepting Raz's argument: (1) there is value in behaving as others do, for it improves the common goods of peace and safety, by reducing friction between citizens; (2) there is value in being ruled by reference to the same authority as others are ruled by; (3) there is value in being guided by a legal and bureaucratic order that has oversight of and integration of quite general matters of social life upon which no individual person could claim to be an authority; (4) there is value in being subject to the same dispute settlement institutions and processes which decide upon matters of immorality and justice; (5) there is value in its being made certain what is the responsibility of each person to the common good.

## VIII.3.

*Acceptance not a datable act of will*: Various writers in the natural law tradition held otherwise, not least Hobbes but also Grotius in passages such as the following: 'For those who had associated themselves with some group, or had subjected themselves to a man or to men, had either expressly promised, or from the nature of the transaction must be understood impliedly to have promised, that they would conform to that which should have been determined, in the one case by the majority, in the other by those upon whom authority had been conferred.' (*DIBP* Proleg § 15.)

*Friendship as a basis of law*: See Stephen Utz, 'Associative Obligation and Law's Authority' 17 (2004) *Ratio Juris* 286: '[A]ssociative obligations cannot be said to arise by consent, express or implied. Family membership and even friendship are, in relevant respects, nonconsensual.'

*Acts and omissions as evidence of opinio iuris*: It may often be that different forms of behaviour, or different omissions from acting, can constitute evidence of *opinio iuris*. Evidence of the emergent rule must therefore arise from commonality of purpose rather than similarity of action: for example, two different state communities may be involved in degrading the environment of a river, the first state overfishing the river, the second polluting it with industrial chemicals. State one's custom-forming act might be the removal of its boats from the river and concentrating resources on its sea-fishing industry instead. State two's custom-forming act might be disposing of its chemicals in an alternative way (not necessarily environmentally friendly!) or in the longer term, its gradual reformation of its industries to use clean energy or hybrid technologies. But the commonality of purpose is the same in both states: to restore the natural environment of the river. Of course, the commonality of purpose may be simply to avoid international pressure or disapprobation of activities that both states would otherwise have continued. This is perhaps not inconsistent with the recognition of a *rule* emerging, but this will not be the case in all situations, in which case it would seem that there is no *opinio iuris* as such.

### VIII.4.

*Constitution of states and authority*: Perhaps a fourth source of legitimacy is that of disputes over a nation's homeland, as tragically played out in the ongoing war in the Middle East.

*Types of foreign warfare that it is legitimate for legal authority to pursue*: The three purposes mentioned in the text could be summarized by the idea of a 'just war'. But both the text and the summary belie the complexity and difficulty of the relevant rules of the international law of armed conflict, from which the main text prescinds. But it is important to mention that the natural law philosophers are divided over the proposition that states may go to war to eliminate a *threat*, rather than actual moves by the aggressor against the innocent state. Preemptive self-defence is therefore not allowed by natural law (though military preparations may be made short of manoeuvring into an attack formation), for self-defence presupposes aggressive acts to which the innocent state responds. It is in this second sense that the proposition in the text speaks of response to threat, that is, to a real and immanent threat of invasion, destruction, or annexation.

## CHAPTER IX

### IX.2.

*All commitments are willed on the basis of what is good for oneself and others*: Is this true of all commitments, or only those that are good? There is some variation in the views of the major natural law theorists, but it seems safe to say that every person acts for the sake of some (perceived) good that they wish to bring about (Aristotle: *NE* I.1). It also seems safe to say that what people commit themselves to is in some way and on some level to do with their fulfilment. Even an ascetic who commits herself to God and renounces worldly pleasures, riches, influence, and pledges obedience to their Order, experiences forms of fulfilment. Even the dictator wishes to bring about some good, again perceived rather than real, that is wholly or partly based on their own fulfilment. But perhaps, it might be objected, the dictator (or to be cynical) persons generally will what is good for themselves without a thought of what is good for others. But the cynicism overreaches itself: for virtually every person seeks the good of at least those to whom one is related, or to whom one is friendly. No person seeks or would wish for the destruction of everyone save themselves. Exterminatory regimes may target increasing numbers or classes of person for the death camps, but not the entire population. Thus the proposition above indeed does hold true of all commitments, though sometimes in a radically reduced and distorted sense.

## IX.3.

*Raz on obligation*: There are numerous challenges to Raz's position, for example that of David Enoch: 'Authority and Reason-Giving' 89 (2014) *Philosophy and Phenomenological Research* 296. See also Margaret Gilbert *A Theory of Political Obligation: Membership, Commitment and the Bond of Society* (OUP 2006) who puts forward the following proposition: 'X has an absolutely conclusive reason for performing some action A iff a consideration C that speaks in favour of A is such that given C, rationality requires that X do A, whatever else is true' (31). Where does this get us? Unlike the notion of a 'sufficient reason', the conclusive reason escapes the balance-sheet conception of practical rationality that bedevils the literature on obligation. For 'to have sufficient reason to do something is not in and of itself to have an absolutely conclusive reason for doing it'. Unfortunately, the majority of laws are not conclusive reasons in this sense because contrary moral values may lead one to conclude that they are not to be obeyed either in part or in full. Whether one has conclusive reasons, or sufficient reasons, or prudential reasons for obeying the law reignites the debate around Finnis's attempt to distinguish between different kinds of attitude toward the law, and his identification of the focal case: that of the person of practical reasonableness, the *phronimos*. This latter figure will scrutinize the moral value of the law, and the strong reasons one has to obey the law even in the face of injustice, in deciding on the question of obedience. One could say that such a person sometimes has conclusive reasons for obedience, and in many cases only sufficient reasons. Now although natural law theory is not primarily concerned with the question of obedience, it obviously must possess such a theory. Thus in addition to the main text we can make the following comments. In order to rid ourselves of the balance-sheet mode of reasoning, and of reflective equilibrium, let us concentrate upon the individual's relationship to the law. The majority of laws do not possess the form of giving reasons to anybody. They merely stipulate that such-and-such is the case, or is to be the case, so that 'reasons' only enter the picture through the generalized disposition to be law-abiding, that is to say, their commitment. Such a commitment can be relatively unconscious, though it is never wholly so: one's decision every day to drive under the speed limit manifests one's commitment to obey the law. But the true measure of whether the law, or a law, deserves to be obeyed, is not that of any one person, but that of the *phronimos*, whose hypothetical commitments are the proper focus of study when such questions of obedience arise: or, as Aquinas would surely say, that of the mature and good Christian who possesses wisdom and the virtues.

## IX.4.

*Commitment is a certain voluntary act*: Crowe argues that social friendship is not a basis for an obligation to the common good (*NLNL* 92). The doubt is misplaced: would one say of a close friendship between two individuals that the one owes no duty to the other to act in ways that operate for the good of both of them? Or would one say that each friend is obligated to assist the other in ways of flourishing that increase the flourishing of both? Crowe's assumption would appear to that the voluntary cannot give rise to the duty. Clearly in some cases this is true. I voluntarily go to a concert or to the cinema; I have no obligation to do so. But other voluntary acts clearly do give rise to obligations: I voluntarily enter into a contract which generates a web of rights and obligations. Finnis rightly pointed to a nexus of social relationships ranging from contracting parties at arm's length to friendship in the highest sense, there being at every point a common good between the persons. See *NLNR* VI.3–4. Thus there seems no compelling reason to accept Crowe's argument.

*Presumptive obligations*: Many of these obligations are strongly presumptive. Yet even in the context of strong presumption, there is the possibility of defeat. One's most intimate moral commitments must be subjected, at least periodically, to the searchings of conscience, even if usually reaffirmed.

*Obligation to pay taxes/being obliged to pay*: A potential response is that the two concepts remain separate, one's obligation to pay being ongoing, whereas one's being obliged to pay comes at the point of being coerced by state machinery. But this objection is surely misconceived: 'obliged' in ordinary language does not refer only to the coercive mechanisms of the law but to the general impression that the law obliges, that even the threat of future coercion if one does not conform is a form of obliging. The defender of Hart may argue that the point of conceptual analysis is in fact to regiment our thoughts rather than to record them, but such a regimentation must reveal something about the deep structure of our language and our commitments. In the case of law this is not the case: when asked by some person, 'why are you paying your taxes?', the response: 'because I am obliged to' is a near-synonym for 'because I am obligated to'. There is no 'deep' difference between each locution which could warrant the imposition of a re-regimentation of language. To repeat: there are situations in which the distinction makes sense, but such situations are limited.

*Equity a matter of general justice*: This appears to be a violation of Aquinas's principle that the law should not seek to govern the inner moral life of citizens but only their outward actions: the law should not expect perfection but only a narrower set of virtues. But in fact equity is simply another form of general justice: the relatability of other virtues, not normally subject to legal regulation, to others and thus matters of justice; here, in particular, the virtues of prudence and honesty. The doctrine is limited: it does not govern mental states as such but such states in conjunction with actions, and then only opposing those interior mental states to the actor so as to block *procedural* avenues that might otherwise be relied upon to evade an obligation.

*People are owed the truth on the majority of occasions*: There is an ambiguity in this phrase which needs to be resolved. The phrase should not be taken as saying that lying is permitted as the best strategy in some cases. Rather it is to be understood negatively, namely that there are circumstances in which certain people (e.g. axe murderers), though not to be lied to, are nevertheless to be deprived of the information they are seeking in order to carry out an injustice (e.g. murdering the family one is hiding in one's basement). See

Finnis *Fundamentals of Ethics* (Georgetown University Press 1983) 151; *Moral Absolutes: Tradition, Revision & Truth* (Catholic University of America Press 1991) 63–67.

*Conscience can be innocently or culpably in error in relation to secondary precepts*: Aquinas uses the phrase 'wrongful promptings' (*malas persuasiones*) in the text, which he compares to error on the part of the mind when reasoning from faulty understandings. Thus Aquinas leaves open the door to the doctrine that would become known as 'invincible ignorance'.

### IX.5.

*Votes for unjust laws*: See the discussion in Finnis, *CEJF* IV.22. This discussion pertains to a rather specialized situation in which the law-maker is faced with a Bill that reduces the immorality of the existing law, without altogether eliminating it (e.g. a Bill that allows abortions to be carried out until the twentieth week, in a situation where currently abortions can be lawfully carried out until the thirtieth week). His conclusion is that a law-maker can morally vote for the unjust law. This is different to the situation contemplated in the main text, in which legislation does not so restrict an unjust situation, but introduces a new injustice *but* alongside some morally good or valuable effects. Here there is no room for the apology that the law-maker does not *intend* the immoral effects, because s/he presumptively has the intention to vote for the legislation that includes those effects. Those uncomfortable with Finnis's conclusions may see little moral difference between the two cases.

## CHAPTER X

### X.1.

*There are no grand theories*: That is to say, no grand theories of 'political morality', yet for an argument that private law rests upon Aristotelian ethics, see James Gordley, *Foundations of Private Law* (Oxford University Press 2006).

### X.2.

*Conclusio and determinatio*: Of relevance here is the classical description of common law as the 'artificial perfection of reason'. This phrase has the potential to underestimate the degree to which the common law is a direct expression of natural law, with no artificiality or (as the phrase implies) imprint of many minds refining and (thus) changing the norm as a kind of *determinatio*.

*Unjust laws*: It should be added that unjust laws (like any other laws) cannot easily be individuated and, as such, surgically removed from the legal system; for such laws can work their way into other extant concepts, definitions, and principles, or otherwise influence their development. To remove an unjust law is not therefore simply to tear out a bad concept or rule. A legal system may very well exhibit structural inequalities to which no easy response can be made.

*Determinatio*: A good example is Hart's public ordinance excluding vehicles from a public park. Hart treats the issue as a linguistic one (the open texture of the word 'vehicle') but the issue is not predominantly one of interpretation. Certain conveyances (toy cars, prams) are permitted because they are (a) not dangerous, (b) not polluting, (c) not creative of excessive noise of disturbance, and (d) unlikely to go out of control ... Other 'vehicles' such as skateboards or racing bicycles may possibly be excluded on one or more of these grounds: each ground gives expression to a moral principle or facet of justice which, while not completely determining a particular solution, nevertheless rationally constrain the thinking that goes into crafting legal judgment.

## X.3.

*The eight desiderata as failures to create law*: To speak more correctly, the 'desiderata' (that which is required but is lacking) are deductions from the deficiencies outlined in 1(i)–(viii); that is, the desiderata are positive characteristics whereas the deficiencies are negative, that is, failures.

*Journey from non-law into law*: It might be objected that many rules of the common law are vague or ambiguous but are not 'non-law'. But vagueness should not be confused with generality, nor with series of highly particularized norms from which a degree of abstraction and re-formulation (or in some instances formulation) is required for the rule to be then reparticularized in application. Further, vagueness must not be confused with the recognition that in law, there are many ways to go wrong but not necessarily only one way of doing right, that is, of giving effect to the *rights* of the litigating parties. Indeed, adjudication is intended to give to the litigating parties what is their *right*, and this can scarcely be accomplished unless there are clear laws in favour of one or other party; but the relevant rules often achieve diamond precision only *through the process of being applied*, by an interpretation of the law in the light of legal principle, common sense, public policy, avoidance of slippery slopes, etc. Common law legal norms may be characterized as being chronically *incomplete* but not chronically *vague*. They are incomplete in the sense that such norms very often appear only in the context of previous judgments from which it is difficult to extract the *ratio decidendi* from obiter remarks. Because of the need for *this* judgment to apply to the facts of *this* case, the common law resists any attempt to freeze a particular form of words as being the final statement of any legal rule. For the judgment handed down in *this* case is itself a consideration (significant or merely persuasive) to be taken up in *future* judgments *ad infinitum*. Legal positivists insist on the idea that law contains lacunae which must be cured through acts of adjudicative legislation for precisely this reason: the majority of laws are not imprecise but rather incomplete, but those that are imprecise do not count as laws unless and until defined in official legal judgments.

*A tax statute that levies duty on transactions that occurred years ago is unjust, but not actually retroactive*: For a retroactive rule (a) governs only past behaviour and (b) punishes persons for not having paid such sums in the past, whereas the contemplated rule (a) applies to conduct now—payment or non-payment, and (b) punishes only conditional on one's present act (of non-payment).

*The rule of law as a form of morality*: John Gardner (*Law as a Leap of Faith* 202) offers a strangulated interpretation of Fuller in which he writes that the desiderata of legality are concerned with the 'how' rather than the 'why' of law. This seems to me evidently false from the many passages in which Fuller insists that the desiderata have a *purpose* (to rescue the human being from the blind play of chance and secure a purposeful and creative way of being) rather than merely a technical interest in *how* this might be achieved.

## X.4.

*Hart on primitive law*: In fact Hart concedes that although the union of primary and secondary rules constitutes the essence of law, nevertheless they are not always found together wherever the word 'law' is used: *CL* 155.

*Nazi law*: As Jews and left-thinking Germans were purged from their official positions within the German legal system, the situation regarding the law became increasingly opaque: the infamous Nuremberg Race Laws were legislated though not through the normal legal channels; the system did not lack lawyers and judges willing to interpret and apply Nazi law through the courts; and so on. No precise analysis can reveal exactly at what stage Nazi law ceased to be 'law', for aside from the opacity that comes from direct dictatorship there is also the fact that the desiderata of legality are not met or not; they are rather fulfilled to a greater or lesser degree. There is no pre-defined point at which rule through existing legal mechanisms becomes the rule of 'men' not law.

*Austin on unjust law*: Austin's famous quotation is as follows: 'Suppose an act, innocuous or positively beneficial, be prohibited by the sovereign under penalty of death; if I commit this act, I shall be tried and condemned, and if I object to the sentence that it is contrary to the law of God ... the court of justice will demonstrate the inconclusiveness of my reasoning by hanging me up, in pursuance of the law of which I have impugned the validity' (*Province* 185). Key to understanding this passage is of course the description of the law-applying agencies as courts *of justice*: if such institutions really did live up to their name, they would take every opportunity to mitigate the harsh effects of unjust laws, or to warn the defendant that they are heading into trouble.

*Is there more to natural law?*: Matthew Kramer writes that natural law theorists 'down the centuries ... from ancient times [to] the present day' assert that 'the status of any norm N as a law in any legal system is always dependent on the norm's satisfaction of some test of moral validity' (*HLA Hart* 157). This would, of course, exclude the possibility of unjust laws, which form a central concern of natural law theory. For the natural law theorist (as much as anyone) wishes to point to laws that are unjust and which therefore may not be binding in conscience or which may even require disobedience. Elsewhere, Kramer defines inclusive positivism as consisting in the following thesis: 'It can be the case, though it need not be the case, that a norm's consistency with some or all of the requirements of morality is a precondition for the norm's status as a law in this or that jurisdiction': 'Throwing Light on the Role of Moral Principles in the Law: Further Reflections' *Legal Theory*, 8 (2002) 115–43. The focal point here is the unqualified sense given to the term 'status' or 'status as a law'. Natural law theory regards even some unjust laws as having 'status as laws', but only in a reduced and attenuated sense, as is made clear in the discussion in the main text. The existence of qualifications in status 'as laws' seems to be the main stumbling block for legal positivists, who appear to think that such 'status' must be binary: present or not. See also Honore, 'The Necessary Connection Between Law and Morality' 22 (2002) *Oxford Journal of Legal Studies* 490: 'It is not plausible to say, with some old fashioned natural lawyers, that the morally objectionable laws are not laws and legal systems'; Richard Stacey 'Democratic Jurisprudence and Judicial Review: Waldron's Contribution to Political Positivism' (2010) *Oxford Journal of Legal Studies* 30 (2010) 755: '*Lex iniusta non est lex* is the familiar refrain of natural lawyers seeking to ground legal validity on notions of justice and right.'

*Hart on natural law*: Gardner suggests that Hart is 'wrongly' associated with the thesis that there are no necessary connections between law and morality; that his statements to this effect are 'bungled' attempts to state his real thesis which is that 'there are no moral standards for law which are such that law automatically satisfies them.' (*Law as a Leap of Faith* 221). But it is difficult to make sense of this thesis. For the relevant natural law thesis is not that laws 'automatically' satisfy certain moral demands, but that certain laws are not laws, or not fully laws, unless they satisfy moral demands. Furthermore, Gardner offers a rather strained interpretation of Hart which involves denying that he meant what he did say and affirming that his view is expressed in a claim that he did not make. Further instances of this can be found in Gardner's theory that Hart denied that rules are practices ('*Law as a Leap of Faith* as others see it' (2014) 33 *Law and Philosophy* 815.) Gardner argues that 'Hart had pretty chaotic thoughts about normativity that do not add up to a worked-out position' (ibid, 816). But it is highly unlikely that a philosopher of Hart's acumen and whose works are centred upon the analysis of concepts would have left such matters in darkness.

*Legal positivism*: The term 'legal positivism' is notoriously ambiguous. Hart himself gave five possible meanings: (i) all laws are commands of human beings (including laws of physics?); (ii) there is no necessary connection between law and morality; (iii) the analysis of the meanings of legal propositions is distinct from historical, sociological, or critical appraisals; (iv) a legal system is a closed logical system; (v) moral propositions cannot be determined by rational argument. (*CL* 302n, see also 268). Neil MacCormick offers a sixth: (vi) there is not a conceptual but a contingent connection between morality and positive law, and neither moral principles nor positive laws are deliverances of reason. ('Natural Law Reconsidered' (1981) 1 *Oxford Journal of Legal Studies* 100); and John Gardner a seventh: (vii) In any legal system, whether a norm is legally valid and hence wither it forms part of the law of that system, depends on its sources not its merits, where its merits ... include the merits of its sources. (*Law as a Leap of Faith* 19–21.)

## X.5.

*Nine purposes of law*: Contrast Dworkin, *LE* 98: the purpose of law is to establish a justifying connection between past political decisions and present coercion. But past rulings and legislative acts are not morally inert norms in search of a justification; they embody a justification. Dworkin's use of the term 'political' is distortive if intended to erode the boundary between the political and the legal. The main text explores some of the dimensions of legal reason that clarify the connection between past and present justifications.

*Practices of recognition*: To the list in the text could be added practices of overruling and establishing a precedent in a case of first impression: see Timothy Endicott, 'Adjudication and the Law' (2007) 27 *Oxford Journal of Legal Studies* 311. On the subject of the rule of recognition, Nigel E Simmonds makes the following apposite remarks: 'Hart also accepts that the rule of recognition may be uncertain: he could scarcely account for the problems of constitutional law and the uncertainties (in our system) surrounding the doctrine of stare decisis if he denied this.' 'The question of the content of the rule of recognition cannot be a question of empirical fact. Although a practice is composed of human actions, and these actions are themselves facts, a practice has a capacity for extension to future occasions which cannot be captured by a factual description of the actions which compose it.' 'Practice and Validity' (1979) 38 *Cambridge LJ* 367 & 369 respectively.

### X.6.

*C's immunity renders inoperative D's otherwise operative power*: Powers may beget further powers: there is every person's ever-present liability to be made a contractual offer—an exercise of a power that bestows a further power on D (to accept or reject the offer) and which may or may not produce intricately intertwined rights and duties under the ensuing contract.

## CHAPTER XI

### XI.1.

*Lex iniusta non est lex*: The equation of natural law theory with the phrase 'an unjust law is not a law' remains depressingly prevalent, despite the efforts of Finnis and others to dispel it. See for example: Richard Stacey, (2010) 30 *Oxford Journal of Legal Studies* 749–73; T Honore (2002) 22 *Oxford Journal of Legal Studies* 489–95; Philip Soper, 'In Defence of Classical Natural Law in Legal Theory: Why Unjust Law Is No Law at All' (2007) 20 *Canadian Journal of Law & Jurisprudence* 201.

### XI.2.

*An unjust law is not a law*: The sense in which this phrase is asserted is actually less extreme than the distinction urged by Austin in *The Province of Jurisprudence Determined*, namely between law 'properly so called' and *law* 'improperly so called', that is, 'law' that is not positive law (*Province* 171).

*An unjust judgment is not a judgment*: The misjudgement is not a kind of judgment to the extent that it lacks proper order of premises to conclusion, but is a kind of judgment generically, that is, inasmuch as a train of reasoning comes to a firm conclusion which becomes the basis of future acts or future chains of reasoning.

*Law makes a person good not absolutely but relative to this or that regime's norms*: But Aquinas seems to overlook the fact that the regime's aims are immoral, corrupt or unreasonable. Hence for a person to become 'good' in relation to such norms (that is, to shape their behaviour in accordance with those norms) is seriously immoral, and should not be attempted by any citizen living under such rules.

### XI.3.

*A ruler acts with an imperfect will and without God's guidance*: Suarez's statement is too strong, for the natural law is part of eternal law, and whist capable of being deflected, human reason is also and typically capable of participating in that eternal law through the natural law, that is, the law of natural reason.

### XI.6.

*Positivist distinction between just and unjust legal systems*: Positivists claim that their theoretical framework allows for greater precision and greater explanatory power. But in fact, a theoretical framework that is incapable of distinguishing between those cases in which there is a corrupt, unjust but functioning legal order, and those in which a purported legal system is not, properly, a legal system but a form of arbitrary governance or tyranny, is distinctly lacking in theoretical power where it most counts.

*The 'good' German judge*: Two points are worthy of mention: (1) the judge's complicity in upholding a total system of horrific injustice, however unwillingly: is a form of both personal and collective guilt, and (2) the often-cited paradox that, if some judges are good and others bad, this decreases the choices open to the law's victims, for they cannot be sure which judge they will face, and in some cases this encourages some victims to break the law in the belief that they may be tried by a good judge; a form of risk-taking that may result in more victims being prosecuted to the full extent of the law than if there were only bad judges.

## CHAPTER XII

### XII.1.

*States envy the resources of other states*: Can one attribute states of mind to 'states'? What is really at stake here is the collective mind (or at least collective responsibility) of a state government; though there is also the phenomena of a 'national mood', especially relating to warfare.

### XII.3.

*Natural laws in human context*: Reed incorrectly states that (a) no specific principles can be derived from natural law, and (b) morality is contextual and never independent of law making activity: see *A Theology of International Law* 60. See also Allott, *Eunomia* 3.29.49.

*States must forgo their rights for the sake of peace*: There are a number of limitations to this doctrine: (1) states are responsible for the flourishing and common good of their citizens, and must shape their international strategies and relations wisely in response to this; (2) by forgoing their rights, states should not communicate to aggressor states the idea that such rights are pseudo-rights, or morally questionable; (3) in this respect states must act as brothers to other states by (a) exhibiting care for their common good, and (b) offering correction of their immoral acts, whether by action or diplomacy.

## XII.4.

*States as intermediating institution*: This standing between individuals and international tribunals does not, obviously, entail any duty or even right of a state to withhold one of its members from an international tribunal to face charges such as war crimes committed during for example a UN-sanctioned armed response to a global threat.

*Outlaw states*: Rawls's concept is troublesome insofar as it suggests that certain nations are beyond or outside international law. The process of 'brotherly correction' requires one to regard the recalcitrant as requiring a reorientation towards the common good, without being fully ostracized from the international community, in the same way that we should not view a neighbour as beyond or beneath the benefits of natural law, however qualified that person's pursuit of the good might be.

## XII.6.

*It is impermissible to conduct a war of religion*: Grotius's position on this matter needs to be correctly understood. He appears to suggest the contrary when he holds that it is permissible—even legitimate—to go to war to redress a crime against God (*DIBP* II.20.44). But he immediately adds that the right to engage in warfare at all has its origin in Divine law, and every injury done to any people is a crime against God.

# Index

*For the benefit of digital users, indexed terms that span two pages (e.g., 52–53) may, on occasion, appear on only one of those pages.*

The manufacturer's authorised representative in the EU for product safety is Oxford University Press España S.A. of el Parque Empresarial San Fernando de Henares, Avenida de Castilla, 2 – 28830 Madrid (www.oup.es/en or product.safety@oup.com). OUP España S.A. also acts as importer into Spain of products made by the manufacturer.

www.ingramcontent.com/pod-product-compliance
Lightning Source LLC
Chambersburg PA
CBHW071102290426
44082CB00004B/104
* 9 7 8 0 1 9 2 8 8 6 9 9 6 *